Celtic Daily Prayer

BOOK ONE

WILLIAM
COLLINS

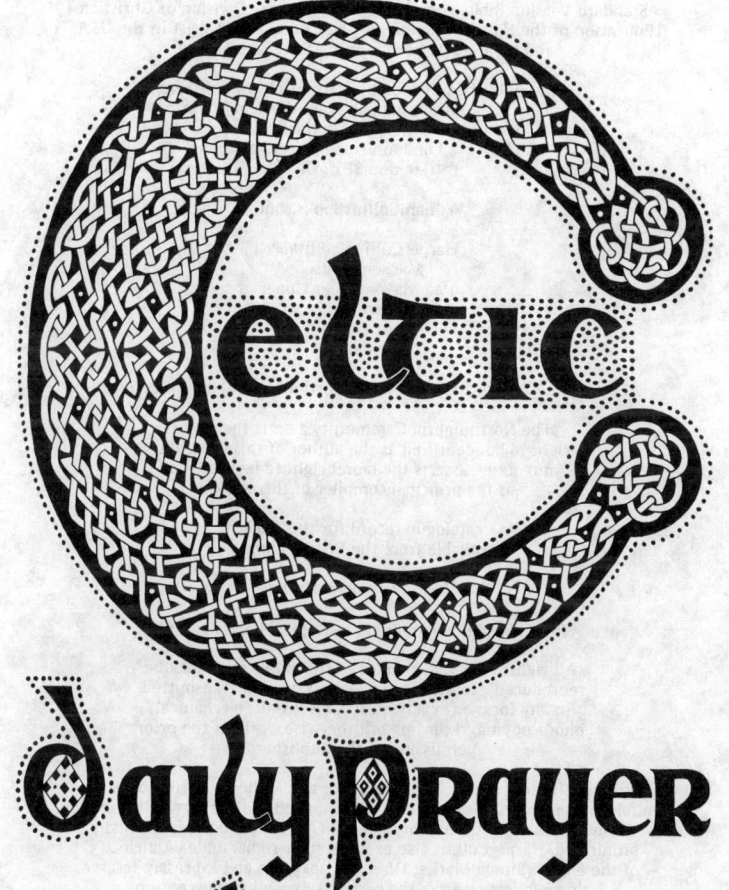

Celtic Daily Prayer

Book One
The Journey Begins

This book contains material from *Celtic Daily Prayer*, first published
in Great Britain in 1994 by Marshall Pickering, and *Celtic Night Prayer*,
first published in 1996 by Marshall Pickering.

The Scripture quotations contained herein are from the New Revised
Standard Version Bible, copyright © 1989, by the Division of Christian
Education of the National Council of the Churches of Christ in the USA,
and are used by permission. All rights reserved.

First published in 2002 by HarperCollins*Publishers*
This 2015 edition published by William Collins
An imprint of HarperCollins*Publishers*
1 London Bridge Street,
London SE1 9GF

WilliamCollinsBooks.com

HarperCollins*Publishers*
Macken House,
39/40 Mayor Street Upper,
Dublin 1
D01 C9W8
Ireland

Copyright © 2000, 2005, 2015 The Northumbria Community Trust

The Northumbria Community asserts the moral
right to be identified as the author of this work and
Andy Raine asserts the moral right to be identified
as the principal compiler of this work.

A catalogue record for this book is
available from the British Library.

ISBN 978-0-00-812302-4

Printed and bound in India by Replika Press Pvt. Ltd.

All rights reserved. No part of this publication may be
reproduced, stored in a retrieval system, or transmitted,
in any form or by any means, electronic, mechanical,
photocopying, recording or otherwise, without the prior
permission of the publishers.

Without limiting the exclusive rights of any author, contributor or the
publisher of this publication, any unauthorised use of this publication to
train generative artificial intelligence (AI) technologies is expressly
prohibited. HarperCollins also exercise their rights under Article 4(3)
of the Digital Single Market Directive 2019/790 and expressly reserve
this publication from the text and data mining exception.

This book contains FSC™ certified paper and other controlled sources
to ensure responsible forest management.

For more information visit: www.harpercollins.co.uk/green

CONTENTS

This book is the first of two volumes of *Celtic Daily Prayer* that are numbered continuously. Pages 837–1668 can be found in *Celtic Daily Prayer Book Two: Farther Up and Farther In*.

Opening invocation	xi
About this book	1
DAILY OFFICE	**11**
How to use Daily Office	13
Morning Prayer	16
Midday Prayer	19
Evening Prayer	21
Meditations for each day of the month	26
Compline (night prayer)	53
How to use Compline	53
Sunday – the Ita Compline	54
Monday – the Aidan Compline	57
Tuesday – the Cuthbert Compline	60
Wednesday – the Felgild Compline	64
Thursday – the Ebba Compline	66
Friday – the Boisil Compline	68
Saturday – the Patrick Compline	70
COMMUNION	**75**
SHABBAT	**89**
Why Shabbat?	89
The Welcoming of Shabbat	91
Shabbat	94
Havdala (end of Shabbat)	97

TIMES AND SEASONS 103

Advent	105
An evening prayer for blessing during Advent	107
A prayer before a Christmas crib	108
The Advent antiphons	108
Christmas	112
New Year	115
The opening door	115
A covenant service	116
Light a candle in the darkness	121
Lent	123
Approaching Easter	125
Foot washing	125
The way of the cross	128
Easter Eve	141
Easter	144
An Easter vigil	144
The Sunday after Easter	154
Ascension	157
Pentecost	160
Harvest	161
Veni creator	161
Awakening	162
A time to gather	162
From the Celtic psalter	163
A harvest offering	163
The gathering of joy and pain	164
A harvest prayer	164
Care of the land, care for the world	165

RITES OF PASSAGE 167

Coming into the light – birth	169
Prayers for the Christening or	
dedication of a child	169
Coming into the light – rebirth	174
A baptismal prayer	174
A confession of faith	174
Marriage – light and shadow	176

A marrying prayer	176
Thigpen's wedding	176
Peace-prayer for a wedding	177
Marriage blessings	178
In difficulties	178
The ultimate answer	179
Prayer for reconciliation	179
In difficult times	**180**
On separation from loved ones	180
A prayer in time of darkness	180
A prayer in brokenness	181
A general intercession for those in trouble	182
Mid-life	**183**
Mid-life appraisal	183
A prayer in 'the middle years' of opportunity	184
Liminal space	**185**
Where earth and heaven meet	185
Prayers for sleepless nights	185
Courage, hope and peace	186
The shadow of death	**187**
Death and dying	187
A prayer on behalf of the dying	188
Facing death with courage	189
Watching with one who is dying	190
The darkness of bereavement	**190**
Walking with grief	190
Come now	191
A caim written as a night prayer for someone recently bereaved	192
Caelan – for the loss of a child	192

BLESSINGS AND GRACES 197

Prayers for blessings	**199**
For a journey	200
Blessings	**200**
On the departure of a well-loved guest	200
Till we meet again	200
A blessing on someone's journey or on a child	201

Just you	201
Nan's blessing	201
My prayer for you	202
Caim prayer (When I do not know what to pray)	203
Graces	205
A Hebridean grace	205
Brigid's grace	205
Shabbat	205
From the Isle of Lewis	206
The stranger's blessing	206
Saranam (refuge)	206
Community thanksgiving	206
Leading up to Christmas	207
Christmas	207

FOLLOW THE EXAMPLE — 209

Calendar and resources for saints' days and festivals	211
Brigid – in welcoming	267
A house-blessing	268
Prayers for a workplace	274
Oswald – in practical ways	277
Prayers for committing our work to God	278
Aidan – in the power of the Spirit	282
Prayers for being sent out with God's blessing	282
Chad – in willing service	286
Prayers for a journey or at a time of change	286
Hild – in the right place	291
Wrestling with the call of God	291
Cuthbert – into a desert place	295
For a solitary retreat	296
Brendan – in exploration of a vision	302
Prayers for a spiritual journey	302
Ninian – in relating to the whole of life	318
Prayers for the blessing of the land and of life	319
Caedmon – in declaration of a dream	321
Prayers about becoming a voice for those who have no voice	322
A litany of saints – The house that John built	326

THE AIDAN SERIES OF DAILY READINGS — 329

January: Consider my meditation — 332
February: Devoted to Him — 352
March: Ask for the old paths — 370
April: The inward journey — 392
May: Crossroads — 409
   All your creatures — 423
   Gift from the sea — 429
June: Desert Fathers — 438
July: Pilgrimage — 453
August: Iona — 482
September: In the shadow of Aidan — 510
October: With understanding — 529
November: Chosen people — 553
December: Deeper life — 580

THE FINAN SERIES OF DAILY READINGS — 599

January: Be Thou my vision — 601
February: Doorkeepers — 619
March: Small beginnings — 637
April: Abandonment — 653
May: To a young disciple — 668
June: Jesus of the scars — 688
July: The city without a church — 706
August: What gives you the right? — 719
   Without walls — 726
September: Standing in the secret — 736
   Broken gold — 745
   Celtic insight — 748
October: Parting and planting — 756
November: The house that John built — 772
December: Enter in — 789

THANKS AND ACKNOWLEDGEMENTS — 811

Cross-references — 813
Sources and acknowledgements — 828
Bibliography — 834
Contact details for the Northumbria Community — 836

Invocation of the Holy Spirit

Most powerful Holy Spirit,
    come down
        upon us
and subdue us.

From heaven,
    where the ordinary
        is made glorious,
    and glory seems
but ordinary,

bathe us
    with the brilliance
    of Your light
like dew.

About this book

If you are beginning this book right here in the introductory pages, you probably have a number of questions in your mind:

- Where do these prayers and liturgies come from?
- Why is it called a *Celtic* daily prayer book?
- What is the Northumbria Community?
- How might I best use this book?
- Is it for personal or group use?
- Is it for me?

We have tried to make this volume as easy as possible to use – and our prayer is that a worthwhile spiritual voyage of exploration may be in store for those who want to embark on it without further introduction. But still the questions remain, begging answers. It is difficult to address each one in isolation, since the story behind the liturgies is also the story of the Northumbria Community itself; and, taken together, they form a closely woven garment created and worn by a large number of very different people who have found themselves companions on similar journeys – alone but yet, to the surprise and delight of the travellers, together.

Whatever the starting points for our very different journeys, and whatever language we use to describe them, there are some common tasks that we all engage in: looking for signposts to tell us where we are; trying to make sense of what we have already experienced along the way; and seeking to know what lies ahead and at journey's end. Life, in short, is a pilgrimage; and the contents of this prayer book, *Celtic Daily Prayer Book One: The Journey Begins*, may justly be taken as songs to sing and stories to tell along the road.

The Upper and Nether Springs

> God will make a watered garden:
> upper springs and nether springs
> in the field that Father's given.

One of the key starting points on this particular journey is Holy Island – the island of Lindisfarne, lying just off the beautiful coastline of north Northumberland, cut off from the mainland at each high tide and in itself a rich storehouse of stories about the development and growth of the Christian faith in Britain and beyond. In 1976, Andy Raine, the main compiler of the material used in this book, came to live on the island. Fairly soon, the rhythm of prayer and attention to Scripture drew his focus to the story of Caleb and his daughter Achsah and her husband Othniel in Judges 1:14-15. As the people of Israel took possession of their promised land, Caleb was able to give land to his daughter and son-in-law; but it was dry land and they needed sources of water. Caleb, we read, not only granted them the 'upper' springs but the lower, hidden or 'nether' ones as well. It seemed to Andy and others that Holy Island itself filled the role of the Upper Springs. But where were the Nether Springs? That quest forms an important part of our story.

At about the same time, John Skinner and his wife Linda, who were to be the driving force in the foundation of the Community, were struck by the passage in Isaiah 58:11-12, which speaks of restoring foundations from times long past; of springs whose waters never fail; and of building out of brokenness. Many visitors came to their home, and for a time Andy Raine lived with them. It was a significant taste, even then, of what community was to mean.

Each year around Easter time a 'Workshop' would be held and friends would gather, both from the local area and from much further afield, seeking answers to the question, 'How then shall we live?' and exploring the ancient paths of Desert and Celtic spirituality. Years of struggle followed as the families and individuals journeying together locally struggled to discover what it meant to live as contemplatives with growing children, financial pressures and a constant stream of visitors. They would take any work that came along (window cleaning, gardening, anything) to survive in the land they felt they had been called to pray for and to live in. John Skinner, in describing this period, says, 'We were just following what we felt was our own call, with no thought of starting something, but people just began to come, and they didn't stop coming. In time we had so many people visiting that we couldn't do our work any more.' Something had indeed started and a place of welcome was needed around its 'Nether Springs'.

It was in October 1992 that the Nether Springs found a home at Hetton Hall, a large house with a central peel tower (testifying to its early history in the days of border warfare) set in grounds that included a lovely prayer garden. It was located close to Cuthbert's Cave in the Kyloe Hills, where the saint's body was carried by the monks from Holy Island fleeing from the Viking invaders. And, yes, the water supply was spring-fed. This was to be the Mother House of the Community for eighteen years, providing a place of retreat and reflection for those in Community – or indeed for anybody else who wished to come. Even though it was in many ways a very ordinary place, it was a haven, a safe place in which to encounter God. Study breaks could be accommodated and teaching courses were held there through the year; and Hetton Hall not only provided a base for Community folk living in north Northumberland, but it was also a focal point for the many dispersed around the country – and around the world. 'Nether Springs' serves as one expression of the monastic heart of the Community's ethos as well as being an administrative centre for much of the mission and work of the wider Community. In 2010 'Nether Springs' relocated to Acton Home Farm, near Felton in Northumberland, and continues its role as the Mother House of the Community. In providing a place of seeking God and of hospitality, it can be a home committed to new monastic formation, and may offer a window into the wider Community's life and work. The Community is not only 'there': it is everywhere where Companions are on their journey.

The liturgies

> I bind unto myself this day
> the strong name of the Trinity.

The liturgies, prayers and meditations you will find in this book were forged on the anvil of hard years of struggle and pain as the journey together unfolded. They draw from a deep well of spiritual experience transcending fashion, culture and denomination. At the heart of them lies the Daily Office – the prayers to be used, either individually or communally, each day in the morning, at midday and in the evening. It was discovered very early that one of the precious gifts handed down to us through the monastic tradition is the persistent rhythm of the daily offices – repeating words of timeless spiritual truth, drawn largely from the Psalms, until they grow into the very core of our being, helping to define who we are and to whom we belong. The prayers came together in time for one of the Easter Workshops, and they immediately felt comfortable – simple and strong.

After the daily prayers the 'Meditations for each day of the month' were chosen. These are thoughts that have come to have special significance to those on the journey, throwing a special light on the way ahead and providing landmarks to help mark the path. These thoughts may be direct from Scripture, or may be inspired by Scripture, or may be prayers and sayings by others that have been found especially relevant and have become part of our own story.

Morning and Evening Prayer call for different passages of Scripture to be read each day; and so series of daily readings were prepared to provide a cycle of these and to add brief commentaries on them. The commentaries were often extracts from writers whose words were found to be particularly helpful. Taken together each day within the discipline of Daily Office, there is a satisfying mix of ingrained liturgy, familiar meditation and fresh inspiration.

Those who have ever used a liturgy of Compline will know how appropriate it can be as a gentle way of rounding off the day. And so a different form of Compline for each day of the week was prepared, drawing especially from the *Carmina Gadelica*, and dedicated to some of the Celtic saints whose lives have been such a strong influence on Northumbria in general and on the Community in particular.

Of course, there are many more Celtic saints than days of the week, and other liturgies inspired by them have been prepared for particular uses. (You will find these in the section called 'Follow the example'.)

The rite of Holy Communion included in this book does not in any way attempt to replicate what would have been familiar to seventh-century Northumbrians. Most of us would find their Eucharistic liturgy very long, very Latin and very laborious, however immediate and accessible the surroundings and manner of celebration! Today on the one hand, we have celebrants in Catholic, Anglican/Episcopal and Orthodox congregations who are glad to find individual prayers that are acceptable for substitution at various points in their regular or occasional liturgies of Mass or Communion; we commend the text of this form of service to them as a resource to dip into. On the other hand, there are congregations who have always shared in the breaking of bread together, but without any written form of words beyond those recorded in Scripture. Some of them have found our experimental forms of Communion helpful; and the version used here is one that benefits from various practical considerations and careful revision into a new framework. The Jewish tradition of Family Shabbat, adapted with prayers from the Celtic tradition, finds its place in our book – moreover, it provides a liturgical means of honouring women. The Community is rather like a big, sprawling family; gatherings are often family reunions! Many means are sought to strengthen the bonds between us (and to provide channels of healing where there is dispute).

As these and the other liturgies in this collection were devised, accepted and recorded, they came to be published initially in Filofax form, with each month's series of daily readings being distributed to subscribers to add into the binder. Somewhat to everybody's surprise, this began to circulate more widely, and the demand led to the publication by HarperCollins first of *Celtic Daily Prayer* and, subsequently, *Celtic Night Prayer*. This in turn led to this current book, a combined volume, now reissued as *Celtic Daily Prayer Book One: The Journey Begins*, which has been sold to many thousands of people and is also being translated into a number of languages. It is our prayer that, whether or not you wish to join us as companions on our journey, you will find material here that will enrich your spiritual life and draw you closer to God.

From the beginning, all the daily prayers have had sung, as well as spoken versions; and many of the meditations, and parts of other liturgies and Complines, also have musical settings. These recordings have played an important part in linking Companions and Friends together wherever they may be – at home, in the workplace or travelling.

Why Celtic?

Here I stand;
and I say a prayer.

Things Celtic are currently very much in fashion – but that was not so much the case when these liturgies were first devised. In order to make sense of the journey, we needed to 'explore the old paths' to find what they could teach us. Often these are neglected in the headlong embrace of everything that is new. The 'old paths' all around us here in Northumbria resound with the startling testimony of the remarkable men and women who simply loved God and followed Jesus wherever the Spirit impelled and empowered them to go; they lit a fire in the so-called 'dark ages' that brought warmth, culture, learning and, most of all, faith to vast numbers of people.

As we researched and studied these saints (and the Desert Fathers and Mothers, who were their spiritual predecessors) we found that many of the lessons they taught gave us hope and coherence on our own journey: that people matter more than things, and relationships more than reputation; that prayer and action, contemplation and involvement, all belong together. Whilst resisting the temptation to hark back to some mythical 'golden age' (which probably never existed), we have attempted to be true to what we have learned and lived in the shadow of the Northumbrian saints and their teachers. We are not trying to say that these prayers and simple liturgies are similar to anything used in seventh-century Northumbria; but we do hope that the relevance and immediacy of their style reflect the faithful and uncompromising lives of those whose example we attempt to follow.

Some of the prayers, stories and illustrations in this book are very old; others are more current. We make no apologies for this mix. If the early Celtic saints (and those whom they taught to follow in similar well-trodden ways of prayer and courageous mission) have much to say to us in our own generation and culture, then it must be interpreted in a more contemporary idiom where necessary.

Northumbria Community

> God called forth a people;
> and we responded to His call.

Northumbria Community in its present form emerged as an expression of the mixed life that embraces both the contemplative and the apostolic in the context of a shared vision and vocation. Historically, Celtic Christian monasticism was noted for its combining of monastery and mission. Ordinary Christian people found ways of weaving disciplines of prayer into their daily life. From the earliest days we were aware of this call to a continuity of purpose which would enable us to help 'rebuild the ancient ruins and raise up the age-old foundations' of our forefathers and mothers in the faith. We were being slowly drawn into a monastic way, but this was a new and different monasticism. Dietrich Bonhoeffer spoke of a similar call when he wrote: 'The renewal of the Church will come from a new type of monasticism which only has in common with the old an uncompromising allegiance to the Sermon on the Mount. It is high time people banded together to do this.'

This understanding of people united by a common vision was central to our formation as a geographically dispersed Community. In effect two groups came together: the one mainly emphasising the monastic, contemplative stream; and the other emphasising the apostolic and the need to take the monastery through mission into the marketplace. The former were represented by the original 'Nether Springs Trust' which was formed to release John and Linda Skinner into establishing this 'new monastic' vision. The latter were Northumbria Ministries, led by Roy Searle, whose vision was to see fires lit all over the ancient kingdom of Northumbria – and to carry the torch of the gospel wherever the Father leads. The merging of the two groups in 1990 formed the Northumbria Community. In our growth and development we have gradually understood that for us this being 'banded together' was expressed in being alone yet together, enriched by our diversity but united in heart by our common commitment to our vows, in which we say 'YES' to Availability and Vulnerability, and in being Companions together in Community.

Although the Community has grown, Companions and Friends, many living geographically distanced from one another, still value opportunities of being at the Mother House or at other Community Houses in the UK and abroad. Also, in some areas, Community groups have been established, meeting monthly, but only if Companions within reach of each other discern that this should be a priority. Inevitably such groups take on a life and form of their own, with each individual contributing to the wide variety of experience and styles of a disparate collection of people finding themselves on a journey together. Friendship and the sharing of stories, music and the arts in general provide the natural means to help us engage with people of all backgrounds and interests in a manner that leaps across the boundaries of church and religion.

Community Teams are sometimes pulled together with opportunities to engage with many beyond the walls of any church, perhaps at festivals, on pilgrimages, in schools and colleges, or invited to journey 'wherever the Father leads' following particular initiatives prompted by listening prayer. Strong emphasis is placed upon creativity and music, dance, storytelling and other expressive arts, evidenced whenever the Community gathers or is 'on the road'.

At 'Nether Springs' and through our website, we sell books, cards, music and other resources to enable the stories and insights to be passed on to a wider audience. This reflects the desert tradition of 'basket-making' and helps raise funds for the Community.

In carrying out all these activities we are very concerned that the Community does not become institutionalised. The rather anonymous, raw and ragged style of the early part of the journey remains a vital part of the Community ethos as we grow and develop. We aspire to measure ourselves constantly against these words of William Stringfellow, which have long been an inspiration to us:

> Dynamic and erratic, spontaneous and radical, audacious and immature, committed if not altogether coherent, ecumenically

open and often experimental, visible here and there, now and then, but unsettled institutionally. Almost monastic in nature, but most of all enacting a fearful hope for human life in society.

If, having used this book, you wish to know more about the Northumbria Community, we invite you to get in touch with us using the contact details given at the end.

The Community Rule of Availability and Vulnerability

> I say 'Yes, my Lord'
> in all the good times,
> through all the bad times.

In the same way as the liturgies emerged from lives actually lived in community, so has the Community's Rule. It is a response to that insistent question: 'How then shall we live?' It is a call to risky living: it is not a comfortable or easy solution to life's problems. Whilst we welcome any who wish to walk with us in seeking God, we ask that those who wish to become Companions with us in Community say 'YES' to Availability and Vulnerability as their way of living. This involves availability to God and to others – expressed in a commitment to being alone with God in the cell of our own heart and to being available for hospitality, intercession and mission. Intentional vulnerability is expressed through being teachable in the discipline of prayer, saturation in the Scriptures and being accountable to one another, often through soul-friendships. It also means 'embracing the heretical imperative' (challenging assumed truth), being receptive to constructive criticism, affirming that relationships matter more than reputation, and living openly among people as 'church without walls'. This is not something to be entered into lightly!

How to use this book

> If you want to live life free,
> take your time, go slowly.
> Do few things, but do them well.
> Simple joys are holy.

Most of this book is best used on an individual basis or in the context of a small family group. The starting-point must be the Daily Office, with its accompanying Meditation and Daily reading. It is strongly recommended that, before using this book, you read the section entitled 'How to use the Daily Office': it will be your best introduction to the style of worship that pervades this prayer book.

Having established the pattern of daily prayer and perhaps incorporated the Complines into daily use, you can dip into the rest of the liturgies as a resource book for worship on specific occasions or to meet particular needs. This can still be on an individual or small-group basis, but these additional liturgies are ideal for use by larger groups. Those with responsibility for leading worship may find material here to dip into or to inspire their own creativity. If you do this, we only ask that you respect the copyright both of the Community in this publication and of those whose work we, in our turn, have used in this compilation (for details see the 'Sources and Acknowledgements' section, p.828). We will be able to advise you on such matters (see the 'Contact details', p.836).

Whether you use this book daily or as an occasional resource to dip into, we pray, with you, in the words of an old Celtic blessing:

> O God, make clear to us each road.
> O God, make safe to us each steep;
> when we stumble, hold us;
> when we fall, lift us up.
> When we are hard-pressed with evil,
> deliver us;
> and bring us at last to Your glory.

Daily Office

DAILY OFFICE

How to use Daily Office

The Daily Office – Morning, Midday and Evening Prayer – is at the core of the life of the Northumbria Community. A regular cycle of daily prayers constitutes the essential rhythm of life around which other activities can take their proper place. In this respect the Community follows the rich tradition of monastic communities through the centuries. At 'Nether Springs', the Mother House of the Community, the Office is said or sung, by guests and Community folk, at set times in the chapel or in other rooms prepared for worship. Saying at least one of the Offices can be a natural part of the rhythm of our day; individuals can work out when it is possible to say Office and some families even achieve saying Office at home together. The Office can be said anywhere, but ideally, for Morning and Evening Prayer, a quiet place, as free from interruptions as possible, is chosen. Our lives are usually too full of noise, so this could be the ideal moment of the day to experience real silence.

Starting and ending

Daily Office (and indeed each liturgy in this prayer book) will be best begun and ended with a few moments of reflective silence; and by affirming that the prayers are said in 'the name of the Father, and of the Son and of the Holy Spirit'. Many (especially those whose church tradition usually scorns such gestures) find that making the sign of the cross at this juncture helps to reinforce the significance of the words.

Sources and music

The words of the Daily Office are drawn from a variety of sources (see 'Sources and Acknowledgements', p.828), such as St Patrick's Breastplate, Teresa's Bookmark, Columba's Blessing and so on – and from Psalm 27 for Morning Prayer, Psalm 90 for Midday Prayer and Psalm 130 for Evening Prayer. There are sung versions of all parts of the Daily Office which are available in CD, MP3 and music-sheet form (for more information see 'Contact details for the Northumbria Community', p.836). Many have found that the use of these recordings whilst travelling to or from work by car can be very helpful, and reinforces the knowledge that we are praying 'alone, together'.

Scriptures, reading and meditation

Morning and Evening Prayer include Scriptures, readings, meditations and prayers. The Aidan and Finan series of Daily readings in this book can be used to provide a coherent pattern of Scripture readings and commentaries for this use. Most of the selected Scriptures are short, and time should be allowed after each reading for its meaning to filter down from the head to the heart, and to seek the significance of each for that day. The relevant meditation for the day of the month follows, and repetition of them month by month turns them into familiar friends – they are worth learning by heart. Again, time should be allowed for new insights to develop in the mind and heart before moving on. Some find that the mornings tend to be too rushed for lengthy silences and that this can best wait till Evening Prayer. The important thing is to find a rhythm that works for you. If you are praying on your own, and have formed the habit of keeping a spiritual journal or prayer diary, this may be the right moment of the day to make entries in it.

Prayer

After the Scripture readings and meditations, there is an opportunity to pray whatever is on your mind and heart, offering to God the concerns of the day, your personal needs and prayers for other people. A 'prayer basket' or 'prayer pot' may be used, from which are selected three names for holding up before God. The basket or prayer pot contains slips of paper on which have been written the names of folk to be remembered in prayer. (It is, of course, important that names are added and removed regularly as circumstances change.) The selected slips may be placed where they can be seen from time to time during the day, or carried around, as a reminder for continued prayer. The Community also uses a regularly produced Prayer Guide. (To request copies of this, use the 'Contact details' on p.836.) At 'Nether Springs', the custom is to have a time of silent prayer after reading the day's entry from the Prayer Guide. When there is no information about the particular needs of the persons, families and situations brought to mind, the following prayer is helpful:

> These dear ones, O Lord,
> bless Thou and keep
> in every place where they are.

Midday prayer

This is specially devised for use in the middle of a busy working day. For this reason it is short, and can be prayed in the time it takes to boil a kettle, especially if committed to memory. Some find it helpful to make a point of saying it whilst moving around (whilst preparing lunch, for instance), as a reminder to pray as we work and work as we pray. Others find it a welcome opportunity to withdraw from the tensions and busyness of the day to spend some time being quiet and alone with God, putting the day's work into a different perspective.

Midday Prayer retains the 'Thee' and 'Thou' forms of speech. This may seem unfamiliar to the many who are used only to modern language, but it is a deliberate attempt to highlight the contemporary relevance of the treasure of prayer from long ago.

Morning Prayer

*Said or sung all together except for the sentences marked
'Call' which are for the Leader only.
+ indicates that you may make the sign of the cross.
All say together the sections in **bold** type.*

+ **In the name of the Father,
and of the Son,
and of the Holy Spirit.
Amen.**

Opening sentences

**One thing I have asked of the Lord,
this is what I seek:
that I may dwell in the house of the Lord
all the days of my life;
to behold the beauty of the Lord
and to seek Him in His temple.**

Call Who is it that you seek?
Response **We seek the Lord our God.**

Call Do you seek Him with all your heart?
Response **Amen. Lord, have mercy.**

Call Do you seek Him with all your soul?
Response **Amen. Lord, have mercy.**

Call Do you seek Him with all your mind?
Response **Amen. Lord, have mercy.**

Call Do you seek Him with all your strength?
Response **Amen. Christ, have mercy.**

Declaration of faith

> **To whom shall we go?**
> **You have the words of eternal life,**
> **and we have believed and have come to know**
> **that You are the Holy One of God.**
>
> **Praise to You, Lord Jesus Christ,**
> **King of endless glory.**

Scripture readings

> Psalm
> Old Testament Scripture
> New Testament Scripture

Daily reading

Meditation for the day of the month (see pages 27–52)

Prayers for others

Canticle

Christ, as a light
illumine and guide me.
Christ, as a shield
overshadow me.
Christ under me;
Christ over me;
Christ beside me
on my left and my right.
This day be within and without me,
lowly and meek, yet all-powerful.
Be in the heart of each to whom I speak;
in the mouth of each who speaks unto me.
This day be within and without me,
lowly and meek, yet all-powerful.
Christ as a light;
Christ as a shield;
Christ beside me
on my left and my right.

Blessing

May the peace of the Lord Christ go with you,
wherever He may send you.
May He guide you through the wilderness,
protect you through the storm.
May He bring you home rejoicing
at the wonders He has shown you.
May He bring you home rejoicing
once again into our doors.

+ In the name of the Father,
and of the Son,
and of the Holy Spirit.
Amen.

Midday Prayer

Said or sung all together.
+ indicates that you may make the sign of the cross.
*All say together the sections in **bold** type.*

+ **In the name of the Father,**
  and of the Son,
  and of the Holy Spirit.
  Amen.

Opening sentences

Let the beauty of the Lord our God be upon us.
Establish Thou the work of our hands;
establish Thou the work of our hands.

The Lord's Prayer

Our Father, who art in heaven,
hallowed be Thy name;
Thy kingdom come;
Thy will be done;
on earth as it is in heaven.
Give us this day our daily bread
and forgive us our trespasses
as we forgive those who trespass against us.
And lead us not into temptation;
but deliver us from evil.
Amen.

Declaration of faith

> We believe and trust in God the Father Almighty.
> We believe and trust in Jesus Christ His Son.
> We believe and trust in the Holy Spirit.
> We believe and trust in the Three in One.

Canticle

> Teach us, dear Lord, to number our days;
> that we may apply our hearts unto wisdom.
> Oh, satisfy us early with Thy mercy,
> that we may rejoice and be glad all of our days.
> And let the beauty of the Lord our God be upon us;
> and establish Thou the work of our hands.
> And let the beauty of the Lord our God be upon us;
> and establish Thou the work of our hands, dear Lord.

Blessing

> Let nothing disturb thee,
> nothing affright thee;
> all things are passing,
> God never changeth!
> Patient endurance attaineth to all things;
> who God possesseth
> in nothing is wanting;
> alone God sufficeth.

+ In the name of the Father,
  and of the Son,
  and of the Holy Spirit.
  Amen.

Evening Prayer

*Said or sung all together except for the sentences marked
'Call' which are for the Leader only.
+ indicates that you may make the sign of the cross.
All say together the sections in **bold** type.*

+ **In the name of the Father,
and of the Son,
and of the Holy Spirit.
Amen.**

Opening sentences

**My soul waits for the Lord
more than those
who watch for the morning,
more than those
who watch for the morning.**

Call   Out of the depths I have cried to You.
Response   **O Lord, hear my voice.**

Call   With my whole heart I want to praise You.
Response   **O Lord, hear my voice.**

Call   If You, Lord, should mark iniquities:
Response   **who could stand? who could stand?**

**I will wait for the Lord.
My soul waits,
and in His word
do I hope.**

Expressions of faith

Lord, You have always given
bread for the coming day;
and though I am poor,
  today I believe.

Lord, You have always given
strength for the coming day;
and though I am weak,
  today I believe.

Lord, You have always given
peace for the coming day;
and though of anxious heart,
  today I believe.

Lord, You have always kept
me safe in trials;
and now, tried as I am,
  today I believe.

Lord, You have always marked
the road for the coming day;
and though it may be hidden,
  today I believe.

Lord, You have always lightened
this darkness of mine;
and though the night is here,
  today I believe.

Lord, You have always spoken
when time was ripe;
and though You be silent now,
  today I believe.

Scripture readings

> Psalm
> Old Testament Scripture
> New Testament Scripture

Daily reading

Meditation for the day of the month (see pages 27–52)

Prayers for others

Canticle

In the shadow of Your wings
I will sing Your praises, O Lord.

The Lord is my light, my salvation;
whom shall I fear?
The Lord is the refuge of my life;
of whom shall I be afraid?

In the shadow of Your wings
I will sing Your praises, O Lord.

One thing I ask of the Lord,
one thing I seek;
to dwell in the presence of my God,
to gaze on Your holy place.

In the shadow of Your wings
I will sing Your praises, O Lord.

I believe I shall see the goodness
of the Lord in the land of the living.
O wait for the Lord!
Have courage and wait,
wait for the Lord.

In the shadow of Your wings
I will sing Your praises, O Lord.

Blessing

> See that you be at peace among yourselves, my children,
> and love one another.
> Follow the example of the wise and the good,
> and God will comfort you and help you,
> both in this world
> and in the world which is to come.

> + In the name of the Father,
> and of the Son,
> and of the Holy Spirit.
> Amen.

Meditations for each day of the month

The 31 meditations presented here for use day by day during each month have particular significance in the life of the Northumbria Community. Each one tells a special part of the Community's story, highlights an essential foundation stone or evokes a key memory. Readers who have not shared the Community's journey are invited to enter into the spirit of them. Using these meditations month by month will, we hope, turn them into dearly loved companions on your own journey too. To make this element of the Daily Office more personal to you, you could add or substitute some of your own special foundational words (e.g. Scripture verses, poetry, extracts from your own spiritual journal or other writings that have touched you deeply), reminding yourself of them month by month.

Many of the meditations have musical versions (another aid to remembering them). For instance, the meditation for Day 25 can be sung to the tune of 'Annie Laurie'.

As these meditations become more familiar, thinking of the date in the month can immediately call to mind the words of the appropriate meditation. Making a conscious habit of this can be a means of making a spiritual connection at any time just by thinking of the date – a very helpful technique for putting the pressures of the day into a wider and deeper perspective.

Day 1

It is a difficult
   lesson to learn today,
to leave one's friends
   and family and deliberately
practise the art of solitude
   for an hour or a day
      or a week.
   For me, the break
is most difficult...

And yet, once it is done,
   I find there is a quality
to being alone that is
   incredibly precious.

   Life rushes back into the void,
      richer,
         more vivid,
            fuller than before!

Anne Morrow Lindbergh

Day 2

There is a contemplative
   in all of us,
almost strangled
   but still alive,
who craves quiet
   enjoyment of the Now,
and longs to touch
   the seamless

garment of silence
   which
makes whole.

Alan P. Tory

Carmelite vow

Let each stay in or near
   their own cell
meditating, day and night
   on the law of the Lord,
     and vigilant in prayer,
   unless otherwise employed
     by the Holy Spirit.

Day 3

The Cry to God as 'Father'
   in the New Testament
is not a calm acknowledgement
   of a universal truth about
God's abstract fatherhood.
It is the Child's cry
   out of a nightmare.

It is the cry of outrage,
   fear, shrinking away,
when faced with the horror
     of the 'world'
   – yet not simply or exclusively
     protest, but trust as well.

'Abba Father'
   all things are possible
     to Thee...

Rowan Williams

Day 4

Prayer of abandonment to God

Father, I abandon myself
   into Your hands.
Do with me what You will,
whatever You do, I will thank You,
I am ready for all, I accept all.
Let only Your will be done in me,
   as in all Your creatures,
and I'll ask nothing else, my Lord.

Into Your hands I commend my spirit;
I give it to You
   with all the love of my heart,
for I love You, Lord,
   and so need to give myself,
to surrender myself into Your hands
   with a trust beyond all measure,
   because You are my Father.

Charles de Foucauld

Day 5

The Methodist covenant prayer

I am no longer my own, but Thine.
Put me to what Thou wilt,
   rank me with whom Thou wilt;
put me to doing, put me to suffering;
let me be employed for Thee
   or laid aside for Thee;
let me be exalted for Thee,
   or brought low for Thee;
let me be full, let me be empty;

let me have all things,
    let me have nothing;
I freely and heartily yield all things
    to Thy pleasure and disposal.

And now, O glorious and blessèd God,
    Father, Son and Holy Spirit,
Thou art mine, and I am Thine.
    So be it.
And the covenant
    which I have made on earth,
    let it be ratified in heaven.
Amen.

Day 6

If I only love Jesus

I praise the wounds
    and the blood of the Lamb
    that heals the weakness
        of my body,
I praise the wounds
    and the blood of the Lamb
    that heals the weakness
        of my soul,
I praise the wounds
    and the blood of the Lamb
    that heals the weakness
        of my spirit!

Praise be to the blood of the Lamb
    in His forgiving power.
Praise be to the blood of the Lamb
    in His cleansing power.
Praise be to the blood of the Lamb
    in His saving power.

Praise be to the blood of the Lamb
  in His releasing power.
Praise be to the blood of the Lamb
  in His victorious power.
Praise be to the blood of the Lamb
  in His renewing power.
Praise be to the blood of the Lamb
  in His protecting power.

For whoever believes
  in the power of the blood of Jesus,
    nothing is impossible.

I praise the blood of the Lamb
  that covers all my sins
    so that they can no
    longer be seen,
I praise the blood of the Lamb
  that cleanses me
    from all my sins
    and makes me
    white as snow,
I praise the blood of the Lamb
  that has power to free me
    from all my bondages
    and chains of sin.

I praise the blood of the Lamb
  that makes all things new.
    Hallelujah! Amen.

M. Basilea Schlink

Day 7

For whoever believes
  in the power
  of the blood of Jesus,
nothing is impossible!

The Lord shall surely
  perfect that thing,
  that thing
  which concerneth thee.

To whoever believes
  in the power
  of the blood
  of the Crucified Lamb,
nothing shall be called impossible!

Blessed be the Lamb
  that was slain before
  the foundation of the world.

Day 8

I find Thee enthroned in my heart,
  my Lord Jesus.
It is enough.
I know that Thou art throned
  in heaven.
My heart and heaven are one.

Alistair Maclean

Day 9

The fast

Is this not the fast that I have chosen:
to loose the bonds of wickedness?
to undo the heavy burden?
and to let the oppressed go free?
that you break every yoke?

Is it not to share your bread with the hungry?
that you bring to your house those who are cast down?
when you see the naked person that you cover them?
and not hide yourself from your own flesh and blood?

Then shall your light break forth as the morning;
healing shall spring forth speedily;
and your righteousness shall go before you;
the glory of the Lord shall be your rearguard.

Then you will call; and the Lord will answer.
You shall cry, and He will say,
   'Here I am.'

Is this not the fast that I have chosen:
to loose the bonds of wickedness?
to undo the heavy burden?
and to let the oppressed go free?
that you break every yoke?

And if you extend your soul to the hungry
and satisfy the afflicted soul,
then shall your light dawn in obscurity
and your darkness shall be as the noonday.

Then shall your light break forth as the morning;
healing shall spring forth speedily;
and your righteousness will go before you;

the glory of the Lord will be your rearguard.
Then you will call; and the Lord will answer.
You will cry, and He will say,
   'Here I am.'
You will cry, and He will say,
   'Here I am.'

The Lord will guide you always;
He will satisfy your needs in a sun-scorched land.
The Lord will strengthen your frame.
You will be like a well-watered garden,
like a spring whose waters never fail.

Your people will rebuild the ancient ruins
and will raise up the age-old foundations;
you will be called
   Repairer of Broken Walls,
   Restorer of Streets with Dwellings.

You will be like a well-watered garden,
like a spring whose waters never fail.

Adapted from Isaiah 58:6-12

Day 10

What mean these stones?

Land of my fathers,
how I long to return,
to touch thy earth,
and find again thy sacred paths,
well-walked with the Gospel of Peace,
veiled now in the shadow of mediocrity.

'What mean these stones'
which beset thy coastline,

who in twisted agony cry out
in praise and supplication of Him
and the renewal of the faith
that bled to secure them there?

Yet we would walk again
    thy sacred paths,
repair thy ancient ruins,
restore thy broken altars,
raise up the foundations
of many generations.

Hear this, you lands of the South
who hold many in captivity
by your empty words
and well-worn myths,
who neglect to see justice
for the poor, the widow,
    the fatherless.

Look to the North –
for lo your Redeemer comes,
clothed in the poverty of the few
who dare to speak His name,
    without vanity,
in a whisper,
    lest the earth should tremble.
Holy, Holy, Holy is the Lord.

Poor of Yahweh, arise,
take up the ancient mantle
which has awaited your day;
clothe yourselves within its humility,
for you have been set
as a stumbling block for many.

Day 11

Jeremiah's field

Weep, weep not for me,
    but weep for yourselves
    for the day has ended.
Weep not for me,
    for the night must come
    before the morning.
This is the time, the time
    for seeking the Lord.
This is the time, the time
    for weeping before Him.
Now is the time, the time
    for returning.

Set up the waymarks!
    turn your hearts
    towards the highway.
Turn again,
    turn again,
O virgin Israel.
Return to the Lord.

Day 12

In returning

In returning to Me,
    and waiting for Me,
    shall you be saved.
In quietness and confidence
    is your strength.
But we would trust ourselves
and stand in our own strength
and we shall be ashamed
    upon that day.

But the Lord still waits for you
  to show to you His love
  as He has said.
And He, He will conquer you
  so that He may bless you
  with Himself.
Blessed are they
who wait upon the Lord
for they shall weep no more,
  neither be afraid.

O my people in Jerusalem,
  weep no more,
for the Lord
  shall be gracious unto you,
  and show to you His love,
  as He has said.
And though He give to you the bread
and water of adversity,
with your own eyes
  you shall see your King,
  and you shall say,
  you shall say:
Blessèd is He! Blessèd is He!
Blessèd is He who comes
  in the name of the Lord!
Blessèd is He! Blessèd is He!
Blessèd is He who comes
  in the name of the Lord!

Tear down your images
and the idols that you have made,
for the Lord has prepared a fire
  to cover the earth.

And the glory of the Lord
  shall descend upon His hill
  upon that day.

And the law of the Lord
   shall go out from Zion
   in His name.
And all the nations of the earth
shall bow before the One
   they have pierced.
And the poor of the earth
   shall rejoice:
   Messiah has come!

Jesus! Emmanuel!
Blessèd is He who comes
   in the name of the Lord.
Lion of Judah!
Blessèd is He who comes
   in the name of the Lord.
Tear down your images
and the idols that you have made,
for the Lord has prepared a fire
   to cover the earth.

Reflections on Isaiah 30

Day 13

Achsah and Othniel

And so it was that Achsah kept urging Othniel her husband to ask from her father a field. She lighted from off her ass, and Caleb said to her, 'What is it that you want?' And she said to him, 'Give me a blessing, for you have given me this dark, desert land; now give me also springs of water.' And her father gave her the upper and the nether springs.

Judges 1:14-15

Day 14

The field

Every curse becomes a blessing
to the people of God's choosing.
He who spoke it shall perform it.
He shall bring on us the blessing,
   though the enemy may fight.
   My Jesus has done all things
      right.

In the dry and desert places
Jesus is our souls' oasis.
He will give us of His plenty,
fill the vessels once so empty,
   pour His waters on the ground,
   living waters gushing round.
See the land so black and barren;
God will make a watered garden:
fruitfulness where once
      was parchedness,
light to break into the darkness,
   upper springs
      and nether springs
   in the field
      that Father's given.

Satan tries, but cannot block it;
powers of Hell could never stop it.
Darkness flees as light is given.
God establishes His heaven
   in our hearts, and in this place
   shows the radiance of His face.

Reflections on Judges 1:14-15;
Numbers 24:1-10; Psalm 126:3-4

Day 15

The unclean spirit

> When an unclean spirit
> > has gone out of someone,
> it wanders through dry places,
> > seeking rest and finding none.
>
> Then it says,
> 'I will return into the house
> I came out of.'
> And when it gets there
> > it finds the house empty,
> > swept,
> > > and put in order.
>
> Then it goes,
> > and brings along
> > seven other spirits
> > more evil than itself,
> > > and they enter in
> > > and settle there:
> and the last state of that person
> > is worse than the first.
>
> Even so shall it be
> > with this evil generation.

Matthew 12:43-45

Legend says that when Satan raised his giant battle-axe against Heaven's gates, God's shaft of lightning struck it from his hand. The flaming axe fell into the North Sea, and was changed into the thousand-acre island of Lindisfarne.

    Through the centuries this bit of lore concerning God's victory inspired those who lived on, or visited the island, to keep Satan's power underfoot...

Lord, show us the things that were binding the work You have called forth on Holy Island, and in other places.
Help us to loose *YOUR* work,
>and let it go
>>in resurrection power.

Day 16

St Aidan's prayer for the Holy Island of Lindisfarne

Lord, this bare island,
>make it a place of peace.

Here be the peace
>of those who do Thy will.
Here be the peace
>of brother serving man.
Here be the peace
>of holy monks obeying.
Here be the peace
>of praise by dark and day.
Be this Island Thy Holy Island.
I, Lord, Thy servant, Aidan,
>make this prayer.
Be it Thy care.
Amen.

Day 17

Here am I, Lord,
>I've come to do Your will.
Here am I, Lord,
>in Your presence I'm still.

Day 18

Primeval fire fused a cradle of rock.

Borne by the rocking tides,
smooth sand folded its hollows;
frail seeds flew
   on the winds' shoulders;
blessed by soft rain
   and warmth of sun,
grass and herb
   bound the shifting dunes.
Lastly, trusted servants came, led by Christ
to build a home for restless souls,
a beacon to shed forth His light.

Lord of rock and tide,
of sun and air,
Bringer of light:
may Your blessing rest
on this Your house

Day 19

A haven

Lord, take this song
   and fill it with Your presence.
Let it bring a word of hope
   to weary care-full hearts.
Take this song
   and fill it, Lord.
Fill it with Yourself.

Lord, take my life
   and fill it with Your praises.

Let me speak a word of peace
   that Jesus brings in me.
Take this life
   and fill it, Lord.
Fill it with Yourself.

Lord, take this place
   and fill it
   with Your blessing.
Let it be a haven
   where the
   poor in spirit
   sing.
Take this place
   and fill it, Lord.
Fill it with Your praise.

Day 20

Even though the day be laden
and my task dreary
and my strength small,
a song keeps singing
in my heart.
For I know that I am Thine.
I am part of Thee.
Thou art kin to me,
and all my times
are in Thy hand.

Alistair Maclean

I trust in Thee, O Lord,
   I say, Thou art my God.
My times are in Thy hand,
   my times are in Thy hand.

Blessed be the Lord,
>   for He hath wondrously shown
His steadfast love to me,
>   His steadfast love to me.

Psalm 31:14-15, 21

Day 21

Seven times a day, as I work upon this hungry farm,
I say to Thee, 'Lord, why am I here? What is there here to stir
my gifts to growth? What great thing can I do for others –
I who am captive to this dreary toil?'

And seven times a day Thou answerest, 'I cannot do without
thee. Once did My Son live thy life, and by His faithfulness did
show My mind, My kindness, and My truth to men. But now He
is come to My side, and thou must take His place.'

From Hebridean Altars

Day 22

Enrich, Lord, heart,
>   hands, mouth in me
with faith, with hope
>   and charity,
that I may run, rise,
>   rest in Thee.

George Herbert

Day 23

As the rain hides the stars,
  as the autumn mist hides the hills,
happenings of my lot
  hide the shining of Thy face from me.
Yet, if I may hold Thy hand
  in the darkness,
it is enough;
since I know that,
  though I may stumble in my going,
Thou dost not fall.

Alistair Maclean

The Lord is thy keeper,
  the Lord is thy shade.
The sun shall not smite thee by day,
  nor the moon by night.
The Lord shall preserve thee,
  thy soul from all evil;
the Lord shall preserve thee,
  thy going and thy coming,
from this time forward,
  and even for evermore.

from Psalm 121

As it was, as it is,
  and as it shall be
evermore, God of grace,
  God in Trinity!
With the ebb, with the flow,
  ever it is so,
God of grace, O Trinity,
  with the ebb and flow.

*Traditional Gaelic prayer learned from
Alexander Macneill (fish salter), Barra*

Day 24

Saviour and friend,
how wonderful art Thou!
my companion upon the changeful way,
the comforter of its weariness,
my guide to the eternal town,
the welcome at its gate.

Alistair Maclean

As the moorland pool images the sun,
so in our hours of self-giving Thou shinest on us,
and we mirror Thee to others.
But of that other land, our heaven to be,
we have no picture at all.
Only we know that Thou art there,
and Jesus the door and the welcome
of each faithful one.

Alistair Maclean

Day 25

Of all in earth and heaven
the dearest name to me
is the matchless name of Jesus
the Christ of Calvary!
    The Christ of Calvary!
    The dearest name to me
    is the matchless name of Jesus
    the Christ of Calvary.
I cannot help but love Him
or tell His love to me
for He became my ransom,
the Christ of Calvary.
    The Christ of Calvary!

>   The dearest name to me
>   is the matchless name of Jesus
>   the Christ of Calvary.
> I could not live without Him,
> His love is life to me.
> My blood-bought life I give Him,
> the Christ of Calvary.
>   The Christ of Calvary!
>   The dearest name to me
>   is the matchless name of Jesus
>   the Christ of Calvary.

Day 26

My Master's face

> No pictured likeness of my Lord
>   I have;
> He carved no record
>   of His ministry
>   on wood or stone,
> He left no sculptured tomb
>   nor parchment dim
> but trusted for all memory of Him
>   the heart alone.
>
> Who sees the face but sees in part;
> who reads the spirit which it hides,
>   sees all,
>   and needs no more.
>
> Thy life in my life, Lord,
>   give Thou to me;
> and then, in truth,
>   I may forever see
>   my Master's face!

William Hurd Hillyer

Day 27

Arise, my love, my fair one,
and come away with me.
Arise, my love, my fair one,
and come away with me.

For lo, the winter is passed
and the rain is gone away.
Come away with me,
   come away with me.
The flowers appear on the earth,
the time for singing has come,
and the voice of the turtle-dove
is heard in our land.

Come away with me.

The fig-tree puts forth its fruit,
the vines are in blossom,
they put forth their fragrance,
O come away with me.

Arise, my love, my fair one,
come away with me.
Arise, my love, my fair one,
come away with me.

O come away with me,
come away
   with me.

John and Ross Harding

Day 28

Psalm 84

How lovely is Thy dwelling-place,
    O Lord of hosts, to me.
My soul is longing and fainting
    the courts of the Lord to see.
My heart and flesh, they are singing
    for joy to the living God.
How lovely is Thy dwelling-place,
    O Lord of hosts, to me.

Even the sparrow finds a home
    where he can settle down,
and the swallow, she can build a nest
    where she may lay her young,
within the courts of the Lord of hosts,
    my King, my Lord, and my God;
and happy are those who are dwelling where
    the song of praise is sung.

And I'd rather be a door-keeper
    and only stay a day,
than live the life of a sinner
    and have to stay away.
For the Lord is shining as the sun,
    and the Lord, He's like a shield;
and no good thing does He withhold
    from those who walk His way.

How lovely is Thy dwelling-place,
    O Lord of hosts, to me.
My soul is longing and fainting
    the courts of the Lord to see.
My heart and flesh, they are singing
    for joy to the living God.
How lovely is Thy dwelling-place,
    O Lord of hosts, to me.

Day 29

Lady Poverty in the eyes of Juniper, friend of Francis, fool of God

If I am truly poor, then I am dependent on others for everything, and I feel useless and worthless, and I realise deep within that everything is a gift from the Father. Then in this attitude of complete dependence, I become useful again, for then I am empty of selfishness and I am free to be God's instrument instead of my own. In poverty I begin to value everything rightly again. I see how little really matters, and I see that only that which glorifies God is of value.

I write these words in pain, Lady Poverty, for I have wept bitter tears because I was poor and had to beg from others, and I felt like a burden to people and to God ... And I have grown weary of Christ's words not to worry about tomorrow. But in His grace I have surrendered to God's sovereignty and providence, and it has made me free...

Lady Poverty, I love you. You, my Lady, take all the sting from being poor. In your embrace I am rich indeed, for I have someone to love. I have you. Perhaps, my Lady, that is why I keep submitting, surrendering my desire to control my life, my need to provide for the future. You have stolen my heart and made me happy, and your love makes up for all the pain that loving you involves ... and we know it is all worthwhile because when we look into your eyes, we see Christ Himself.

Murray Bodo

Day 30

Saranam (refuge)

Receive our thanks
    for night and day,
for food and shelter,
    rest and play.

Be here our guest,
>	and with us stay,
saranam, saranam, saranam.

For this small earth
>	of sea and land,
for this small space
>	on which we stand,
for those we touch
>	with heart and hand,
saranam, saranam, saranam.

In the midst of foes
>	I cry to Thee,
from the ends of earth,
>	wherever I may be,
My strength in helplessness,
>	oh, answer me!
saranam, saranam, saranam.

Make my heart to grow
>	as great as Thine,
so through my hurt
>	Your love may shine,
my love be Yours,
>	Your love be mine,
saranam, saranam, saranam.

For those who've gone,
>	for those who stay,
for those to come,
>	following the Way,
be guest and guide
>	both night and day,
saranam, saranam, saranam.

(See p.99 for the music for this meditation.)

Day 31

L'Abri

But in addition to these conversations and discussions, something else was happening. People were finding it hard to 'shake off' what they were living through.
They were there while we were praying for things that they later found had been given...
They were being given (not by us, but by God's answers to prayers) a demonstration that God exists...
It was a combination which could never be 'planned' or 'put on' as an exhibit ... it had to be real.
...a completely new work ... would never have been possible if we had not been uprooted completely in every way, and if in that uprooting we had not decided to pray for God's solution and leading every step of the path as it wound through unknown territory.
We also prayed that if it grew, God would send us the workers of His choice, rather than our trying to advertise or get people to help us ... So not to advertise, but simply to pray that God will send those of His choice, and keep others away, is a different way of doing things.
We don't say everyone ought to work this way, we simply say we feel we were led by God to do this as a demonstration that He is able to bring the people to a place – even a tiny out-of-the-way place ... and only to bring the ones He wants to have there for His purposes.

Edith Schaeffer

Compline (night prayer)

How to use Compline

'Shall we say Compline tonight?' Compline is used in the Northumbria Community as an optional extra to the Daily Office, but brings a perfect end to the day. Many use it on a regular basis, usually just before retiring to bed. On retreats it can be used to bring time together to a close as the whole household goes into quiet until next morning. These prayers are not lengthy and can be offered in just a few minutes.

It is recommended that a time of quietness should precede Compline, emptying out all the tensions and concerns of the past day and shifting the focus of our attention back to God. Then the sign of the cross can be made silently before starting the spoken prayers.

If you have young children, Compline can be used as bedtime prayers with them or over them, substituting the child's or children's names in the boxed sections whenever they cannot say the prayer for themselves. For example: 'In peace will *Martha* lie down, for it is You, O Lord, You alone who makes *her* to rest secure.'

There is a different form of Compline for each day of the week. Each is named after an individual from the era of the Celtic and the Northumbrian saints, serving as another reminder of the example set by 'the wise and the good' who inspire us to seek God as they did.

Sunday – the Ita Compline

Ita, who died in about 570, was abbess of a women's community at Killeedy, County Limerick, in Ireland. She ran a school for boys where she taught:

Faith in God
with purity of heart;
simplicity of life
with religion;
generosity
with love.

Among those schooled by Ita was Brendan, who honoured her as his foster-mother and adviser. The Compline that follows is named after her because of its emphasis on examination of the heart, and the prayers of care and protection for each soul who crosses our path.

+ *indicates that you may make the sign of the cross.*
* *indicates a change of reader.*
All say together the sections in **bold** *type.*
*The words in **bold italic** type set between lines should be said by each in turn.*

+ *(silently.)*

> **The Sacred Three**
> **to save**
> **to shield**
> **to surround**
> **this hearth**
> **this home**
> **this night**
> **every night.**

COMPLINE (NIGHT PRAYER) | SUNDAY

* Search me, O God, and know my heart.
  Test me and know my thoughts.

* See if there is any wicked way in me,
  and lead me in the way everlasting.

  **O Father, O Son, O Holy Spirit,
  forgive me my sins.
  O only-begotten Son of the heavenly Father,
  forgive.
  O God who is one,
  O God who is true,
  O God who is first,
  O God who is one substance,
  O God only mighty,
  in three Persons, truly merciful,
  forgive.**

* O God of life, this night,
  O darken not to me Thy light.

* O God of life, this night,
  close not Thy gladness to my sight.

* Keep Your people, Lord,
  in the arms of Your embrace.
  Shelter them under Your wings.

* Be their light in darkness.
  Be their hope in distress.
  Be their calm in anxiety.

* Be their strength in weakness.

* Be their comfort in pain.

* Be their song in the night.

> *In peace will I lie down, for it is You, O Lord,*
> *You alone who makes me to rest secure.*

* Be it on Your own beloved arm,
  O God of grace, that I in peace shall awake.

  Be the peace of the Spirit mine this night.
  Be the peace of the Son mine this night.
  Be the peace of the Father mine this night.
  The peace of all peace be mine this night
+ in the name of the Father,
  and of the Son,
  and of the Holy Spirit.
  Amen.

Monday – the Aidan Compline

Aidan came to Lindisfarne from Iona in the year 635 at the request of King Oswald. He was a man of deep prayer who meditated on the words of Scripture, equipping himself in quiet for an active and highly effective apostolate. He remained at Lindisfarne for sixteen years.

In 651, Aidan was taken ill at Bamburgh and died. Cuthbert, who was at that moment looking after a flock of sheep on the Lammermuir hills, saw a vision of angels taking Aidan's soul to heaven.

+ *indicates that you may make the sign of the cross.*
* *indicates a change of reader.*
*All say together the sections in **bold** type.*
*The words in **bold italic** type set between lines should be said by each in turn.*

+ *(silently.)*

> * O Christ, Son of the living God,
> may Your holy angels guard our sleep,
> may they watch over us as we rest
> and hover around our beds.
>
> * Let them reveal to us in our dreams
> visions of Your glorious truth,
> O High Prince of the universe,
> O High Priest of the mysteries.
>
> * May no dreams disturb our rest
> and no nightmares darken our dreams.
> May no fears or worries delay
> our willing, prompt repose.
>
> * May the virtue of our daily work
> hallow our nightly prayers.
> May our sleep be deep and soft
> so our work be fresh and hard.

**I will lie down and sleep in peace
for You alone, Lord, make me dwell in safety.**

---

*My dear ones, O God, bless Thou and keep,
in every place where they are.*

---

* Into Your hands I commit my spirit;
I give it to You with all the love of my heart.

* How precious to me are Your thoughts, O God!
How vast is the sum of them!
Were I to count them,
they would outnumber the grains of sand.
When I awake, I am still with You.

**I make the cross of Christ upon my breast,
+ over the tablet of my hard heart,
and I beseech the Living God of the universe –
may the Light of Lights come
to my dark heart from Thy place;
may the Spirit's wisdom come to my heart's tablet
from my Saviour.**

* Christ without sin, Christ of wounds,
I am placing my soul and my body
under Thy guarding this night,
Christ of the poor, Christ of tears.
Thy cross be my shielding this night,
O Thou Son of tears, of the wounds, of the piercing.

**I am going now into the sleep:
O be it in Thy dear arm's keep,
O God of grace, that I shall awake.**

* My Christ! my Christ!
  my shield, my encircler,
  each day, each night,
  each light, each dark.

* My Christ! my Christ!
  my shield, my encircler,
  each day, each night,
  each light, each dark.
  Be near me, uphold me,
  my treasure, my triumph.

Circle me, Lord,
keep protection near
and danger afar.

---

* Circle me, Lord,
  keep light near
  and darkness afar.

* Circle me, Lord,
  keep peace within;
  keep evil out.

The peace of all peace
be mine this night
+ in the name of the Father,
and of the Son,
and of the Holy Spirit.
Amen.

Tuesday – the Cuthbert Compline

Cuthbert's angelic vision, which coincided with the death of Aidan, convinced him that he was meant to follow Christ just like the beloved founder of the monastery on Lindisfarne.

Cuthbert became a monk at Melrose Abbey, under the guidance of Boisil, the prior. Cuthbert succeeded him, and later in his life became bishop at Lindisfarne. He died in 687.

+ *indicates that you may make the sign of the cross.*
* *indicates a change of reader.*
All say together the sections in **bold** *type.*
The words in ***bold italic*** *type set between lines should be said by each in turn.*

+ *(silently.)*

> * I will lie down and sleep in peace
> for You alone, Lord,
> make me dwell in safety.
>
> **O God, and Spirit, and Jesu, the Three,**
> **from the crown of my head, O Trinity,**
> **to the soles of my feet mine offering be.**
> **Come I unto Thee, O Jesu, my King –**
> **O Jesu, do Thou be my sheltering.**

> ***My dear ones, O God, bless Thou and keep,***
> ***in every place where they are.***

> * Whoever has chosen to make
> the shelter of the Most High their dwelling place
> will stay in His over-shadowing.
>
> * He alone is my refuge, my place of safety;
> He is my God, and I am trusting Him.

* He will rescue you from the traps laid for your feet,
  and save you from the destroying curse.

* His faithful promises are your armour.
  You need no longer be afraid of any terror by night,
  or the death-arrow that flies by day.

* The Lord Himself is your refuge;
  you have made the Most High your stronghold.

* Be my strong rock, a castle to keep me safe,
  for You are my crag and my stronghold.

* How precious to me are Your thoughts, O God!
  How vast is the sum of them!
  Were I to count them,
  they would outnumber the grains of sand.
  When I awake, I am still with You.

---

*I will not lie down tonight with sin,
nor shall sin,
nor sin's shadow,
lie down with me.*

**O God of life, this night,
O darken not to me Thy light.
O God of life, this night,
close not Thy gladness to my sight.
O God of life, this night,
Thy door to me, O shut not tight,
O God of life, this night.**

* Be it on Thine own beloved arm,
  O God of grace,
  that I in peace shall waken.

(For optional use, sung as a hymn or spoken reflectively by individual readers.)

> As the bridegroom to his chosen,
> as the king unto his realm,
> as the keep unto the castle,
> as the pilot to the helm,
> so, Lord, art Thou to me.
>
> As the fountain in the garden,
> as the candle in the dark,
> as the treasure in the coffer,
> as the manna in the ark,
> so, Lord, art Thou to me.
>
> As the music at the banquet,
> as the stamp unto the seal,
> as the medicine to the fainting,
> as the wine-cup at the meal,
> so, Lord, art Thou to me.
>
> As the ruby in the setting,
> as the honey in the comb,
> as the light within the lantern,
> as the father in the home,
> so, Lord, art Thou to me.
>
> As the sunshine in the heavens,
> as the image in the glass,
> as the fruit unto the fig-tree,
> as the dew unto the grass,
> so, Lord, art Thou to me.

* Jesu, Son of Mary!
my helper, my encircler.
Jesu, Son of David!
my strength everlasting.
Jesu, Son of Mary!
my helper, my encircler.

**The peace of all peace
be mine this night
+ in the name of the Father,
and of the Son,
and of the Holy Spirit.
Amen.**

Wednesday – the Felgild Compline

Felgild lived in the late seventh century. After Cuthbert died Ethilwald took his place as hermit of the Inner Farne. Twelve years later, having never left the island, he also died. Felgild was the next hermit to come there, but the rigours of his life in the cell aggravated a swelling on his face. The condition was suddenly healed, allowing him to continue the life of a solitary.

The Compline is dedicated to him because he represents so many whose names we never hear who faithfully follow the example of good men and women of old, continuing in their devotion to prayer and their battles against the power of evil.

+ *indicates that you may make the sign of the cross.*
* *indicates a change of reader.*
*All say together the sections in **bold** type.*
*The words in **bold italic** type set between lines should be said by each in turn.*

+ *(silently.)*

> **Calm me, O Lord, as You stilled the storm.**
> **Still me, O Lord, keep me from harm.**
> **Let all the tumult within me cease.**
> **Enfold me, Lord, in Your peace.**

* Father, bless the work that is done,
and the work that is to be.

* Father, bless the servant that I am,
and the servant that I will be.

> ***Thou Lord and God of power,***
> ***shield and sustain me this night.***

**I will lie down this night with God,
and God will lie down with me;
I will lie down this night with Christ,
and Christ will lie down with me;
I will lie down this night with the Spirit,
and the Spirit will lie down with me;
O God and Christ and the Spirit,
be lying down with me.**

* The peace of God
  be over me to shelter me,

* under me to uphold me,

* about me to protect me,

* behind me to direct me,

* ever with me to save me.

**The peace of all peace
be mine this night
+ in the name of the Father,
and of the Son,
and of the Holy Spirit.
Amen.**

Thursday – the Ebba Compline

Ebba died in the year 683. She was the sister of Oswald and Oswy, who were both kings of Northumbria. She founded the 'double' monastery (where there were both men and women there) at Coldingham, situated on St Abb's Head, and it was subsequently named after her.

Ebba was consecrated a nun by Aidan. Bede described her as 'a pious woman and a handmaid of Christ'.

+ *indicates that you may make the sign of the cross.*
* *indicates a change of reader.*
All say together the sections in **bold** *type.*
The words in ***bold italic*** *type set between lines should be said by each in turn.*

+ *(silently.)*

> * Find rest, O my soul, in God alone:
> my hope comes from Him.
>
> **Come I this night to the Father,**
> **come I this night to the Son,**
> **come I to the Holy Spirit powerful:**
> **come I this night to God.**
> **Come I this night with Christ,**
> **come I with the Spirit of kindness.**
> **Come I to Thee, Jesus.**
> **Jesus, shelter me.**
>
> * I will lie down and sleep.
> I wake again,
> because the Lord sustains me.
>
> * By day the Lord directs His love;
> at night His song is with me –
> a prayer to the God of my life.

* Be strong and take heart,
all you who hope in the Lord.

* This dwelling, O God, by Thee be blest;
and each one who here this night does rest.

* May God be in my sleep;
may Christ be in my dreams.
May the Spirit be in my repose,
in my thoughts, in my heart.
In my soul always
may the Sacred Three dwell.

---

*May the Father of heaven
have care of my soul,
His loving arm about my body,
through each slumber
and sleep of my life.*

**The Son of God be shielding me from harm,
the Son of God be shielding me from ill,
the Son of God be shielding me with power.
The Son of God be shielding me this night.**

* Sleep, O sleep in the calm of each calm.
Sleep, O sleep in the guidance of all guidance.
Sleep, O sleep in the love of all loves.
Sleep, O beloved, in the Lord of life.
Sleep, O beloved, in the God of life.

**The peace of all peace
be mine this night**
+ **in the name of the Father,
and of the Son,
and of the Holy Spirit.
Amen.**

Friday – the Boisil Compline

Boisil, Prior of Melrose Abbey, died in 661. Bede described him as 'a priest of great virtue and prophetic spirit'. Boisil, on his first meeting with Cuthbert, who was to be his pupil, exclaimed, 'Behold, the servant of the Lord!' – recognising the call of God on the young man's life.

+ *indicates that you may make the sign of the cross.*
* *indicates a change of reader.*
*All say together the sections in **bold** type.*
*The words in **bold italic** type set between lines should be said by each in turn.*

+ *(silently.)*

> * Lord, You will keep us safe
> and protect us forever.
>
> **I am placing my soul and my body
> in Thy safe keeping this night, O God,
> in Thy safe keeping, O Jesus Christ,
> in Thy safe keeping, O Spirit of perfect truth.
> The Three who would defend my cause
> be keeping me this night from harm.**
>
> * I call on You, O God,
> for You will answer me;
> give ear to me and hear my prayer.
>
> * Show the wonder of Your great love,
> You who save by Your right hand
> those who take refuge in You from their foes.
>
> * Keep me as the apple of Your eye;
> hide me in the shadow of Your wings.

Lighten my darkness, Lord.
Let the light of Your presence
dispel the shadows of night.

* Christ with me sleeping,
  Christ with me waking,
  Christ with me watching,
  each day and each night.

* Save us, Lord, while we are awake,
  guard us while we are asleep;
  that, awake, we may watch with Christ,
  and, asleep, may rest in His peace.

God with me protecting,
the Lord with me directing,
the Spirit with me strengthening
for ever and for evermore.

* In the name of the Father precious,
  and of the Spirit of healing balm.
  In the name of the Lord Jesus,
  I lay me down to rest.

The peace of all peace
be mine this night
+ **in the name of the Father,**
  and of the Son,
  and of the Holy Spirit.
  Amen.

Saturday – the Patrick Compline

Patrick (389–461) was a Briton and a former slave in Ireland. He became the 'Apostle to Ireland', travelling widely, evangelising tirelessly and organising churches and monasteries. He established his episcopal seat in Armagh, which became the centre of Christianity for the whole of Ireland.

Patrick was fearless in pursuit of his aim: to destroy paganism and to exalt the name of the Triune God.

+ *indicates that you may make the sign of the cross.*
* *indicates a change of reader.*
All say together the sections in **bold** *type.*
The words in ***bold italic*** *type set between lines should be said by each in turn.*

+ *(silently.)*

> **In the name of the King of life;**
> **in the name of the Christ of love;**
> **In the name of the Holy Spirit:**
> **the Triune of my strength.**

* I love you, O Lord my strength.
The Lord is my rock,
my fortress and my deliverer.
My God is my rock
in whom I take refuge.

* I will praise the Lord who counsels me;
even at night my heart instructs me.

* I have set the Lord always before me.
Because He is at my right hand,
I shall not be shaken.

*I am placing my soul and my body
under Thy guarding this night, O Christ.
May Thy cross this night be shielding me.*

---

* Into Your hands I commit my spirit;
  redeem me, O Lord, the God of Truth.

* The God of life with guarding hold you;
  the loving Christ with guarding fold you;
  the Holy Spirit, guarding, mould you;
  each night of life to aid, enfold you;
  each day and night of life uphold you.

  **May God shield me;
  may God fill me;
  may God keep me;
  may God watch me;
  may God bring me this night
  to the nearness of His love.**

* The peace of the Father of joy,
  the peace of the Christ of hope,
  the peace of the Spirit of grace,

  **the peace of all peace
  be mine this night**
+ **in the name of the Father,
  and of the Son,
  and of the Holy Spirit.
  Amen.**

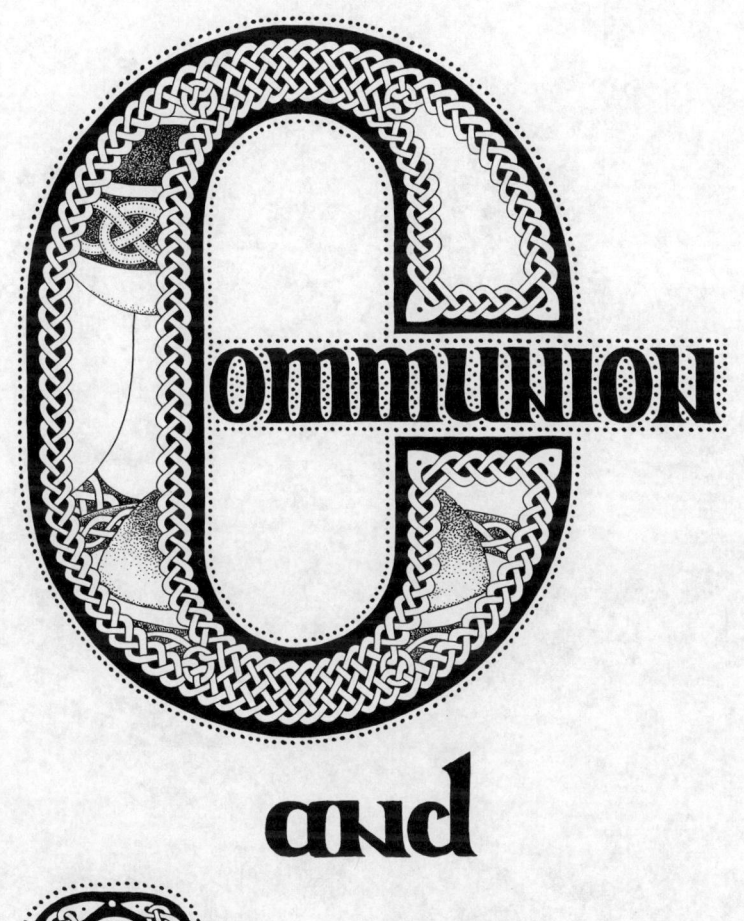

Communion and Shabbat

COMMUNION

How to use this Communion liturgy

This form of Holy Communion does not in any way attempt to replicate what would have been familiar to seventh-century Northumbrians. Most of us would find their eucharistic liturgy very long, very Latin and very laborious, however immediate and accessible the surroundings and manner of celebration! Today, on the one hand, we have celebrants in Catholic, Anglican/Episcopal and Orthodox congregations who are glad to find individual prayers that are acceptable for substitution at various points in their regular or occasional liturgies of Mass or Communion; we commend the text of this form of service to them as a resource to dip into. On the other hand, there are congregations who have always shared in the breaking of bread together, but without any written form of words beyond those recorded in Scripture. Some of them have found our experimental forms of Communion helpful; and the version used here is one that benefits from various practical considerations and careful revision into a new framework.

No instructions are given for standing, sitting or kneeling, nor any suggestions for the arrangement of physical surroundings; but the overall atmosphere should be one of inclusion and community, not of 'president and spectators'. Where possible, individual readers can share the leading of the service prior to the actual consecration, but this is obviously dependent upon circumstances and time for preparation. Ideally, there is space for creativity of every kind in this gathering as the family of God to celebrate His presence as Emmanuel – God with us.

(See also the Finan reading for 30 July.)

Communion

*All say together the words in **bold** type.*

The gathering

There is one God
and one mediator between heaven and earth,
the man Christ Jesus,
who gave Himself as a ransom for all people.

Whoever is on the Lord's side,
let them join with me,
that we may come to the visions of God.

Choose option A or B.

Option A
Create a clean heart within me, O God,
so that it may become Your chosen shelter
and the resting place of the Holy Spirit.

I make the cross of Christ upon my breast,
+ **over the tablet of my hard heart,**
and I beseech the living God of the universe,
may the Light of lights come to my dark heart
so that I may live in the power of Your love.

COMMUNION | THE GATHERING

Option B
Lord, I come to You.
Let my heart be changed, renewed,
flowing from the grace
that I've found in You.
And, Lord, I've come to know
the weaknesses I see in me
will be stripped away
by the power of Your love.

Hold me close,
let Your love surround me.
Bring me near,
draw me to Your side;
and, as I wait,
I'll rise up like the eagle,
and I will soar with You.
Your Spirit leads me on
by the power of Your love.

Lord, unveil my eyes,
let me see You face to face:
the knowledge of Your love
as You live in me.
Lord, renew my mind
as Your will unfolds in my life,
in living every day
in the power of Your love.

Hold me close,
let Your love surround me.
Bring me near,
draw me to Your side;
and, as I wait,
I'll rise up like the eagle,
and I will soar with You.
Your Spirit leads me on
by the power of Your love.

Pause.

> I know indeed that You are beautiful.
> Put forth to me the power of Your love,
> be leaping over the mountains of my transgressions,
> and wash me in the true blood of conciliation.
>
> Pour down upon us from heaven
> the rich blessing of Your forgiveness.
> Grant to us, O Saviour of Glory, the fear of God,
> the love of God and His affection,
> and the will of God to do on earth at all times
> as angels and saints do in heaven.
>
> In the name of Father, Son and Holy Spirit. Amen.
>
> **I praise the wounds and the blood of the Lamb**
>   **that heals the weakness of my body.**
> **I praise the wounds and the blood of the Lamb**
>   **that heals the weakness of my soul.**
> **I praise the wounds and the blood of the Lamb**
>   **that heals the weakness of my spirit.**
>
> **Praise be to the blood of the Lamb**
>   **in His forgiving power.**
> **Praise be to the blood of the Lamb**
>   **in His releasing power.**
> **Praise be to the blood of the Lamb**
>   **in His victorious power.**
> **Praise be to the blood of the Lamb**
>   **in His renewing power.**
> **Praise be to the blood of the Lamb**
>   **in His protecting power.**
>
> **I praise the blood of the Lamb**
> **that makes all things new.**
> **Hallelujah! Amen.**

Scripture readings

Old Testament reading
New Testament reading
Gospel reading

I pray You, good Jesus,
that as You have given me the grace
to drink in with joy
the Word that gives knowledge of You,
so in Your goodness You will grant me
to come at length to Yourself,
the source of all wisdom,
to stand before Your face for ever.

The breaking and sharing of the Word

A sharing of reflections on the Word of God just heard.

Declaration of faith

For occasional use.

There is no other God,
there never was and there never will be,
than God the Father,
unbegotten and without beginning,
the Lord of the Universe,
as we have been taught,
and His Son, Jesus Christ,
whom we declare to have always been
with the Father
and to have been begotten spiritually
by the Father
in a way that baffles description,
before the beginning of the world,

before all beginning;
and by Him are made all things
visible and invisible.
He was made man, defeated death
and was received into heaven by the Father,
who has given Him power over all names
in heaven, on earth, and under the earth;
and every tongue will acknowledge to Him
that Jesus Christ is the Lord God.
We believe in Him
and we look for His coming soon
as judge of the living and the dead
who will treat everyone according to their deeds.
He has poured out the Holy Spirit upon us
in abundance:
the gift and guarantee of eternal life,
who makes those who believe and obey
children of God and joint heirs with Christ.

**We acknowledge and adore Him as one God
in the Trinity of the Holy Name.**

Prayers for others

Having reflected on His Word,
let us call upon the name of the Lord,
trusting in the Holy Spirit to lead and guide us.

Individuals bring bidding prayers. After each one, all respond with one of the following said or sung responses:

Choose option A, B or C.

COMMUNION | PRAYERS FOR OTHERS

Option A
**Listen, Lord,
listen, Lord,
not to our words
but to our prayer.
You alone, You alone
understand and care.**

Option B
**O Lord, hear my prayer;
O Lord, hear my prayer;
when I call, answer me.
O Lord, hear my prayer;
O Lord, hear my prayer;
come and listen to me.**

Option C
**Through our lives,
and by our prayers,
Your Kingdom come.**

(An example of prepared bidding prayers can be found on p.182, 'A general intercession for those in trouble'.)

**Through our lives,
and by our prayers,
Your Kingdom come.**

The Lord's Prayer

Choose option A or B.

> *Option A*
> **Our Father who art in heaven,**
> **hallowed be Thy name;**
> **Thy Kingdom come,**
> **Thy will be done**
> **on earth as it is in heaven.**
> **Give us this day our daily bread**
> **and forgive us our trespasses**
> **as we forgive those who trespass against us:**
> **and lead us not into temptation,**
> **but deliver us from evil.**
>
> **Deliver us, Lord, from every evil,**
> **and grant us peace in our day.**
> **In Your mercy keep us free from sin**
> **and protect us from all anxiety**
> **as we wait in joyful hope**
> **for the coming of our Saviour, Jesus Christ;**
> **for the Kingdom, the power**
> **and the glory are Yours**
> **now and for ever. Amen.**
>
> *Option B*
> **Our Father in heaven,**
> **hallowed be Your name.**
> **Your Kingdom come,**
> **Your will be done**
> **on earth as in heaven.**
> **Give us today our daily bread.**
> **Forgive us our sins**
> **as we forgive those who sin against us.**
> **Lead us not into temptation,**
> **but deliver us from evil;**
> **for the Kingdom, the power**
> **and the glory are Yours,**
> **now and for ever. Amen.**

The peace

All stand, ready to exchange the peace.

> Christ, King of Tenderness,
> Christ, King of Tenderness,
> bind us with a bond
> that cannot be broken.
> Bind us with a bond of love
> that cannot be broken.

> My brothers and sisters,
> the peace of our Lord Jesus Christ
> be with you.
> **And also with you.**

All now exchange a sign of peace.

The presentation of the gifts

Gifts of bread and wine may be brought forward.

> The Lord is with us
> **and His Spirit is here.**

Choose option A or B.

> Option A
> Look with kindness on Your people
> gathered here before You.
> Send forth the power of Your Spirit
> so that these gifts may become for us
> the Body and Blood of Your beloved Son,
> Jesus, the Christ,
> in whom we have become Your own.

Holy, holy, holy Lord,
God of power and might,
heaven and earth are full of Your glory,
hosanna in the highest.

Option B
Blessed are You,
Lord God of the universe,
our Father for ever and ever;
for through Your goodness
we have these gifts of bread and wine
which earth has given
and human hands have made.
May they become for us
the food and drink of eternal life.

Bless the King of all the earth!
Holy, holy, holy Lord.
God of power and might.

('A litany of saints' from pp.326–8 may be inserted when required.)

Eucharistic Prayer

Choose Option A or B.

Option A
O God, You are always
  thinking about Your people.
You never forget us.
You sent Your Son, Jesus,
who gave His life for us
and who came to forgive us
and taught us to forgive each other.

**Blessèd is He
who comes in the name of the Lord.
Hosanna in the highest.**

Option B
When the Saviour of the world
was stretched out on the tree of death,
the elements erupted
and earth gave up its dead.
His blood, spilled on the earth,
transformed earth and heaven.
May His body and blood
change us and transform us.

**Blessèd is He
who comes in the name of the Lord.
May His body and blood
change us and transform us.**

On the very night He was betrayed,
Jesus took bread and gave You thanks.
He broke it and gave it to His disciples, saying,
'Take, eat, this is My body
which is given to you;
do this in remembrance of Me.'

In the same way, after supper
He took the cup and gave You thanks.
He gave it to them, saying,
'Drink this, all of you;
this is My blood of the new covenant,
which is shed for you and for many
for the forgiveness of sins.
Do this as often as you drink it,
in remembrance of Me.'

Christ has died;
Christ is risen;
Christ will come again.

Communion

Almighty God,
our Heavenly Father,
in Your tender mercy,
send us the Spirit of the Lamb.

**Jesus, Lamb of God:
have mercy on us.
Jesus, bearer of our sins:
have mercy on us.
Jesus, redeemer of the world,
give us Your peace.**

If you are thirsty,
drink the Fount of Life.
If you are hungry, eat the Bread of Life.
Blessed are all who hunger for this Bread
and thirst for this Fount.

The receiving of Communion.

After Communion

**Almighty Father, Son and Holy Spirit,
eternal, ever-blessèd, gracious God:
to me, the least of saints, to me allow
that I may keep a door in Paradise;
that I may keep even the smallest door,
the furthest door, the darkest, coldest door,
the door that is least used, the stiffest door,
if so it be but in Your house, O God!**

If so it be that I can see Your glory, even afar,
and hear Your voice, O God!
and know that I am with You,
You, my God.

Blessing and dismissal

I bless you
in the name of the Father, the Son
and the Sacred Spirit:
the One and the Three.
May God give you to drink of His cup;
may the sun be bright upon you;
may the night call down peace;
and when you come to His household
may the door be open wide
for you to go in to your joy.

Go in peace to love and serve the Lord.
In the name of Christ. Amen.

SHABBAT

Why Shabbat?

We need to stop. We are made that way. If we don't stop, eventually we break down. That is why we are commanded to experience Sabbath. It is right up there with telling the truth and not killing anyone. For 24 hours in each week we are to stop. (Wait, better make that 25 hours to be on the safe side, in case it gets eaten into, chipped away at or gradually eroded.) God commands it not as a way of pleasing Him, but as His gift to us.

The danger is that we turn Sabbath-keeping into another thing to do, and become rigid about what we are resting from rather than relaxed. (We may choose to keep the computer turned off, have a rest from the TV, avoid chores or having to drive anywhere. What is helpful for you? Sleeping longer? Or taking off to go walking in the countryside? Weekends can be filled with family, social events, sports or even with conferences! They continue to be the time when most people have more flexibility.)

The key to really opening up 'Shabbat' is this: *'Carry no burdens on this Sabbath day.'* We take time on a Friday evening to stop, let all the stress and struggle and worry and responsibility slip from our shoulders. Even the things we need to pick up again later are carried more lightly because of this decision to stop.

The scripture counts each day as beginning at dusk, so Friday-into-Saturday was the Sabbath. Celtic Christians respected the Sabbath as 'entering into the rest'. (Read Leslie Hardinge's *The Celtic Church in Britain* for all the clear evidence of this.)

Keeping Sunday as 'the Sabbath Day' has a rather different history. We think of 'doing one's duty' by going to church, wearing stiff collars and Sunday-best, avoiding worldly music, or focusing on 'improving' reading ... For those who 'do' church, Sunday can be far from restful. Sometimes it becomes so exhausting anyone would need a week to recover!

Whether the 'day off' is Saturday, Wednesday or whenever, we need it.

These prayers honour the centuries-old traditions of stopping, lighting candles, loosing burdens, sharing bread and wine and a meal together. Enjoy them. Breathe them in. Receive the gift.

We are sometimes asked how the Shabbat liturgies could be adapted for use by someone on their own, and obviously it's hard to be prescriptive. One Jewish perspective would be that 'the alone He sets in families', which means that families could take the opportunity to offer hospitality to those who'd otherwise be on their own. Certainly a Shabbat meal tends to be one of the nicest meals of the week and is taken in an unhurried way. People who are alone may also consider using that as an opportunity to invite others to eat with them. Some discussions about single people and Shabbat suggest lighting a candle early if you were going to be going out and leaving it burning in a safe place so the Shabbat light is already lit to welcome you on your return. When we have men's groups together for a weekend, and want to keep Shabbat, we will often invite a woman to bless us by lighting candles for us, then leaving us to it. The women really do preside over these prayers, and it's a shame not to celebrate and honour them in this way wherever possible. But being creative about these things is part of the joy – legislating about them really isn't!

The Welcoming of Shabbat

Prayers read by individual women, taking turns.
* indicates a change of reader.

* Creator Spirit
  mighty wind of God,
  You brood over our lives,
  and speak new life into our chaos.

* Blessed is the Holy One, our God,
  who kindles light in the darkness,
  and who sanctifies the Sabbath.

One woman lights a single Shabbat candle (or pair of candles, if that is already your family custom) on behalf of everyone.

* Your Sabbath
  celebrates the flowering of creation,
  the wedding of our hopes
  to Your divine yearning.
  In the light of Your holy Sabbath
  each day is holy:
  in the overflowing of Sabbath joy,
  each moment is sacred.

All women:

**Blessed be God
who gives us the Sabbath
and leads us to the waters of stillness.**

* The day is not a day but an attitude, a disposition,
  a rest in the human heart.
  So carry no burdens on this Sabbath day,
  rather, when God rests in you,
  so you also rest in Him.

And when God does His work in you,
so you also do your work in Him.

All women:

> Welcome the day,
> receive the gift.
> Remember the Sabbath and keep it.
> It is made for you:
> your freedom,
> your joy,
> your healing.
>
> Blessed be God,
> Father, Son and Holy Spirit,

* who restores our soul
  and commands us to rest.

Then during this song, 'Shabbat Welcome' (or some similar piece of music), we each allow all the burdens we carry to slip from us, and consciously cast down and cast off any that persistently try to remain attached ... Let go! ... Let God! ... Shalom!

Song

Light the candle, keep a Sabbath to the Lord.
Light the candle, come, be restored.
Light the candle, welcome the day.
Receive it ... hold it ... treasure it.

Welcome the day,
welcome the day.

Light the candle as the evening falls.
Loose your burdens, look to the Lord.
As we honour Him, peace is restored.
Receive it ... hold it ... treasure it,
the peace of the Lord,
the peace of the Lord.

Light the candle, see its gentle flame.
Anxious thoughts recede – stillness will stay.
Like the candle burns, so love remains,
receiving, holding, treasuring.

Evening and morning say,
Welcome the day!

Shabbat

1. The lighting of candles

These prayers are only to be used by a woman (or girl): this is her privilege exclusively. A single candle may be used for simplicity, with one of the women present lighting it on behalf of all; but if you have enough candles and holders the following is the normal practice.

Each woman or girl lights a candle of her own, setting it in front of her (remembering to pray for, or give thanks for, her own mother). A married woman also lights another candle for her husband, and one for each of her children. A single or divorced woman, or a widow, will light only one candle, plus ones for any children she may have who are still living. If appropriate she could light an extra candle to commit to God a child she has miscarried or aborted, or a child who has died or been adopted. A widow could light a candle for her late husband.

The prayers over the lighting of the candles (the ones with the actions) are said by all the women and girls present.

The other prayers are usually said by the woman in whose home you are gathered, but any woman present may say them. A small girl could repeat them if desired.

Do all this as quickly or as slowly as you feel is appropriate to the occasion or suitable to your needs as a household. It need only take a few moments.

> Blessed are You, Lord,
> High King above all kings,
> our Father for ever and ever.
> Thine, O Lord, is the greatness,
> the power, the glory,
> for ever and ever.
> Amen.

Lighting candles individually or together:

Let Thy face, O Lord, shine forth upon us,
and be Thou merciful unto us.

Individually or together moving hands over the candles, palms-down, with circular motion inwards towards the eyes, three times:

The peace of God...
and of Christ...
and of the Holy Spirit...
be upon us *[and upon us and our children]*
for ever more.

Individually or together, covering eyes with hands:

I do not think that I shall fear Thee
when I see Thee face to face.

All women together, removing hands from eyes, and looking at the candles:

Thou art our trust, O King of kings.

I pray that no envy and malice,
no hatred or fear, may smother the flame.
I pray that indifference and apathy,
contempt and pride,
may not extinguish its light.
Be with us by day,
be with us by night,
and as darkness covers the earth
keep our lights shining brightly.
We are on a journey,
for our hearts have run before us
to Your kingdom;
once far off,
we have now been brought near.

See how good and joyful a thing it is to dwell
together in unity!

2. The breaking of bread

These prayers should only be used by the menfolk, and a man or boy should have the bread or wine before him, breaking the bread and passing it to the next person. He may eat first or last as desired.

The same procedure is followed with passing and drinking the wine.

Taking the bread:

> Blessed are You, Lord,
> High King above all kings,
> for through Your goodness we have this bread.
> You have given us Your peace,
> and set a hunger in our hearts.
> Restore our strength.
> Give new energy to tired limbs,
> new thought to weary minds.

The bread is shared with everyone, usually with salt to sprinkle on it.

Taking the wine:

> Blessed are You, Lord,
> High King above all kings,
> for through Your goodness we have this wine.
> We thank You for Your loving kindness
> which has filled our days
> and brought us to this time and place.
> May the wine restore our souls,
> giving new vision to dry spirits,
> new warmth to cold hearts.

The wine is shared with everyone.

3. Thanksgiving before sharing a meal

Food may have been prepared for the guests, or they may even have brought food as well to contribute to the shared meal, but in any case you should endeavour to sit at one table, and leave one spare place-setting, or one seat free. This is to welcome the Christ who comes in the guise of the stranger or 'unexpected' visitor. This reminds us that we long for the coming of Christ – His returning – and yet honour His presence with us. Also, it teaches us to treat with honour whoever may come and be given the place prepared as His.

Before eating:

> Bless, O Lord,
> this food we are about to eat,
> and we pray You, O God,
> that it may be good for our body and soul,
> and if there is any poor creature
> hungry or thirsty walking the road,
> may God send them in to us
> so that we can share the food with them,
> just as Christ shares His gifts with all of us.

Havdala (end of Shabbat)

If the Shabbat prayers have been used to welcome a full 25 hours where burdens were laid down, you may wish to mark the transition into the busyness of another week. These rituals would be used on the Saturday evening. The period of rest is officially 25 hours, in case we should inadvertently short-change that time!

And while we still can, we greet each other saying:

Shabbat Shalom

On special occasions each person may be invited to go and find a stone from outdoors and write the word SARANAM on it in red marker pen.

The stones are piled to build a cairn or heap. Within a family you may wish to keep each individual's stones to use on another occasion.

If it has not been kept burning continuously, the Shabbat candle is now re-lit by one of the women.

If there is a cairn of stones a man, or all the men, say:

> What do these stones mean?
> When your sons ask you, you can say,
> 'These stones speak of where we have come from!
> Each of us carried a stone;
> it represents the life we live
> – and all that we have celebrated and observed,
> all that we have suffered, carried and endured.
> This has been our life.
> We lay it here, and honour it.'

Then everybody removes their individual stone and holds it as the song 'Saranam' is said or sung.

1. Saranam (Refuge)

> Receive our thanks for night and day,
> for food and shelter,
> rest and play.
> Be here our guest
> and with us stay,
> saranam ... saranam ... saranam.
>
> For this small earth of sea and land,
> for this small space
> on which we stand,
> for those we touch
> with heart and hand,
> saranam ... saranam ... saranam.
>
> In the midst of foes I cry to Thee,
> from the ends of earth,

wherever I may be,
my strength in helplessness,
oh, answer me,
saranam ... saranam ... saranam.

Make my heart to grow as great as Thine,
so through my hurt
Your love may shine,
my love be Yours,
Your love be mine,
saranam ... saranam ... saranam.

For those who've gone, for those who stay,
for those to come,
following the Way,
be guest and guide
both night and day,
saranam ... saranam ... saranam.

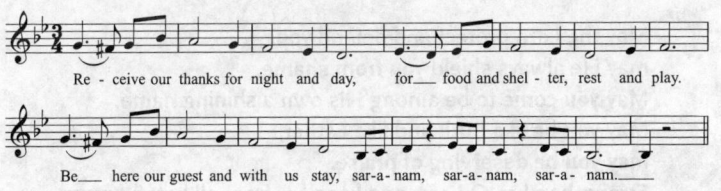

Re-ceive our thanks for night and day, for food and shel-ter, rest and play.
Be here our guest and with us stay, sar-a-nam, sar-a-nam, sar-a-nam.

2. A six-stemmed candle

With a light taken from the Shabbat candle a six-stemmed candle is lit. (These may be bought from any Jewish supplier, are found easily online or may be plaited from 'spaghetti' candles. An improvised substitute would be six small upright candles in a bowl of sand.)

Once all six wicks are lit, the Shabbat candle is removed and blown out. This tells us that the peace and prayer of Shabbat must be carried into the busyness of the next week.

Then a cup of wine on a bowl or deep saucer is filled to overflowing. The cup is passed clockwise from person to person to drink until it is finished.

The joy of Shabbat flows into the week ahead. (The spilt wine in the dish/ saucer may be reserved for extinguishing the six-stemmed candle if it becomes dangerous.)

3. The blessing of children

Then the blessing of children is said (or it may be sung to the tune of Sabbath Prayer from Fiddler on the Roof*) and may include blessing of any children, and the children of anyone with you, even if those children are by now adults or are not present. They still get remembered, blessed and prayed for.*

Each parent of any girls says in turn:

**(Name), my daughter
(and name, my daughter),**

Parents of any girls sing/say all together:

**May the Lord protect and defend you,
may He always shield you from shame.
May you come to be among His own a shining name.
May you be like Ruth and like Esther,
may you be deserving of praise.
Strengthen *her*, O Lord, and keep *her* from all hateful ways.
Daughter(s) of my heart,
in everything you do, may the Lord preserve you from pain.
Favour *her*, O Lord, with happiness and peace.
We give *her* back to you.
Amen.**

Parents of any boys all together say:

May God bless you, the God of Abraham, Isaac and Jacob.

They sing/say together:

> Here, O Lord, our *son* await(s) Your blessing.
> May *he* walk before You all *his* days.
> Everywhere *he goes* be Yours the Name *he knows*
> and may *he* come to know Your ways.
>
> Here we stand like Abraham with Isaac,
> saying to the Lord, 'Here am I'.
> In everything, Amen,
> we look to You again,
> and bless him in Your Name,
> our God.

Each parent of each boy present says in turn:

> *(Name), my son,*
> *may the joy of God be upon you,*
> *and on your face!*

4. A sweet fragrance

Now spices or incense will be lit. It can be in a special spice jar or with lit charcoal on a stone and grains of incense on top. When it is smoking, the plate of incense should be handed around clockwise so each person can waft it over themselves and breathe it in deeply. The sweet savour of Shabbat should linger on us as we walk into the world outside.

5. Recollection ('Best thing')

Everyone is given time to think through the last 25 hours or so since the Shabbat Welcome. What is their 'best thing'? (Sometimes the children will say, 'Can I have two best things?') Once everybody has decided, we go around clockwise and each in turn say what the best thought, experience or memory of the time has been.

If you prefer, the very first 'best thing' can be introduced with these words, said or sung:

> We give You thanks.
> Your Name is near.
> You're not just over there
> or over here.
> You're very near.

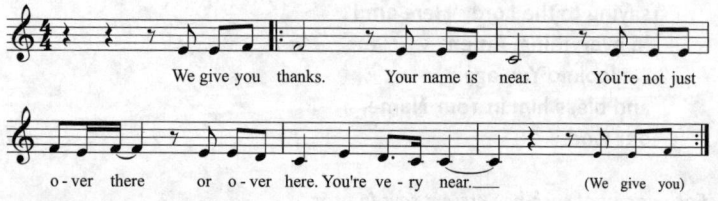

6. Anointing oil

Next a small bottle or saucer of oil is passed around. This may be olive oil, or some appropriate fragrant oil. A small amount is put on the heel of the hand and placed gently but firmly on the forehead of the person to the left. The words, 'Go peacefully' are said, perhaps with the person's name. The Shalom we have experienced is part of us, and goes with us.

7. The sweetness

Finally a bowl is passed round with parcels of 'the sweetness'. It may be sultanas, raisins, marshmallows, chocolate or small sweets, wrapped to open, trade with or consume. But the sweetness of this day and this time together becomes part of us and is carried with us.

Times and seasons

TIMES AND SEASONS

Advent

Advent is traditionally a time of preparation for Christmas. It is said that the door to the stable where the Christ-child has been born is very low – and only those who kneel find access. Being ready for Christmas should mean that our thoughts are focused not just on letters, cards and presents, but on repentance, humbling and interior 'housecleaning'. John the Baptist warned his hearers to prepare a way for the Lord – to make a clear and level pathway. This involves removing any boulders that stand in the way, and filling in any potholes. The boulders are the things we have done that we should not have done; the potholes are the things we have failed to do which we obviously should have done. The more, as individuals, family or congregation, we are focused in this way, the less we will be overwhelmed by the commercialisation of Christmas.

In the run-up to Christmas we remember especially Zacharias and Elizabeth, and the child John who, still in the womb, leapt in anticipation of the coming of the Lord. Christ has come; Christ has died and is risen; Christ will come again.

A number of customs help us in our preparation for the coming of the Lord:

1. Celtic Advent was always a full 40 days of preparation, matching the 40 days of fasting and prayer observed before Easter. A candle can be chosen and lit every evening from the beginning of Celtic Advent; this may be dark blue, purple or white. A suggested prayer is included as a blessing for evenings during Advent.

2. The Jesse Tree is a branch decorated with ornaments signifying characters in the genealogy of Jesus, Mary and Joseph through the line of David, son of Jesse. It may also have ornaments signifying prophecies foretelling the coming of the Messiah. One evening in Advent may be chosen to add the ornaments one by one, remembering the stories behind them; or one ornament may be added each day, perhaps from the beginning of December.

3. Many households have some kind of Christmas crib with figures of Mary, Joseph, animals and so on. This can be enjoyed more fully by waiting to place the child in the manger during the night of Christmas Eve, and then bringing the shepherds to the stable (later they can be removed and the Magi positioned at some distance from the crib, finally arriving on 6 January). If the child is not placed in the manger until Christmas, then the 'Prayer before a Christmas crib' would be appropriate between Christmas Day and 6 January. Some crib scenes already have all the figures in place; so, in either case, from the time the child is in the stable, a small night-light can be placed in front of him and a card with the 'Prayer before a Christmas crib' can be positioned nearby so it can be read each time the candle is lit.

4. The Advent antiphons are ancient prayers traditionally used from 17 to 23 December. On Antiphon Day (17 December) a pilgrimage walk may be planned, breaking the journey occasionally to say the next of the antiphons in turn, and saying or singing the accompanying verse of the popular Advent hymn, 'O come, O come, Immanuel', which is based upon the antiphon prayers.

5. A seven-stemmed candle, known as a *menorah*, may also be used, preferably set in a window. One light is lit on the first evening (17 December), two on the second evening and so on, and the appropriate antiphon for that day may be said or sung. This is also reminiscent of the lighting of household *hanukkah* candles in the Jewish festival which falls close to Christmas time. This commemorates a miracle in the days of the Maccabees when a single day's supply of oil burned on and on until more could be supplied for the *menorah* in the Temple.

An evening prayer for blessing during Advent

* denotes a change of reader.
*All say together the words in **bold** type.*

* God of the watching ones,
  give us Your benediction.

* God of the waiting ones,
  give us Your good word for our souls.

* God of the watching ones,
  the waiting ones,
  the slow and suffering ones,
  give us Your benediction,
  Your good word for our souls,
  that we might rest.

* God of the watching ones,
  the waiting ones,
  the slow and suffering ones,

* and of the angels in heaven,

* and of the child in the womb,

  give us Your benediction,
  Your good word for our souls,
  that we might rest and rise
  in the kindness of Your company.

A prayer before a Christmas crib

I open the stable door;
I kneel before the infant;
I worship with the shepherds;
I adore the Christ child.
I give my love with Mary and Joseph;
I wonder at the 'Word made flesh'.
I am aware of the love of God;
I sing glory with the angels;
I offer my gifts with the wise men.
I receive the living Lord;
I hold Him in my hands;
I go on my way rejoicing,
glorifying and praising God.

David Adam

The Advent antiphons

The words in **bold**, *from the Advent hymn, may be sung.*

1. (17 December)
O Wisdom,
You come forth from the mouth of the Most High.
You fill the universe and hold all things together
in a strong yet gentle manner.
O come to teach us the way of truth.

O come, O come, Thou wisdom from above;
the universe sustaining with Thy love.
Thou springest forth from the Almighty's mouth.
Subdue us now, and lead us in Thy truth.

Rejoice! Rejoice! Immanuel
shall come to thee, O Israel.

2. (18 December)

O Adonai and leader of Israel,
You appeared to Moses in a burning bush
and You gave him the law on Sinai.
O come and save us with Your mighty power.

O come, O come, Thou Lord of might,
who to Thy tribes on Sinai's height,
in ancient times didst give the law
in cloud, and majesty and awe:

Rejoice! Rejoice! Immanuel
shall come to thee, O Israel.

3. (19 December)

O Stock of Jesse,
You stand as a signal for the nations.
Kings fall silent before You whom the peoples acclaim.
O come to deliver us, and do not delay.

O come, Thou rod of Jesse, free
thine own from Satan's tyranny;
from depths of hell Thy people save,
and give them vict'ry o'er the grave:

Rejoice! Rejoice! Immanuel
shall come to thee, O Israel.

4. (20 December)

O Key of David and sceptre of Israel,
what You open, no one can close again;
what You close, no one can open.
O come to lead the captive from prison;
free those who sit in darkness and in the shadow of death.

**O come, Thou Key of David, come,
and open wide our heav'nly home;
make safe the way that leads on high,
and close the path to misery:**

**Rejoice! Rejoice! Immanuel
shall come to thee, O Israel.**

5. (21 December)
O Rising Sun,
You are the splendour of eternal light
and the sun of justice.
O come and enlighten those who sit in darkness
and in the shadow of death.

**O come, Thou Day-spring, come and cheer
our spirits by Thine advent here;
disperse the gloomy clouds of night,
and death's dark shadows put to flight:**

**Rejoice! Rejoice! Immanuel
shall come to thee, O Israel.**

6. (22 December)
O King whom all the peoples desire,
You are the cornerstone which makes all one.
O come and save us whom You made from clay.

**O come, Desire of Nations, bind
all peoples in one heart and mind.
Bid the strife and quarrels cease.
Fill all the world with heaven's peace.**

**Rejoice! Rejoice! Immanuel
shall come to thee, O Israel.**

7. (23 December)
O Immanuel,
You are our King and judge,
the One whom the peoples await, and their Saviour.
O come and save us, Lord, our God.

**O come, O come, Immanuel,
and ransom captive Israel
that mourns in lonely exile here
until the Son of God appear:**

**Rejoice! Rejoice! Immanuel
shall come to thee, O Israel.**

Christmas

* indicates a change of reader.
*All say together the words in **bold** type.*

Christmas Eve at dusk and/or before midnight

* * This night is the long night
  when those who listen await His cry.

* * This night is the eve of the great nativity
  when those who are longing await His appearing.

* * Wait, with watchful heart.

* * Listen carefully, through the stillness;
  listen, hear the telling of the waves upon the shore.

* * Listen, hear the song of the angels glorious –
  ere long it will be heard
  that His foot has reached the earth:
  news – that the glory is come!

* * Truly His salvation is near
  for those who fear Him,
  and His glory shall dwell in our land.

* * Watch and pray, the Lord shall come.

* * Those who are longing await His appearing.

* * Those who listen await His cry.

* * Watch...

* Wait...

* Listen...

This night is the long night.

After midnight as Christmas Eve turns to the Feast of the Christ Mass, the Nativity of the Christ Child

**This night is born Jesus,
Son of the King of glory.
This night is born to us
the root of our joy.
This night gleamed sea and shore
   together.
This night was born Christ,
the King of greatness.**

* Though laid in a manger,
  He came from a throne;
  on earth though a stranger,
  in heaven He was known.

  **How lowly, how gracious
  His coming to earth!
  His love my love kindles
  to joy in His birth.**

* Sweet Jesus, King of glory!

* Now You sleep in a manger,
  in a stable poor and cold;

* but for us You are the highest King,
  making our hearts into Your palace.

Christmas Day (after it has grown light)

* All hail! let there be joy!

   **Hail to the King, hail to the King.
   Blessed is He, blessed is He.**

* The peace of earth to Him;

* the joy of heaven to Him.

* The homage of a King be His,
  King of all victory;

* the welcome of a Lamb be His,
  Lamb of all glory:
  the Son of glory down from on high.
  All hail, let there be joy.

* Deep in the night
  the voice of the waves on the shore
  announced to us: Christ is born!
  Son of the King of kings
  from the land of salvation,
  the mountains glowed to Him,
  the plains glowed to Him,
  then shone the sun on the mountains high to Him.
  All hail, let there be joy.

* God the Lord has opened a Door.
  Christ of hope, Door of joy!
  Son of Mary, hasten Thou to help me:

   In me, Lord Christ, let there be joy.

New Year

The opening door

This is to be used as a 'first-footing' prayer. In Scotland and the northern parts of England, New Year is given much importance: folk go from house to house wishing each other a good year ahead, and celebrate their good wishes with food and plenty of drink. It is often seen as important who should be the first to cross the threshold and 'bring in the year' once midnight has passed.

This song (spoken or sung) asks Christ Himself to come and 'first-foot' for us. The door is opened to welcome Him in and invite His blessing, whether He comes in silence or in the company of other guests.

> This day is a new day
> that has never been before.
> This year is a new year,
> the opening door.

Open the door.

> Enter, Lord Christ –
> we have joy in Your coming.
> You have given us life;
> and we welcome Your coming.

> I turn now to face You,
> I lift up my eyes.
> Be blessing my face, Lord;
> be blessing my eyes.
> May all my eye looks on
> be blessed and be bright,
> my neighbours, my loved ones
> be blessed in Your sight.

You have given us life
and we welcome Your coming.
Be with us, Lord,
we have joy, we have joy.
This year is a new year,
the opening door.
Be with us, Lord,
we have joy, we have joy.

A covenant service

This may be used at the first opportunity at the beginning of a year, or at some other appropriate time of new beginnings. This may be for a community, a household or a small group of friends. Because the service is long, it is important to take time to pray it reflectively, going through it slowly.

* denotes a change of reader. Some groups will wish to have each person take a turn in reading; a larger group or congregation will focus more easily if a few people who can read clearly are selected on their behalf.
*All say together the sections in **bold** type.*
*The words in **bold italic** type set between lines should be said by each person in turn.*

> **I bind unto myself this day**
> **the strong name of the Trinity.**
> **I humbly praise the aweful name:**
> **the Three in One, the One in Three,**
> **of whom all nature hath creation –**
> **eternal Father, Spirit, Word.**
> **Praise to the God of my salvation!**
> **Salvation is of Christ the Lord.**
>
> **I bind this day to me for ever**
> **by power of faith: Christ's incarnation,**
> **His baptism in the Jordan river,**
> **His death on cross for my salvation.**

His bursting from the spicèd tomb,
His riding up the heavenly way,
His coming on the day of doom,
I bind unto myself today.
**Christ be with me, Christ within me,
Christ behind me, Christ before me,
Christ beside me, Christ to win me,
Christ to comfort and restore me.
Christ beneath me, Christ above me,
Christ in quiet, Christ in danger,
Christ in hearts of all that love me,
Christ be with me this day.**

* O God, You have been good.
  You have been faithful;
  You have been good.

* You have shown us Your love,
  not just in the year that is past,
  but through all the years of our lives.

  **O God, You have been good.
  You have been faithful;
  You have been good.**

* You have given us life and reason,
  and set us in a world which is full of Your glory.

* You put family around us
  and comfort us with friends.
  You touch us through the thoughtfulness
  and warmth of other people.

  **O God, You have been good.
  You have been faithful;
  You have been good.**

* In darkness You have been our light,
  in adversity and temptation a rock of strength.
  You are the source of our joy,
  and all the reward we ever need.

Your loving kindness is everlasting.
Your loving kindness is everlasting.

* You remembered us when we had forgotten You,
  followed us when we ran away,
  met us with forgiveness
  whenever we turned back to You.

Your loving kindness is everlasting.
Your loving kindness is everlasting.

* God our Father,
  You have set forth the way of life
  for us in Your beloved Son.
  We confess with shame
  our slowness to learn from Him,
  our reluctance to follow Him.

* You have spoken and called,
  and we have not given heed.
  Your beauty has shone forth,
  and we have been blind.

Be tender in Your mercy, Lord,
be tender in Your mercy.

* Forgive us,
  that we have not loved You
  with all our heart,
  with all our soul,
  with all our mind,
  with all our strength.

* We have taken much, and returned little thanks;
  we have been unworthy of Your unchanging love.

* Forgive us
  our coldness and indifference,
  our lack of constant love,
  our unbelief,
  our false pretences,
  our refusal to understand Your ways.

  Be tender in Your mercy, Lord,
  be tender in Your mercy.

* Teach us Your ways, O Lord,
  and let us walk in Your truth.
  We put behind us
  our stubborn independence,
  and turn again to You.

* Now let us willingly fasten ourselves
  to the God of covenant:
  that we be Christ's,
  and Christ be ours.

* Christ has many tasks for us.
  Some are easy; others are difficult.
  Some bring honour; others bring reproach.
  Some are to our liking, and coincide
  with our own inclinations, and are
  in our immediate best interest;
  some are just the opposite.
  In some we may please Christ
  and please ourselves;
  in others we cannot please Christ
  except by denying ourselves.
  Yet the power to take on all of these
  is most definitely given us in Jesus;

for it is He who strengthens us,
and comes to help us when we are weak.

* Let us say Yes to the covenant
that He makes with us.

I am no longer my own, but Yours.
Use me as You choose;
rank me alongside whoever You choose;
put me to doing, put me to suffering;
let me be employed for You, or laid aside for You,
raised up for You, or brought down low for You;
let me be full, let me be empty;
let me have all things, let me have nothing;
with my whole heart I freely choose to yield
all things to Your ordering and approval.

So now, God of glory,
Father, Son and Holy Spirit,
You are mine, and I am Your own.

(Holy Communion may now follow, beginning at the peace – or a simple meal of bread and wine. This is to remind us that the new covenant was sealed with the blood of Christ.)

Light a candle in the darkness

This is especially suitable for use on:
- New Year's Day, or the first suitable opportunity in early January;
- All Hallows' Eve (31 October) or All Saints' Day (1 November).

Small night-lights are lit one at a time in memory of Christian martyrs. A quote from the person or from the story of their life is read, and then the candle is lit. For example, choose from the following: Dietrich Bonhoeffer, Charles de Foucauld, Jean Donovan, Martin Luther King Jr, Oswin, Polycarp, Oscar Romero, Telemachus, Thomas Merton (see 'Calendar and resources for saints' days and festivals', p.211).

A song may be sung or played about candles in darkness. This could be 'Light a candle in the darkness' (see below), or 'Light one candle' (see below).

A suitable Scripture reading would be Hebrews 11:36—12:2.

A larger candle could then be lit and placed among the night-lights, and 'A confession of faith' from 'Coming into the light — rebirth' (see p.174) could be said together.

Light a candle in the darkness

> Light a candle in the darkness
> Light a candle in the night
> Let the love of Jesus light us
> Light a candle in the night.

From the album Alien Brain *by Garth Hewitt*

Light one candle

> Light one candle for the Maccabee children
> with thanks that their light did not die;
> and light one candle for the pain they endured
> when their right to exist was denied.
> Light one candle for the terrible sacrifice
> justice and freedom demands;

and light one candle for the wisdom to know
when the peacemakers' time is at hand.

> *Chorus:*
> Don't let the light go out;
> it's lasted for so many years.
> Don't let the light go out;
> let it shine through our love and our tears.

Light one candle for the strength that we need
to never become our own foes.
Light one candle for those that are suffering
the pain we learned so long ago.
Light one candle for all we believe in;
let anger not tear us apart.
Light one candle to bind us together
for this is the song in our heart:

> *Chorus.*

What is the memory that's valued so highly
that we keep it alive in that flame?
What's the commitment to those who have died
when we cry that they've not died in vain?
We have come this far always believing
that justice will somehow prevail.
This is the burden, this is the promise,
this is why we will not fail:

> *Chorus.*

Don't let the light go out!

A song about Hanukkah by Peter Yarrow.
Sung by Peter, Paul and Mary on the album No Easy Road

Lent

The following may be useful for meditation and reflection during this season.

> The other morning some of us were together in a church where the rector was saying Morning Prayer, and leading us in guided silent prayer. He said, 'Let us pray for those whom we love.' And that was easy. Then he said, 'Let us pray for those whom we do not love.' And there rose up before my mind three men for whom I had to pray. They were men who have opposed my work. In this they may have been wrong. But my wrong was in resentment and a feeling of letting myself be cut off from them, and even from praying for them, because of it. Years ago I read a quotation from Mary Lyon that recurs to me again and again: 'Nine-tenths of our suffering is caused by others not thinking so much of us as we think they ought.' If you want to know where pride nestles and festers in most of us, that is right where it is; and it is not the opposition of others, but our own pride, which causes us the deepest hurt. I never read a word that penetrated more deeply into the sin of pride from which all of us suffer, nor one which opens up more surgically our places of unforgiveness.
>
> *Samuel Moor Shoemaker*, And Thy Neighbour

O Son of God,
do a miracle for me
and change my heart.
Thy having taken flesh
to redeem me
was more difficult
than to transform
my wickedness.

Irish, 15th century

Thy measure of prayer shall be until thy tears come;
or thy measure of work or labour till thy tears come;
or thy measure of work or labour, or of thy genuflections,
until thy perspiration come often, if thy tears are not free.

From the Rule of St Columba of Iona

(See also the Aidan readings for 21–22 April.)

Approaching Easter

Foot washing

This is particularly appropriate for Maundy Thursday.

A towel, some soap and a basin are needed – perhaps several of each.
'The Basin and the Towel' and 'Let me be your Servant' may be said or
sung all together, or said with a different reader for each verse.
*All say together the words in **bold** type.*

> Jesus said,
> **'A new commandment I give to you,**
> **that you love one another, as I have loved you.'**

The basin and the towel

> In an upstairs room a parable
> is just about to come alive;
> and while they bicker about who's best
> with a painful glance He'll silently rise.
> Their Saviour-servant must show them how,
> through the will of the water
> and the tenderness of the towel.
>
> And the call is to community,
> the impoverished power that sets the soul free
> in humility to take the vow
> that day after day
> we must take up the basin and the towel.
>
> In any ordinary place,
> on any ordinary day,
> the parable can live again
> when one will kneel and one will yield.

Our Saviour-servant must show us how,
through the will of the water
and the tenderness of the towel.
And the space between ourselves, sometimes,
is more than the distance between the stars.
By the fragile bridge of the servant's bow,
we take up the basin and the towel.

And the call is to community,
the impoverished power that sets the soul free
in humility to take the vow
that day after day
we must take up the basin:
and the call is to community;
and day after day
we must take up the basin and the towel.

Michael Card

I was dreaming that I was treading the streets of the Holy City, pottering about like a tourist. In my wandering I came upon the museum of that city of our dream. I went in, and a courteous attendant conducted me round. There was some old armour there, much bruised with battle. Many things were conspicuous by their absence. I saw nothing of Alexander's, nor of Napoleon's. There was no Pope's ring, nor even the ink-bottle that Luther is said to have thrown at the devil, nor Wesley's seal and keys. I saw a widow's mite and the feather of a little bird. I saw some swaddling clothes, a hammer, and three nails, and a few thorns. I saw a bit of a fishing-net and the broken oar of a boat. I saw a sponge that had once been dipped in vinegar, and a small piece of silver. But I cannot enumerate all I saw, nor describe all I felt. Whilst I was turning over a common drinking cup which had a very honourable place, I whispered to the attendant, 'Have you not got a towel and basin among your collection?' 'No,' he said, 'not here; you see they are in constant use.' Then I knew I was in Heaven, in the Holy City, and amid the redeemed society.

Knowing that He came from God and went to God

…Jesus took a towel and basin.

A. E. Whitham

Let me be your servant

In the following song 'Sister' or the name of the person addressed may be inserted in place of 'Brother'. Alternatively, the first line of verses 1 and 6 can be changed to 'Brother, sister, let me serve you…'.

1. *Brother*, let me be your servant,
   let me be as Christ to you.
   Pray that I may have the grace to
   let you be my servant, too.

2. We are pilgrims on a journey,
   and companions on the road.
   We are here to help each other
   walk the mile and bear the load.

3. I will hold the Christ-light for you
   in the night time of your fear.
   I will hold my hand out to you,
   speak the peace you long to hear.

4. I will weep when you are weeping;
   when you laugh I'll laugh with you.
   I will share your joy and sorrow,
   till we've seen this journey through.

5. When we sing to God in heaven
   we shall find such harmony,
   born of all we've known together
   of Christ's love and agony.

6. *Brother*, let me be your servant,
   let me be as Christ to you.
   Pray that I may have the grace to
   let you be my servant, too.

Each in turn washes another person's feet, until all who wish to have had a chance to participate. This is an informal time; songs may be sung, music played, coffee served!

The way of the cross

At each point or station on the journey a reading is provided which acts as a narration. A second reader can be chosen for the prayer which follows, with everyone joining in for the final phrase in **bold** *type.*

1. Jesus is condemned to death

His accusers brought many false charges against Jesus, but He spoke not a word in His own defence. 'Crucify him!' they shouted.

Pilate washed his hands, to show the decision was not his own, but he did not dare to side publicly with Jesus; instead, he was willing to content the people.

So Jesus was condemned to death.

> Lord, when You were misunderstood,
> You silently forgave;
> but we so often respond in anger.
> Lord, have mercy.
> **Lord, have mercy.**
>
> Lord, You gave us opportunity to choose Jesus,
> but for so long we have chosen the rebellion
> that demanded Your death.
> Lord, have mercy.
> **Lord, have mercy.**

2. Jesus receives the cross

Jesus was scourged. The whips cut His back until it was shredded and bathed in His blood. A crown of thorns was set upon His head in mockery. Then they returned His robe to Him, and brought Him to the cross on which He was to die.

Jesus embraced the cross, resting it painfully on the smarting wounds on His back.

> Lord, You were scourged and wounded;
> You deserved no punishment,
> but were punished in our place.
> Thank You, Jesus.
> **Thank You, Jesus.**
>
> When You were already hurting,
> You embraced the cross.
> Thank You, Jesus.
> **Thank You, Jesus.**

3. Jesus falls for the first time

Jesus had willingly embraced the cross, but His physical body was weak from lack of sleep, from the pressures of arrest and trial, and from torture and beating.

The spirit is willing, but the flesh is weak. Jesus said, 'Yes', but His body hesitated and He fell to His knees, determining to rise again even in His weakness.

> Lord, You embraced and shouldered Your cross,
> but Your body was weak.
> Your Body still is weak:
> Your people shrink from the weight of suffering.
> In our weakness, Lord, let us pray:
> Your will be done.
> **Your will be done.**

Jesus, You were first a carpenter:
build us into what You desire,
and secure every joint tightly,
that we may hold together.
Plane the rough surfaces of our relationships.
We are Your workmanship –
Your will be done.
Your will be done.

Jesus, You said 'YES' to the Father's will;
and only Your body hesitated.
May we, Your Body, no longer hesitate,
but follow You in Your obedience, saying:
Your will be done.
Your will be done.

4. Jesus is met by his blessed mother

As Jesus again shouldered the cross and bore its burden, He glanced ahead and saw His mother. He could not stop to talk, to explain, to gather her in His arms and comfort her. All His energy was being soaked into that cross.

Who are My mother and brothers? Those who do the will of My Father.

Not My will, Father, but Yours.

Lord, You had to leave the security
of home and family, twice.
You left Your Father to be a man with us,
and left Your human family to die for us.
You had to pray to Your Father:
My God, I trust in You.
My God, I trust in You.

Lord, when we leave all and follow You
and it hurts those we love,
help us to know that You have been there, too;

that no one leaves behind father, mother or loved one
but is more than rewarded in the end.
Help us to pray:
My God, I trust in You.
My God, I trust in You.

Lord, when Your cross pierces
our own desires,
and makes us call out,
let our cry be, through our pain:
My God, I trust in You.
My God, I trust in You.

5. The cross is laid on Simon of Cyrene

Simon carried the cross of Christ. At first it was just a tiresome and unwelcome task he was forced into by the soldiers; only later did he recognise his privilege in shouldering the burden of the One who made the worlds.

He was compelled to carry the cross part of the way for Jesus. Simon, himself a stranger, an outcast, often misunderstood, perhaps identified with Jesus, and felt the gratitude of this Man above all men; and amid the pity Simon felt for Him, he felt a burning compassion flowing back to him from Jesus, a burning, life-changing love. Simon carried the cross of Christ.

As Simon took the weight of the cross from Jesus,
You have taught us that we must bear one another's
burdens, and so fulfil the law of Christ.
May we carry Your cross.
May we carry Your cross.

Simon was one just passing by,
but suddenly he was compelled to change direction,
and, with all his strength given
to the carrying of the cross,
pressed through the crowds

to the Place of the Skull,
Golgotha, Calvary.

Sweet Jesus, like Simon,
may we carry Your cross.
May we carry Your cross.

6. Veronica wipes the face of Jesus

An act of compassion. A woman called Veronica places a cool cloth upon His hot and tired face. He feels the coolness of the cloth, and the love with which it is offered. And through His pain He smiles – a smile never to be lost, never to be extinguished. She reaches out to touch His face, and He leans His head into her hands, within her reach.

Oh, blessed day! The Master touched her life, her heart, her outstretched hands. What faith! What lovely face! What timeless meeting ... O blessed Christ.

Christ of the human road, let us,
like Veronica, reach out to touch You,
and, sweet Christ,
show us Your lovely face.
Show us Your lovely face.

Legend or living person, Veronica, by example,
teaches us to be Your witness,
that others may gaze into Your loving eyes
and know Your smile.
Show us Your lovely face.
Show us Your lovely face.

As we see Your face by faith,
we learn to become like You, Lord Christ.
That the world may see Your glory:
show us Your lovely face.
Show us Your lovely face.

7. Jesus falls the second time

The pain, the exhaustion, the love that drives Him on – but the cross is so heavy. Again He falls beneath the weight; and in bitter resolution – Thy will be done – and in fatigue, Jesus again drives Himself up against the cross, and carries it on towards the fateful Hill of Death.

> Will it never end?
> I'm not as sure as when I started.
> I never knew it would be like this.
> But this is my firm choice:
> Lord, I will go on with You.
> **Lord, I will go on with You.**
>
> Lord, often I fall,
> and the temptation is not to rise again
> and continue with You.
> When I fall and others watch and laugh,
> or say, 'I told you so, you'll never make it,'
> give me the strength to fulfil my promise:
> Lord, I will go on with You.
> **Lord, I will go on with You.**

8. Jesus meets the women of Jerusalem

As Jesus continued, painfully stumbling along the road to Calvary, a group of women joined themselves to the procession, wailing in the manner normally considered appropriate for a funeral procession. But Jesus told them instead to cry out to God for themselves and their own children.

> Lord, some of us are never far from tears,
> and some of us have forced ourselves not to cry.
> Bring our tears into Your captivity and direction,
> that they respond to Your voice.
> You have the words of eternal life.
> **You have the words of eternal life.**

Lord, You have the words of eternal life.
You have the words of eternal life.

9. Jesus falls the third time

Jesus fell again. Oh God, how many times must I fall and pick up that cross again? As many as seven times? Or seventy times seven times? For ever; until this never-ending road is ended; until the impossible is completed, the unbearable borne through all eternity.

For the sake of My children, My sons, My loved ones, My bride, My people, I must go on. I will not, I must not, give up now. The way of sorrows, the way of pain, the way of self-renunciation, the way of My cross.

> How long the road You came for us, Lord,
> with Your smarting burden! O Lord,
> Your love has no limits.
> **Your love has no limits.**

> You picked up the weight of Your cross,
> the weight of our sins.
> We are Your burden, an overwhelming burden;
> but that burden is sweet to You
> because of the love You also bear to us,
> an overwhelming love.
> Your love has no limits.
> **Your love has no limits.**

> Lord, I know You can forgive me:
> Your love has no limits.
> **Your love has no limits.**

10. Jesus is stripped of his garments

At the place of death the King of life is stripped of His clothes. Naked, He came into the world; naked, He is taken from the world.

Vulnerable, exposed, God became man. He was a crying, helpless, dependent baby. Now, vulnerable, exposed, His heart, His life, His body all bared before the world, He will be hung up to be mocked. But God is not mocked – His very nakedness is a parable, a sacrament, a picture of the Father's hurting heart exposed in love to us.

> Lord, You were stripped of the robes You wore,
> but You were the same – it didn't change You.
> Things meant little to You; You never hid behind them.
> You showed us the Father's heart,
> so open and broken:
> may we be open to You, and to each other.
> **May we be open to You, and to each other.**
>
> Lord, for our sake You left the riches of heaven
> and became poor.
> You came within our reach.
> May we be open to You, and to each other.
> **May we be open to You, and to each other.**
>
> You did not hold on to even the little
> You had left to call Your own.
> May we be open to You, and to each other.
> **May we be open to You, and to each other.**
>
> The nakedness of God was exposed before the world.
> Lord, O lovely Christ,
> may we be open to You, and to each other.
> **May we be open to You, and to each other.**
>
> No robe was left now upon Your tired shoulders,
> just a crown of mockery on Your head.
> You were still a King.
> You loved, and won rejection and pain –
> but still You loved.
> May we be open to You, and to each other.
> **May we open to You, and to each other.**

11. Jesus is nailed to the cross

The journey was at an end. Jesus was quickly thrown backward with His shoulders against the wood. The soldier felt for the depression at the front of the wrist; he drove a heavy, square, wrought-iron nail through the wrist and deep into the wood. Quickly, he moved to the other side and repeated the action, being careful not to pull the arms too tightly. The title 'Jesus of Nazareth, King of the Jews' was nailed into place, and the cross-bar lifted into position. The left foot was pressed backward against the right foot. With both feet extended, toes down, a nail was driven through the arch of each, leaving the knees moderately flexed.

The victim was now crucified.

'Jesus of Nazareth, King of the Jews.'

He is our peace.

> Jesus, our sin put the nails in Your hands.
> It was love that held You there.
> **It was love that held You there.**
>
> Jesus, our sin put the nails in Your feet.
> It was love that held You there.
> **It was love that held You there.**
>
> The soldiers hoisted Your cross on high.
> You were their prisoner;
> but no one took Your life away from You.
> You gave it willingly, freely.
> It was love that held You there.
> **It was love that held You there.**
>
> You were lifted high upon that cross,
> even as You had prophesied when You promised:
> 'I, if I be lifted up from the earth,
> will draw all people to Me.'
> It was love that held You there.
> **It was love that held You there.**

12. Jesus dies upon the cross

As Jesus slowly sagged down with more weight on the nails in the wrists, excruciating, fiery pain shot along the fingers and up the arms to explode in the brain. As He pushed Himself upward to avoid this stretching torment, He placed His full weight on the nail through His feet. Again there was searing agony as the nail tore through the nerves. As the arms fatigued, great waves of cramps swept over the muscles, knotting them in deep, relentless, throbbing pain. Jesus fought to raise Himself, in order to get even one short breath. 'Father, forgive them, for they know not what they do.'

To the thief dying at His side: 'Today thou shalt be with Me in Paradise.'

To His mother and His closest friend: 'Woman, behold thy son' – 'Behold thy mother.'

In the words of the psalm foretelling the death of Messiah, He cried: 'My God, why hast Thou forsaken Me?'

> Father God, You waited
> through the long hours of agony,
> when He was robbed even
> of the sense of Your love, Your presence,
> when the sin and disease and hatred
> and darkness overwhelmed Him so greatly.
> He was wounded for my transgressions.
> **He was wounded for my transgressions.**
>
> Father, what love is this of His?
> What love is this of Yours
> that His dying love reflects?
> Your forgiveness for me,
> as we gaze upon His sacrificial death,
> is as truly an undeserved gift
> as the pardon He spoke to the dying thief.
> It is mine if I will only receive:
> He was wounded for my transgressions.
> **He was wounded for my transgressions.**

13. Jesus is taken from the cross

Jesus could now feel the chill of death creeping through His tissues. And with a loud voice He cried: 'It is finished.' His mission of atonement had been completed. Finally, He could allow His body to die. With one last surge of strength, He once again pressed His torn feet against the nail, straightened His legs, took a deeper breath, and uttered His seventh and last cry: 'Father, into Thy hands I commit My spirit.' A while later, the soldier pierced a long spear into the side of the dead man, to His heart. The watery fluid and blood that flowed out show us He had literally died of a broken heart – not the usual crucifixion death of suffocation. The friends of Jesus were allowed to remove His holy body, and for a moment his mother held Him again upon her lap, cradled in her arms.

Let Him sleep now. It is finished.

> See from His head, His hands, His feet,
> sorrow and love flow mingled down!
> Did e'er such love and sorrow meet?
> or thorns compose so rich a crown?
> It was for me.
> **It was for me.**
>
> Forbid it, Lord, that I should boast
> save in the death of Christ my God.
> All the vain things that charm me most,
> I sacrifice them to His blood:
> It was for me.
> **It was for me.**

14. Jesus is laid in the sepulchre

Laid in a borrowed tomb, awaiting the sign of Jonah
– the only sign that would be given to His generation
– that after three days and nights in the womb of the earth,
the belly of the fish, the grave and hell,
He would come forth to do His Father's will

– Jesus the humble Son of God, the exultant Son of Man,
the eternal contradiction, the Blessed One.
The end is not yet. Weeping endures for a night,
but joy comes in the morning.
The good news – 'He is risen' –
will burst upon the Son-rise.

Therefore with joy shall we draw water
out of the wells of salvation.

> When all is dark,
> and Hope is buried,
> it is hard to trust His words
> that promised, before the pain:
> He died that I might live.
> **He died that I might live.**
>
> In His death is my birth.
> He died that I might live.
> **He died that I might live.**
>
> In His life is my life.
> He died that I might live.
> **He died that I might live.**
>
> My Jesus! He died that I might live.
> **He died that I might live.**

15. Jesus is risen!

Where is my Lord?
They have taken Him away.
All I see is a tomb, a place that is empty.
And just when I need Him,
and long for His voice,
even His body would not wait for my tears.

Shut away in a box, He has conquered their coffin.
Shut away in a book, He fulfils, Living Word.
Shut away in our concepts, He shatters such shackles.
No prison can hold Him; no tomb thwart the miracle.
His life is our liberty; His love changed my life.
No dying can rob me of what He has given:
once blind, now I see.
Hallelujah! His promise:
'In the day when the hearts of men
fail them for fear,
then look up, little flock,
your redemption draws near.'

> Let all creation
> give thanks to the Risen Lord.
> **Give thanks to the Risen Lord!**
>
> Filled with His praises,
> give thanks to the Risen Lord.
> **Give thanks to the Risen Lord!**
>
> He is our Shepherd, and we are His sheep.
> Give thanks to the Risen Lord.
> **Give thanks to the Risen Lord!**
>
> Stepping out boldly, we claim resurrection.
> Give thanks to the Risen Lord.
> **Give thanks to the Risen Lord!**

Easter Eve

The following passage is taken from chapters 15 and 16 of the *Book of Nicodemus*, one of the manuscripts circulated early in the life of the Christian community. It is not, of course, accepted as canonical, but is rather in the style of the medieval mystery plays which teach through recounting the stories dramatically. This section, which may be used as a spur to meditation during the strange period of waiting between Good Friday and Easter Sunday, vividly illustrates the statement in the creeds that Jesus descended into hell, and imagines what happens when He gets there!

> Satan, the prince and captain of death, said to the prince of hell: 'Prepare to receive Jesus of Nazareth Himself, who boasted that He was the Son of God, and yet was a man afraid of death and said, "My soul is sorrowful even to death." Besides, He did many injuries to me and to many others; for those whom I made blind and lame and those also whom I tormented with several devils, He cured by His word; yea, and those whom I brought dead to thee, He by force takes away from thee.'
>
> To this, the prince of hell replied to Satan, 'Who is that so-powerful prince, and yet a man who is afraid of death? For all the potentates of the earth are subject to my power, whom thou broughtest to subjection by thy power. But if He be so powerful in His human nature, I affirm to thee for truth that He is almighty in His divine nature, and no man can resist His power. When therefore He said He was afraid of death, He designed to ensnare thee, and unhappy it will be to thee for everlasting ages.'
>
> Then Satan, replying, said to the prince of hell, 'Why didst thou express a doubt, and wast afraid to receive that Jesus of Nazareth, both thy adversary and mine? As for me, I tempted Him and stirred up the people of the Jews with zeal and anger against Him. I sharpened the spear for His suffering; I mixed the gall and vinegar, and commanded that He should drink it; I prepared the cross to crucify Him, and the nails to pierce

through His hands and feet; and now His death is near to hand, I will bring Him hither, subject both to thee and me.'

Then the prince of hell answering, said, 'Thou saidst to me just now, that He took away the dead from me by force. They who have been kept here till they should live again upon the earth, were taken away hence, not by their own power, but by prayers made to God, and their almighty God took them from me. Who then is this Jesus of Nazareth that by His word hath taken away the dead from me without prayer to God? Perhaps it is the same who took away from me Lazarus, after he had been four days dead, and did both stink and was rotten, and of whom I had possession as a dead person, yet He brought him to life again by His power.'

Satan answering, replied to the prince of hell, 'It is the very same person, Jesus of Nazareth.'

Which, when the prince of hell heard, he said to him, 'I adjure thee by the powers which belong to thee and me, that thou bring Him not to me. For when I heard of the power of His word, I trembled for fear, and all my impious company were at the same time disturbed. And we were not able to detain Lazarus, but he gave himself a shake, and with all the signs of malice, he immediately went away from us; and the very earth, in which the dead body of Lazarus was lodged presently turned him out alive. And I know now that He is almighty God who could perform such things, who is mighty in His dominion, and mighty in His human nature, who is the Saviour of mankind. Bring not therefore this person hither, for He will set at liberty all those whom I hold in prison under unbelief, and bound with the fetters of their sins, and will conduct them to everlasting life.'

And while Satan and the prince of hell were discoursing
thus to each other, of a sudden there was a voice as of
thunder and rushing of winds, saying, 'Lift up your gates,
O ye princes; and be ye lifted up, O everlasting gates – and
the King of Glory shall come in.'

When the prince of hell heard this, he said to Satan,
'Depart from me, and begone out of my habitations; if thou
art a powerful warrior, fight with the King of Glory. But
what hast thou to do with Him?' And he cast him forth
from his habitations.

And the prince said to his impious officers, 'Shut the brass
gates of cruelty, and make them fast with iron bars, and fight
courageously, lest we all be taken captives.'

But when all the company of the saints heard this they spake
with a loud voice of anger to the prince of hell: 'Open thy gates
that the King of Glory may come in!'

(See also part 14 of 'The way of the cross', p.138.)

Easter

See part 15 of 'The way of the cross', p.139.
See also the Aidan reading for 12 May.

An Easter vigil

Ideally a fire should be lit outdoors. The church building or other meeting place is left in complete darkness. Each person is given an unlit candle (with a tightly fitting holder to catch dripping wax). A large white candle waits in readiness to be lit from the fire. As the fire is lit, it is blessed with the singing of 'Christ, as a light' (see p.18; music can be found in Book Two, p.866). You may omit the section, 'Be in the heart...' for brevity's sake, unless the fire does not catch easily!

* *indicates a change of reader.*
All say together the sections in **bold** *type.*

Piercing the candle

* Christ behind us in all of our yesterdays.
Christ with us in our today.
Christ before us in all of our tomorrows,
Alpha and Omega, Christ, Lord of all!

**By the wounds and the blood of the Lamb,
may God guard and keep us. Amen.**

The celebrant or other designated person now hammers small nails into the side of the large white candle – four nails in the shape of a cross, signifying wounds in hands, head and feet, then one longer nail in the centre of the cross, signifying the spear piercing the heart of Jesus. This is in time with the next five acclamations:

* Praise be to the blood of the Lamb
  in His forgiving power.

* Praise be to the blood of the Lamb
  in His cleansing power.

* Praise be to the blood of the Lamb
  in His saving power.

* Praise be to the blood of the Lamb
  in His releasing power.

* Praise be to the blood of the Lamb
  in His victorious power.

**By the wounds and the blood of the Lamb,
may God guard and keep us. Amen.**

The Easter candle is lit from the fire, then the other candles are lit from the Easter candle, and light is passed from one to another as 'Christ, as a light' is sung again in its entirety. If the weather is dreadful all may process indoors at this stage.

* Christ is risen!
  **He is risen indeed!
  Alleluia!**

Exsultet

* Leap and spin, you powers of heaven.
  Burst into explosive songs of joy,
  all you companies of angels.
  Let the throne of God be surrounded
  with the praises of all that has life.

* The earth glories in her Maker.
  Now mountain and valley glow in splendour;
  the sea on the shore whispers the praises of Jesus.
  Rivers stream through thirsty soil,
  bringing news of gladness –
  the Redeemer is risen. His glory fills the earth.
  The trees thunder their praises,
  and loudly clap their hands.

* Sound a trumpet through all the earth.
  Our Morning Star is alive!
  Risen in splendour, He is among us;
  the darkness is driven back.
  We, His people, join in the dance of all creation.

**We praise the blood of the Lamb
that has bought our freedom
and reversed the curse of disobedience
and wilfulness.**

**Jesus is the true Lamb that was slain,
whose blood is on the door of our hearts,
whose blood is the protection of the homes
of all believers.**

The symbolism of the following prayers recollects the story of the Passover, when a lamb was killed and its blood was smeared on the doorposts of each Jewish home, protecting those within from the angel of death. Soon their journey began, led through the desert by the presence of God in a pillar of cloud by day and fire by night. This night, the breaking of the Easter dawn recollects Christ's victory over death, and our freedom from slavery to self-will. The actual Passover would be celebrated on the night of the crucifixion, not at the first stirrings of the resurrection, but the symbolism still remains true, and recalls the question asked by the youngest male child at every Passover remembrance meal: 'Why is this night different from any other night?'

* This is now the night
  when first You freed Your people,
  and led Israel's children
  out from slavery in Egypt.
  Dry-shod, they walked through the sea.

* This is now the night when the pillar of fire
  destroyed the darkness of sin!

* This night, Christians everywhere,
  washed clean, and free from any blemish,
  are renewed in hope,
  and learn to grow together as one.

* This night, Jesus our mighty Lord
  broke the chains of death,
  and returned to us, undefeated.
  He is become our Champion.

* What good would life have been to us,
  had the Son of the Most High not come
  to redeem us from
  our helplessness?

* The power of this holy night
  drives away evil and washes guilt away,
  restores lost innocence,
  and turns our mourning into joyful dancing.
  It humbles the proud of heart,
  overturns hatred, and quickens us to peace.

* In the joy of this night,
  Father, receive our offering:
  this holy fire, this Easter light.
  Let its flame ever-burning
  break through the darkness of our times.
  Let it be a pillar of fire,
  leading us forward in Your truth.

May the Sun of Justice which never sets
find this flame still burning;
may Christ the Morning Star
who came again from the dead
find His light brightly burning
in our hearts.

In me, Lord, let there be light.

An optional song as all process indoors:

**He has done so much for me, I cannot tell it all.
I cannot tell it all, no, I cannot tell it all.
He has done so much for me, I cannot tell it all.
He has taken all my sin away.**

**Praise God! Praise God!
Praise God! Praise God!
Praise God! Praise God!
He has taken all my sin away.**

**O death, where is thy sting?
O grave, where is thy victory?
Grave, where is thy victory?
O death, where is thy sting?
For the sting of death is sin,
and the strength of sin is law,
but He's taken all my sin away.**

**Praise God! Praise God!
Praise God! Praise God!
Praise God! Praise God!
He has taken all my sin away.**

Blow out the candles.

Scripture readings

Any of these seven readings may be omitted except the third:

* 1. Creation: selected verses from Genesis 1.
* 2. Abraham and Isaac: selected verses from Genesis 22.
* 3. The Red Sea: Exodus 14:15–22.

All sing 'The song of Miriam' or 'The song of Moses':

The song of Miriam

> The Lord is my strength and song,
> and He is become my salvation.
>> He is my God, and I will prepare Him an habitation;
>> my father's God, and I will exalt Him.
>
> He hath triumphed gloriously: I will sing unto the Lord.
> He hath triumphed gloriously:
> the horse and his rider hath He thrown into the sea.
>
> The Lord is a man of war; the Lord is His name.
> Pharaoh's chariots and his host
> hath He cast, hath He cast into the sea.
>
> Thy right hand, O Lord, is become glorious in power;
> Thy right hand, O Lord, hath dashed in pieces the enemy.
>
> Who is like unto Thee, O Lord, among the gods?
> who is like Thee, glorious in holiness,
> fearful in praises, doing wonders?
>
> The Lord is my strength and song,
> and He is become my salvation.
> He is my God, and I will prepare Him an habitation;
> my father's God, and I will exalt Him.

The song of Moses

> I will sing unto the Lord for He has triumphed gloriously.
> The horse and rider are thrown into the sea.
>
> The Lord my God, my strength, my song,
> is now become my victory.
>
> The Lord is God, and I will praise Him;
> my father's God and I will exalt Him.

Resume the scripture readings:

* 4. A way through: Isaiah 43:16-21.
* 5. God, our husband: Isaiah 54:5-14.
* 6. A new heart: Ezekiel 36:24-28, 33-36.

A Peruvian gloria

(a sung Gloria with a cantor leading and all echoing.)

> Glory to God, glory to God, glory to the Father...
> To Him be glory for ever...
> Allelujah, amen...
> Allelujah, amen...
>
> Glory to God, glory to God, Son of the Father...
> To Him be glory for ever...
> Allelujah, amen...
> Allelujah, amen...
>
> Glory to God, glory to God, glory to the Spirit...
> To Him be glory for ever...
> Allelujah, amen...
> Allelujah, amen...

Resume the Scripture readings:

* 7. Put on Christ: Colossians 3:1-5.

* As we now listen to the story of the events and experiences that led to our Lord's death and resurrection, we are drawn deeper into the stories – we participate in them.

We are in the room as Jesus takes the towel and basin; we listen as Jesus shares His heart with His friends. We hear Jesus pray for us, you and me. We enter into the confusion, the disappointment, the fear and raw emotion as we witness the events. We agonise at His death, and feel the darkness of bereavement, before the mystery of His coming to us that dispels our doubts and rekindles faith and hope, love and trust.

As we listen, may Jesus the Lord of Life speak to us, and touch us with His resurrection power.

There now follow readings or memorised chapters from the Gospel of John. This may be just chapters 20 and 21, or if desired, from chapter 13 through to 21, with a new reader or storyteller for each chapter. At the beginning of the reading of chapter 20 commence relighting the candles.

A short silence is kept.
'The house that John built' (A litany of saints) may follow (see p.326).

The blessing of water

* Scripture reading: Isaiah 55:1-11.

* Lord, Your Spirit brooded over the face
  of the deep, and out of the chaos
  brought forth life and beauty.
  All we have to bring You is our brokenness.

  In me, O Lord,
  let there be life.

   * Blessed are You, O Lord,
     King of the Universe.
     Jesus, You are the Living Water,
     pouring Yourself out, for us, like a flood,
     quenching our thirst with Your love.
     Bless this water;

     let it be a sign to us *(sign with a cross)*
     of the Prince who stands in the streets,
     saying, 'Come to Me, receive freely
     the waters of life!'

The song 'Come to the water' may be sung while the water that has been blessed is splashed over those present.

Come to the water

> **O, let all who thirst,**
> **let them come to the water.**
> **And let all who have nothing,**
> **let them come to the Lord:**
> **without money, without price.**
> **Why should you pay the price,**
> **except for the Lord?**
>
> **And let all who seek,**
> **let them come to the water.**
> **And let all who have nothing,**
> **let them come to the Lord:**
> **without money, without strife.**
> **Why should you spend your life,**
> **except for the Lord?**

And let all who toil,
let them come to the water.
And let all who are weary,
let them come to the Lord:
all who labour, without rest.
How can your soul find rest,
except for the Lord?

And let all the poor,
let them come to the water.
Bring the ones who are laden,
bring them all to the Lord:
bring the children without might.
Easy the load and light:
come to the Lord.

Baptisms, if any, follow at this point.
Then a renewal of vows, using 'A confession of faith' from 'Coming into the light' (see p.174). All renew these promises at this time, not just the new believers.
A Communion service may now follow, if desired, beginning from 'The presentation of the gifts' (see p.83).

The Sunday after Easter

Jesus says, 'Blessed are those who have not seen and yet believe.' But many of us are much heartened by His special appearing to Thomas, who, in his integrity, needed to question in order to firmly believe. In a sense he is the true apostle of the 'heretical imperative'.

* indicates a change of reader.
*All say together the sections in **bold** type.*

* The disciples were assembled behind closed doors
when suddenly You entered, O Jesus our almighty God.
You stood in their midst, and gave them Your peace;
You breathed the Holy Spirit on them.
You commanded them to wait in Jerusalem
until they would be clothed with power from on high.

And so we cry to You:
Glory to You,
our resurrection,
our light,
and our peace!

* Eight days after Your resurrection, O Lord,
You appeared to Your disciples in the upper room.
You greeted them: Peace be with you!
You showed Your hands and feet to the doubting disciple.
Then in faith he cried to you:
'Glory to You, my Lord and my God!'

* Thomas, called the twin, was absent
when You came to Your disciples through closed doors,
    O Christ.
He refused to believe what they told him;
but You did not reject him for his faithlessness.

When he saw Your side, and the wounds in Your hands and feet,
his doubts vanished and his faith was confirmed.

* After both seeing and feeling You,
  he confessed You to be neither an abstract god,
    nor merely a man.
  He cried: 'Glory to You, my Lord and my God!'

* After Your resurrection, O Lord,
  Your disciples gathered behind closed doors.
  You appeared in their midst, and gave them Your peace.
  When Thomas saw Your hands and side he believed.
  He confessed You to be his Lord and God,
  the Saviour of those who trust in You.

* Though the doors were locked,
  Jesus suddenly appeared to the disciples.
  He calmed their fears and gave them peace.
  Then He said to Thomas:
  Why do you not believe that I am risen from the dead?
  Bring your hand here. Thrust it into My side and see.
  Your doubt will teach My passion and resurrection to all,
  and everyone will join your shout:

'Glory to You, my Lord and my God!'

* Oh, most strange wonder!
  doubt has given birth to faith.
  Thomas said: 'Unless I see, I will not believe.'
  But when he touched the Saviour's side,
  he understood.
  He realised that God has suffered in the flesh.

* He cried to the risen Lord with joyful voice:
  Glory to You, my Lord and my God!

* Oh, most strange wonder!
  grass was not scorched by touching fire:

Thomas thrust his hand into the fiery side
of Jesus Christ our God;
he touched Him, yet was not consumed.

* Stubbornness of soul was changed to fervent faith.
He cried from the depths of his soul:
'You are my Master, who rose from the dead.
Glory to You, my Lord and my God!'

* Oh, most strange wonder!
John the apostle leaned on the bosom of the Word,
but Thomas was made worthy to touch His side.

Glory to You, my Lord and my God!

* How great and boundless
is the multitude of Your compassions.

**Give us understanding,
that with Thomas we may cry to You:
'Glory to You, my Lord and my God!'**

Ascension

This liturgy combines material from a variety of sources: a traditional Scottish prayer ('May Jesus Christ Mac David guide our flight, and give us lodging in His peace-bright hall') is blended with the imagery of Jewish betrothal custom and Catherine de Hueck Doherty's vision of the bride as a 'servant of the poor'. The scriptures used are from the Song of Solomon and St John's Gospel.

* indicates a change of reader.
*All say together the sections in **bold** type.*

* Jesus betrothed His followers to Himself. He offered His love, His own body and all His Kingdom. He looked for our love, our willingness to follow Him, our promise to be His alone, to wait for Him.

* 'You have not chosen Me,' He said, 'but I have chosen you. Receive My love. Do not be afraid. Drink from My cup as the sign of your betrothal to Me. Trust in My love and believe in Me. If only you could see Me for who I am!'

* 'My Father is rich in houses and land. I am going to prepare such a wonderful place for you, so where I am you can be with Me. When all is ready, I will return and take you to Myself.'

* 'Walk as My own in the world, and remember how I have loved you. It is better that I leave you now – for time is short, and you have much to do as you prepare for My returning.'

* Clouds of heaven covered Him as He was taken up out of their sight.

* When the people of heaven welcomed their heart-love, Mary's beautiful Son broke into tears before them.

* 'I am My beloved's,' He said, 'and she will be Mine. My desire is towards her, and she will not fail Me. Soon she will shine as brightly as the sun, reaching out for Me, urgent as a mighty army, radiant and terrifying. My sister, my Bride, she is Mine!'

* The Spirit of promise gave this vision, the Spirit He said would lead us deeper into truth. It is a vision of what we, as His own, can become.

* There she stands, above the treeline, shining in the rays of the noonday sun.

* She is beautiful and simple, with her doors wide open; and into her stream the rich and poor alike.

* She is the Bride of Christ. She is His beloved and He is all tenderness, all love, towards her.

* Not only is she His beloved, but she serves the people whom He loved, the poor. The people whom He fed with loaves and fishes, she now feeds with bread and wine.

* From her heart rises an immense cry of adoration:

   My Lord has died.
   Jesus, my Lord is risen.
   Jesus our Lord will come again
   to take us to Himself –
   that where He is
   we may be also.

* Give us the safe home, God, for which we long, in Your Kingdom's lovely gates to sing.

* May Christ the son of David guide our flight, and give us lodging in His peace-bright hall.

Even so, come, Lord Jesus.

* We look for You

   and long for Your returning.

* When all is ready

* and time is ripe

   gather us into Your arms.

* Lord, hasten the day when those who seek You in every nation will come from the east and west, from north and south, and sit at table in Your Kingdom.

   We long for Your appearing!
   We long for Your appearing!
   We long for Your appearing!
   We believe.

Pentecost

An invocation of the Holy Spirit

Most powerful Holy Spirit,
come down
upon us
and subdue us.

From heaven,
where the ordinary
is made glorious,
and glory seems
but ordinary,

bathe us
with the brilliance
of your light
like dew.

Harvest

If you want to know the Creator, understand created things.

Columbanus

(See also 'A call to bless' (the Ninian liturgy) on p.318 and Finan reading for 17 September).

Veni creator

Come Lord, come down,
come in, come among us.
Come as the wind to move us;
come as the light to prove us;
come as the night to rest us;
come as the storm to test us;
come as the sun to warm us;
come as the stillness to calm us;
come Lord, come down,
Come in, come among us.

To God the Father, who created the world;
to God the Son, who redeemed the world;
to God the Holy Spirit, who sustains the world;
be all praise and glory, now and for ever. Amen.

David Adam

Awakening

Awaken us to Your glory.
Restore a gentleness of touch.
Awaken us to Your glory.
Bring us an awareness of You.
Awaken us to Your glory.

David Adam

A time to gather

A time to gather, a time to reap
the fruits we've planted, hoping to bear peace.
The seeds have fallen so many months ago:
the harvest of our life will come.

In tenderness is life's beauty known;
and as we listen the morning star will shine.
The days go by; why not let them be filled
with new and surprising joys?

A time for kneading love's leaven well,
to open up and go beyond ourselves;
and as we reach for this moment, we know
that love is a gift born in care.

A time for hoping and being still,
to go on turning away from brittle fear.
A time to come back with all of one's heart
and bending to another's call.

This is our journey through forests tall;
our paths may differ; and yet among them all
life's dreams and visions sustain us on our way,
as loving gives birth to joy, gives birth to joy.

Gregory Norbert, Weston Priory

From the Celtic psalter

My dear King, my own King,
without pride, without sin,
You created the whole world,
eternal, victorious King.

King of the mysteries,
You existed before the elements,
before the waters covered the ocean floor;
beautiful King,
You are without beginning and without end.

King, You created the land out of shapeless mass,
You carved the mountains and chiselled the valleys,
and covered the earth with trees and grass.

King, You measured each object
and each span within the universe:
the heights of the mountains
and the depths of the oceans;
the distance from the sun to the moon,
and from star to star.

And You created men and women
to be Your stewards of the earth,
always praising You for Your boundless love.

9th century

A harvest offering

Man offers the first-fruits of his labour to the creator of everything in the universe, stars and cornstalks and grains of dust. This is not to say however that man is simply a brutish breaker of furrows, but he labours well in a variety of trades also, with stone and with loom and with oar and with harp and with law-book and with sweet ordering of words and with prism, towards some end which is likewise a kind of harvest. Well he knows that he could not call himself man at all unless he labours all his time under the sun to encompass the end for which his faculties were given to him. This end, whatever the nature of his occupation, is his harvest time; and he would be a poor labourer that would not wish, among all that broken gold, to offer back a tithe or a hundredth into the hands that formed the original fecund dust.

George Mackay Brown, Magnus

The gathering of joy and pain

To the singing of the harvest-song goes the life of a year, or of all the years – the summer that is gone, the winter that is coming; the ones who have sown but are not here to reap; the ones who will sow when the reapers that are have been forgotten; the Good Being who makes the sun shine and the corn ripen. There may be the breath of a sigh in that song, but there is also in it a whole storm of rapture.

Gladness must come to its own some time; for the sorrows, there are all the times. To the harvest-field go we, then, for life as it ought to be. The sickle is fate, the hand that holds it is ours, and for once we will be the conqueror. Cut we down a sorrow here and a pain there, bind them, and make them our slaves.

Kenneth McLeod, The Road to the Isles

A harvest prayer

> May the holy and life-giving God
> teach us to reverence all His works,
> to praise Him in all we do,
> to live in His image and to His glory.

Care of the land, care for the world

Land is a gift of God to His people.
The Scriptures remind us
that the people of God
are charged with tending, caring,
resting and stewarding the land.
But when people violate God's laws
then the land is spoiled.

We confess our sin
in penitence
and with sorrow.

We grieve at the polluted seas,
poisoned atmosphere,
all ugliness, misuse and greed,
at arrogant exploitation
and indifference to consequences.

Have mercy on us, Lord.
Heal our lives,
and Your world.

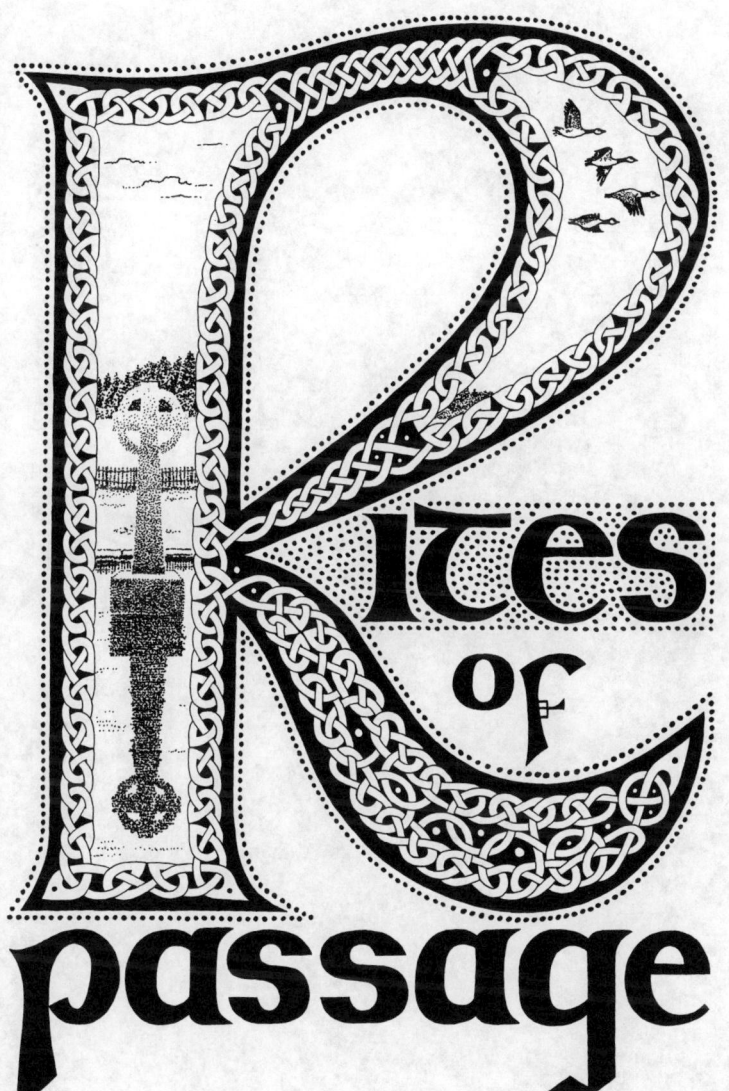

Rites of Passage

RITES OF PASSAGE

Coming into the light – birth

These are prayers which may be used at the christening or dedication of a child.

Two alternative forms are provided. In the past we have always used Option A when the child is a boy and Option B when the child is a girl; but the distinction seemed quite arbitrary. Either can be used as preferred, but the wording of Option B will need adjusting if used for a boy. Sections in square brackets should be omitted where parents are not both believers.

If a Scripture is to be read for the occasion before the prayers, the following are suggested options:
- Psalm 127:1-5;
- 1 Samuel 1:9-20, 24-28; 2:1-2, 9, 18-19;
- Mark 10:13-16.

Prayers for the Christening or dedication of a child

Option A

Celebrant (or friend or godparent):
> The blessing of Christ
> comes to you in this child.
> His blessing is mercy
> and kindness and joy.
> Blessing comes to home
> and to family.

Celebrant (or friend or godparent):
>Welcome, *(name of child)*,
>child of love.
>God is here to bless you.
>And blessed are you,
>beyond telling,
>to be born to parents
>who love you
>and love each other
>[servants of the
>great King Jesus].

Godparent (or celebrant or friend):
>Grow gently, *(name of child)*,
>in love of God.
>We bless you,
>and pray
>Christ be near you,
>now and each hour
>of your life.
>
>**God be with you**
>**in this your day,**
>**every day and every way,**
>**with you and for you**
>**in this your day,**
>**and the love**
>**and affection**
>**of heaven**
>**be toward you.**

Celebrant (or friend or godparent):
>As a tiny baby your parents cover
>and clothe you
>in their love
>[and with their faith].

RITES OF PASSAGE | COMING INTO THE LIGHT – BIRTH

> As you grow
> may faith grow with you.
> May you find the presence
> of Christ your clothing
> and protection.
> And year by year may the
> knowledge of His presence
> be greater for you,
> that daily you may put on Christ
> and walk as His own in the world.

Parents:

> *(Name of child)*,
> may God make clear to you each road;
> may He make safe to you each steep;
> should you stumble, hold you;
> if you fall, lift you up;
> when you are hard pressed with evil,
> deliver you –
> and bring you at last to His glory.

Celebrant (or friend or godparent), facing the parents:

> The blessing of Christ
> comes to you in *(name of child)*;
> this blessing is mercy
> and kindness and joy.
> Blessing comes to home
> and to family.

Option B

Celebrant (or friend or godparent):

> The blessing of Christ
> comes to you in this child.
> His blessing is mercy
> and kindness and joy.
> Blessing comes to home
> and to family.

Parents:
>*(Name of child)*, Lord,
>Your gift to us:
>we lift *her* up to You.
>Always You hold *her*:
>This life You entrusted to us,
>a sign of Your love and Your faith.
>
>[Our names are inscribed upon Your palms.
>You pour blessing on the details of our days.]
>
>We are giving *her* back to You, dear Lord.
>We are giving *her* back to You.
>
>[Your Kingdom come
>and Your will be done
>in everything that we do.
>We are giving *her* back to You.]
>
>Of Your tenderness and healing and patience
>there is no end at all.
>We know we can trust You, Lord;
>We know we can trust You.

Celebrant (or friend or godparent):
>Welcome, *(name of child)*,
>child of love.
>God is here to bless you.
>And blessed are you,
>beyond telling,
>to be born to parents
>who love you
>and love each other
>servants of the great King Jesus].

Godparent (or celebrant or friend):
>	Grow gently, *(name of child)*,
>	in love of God.
>	We bless you,
>	and pray
>	Christ be near you,
>	now and each hour
>	of your life.
>
>	**God be with you**
>	**in this your day,**
>	**every day and every way,**
>	**with you and for you**
>	**in this your day,**
>	**and the love**
>	**and affection**
>	**of heaven**
>	**be toward you.**

Celebrant (or friend or godparent), facing the parents:
>	The blessing of Christ
>	comes to you in your *(name of child)*;
>	this blessing is mercy
>	and kindness and joy.
>	Blessing comes to home
>	and to family.

(See also 'Blessing on a child', p.201.)

Coming into the light – rebirth

A baptismal prayer

To be said by the one being baptised.

> Lord,
> through the hand
> of Your friend and servant,
> place Your hand upon my head.
>
> Place Your right hand
> upon my head, Lord,
> and claim me as Your own.
>
> I call on all heaven to witness today
> that I have put on Christ.

A confession of faith

This may be used:
- at the baptism of a believer;
- at confirmation or its equivalent;
- for the renewal of baptismal vows.

> I call all heaven to witness today
> that I have put on Christ.
>
> I choose no other Lord
> than the Maker of heaven and earth.
>
> This day I walk with Him
> and He will walk with me.

I fasten close to me this day
that same Jesus
who came to us as flesh and blood
and was Himself baptised in the Jordan river.

He died upon a cross to rescue me,
broke free from death, its conqueror.
He left us, to return the more certainly.
All these truths and their power
I fasten close to me this day.

Resisting my own selfishness and sin,
refusing to live as a slave to riches,
pleasure or reputation,
rejecting Satan and all his lies,
I call on heaven to witness today
that I have put on Christ.

Marriage – light and shadow

A marrying prayer

All we have came only from You.
Everything we hope for
will only come from Your love.
All that we enjoy You gave us freely.
Everything we ask for
is only Yours to give.

Give us the light to understand.
Put fire behind our will.
Be at the beginning of all we begin.
Excite our love,
strengthen our weakness,
encompass our desire.

Shield our thoughts,
and cradle our bodies,
and as we breathe this prayer,
in our hearts may we feel
Your presence.

Thigpen's wedding

Here I set my face unto you.
Here I speak my heart's true vow.
Here I choose to walk beside you,
loving only you,
my heart speaks true,
for evermore from now.

I will love you in the dawning
and in the bright noon-day.

I will love you in the even.
Every day I live,
my heart I'll give.
I'll love you from my grave.

I have heard God in your laughter.
I have seen Him on your face.
And it's clear now what He's after,
for He wrote your name
on my heart in flame;
it's a wound I'll not erase.

We will mount the wings of morning.
We will fly before the wind.
We will dwell within the mystery
of the glories of Jehovah's love:
a circle with no end.

We will pitch our tents towards Zion
in the shadow of His love.
We will covenant between us.
We will covenant with the earth below
and with heaven up above.
We will covenant with the dust below
and the Spirit up above.

From the album The Vigil
by Kemper Crabb

Peace-prayer for a wedding

Christ, King of tenderness,
Christ, King of tenderness,
bind *us* with a bond
that cannot be broken.
Bind *us* with a bond of love
that cannot be broken.

'Us' may be changed to 'them'. The 'Caim prayer' (p.203) may also be appropriate at a wedding.

Marriage blessings

1.

May God and your marriage
bring you joy.
God give you joy of one another!

2.

Be ever
in the embrace of the Father.
Be ever
in the embrace of the Son.
Be ever
in the embrace of the Spirit.
Be ever
in the embrace of one another.

3.

May the Lord
tie a bond of your love
between you for ever
without loosening.

In difficulties

O God, make clear to us each road.
O God, make safe to us each steep;
when we stumble, hold us;
when we fall, lift us up.
When we are hard pressed with evil,
deliver us;
and bring us at last to Your glory.

The ultimate answer

Oh, you lovers everywhere
who are parted and troubled,
or near and discordant,
go quickly to Him who waits
on the hilltops of your souls,
for there you will find peace,
and your hidden love.

Let Christ always be
the third person at the feast,
the white passion at the bridal,
the constant companion on the road.

He is the ultimate answer
and even now
is nearer than breath
or as far away
as your stubborn will.

Ruth St Denis, An Unfinished Life

Prayer for reconciliation

Lord,
let our memory
provide no shelter
for grievance against each other.

Lord,
let our heart
provide no harbour
for hatred of each other.

Lord,
let our tongue
be no accomplice
in the judgement of each other.

In difficult times

See also the Caim prayer on p.203.

On separation from loved ones

> Give *them* peace
> to know I am unharmed.
> Give *them* hope
> to know I will return.
> Give *them* patience to wait
> and courage to endure the waiting.
> Give *them* strength
> so that *they* will not grow weary.

Stephen Lawhead

Nothing can fill the gap when we are away from those we love, and it would be wrong to try and find anything. We must simply hold out and win through. That sounds very hard at first, but at the same time it is a great consolation, since leaving the gap unfilled preserves the bonds between us. It is nonsense to say that God fills the gap; He does not fill it, but keeps it empty so that our communion with another may be kept alive, even at the cost of pain.

Dietrich Bonhoeffer

A prayer in time of darkness

> All that I love
> into Your keeping.
> All that I care for
> into Your care.

Be with us by day,
be with us by night;
and as dark closes
the eyelids with sleep,
may I waken
to the peace of a new day.

A prayer in brokenness

O God,
I cannot undo the past,
or make it never have happened!
– neither can You. There are some things
that are not possible even for You
– but not many!

I ask You,
humbly,
and from the bottom of my heart:
Please, God,
would You write straight
with my crooked lines?
Out of the serious mistakes of my life
will You make something beautiful for You?

Teach me to live at peace with You,
to make peace with others
and even with myself.

Give me fresh vision. Let me
experience Your love so deeply
that I am free to
face the future with a steady eye,
forgiven,
and strong in hope.

A general intercession for those in trouble

These may be used as bidding prayers during Communion (see p.81).

* indicates a change of reader (if desired).

* We hold before God:
  those for whom life is very difficult;
  those who have difficult decisions to make, and who honestly do not know what is the right thing to do.

* We hold before God:
  those who have difficult tasks to do and to face, and who fear they may fail in them;
  those who have difficult temptations to face, and who know only too well that they may fall to them, if they try to meet them alone.

* We hold before God:
  those who know that they can be their own worst enemies.

* We hold before God:
  those who have difficult people to work with; those who have to suffer unjust treatment, unfair criticism, unappreciated work.

* We hold before God:
  those who are sad because someone they loved has died; and any who are disappointed in something for which they hoped very much.

William Barclay

Mid-life

Mid-life appraisal

Is it not possible that middle age can be looked upon as a period of second flowering, second growth, even a kind of second adolescence? It is true that society in general does not help one accept this interpretation of the second half of life. And therefore this period of expanding is often tragically misunderstood. Many people never climb above the plateau of forty-to-fifty. The signs that presage growth are so similar, it seems to me, to those in early adolescence: discontent, restlessness, doubt, despair, longing. But now these are interpreted falsely as signs of decay. In youth one does not as often misinterpret the signs: one accepts them, quite rightly, as growing pains. One takes them seriously, listens to them, follows where they lead. One is afraid. Naturally. Who is not afraid of pure space – that breathtaking empty space of an open door? But, despite fear, one goes through to the room beyond.

But in middle age, because of the false assumption that it is a period of decline, one interprets these life-signs, paradoxically, as signs of approaching death. Instead of facing them, one runs away. Anything, rather than face them. Anything rather than stand still and learn from them. One tries to cure the signs of growth: to exorcise them, as if they were devils, when really they might be angels of annunciation.

Angels of annunciation of what? Of a new stage in living when, having shed many of the physical struggles, the wordly ambitions, the material encumbrances of active life, one might be free to fulfil the neglected side of one's self. One might be free for growth of mind, heart and talent; free at last for spiritual growth.

So beautiful is the still hour of the sea's withdrawal, as beautiful as the sea's return when encroaching waves pound up the beach, pressing to reach those dark rumpled chains of seaweed which mark the last high tide.

We have so little faith in the ebb and flow of life, of love, of relationships. We leap at the flow of the tide and resist in terror its ebb. We are afraid it will never return. We insist on permanence, on duration, on continuity; when the only continuity possible, in life as in love, is in growth, in fluidity – in freedom, in the sense that dancers are free, barely touching as they pass, but partners in the same pattern. The only real security is not in owning or possessing, not in demanding or expecting, not in hoping even. Security in a relationship lies neither in looking back to what it was in nostalgia, nor forward to what it might be in dread or anticipation, but living in the present relationship and accepting it as it is now.

Anne Morrow Lindbergh,
Gift from the Sea

A prayer in 'the middle years' of opportunity

> Lord, help me now to unclutter my life,
> to organise myself in the direction of simplicity.
> Lord, teach me to listen to my heart;
> teach me to welcome change, instead of fearing it.
> Lord, I give You these stirrings inside me,
> I give You my discontent,
> I give You my restlessness,
> I give You my doubt,
> I give You my despair,
> I give You all the longings I hold inside.
> Help me to listen to these signs of change, of growth;
> to listen seriously and follow where they lead
> through the breathtaking empty space of an open door.

Liminal space

Where earth and heaven meet

Allow more and more thoughts
of Your thinking to come into our hearts,
day by day,
till there shall at last be an open road
between You and us,
and Your angels may go up and down amongst us,
so that we may be in Your heaven,
even while we are upon Your earth.
Amen.

Adapted from a passage in David Elginbrod
by George MacDonald

Prayers for sleepless nights

You who keeps the stars alight,
and our souls burning
with a light beyond that of the stars,
grant that they may shine before You
as the stars for ever and ever.

And as You hold the stars burning in the night
when no one sees them,
so hold the light burning in our souls
when we see neither You nor that light,
but are buried in the grave of sleep and forgetfulness.
Amen.

Adapted from a passage in David Elginbrod
by George MacDonald

The sky is bright with uncountable stars.
I know they are uncountable:

I have tried this impossible task
these sleepless nights.

Where are You, Lord,
as the fog of fatigue
numbs me of all
but the desperate desire to sleep?

Comfort me, Lord, with Your presence
as the ever-watchful mother
soothes the fretful, feverish child.

Grant me the gift of sleep;
and be the guardian of my dreams,
that I may know You through them also.
Or if I must watch with You through
the long, hard night,
share with me the burden of Your heart
that my sleepless hours
be spent in purposeful prayer.

And if You bless me once more with the
gift of the morning,
may I rise,
grateful to greet You,
ready to walk with You
into the tasks of the day.

Anne Wadey

Courage, hope and peace

O God, we belong to You utterly.
You are such a Father
that You take our sins from us
and throw them behind Your back.
You clean our souls,
as Your Son washed our feet.

We hold up our hearts to You:
make them what they must be.

Adapted from a passage in Malcolm
by George MacDonald

The shadow of death

Some day I must die;
I know not the time nor the place.
Let me not die in sin,
but wrapped in Your loving grace.

Death and dying

Preparing for what may be just ahead

Tonight, as on other nights,
I'm walking alone
through the valley of fear.
O God, I pray
that You will hear me,
for You alone know
what is in my heart.
Lift me out of the valley of despair
and set my soul free.

Anne Wadey

Bright King of Friday and Father Almighty,
make a roof for me by night and guard me by day.
If You are to bring me along the path
I have never seen before,
make it a pathway for me to the life of glory.

Irish prayer

Evening comes when You call,
and all nature listens to You
because You hold it all.
And now You hold me.

Blessed are You, O Lord our God,
King of the universe!
At Your word night falls.
In Your wisdom You open heaven's gates.
You set the stars in the vault of heaven.
You created night and day.

Blessed are You, O Lord,
at whose word night falls.
All nature listens to You,
because You hold it all.
And now You hold me.

From the Talmud *and a song by*
Annie Herring and Matthew Ward

I am going home with You,
to Your home.
I am going home with You
to Your home of mercy.
I am going home with You
to the fount of all blessing.

From Carmina Gadelica

A prayer on behalf of the dying

Change 'woman' to 'man' etc. as appropriate.

God, omit not this *woman* from Your covenant.
The many evils that in this life *she* has committed
she cannot count or list this night.
Gather this soul with Your own arm, O Christ,
great King of the City of Heaven.

It was Your work, O Christ,
the buying of the soul
at the time of the balancing of the beam,
at the time of bringing of judgement.
Be this soul hidden in Your right hand.

May Michael, prince of angels,
come to meet *her* soul,
leading it home
to the heaven of the Son of God.

Facing death with courage

The name of the dying person should be inserted where indicated.

Lord,
so strange to us
this doorway labelled death!
– a door of darkness
still closed to protect us
from the brilliance of eternal life;
a final obstacle
to the fullness of Your presence.

We stand together at the threshold,
(name),
and I who pray this prayer
for this Your child.

Give courage, Lord,
for this uncharted journey,
peacefulness at parting
from all that must be left behind,
and an inner vision of invitation
for all that is better that awaits.

And I also must release *(name)*
from my own flawed embrace
to Your precious and perfect presence.
Soon enough,
I too must follow,
placing my footsteps
in those of the Christ Himself.

Watching with one who is dying

Sleep now, sleep, and away with your sorrow,
Sleep now, sleep, and away with your sorrow,
Sleep now, sleep, and away with your sorrow;
Sleep, my loved one, in the Rock of the fold.

Sleep, O sleep in the calm of all calm.
Sleep, O sleep in the guidance of guidance.
Sleep, O sleep in the love of all loves.
Sleep, my loved one, in the Lord of life.
Sleep, my loved one, in the God of life.

The shade of death lies upon your face, my loved one,
but the Jesus of grace has His hand round about you;
in nearness to the Trinity farewell to your pains;
Christ stands before you and peace is in His mind.

The darkness of bereavement

Walking with grief

Do not hurry
as you walk with grief;
it does not help the journey.

Walk slowly,
pausing often:
do not hurry
as you walk with grief.
Be not disturbed
by memories that come unbidden.
Swiftly forgive;
and let Christ speak for you
unspoken words.
Unfinished conversation
will be resolved in Him.
Be not disturbed.

Be gentle with the one
who walks with grief.
If it is you,
be gentle with yourself.
Swiftly forgive;
walk slowly,
pausing often.

Take time, be gentle
as you walk with grief.

Andy Raine

Come now

Come now
live in us.
Let us stay in You,
since if we be all in You,
we cannot be far from one another,
though some may be in heaven
and some upon earth.

Adapted from a passage in David Elginbrod
by George MacDonald

A caim written as a night prayer for someone recently bereaved

(See p.203 for an explanation of caim prayer.)

> This night and every night
> seems infinite with questions,
> and sleep as elusive
> as answers.
>
> Pain and longing are always present,
> dulled only a little
> by the distractions of day.
> I am weary; I am angry.
> I am confused.
>
> Circle me, Lord.
> Keep despair and disillusion without.
> Bring a glimmer of hope within.
>
> Circle me, Lord;
> keep nightmare without.
> Bring moments of rest within.
>
> Circle me, Lord;
> keep bitterness without.
> Bring an occasional sense
> of Your presence within.

Caelan – for the loss of a child

Caelan is the Gaelic word for 'little one' – the name given by Nick and Anita Haigh to their second unborn baby. The traumatic experience of losing two babies led Anita to the realisation that there are few specific liturgical resources available for parents and families seeking spiritual strength at a time of such great need; hence this liturgy.

RITES OF PASSAGE | THE DARKNESS OF BEREAVEMENT

This form of prayer may be used:
- on the loss of a baby through miscarriage;
- after a stillbirth or loss of a newborn baby;
- by those coming to terms with an abortion.

All who wish may read in turn.
* indicates a change of reader.
*All say together the sections in **bold** type.*

**We have come to seek You, O God
just as we are we come.**

**We have come to be sought by You;
just as we are we come.**

* We come as we are,
with our anguish and pain.

* We come as we are,
with our anger and disappointment.

* We come as we are,
in our loss and confusion.

* We come as we are,
with our hopes dashed,

* our faith shaken,

* and our spirits wearied.

**O God, who is close to the broken-hearted,
bind up our wounded hearts.**

**O God, who saves those crushed in spirit,
bring peace to our troubled souls.**

Scripture readings

* How long, O Lord? Will You forget me forever?
  How long will You hide Your face from me?
  How long must I wrestle with my thoughts
  and every day have sorrow in my heart?

* But I will trust in Your unfailing love;
  I will rejoice in Your salvation.
  I will sing to the Lord
  for He has been good to me.

Psalm 13:1-2a, 5-6

* Come to Me, all you who are weary and heavy laden,
  and I will give you rest.

* Take My yoke upon you and learn from Me;
  for I am gentle and humble in heart,
  and you will find rest for your souls.

Matthew 11:28-29

Committal

The following is said by the parents together:

We thank You for the gift of life.

We acknowledge that all life comes from You,
and is known and cherished by You.

Into Your loving care, we commit our little one *(name)*,
as we entrust to You the life so briefly entrusted to us.

We ask for the strength to hold on to our faith,
for the desire to forgive when we do not comprehend
Your ways,

for the vision to look forward in hope,
and for peace born of a surrendered spirit.

In Your goodness and mercy, hear our prayer.

Then follows some symbolic gesture of committal. It could be the planting of a tree, throwing of flowers into the sea ... Appropriate music may be used; perhaps Nick and Anita's own 'Song for Kim' from their album Celtic Roots & Rhythms.

Reading

I am bewildered by so many things. I ask myself why the little one is taken from the breast; why the dreams Thou hast sent us reach not their haven of fulfilment. Jesus, Light in my darkness, bring me out of my groping into the radiance of Thy truth. Yet, if Thou withhold Thy light from me because my eyes cannot bear its brightness, still give me what is needful to make my dark be gone. Amen.

Adapted from Hebridean Altars *by Alistair Maclean*

Declaration

> You're the voice that calms our fears.
> You're the laughter – dries our tears.
> You're our music, our refrain.
> Help us sing Your song again.
>
> Lord have mercy,
> Christ have mercy,
> Lord have mercy.
>
> In the name of the Father,
> and of the Son,
> and of the Holy Spirit.
> Amen.

for the strength to look forward in hope,
and for peace borne in surrendered sleep.

In Your goodness and mercy, hear our prayer.

Insert your own symbolic gesture of committal. If possible, let the blessing of a tree, the lighting of incense, a candle, or a simple prayer of thanksgiving be enough. Pets and Angels over Soughbones, from Inspired Gifts & Roots & Fruit, Ine.

Reading

I am besieged by so many things I ask myself why the little one is taken from the breast, why the dream. Thou hast sent is ready for their haven of fulfilment. Jesus, light of my darkness, bring me out of my stepping into the radiance of Thy truth, yet if Thou withhold Thy light from me, I cast my eyes cannot bear the brightness, still give me that which needs to make my dark perfect. Amen.

Adapted from Meditations Before Mass, Romano Guardini

Declaration

You're the voice that calms our fears.
You're the laughter—drives our tears.
You're our music, our refrain.
Help us sing Your songs again.

Lord, have mercy.
Christ, have mercy.
Lord, have mercy.

In the name of the Father,
and of the Son,
and of the Holy Spirit.
Amen.

Blessings and Graces

BLESSINGS AND GRACES

Prayers for blessings

The telling place

> Bless us, Lord, this day with vision.
> May this place be a sacred place,
> a telling place,
> where heaven and earth meet.

For work

> Lord, bless the work that we do;
> bless it,
> and keep us in Your power.

On foot

> Bless to me, O Lord,
> the earth beneath my feet;
> bless to me, O Lord,
> the path I tread:
> my walk this day with the Father,
> my walk this day with Christ,
> my walk this day with the Spirit.

For a journey

Let me not undertake this journey begrudgingly,
but instead with love and thankfulness, saying,
as Columba said:
I thank You for this, my God:
I am a traveller
and stranger in the world,
like so many of Your people
before me.

Blessings

On the departure of a well-loved guest

Would it not be the beautiful thing now,
if you were just coming instead of going?

Till we meet again

May the road rise to meet you;
may the wind be always at your back.
May the sun shine warm upon your face
and the rain fall softly on your fields.
Until we meet again
may God hold you
in the hollow of His hand.

A blessing on someone's journey or on a child

I bless you, *(name)/darling one*,
in the name of the Holy Three,
the Father, the Son and the Sacred Spirit.
May you drink deeply
from God's cup of joy.
May the night bring you quiet.
And when you come
to the Father's palace
may His door be open
and the welcome warm.

Just you

You are not an accident.
Even at the moment of your conception,
out of many possibilities
only certain cells combined,
survived, grew to be you.
You are unique.
You were created for a purpose.
God loves you.

Nan's blessing

I'll never understand the love
the Lord Jesus has for you, *(name)*,
I'll never understand
how much He loves you.
But this much I know:
that He loves you,
He loves you
with all of His heart,
and you are so precious to Him.

My prayer for you

May the Father of Life pour out His grace on you;
may you feel His hand in everything you do
and be strengthened by the things He brings you through:
this is my prayer for you.

May the Son of God be Lord in all your ways;
may He shepherd you the length of all your days,
and in your heart may He receive the praise:
this is my prayer for you.

And despite how simple it may sound,
I pray that His grace will abound
and motivate everything you do;
and may the fullness of His love be shared through you.

May His Spirit comfort you, and make you strong,
may He discipline you gently when you're wrong,
and in your heart may He give you a song:
this is my prayer for you.

May Jesus be Lord in all your ways,
may He shepherd you the length of all your days,
and in your heart may He receive the praise:
this is my prayer for you, my prayer for you.

Caim prayer (When I do not know what to pray)

When words get in the way and it seems impossible to focus, the caim or 'encircling' prayer can often be helpful. Draw a circle clockwise around yourself, using the right index finger as you say the prayer; this symbolises the encircling love of God. (The situation may make this physical action impractical; in which case see the action in your mind's eye as you pray.) See yourself and others encircled and be aware that the living God surrounds and encloses with His love, care and protection.

The caim prayer can be adapted to many different situations (for instance, see its use with somebody recently bereaved, p.192). Sometimes a particular form of the prayer that has been found to be helpful can be written down for repeated use when praying again for the same person or for another person in similar circumstances.

Different examples of caim prayers are given here. Insert *him*, *her* or *them* instead of *name* if appropriate, and change the wording to suit the circumstances.

1.
Circle *(name)*, Lord.
Keep *(comfort)* near
and *(discouragement)* afar.
Keep *(peace)* within
and *(turmoil)* out.
Amen.

2.
Circle *(name)*, Lord.
Keep protection near
and danger afar.

Circle *(name)*, Lord.
keep hope within,
keep despair without.

Circle *(name)*, Lord.
Keep light near
and darkness afar.

Circle *(name)*, Lord.
keep peace within
and anxiety without.

The eternal Father, Son and Holy Spirit
shield *(name)* on every side.
Amen.

3.
The compassing of God be upon you,
the compassing of the God of life.

The compassing of Christ be upon you,
the compassing of the Christ of love.

The compassing of the Spirit be upon you,
the compassing of the Spirit of grace.

The compassing of the Sacred Three be upon you,
the compassing of the Sacred Three protect you,
the compassing of the Sacred Three preserve you.
Amen.

Graces

A Hebridean grace

Lord God, giver of all good things,
may we who share at this table,
like pilgrims here on earth,
be welcomed with Your saints
to the heavenly feast.
Amen.

Brigid's grace

God bless our food;
God bless our drink.
And keep our homes
and ourselves
in Your embrace,
O God.
Amen.

Shabbat

Bless, O Lord,
this food we are about to eat;
and we pray you, O God,
that it may be good
for our body and soul;
and, if there is any poor creature
hungry or thirsty walking the road,
may God send them in to us
so that we can share the food with them,
just as Christ shares His gifts
with all of us.
Amen.

From the Isle of Lewis

Our God, we are Your guests,
and 'tis You who keeps the generous table.
We thank You.
Amen.

The stranger's blessing

The Sacred Three be blessing thee,
thy table and its store.
The Sacred Three be blessing
all thy loved ones evermore.
Amen.

Saranam (refuge)

Receive our thanks for night and day,
for food and shelter, rest and play.
Be here our guest and with us stay,
saranam, saranam, saranam.

(See p.99 for a musical setting)

Community thanksgiving

O Lord, everybody's home,
eating, drinking,
breathing in the Lord.
Now rejoice: the family's all together.

Leading up to Christmas

Watch and pray:
the Lord shall come.
Those who are longing
await His appearing.
Those who listen
await His cry.
Watch ... Wait ... Listen.

Christmas

The blessing of Christ
comes to cave and to hillside.
His coming is mercy
and kindness and joy.
Hope is born
in this, His birthing.

Follow the example

FOLLOW THE EXAMPLE OF THE WISE AND THE GOOD

Calendar and resources for saints' days and festivals

A saint is not someone who identifies his own mood, suppresses it and then does the opposite: but someone who lives to a heroic level – loving God, others and themselves heroically. There are thousands of named saints; and many more saints who all gave themselves wholly to the task of loving.

We are not to imitate the departed saints – they are unlikely to be of our own personality or temperament so it would not be appropriate. We should not ask: 'What can I learn and imitate?' No, instead we should ask: 'What can I learn about God?' The life of a saint is not the life of a great man or woman, but of God's life in an ordinary man or woman. Saints' days are not all about that saint: but about a celebration of Christ.

Remembering the saints gives us a bigger idea of the things of God. When Elisha's servant saw the enemy chariots (2 Kings 6:15-16), he had to have his eyes opened so that he could see God's chariots of fire. It was such a big view of God that Elisha had, and now his servant could share in that. This is exactly how the saints can help us: if ever we feel outnumbered, remember that we never get to see the whole church.

Kate Tristram

The saints chosen here have particular significance for us in the Community. Some are Celtic, some modern – and the choice of who is included or excluded may seem arbitrary. This calendar is, however, offered with sincerity and without desire to cause offence. (We could have included John the Baptist, Julian of Norwich, Janani Luwum and so on – but we had to stop somewhere!)

Saints' days Scripture readings

A saints' day usually marks not their birthday but the date of their death (promotion to glory!).

The following readings have been selected for use at Holy Communion or Mass on a saint's day; they could also be used for a pilgrimage or themed service. The bold bracketed verse (or part of a verse) notation in the Psalm readings suggests a verse containing a phrase that can be used as a response and interspersed intelligently amongst the other Psalm verses chosen. As an example, for Aidan on 31 Aug the response would be part of verse 19 of Psalm 77 – 'Your path led through the sea' – which is short enough for a congregation to remember and repeat.

FOLLOW THE EXAMPLE | SAINTS' DAYS SCRIPTURE READINGS

DATE	SAINT	OT READING	PSALM READING	NT READING	GOSPEL READING
1 Jan	New Year	Isaiah 42:5, 9, 12	Psalm 68:1, 3-10, 28, 32-35 (**9**)	Philippians 3:7-16	John 1:35-50
1 Jan	Telemachus	Isaiah 59:15-16	Psalm 84:4-12 (**12B**)	Romans 12:20-21	Matthew 5:2-3, 8-9
4 Jan	Juniper	Jeremiah 17:7-8	Psalm 1:1-3 (**1A**)	1 Corinthians 1:26-31	Matthew 18:1-5
6 Jan	Three Kings' Day	Job 9:1-12	Psalm 72:1-2, 4-6, 10-12, 15, 17-19 (**11**)	Acts 17:24-27	Matthew 2:1-2 or Matthew 1:18-25; 2:1-2, 13-14
13 Jan	Hilary of Poitiers	Isaiah 32:2-6	Psalm 119:41-46 (**42B**)	2 Timothy 1:13-14; 2:1-2	Matthew 18:24-28
13 Jan	Kentigern	Ecclesiastes 11:5	Psalm 19:1-4, 7-8 (**14A**)	Acts 18:24-27	Mark 4:3-9
15 Jan	Ita	Proverbs 24:3-4	Psalm 119:9-16 (**11A**)	1 Thessalonians 2:7-8, 10, 12-13	Matthew 5:1-3, 7-8
15 Jan	Paul of Thebes	Isaiah 61:8-9	Psalm 63:1, 7-8 (**1A**)	1 Thessalonians 4:11-12	Matthew 6:5-6
17 Jan	Antony of Egypt	Isaiah 35:1-2	Psalm 91:2-7 (**2B**)	Ephesians 6:11-18	Matthew 19:16-21
28 Jan	Canaire	Exodus 13:20-21	Psalm 99:3-5, 7 (**3B**)	Galatians 3:26-29	Luke 24:9-11
1 Feb	Brigid	Leviticus 9:23-24	Psalm 104:13-15, 24-34 (**34B**)	2 Corinthians 9:6-13	John 2:3-11
8 Feb	Elfleda	1 Samuel 2:8-19, 26; 3:3-4	Psalm 16:1-2, 5-8 (**1**)	Philippians 4:4-7	John 15:1-5
9 Feb	Teilo	Exodus 22:26-27	Psalm 119:145-149 (**145B**)	James 1:19-20, 26	Matthew 5:21-22; 7:1-2
11 Feb	Caedmon	Judges 6:11-12	Psalm 147:7-9, 11-19 (**7A**)	Acts 2:16-18	Luke 1:64-66, 76-79
17 Feb	Finan	Genesis 22:14-18	Psalm 145:3, 4-7 (**4A**)	Romans 12:16-18	Matthew 5:14-16

FOLLOW THE EXAMPLE | SAINTS' DAYS SCRIPTURE READINGS

DATE	SAINT	OT READING	PSALM READING	NT READING	GOSPEL READING
17 Feb	John Hyde	1 Kings 18:42-45	Psalm 144:3-4 (**4**)	1 Thessalonians 5:16-19	John 16:20-24
18 Feb	Colman	Ecclesiastes 7:8-14	Psalm 31:3-6, 14-15 (**6B**)	2 Timothy 4:6-8	Mark 9:35-42
23 Feb	Polycarp	Daniel 3:13-25	Psalm 116:12, 14-15 (**15**)	Revelation 2:8-11	John 17:11, 13-17
1 Mar	David	1 Chronicles 16:8-11	Psalm 89:1-3, 15-16 (**1A**)	Ephesians 2:4-10	Mark 4:26-29
2 Mar	Chad	Exodus 3:2-5	Psalm 103:19-22 (**19A**)	2 Timothy 4:7-8	Luke 14:7-11
4 Mar	Owini	Jeremiah 31:9, 20-21	Psalm 139:1-10 (**2A**)	1 Thessalonians 4:11-14	John 21:24-25
5 Mar	Piran	Deuteronomy 33:1, 18-19	Psalm 139:1-6, 15-18 (**17b-18a**)	Hebrews 11:12-15	Luke 3:4-6, 8
6 Mar	Baldred	1 Kings 19:11-13A	Psalm 18:25, 30-32 (**10A**)	1 Thessalonians 1:2-3	Matthew 21:18-22
6 Mar	Billfrith	Exodus 35:30-36:2	Psalm 119:72-74, 77 (**77B**)	Revelation 21:10-11, 19-23	Matthew 13:44-46
8 Mar	Senan	1 Chronicles 12:17-18, 21-22	Psalm 116:5, 7-9, 12-13 (**5**)	Hebrews 5:11-6:3	John 4:7-11
12 Mar	Paul Aurelian	Job 11:7-9	Psalm 84:5, 7-8, 11-12 (**5**)	Acts 20:1-2, 4-5, 13-15, 17-18, 32-36; 21:1-2	John 3:8-10, 12
17 Mar	Patrick	1 Kings 18:21-39	Psalm 18:30-33 (**32**)	1 Corinthians 9:19-23	Matthew 28:18-19
17 Mar	Joseph of Arimathea	1 Kings 8:27-30	Psalm 116:7-9, 12-13 (**13**)	Galatians 6:9-10	John 19:38-42

FOLLOW THE EXAMPLE | SAINTS' DAYS SCRIPTURE READINGS

DATE	SAINT	OT READING	PSALM READING	NT READING	GOSPEL READING
20 Mar	Cuthbert	Ezekiel 34:5-6, 11-12, 15	Psalm 4:1, 3, 6-8 (**8**)	2 Corinthians 5:16A, 17-20A	John 21:16-18
20 Mar	Herebert	Amos 3:3	Psalm 133:1-3 (**1**)	Hebrews 4:16; 5:2, 7	Matthew 18:19
21 Mar	Enda	Isaiah 32:2-4	Psalm 32:1-8 (**Psalm 33:22**)	Hebrews 11:38–12:2	Matthew 13:45-46
23 Mar	Ethilwald of Farne	1 Kings 8:28-29	Psalm 107:29-31 (**29A**)	Acts 27:25-26	Matthew 8:23-27
23 Mar	Felgild	Lamentations 3:56-57	Psalm 55:1-2, 17-18 (**1**)	Acts 27:20, 26	Luke 4:1-13
24 Mar	Oscar Romero	Job 29:11-16	Psalm 10:2, 5-12 (**12**)	James 2:5-9, 12-13	John 12:23-24, 26-28
1 Apr	Mary of Egypt	Hosea 2:14-15	Psalm 56:8-11, 13 (**13**)	Colossians 3:2-5; 4:2	Luke 7:37-48
4 Apr	Martin Luther King Jr	Deuteronomy 32:44-52; 34:1-5	Psalm 119:120-126 (**126A**)	Galatians 3:26-28	Luke 23:26-27
7 Apr	Roland Walls	Isaiah 30:20-21	Psalm 27:1, 4-9, 13-14 (**8**)	Colossians 3:12-15	Mark 9:1-8, 14-16
9 Apr	Dietrich Bonhoeffer	Numbers 13:17-18, 30-32	Psalm 144:1-4 (**1A, B**)	1 John 4:18-19, 21	Matthew 13:51-54
12 Apr	Aldwin	Isaiah 58:6-8, 11-12	Psalm 126:1-3 (**Hebrews 3:4**)	Hebrews 3:1-6, 13-14	Luke 13:18; 14:28-29, 33
11 May	Comgall	Proverbs 8:3-12	Psalm 113:1-3 (**3A**)	Revelation 3:18-19	Matthew 4:13-17
14 May	William Walcher	1 Samuel 3:13-18	Psalm 69:4-6, 19-20 (**19**)	1 Corinthians 3:8-13	Matthew 10:26-28A, 39-42
14 May	Elfwy	Genesis 26:17-25	Psalm 34:1-5 (**Jude 20**)	3 John 2-4, 14	Luke 4:16-18; 19:28-40

FOLLOW THE EXAMPLE | SAINTS' DAYS SCRIPTURE READINGS

DATE	SAINT	OT READING	PSALM READING	NT READING	GOSPEL READING
16 May	Brendan	Isaiah 49:8-9	Psalm 107:23-31 (**24**)	Acts 14:22B, 26, 28	John 2:22—3:2
21 May	Godric	Isaiah 48:15-18	Psalm 23:1-5 (**3**)	1 Corinthians 1:25-29	John 1:22-23
26 May	Bede	Jeremiah 9:23-24	Psalm 37:3-6, 31 (**3B**)	1 Corinthians 1:20-24	John 20:29-31; 21:25
3 Jun	Kevin	2 Kings 6:1-4	Psalm 84:2-4, 12 (**12**)	Romans 1:16, 18-21	Matthew 13:1-2, 31-32
4 Jun	Eadfrith	Habakkuk 2:1-2	Psalm 51:6, 12, 15, 18 (**6B**)	Galatians 6:4, 10-11	Luke 24:45-48, 50
4 Jun	Petroc (Pedrog)	1 Samuel 26:5-17, 21-25	Psalm 46:1-3, 8-10 (**9**)	James 3:13-15, 17-18	John 19:30-35
9 Jun	Columba	Jeremiah 9:17-19, 22-24	Psalm 45:1-2, 3-4, 17 (**1B**)	Revelation 1:9-19	Luke 2:47-52
24 Jun	Bartholomew of Farne	Ecclesiastes 2:10-11, 13	Psalm 42:1-2 (**2B**)	1 Corinthians 1:31—2:3	Matthew 7:24-25
28 Jun	Irenaeus	Isaiah 24:14-16A; 25:4-9	Psalm 11:1-3, 7 (**1A**)	2 Peter 1:16-21	John 16:13-14
3 Jul	Thomas	1 Kings 10:1-9	Psalm 8:1, 3-8 (**1A**)	Acts 1:1-5, 7-8	John 20:4-28
7 Jul	Boisil	1 Kings 2:2-4	Psalm 143:5-8, 10 (**5B, C**)	1 Thessalonians 5:12-14, 16-20, 24	John 3:26-30
23 Jul	John Cassian	Jeremiah 17:9-10	Psalm 34:11, 14-15, 17-19 (**11**)	3 John 3-4	Matthew 21:28-32
31 Jul	Ignatius of Loyola	Isaiah 11:2-3	Psalm 19:7-9, 11-12, 14 (**14A, B**)	1 Corinthians 2:9-16	Luke 15:20-25, 28, 31

FOLLOW THE EXAMPLE | SAINTS' DAYS SCRIPTURE READINGS

DATE	SAINT	OT READING	PSALM READING	NT READING	GOSPEL READING
5 Aug	Oswald	Ecclesiastes 9:7, 10, 12	Psalm 21:1-3, 6-7 (**7A**)	1 Peter 4:12-16	John 16:29-33
11 Aug	Clare	Song of Songs 8:6-7, 13	Psalm 45:10-11 (**10A, C**)	1 Thessalonians 5:16-25	Luke 12:32-33
15 Aug	Mary, mother of Jesus	Isaiah 7:14	Psalm 40:5, 8, 16 (**5B, C**)	Acts 1:14	Luke 1:30-35, 37-38, 46-55
16 Aug	Brother Roger of Taizé	Micah 4:2-5	Psalm 27:1, 4, 7-8, 13 (**Luke 23:42**)	1 John 1:2-7	John 3:6-9, 19-21
20 Aug	Oswin	Esther 6:7-9	Psalm 147:3, 5, 10-11 (**5**)	1 John 2:6, 15, 17	Matthew 25:34-40
25 Aug	Ebba	Proverbs 31:30	Psalm 45:3, 6-7, 9A, 10 (**6A**)	Romans 14:1, 4, 7-13, 19	Luke 12:2-3, 32, 35
26 Aug	Ninian	Isaiah 54:2, 10, 17	Psalm 139:1, 4-5 (**5A**)	James 1:17-18	Matthew 5:14-16
28 Aug	Pelagius	Ecclesiastes 3:9-14	Psalm 36:7-9 (**9A**)	Hebrews 12:2-3, 7-15	Luke 6:20-23
28 Aug	Arthur Burt	1 Samuel 17:40-42	Psalm 20:1-2, 4-7 (**Psalm 72:19b**)	1 John 4:4, 18-19	John 5:19-20, 30
31 Aug	Aidan	Isaiah 6:1-8	Psalm 77:11-14, 16-19 (**19A**)	Hebrews 5:12-14	John 4:34-35
5 Sep	Teresa of Calcutta	Isaiah 40:28-31	Psalm 147:1-3, 11, 14 (**3**)	James 1:17-18, 22, 27	Matthew 18:10-11
6 Sep	Madeleine L'Engle	Isaiah 49:8-10, 23b	Psalm 69:2-3, 13 (**13**)	John 4:23-30	John 4:23-30
18 Sep	George MacDonald	Isaiah 64:1-5, 8	Psalm 68:3-5 (**5**)	1 John 2:12-14; 3:1-3	Luke 15:11-13, 17-28

FOLLOW THE EXAMPLE | SAINTS' DAYS SCRIPTURE READINGS

DATE	SAINT	OT READING	PSALM READING	NT READING	GOSPEL READING
21 Sep	Henri Nouwen	Hosea 6:1-3	Psalm 71:1-3 (**3A**)	Philippians 3: 7-11	Luke 4:17-20, 30; 5:15-16
23 Sep	Adamnan	Proverbs 15:18, 33	Psalm 120:1, 6-7 (**1**)	1 Corinthians 4:1-5	Luke 8:40-42, 54-55
25 Sep	Cadoc	Isaiah 26:7-9	Psalm 121:2-3, 5-8 (**2**)	Ephesians 6:2-3, 18-19	Matthew 6:6
29 Sep	Michael and All Angels	Daniel 12:1-3	Psalm 103:19-22 (**19A**)	Revelation 12:7-12	Matthew 26:52-54
3 Oct	Thérèse of Lisieux	Song of Songs 2:10-14	Psalm 5:1-6, 13, 15, 17 (**6B**)	Galatians 5:22, 25; 6:2	Matthew 18:1-4
4 Oct	Francis of Assisi	Genesis 32:23-31	Psalm 148:1-3, 7-13 (**3A**)	Galatians 6:14, 16-18	Luke 12:22-34
10 Oct	Paulinus	Ecclesiastes 11:6	Psalm 97:1-2, 6, 11-12 (**1A, C**)	1 Corinthians 3:5-9	Mark 4:26-29
12 Oct	Wilfrid	Isaiah 40:12-15, 17, 23-24	Psalm 27:7-8, 13-14 (**13B, C**)	1 Corinthians 3:9-15, 20-23	Matthew 6:6, 17, 34
15 Oct	Teresa of Avila	Nehemiah 2:17-18	Psalm 77:1-3, 6, 12-13 (**3**)	Romans 8:26-27	Matthew 25:1-10
16 Oct	Gall	Proverbs 27:5-6, 11	Psalm 115:3-8 (**4**)	Acts 15:32-41	Matthew 28:19-20
21 Oct	Tuda	Proverbs 22:17-19	Psalm 88:2-3, 9, 12-13 (**9B**)	Ephesians 4:2-6, 26-27, 29	Matthew 5:44-45, 48
26 Oct	Cedd	Proverbs 22:2, 6, 19	Psalm 22:26-31 (**31**)	1 Peter 2:2-9	John 1:35-42
26 Oct	Eata	Proverbs 15:33; 16:7-8	Psalm 104:19, 25, 27-31, 33-34 (**31B**)	Hebrews 12:12-15	John 6:63, 65, 67-69
31 Oct	All Hallows' Eve	Isaiah 45:5-8	Psalm 91:1-2, 7, 9-10, 11 (**1**)	1 John 4:7-9	John 9:4-5; 10:1-10

FOLLOW THE EXAMPLE | SAINTS' DAYS SCRIPTURE READINGS

DATE	SAINT	OT READING	PSALM READING	NT READING	GOSPEL READING
31 Oct	Bega	Ezra 3:11-13	Psalm 56:8, 10-12 (**12**)	Philippians 4:4-6	John 11:25-28
31 Oct	Reinfrid	2 Kings 6:1-4	Psalm 122:1, 7-9 (**1**)	2 Corinthians 5:17-19	Matthew 5:4-9
1 Nov	All Saints' Day	2 Samuel 12:16-23	Psalm 133:1-3 (**Psalm 134:3**)	Revelation 7:9-10, 16-17	John 14:1-6
6 Nov	Illtyd	2 Samuel 22:20, 32-34	Psalm 34:11-15 (**11**)	Philippians 3:7-9	Mark 1:35-37
7 Nov	Willibrord	Nehemiah 8:9-11	Psalm 30:4-5, 11-12 (**5B**)	2 Timothy 3:14; 4:2	John 1:14, 16-18
11 Nov	Martin of Tours	2 Kings 6:1-4	Psalm 111:1-5, 10 (**10B, C**)	1 Corinthians 2:9-16	Matthew 25:37-40
16 Nov	Celtic Advent Begins	Isaiah 40:3-5, 9-11	Psalm 72:4-11, 17, 19 (**11**)	1 John 2:24-25, 27-28	Matthew 4:13-17
17 Nov	Hild	Proverbs 8:12-17	Psalm 37:3-7, 11 (**8B**)	Ephesians 4:10-13	Matthew 13:44-46, 31-33
22 Nov	C.S. Lewis	Jeremiah 29:11-13	Psalm 40:5, 8, 10-11 (**10A, B**)	1 Corinthians 2:9-10	John 9:17-30
23 Nov	Columbanus	Isaiah 30:18, 20-21	Psalm 84:5:8 (**5**)	Acts 2:42-47	Matthew 12:46-50
24 Nov	Eanfleda	Proverbs 31:11-12, 14-15, 25-26	Psalm 5:3, 7, 11-12 (**7A**)	James 1:17-20	Matthew 7:13-14
1 Dec	Charles de Foucauld	Job 23:8-12	Psalm 131:1-2 (**1C, D**)	Ephesians 3:7-9	Luke 23:39-49
2 Dec	Jean Donovan	Proverbs 31:8-9	Psalm 142:2, 4-6 (**2**)	Galatians 5:13-14	Luke 14:8-14

DATE	SAINT	OT READING	PSALM READING	NT READING	GOSPEL READING
7 Dec	Diuma	Ecclesiastes 11:4-6	Psalm 62:5-8 (**8A, B**)	1 John 5:3-8, 11	John 17:18-23
11 Dec	Thomas Merton	1 Kings 19:11-12	Psalm 17:5-8, 15 (**8**)	2 Corinthians 10:3-5	Mark 13:32-39
12 Dec	Finnian of Clonard	Ezekiel 47:3-7, 12	Psalm 135:1-2, 6-7, 13 (**13**)	1 Peter 5:2-3, 5-6	Luke 24:45-48
14 Dec	John of the Cross	Song of Songs 6:2-3; 7:10; 8:5A, 6	Psalm 88:1-2, 6, 9, 13, 18 (**18B**)	Philippians 4:11-12	Matthew 10:26-27, 34-39
14 Dec	Catherine de Hueck Doherty	Isaiah 58:10	Psalm 40:10, 17 (**10A, B**)	1 Corinthians 7:29-31	Matthew 19:21
17 Dec	Antiphon Day	Ecclesiastes 7:5, 8-9, 29; 8:1	Psalm 90:1-2, 4-6, 9-10, 12, 14, 16-17 (**2**)	James 3:13, 17	Luke 2:25-32, 329-40
18 Dec	Samthann	1 Kings 8:54-56	Psalm 119:147-148, 151-152 (**151**)	Hebrews 4:12	Mark 11:24-25
24 Dec	Christmas Eve	Isaiah 1:2-3; 9:1-2, 6-7	Psalm 95:1-7a (**6**)	1 John 4:7-9	Luke 2:8-25
25 Dec	Christmas Day	Isaiah 11:1-4a, 6-10	Psalm 96:1-13	Philippians 2:4-7, 9-11	John 1:1-5, 9-14
26 Dec	Stephen	2 Chronicles 24:19-21	Psalm 131:1-2 (**1A**)	Acts 6:1-15; 7:52-60	Matthew 23:34-39
27 Dec	John the Beloved	Habakkuk 2:2-3, 20	Psalm 71:5, 7-8 18-19, 23-24 (**18A, C**)	1 John 2:7-10	John 21:20-25
28 Dec	Holy Innocents	Jeremiah 31:12-13, 15-17	Psalm 71:13-14 (**14**)	Romans 8:34, 38-39	Matthew 2:13-18
31 Dec	John Wycliffe	Nehemiah 8:8-12	Psalm 119:46-49 (**46**)	2 Timothy 4:1-5	John 15:20; 16:12-15

Adamnan (?–704): 23 September

Ninth abbot of Iona, in 688 he visited Coelfrid in Wearmouth, who persuaded him to adopt Roman customs. Adamnan could not persuade all his monks to adopt the reforms, and for many years on the tiny island of Iona two tonsures and two dates for Easter persisted. It was to persuade these monks that he intended no dishonour to Columba that Adamnan wrote his famous biography of that much-loved saint. Ironically, Adamnan was a peace-loving man, and worked for Irish law to be changed, exempting women, children and clergy from military service.

Aidan (?–651): 31 August

For Aidan's biography see the introduction to 'The Aidan Compline' (p.57) and 'Aidan – in the power of the Spirit' (p.282).

Scriptures:
Isaiah 6:1-8;
Hebrews 5:12-14

Aldwin (?–1087): 12 April

In 1068, after the turmoil of the Norman conquest, Aldwin was prior of Winchcombe Abbey but began dreaming of the monastic communities he read of in Bede. Soon he set out north with Elfwy and Reinfrid from nearby Evesham Abbey hoping to rebuild the ancient monastic sites. The dream became a reality and a new monasticism took root in previously prayed-in places.

Scriptures:
Isaiah 58:6-8, 11-12;
Hebrews 3:1-4

All Hallows' Eve: 31 October

This night is known in popular culture as Halloween, a time of witches, pumpkins, hobgoblins and ghosts. It is a popular and highly commercialised holiday in America, imported long ago from Ireland. The old pagan festival was Samhain; in pastoral terms, this marked the ending of the old year and the beginning of the new, the passing of summer and the beginning of winter. The livestock were brought in, and any surplus animals were slaughtered soon afterwards – so bone-fires were lit.

The old belief was that there was danger and vulnerability at this time of transition, which was neither in one year nor in the next. Spiritual barriers could be dissolved. These old beliefs were never quite eradicated by the coming of Christianity, but lingered as a persistent superstition, a residual folk-memory. The real Christian festival is All Hallows or All Saints on 1 November.

Tonight light a large candle and gather round to say Compline. The candle could be left shining in a window. Or plan to recall the martyrs of the faith with 'Light a candle in the darkness' (p.121).

Scripture:
Psalm 91:9-11

All Saints' Day: 1 November

All Saints or All Hallows is the feast of the known and unknown believers who are redeemed and now in heaven. It has been celebrated for centuries on this date. Those who have gone before us cheer us on, and encourage us to live faithfully.

Scriptures:
Hebrews 12:1-2, 22-23;
Revelation 7:9-10, 16-17;
19:5, 9

Antiphon Day: 17 December

This day is traditionally known by its Latin name 'O Sapientia', meaning 'O Wisdom'. In the lead-up to Christmas Eve a particular prayer is used for each of the preceding seven days. The Advent carol 'O come, O come, Immanuel', is based on them. For many years we have walked the Pilgrims' Way over the sands to Holy Island on this day in all kinds of weather, pausing to say the prayers and sing the verses. The same tradition could be followed in different locations on Antiphon Day.

Antony of Egypt (251–356): 17 January

It was about 285 when Antony went into the Egyptian desert to live in complete solitude. His reputation attracted followers who settled near him. Around 305 he came out of the hermitage to act as their Abba. Five years later he retired again into solitude. He is looked upon as the founder of monasticism. Athanasius' *Life of Antony* had enormous influence for hundreds of years, inspiring others to imitate his life as a hermit and soldier for Christ.

Baldred (eighth century): 6 March

A Northumbrian hermit. He lived in Tyninghame and then lived as a solitary on the Bass Rock. (St Baldred's Rock is reputed to have been shifted to its present location by the power of his prayers, having previously been a dangerous reef!)

Bartholomew of Farne (?–1193): 24 June

Monk and hermit, born of Scandinavian parents at Whitby and named Tostig; he changed his name to William to avoid ridicule. He had a wild youth, but suddenly refused marriage, went to Norway and became a priest there. He spent three years in English parish ministry, and became a monk at Durham in the late 1140s, taking the name of Bartholomew. He had a vision of Christ on the Rood turning His head towards him and stretching out His arms to embrace him. Bartholomew went as a hermit to Inner Farne and remained there for most of the next 42 years. He prayed, worked and sang. His most difficult times were the two periods when he had to share the island with another hermit, but he was otherwise always cheerful and generous in welcoming his many visitors.

Bede (673–735): 26 May

Educated at Jarrow from the age of seven, he became a monk, priest and scholar there. He rarely travelled, but was widely known through his writings. In his day it was his Scripture commentaries that he was famed for, but his *History of the English Church and People* has been his enduring legacy, and with it the accounts of Aidan, Cuthbert and others that are so important for us. His irritating disapproval of the Celtic practices that were overturned at the Whitby Synod is balanced by his admiration for the holy lives of the Irish missionaries from Iona. He died, singing 'Glory be to the Father and to the Son and to the Holy Ghost', after finishing his work on a vernacular translation of John's Gospel. A devoted gathering of the community surrounded him as his long life came to its end.

Bega (seventh century): 31 October

A nun at Hackness (near Scarborough), the daughter community of Whitby. In a vision she heard a bell, saw the roof of the nunnery at Whitby being rolled back and flooded with light, and witnessed the soul of Hild being taken to heaven by angels. This vision coincided with Hild's death at Whitby.

Billifrith (eighth century): 6 March

A hermit (perhaps on Lindisfarne) who 'adorned the Lindisfarne Gospels with gold, silver and gems on the binding'.

Scripture:
Exodus 35:30–36:2

Boisil (?–661): 7 July

A prior at Melrose who first welcomed Cuthbert and recognised how greatly God's hand would be upon him. Whilst dying of the plague he asked to spend a week with Cuthbert in reading John's Gospel, and prophesied that God wanted Cuthbert to be a bishop one day.

Dietrich Bonhoeffer (1906–45): 9 April

Bonhoeffer was hanged in Flossenburg concentration camp three weeks before Hitler's suicide and the end of the Second World War. He had studied theology, and before ordination did a student exchange to the USA. There he saw at first hand the evils of racism, little guessing how relevant it would soon become to life in Germany.

He was ordained, then lectured at Berlin University, where his talk of peace was unpopular; but his heart lay with a confirmation class of 50 boys from a slum estate. The Church in Germany was riddled with nationalism, anti-Semitism and compromise. Bonhoeffer withdrew to a Lutheran church in London, but he knew that he must return to Germany.

He became the director of a Confessing Church seminary, and was responsible for 25 young men, whom he tried to raise in community. They dispersed when the Nazis closed the seminary, but they secretly studied under Bonhoeffer, assessing the 'cost of discipleship'. The net tightened around the Jews as Bonhoeffer withdrew to America, knowing that he must return again – as a pacifist almost certainly to face death.

He became a resistance worker, and was part of a failed plot to assassinate Hitler. But it was his evasion of the call-up for military service that led to his arrest. He wrote to his parents and his fiancée when he was allowed to do so. He supported and prayed for his fellow prisoners. Perhaps he died because of his political convictions and not as a Christian martyr, but he would have said that there was no distinction between the two.

Brendan (486–575): 16 May

He is remembered with great affection for his great sea voyages, which captured the imagination of the people of his own time – and many in every age since. The accounts seem to read partly as travelogue and partly as a spiritual journal or allegory. He was fostered by Ita. He founded some large monasteries, including that of Clonfert in Galway, where he was eventually buried.

Brigid (c.450–523): 1 February

For Brigid's biography see 'Brigid – in welcoming' (p.267).

Arthur Burt (1912–2014): 28 August

Arthur looked for a day when the glory of the Lord will flood the earth, when people will find faith without human intervention, and the Spirit moving within us will wake and shake us, mobilise and connect us with these missing limbs as we surrender at last to an overwhelming love. He never let failure be an impediment to God moving through him. He was deliciously human. He hitchhiked everywhere, and travelled the world at God's bidding. If he arrived at a meeting he might preach, but only if God gave him something to say, believing that if God didn't reveal truth, he certainly couldn't.

'There's a power in the word greater than the word to reveal the Word', so he'd pause expecting more revelation to occur in between!

His teaching was always practical – small memorable phrases he called pebbles to slay Goliath: 'Fear is always built on a lie. Always! You can never adequately deal with fear unless you deal with the lie behind it. Deal with the lie and the fear will die.'

> Not only in the words you say,
> not only in your deeds confessed,
> but in the most unconscious way
> is Christ expressed.
>
> Is it a beatific smile? a holy light upon your brow?
> Oh no, I felt His presence when you laughed just now.
>
> For me 'twas not the truth you taught,
> to you so clear, to me so dim;
> but when you came to me, you brought a sense of Him.
>
> And from your eyes He beckons me;
> from your lips His love is shed, 'til I lose sight of you
> and see the Christ instead.

Beatrice Clelland
from *Portrait of a Christian*

Scriptures:
Psalm 105:17-22;
Genesis 50:19-20;
James 4:6-12

Cadoc (early sixth century): 25 September

Cadoc probably trained in Ireland. Returning to Wales, he profoundly influenced the faith-life of his own parents, and then founded the monastery at Llancarfan, west of Cardiff. Finnian of Clonard became his pupil. He seems to have visited Cornwall and Scotland also. He loved the simple life of a hermit.

Caedmon (?–680): 11 February

For Caedmon's biography see 'Caedmon – in declaration of a dream' (p.321).

Canaire (?–530): 28 January

Canaire lived as a hermit near Bantry Bay in the south of Ireland. In a vision she saw Inis Cathaig, the island we now call Scattery Island. She saw a pillar of fire rising above it where Senan lived and prayed. She became convinced that this was to be her place of resurrection, and so began the journey at once, completing the last stretch by walking across the waters.

Senan met her, but insisted that only men were allowed on the island, even as visitors.

'Christ came to redeem women no less than to redeem men,' she said. 'No less did he suffer for the sake of women than for the sake of men. No less than men, women enter into the heavenly kingdom.'

In honour of her stubbornness Senan gave her what she asked for: communion from his hand, and a place for her to lie. The moment she gladly received the sacrament she was taken to heaven.

Teach us to follow in Your steps
across the icy waters of prejudice and fear
to the perfect communion of God's Kingdom.

Mary Low

Scriptures:
Luke 8:1-3;
Galatians 3:26-29

John Cassian (360–435): 23 July

A monk in Bethlehem and in Egypt, John Cassian later settled in Marseilles, where he founded two monasteries, one for men and one for women. His writings about monastic life were enormously influential, and he strongly refuted some of the teachings of Augustine.

See:
Finan readings for 10 and 21 March.

Cedd (?–664): 26 October

An abbot and bishop, and a brother of Chad. He was trained with his brothers by Aidan on Lindisfarne. He founded the abbey at Lastingham and the monastery at Bradwell-on-Sea (where the present-day Othona Community is based).

Celtic Advent Begins: 16 November

The beginning of the traditional period of monastic fasting and preparation for the feast of Christmas. We seek to prepare the way for the Lord to come right into the centre of our lives. Every valley and pothole should be filled in, every mountain levelled and every obstacle removed. The mountains are the wrongs we do, and the potholes are the good things we fail to do. Prepare a way for the Lord!

Chad (?–672): 2 March

For Chad's biography see 'Chad – in willing service' (p.286).

Charles de Foucauld (Brother Charles of Jesus) (1858–1916): 1 December

Brother Charles of Jesus, who lived and died in poverty among the tribespeople of the Sahara, was from a rich French family and had been a playboy, a soldier and an explorer at earlier stages in his life. Dramatically converted to Christ, he became a monk, but found even the Trappist Order not demanding enough, and lived out his vocation as a hermit, and finally also as a priest. The Communities of Little Brothers and Sisters of Jesus sprang up only after his death. He was betrayed by his own servant and murdered by bandits from a fanatical Muslim sect.

Clare (1194–1253): 11 August

Clare of Assisi decided at the age of 18 to join Francis and his brothers. She lived an enclosed life of poverty and prayer, leading a community of women.

> **Scriptures:**
> Luke 18:28-30;
> 12:32-33

Colman (?–676): 18 February

Colman was an Iona monk and an Irishman. He was bishop at Lindisfarne from 661 to 664, following Aidan and Finan. He spoke for the Celtic party at the Synod of Whitby, but seems to have been genuinely surprised by its outcome, expecting only to have to yet again explain the usual difficulties. He withdrew to Iona, with a large company of English and Irish monks. Some years later he returned with them to his home in the west of Ireland and founded a monastery on Inis Bofin in 667, and eventually a separate one for the English monks in Mayo, which became a famous college. (He died during the 670s, but the exact year is in question.)

Columba (521–97): 9 June

An Irish prince who chose the monastic life. He was trained by Finnian of Moville, then by Finnian of Clonard. He founded monasteries at Derry, Durrow and Kells. He left Ireland in 563 and settled on Iona in Scotland. He was a large man with a big, resonant singing voice. He was also an excellent scribe and illuminator of manuscripts.

A much-loved abbot, he had a missionary zeal and great prophetic insight. The tribute written at his death (see the Finan reading for 26 September) by one of the bards of Ireland (whose calling he had defended) speaks eloquently of a prince among saints, gifted but always accessible – and disarmingly human.

Columbanus (543–615): 23 November

A tireless Irish missionary monk working in Europe. His chief foundations were in Luxeuil and Bobbio. He was no stranger to hardship, persecution and controversy. He was known also for the strictness of the Rule of Life that he and his followers observed; this rule was widely adopted. The headings to the Finan readings for May are taken from his *Letter to a Young Disciple*.

Comgall (516–601): 11 May

Born in Ulster, he was a warrior as a young man, and was then discipled by Fintan before living a severely ascetic life on the island of Lough Erne. Later he founded Bangor Monastery on the south shore of Belfast Lough, where Columbanus and others were trained. He visited Inverness with Columba and Kenneth, where they challenged King Brude and his druids. Bangor had a famous perpetual choir which for 150 years sang continuous praises on a shift system.

Cuthbert (634–87): 20 March

For Cuthbert's biography see 'The Cuthbert Compline', p.60 and 'Cuthbert – into a desert place' (p.295).

David (?–588): 1 March

The founder of ten monasteries, mostly in Wales, David (Dewi) imitated the ascetic ways of the Desert Fathers. His main monastery was at Menevia, now called St David's, in Pembrokeshire. His monks did heavy manual work and were fed only bread, vegetables and water. David said, 'They should labour so hard that they want only to love one another. There should be no conversation beyond what is necessary.' He taught that someone asking to join a monastery should be made to wait at the door for ten days and treated with hostility; then, if he were patient throughout this treatment, he should be welcomed warmly.

Diuma (?–658): 7 December

Diuma, Cedd, Betti and Adda were sent together as missionary priests to Mercia by Finan of Lindisfarne. Diuma became the first bishop of the Middle Angles and the Mercians.

Catherine de Hueck Doherty (1896–1985): 14 December

Catherine was the child of wealthy Orthodox parents in Russia. She was steeped in the spirituality of her country, but during her father's long diplomatic/business assignments abroad she was at times educated in Catholic convent schools. She was married at the age of 15 to Boris de Hueck, and the couple fled to Finland at the time of the Bolshevik revolution. They went on to England and then settled in Canada as refugees. Their son George was born there. In England Catherine had formally identified herself as a Catholic.

She now experienced great poverty, and the disintegration and, finally, the annulment of her marriage. Her gift for lecturing eventually brought her financial security and success, but she was haunted by the call of God to forsake security and work among the very poor. For some years 'Friendship House' worked primarily among poor immigrants, and she became closely associated with Dorothy Day and the young Thomas Merton. In 1943 she married Eddie Doherty, and in 1947 they moved to Combermere, nearly 200 miles from Toronto, where a large community called 'Madonna House' grew up, united in prayer and service to the poor. The community moved towards formal vows and lifelong commitments, and in 1955 Eddie and Catherine chose to avow celibacy together.

Catherine's persuasive advocacy of the richness of Russian spirituality and of the relentless call of Jesus to preach the gospel without compromise has had a profound impact on many people throughout the West. Her humour and disarming directness showed that true holiness can have a very human face.

> Little, be always little, simple, poor, childlike.
> Do little things exceedingly well, for love of Me.
> Love, love, love, never counting the cost.
> Go into the marketplace and stay with Me.
> Pray, fast, pray always, fast.
> Be hidden, be a light to your neighbour's feet.

From 'The Little Mandate' at Madonna House

Jean Donovan (1953–1980): 2 December

Jean Donovan, a member of an affluent American family, was a college graduate and a successful accountant, but she quit her job to spend two years as a lay missionary in El Salvador. She sorted out the mission accounts, distributed food, and eventually led Scripture discussions and buried whoever had been shot that day. In the first five months of 1980 over 2,000 ordinary Salvadoreans were killed. Priests who lived alongside the peasants, introducing basic literacy and caring for the people, became targets for the death squads. Mission teams of nuns and laypeople like Jean attempted to look after the parishes that the priests had been forced to abandon. She said:

> I'm never sure if I've got enough to share with people and then
> I realise that I do, it's God that helps us, He sort of carries us,
> because I couldn't do this by myself.

And she wrote in a letter to a friend:

> Several times I have decided to leave El Salvador. I almost
> could except for the children, the poor, bruised victims of this

insanity. Who would care for them? Whose heart could be so staunch as to favour the reasonable thing in a sea of their tears and loneliness? Not mine, dear friend, not mine.

Two weeks later, Jean Donovan and three nuns were driving from the airport when their van was ambushed by six guardsmen who raped and shot them. The soldiers were paid hundreds of dollars – they had been ordered to do this so as to humiliate and destroy 'subversives'.

> **Scripture:**
> Proverbs 3:27;
> 31:8-9

Eadfrith (?–721): 4 June

The scribe of the Lindisfarne Gospels and, later, bishop at Lindisfarne. He restored Cuthbert's oratory on Inner Farne for Felgild's use.

Eanfleda (626–704): 24 November

A daughter of King Edwin of Northumbria, she was baptised a Christian as a new baby in thanksgiving for Edwin's escape from assassination. After Edwin's death in battle seven years later she and her mother and the other children returned to Kent with Paulinus. She came back to Northumbria to marry Oswy when she was 16. After his death she joined her daughter Elfleda at Hild's monastery in Whitby which, after Hild's death, they ruled jointly.

Eata (?–686): 26 October

One of the original 12 boys trained by Aidan, he was sent to Melrose to be its first abbot. He became Abbot of Lindisfarne after the Synod of Whitby, and subsequently bishop. He then swapped appointments with Cuthbert, and so became Bishop of Hexham.

Ebba (?–683): 25 August

A sister of Oswald and Oswy, she probably married into the royal house of Wessex. Having been widowed, she returned to Northumbria, where she became a nun and lived at the monastery at Ebchester near Newcastle. She was the founder and abbess of a double monastery at Coldingham, situated on what is now called St Abb's Head (the land having been given to her by her brother Oswy as an offering that he hoped would atone for his murder of Oswin). She ruled there for 30 years, but not very strictly; so when the abbey burned down soon after her death, this was seen as a judgement on the prayerlessness of the remaining nuns and brothers. Ebba is described by Bede as 'a pious woman, and a handmaid of Christ'.

Scriptures:
Genesis 18:23-32;
Psalm 45:9a;
Proverbs 31:30

Elfleda (653–714): 8 February

A daughter of Eanfleda and Oswy. Consecrated to God from infancy in thanksgiving for Oswy's victory in battle over Penda of Mercia in 654, she was given to the care of Hild at Hartlepool. She eventually became joint-abbess at Whitby with her mother Eanfleda. A friend of Cuthbert, she met with him on Coquet Island to ask his insights. She was also a mediator and advocate on behalf of Wilfrid, and is described by Eddius Stephanus as 'comforter, and best counsellor of the whole province'.

Elfwy (eleventh century): 14 May

After the Norman conquest Aldwin, Reinfrid and Elfwy set out north from Evesham with one donkey, but also with a determination to see the blackened barren land of Northumbria watered again, its holy places restored and communities rebuilt. These three men were consumed with the vision of restoring the ruined places where earlier monasteries had been. They had seen and met the refugees heading south, some of them arriving in the Evesham area. Aldwin, recognising the names of the places these starving folk had come from, determined to journey there, and spoke of this to the monks at Evesham. Elfwy just knew he would go with him and help in whatever way he could. He had a care and compassion for people, and was 'memorable for the simplicity and innocence of his life, and for his constancy in prayer and tears'. They began rebuilding at Jarrow, where Elfwy settled and remained. His exact date or year of death are not recorded, so we remember his life on the anniversary of the death of his friend Walcher, who had hoped to join their community.

Scripture:
Jude 20, 24-25

Enda (?–530): 21 March

On the death of his father Conall, Enda inherited control of a large territory in the north of Ireland, and battled with various enemies to defend it. His sister, Fanchea, had already embraced consecrated religious life with a community in Meath, and was not thrilled when he and his noisily triumphant men called in to visit, his hands still stained with the blood of battle. He agreed to live quietly and settle down, on condition that she released a girl in her care to him to be his bride. But soon after this Fanchea sent for him quickly: the girl promised to him had died, and Fanchea bravely forced him to look at her body and face his own mortality. He left Ireland for several years, entered monastic life and was ordained at Candida Casa in Scotland.

On his return he eventually begged from his brother-in-law, Aengus King of Munster, land for a monastic settlement in an austere setting near Galway Bay off Ireland's west coast on the Aran Islands, which he thought as beautiful as 'a necklace of pearls God has set upon the bosom of the sea'.

This was in 484. Enda's early island mission had around 150 monks, but later when the community grew he divided up the territory between his disciples, who founded their own monasteries to accommodate the large number of vocations. These monks imitated the asceticism and simplicity of the earliest Egytian desert hermits, and were renowned for their passionate love for God. Enda was a father to all in these settlements. 'Aran of the Saints' became a miniature Mount Athos, with a dozen monasteries scattered over the island. Killeany, where Enda himself lived, was the most famous. A great tradition of austerity, holiness and learning was begun that was to enrich Europe for the next thousand years.

The monks of Aran lived alone in their stone cells, slept on the ground, ate together in silence, surviving on what they could harvest from the land and the sea. They were known as 'men of the caves' but were eager to be 'men of the cross'. Enda's monastic Rule set aside many hours for prayer and the study of scripture. It is said that no fire was ever lit to heat the cold stone cells, but they somehow gave hospitality to many seeking wisdom and the spiritual life.

In his own lifetime, Enda's monastic settlement on the Aran islands became an important pilgrimage destination, as well as a centre for the evangelisation of surrounding areas, all on account of the one-time-warrior's response to God's surprising call. Enda died in his little rock cell by the sea as a very old man, and it is said we will never know until the day of judgement the number of saints whose bodies lie in the soil of Aran.

> Perhaps the calling within us all becomes most real when it grows in response to a wounding of spirit, the healing like that layering of a pearl, bringing something beautiful out of hurt. Out of the bosom of this sea grew many pearls; each one responding as the oyster responds to injury; not through violence, or resentment, but by surrounding it with layers of resilience, spiritual strength and prayer. Upon such wisdom who could put a price?
>
> *Marie Gelling*

Enda is seen as the father of Irish hermits.

Scripture:
Matthew 13:45-46

Ethilwald of Farne (?–699): 23 March

A monk and priest of Ripon, he succeeded Cuthbert at the hermitage on Inner Farne in 687. He remained there for 12 years until his death and was replaced by Felgild. Cuthbert's work of prayer continued...

Felgild (651–725): 23 March

We have no record of the precise date of his death, but we remember him with Ethilwald, whom he followed to the Inner Farne. (For further biographical details see 'The Felgild Compline', p.64 and 'Felgild – in persisting in prayer', which can be found in Book Two, p.1128.)

Finan (?–661): 17 February

An Irish monk from Iona, Finan was Aidan's successor as bishop at Lindisfarne. With a strong base now established, in his day came the great missionary expansion throughout England.

Finnian of Clonard (?–549): 12 December

The abbot and founder of Clonard, where, reputedly, the 'twelve apostles of Ireland' were trained. He was the author of the earliest surviving Irish penitential manual. He founded monasteries at Rossacurra, Drumfea and Kilmaglush, then went to Wales to study the monasticism of David, Cadoc and Gildas. Returning to Ireland, he founded monasteries at Aghowle, Magna Sulcain and finally Clonard. Here he was known as 'the teacher of the saints of Ireland'. He died of the yellow plague. He should not be confused with his contemporary, Finnian of Moville.

Francis of Assisi (1181–1226): 4 October

John Bernardone was nicknamed Francesco ('Frenchie') because his mother was from Provence. His father was a wealthy cloth-merchant.

Francis was ill after a year's imprisonment during a local war. As he recovered he began to care for the poor and the lepers. He began to give away his father's goods.

The painted crucifix in the derelict church of San Damiano seemed to say to him, 'Build My Church, which, as you see, is in ruins.' He began to rebuild the chapel, stone by stone. But the word he had received there also spoke prophetically about a renewal and rebuilding of the larger Church of his day – a rebuilding through a simple loyalty and obedience to Christ and a rejection of all the Church's clutter, corruption and compromise.

Francis brought conversion by example. Taking off the clothes that his natural father had paid for, he stood naked and asked for the Church's covering and protection. With some embarrassment it was given. Francis and his order of Brothers Minor in absolute poverty continued to embarrass and energise the Church. Like Jesus, it was said of Francis that the poor 'heard him gladly'.

Because so many of his followers were clever, well-educated men, many of his sayings and numerous accounts of the incidents of his life have survived. The most famous prayer that is ascribed to him was not in fact his own, but aptly sums up his spirituality: 'Lord, make me an instrument of Your peace.'

Gall (?–640): 16 October

Faithful friend and disciple of Columbanus, Gall unwittingly offended him – yet then carefully obeyed his injunction to no longer celebrate Communion while Columbanus lived. Both continued to work tirelessly for the gospel. As Columbanus died, he sent Gall his pastoral staff as a sign of final reconciliation.

Godric (c.1065–1170): 21 May

Godric, by turn a pedlar, sailor and entrepreneur, eventually went by boat to Lindisfarne where he encountered a vision of Cuthbert that altered his life, until at Finchale near Durham he also became a hermit, remaining there for the final sixty years of his life, increasingly esteemed as an unpredictable yet wise and holy man.

Scriptures:
1 Corinthians 1:25-29;
John 1:22-23

Herebert (?–687): 20 March

Cuthbert of Lindisfarne and Herebert of Derwentwater were friends. Once a year they would meet for spiritual support and conversation. Herebert was a hermit and so (when he was allowed to be) was Cuthbert. Once, on hearing that Cuthbert was visiting Carlisle, Herebert arranged to meet him there. Then Cuthbert confided that they should not use their time together unwisely, since before many months passed he would depart this life. Herebert suggested that they should leave together, and they agreed upon this. Months later they died on their separate islands on the same day and companionably passed into glory.

Scriptures:
Psalm 133:1-3;
Amos 3:3;
Matthew 18:19

Hilary of Poitiers (315–68): 13 January

Born at Poitiers of pagan parents, he married and had a daughter. In 350 he became a Christian through a long process of study. In 353 he was made a bishop, and subsequently became famous as a teacher. Martin of Tours became his disciple. Hilary contested strongly against the Arian heresy and so was alternately applauded or banished, as fashions and power-bases changed. He was a fearless role model for Martin.

Hild (614–80): 17 November

For Hild's biography see 'Hild – in the right place' (p.291).

Holy Innocents: 28 December

This feast commemorates the Bethlehem children, aged two years and under, who were massacred by Herod the Great in his attempt to eliminate any rival king of the Jews. It speaks also of the unborn children whose lives are taken through abortion. We pray also for healing and forgiveness for all parents of aborted babies.

> Where is the sound of hope,
>   the cry of a child that wakes?
> The dull, aching, continued breathing
>   of the mother
> becomes a wail of grief,
>   a weeping for the children
>   who are no more.
> The silent landscape shudders.
>   God of mercy, light in darkness,
> hold gently to Your heart
>   the tiny ones we cradle in our prayer
> whose life was over
>   before it had begun.

Scriptures:
Jeremiah 31:12-13, 15-17;
Matthew 2:13-18;
Romans 8:34, 38-39

John Hyde (1865–1912): 17 February

'Praying Hyde', a missionary to India, was one of six children of a Presbyterian minister from Illinois. He remained single because, as he explained, 'I felt that I wanted to give something to Jesus

Christ who loved me so. I told the Lord that I would not marry, but be His altogether.'

His main work was not as a teacher or an evangelist, but as an intercessor on location. However, his health was not robust. Eventually a doctor said, 'His heart is in an awful condition. It has been shifted out of its natural position on the left side to a place over on the right side.' After 19 years in India he was sent back to England and America.

One woman said of him, 'I do not remember that he ever talked about prayer: he prayed. Speaking sometimes four or five times a day, he would then spend half the night in prayer.' A missioner in England prayed once with him. Hyde fell to his knees, was five minutes in silence, then both men looked up with faces streaming with tears. Hyde said, 'Oh, God!' and then was still again for five minutes. 'Then came up from the depths of his heart such petitions for men as I have never heard before, and I rose from my knees to know what real prayer was.'

Ignatius of Loyola (1491–1556): 31 July

He was born in Loyola in Spain, the youngest of 13 children. While serving as a soldier he received a bullet wound in the leg, and during convalescence he began spiritual reading. He soon came to God, and before long wrote the first draft of the *Spiritual Exercises*. He went on pilgrimage to Jerusalem, was persuaded by the Franciscans there to renounce his plan to convert the local Muslims, and finally, in Paris, gathered six disciples and taught the *Exercises*. This band became the Society of Jesus, or the Jesuits, who made themselves available to work for the spread of the faith anywhere in the world. They were instructed to visit the sick and poor and to avoid argument and displays of learning.

Illtyd (fifth–sixth centuries): 6 November

Most of the accounts of the incidents in his life are unreliable, but he was clearly a major influence on Christianity in Wales. He was at one time a soldier and perhaps had been married, but, influenced by Cadoc and/or Dyfrig, he became a monastic and hermit. Other men gathered round him and were discipled by him. David, Samson, Gildas and Paul Aurelian were among his students at Llantwit Major (Llanilltyd Fawr) in Glamorgan. He is said to have disappeared without warning to become a hermit again. Some legends link him with Arthur or name him and Cadoc as keepers of the Grail.

Irenaeus (130–200): 28 June

Probably from Smyrna, where as a boy he knew Polycarp. He studied at Rome, then became a priest at Lyons at the invitation of the first bishop there, Pothinus. He was sent to Rome with a letter for the Roman bishop during a time of persecution. On his return he found that Pothinus had been killed in the persecution. Irenaeus himself was made the new bishop. He was an important theologian and writer.

Ita (?–570): 15 January

For Ita's biography see 'The Ita Compline' p.54 and 'Ita – in fostering courage', which can be found in Book Two, p.1109.

John of the Cross (1542–91): 14 December

A tiny man, but a giant in the Spirit, John of the Cross was the greatest of the Spanish mystics. A Carmelite friar, he was persuaded by Teresa of Avila to join a reform movement within the Carmelites known as the Discalceds. He was seized and thrown into prison by repressive calced Carmelites, but finally he escaped. The Discalceds won their independence, but towards the end of his life John was to suffer further persecution, this time from the vicar-general of his own Discalced order. He was stripped of rank and responsibility and banished to a remote area, where he died. His most famous work was *The Dark Night of the Soul* – a poem with a prose spiritual commentary. The 'night' which seems unwelcome becomes sweeter than the dawn, and unites the Divine Lover and His beloved until each is transformed into the other. Eventually even the senses depart:

> I lay quite still, all memory lost,
> I reclined on my Loved One's breast;
> I knew no more, in my abandonment
> I threw away my care,
> and left it all forgotten among the lilies fair.

John the Beloved (first century): 27 December

John was Jesus' closest disciple and is traditionally believed to be the only one of the Twelve who was not martyred. He ended his days at an advanced age in Ephesus, and his tomb is in modern Selçuk. He was revered by the desert hermits and was thought of as the father of the emerging Celtic branch of the Church.

Eusebius speaks of his exile to Patmos and disputes over the authenticity of his writings. He also tells of John's concern for a particular young man – a believer who fell into sin and finally became a bandit leader. John rode after him and was captured by his men. He declared his willingness to even give his life for this man if he would only be saved. The man finally threw down his weapons and, falling into the old man's arms, wept so greatly that it was as if he were baptised a second time in tears. John led him back, forgiven by God and restored.

Scripture:
John 21:20-25

Joseph of Arimathea (first century): 17 March

A wealthy Israelite who was a secret believer in Jesus, Joseph laid the Master's body in his own tomb. Tradition says that he came to the island which is now Glastonbury Tor, where he and his companions built a wattle chapel.

Scripture:
John 19:38-42

Juniper (?–1258): 4 January

An early brother of Francis of Assisi, he was grieved at the relaxation of their rule of absolute poverty which followed the death of Francis, and with some others he withdrew to live more simply among the mountain caves.

Many stories persist about the absurd actions and sayings of Juniper which became thought-provoking parables. He chose to play the fool 'lest he become a real fool by allowing others to invest him with a holiness and wisdom that belongs only to God'.

Francis said, 'Juniper, so please it God that upon your branches thousands of souls shall build their nests. I wish I had a forest of such junipers!'

Kentigern (?–612): 13 January

Also affectionately know as Mungo, he was a monk and bishop and worked as an evangelist in Strathclyde and Cumbria. He also founded Glasgow.

He was a contemporary of Columba. Once, with their respective companies of missionaries, they met up, singing psalms back and forth as they approached. They embraced and blessed each other and exchanged pastoral staffs, before continuing with their journeys and their work.

Kevin (498–618): 3 June

Kevin lived as a hermit at Glendalough. There disciples gathered round him and a monastery grew up. He is said to have lived to be 120. One much-loved story tells of a blackbird building its nest in his outstretched praying hands. He kept perfectly still until the eggs hatched. Regardless of whether the story is true, it paints a beautiful word-picture of his spirituality.

> **Scriptures:**
> Psalm 84:3;
> Mark 3:7

Martin Luther King Jr (1929–68): 4 April

King was a black American preacher who became a civil rights activist, teaching 'active non-violent resistance to evil' and opposing racism and segregation. In many ways he was a flawed hero, but he was a committed and sincere man who died for his faith and for the freedom of his people. The day before he was shot he said:

> I want you to say that I tried to love and serve humanity. I won't have any money to leave behind. I won't have the fine and luxurious things of life to leave behind. But I just want to leave a committed life behind. Like anybody, I would like to live a long life. But I just want to do God's will. With this faith I will go out and carve a tunnel of hope from a mountain of despair. He's allowed me to go up the mountain. And I've looked over. And I've seen the Promised Land. And I may not get there with you. But I want you to know that we as a people will get to the Promised Land. Black men and white men, Jews and Gentiles, Protestants and Catholics will be able to join hands and sing with the Negroes in the spiritual of old:
>
> > Free at last,
> > free at last.

Thank God Almighty
we are free at last.

Madeleine L'Engle (1918–2007): 6 September

A gifted writer, she was also a perceptive thinker and praying person who learned to expect the unexpected. She tried to write every day and pray regularly, and liked to have soup, and other meals, in progress to be added to when passing by the stove. Seemingly unconnected ingredients would creatively combine to be ready to greet the apparently unanticipated guest.

Prayer and writing came about in a similar way; by welcoming the unexpected you prepare for all your life. Her many novels, journals, poems and theological reflections delight children and adult readers by combining science and art, story and reality, God, loneliness and love, in a way that transcends category so that bookshops and libraries have no idea where exactly to place her!

C.S. Lewis (1898–1963): 22 November

Clive Staples Lewis, known to family and friends as Jack, was born in Belfast. His father was a solicitor and his mother, who died when he was a child, was a clergyman's daughter. His time as a boy was spent with his brother, or more often reading alone in an attic full of books. As an academic in Oxford he taught English at Magdalen College. As he tells in *Surprised by Joy*, he recognised God's existence in 1929 and came to belief in Jesus in 1931.

He was a brilliant Christian apologist. His radio broadcasts, now collected as *Mere Christianity*, made theology practical and accessible for ordinary people when much of the Church was awash with modernism and scepticism. His *Screwtape Letters* – the writings of a fictional demon – alerted a whole generation to the stratagems of hell, the existence of which many Christians no longer retained the courage to believe in.

His science-fiction trilogy and the seven *Chronicles of Narnia* allow all who have been scared by the 'watchful dragons' of religion to experience awe, joy and wondering love in the presence of One who, in our world, is known by a different name. Lewis was a close friend of J.R.R. Tolkien and Charles Williams and was profoundly influenced by the writings of George MacDonald.

As a middle-aged professor he married, and then fell in love with, Joy Davidman, an American divorcée with two young sons. Her death devastated and deepened him, prompting the poem 'As the ruin falls'.

George MacDonald (1824–1905): 18 September

Scottish author, poet and Christian minister, his writings draw deeply on the indigenous spirituality of the pre-clearances Highlands and the folk memory of the people. He was friends with many important authors of his day, and inspired others to see the vividly apprehended imaginative and spiritual experience as something that can be conveyed through frank conversation, writing, preaching or the arts. He has the capacity to give us a vivid picture of the unseen, so we can 'believe in the wide-awake real ... where joy is but a form of love'. His ever-present concern was for his wife Louisa and their eleven children, and sometimes his beliefs were revolutionary, especially when he challenged the strict Calvinism of his upbringing. His understanding of God is vividly portrayed as the warmth of a much-loved father whose company is to be deeply desired.

Martin of Tours (316–97): 11 November

Martin won a discharge from the Roman army to become a hermit. A community grew up around him in France, and whole areas were evangelised as teams of his followers occupied sites previously dedicated as heathen shrines. Martin was a hermit and then a monastic in the desert tradition, but, with this sending out of teams, we have the beginnings of a missionary monastic movement that was to be characteristic of Celtic Christianity.

Mary, Mother of Jesus (first century): 15 August

She was married to Joseph whilst carrying Jesus, who had been conceived within her by the Holy Spirit. On the cross Jesus entrusted her to the care of John the Beloved, and they made their home in Ephesus. John's tomb and Mary's house are situated near present-day Selçuk.

The key words of Mary's life could be said to have been: *'Let it be* to me according to Your will' and, pointing to Jesus, 'Whatever He says to you, *do it.'*

* *indicates a change of reader if used in a group.*

> * Welcome, Mary, sister in faith;
> the Lord has surely chosen you.
> The life leaps within me
> to herald the fruit of your womb
> which is Jesus!
> Who am I
> that the mother of my Lord
> should come to me?
> Pray with me now,
> and always.
> Amen.
>
> * Weep, Mary, a mother's tears.
> Your son must die,
> thrust high in agony.
> Alone in suffering,
> separated from His Father's smile
> by sin we laid upon Him.
> Blessed is He
> who comes in the name of the Lord.
> Now, Mary, be mother to John
> and all who will lean, like him,
> close to the heart of Christ,
> and watch with Him in the hour of death.
> Amen.

> * You, Mary, who knew His grace,
> now you're with the Lord.
> Blessed is any who walks with God,
> then is not here, but taken – to Jesus!
> Hold us, Mary, at peace with God;
> join with the prayers of the penitent,
> now and at the gate to life.
> Amen.

Andy Raine, Picking up the Rosary

Scriptures:
Isaiah 7:14;
Luke 1:30-35, 37-38, 46-55;
John 2:1-11;
19:25-27

Mary of Egypt (fifth century): 1 April

One of the many Ammas (or 'mothers') of the desert. She ran away from her home in Egypt, and from the age of 12 she was a prostitute in Alexandria. Then, aged 29, just out of curiosity she joined a pilgrimage to Jerusalem, paying her passage by offering herself to sailors. An invisible force kept her from entering the Church of the Holy Sepulchre with other pilgrims, so she crossed the Jordan and lived for 47 years as a penitent.

A monk called Zosimus discovered her in the desert and heard her story. Later he returned to bring her Communion. Zosimus never forgot her, and planned to meet up with her a year later. He arrived to find her dead, and was on hand to bury her.

In the Eastern churches this story is read as part of the liturgy for the last Thursday in Lent. Mary is chosen here to represent all the named and unnamed Desert Mothers, hermits and penitents.

Scripture:
Hosea 2:14-15

Thomas Merton (1915–68): 11 December

As Merton found God, his loneliness became solitude. This led him to a monastic life of contemplation and compassion. He became a spiritual guide for Trappist scholars and novices – and for his reading public. He was hungry for human intimacy, but even more hungry for intimacy with God. 'True solitude is deeply aware of the world's needs. It does not hold the world at arm's length,' he wrote. The actual Christian task involves 'accepting ourselves as we are in our confusion, infidelity, disruption, ferment, and even desperation'.

Michael and All Angels: 29 September

This feast recollects that we live in 'this vale of sorrows' in a place of spiritual conflict between heaven and the powers of darkness. Perhaps because they are physically close to the skies, high places have been seen by Christians as strategic sites to claim or capture. (Hills, mountains and churches at high altitude are often named after or dedicated to Michael.) In such places believers stand against the 'prince of the power of the air' – the fallen angel Satan. Michael and all good angels are called on to contend on our behalf.

His intervention is also called to mind at the time of dying, to carry the soul safely to the Kingdom of light, or to contend with the Accuser. This explains Michael's frequent occurrence in the orally preserved prayers and invocations of the Hebridean people. This idea of Michael as the receiver of the souls of the dead is also reflected in the American Negro spiritual 'Michael, row the boat ashore'.

If the Accuser reminds sinners of their past, Michael teaches us to remind the enemy of his future!

> Holy Michael, archangel, defend us in the day of battle; be our safeguard against the wickedness and snares of the Devil. May God rebuke him, we humbly pray: and do thou, prince of the heavenly host, by the power of God thrust down to Hell Satan and all wicked spirits who wander through the world for the ruin of souls. Amen.

Scriptures:
Genesis 28:10-12, 16-17;
Genesis 32:1-2;
2 Kings 6:8-17;
Psalms 103:19-22; 118;
Daniel 12:1-3;
Jude 9;
Revelation 12:7-12

Ninian (?–432): 26 August

For Ninian's biography see 'Ninian – in relating to the whole of life' (p.318).

Henri Nouwen (1932–96): 21 September

Dutch Catholic priest and Professor of Psychology at both Yale and Harvard, he became a living example of 'downward mobility' and Christlikeness. Making himself of no reputation, he left the public eye to work 'as a priest for the poor' in both Latin America and in the L'Arche Daybreak Community in Canada. He was a 'wounded healer' whose restless seeking for God has left a legacy to the world through his prolific writings on the spirituality of brokenness and vulnerability.

Oswald (605–42): 5 August

For Oswald's biography see 'Oswald – in practical ways' (p.277).

Oswin (?–651): 20 August

A Christian king of the southern part of Northumbria known as Deira, Oswin was 'a man of handsome appearance and great stature, pleasant in speech and courteous'. He was a great friend of Bishop Aidan and tried to give him a horse to speed him on his journeys. Aidan gave the horse away to the first beggar asking for alms!

Oswin was assassinated on the order of his cousin King Oswy, who wanted to be king of all Northumbria. Aidan was heartbroken at his death, and Oswin in time came to be revered as a martyr. The sites of 12 monasteries, including Whitby, were given by Oswy as a hopeful reparatory gesture for this killing!

Owini (?–670): 4 March

Owini came from a noble family in East Anglia and was a servant to Princess Etheldreda (who was briefly married to an old man, then to a boy prince, Egfrith of Northumbria).

When Etheldreda joined her aunt Ebba at the monastery of Coldingham, Owini joined the monastery at Lastingham under Chad. He journeyed there on foot, working his keep as he travelled. The journey was so difficult and dangerous that afterwards he set up wooden crosses along the route to serve as waymarks for pilgrims and travellers.

At Lastingham he begged to work hard on the land, rather than study. He became Chad's companion and biographer and followed him to Lichfield.

Patrick (389–461): 17 March

For Patrick's biography see 'The Patrick Compline', p.70 and 'Patrick – in resolute discipleship', which can be found in Book Two, p.1101.

Paul Aurelian (sixth century): 12 March

The son of a British chieftain, he was a hermit and a disciple of Illtyd. He was identified as *peregrinus pro Christo*, one for whom 'the coracle is on the sea'. With 12 companions he travelled from Wales to Brittany and founded churches there. He is known also as Paulinus of Wales and in Brittany as Pol de Léon. He also stayed with his sister in Cornwall. For some years he lived as a hermit near Llandovery and founded a monastery at Llanddeusant. The order of the events prior to his death is not clear. He was 104 years old at his death.

Paulinus (?–644): 10 October

He accompanied the Christian princess Ethelburga of Kent when she went to Northumbria to marry King Edwin. He presented the faith to Edwin, who listened carefully but remained uncertain. However, his pagan high priest, Coifi, was so soundly converted that he rode off to torch his own temple. Paulinus is said to have baptised thousands of people in the Swale near Catterick and in the Glen, near the royal summer residence of Yeavering (not far from Wooler) and at Holystone (near Rothbury).

When Edwin was killed in battle in 633 all was thrown into confusion. Paulinus returned to Kent with the queen and her children, and was appointed Bishop of Rochester, where he remained until his death.

Paul of Thebes (?–345): 15 January

He fled to the Egyptian desert during a time of persecution and became the first Christian hermit. He lived for well over 100 years and was buried in the desert by Antony.

Pelagius (c.350–418): 28 August

We have chosen to mark Pelagius' memory on the feast day normally assigned to Augustine of Hippo, who did so much to malign Pelagius and who is the source of many erroneous teachings and emphases that still dog Christian thinking today!

Pelagius was a British theologian, teacher, writer and soul-friend who settled in Rome. He was highly spoken of at first – even by Augustine. He taught about the value of soul-friendship. He celebrated the fact that the goodness of God cries out through all of creation, for 'narrow shafts of divine light pierce the veil that separates heaven from earth'.

But soon he was criticised for teaching women to read Scripture, and for believing that the image of God is present in every newborn child, and that sex is a God-given aspect of our essential creation. He did not deny the reality of evil or its assault on the human soul, or the habitual nature of sin. Augustine's own peculiar ideas were in stark contrast, seeing humanity as essentially evil, and polluted by the sexual activity which causes conception to occur.

Augustine tried twice in 415 to have him convicted of heresy – on both occasions Pelagius was exonerated in Palestine. In 416 Augustine and the African bishops convened two diocesan councils to condemn him and Celestius, another Celt. In 417 the Bishop of Rome called a synod to consider the conflict, and declared Pelagius' teaching entirely true, and urged the African bishops to love peace, prize love and seek after harmony. They ignored this, and in 418 they persuaded the State to intervene and banish Pelagius from Rome for disturbing the peace. The Church then was obliged to uphold the Emperor's judgement, and excommunicated and banished him, though no reasons were made clear. He returned to Wales, probably to the monastery of Bangor.

Two centuries later all the same ideas were still to be found in Celtic Christianity. History is written by the victors, so most reports of what Pelagius said are given from Augustine's viewpoint, not in his own balanced and sensible words. He was also criticised by Jerome for being a big, enthusiastic man, stupid from eating porridge and over-confident in his own strength, and for wearing his hair in an inappropriate style!

Petroc (?–c.564): 4 June

In Welsh tradition, 'Pedrog' is named as one of three just knights contending against whoever did wrong to the weak. But sickened and traumatised by all the slaughter in the futile battle of Camlan, he broke his spear and dedicated himself to the peaceful service of God. He is said to have travelled to India, returning years later with a tame wolf that guarded his staff and sheepskin. 'Petroc' is revered as a saint in Cornwall where he founded an abbey at Bodmin. His two symbols are a broken spear in his hand and the tame wolf at his side, signalling the power of love to tame the forces of chaos and destruction.

Scripture:
Psalm 46:8-10

Piran (early sixth century): 5 March

Tied to a millstone, Piran is said to have floated safely across the Irish Sea to the sands of Perranporth on the north coast of Cornwall. Keiran of Saighir was a prominent Irish hermit/bishop, whose story ends abruptly, just as Piran appears in Cornwall, and the two saints seem to have been the same person. Piran built an oratory on the sands, and made a fire which he surrounded with stones. A stream of white liquid trickling from the dark rocks showed him how to smelt tin!

Polycarp (69–155): 23 February

Polycarp was taught by John, the Lord's own disciple, who made him a bishop in Smyrna in 96. In his time the date for celebrating Easter was already a matter of controversy. He visited Anicetus, the Bishop of Rome, to discuss a uniform practice, but they could not agree, except to differ. Before they parted, Polycarp celebrated Communion in Anicetus' own chapel at his invitation. He was much loved and respected by all who knew him. He was martyred as a very old man, being burnt alive in a stadium during one of the waves of persecution. The letter describing his ordeal is the first narrative account of a Christian martyrdom after that of Stephen.

Scripture:
Daniel 3:23-25

Reinfrid (?–1084/5): 31 October

Reinfrid spent much of his life as a ruthless mercenary in the service of William of Normandy but gradually became sickened by the destruction of which he had been part, and was haunted by recurring dreams of burning crops and homesteads. After a particularly disturbing assignment in Whitby he retired in search of peace, and was admitted to the monastery at Evesham.

There he met with Prior Aldwin of Winchcombe and went north with him to rebuild ruined monastic sites in Northumbria, including Hild's foundations at Whitby and Hackness. While peacefully repairing a broken bridge over the river at Hackness he was hit by a falling timber, and died in the midst of the work he loved. (We remember him on the feast day of Bega who was a nun at Hackness in Hild's time.)

Scriptures:
2 Corinthians 5:17-19;
Isaiah 58:6-12

Brother Roger of Taizé (1915–2005): 16 August

Brother Roger (Frère Roger) was the founder and first prior of the Taizé Community, an ecumenical monastic community. From 1937 to 1940, Roger Schütz-Marsauche studied Reformed Theology in Strasbourg and Lausanne, and was a leader in the Swiss Student Christian Movement. During his recovery from tuberculosis, he began to feel drawn to a monastic way of life.

Then in 1940, at the start of World War II, he felt called to serve those suffering from the conflict. He rode a bicycle from Geneva to Taizé, a small town in unoccupied France, just beyond the line of demarcation from the zone occupied by German troops. He bought an empty house there and for two years he and his sister hid Christian and Jewish refugees. When the Gestapo became aware of their activities they left. In 1944, he returned to Taizé to found the Community, initially a small quasi-monastic community of men living together in poverty and obedience, open to all Christians. He explains, 'I found my own identity as a Christian by reconciling within myself my protestant origins and the mystery of the Catholic faith, without breaking fellowship with anyone...'

Since the late 1950s, many thousands of young adults from many countries have found their way to Taizé to take part in meetings of prayer and reflection. At one Taizé gathering in Paris in 1995, he spoke to more than 100,000 young people sitting on the floor. 'We have come here to search, or to go on searching through silence and prayer, to get in touch with our inner life. Christ always said, "Do not worry, give yourself."'

Brother Roger received Eucharist at the Catholic Mass celebrated every morning in his monastery by Catholic priests of his community, and entered progressively into a full communion with the faith of the Catholic Church without a 'conversion' that would imply a break with his origins.

'Living God, You want us to have hearts that are completely simple, so the complicated things in life do not bring us to a halt. Through the Holy Spirit, the spirit of the Risen Christ, You come to open the way for us. You loved us first, before we loved You.' With his idealism and moving prayers such as these, he successfully steered the high revolt of many from the 1968 generation away from revolutionary violence into the calmer waters of spirituality.

'Taizé's strength is still in the poetry of its message,' writes Alain Woodrow, 'and Brother Roger loved paradoxes. Taizé used to be unfashionably opposed to doubt and contention; now it is unfashionably opposed to certainty as a test of Christian identity.'

'It is our resistance to what we experience that makes creativity possible. So don't get rid of resistance like that by going around it or trying to eliminate it,' said Brother Roger. 'I say to myself, go on seeking, be glad for being sensitive, be glad you're able to go beyond the resistance inside you.'

It was during the evening prayer service in Taizé on 16 August 2005 that Brother Roger was attacked by a young Romanian woman, later declared mentally ill. She stabbed him several times and, though one of the brothers carried him from the church, he died shortly afterward.

The Taizé community is unashamedly ecumenical, welcoming seekers from all over Europe and beyond to grow in prayer or explore what faith would look like and be open to an encounter with Christ. Brother Roger used to say whenever young people were leaving to go home that they might not find there anything very similar to life at Taizé, but they could look at the tiny area of even a few streets around where they lived or worked, and there discover any sign of the Spirit of God at work in their world, and whatever it was throw their energies into supporting it.

Scripture:
John 13:35

Oscar Romero (1917–80): 24 March

Romero was a safe appointment as archbishop in El Salvador – he was a conservative and religious man, unlikely to align himself directly with the poor in a country on the brink of civil unrest and political turbulence. But the murder of a Jesuit priest and the army opening fire on a peaceful protest gathering soon made him take sides and become identified with the oppressed.

He urged his priests to shelter anyone in terror of their lives. He moved out of his palace and lodged at a cancer hospital for the poor. He began his sermons by reading the names of the murdered and the missing. He condemned the use of violence in pursuit either of justice or self-interest. He spoke out against the institutional violence of economic oppression.

For three years he was a voice for the voiceless, and then he was shot whilst saying Mass. The Gospel of the day read: 'If a seed of wheat falls into the ground and dies it will bear much fruit.' A newspaper released a message he had already prepared for this eventuality: 'I have often been threatened with death. But, as a Christian, I do not believe in death without resurrection. If they kill me, I shall rise again in the Salvadorean people, a witness of hope in the future.'

> **Scriptures:**
> Job 29:11-16;
> Proverbs 31:9;
> John 12:23-24, 26-28

Samthann (?–739): 18 December

Samthann was the Abbess of Clonbroney in Ireland and was renowned for her prayer and her wisdom. When asked what position prayer should be made in – lying down, sitting or standing – she replied: 'In every position, a person should pray!' To someone who spoke of pilgrimage, but was really only anxious to travel and was dressing this with excuses, she said: 'God is near to all who call on Him, and the Kingdom of Heaven can be reached from every land.'

Senan (?–544): 8 March

An Irish monk and the founder of several monasteries, all on islands. He finally settled on Inis Cathaig, which we now know as Scattery Island (where Aidan was a monk before moving to Iona).

Stephen (?–35): 26 December

The first Christian martyr. It is said that Jesus sat at the Father's side, but rose to greet Stephen.

> **Scriptures:**
> 2 Chronicles 24:19-21

Teilo (sixth century): 9 February

A pupil of Dyfrig and Paul Aurelian. During the plague he spent seven years away from Wales with Samson at Dol in Brittany. His main foundation was at Llandeilo Fawr. One of the sayings attributed to him is 'Do not do injury, if you can possibly avoid it' – a challenging admonition.

Telemachus (?–391): 1 January

A monk from the East who lived alone as a hermit, devoting his life to prayer. Sent by God to Rome, he entered the Colosseum where the Games were to be held that day. He ran out between the gladiators, trying to separate them, and was killed. The Emperor Honorius was present, and in consequence abolished the Games soon afterwards. Telemachus was revered as a martyr.

Teresa of Avila (1515–82): 15 October

From a Spanish family of converted Jews, she became a Carmelite nun and founded the Reformed or Discalced Carmelites. John of the Cross was her protégé. She was given to mystical experiences in prayer. She taught an openness to such possibilities, but she did not encourage undue dependence on them. Times of experiencing God's presence were to be received with gratitude and joy, but were not to be treated as a right or allowed to become disruptive.

Her order's way of life was austere and her reforms were radical, but she is now honoured as a Doctor of the Church. 'God made me pleasing,' she wrote. She would perhaps have made even more enemies than she did, had He not blessed her with the gift of being likeable!

Teresa of Calcutta (1910–97): 5 September

Born in Serbia to Albanian parents, she became a nun and longed for permission to move outside the convent walls and work with the poorest of the poor in India. In later years she received great recognition and various 'peace prizes', but challenged all kinds of people to compassion and discipleship through her media exposure. 'Do you know and love the poor?' she asked. 'If you do not know them, how can you love them?'

Working among the slums of Calcutta, she remained radiant. She commented pragmatically, 'The surest way to preach Christianity to the pagan is by our cheerfulness, our happiness. What would our life be if the Sisters were unhappy? We would do the work, but we would attract nobody.'

Thérèse of Lisieux (1873–97): 3 October

Thérèse's mother died when she was four and her father moved with his daughters to Lisieux in Normandy. At 15 she was allowed to become a Carmelite nun, though she had longed to do so earlier. Ironically, she had only nine years of convent life before she died of tuberculosis. She had intended to offer herself as a missionary nun to work in Hanoi in Vietnam, but the onset of the disease convinced her that this would not be possible. Her own written story of her interior life was reworked after her death by her sister and was published. It had instant appeal, and was translated into various languages. In 1952 her own original version, *The Story of a Soul*, was made available. We include her here because of the profound impact of some of her reflections, which are used in our readings.

Thomas (first century): 3 July

Persistent tradition links Thomas with missionary work in India, and the Syriac Christians of Malabar claim that they were evangelised by Thomas, who was killed by a spear and buried at Mylapore, near Madras.

Three Kings' Day: 6 January

6 January is Three Kings' Day for many countries in Europe and beyond. It is marked in Holland, the Czech Republic and India, and the date is celebrated by Hispanic communities everywhere. This is the Epiphany of the church calendar, the twelfth day after Christmas, when the Magi arrived bearing gifts for baby Jesus. On this day, rather than Christmas itself, children in Latin America would traditionally receive their gifts, brought by the three kings, Melchior, Gaspar and Balthazar. A cake or sweetbread is often baked, shaped as a wreath or a crown with candied jewels.

Tuda (?–664): 21 October

Educated in the southern part of Ireland, Tuda was chosen as bishop to replace Colman after the famous Whitby Synod. So at Lindisfarne Tuda was bishop and Eata was abbot (though Eata also continued to be Abbot of Melrose). We know from Cuthbert's later difficulties that the reforms were not accepted easily, so it must have been a difficult appointment. Tuda was a 'good and devout' man, and might have done much to reconcile opposing factions; but it was just at this time that the plague struck, and he was one of the fatalities as it ravaged the whole land.

Scripture:
Matthew 5:44-45, 48

William Walcher (?–1080): 14 May

After six years as a good friend and wise benefactor to Aldwin and his companions, William Walcher, Bishop of Durham, was ambushed and brutally killed in a riot at Gateshead. Walcher had also been made Earl of Northumbria, and was blamed for the random cruelties of various overlords for whom he was nominally responsible. The local populace still resented the Normans, and the indignant crowd inflicted so many wounds on Walcher that his naked body could scarcely be identified. His friends from the monastery at Jarrow brought a little boat to carry his body away and prepare it for burial. In a difficult and turbulent time, Walcher was a gentle soul who sincerely followed Christ.

> **Scriptures:**
> Psalm 69:4-6, 19-20;
> Matthew 10:26-28a, 39-42

Roland Walls (1918–2011): 7 April

A constant throughout the history and formation of the Northumbria Community has been the influence and example of Father Roland Walls of the monastic Community of the Transfiguration. The Community (now Hermitage) of the Transfiguration has its home some 400 yards from Rosslyn Chapel, situated in the village of Roslin, near Edinburgh. Its main building is a rather rundown ex-Miners' Welfare Institute, beyond which is a silent enclosure consisting of a chapel and four huts. The whole place is inconspicuous and minimalist with simplicity a prominent feature. The vocation of Northumbria Community was initiated and shaped here, a deliberately unpublicised, understated place of prayer and hospitality.

Roland, a theologian who had taught in the Divinity faculty at both Cambridge and Edinburgh Universities, became mentor to the early pioneers and remained (along with his colleague Brother John Halsey) a key spiritual director to the Northumbria Community for decades. He introduced Northumbria Community to 'Desert' and 'monastic spirituality' and their teaching, insight and wisdom has been handed down and passed on as example and life. Simplicity, humility, the place of laughter, teasing and absurdity, incarnational living that is real, messy, unpretentious and deeply authentic. In the words of Rowan Williams, there are few people in the past half-century who have 'brought God so vividly alive to so many'.

Scriptures:
Psalm 27;
Mark 9:1-9, 15;
Isaiah 30:20-21

Wilfrid (633–709): 12 October

He resented his years on Lindisfarne and longed for Rome's ways. Power, prestige and recognition were his goals – but only so that the Church would be taken seriously as a force for good. He was at various times deposed from his office as bishop, exiled and imprisoned, but these troubles were mostly of his own making. Shipwrecked in Frisia (northern Holland), he won the love of the local people by his Lindisfarne-gained knowledge of fishing, and was able to evangelise them effectively. Once, in exile, he also evangelised the fierce South Saxons, a farming people whose crops had failed. He taught them to harvest the sea, and also soon baptised large numbers of them. His time at Lindisfarne had not been wasted.

Willibrord (658–739): 7 November

Born in Yorkshire, he studied in Ireland and was ordained there. He returned to England and led a mission to Frisia. He was based in Utrecht, and later founded a monastery at Echternach. He is an important saint to the people of Holland and Luxembourg. A step-dance has persisted at Echternach in which the clergy participate. Willibrord was noted for his graciousness and joy, and for his faithful preaching. The inspiration for his mission and his life's work was probably hearing Wilfrid at Ripon reminiscing about his own time among the people of Frisia.

John Wycliffe (1324–84): 31 December

Born at Wycliffe (near Barnard Castle), he was educated locally at Eggleston Abbey, then at Oxford. A Catholic, a theologian and a Bible translator, he recognised the need for the Bible to be in the language of the people. He was very influential, especially in the years following the plague whilst based in Oxford. He taught at Balliol College, but then retired to Lutterworth because of ill health and increasing controversy over his teachings. He taught consubstantiation – that the consecrated host 'is naturally real bread and sacramentally the Body of Christ' (which was at the time considered a shocking idea).

In his last two years he wrote prolifically before dying of a stroke; but he was posthumously condemned and his remains were dug up, burned and scattered. This was because he had protested that such a high proportion of parish giving was required to go overseas to swell Vatican funds, and because of his objection to the sale of indulgences. The Roman authorities disliked his teachings on consubstantiation and his policy of encouraging others to learn and tell Bible stories in English.

Brigid – in welcoming

Brigid of Kildare (c.450–523)

A call to recklessness

Many legends and few facts survive about this Irish woman who founded a community at Kildare, primarily for women. She was famed for her generosity and hospitality, and her influence was widespread; but she remained eminently practical.

As a young woman, Brigid was in the habit of giving freely of her father's possessions and food to the poor and needy. Her father became so frustrated that he decided to sell her to the king and bundled her into his chariot. He left her at the castle gate while he consulted with the king, and Brigid was approached by a beggar asking for alms. She gave him her father's sword. Brigid's father and the king were amazed, and the king said he could not buy her from her father: 'She is too good for me – I could never win her obedience.'

Once Brigid was the guest at a house when lepers came begging for food. Brigid could find no one about but a young dumb boy. So she asked him for the key to the kitchen. He turned to her and was able to say, 'I know where it is kept,' and together they fetched food and attended to the guests.

Brigid led a group of women who had decided to become holy nuns, and she asked Bishop Mel to bless their taking of the veil. Brigid held back out of humility, but the bishop saw the Spirit of God descend upon her and called her forward. Laying hands upon her, he said, 'I have no power in this matter. God has ordained Brigid.' And so it came to pass that by the intervention of the Holy Spirit the form of ordaining a bishop was read over Brigid.

A poor leper came to Brigid one day and asked her for a cow. Brigid looked at him and asked, 'Which would you rather – to take a cow or to be healed of your leprosy?' The man chose: 'I would rather be healed than own all the cows in the world.' So Brigid prayed, stretched out her hand, and the leper was made whole.

May God our Father, our strength and light, bless you with what you most need, beyond even all you would ask. For the weather is always right for the sowing of good seed.

A house-blessing

This form of prayer may be used:

- on 1 February, Brigid's feast day, to pray a blessing on the home (a group of friends or neighbours may even go from one house to the next);
- whenever a Brigid's cross or other cross is put up by the door or on the wall;
- on moving into a new house or blessing a house at any time (the prayers can be taken out and used singly as often as you like).

You will find that the prayers take you round the house, beginning outside the doorway, then in the living room. If the house has an open fire or a wood-stove there are extra prayers 'At a warm place' for use in whichever room it is situated. Next you move to the kitchen.

There is a blessing to use in each bedroom; but special blessings are also included for use in a single person's room, a couple's room, a guest room, a child's room, and the room of an older son or daughter. Read them carefully beforehand and decide which will be appropriate.

Finally you pray a blessing at the door or at any place where a cross or Brigid's cross may be.

The leader (usually the householder) reads the parts in ordinary type, and everyone reads together the sections in **bold** *type.*

At the doorway

> May God give His blessing to the house that is here.
> **God bless this house from roof to floor,**
> **from wall to wall,**
> **from end to end,**
> **from its foundation and in its covering.**

In the strong name of the Triune God
all evil be banished,
all disturbance cease,
captive spirits freed,
God's Spirit alone
dwell within these walls.

**We call upon the Sacred Three
to save, shield and surround
this house, this home,
this day, this night,
and every night.**

In the living room

There is a friend's love
in the gentle heart of the Saviour.
For love of Him we offer friendship
and welcome every guest.
Lord, kindle in my heart
a flame of love to my neighbour,
to my enemies, my friends, my kindred all,
from the lowliest thing that liveth
to the name that is highest of all.

At a warm place

Come to a warm place in this house,
come in the name of Christ.
My heart and I agree,
welcome in the name of the Lord.

**There is a fiery power
in the gentle heart of the Spirit.
Our hearts are agreed
as we kneel by the hearth,**

**and call on the Sacred Three
to save, shield and surround
us and our kin,
this house, this home,
this day, this night
and every night,
each single night.**

In the kitchen

I would welcome the poor
and honour them.
I would welcome the sick
in the presence of angels
and ask God to bless and
embrace us all.

Seeing a stranger approach,
I would put food in the eating place,
drink in the drinking place,
music in the listening place,
and look with joy for the blessing of God,
who often comes to my home
in the blessing of a stranger.

**We call upon the Sacred Three
to save, shield and surround
this house, this home,
this day, this night,
and every night.**

For a bedroom

> Peace be here in the name of the King of life;
> the peace of Christ above all peace,
> the Lord's blessing over you.

For the bedroom of a single person

> Peace be here in the name of the King of life;
> the peace of Christ above all peace,
> the Lord's blessing over you.

May God the Father be the guardian of this place
and bring His peace,
that fear may find no entry here.
May Christ be a chosen companion and friend.
May loneliness be banished.
May the Spirit bring lightness and laughter,
and be the comforter of tears.
Courage be at each going out;
rest be present at each return;
each day, each night,
each going out and each returning.

For the bedroom of a married couple

> Peace be here in the name of the King of life;
> the peace of Christ above all peace,
> the Lord's blessing over you.

Peace between person and person;
peace between husband and wife.
The peace of Christ above all peace,
peace between lovers
in love of the King of life.

For a guest room

**Peace be here in the name of the King of life;
the peace of Christ above all peace,
the Lord's blessing over you.**

May all be welcomed here
as the Christ-child at the stable:
in simplicity and joy,
and as Brigid welcomed the poor,
may the smile of the Son of Peace
be found here
whenever the door is opened.

For the room of a young child

To be said by the parent(s) if possible:
Peace be here in the name of the King of life;
the peace of Christ above all peace,
the Lord's blessing over you.
They say nothing is given birth without pain.
I have a secret joy in Thee, my God,
for, if Thou art my Father,
Thou art my Mother too,
and of Thy tenderness, healing and patience
there is no end at all.
I pray for *(name)*.
(name), may the joy and peace of heaven
be with you.
The Lord bless you.

For the room of an older son or daughter, present or absent

To be said by the parent(s):
>Peace be here in the name of the King of life,
>the peace of Christ above all peace;
>the Lord's blessing over you.

>*Son of my breast/daughter of my heart,*
>the joy of God be in thy face,
>joy to all who see thee.
>The circle of God around thee,
>angels of God shielding thee,
>angels of God shielding thee.
>Joy of night and day be thine;
>joy of sun and moon be thine;
>joy of men and women be thine.
>Each land and sea thou goest,
>each land and sea thou goest,
>be every season happy for thee;
>be every season bright for thee;
>be every season glad for thee.
>Be thine the compassing of the God of life;
>be thine the compassing of the Christ of love;
>be thine the compassing of the Spirit of grace:
>to befriend thee and to aid thee,
>*(name), thou beloved son of my breast/*
>*thou beloved daughter of my heart.*

At the door (or at a cross)

> Christ, in our coming
> and in our leaving,
> the Door and the Keeper;
> for us and our dear ones,
> this day and every day,
> blessing for always. Amen.

Prayers for a workplace

All the above prayers could be adapted as appropriate for use in different locations. For example, the following adaptations are for use in the workplace.

* indicates a change of reader.

Outside the doorway

> * May God give His blessing on this place.
> God bless it from roof to floor,
> from wall to wall, from end to end,
> from its foundation and in its covering.
> In the strong name of the Triune God:
> all evil be banished,
> all disturbance cease,
> captive spirits freed.
> God's Spirit alone
> dwell within these walls.
>
> **We call upon the Sacred Three**
> **to save, shield and surround**
> **this place, this day, and every day.**

In the entrance or reception room

* May all be welcomed here,
  friend and stranger, from near and far.
  May each be blessed and honoured
  as they enter.

  **There is a friend's love
  in the gentle heart of the Saviour.
  For love of Him we offer friendship
  and welcome every guest.**

In each room and work area

  **Peace be here in the name of the King of life,
  the peace of Christ above all peace;
  the Lord's blessing over all.**

* May God the Father
  be the guardian of this place
  and bring His peace.

* May His love be shared,
  and His will be found here,
  and peace between all people.

* May the Spirit bring lightness and laughter here.

* May He be the strengthener and comforter
  in times of difficulty.

* May the Lord give peace
  but never complacency.

* Here may encouragement be found
  and relationships strengthened.

Each day, every day,
each going out, and each returning,
the Lord bless you and keep you.

* Peace between person and person;
  peace between all who work here;
  the peace of Christ above all peace;
  peace between friends
  each day and every day.

* I pray for all who work here: *(Names)*.
  May the joy and peace of heaven
  be with you and around you.
  The Lord bless you.

At the door

Christ, in our coming
and in our leaving,
be the Door and the Keeper
for us
and all who work within this place,
this day and every day,
ever and always.
Amen.

Oswald – in practical ways

Oswald of Northumbria (605–42)

A call to humility

Long ago on the Isle of Iona a young man knelt in prayer, his heart and hands raised in question to the God whom he loved and served. Oswald was his name, and he had been schooled by the saints of Iona to follow the old paths, in the steps of those who long ago had walked with Christ in His way.

A difficult decision was made. Oswald would return to Northumbria, the land of his heritage, and make it his, reclaiming the throne and crown by battle. He would put an end to the years of fighting and division so that his people might live. Oswald planted a wooden cross in the good ground of Heavenfield, setting it up as a waymark. And so Oswald and his companions knelt together at the turn of the road, at the foot of the cross, and prayed.

The battle was decisive, Oswald was victorious, and Northumbria was united under his kingship. Many of those who fought were intrigued by this new deity, the God of the Christians, who had won Oswald's allegiance. Oswald sent for missionaries from Iona to teach his people, but everything went wrong and the team withdrew, admitting to failure. The king prayed and trusted and waited, and reached out his hands to his God.

Then came Aidan from Iona with a band of helpers. This time the work began in earnest, and Oswald the king, Oswald the Christian, went out into the villages and marketplaces where Aidan preached, and he worked willingly as the interpreter.

Prayers for committing our work to God

This form of prayer may be used:
- on 5 August, Oswald's feast day;
- on pilgrimage to Heavenfield or Bamburgh;
- as a way of committing our work to God;
- for those who live out their Christianity in ordinary life.

All who wish to may read in turn.
* indicates a change of reader.
With a large group, split into two halves and read alternately.
*All say together the sections in **bold** type.*

* This day is Your gift to me;
I take it, Lord, from Your hand
and thank You for the wonder of it.

God be with me
in this Your day,
every day
and every way,
with me and for me
in this Your day;
and the love
and affection
of heaven
be toward me.

* All that I am, Lord,
I place into Your hands.
All that I do, Lord,
I place into Your hands.

* Everything I work for
I place into Your hands.
Everything I hope for
I place into Your hands.

* The troubles that weary me
  I place into Your hands.
  The thoughts that disturb me
  I place into Your hands.

* Each that I pray for
  I place into Your hands.
  Each that I care for
  I place into Your hands.

* I place into Your hands, Lord,
  the choices that I face.
  Guard me from choosing
  the way perilous
  of which the end is heart-pain
  and the secret tear.

* Rich in counsel,
  show us the way
  that is plain and safe.

* May I feel Your presence
  at the heart of my desire,
  and so know it for Your desire for me.
  Thus shall I prosper,
  thus see my purpose is from You,
  thus have power to do the good which endures.

* Show me what blessing it is
  that I have work to do.
  And sometimes,
  and most of all
  when the day is overcast
  and my courage faints,
  let me hear Your voice, saying,
  'You are my beloved one
  in whom I am well pleased.'

* Stand at the crossroads and look,
  ask for the ancient paths,
  ask where the good way is,
  and walk in it,
  and you will find rest for your souls.

* In the name of Christ we stand,
  and in His name
  move out across the land
  in fearfulness and blessing.

* To gather the kingdom to the King
  and claim this land for God:
  a task indeed.

* Give us to see Your will,
  and power to walk in its path;
  and lo! the night is routed and gone.

* Lord, hasten the day
  when those who fear You in every nation
  will come from the east and west,
  from north and south,
  and sit at table in Your Kingdom.
  And, Lord,
  let Your glory be seen in our land.

* He has shown you, O man, what is right;
  and what does the Lord require of you,
  but to do justly, and to love mercy
  and to walk humbly with your God?

* Keep me close to You, Lord.
  Keep me close to You.
  I lift my hands to You, Lord,
  I lift them up to You.

**Hands, Lord, Your gift to us,
we stretch them up to You.
Always You hold them.**

* Help me to find my happiness
  in my acceptance
  of what is Your purpose for me:
  in friendly eyes, in work well done,
  in quietness born of trust,
  and, most of all,
  in the awareness of Your presence
  in my spirit.

(Pause for reflection before resuming your activity.)

Aidan – in the power of the Spirit

Aidan of Lindisfarne (?–651)

A call to mission

Long ago, on the island of Iona, a meeting had been called. An angry brother spoke about his failure, telling of the hardness of heart in the kingdom of Northumbria – a land of darkness refusing the life-giving light, inhabited by a stubborn, unreachable people. And one man heard, and his heart was stirred with compassion for that land and its people. To open his heart to this could cost him everything: leaving the island he loved, the companionship of his brothers, their prayer and work. Were there not others still to be reached much closer to home? If he stayed seated among his brothers no one would notice him, no one would know what he had heard in his heart: the cry of the desert, 'Come over to Northumbria and help us.'

'O Lord,' he prayed, 'give me springs and I will water this land. I will go, Lord. I will hold this people in my heart.' A moment later it was his own voice, the voice of Aidan, that broke the awkward silence. 'Perhaps, my brother, if you had spoken with more gentleness, and of the love of Christ, giving them the gospel to nourish them like milk is given to a tiny baby, then you would have won them and remained among them.'

Prayers for being sent out with God's blessing

This form of prayer may be used:
- on 31 August, Aidan's feast day;
- on pilgrimage to Holy Island or Bamburgh;
- for sending out anyone going away on mission;
- by any mission team while they are away.

* *indicates a change of reader.*
With a large group, split into two halves and read alternately.
All say together the sections in **bold** *type.*

* Then I heard a voice in heaven saying,
'Whom shall I send?
and who will go for us?'
Then said I,
'Here am I; send me.'

* I will go, Lord, if You lead me:
I will hold Your people in my heart.

* Deeper in my heart I will hear Your call;
I will cry for the desert
until my eyes run with tears
because people do not obey Your laws.

* If I open my eyes to the world around me,
if I open my heart to the people
that surround me,
then I feel pain and brokenness,
I see suffering and injustice.

* Lord, see what evil
the prince of this world is devising.
Let the wind of Your Spirit blow
and reverse the works of darkness:
and Your fire will cover the earth.

Deliver us, Lord, from every evil
and grant us peace in our day.
In your mercy, Lord,
keep us free from sin,
and protect us from all anxiety
as we wait in joyful hope
for the coming of our Saviour,
Jesus Christ.
Let Your Kingdom come, Lord, in me.

**I pray the protection of Christ to clothe me,
Christ to enfold me,
to surround me and guard me
this day and every day,
surrounding me and my companions,
enfolding me and every friend.**

* We pray for ourselves,
  for the gift of friendship
  and of faithfulness;
  and that we would be freed
  from selfishness.

**We will journey
with the kind-hearted Saviour.
If we have fed the hungry
from our own table,
God will feed us with all good gifts.**

* We will keep before us
  the deepening and strengthening
  of our companions' faith,
  assisting each other
  in meditation and prayer.

* May we protect
  each other's times for silence.
  Give us the courage to say:

**Leave me alone with God
as much as may be.
As the tide draws the waters
close in upon the shore,
make me an island, set apart,
alone with You, God,
holy to You.**

**Then with the turning of the tide,
prepare me to carry Your presence
to the busy world beyond,
the world that rushes in on me,
till the waters come again
and fold me back to You.**

Pause for reflection.

* Lord, give us the desire to love goodness,
  to passionately love goodness;
  teach us moderation in all things;
  teach us to love wisdom,
  and to greatly love Your law.

* So often we hold too lightly to our belief.
  May we plant the faith patiently,
  calmly and untiringly
  in the good ground of hungry hearts.

**God and the angels guard us!
May He bring us home rejoicing!**

Chad – in willing service

Chad of Lichfield (?–672)

A call to readiness

Chad and his brothers were early pupils in Aidan's school at Lindisfarne. Chad continued his studies by journeying to Ireland; but when his brother Cedd died, he returned to take his place as abbot of Lastingham. Then for a time he was bishop at York, but was soon removed over a technicality. This he accepted with no reproach, and was sent instead as bishop to the people of Mercia. At that time Chad spoke warily of the honour of being recognised as a bishop: 'I never thought myself worthy of it,' he said, 'but, though unworthy, I consented to undertake it for obedience's sake.'

Even as a bishop he lived in a small cell and travelled barefoot. His obvious simplicity embarrassed Bishop Theodore of Canterbury, who often urged Chad to ride, not walk. Once he was so frustrated that he bodily lifted Chad onto a horse and sent him on his journey!

For just three years Chad lived among the Mercians as their bishop, and then he died. Addressing his community, he urged them to always be prepared for death, 'for death may call for us at any time'.

Prayers for a journey or at a time of change

This form of prayer may be used:
* on 2 March, Chad's feast day;
* on pilgrimage to Stowe or Lichfield or Lastingham;
* by anyone in a time of transition or great change;
* by someone going on a journey.

All who wish to may read in turn.
* indicates a change of reader.
With a large group, split into two halves and read alternately.
*All say together the sections in **bold** type.*
*The words in **bold italic** type set between lines should be said by each in turn (or the leader reads, then all repeat together).*

> **My soul thirsts for God, for the living God.**
> **As the deer pants for streams of water,**
> **so my soul pants for You, O God.**

* In the name of the Father.
  Amen.

* In the name of the Son.
  Amen.

* In the name of the Spirit.
  Amen.
  Father, Son and Spirit.
  Amen.
  Father, Son and Spirit.
  Amen.
  Father, Son and Spirit.
  Amen.

* Thanks to You,
  O ever-gentle Christ,
  for raising me freely
  from the black and darkness of last night
  into the kindly light of this day.

  **You pour life into me,
  giving me speech, sense, desire,
  giving me thought and action.
  My fame or repute will be
  just as You allow:
  You mark the way before me.
  As I remember saints
  who have journeyed before me,
  Lord, teach me the way of their simplicity:
  strength with humility,
  at peace in the fear of God.
  May I also go wherever I am led.**

  **The keeping of Christ about me,
  the guarding of God with me
  to possess me, to protect me
  from drowning and danger and loss,
  the gospel of the God of grace
  from brow of head
  to sole of foot,
  the gospel of Christ,
  King of salvation,
  be as a mantle to my body.**

  All I speak
  be blessed to me, O God.
  All I hear
  be blessed to me, O God.
  All I see
  be blessed to me, O God.
  All I sense
  be blessed to me, O God.

All I taste
be blessed to me, O God.
Each step I take
be blessed to me, O God.

Peace between me and my God.
Peace between me and my God.

May I tread the path to the gates of glory;
may I tread the path to the gates of glory.

On your path, O my God,
and not my own,
be all my journeying.
Rule this heart of mine
that it be only Yours.

* We look for solitude.
  In solitude we learn to grow and love,
  to grow in love for God,
  to grow in love for others.

* Christ's cross would I carry,
  my own struggle forget.

* Christ's death would I ponder,
  my own death remember.

* Christ's agony would I embrace,
  my love to God make warmer.

* The love of Christ would I feel,
  my own love waken.

Great God of wisdom,
Great God of mercy,
give me of Your fullness
and of Your guidance
at the turning
of each pass.

Great God of shielding,
Great God of surrounding,
give me of Your holiness
and of Your peace
in the fastening of my death;
give me Your surrounding,
and Your peace upon my death.

Peace between me and my God.
May I tread the path
to the gates of glory.
Rule this heart of mine
that it be only Yours.
God's path would I travel,
my own path refuse.
May I tread the path
to the gates of glory.

Hild – in the right place

Hild of Whitby (614–80)

A call to obedience

Hild was a great-niece of King Edwin of Northumbria and was baptised by Paulinus at the age of 13. She became a nun 20 years later and was urged by Aidan to live out her vocation in her homeland of Northumbria. After founding a small community at Wearmouth, she succeeded Heiu as Abbess of Hartlepool, a double monastery where men and women celibates lived side by side under her rule. Eventually she founded the great double monastery at Whitby, and there she was sought out for her wise counsel by ordinary folk and rulers alike.

Wrestling with the call of God

This form of prayer may be used:
- on 17 November, Hild's feast day;
- on pilgrimage to Whitby, Monkwearmouth or Hartlepool;
- by women who wish to be taken seriously;
- by anyone, man or woman, who is wrestling with a sense of vocation.

* indicates a change of reader.
With a large group, split into two halves and read alternately.
*All say together the sections in **bold** type.*
*The words in **bold italic** type set between lines should be said by each person in turn (or the leader reads, then all repeat together).*

* Take me often from the tumult of things
  into Thy presence.
  There show me what I am,
  and what Thou hast purposed me to be.
  Then hide me from Thy tears.

---

*O King and Saviour,
what is Thy gift to me?
And do I use it to Thy pleasing?*

---

* Now we must praise the guardian of heaven,
  the might of the Lord
  and His purpose of mind,
  the glorious all Father,
  for He, God eternal, is kind.

* The will of God be done by us,
  the law of God be kept by us,

* our evil will controlled by us,
  our sharp tongue checked by us,

* quick forgiveness offered by us,
  speedy repentance made by us,

* temptation sternly shunned by us,

* blessed death welcomed by us,
  angels' music heard by us,

* God's highest praises sung by us.

* Christ, You are the Truth;
  You are the light.

* You are the Keeper of the treasure
  we seek so blindly.

* My soul's desire is to see the face of
  God and to rest in His house.
  My soul's desire is to study the Scriptures
  and to learn the ways of God.
  My soul's desire is to be freed from
  all fear and sadness, and to share Christ's risen life.
  My soul's desire is to imitate my King,
  and to sing His purposes always.
  My soul's desire is to enter the gates
  of heaven
  and to gaze upon the light
  that shines forever.

  **Dear Lord, You alone know
  what my soul truly desires,
  and You alone
  can satisfy those desires.**

* I have prepared a place for you,
  says the Lord, a place that is for you,
  and only you, to fill.
  Approach My table,
  asking first that you might serve.
  Look even for the lowest tasks.
  Then, the work of service done,
  you may look for your own place at table.
  But do not seek the most important seat
  which may be reserved for someone else.
  In the place of My appointing will be your joy.

---

*Lord, show me the right seat;
find me the fitting task;
give me the willing heart.*

---

* May I be equal to Your hope of me.
If I am weak,
I ask that You send only what I can bear.
If I am strong,
may I shrink from no testing
that shall yield increase of strength
or win security for my spirit.

I trust in Thee, O Lord.
I say, 'Thou art my God.
My times are in Thy hand,
my times are in Thy hand.'

Cuthbert – into a desert place

Cuthbert of Northumbria (635–87)

A call to prayer

Cuthbert was called by God to follow Him on the very night when Aidan died. He entered the monastery at Melrose, where he was welcomed by Boisil. Cuthbert's faithfulness was demonstrated in his years at Melrose, then as guest-master at Ripon. After Boisil departed to the Lord, Cuthbert was made Prior of Melrose, and many were instructed by the authority of his teaching and the example of his life. It was also his custom to travel and preach, particularly in those remote districts and villages which were situated in high and rugged hills, which others shrank from visiting.

Many miracles followed Cuthbert's preaching, and he was given grace to see into people's hearts. As a result, many were converted from a life of foolish custom to the love of the joys of heaven.

After the Synod of Whitby, at which it was ruled that the Northumbrian Church must adopt Roman practices, Abbot Eata transferred Cuthbert from the monastery at Melrose to that on Lindisfarne, where he had to teach the revised rule of monastic life. Gradually he won the love and obedience of the brothers.

After many years in the monastery he finally entered with great joy, and with the goodwill of the abbot and monks, into the remoter solitude that he had so long sought, thirsted after and prayed for. To learn the first steps of solitude he retired to a place in the outer precincts of the monastery. (This is believed to be the tiny tidal island adjoining Lindisfarne which is now known as St Cuthbert's Island.) Not until he had first gained victory over our invisible enemy by solitary prayer and fasting did he seek a more remote place on the island of Inner Farne.

Bede tells us that the island was inhabited by demons; and Cuthbert was the first man brave enough to make his home there. Indeed, the demons fled at the entry of this soldier of Christ, clothed fully in the armour of God.

After nine years he was prevailed upon to leave his solitude to become a bishop. Exchanging places with Eata, he avoided removing to Hexham and for two years was bishop at Lindisfarne. Then he returned to the Inner Farne to resume his life of prayer. On his death one of the monks watching nearby lit two candles, and went up to a piece of high ground, signalling with the candles held one in each hand, to let the Lindisfarne brethren know that Cuthbert's holy soul had gone to the Lord.

For a solitary retreat

This form of prayer may be used:
- on 20 March, Cuthbert's feast day;
- on pilgrimage to Cuthbert's Cave or at Lindisfarne, St Cuthbert's Island, Melrose, Ripon, Durham Cathedral or the Inner Farne;
- on solitary retreat anywhere;
- by those drawn to the solitary life.

On an individual retreat the sections could be used as a focus one day at a time, encouraging the experience of prayer, abandonment, reconciliation, resisting evil, and then prayer of the heart.

1. Prayer

> Hear my voice when I call, O Lord;
> be merciful to me and answer me.
> My heart says of You, 'Seek His face!'
> Your face, Lord, I will seek.
> Do not hide Your face from me,
> do not turn Your servant away in anger;
> You have been my helper.
>
> Do not reject me or forsake me,
> O God my Saviour.
> Though my father and mother forsake me,
> the Lord will receive me.

Teach me Your way, O Lord;
lead me in a straight path.
Amen.

Lord, I have heard Your voice
calling at a distance.
Guide my steps to You, Lord,
guide my steps to You.
Lord, I have heard Your voice
calling at a distance.
Guard my way to You, Lord,
guard my way to You.

Lord, I have heard Your voice
calling at a distance.
Keep my heart for You, Lord,
keep my heart for You.
Lord, I have heard Your voice.
Amen.

2. Abandonment

Softly as the dew-fall of heaven,
may the Holy Spirit come upon me
to aid me and to raise me,
to bind my prayer firmly
at the throne of the King of life.

God's will would I do,
my own will bridle;
God's due would I give,
my own due yield;
God's path would I travel
my own path refuse.

All whom I love,
into Your safe keeping;

all that I am,
into Your tender care;
all that will be,
into Your perfect will.
Amen.

3. Reconciliation

O King of Kings,
O King of the universe,
King who will be, who is,
may You forgive us each and every one.
Accept my prayer, O King of grace.

Anyone who claims to be in the light,
but hates their brother or sister,
is still in the darkness.
Whoever loves their brother or sister
lives in the light;
and there is nothing
to make that person stumble.

Examine your own heart.

Lower my vengeance,
my anger and my hatred,
and banish my wicked thoughts from me;
send down a drop from heaven
of Your holy Spirit
to vanquish this heart of rock of mine.
Amen.

Lord,
let our memory
provide no shelter
for grievance against another.

Lord,
let our heart
provide no harbour
for hatred of another.

Lord,
let our tongue
be no accomplice
in the judgement of a brother.

4. Resisting evil

Under the protection of the King of life,
a protection that will not betray us.
May the Holy Spirit come upon us;
may Christ deliver us, bless us.

Do not put out the Spirit's fire;
do not treat prophecies with contempt.
Test everything.
Hold on to the good.
Resist every kind of evil.

Jesus, great Son of Mary,
I call on Your name,
and on the name of John the Beloved,
and on the names
of all the saints in the wide world,
to shield me in the battle to come.
Amen.

Jesus, only Son of the Father, and Lamb,
who shed Your heart's true
blood,
dearly to buy us,
protect me, accompany me,
be near me ever.

Jesus, only Son of the Father and High King,
Your name is above every name,
In the name of Jesus
let no evil be welcome in our hearts,
or in this place.

5. Prayer of the heart

My eyes, my eyes
have seen the King.
The vision of His beauty
has pierced me deep within.
To whom else can I go?

My heart, my heart
desires Him.
He's touched something inside of me
that's now reaching out for Him.
And I know that I must go.

My God is my love,
my guard, my healing one;
my bright love
is my merciful Lord;
my sweet love is Christ;
His heart is my delight;
all my love are You,
O King of glory.
Amen.

6. Commitment

> In the true faith may we remain;
> in Jesus may we find hope;
> against exploitation of the poor may we help;
> against our faults may we fight,
> our bad habits abandon;
> the name of our neighbour may we defend;
> in the work of mercy may we advance;
> those in misery may we help;
> every danger of sin may we avoid;
> in holy charity may we grow strong;
> in the well of grace in confession may we wash;
> may we deserve the help of the saints,
> the friendship of our brother Cuthbert win.
> Amen.
>
> + In the name of the Father,
> and of the Son,
> and of the Holy Spirit.
> Amen.

Brendan – in exploration of a vision

Brendan the Navigator (c.486–575)

A call to risky living

Brendan is one of the best loved of all the Celtic saints. The story of his sea-voyages has held a special fascination for every generation.

In the accounts that have been handed down to us the distinction between actual events and interior vision and experiences is not always clear. The hauntingly vivid images of the tree full of angels (see Part IV) and the vision of Judas (Part VII) are good examples. Yet real voyages were undertaken, and Tim Severin's *Brendan Voyage* makes interesting reading, as time and again Severin and his crew found that they were replicating experiences, described so poetically in the Brendan accounts, that others had dismissed as fantasy. The voyage of adventure is an appropriate analogy of the spiritual journey that each of us is challenged to undertake.

Prayers for a spiritual journey

This liturgy follows some of the incidents of Brendan's life as a series of meditations. They may be used:
- on 16 May, Brendan's feast day;
- on pilgrimage to Clonfert, or any other of Brendan's foundations;
- by an individual as a springboard for prayer;
- as the basis for a retreat;
- by a group, reading a section at a time, with pauses for silent prayer or shared reflection;
- on a coracle-making course.

Part I

Brendan's companions notice that his heart has been stirred. He is caught by a vision. A place beyond his present shores is calling to his yearning spirit. Does he know with a certainty that he must go?

'We will go with you,' they say. 'We will journey where you journey. Your God is our God – for life or death, we follow.'

Brendan climbs the mountain alone and searches his heart to test the truth of what he feels.

And this was Brendan's mountain prayer:

> Shall I abandon the comforts and benefits of my home,
> seeking the island of promise our fathers knew long ago,
> sail on the face of the deep where no riches or fame
> or weapons protect you, and nobody honours your name?
> Shall I take leave of my friends
> and my beautiful native land,
> tears in my eyes
> as my knees mark my final prayer in the sand?
> King of the mysteries, will You set watch over me?
> Christ of the mysteries, can I trust You on the sea?
>
> Christ of the heavens,
> and Christ of the ravenous ocean wave,
> I will hold fast to my course
> through the dangers I must brave.
> King of the mysteries, angels will watch over me,
> Christ of the mysteries, when I trust You on the sea.
>
> Brendan's example speaks to us each:
> Have I the courage to leave the familiar
> and journey into the unknown?
> to journey beyond the way I have prayed,
> the life I have lived, the sensible and the secure?
> to trust God to take me beyond these familiar shores?
>
> Christ of the mysteries, can I trust You on the sea?

Part II

O Lord, I pray that in You,
I'll break ground both fresh and new.
As a student let me stand.
Break the hardness of the land
with Your forgiving Father-hand.

In his generation new territories open to God;
all he has learnt will prepare him for challenges now.
His own disciples have followed as he obeyed God.
Barriers crumbled, and heathen before Jesus bow.
Brendan will go in adventure with God on the seas.
With care he will choose who his closest companions will be.
All that he learns he will teach those who wait for his word.
This risky enterprise will be preparing a way.
Prepare the way! Prepare the way!
Prepare a way for the Lord.

Have I the faith to leave old ways
and break fresh ground with God?

Part III

They sailed over the loud-voiced waves
of the rough-crested sea
and over the billows of the greenish tide,
and over the abysses
of the wonderful,
terrible, relentless ocean.

I beseech the Father through the Son,
I beseech the Son through the Father,
I beseech the Holy Spirit through the Father and the Son,
and through every creature that praises the Lord,
that all vice may be removed from me
and that every saintly virtue may take root in my soul.

It is enough, O mighty sea,
that you should drown me;
but let these others escape in safety.

Brendan prayed,
and as the vehemence of the storm increased,
his friends watched closely for the firmness of his face
against the blackness of the deep,
its sickening currents
that would threaten
oft to drown them.

We were alone on the wide, watery waste –
nought broke its bright monotony of blue,
save where the breeze the flying billows chased,
or where the clouds their purple shadows threw.

We were alone – the pilgrims of the sea –
one boundless azure desert round us spread;
no hope, no trust, no strength except in Thee,
Father, who once the pilgrim people led.

We breathed aloud the Christian's filial prayer,
which makes us brothers even with the Lord:
'Our Father,' cried we, in the midnight air,
'in heaven and earth be Thy great name adored;
may Thy bright Kingdom where the angels are
replace this fleeting world, so dark and dim.'
We ceased from toil and humbly knelt to pray;
the tranquil hour we hailed with vesper hymn.

Do I assume that the storms will be stronger than me?
Christ of the mysteries, can I trust You on the sea?

Part IV

The whole of earth and heaven waits
to see the sons of courage rise.
Imprisoned spirits sing God's praise
and glimpse His glory through the skies.

White flocks of birds and far-off islands
in psalms lament captivity.
Their antiphon to heaven rises
with groans that new life long to see.

The travail of redemption chorused,
Christ's resurrection brings us here,
the Bird of Heaven still awaiting,
the paraclete our ship to steer.

Psalms of the Scripture,
telling landscapes of the heart!
Am I unsatisfied, longing for heaven
to break through my darkness?
longing for glory of heaven to waken in me?

Part V

After years on this adventure,
Brendan sails in sight of home,
not the home he yearned and sought for,
but familiar sights and people,
those who held and hold him dear.
He is questioned – why the journey?
what its profit? what adventures?
will he stay and share his blessing?

Emptiness now metes out fullness,
days despairing bringing joy,
as bodies healed, belief enkindled

and tortured ones deliverance finding,
prove the power of faithful journeying.
Stormy seas make weathered sea-men,
those who proved God in the deep.

Will I share God's might with others?
show the care He's shown to me?

Part VI

After this season of blessing and usefulness, Brendan continues his journey. The journey should never be undertaken begrudgingly, but with love and thankfulness.

I thank You for this, my God,
I am a traveller and stranger
in the world,
like so many of Your people
before me.

There is a sense of adventure,
of openness to possibilities,
abandonment to God
and expectation
of fulfilling His will.

I accept the responsibility,
I'll hear and obey,
and trust it is Your voice I hear,
the call of the Spirit,
the cry of the Bird of Heaven.

It is a Yes to risky living...

The sea takes me;
where I do not know,
but I gladly go.

> And I can only trust
> every word You say,
> and obey.

Brendan and his brothers visit other communities. One of his companions is called to leave them and remain in a place they visit. The voyage continues through corridors of wonder; vast walls of silent ice hem them in on either side. Then, as suddenly, their path through the seas draws them close to an island that burns with volcanic heat. Fearfully they pass it by, continuing in safety.

> Through the unknown, help me, Lord.
> I will trust, and obey!

Part VII

In vision before them, a sorry figure clings to sea-drenched rocks: Judas Iscariot who in all his weakness betrayed God.

> Tortured in hell,
> but tortured much more by regret.

> I need not live with regrets
> if the Lord made me free.
> Am I like Judas, or can I let God
> comfort me?

Part VIII

> All along their journey,
> Brendan and his friends find those who understand;
> food is provided,
> and needful encouragement to trust God.
> Sometimes in silence the Lord will restore
> and strengthen them,
> sometimes return them to one who can guide them

and be their friend.
Slight explanation surrounds
all these happenings in the deep.
Was Brendan's voyage
just vivid imaginings in his sleep?
He and his friends were gone;
then they returned to testify
God had gone with them,
and shown them His faithfulness again.

If I am obedient
can I trust that God Himself will provide?

Part IX

Year after year
they continue in circles over the waves.
Psalms mark the hours
as sunrise and darkness edge their days.
Ever the land they seek
somewhere across the deep
whispers its promise,
but holds itself hidden from their gaze.

Then as they journey exactly
the way they had before,
waiting a glimpse of its beautiful,
still far-distant shore,
darkness intensifies until before their eyes
the land of promise they saw.

I trust in Thee, O Lord.
I say, Thou art my God.
My times are in Thy hand,
my times are in Thy hand.

Blessèd be the Lord,
for He has wondrously shown
His steadfast love to me,
His steadfast love to me.

Can I believe God would hide His goodness from me?
and in His time would open my eyes so I can see?

Part X

So Brendan found the place he was seeking,
the promise fulfilled, and the day without night.
It seemed a place that had no end or boundary
until they reached a river broad, perhaps unpassable.
The land continued rich and fertile on the other side.
Then came a messenger
who spoke to them by name, explaining:

Yes, they have found this place, but only for a time.
People of Ireland and other lands will hear the story
of their adventure, and be baffled or inspired.

He said:

> Return, your mission now is over.
> God who did call you here, now bids you go.
> Return in peace, then, to your native shore
> and tell the mighty secrets that you know.
>
> Seek your own isle – Christ's newly-bought domain
> which nature with an emerald pencil paints.
> Such as it is, long, long shall it remain,
> the school of truth, the college of the saints,
> the student's bower, the hermit's calm retreat,
> the stranger's home, the hospitable hearth,
> the shrine to which shall wander pilgrim feet
> from all the neighbouring nations of the earth.

Now they move on to tell the story
of what has been and is, but also is to come.
God in the now prepares us for the future;
the end is not yet – with Him it's just begun.

Part XI

After all his adventures,
Brendan's wisdom still was not perfected.
There was plenty God had to teach him,
and many others whose example he could learn by.
It is said it was the overheard exchange
between two sea-monsters
which sent Brendan searching for Brigid of Kildare.

Eager to know, he consulted her wisdom
and asked her the reason the monsters revered her,
who spoke of the power of her fervent prayer.
'For myself,' he said, 'since I came to live devoutly,
I cannot go seven steps
without my mind being set on God.'
'That is good,' smiled Brigid,
'but, if I should answer truly,
I'd say that since the hour
I first set my mind on God
never for one moment have I taken it away.'
Brendan laughed.
'It seems the monsters of the deep spoke truly –
the Son of Mary-virgin found a welcome in your heart;
and His power and your thought of Him
are rooted both in love.'

O Jesu Christ, focus my attention on You.
O Son of Mary, be cradled in my heart.
O Most Holy, fix my mind and my heart's gaze
upon You.

Part XII

Brendan returned to his earlier task
of the founding of monasteries,
schools for the gospel, support for the faithful.
Still he would follow the flight of the wild goose,
the call of the Spirit to seek God's adventures;
and so for ten years around Britain he travelled,
engaging in mission and visiting others
to strengthen in service and learn from their wisdom;
and then he returned to his early foundations.
Ardfert was one of these, and Bright Gleam Kilmore.

But after the time of his famous sea-voyage,
offerings were brought him, supporting the houses;
and men and women sought religious life.
Inis- (or Island)-da-dromand was in Shannon river;
there a community flourished and grew.
All in all, three thousand were monastics
under Brendan's rule.
But when he founded Clonfert,
he said, in words of Scripture,
'Here is my rest for ever, here will I dwell.'

Strengthened in faith, may my work be Yours.
Give me Your task, Your blessing,
and establish what my hands can do.

Part XIII

Life in community is not easy.
Sharing life with others
makes holiness hard to find.
Brendan would not be surprised
at difficulty between
five monks he sent
to Inis-da-dromand

to live together there.
Some of them came to him,
telling their trouble.
Strife had developed
between them; and one
had an axe in the head
from behind, and died.

'Return,' Brendan said,
'to your brother, and tell him to wake.
I would speak with him here.'
They returned, and the dead man arose
and went to meet Brendan, the weapon,
with which he was wounded,
still lodged in his head.

Brendan remembered how on his sea-voyage
he often
had brought peace to souls,
who then had speeded God-ward.
So now he asked this brother the question,
'Would you now rather remain in this life
or go to Christ in heaven?'
He chose for home and gladly died.

Am I surprised by the evil
I sometimes encounter
in me or in others?
Help me to live as one glad to die.
Teach me to live with eternity in view.

Part XIV

Once a student came and visited Clonfert,
and played his harp at mid-day in refectory.
The brothers blessed and welcomed all his music;
and he only then expressed regret
that Brendan was not present.
'He would not allow you to play for him,' they said.
'At least he would not hear, since
for seven years or so he's carried balls of wax around
to stick inside his ears whenever music sounds.'
The student followed Brendan into church,
and begged the abbot there to let him play.
The harp was ready – and the balls of wax.
The student remonstrated, and insisted
Brendan listened while he played two or three tunes.

For his insistence he won Brendan's blessing,
but also explanation for the little balls of wax;
for seven years previously, as Brendan prayed there,
the angel Michael came, as if a tiny bird
to bring God's blessing, and make music for his Lord.

The bird placed its beak under the shadow of the wing,
and sang and sang heaven's tune.
All music after that had seemed discordant;
but silence sometimes harmony can hold.

And so,
is heaven's music real to me?
causing my spirit to be stirred
and to put off its weariness?

Part XV

One day as Brendan sailed by coracle across Dingle Bay
a man shouted to him from headland of Valentia Isle.
He turned his craft to shore, and followed
until the stranger brought him
to two men about to die.
Waters of baptism, bread and body, wine and blood.
He almost heard the trumpet of the angel
as he watched them leave this life.
And now his time was coming.
Carefully he gathered chosen friends
to be around him, went to visit, last of all,
his sister Bryg. There in safety at her convent
Brendan leaves detailed instructions of his burial,
for his body must be taken to Clonfert.
Even in death this focus gives direction –
firm foundations will be laid
for generations yet to come.

Nothing must interfere with this,
his body be placed quietly in a wagon,
in charge of only one brother, unnoticed.

But heaven notices.
And as Brendan, unafraid through great adventures,
for a moment now has fear of passing all alone,
leaving his friends behind him,
upon his darksome journey
to the presence of the King,
in far Iona good Columba
calls to Dermot, 'Hurry, now we celebrate:
this is the day of birth for blessèd Brendan
and I see the heavens open, angel choirs
hasten now to greet his soul, and bear him
to the throne of God Himself.
They shout. God stoops, and Brendan cries...

The mist returns. The land of promise fades from view.
Our work awaits, and bread and wine.'

Part XVI

Lord, I will trust You,
help me to journey beyond the familiar
and into the unknown.

Give me the faith to leave old ways
and break fresh ground with You.

Christ of the mysteries, can I trust You
to be stronger than each storm in me?

Do I still yearn for Your glory to lighten on me?

I will show others the care You've given me.

I determine amidst all uncertainty
always to trust.

I choose to live beyond regret,
and let You recreate my life.

I believe You will make a way for me
and provide for me,
if only I trust You
and obey.

I will trust in the darkness and know
that my times are still in Your hand.

I will believe You for my future,
chapter by chapter, until all the story is written.

Focus my mind and my heart upon You,
my attention always on You without alteration.
Strengthen me with Your blessing
and appoint to me the task.

Teach me to live with eternity in view.

Tune my spirit to the music of heaven.

Feed me,
and, somehow,
make my obedience count for You.

Ninian – in relating to the whole of life

Ninian of Whithorn (?–c.432)

A call to bless

Ninian returned to Scotland after travelling and studying in Europe. At Whithorn he and a team of skilled builders built a gleaming white-stone monastery which became famous throughout the land for education, prayer and mission.

Sometimes he liked to visit the shepherds and herdsmen who tended the flocks and cattle belonging to the monastery. Once he had all the animals gathered into one place so that he could pray a blessing on them. Last of all, he came to the cattle, and with his staff drew around them a circle of protection. Everyone ate, listened to Ninian, then went off to their sleep. The cattle remained, and were noticed by thieves. No wall. No hedge. No ditch. No barking dogs! Just lots of cattle waiting to be carried away!

The thieves rushed inside the circle that Ninian had drawn. The bull of the herd rushed at the men and, attacking their leader, pierced his belly with its horns so that the entrails were torn from him. The bull's hoof tore at the earth and dug its imprint into a stone there, so that place became known as 'The Bull's Print'.

Meanwhile Ninian, finishing his prayer, came past that place and saw the man lying dead and the other thieves running hither and thither nearby. He prayed to God to restore the man to life and health, and did not cease his tears and entreaties till it was so. The other thieves had found themselves unable to leave the confines of the circle until, begging Ninian's forgiveness and being scolded by him, he bade them depart. And only then could they cross the circle.

Prayers for the blessing of the land and of life

This may be used:
* on 26 August, Ninian's feast day;
* on pilgrimage to Whithorn;
* at a Harvest Festival;
* on the blessing of any land.

* *indicates a change of reader.*
All say together the sections in **bold** *type.*

> * As gulls
> in hunger's flight
> keep to the boat's track,
> may we follow
> in Ninian's wake.
>
> As we hunger
> and thirst
> for truth,
> may we follow
> in Ninian's wake.
>
> May we sound the depths of love
> for Ninian's
> and for Christ's sake.
>
> * In the strong name of Jesus
> we bless all that is living,
> and recognise in all that lives
> the reflection of the Word
> who said,
>
> **'Let there be life'**,
> and it lives.

* Teach us to care for
 all that is entrusted to us,
 and nurture every sign of Your presence.

* Circle our dear ones in Your love
 and blessing; and protect us all
 from evil and from danger.

* Give us open eyes to see beyond what
 others say is possible.
 Give us the insight
 to recognise and name deceit.

**May the blessing of our love
and our strong joy in blessing
call out new growth
in everyone we know and meet.**

* Give us a generosity
 that pushes back the boundaries,
 for even death
 by You has been defeated.
 With all our powers
 we find our power in You.

**The Light shines on,
and life is lived in You.**

Caedmon – in declaration of a dream

Caedmon of Whitby (?–680)

A call to be good news to the poor

Caedmon loved to listen. Music thrilled him, and other people's stories, songs and ballads carried him along as helplessly as a small boat on a rising tide. But he couldn't play a note on the harp. Nor could he sing a note in tune. If he tried to join in with a song when he was a child everyone else was unable to keep singing. Besides, he could never remember any words. He couldn't even tell a joke and get it right. His head got all confused, and the words tumbled out back to front.

So a night like tonight was torture for him. Heaven and hell, that's what it was. To hear each person share a song, to listen to the music of the harp as it was passed along, strummed by one, touched gently by another – nothing could be sweeter. But the nearer it came to Caedmon's turn, the more a sickness rose from his stomach and his bowels stirred uneasily. At the last possible moment he ran out of the hall.

Once outside, he went straight to the cattle shed to check on his beasts, then threw himself down on his bed and passed into a fitful sleep.

In his dreams a man stood before him. 'Sing for me, Caedmon,' he said. 'Sing for me.'

'I can't sing,' Caedmon protested. 'Why do you think I'm out here in the cattle shed, instead of inside at the feast?'

'Sing anyway. Sing for me.'

'I don't know what to sing.'

'Sing about the beginning of the world, and sing about creation.'

So Caedmon sang a song of praise to the Guardian of heaven, the Father of glory. And in his dream he was able to sing a song so beautiful that it could make you cry.

When he awoke, the song was still with him, and he sang it for God and for himself. He sang it for the steward of all the farmlands of the abbey. He sang it for Abbess Hild herself when the steward told her what had happened. He sang it for all the scholars and holy men and women of the abbey whom the Lady Hild had called for. He sang it for the people of Whitby and everyone in the countryside round about.

Now someone else looked after the cattle, while whoever could read aloud translated the Scriptures for Caedmon. Each night he sang aloud the things he had heard until a new song was prepared, explaining the Bible to his people in their own language. And for the rest of his life his mouth spoke out the truths that filled his heart.

Prayers about becoming a voice for those who have no voice

This form of prayer may be used:
* on 11 February, Caedmon's feast day;
* on pilgrimage to Whitby;
* by any storyteller, singer or songwriter;
* by those concerned to be a voice for those who have no voice;
* by those committed to solidarity with the poor and disadvantaged.

* indicates a change of reader.
With a large group, split into two halves and read alternately.
*All say together the sections in **bold** type.*
*The words in **bold italic** type set between lines should be said by each in turn (or the leader reads, then all repeat together).*

* I cannot speak,
unless You loose my tongue;
I only stammer,
and I speak uncertainly;
but if You touch my mouth,
my Lord,
then I will sing the story
of Your wonders!

FOLLOW THE EXAMPLE | CAEDMON

* Teach me to hear that story,
  through each person,
  to cradle a sense of wonder
  in their life,
  to honour the hard-earned wisdom
  of their sufferings,
  to waken their joy
  that the King of all kings
  stoops down
  to wash their feet,
  and looking up
  into their face
  says,
  'I know – I understand.'

* This world has become
  a world of broken dreams
  where dreamers are hard to find
  and friends are few.

* Lord, be the gatherer of our dreams.
  You set the countless stars in place,
  and found room for each of them to shine.
  You listen for us in Your heaven-bright hall.
  Open our mouths to tell our tales of wonder.

* Teach us again the greatest story ever:
  the One who made the worlds
  became a little, helpless child,
  then grew to be a carpenter
  with deep, far-seeing eyes.

* In time, the Carpenter began to travel,
  in every village challenging the people
  to leave behind their selfish ways,
  be washed in living water,
  and let God be their King.

* The ordinary people crowded round Him,
  frightened to miss
  a word that He was speaking,
  bringing their friends, their children,
  all the sick and tired,
  so everyone could meet Him,
  everyone be touched and given life.

* Some religious people were embarrassed
  – they did not like the company He kept,
  and never knew just what He would do next.

* He said:
  'How dare you wrap God up
  in good behaviour,
  and tell the poor that they
  should be like you?
  How can you live at ease
  with riches and success,
  while those I love go hungry
  and are oppressed?
  It really is for such a time as this
  that I was given breath.'

* His words were dangerous,
  not safe or tidy.

* In secret His opponents said:
  'It surely would be better that
  one person die.'
  'I think that would be better,
  if he could.'
  Expediency would be the very death of Him.
  He died because *they* thought it might be good.

* You died that we might be forgiven,
  Lord; but that was not the end.
  You plundered death,

and made its jail-house shudder
– strode into life
to meet Your startled friends.

* I have a dream
that all the world will meet You,
and know You, Jesus,
in Your living power,
that someday soon
all people everywhere will hear Your story,
and hear it in a way they understand.

---

*I cannot speak,
unless You loose my tongue;
I only stammer,
and I speak uncertainly;
but if You touch my mouth,
my Lord,
then I will sing the story
of Your wonders!*

---

* So many who have heard
forget to tell the story.

    **Here am I, my Jesus:
    teach me.**

A litany of saints

The house that John built

This may be used:
- as pilgrimage prayers;
- on appropriate saints' days;
- in a Communion service.

indicates a change of reader (if desired).
*All say together the sections in **bold** type.*

* John, beloved disciple of the Lord:
  pray with us.

* Polycarp, faithful and resolute,
  unafraid in the heart of the fire:
  pray with us.

* Irenaeus of Lyon,
  careful teacher,
  tearing off the coat of lies;
  compassionate one,
  revealing the glory of God:
  pray with us.

* Fathers and mothers of the Desert,
  people of prayer and bringers of wisdom:
  pray with us.

* Martin, saint of Tours,
  builder of communities of hermits,
  living simply, loving God;
  Martin, soldier of Christ:
  pray with us.

FOLLOW THE EXAMPLE | A LITANY OF SAINTS

* Ninian of Whithorn,
  apostle and example:
  pray with us.

* Patrick of Britain,
  missionary to the land of Ireland:
  pray with us.

* Brigid, compulsive giver,
  lover of the poor, Brigid of Kildare:
  pray with us.

* Columba of Iona, exiled from Ireland,
  abbot and scribe, lover of Christ;
  Columba now the gentle;
  Columba of the Church:
  pray with us.

* Oswald, king and saint,
  willing interpreter of the Gospel truth;
  Oswald, man of prayer:
  pray with us.

* Aidan, emissary from Iona;
  gentle and straightforward;
  torchbearer; liberator of slaves;
  Aidan of Lindisfarne:
  pray with us.

* Hild of Whitby,
  firm leader of both men and women;
  renowned for your counsel and insight,
  releasing others in their giftedness;
  Hild, woman of courage and faith:
  pray with us.

* Cuthbert of Northumbria,
  hermit and joyous worshipper;

man of prayer and spiritual warfare;
patient minister of reconciliation;
Cuthbert of the people:
pray with us.

* Aldwin, Reinfrid and Elfwy,
keeper of memories, bridge-builder, shepherd,
restorers of ruined places,
guardians of a vision:
pray with us.

(optional:)

* Lord, hasten the day
When those who seek You
in every nation
and from every generation
will come from the east and the west,
from north and south,
and sit at table
in Your Kingdom.

**And, Lord, Let your glory
be seen in our day
and in this land.**

the Aidan series of Daily Readings

About the daily readings

Two complete years of readings are provided in this book: the Aidan series and the Finan series. Two further years of readings, the Colman series and the Eata series, are published separately in *Celtic Daily Prayer Book Two: Farther Up and Farther In*. The names given to all these series are those of the abbots and bishops of Lindisfarne and have no other significance beyond providing a useful label for reference – though they are, of course, familiar and well-loved names to the Northumbria Community.

The readings could be used consecutively over two years. Alternatively, one series could be used with Morning Prayer and the other with Evening Prayer.

Each daily reading provides three Scriptures: one from the Psalms; one from the Old Testament; and one from the New. If the Daily Office is being used by a group, a different reader could be used for each. A Bible may be left open until the next day, placed where it can easily be referred to, at the reading which seems most relevant to the needs of the moment.

THE AIDAN SERIES OF DAILY READINGS

January
Consider my meditation

1 January New Year *(see p.115)*   Telemachus *(see p.261)*

Psalm 46:6-11   Ezekiel 10:6-18   Mark 1:35-37

This month the scripture passages have been chosen to complement the meditations we use each month on that particular date. Instead of study notes there are songs or quotations to stimulate us to action or to quiet.

> The world gives itself
> up to incessant activity
> merely because
> it knows of nothing
> better.
> The inspired man
> works among
> its whirring wheels
> also, but he knows
> whither the wheels
> are going.
> For he has found
> the centre
> where all is
> stillness...
>
> *Paul Brunton*

2 January

Psalm 1:1-3   1 Samuel 1:12-17   Luke 8:40-46

These verses may be sung to any of the tunes used for 'When I survey the wondrous cross', and are brought to us by Wild Goose of Iona.

Inspired by love and anger

When trouble strikes and fear takes root
and dreams are dry and sense unsound,
when hope becomes a barren waste,
then doubts like mountains soar around.

Our wandering minds believe the worst
and ask, as faith and fervour fade,
'Has God now turned His back on us,
forsaking those He loved and made?'

God says, 'See how a woman cares,
can she forget the child she bore?
Even if she did, I shan't forget.
Though feeling lost, I love you more.'

3 January

Psalm 27:7-10   Isaiah 49:13-16   Romans 8:15

God says, 'See how a woman cares,
can she forget the child she bore?
Even if she did, I shan't forget.
Though feeling lost, I love you more.
'My dearest daughter, fondest son,
My weary folk in every land,
your souls are cradled in My heart,
your names are written on My hand.'
Then praise the Lord through faith and fear,

in holy and in hopeless place,
for height and depth and heaven and hell
can't keep us far from His embrace.

4 January Juniper *(see p.245)*

Psalm 119:105-109   Jeremiah 31:6-9   Luke 23:39-46

> A healthy child is
> somehow very much
> like God. A hurting
> child, His son.
>
> *Calvin Miller*, The Singer

In *The Singer* Earthmaker and His Troubadour sit down on the outer rim of space and look at our planet. Earthmaker holds it to His ear...

'They're crying, Troubadour,' He said. 'They cry so hopelessly.' He gave the tiny planet to His Son who also held it by His ear. 'Year after weary year they all keep crying. They seem born to weep then die.'

Then with His nail He scraped the atmosphere and both of them beheld the planet bleed. Earthmaker set earth spinning on its way and said, 'Give Me your vast infinity, My Son; I'll wrap it in a bit of clay.'

And so the Son became a one-of-us.

5 January

Psalm 89:19-29   1 Samuel 16:17-22   Philippians 4:12-13

A covenant sealed with blood commits both parties to each other for ever. All they have belongs to the other, and they will lay down their life on the other's behalf.

> Christ has many services to be done;
> some are easy, others are difficult;
> some bring honour, others bring reproach;
> some are suitable to our natural
> inclinations and temporal interest,
> others are contrary to both.
> In some we may please Christ and please ourselves,
> in others we cannot please Christ except by denying
>   ourselves.
> Yet the power to do all these things is assuredly given us
>   in Christ, who strengthens us.
>
> Therefore let us make
>   the Covenant of God our own.
> Let us engage our heart to the Lord,
> and resolve in His strength never to go back!

The Covenant Service

6 January Three Kings' Day *(see p.263)*

Psalm 116:12-14   Genesis 49:10-11   Luke 7:42-48

The Love of Jesus took Him to Calvary where He forgave, and offered hope even as He suffered.

We need to receive His mercy, but also to show it to others. Jesus is Shiloh, the Awaited One to whom all will gather. His wounds are for our cleansing, His blood the cup of our salvation.

Hear the challenge of this Chuck Girard song:

Don't shoot the wounded,
they need us more than ever.
Sometimes we just condemn them,
and don't take time to hear their story.
Don't shoot the wounded,
some day you might be one.

7 January

Psalm 18:25-29 Isaiah 35:3-8 Philippians 3:12—4:1

Why do we call impossible what God calls possible?
Why do we call unforgivable what God has forgiven?
Why do we compromise with what God calls sin?
How we need to know God's heart, and reach out in His love and wisdom to others.

It's easy to love the people who are standing hard and fast,
pressing on to meet that higher calling.
But the ones who might be struggling, we tend to judge too harshly
and refuse to try and catch them when they're falling.
We put people into boxes and we draw our hard conclusions
and when they do the things we know they should not do
we sometimes write them off as hopeless and we throw them to the dogs.
Our compassion and forgiveness sometimes seem in short supply...

Chuck Girard

8 January

Psalm 78:70-72   Exodus 2:11-15   Matthew 18:32-35

We can love them and forgive them
    when their sin does not exceed our own
for we too have been down bumpy roads before.
But when they commit offences outside the
    boundaries we have set,
we judge them in a word and we turn them out,
    and we close the door.
Myself, I've been forgiven for so many awful things,
I've been cleansed and washed and bathed so many times
that when I see a brother who has fallen from the way,
I just can't find the licence to convict him of his crimes.

Chuck Girard

9 January

Psalm 147:1-3   Proverbs 23:12-17   Matthew 18:12-22

Don't shoot the wounded!

That doesn't mean we turn our heads when we
    see a brother sin
and pretend that what he's doing is all right.
We must help him see his error, we must lead
    him to repent,
cry with those who cry, but bring their deeds into the light.
For it's the sick that need the doctor, and it's the
    lame that need the crutch;
it's the prodigal who needs the loving hand.
For a man who's in despair there should be
    kindness from his friends,
lest he should forsake the fear of almighty God
and turn away from God and man.

Chuck Girard

10 January

Psalm 106:7-12   Joshua 4:1-24   Mark 9:17-24

Stumbling blocks and stepping stones

(a song from Wild Goose of Iona)

Unsure, when what was bright turns dark
and life, it seems, has lost its way,
we question what we once believed
and fear that doubt has come to stay.
We sense the worm that gnaws within
has withered willpower, weakened bones,
and wonder whether all that's left
is stumbling blocks or stepping stones.

11 January

Psalm 31:9-1   Jeremiah 32:6-15   Luke 22:54-65

In the midst of negative circumstances we have to try hard to remember God's promises, remain true to Him, make sure there is something left to come back to and hold on to.

In Jeremiah's case he bought a field when it seemed a foolish step.

Where minds and bodies reel with pain
which nervous smiles can never mask,
and hope is forced to face despair
and all the things it dared not ask;
aware of weakness, guilt or shame,
the will gives out, the spirit groans,
and clutching at each straw we find
more stumbling blocks
   than stepping stones.

12 January

Psalm 127:1-2   Isaiah 30:15-18   James 5:11

To have confidence in God is a hard lesson to learn. When all goes well our gratitude quickly evaporates and becomes carelessness. When life is troubled our reflex is to try and right things ourselves, employing only human reckoning of resources available. Our greatest strength is not to struggle, but to trust there will be a way forward.

> Where family life has lost its bliss
> and silences endorse mistrust,
> or anger boils and tempers flare
> as love comes under threat from lust;
> where people cannot take the strain
> of worklessness and endless loans
> what pattern will the future weave –
> just stumbling blocks?
>   no stepping stones?

13 January   Hilary of Poitiers *(see p.240)*   Kentigern *(see p.245)*

Psalm 126:4-6   Isaiah 43:18-21   Jude 20-23

As Caleb's daughter was an asker, so we need to take courage and seek for springs not only for our own survival, but that others may know the life of God. The life ahead of us is new, and it is even the ancient springs which will bring waters that are always fresh and new.

We must ask boldly of our Father.

> Where hearts that once held love are bare
> and faith, in shreds, compounds the mess;
> where hymns and prayers no longer speak
> and former friends no longer bless;
> and when the church where some belonged
> no more their loyalty enthrones,

the plea is made, 'If You are there,
turn stumbling blocks
    to stepping stones.'

14 January

Psalm 109:25-29   Numbers 23:5-12   1 Corinthians 1:20-31

God loves paradoxes and contradictions. When we are weak, we are strong. Every curse becomes a blessing, and stumbling blocks can be turned to stepping stones; the valley of Achor where all was destroyed can be a doorway of hope.

> Ah God, You with the Maker's eye,
> can tell if all that's feared is real,
> and see if life is more than what
> we suffer, dread, despise and feel.
> If some by faith no longer stand
> nor hear the truth Your voice intones,
> stretch out Your hand to help Your folk
> from stumbling blocks to stepping stones.

15 January   Ita *(see p.54)*   Paul of Thebes *(see p.254)*

Psalm 142:5-7   Numbers 24:2-9   Matthew 21:18-22

The following song from the third chapter of the book of Malachi was given in 1978 as a prayer for the Islanders. Lindisfarne, long dubbed the 'Holy Island', still needs a witness to each succeeding generation, and God will have a presence there in His people.

The Island's inhabitants walk often unknowingly in the field of an ongoing spiritual conflict.

> When the work is done,
> when comes the day of the Refiner's fire,
> when they are purged like gold and silver

to offer Me an offering in righteousness
then shall the offering of My people in My holy place
be pleasant unto Me, the Lord your God,
as in the days of old,
>   and as in former years:
a place of peace,
>   a dwelling-place for man and God.

16 January

Psalm 107:35-37   Malachi 3:2-12   Luke 10:17-21

Why should the former glory of these holy places be greater than what can happen in these latter days? Look at Haggai chapter 2, and you find it need not be so. There again God reminds us the first tenth of our income, at least, must be dedicated to Him – or we are robbing Him.

Can we afford to do this?

Can we afford not to?

When the time is come,
when they return to Me in everything they do
and I am first,
>   then will heaven's windows open wide
and pour a blessing bigger than you can contain.
Then shall the offering
>   of My people in My holy place
be pleasant unto Me, the Lord your God,
as in the days of old,
>   and as in former years:
a place of peace,
>   a dwelling-place for man and God.

17 January Antony of Egypt *(see p.223)*

Psalm 17:5-7   Isaiah 40:3-5   Mark 1:15-18

It is by God's grace that our feet don't lose contact with the path we set out to follow. We say, 'Here I am, Lord,' when He calls. He calls continually to the willing and the unwilling. It is not so much our ability He has need of, but our availability.

> Jesus stands on the shore and whistles
> for His people to respond, wave upon
> wave. He calls them to bind the
> broken-hearted, and build up waste places.

Bryan Pollard

> I see a Man walking by the seashore,
> whistling gently to the waves of those
> who will come to restore the ruined
> places, who're crying,
>
> 'PREPARE THE WAY!
> Prepare the way, Prepare the way.
> Prepare the way for the Lord!'

18 January

Psalm 84:3-7   Malachi 3:16-18   Romans 8:14-17

Each of us has the potential to become a son of God, an heir to all that is His, for each of us, male or female, in every place, has been made in His image, with chance to choose Him.

Only after we have yielded to Him can we reflect the face of Christ.

What kind of stones will Holy Island offer on His return?

When I the Lord shall come
to gather jewels for My diadem
shall I find stones, resistant, hard and rough?
or gems prepared and radiant with My glory?
And shall the offering of My people in My holy place
be pleasant unto Me, the Lord your God?
as in the days of old,
    and as in former years:
a place of peace,
    a dwelling-place for man and God?

So hearken unto Me
    and follow Me with all your heart.

19 January

Psalm 107:28-31   2 Kings 4:8-10   Mark 6:30-31

Time for everything but prayer

Why is there so little anxiety to get time to pray? Why is there so little forethought in the laying out of time and employments so as to secure a large portion of each day for prayer?

Why is there so much speaking, yet so little prayer? Why is there so much running to and fro, yet so little prayer? Why so much bustle and business, yet so little prayer? Why so many meetings with our fellow-men, yet so few meetings with God?

Why so little being alone, so little thirsting of the soul for the calm, sweet hours of unbroken solitude, when God and His child hold fellowship together as if they could never part?

It is the want of these solitary hours that not only injures our own growth in grace but makes us such unprofitable members of the church of Christ, and that renders our lives useless.

Horatius Bonar

20 January

Psalm 87:5-7   2 Kings 4:1-6   Ephesians 5:15-21

In one single quiet hour of prayer the soul will often make more progress than in days of company with others. It is in the desert that the eye gets the clearest, simplest view of eternal certainties; it is in His presence alone, it is then that the soul gathers in wondrous refreshment and power and energy.

And so it is also in this way that we become truly useful to others. It is when coming out fresh from communion with God that we go forth to do His work successfully.
In nearness to God we get our vessels so filled with blessing, that, when we come forth, we can not contain it to ourselves but must, as by a blessèd necessity, pour it out whithersoever we go.

Horatius Bonar

21 January

Psalm 55:16-17   Daniel 6:10-14   1 Thessalonians 5:16-18

O God our Father, who hast set forth the way of life for us in Thy beloved Son: We confess with shame our slowness to learn of Him, our reluctance to follow Him. Thou hast spoken and called, and we have not given heed; Thy beauty has shone forth and we have been blind; Thou hast stretched out Thy hands to us through our fellows and we have passed by. We have taken great benefits with little thanks; we have been unworthy of Thy changeless love.

Have mercy upon us and forgive us, O Lord.

From the Covenant Service

22 January

Psalm 3:3-5   2 Samuel 22:20-21   1 Corinthians 13:12-13

It was only Nicodemus who was told to be born again, the adulteress who was told 'Neither do I condemn you, go, and sin no more', but we all identify with them and learn from the conversation Jesus had with them.

This song was a prophecy for one man, but we can all learn from it:

Reservoir

You place my feet upon a larger place, Lord,
You give my hands a greater task for You.
You set my eyes upon the far horizon
and in my heart I know Your word is true.

You place a reservoir within my heart, Lord,
   that all my tears
      would come from a different place:
that all my ways would minister Your grace
   to those who long
   to see Your face.

23 January

Psalm 121:1-4   Isaiah 42:1-4   John 12:20-21

Even as the tide comes in and goes out again, so we are drawn to retreat into silence and aloneness with God, then released to be involved in the going and activity again.

Most of the world would like to see something of Jesus, but how we fail to show Him through our life! How seldom when we speak is it what He has given us to be said!

So in my life may I know Your approval;
so may I move out with Your commendation,

that my words may be filled with Your grace and truth
from the reservoir within my heart.

You place a reservoir within my heart, Lord,
    that all my tears
        would come from a different place:
that all my ways would minister Your grace
    to those who long
        to see Your face.

24 January

Psalm 18:30-36   Habakkuk 3:17-19   Luke 19:37-41

I'm not defeated. I'm an overcomer. I want to live to give glory to You, God. All creation resounds with Your praise and longs to be finally reconciled. I am part of Your purposes.

You cause my heart to soar like an eagle,
You teach my feet to conquer like a deer.
All I survey shall echo with Your praise,
and Lord,
    I know that *I* must know You here.

You place a reservoir within my heart, Lord,
    that all my tears
        would come from a different place:
that all my ways would minister Your grace
    to those who long
        to see Your face.

Teach us, Lord, to cry with Your tears, as well as our own.

25 January

Psalm 119:111-112   Ezekiel 3:1-3   Luke 9:24-38

God's life in our life is always a miracle.

> Something which is known to have been from the beginning,
> this we have heard, and seen with our own eyes, something we
> have touched and have carefully watched, the Word who is life,
> this we share with those whose lives touch our own.
>   Suddenly the miracle seems possible – to them, and once
> again to us also.
>
> I knew a blind man
> whom a surgeon
> helped to see.
> The doctor never had a
> lover such as he.
> It is in such a way
> that singers love
> composers.
>
> *Calvin Miller*

26 January

Psalm 115:2-8   Numbers 6:24-26   John 6:66-68

If we have truly looked at God then we are different – there is a difference for always. An old man and his wife had been married for many years. Content in each other's company they rarely needed to speak.

Another man, speaking of his way of praying, has said, 'I looks at Him, and He looks at me, and we're happy together.'

> My eyes, my eyes have seen the King.
> My eyes, my eyes have seen the King.

The vision of His beauty
  has pierced me deep within;
to whom else can I go?

John Skinner, The Lord's Song

27 January

Psalm 45:10-11   Song of Songs 2:8-14   Revelation 19:6-8

His Bride is a corporate Bride made up of all those who love Him and put Him before everything else. He loves us and longs to spend time alone with us. He loves to hear us speak to Him, and we love Him because He loves us first, and drew us to Him.

My heart, my heart desires Him,
my heart, my heart desires Him.
He's touched something inside of me
that's now reaching out for Him,
and I know that I must go.

John Skinner, The Lord's Song

28 January   Canaire *(see p.228)*

Psalm 36:5-9   Nehemiah 13:19-22   Luke 12:32-34

The following passage is from *The Last Battle*, the seventh and final Narnia story by C.S. Lewis:

Farewell to shadowlands

'Farther up and farther in!' roared the Unicorn, and no one held back. They charged straight at the foot of the hill and then found themselves running up it almost as water from a broken wave runs up a rock out at the point of some bay. Though the slope was nearly as steep as the roof of a house and the grass was smooth as a bowling green, no one slipped.

Only when they had reached the very top did they slow up; that was because they found themselves facing great golden gates. And for a moment none of them was bold enough to try if the gates would open. They all felt just as they had felt about the fruit – 'Dare we? Is it right? Can it be meant for *us*?'

But while they were standing thus a great horn, wonderfully loud and sweet, blew from somewhere inside that walled garden and the gates swung open.

29 January

Psalm 141:1-2   1 Kings 17:6-16   Matthew 10:38-42

Francis of Assisi said that he was in love with a lady whose name was Poverty. In the meditation for today Brother Juniper talks about his own more stormy relationship with Lady Poverty.

He has learnt to trust God and catches glimpses, in this trust, of a deeper reality, of heaven itself.

Farther up and farther in

Perhaps you will get some idea of it if you think like this. You may have been in a room in which there was a window that looked out on a lovely bay of the sea or a green valley that wound away among mountains. And in the wall of that room opposite to the window there may have been a looking-glass. And the sea in the mirror, or the valley in the mirror, were in one sense just the same as the real one: yet at the same time they were somehow different – deeper, more wonderful, more like places in a story: in a story you have never heard but very much want to know.

C.S. Lewis

30 January

Psalm 46   1 Kings 18:4   John 6:31-34

We cry out to God to be our refuge and strength, our hiding place. We find others who have also taken refuge in Him, and are beginning to build from what is broken.

Gerry Tuohy's song has captured the flavour of what God had built in Ireland, but has spoken also to us concerning Northumberland:

> God called forth a people
> and we responded to His call,
> 'Rebuild this ancient ruin,
> restore My city walls.'
>
> He has led us day by day,
> as we listened to His voice,
> and we were fed on finest wheat,
> and manna from the skies.
>
> When we started, we were strangers,
> we hardly knew each other's names.
> Now we are brothers and sisters,
> and we will never be the same.

31 January

Psalm 118:22-26   Isaiah 28:16   John 2:22–3:2

> God called forth a people
> and we responded to His call,
> 'Rebuild this ancient ruin,
> restore My city walls.'

As we built, brick by brick,
we discovered the cornerstone,
and as we let Him mould and fashion us,
He built us up in love.

Now we have seen,
and we have heard,
that the Lord our God is great
for a wilderness has been transformed
into His holy place.

February
Devoted to Him

1 February Brigid's Day *(see p.267)*

Psalm 80:17   Judges 6:14-24   Revelation 3:20

This month the readings are from the writings of different Christians, both contemporary and from the past, all of them devoted to Him.

> Pray remember what I have recommended to you, which is, to think often of God, by day, by night, in your business, and even in your diversions. He is always near you and with you; leave Him not alone. You would think it rude to leave a friend alone who came to visit you: why then must God be neglected? Do not then forget Him, but think of Him often, adore Him continually, live and die with Him; this is the glorious employment of a Christian; if we do not know it we must learn it.

Brother Lawrence,
The Practice of the Presence of God

2 February

Psalm 139:7-8   Ruth 1:16   1 John 4:16-18

> Lord, You seized me and I could not resist You.
> I ran for a long time, but You followed me.
> I took by-paths, but You knew them.
> You overtook me. I struggled. You won.
> Here I am, Lord, out of breath, no fight left in me,
>   and I've said 'yes' almost unwillingly.

When I stood there trembling
   like one defeated before his captor,
   Your look of love fell on me.
The die is cast, Lord, I can no longer forget You.
In a moment You seized me,
   in a moment You conquered me.
My doubts were swept away, my fears dispelled.
Nothing matters to me,
   neither my comfort, nor even my life.
I desire only You, I want nothing but You.

Michel Quoist, Prayers of Life

3 February

Psalm 149:1-4   Song of Songs 1:4   Matthew 11:16-17

Christ 'in giving Himself to us has become our fellow-pilgrim on life's journey.' But He said 'I piped to you and you would not dance.' In the face of this Christ I felt myself 'so heavy footed and drowsy.' I asked Him, therefore, to wake me, 'rouse me, let me dance hour by hour to Your piping in all I do all day long,' concluding, 'I have trusted in Him and I am helped, therefore my heart danceth for joy and in my song I will praise Him. So make us Thine that we may be a chalice of joy.'

Marjorie Milne, as quoted in Glastonbury Journey,
a biography by Brian Frost

4 February

Psalm 119:105   Isaiah 11:1-2   John 5:30

I am forever speculating about how much Jesus knew. As God, of course, He would know everything. Did that knowledge affect His human knowledge? I tend to side with those who say that His human knowledge was incomplete. I find comfort in thinking of Him also in the dark, following blindly the Father's will. He was asked to fail, to be conquered, to be hounded out of the city and to die as a criminal. Could He see through all that to the victory to follow? It is difficult to tell. I find it good to wrestle with such questions, and in prayer to ask the Lord to enlighten me. What happened to the Master will surely happen to the disciple; we, too, will suffer hardship, and perhaps for no apparent reason.

Ian Petit, The God who Speaks

5 February

Psalm 119:107   Isaiah 53:11   Mark 1:16-17

When Jesus looked o'er Galilee,
so blue and calm and fair,
upon her bosom, could He see
a Cross reflected there?

When sunrise dyed the lovely deeps,
and sparkled in His hair,
Oh, did the light rays seem to say:
A crown of thorns He'll wear?

When in the hush of eventide,
cool waters touched His feet
was it a hymn of Calvary's road
He heard the waves repeat?

But when the winds triumphantly
swept from the open plain,
the Master surely heard the song:
The Lord shall live again!

Catherine Baird

6 February

Psalm 119:96   Judges 6:11-16   John 1:43-50

We are all asked to do more than we can do. Every hero and heroine of the Bible does more than he would have thought it possible to do, from Gideon to Esther to Mary. Jacob, one of my favourite characters, certainly wasn't qualified. He was a liar and a cheat; and yet he was given the extraordinary vision of angels and archangels ascending and descending a ladder which reached from earth to heaven.

In the first chapter of John's Gospel, Nathanael is given a glimpse of what Jacob saw, or a promise of it, and he wasn't qualified either. He was narrow-minded and unimaginative, and when Philip told him that Jesus of Nazareth was the one they sought, his rather cynical response was, 'Can anything good come out of Nazareth?' And yet it was to Nathanael that Jesus promised the vision of angels and archangels ascending and descending upon the son of man.

Madeleine L'Engle, Walking on Water

7 February

Psalm 119:112   Joshua 24:15   Matthew 10:29

Every hour a kingdom

Every hour a *kingdom* is coming in your heart, in your home, in the world near you, be it a kingdom of darkness or a kingdom of light.

The Bible does not say

The Bible does not say that everybody who is not a Christian is a notorious sinner; but it says that the one who lives outside that is wasting their life. They may not be doing wrong, but their life is lost.

No small sin

There is no such thing in the world as a great sin, but there is no such thing as a small sin. The smallest sin is a fall, and a fall is a fall from God, and to fall from God is to fall the greatest height in the universe.

Henry Drummond,
A Mirror Set at the Right Angle

8 February Elfleda *(see p.235)*

Psalm 91:1   Jeremiah 33:3   Romans 8:38-39

So, precisely because I am a sinner, I have fled to Thee; since there is nowhere I can flee from Thee save to Thee, Thou dost stretch out Thine arms to receive me and bend down Thy head to kiss me; Thou dost bleed that I may have drink, and open Thy side in Thy desire to draw me within.

What then shall separate me from the love of Christ, and prevent me from casting myself into His embrace, when He stretches out His hands to me all day long? Shame at the sinfulness and impurity which defile me? No, indeed; a shame that would separate me from my Lord would be fatal. I will rather run to Him as He beckons me to come, and by touching Him I shall be cleansed from all impurity of body and soul. Should I fail to do so I would hear the words of Wisdom reproaching me: 'I stretched out My hand and thou didst not look; thou hast despised all My advice, and I shall laugh at thy destruction.' No, Lord, not so! I will gladly run to Thee albeit a sinner, albeit unclean, for with Thee there is merciful forgiveness; Thou wilt wash me in Thy blood, and I shall be made whiter than snow. I will enter into Thee and not stay without, for outside Thee there is no salvation.

The Monk of Farne

9 February Teilo *(see p.261)*

Psalm 91:2   Daniel 4:29-37   John 8:36

Yes

Yes, I deal with guilt every day.
  What counts is my heart's desire,
  only that my heart's motives be pure,
  and that I strive for that ... day after day.

The devil must know guilt is my most vulnerable
  place. Some days he is most successful in
  destroying my creative energy and vitality
  – just in that very way.

Yes to the fact that Jesus understands it all.
  He has never willed me to carry guilt.

Yes to realising that carrying guilt is a greater
  sin than the failures that caused it...
  that it negates all Christ paid to set us free.

Yes to surrendering this area of my life to God,
  and not picking it up...
  over and over again.

Ann Kiemel

10 February

Psalm 91:9-10   Nehemiah 9:1-3   John 8:2-11

How easy it is to denounce structural injustice,
institutionalised violence, social sin. And it is true, this sin
is everywhere, but where are the roots of this social sin?
In the heart of every human being. Present-day society is
a sort of anonymous world in which no one is willing to
admit guilt and everyone is responsible.

Because of this, salvation begins with the human person, with human dignity, with saving every person from sin. Individually there are among us here no two sinners alike. Each one has committed his or her own shameful deeds, and yet we want to cast our guilt on the other and hide our own sin. I must take off my mask; I, too, am one of them, and I need to beg God's pardon because I have offended God and society. This is the call of Christ.

How beautiful the expression of that woman upon finding herself pardoned and understood: 'No one, Sir. No one has condemned me.' Then neither do I, I who could give that truly condemning word, neither do I condemn; but be careful, brothers and sisters, since God has forgiven us so many times, let us take advantage of that friendship with the Lord which we have recovered and let us live it with gratitude.

Oscar Romero of El Salvador

11 February Caedmon (see p.321)

Psalm 18:6   Genesis 1:20   Acts 8:14-17

In Your presence there is an absence
silencing my greatest fear.
It is with You that I know the essence
of what is life, now that You're near.

It is in the absence of Your presence
that I rekindle my desire;
and it is when I am without You
that I burn, an inextinguishable fire.

In Your presence there is an absence
of all that preys upon my mind;
for my heart's desire's before me,
and I leave all else behind.

It is in the absence of Your presence
that I have learned to be apart.
It is without You that I am with You;
for You are Joy within my heart.

Janet Rimmer

12 February

Psalm 35:27-28   Song of Songs 5:4   Luke 13:29

I still believe in the power of the priesthood, where sinful men are helped by sinful men. I believe in an authority that stoops to wash a poor man's feet. I believe in a banquet where sinners learn to love, eating in company with their God. I believe in parents who teach their children the beauty that is life. I believe in the words that God has left for man, words that can fashion hope from darkness and turn bitter loneliness into love. And I believe in man, fashioned in mystery by God. I believe in the beauty of his mind, the force of his emotions, the fire and loyalty of his love. I know his weakness, his cowardice, his treachery, his hate. But I believe in him and his thirst for acceptance and love.

Most of all I believe in God and the power of His victory in Christ. I believe in a Resurrection that rescued man from death. I believe in an Easter that opened man to hope. I believe in a joy that no threat of man can take away. I believe in a peace that I know in fleeting moments and seek with boldness born of God. I believe in a life that lingers after this, a life that God has fashioned for His friends.

I believe in understanding, in forgiveness, in mercy, in faith. I believe in man's love for woman, and hers for him, and in the fervour of this exchange I hear the voice of God. I believe in friendship and its power to turn selfishness to love. I believe in eternity and the hope that it affords.

Fr James Kavanagh,
A Modern Priest Looks at his Outdated Church

13 February

Psalm 35:14   Ezekiel 22:29-30   Romans 12:21

How can you hope to make the imperfect things perfect, unless you keep before your eyes the vision of God, who is perfection? The prayer that is only against evil destroys itself. If you look at nothing but sorrow and sin, your heart may be at first full of love and pity, but presently anger – righteous perhaps, but still anger – will enter and begin to crowd out love; and then despair will come and deaden pity, and at last will even smother righteous anger. And then there will be silence for the heart that is filled with despair cannot pray.

It is not enough to know that the world is full of evil, we must know also that God is good.

Christ is a part of all the poverty and misery because He was born into it and didn't try to get away from it. If you put Him in the background, with the sin and sorrow all in front, how He shines and makes courage and hope! Yes! And if you put Him in the front, with the darkness all around Him, how He shines again! Either way, He is the light in the picture.

Florence Converse, The House of Prayer

14 February

Psalm 8:4-5   1 Samuel 3:4-7   Luke 11:1-4

Notice that not once did Jesus make His disciples pray. He just kept praying until at last they could contain their hunger no longer and asked Him to teach them how to pray. The question came from the twelve, indicating that they were now ready to listen and to hear. Jesus must have jumped at this opportunity of holding before them His model of prayer. It is interesting to note that He gave them a formula, neat and tidy. It was almost as if He was getting them into practice so that later on their own prayer life could develop. It is also interesting to note that in this first prayer taught by Jesus there is no sentimentality, piousness or rhetoric. It is simple, direct and filled with nobility and sureness. It contains simple praise and intercession.

Pat Lynch, Awakening the Giant

15 February

Psalm 8:6   Genesis 8:22   Philippians 4:8

After a farmer plants wheat he does not lie awake nights worrying lest radishes come up. He knows that it is the nature, or we might say the virtue, of wheat to grow wheat. It is the virtue of acorns to grow oak trees. And it is the virtue of prayers that are based upon that which is true, honest, just, pure, lovely and of good report, to come to fulfilment. Such a fulfilment is in accord with the inevitable unfoldment of all moral law. We do not have to argue or get excited or perspire over trying to make four plus four equal eight. It is the virtue of such a combination to become eight. It is the law of mathematics, irresistible and inevitable as the tides.

In the same irresistible, tidal way, trust to the inborn virtue residing in these laws of the true, the honest, the just, and the pure in your list of desires, and give them completely to God. Relinquish them into His hands, and go off and leave them. Do not worry about them, do not even pray for them for the next few weeks. Give them as completely as the farmer gives his wheat to the soil, after the soil has been properly ploughed and harrowed. Later on, when the weeds begin to come up, we may have to get into these prayers with a cultivator and re-mellow the soil of our faith a bit, but now, go off and leave them entirely.

Glenn Clark, I Will Lift up Mine Eyes

16 February

Psalm 8:3-9   1 Kings 19:11-12   Matthew 6:28-30

I find it good just to let my gaze wander, without any concern for time and without any attempt to force concentration. Gradually one part of the woods catches my attention, and then one tree, and eventually one branch on the tree. My scattered thoughts come to focus on a single experience, and then dive deeper and deeper into that one reality (the universe in a blade of grass). Oftentimes the result is that my attention is absorbed by some small flower or leaf at my feet which I had not even noticed before – and I am at peace!

Thomas H. Green, Opening to God

17 February Finan *(see p.238)* John Hyde *(see p.241)*

Psalm 63:1, 8   Song of Songs 7:11   Luke 9:10

Why is there so little anxiety to get time to pray? It is the want of these solitary hours that not only injures our own growth in grace but makes us such unprofitable members of the church of Christ, and that renders our lives useless.

It is not in society – even Christian society – that the soul grows most rapidly and vigorously. In one single quiet hour of prayer it will often make more progress than in days of company with others. It is in the desert that dew falls freshest and the air is purest. So with the soul. It is when none but God is nigh; when His presence alone, like the desert air in which there is mingled no noxious breath of man, surrounds and pervades the soul; it is then that the eye gets the clearest, simplest view of eternal certainties; it is then that the soul gathers in wondrous refreshment and power and energy.

And so it is also in this way that we become truly useful to others. It is when coming out fresh from communication with God that we go forth to do His work successfully.

Horatius Bonar, Words to Winners of Souls

18 February Colman *(see p.230)*

Psalm 63:1-2   Ezekiel 47:3-5   Acts 4:15-21

> Anyone who has
> a great God
> is little in their own eyes
> **but**
> whoever comes
> to know God as He is,
> becomes nothing
> in their own eyes!
>
> **The Christian life** is not hard to live
> — it's utterly impossible to live!
> Only One can live it!
> **Let Him! In *you*.**
>
> If you were arrested for being a Christian,
> is there enough evidence to convict you?
> **Are you committed as a Christian?**
> Have you gone beyond the point of no return?

Arthur Burt, Pebbles to Slay Goliath

19 February

Psalm 63:3-7   1 Samuel 10:10-11   Acts 17:28

Some persons, when they hear of the 'prayer of quiet,'
falsely imagine the soul remains stupid, dead, and inactive.
But unquestionably it acteth therein, more nobly and more
extensively than it had ever done before, for God Himself is the
Mover and the soul now acteth by the agency of His Spirit ...
Instead, then, of promoting idleness, we promote the highest
activity, by inculcating a total dependence on the Spirit of God as
our moving principle, for in Him we live and move and have our
being ... Our activity should therefore consist in endeavouring to

acquire and maintain such a state as may be most susceptible of divine impressions, most flexible to all the operations of the Eternal Word. Whilst a tablet is unsteady, the painter is unable to delineate a true copy: so every act of our own selfish and proper spirit is productive of false and erroneous lineaments, it interrupts the work and defeats the design of the Artist.

Mme Jeanne Guyon

20 February

Psalm 62:11-12   Isaiah 58:5-6   Matthew 6:5

Sometimes contemplatives think that the whole end and essence of their life is to be found in recollection and interior peace and the sense of the presence of God. They become attached to these things. But recollection is just as much a creature as an automobile. The sense of interior peace is no less created than a bottle of wine. The experimental 'awareness' of the presence of God is just as truly a created thing as a glass of beer. The only difference is that recollection and interior peace and the sense of the presence of God are spiritual pleasures and the others are material. Attachment to spiritual things is therefore just as much an attachment as inordinate love of anything else. The imperfection may be more hidden and more subtle: but from a certain point of view that only makes it all the more harmful because it is not so easy to recognise.

Thomas Merton, Seeds of Contemplation

21 February

Psalm 62:4, 8   Isaiah 53:7   1 Thessalonians 3:1-8

Suppose there is friction and bad feeling in your church – what should you do, especially if you are involved in the arguments and divisions yourself? Further, let's suppose that you are in the right, that the trouble is not your fault, and that you are a mature and compassionate person. In that case, I suggest that you should say to the elders and members of the church: 'If I am in any way the cause of this trouble, even if unwittingly, or if my presence will in any way serve to perpetuate it, I will move to another congregation ... I will go away anywhere you wish, and do anything the congregation says – anything, if it will contribute to peace among Christ's flock and its pastors.'

Anyone who adopts this attitude will deserve a high reputation amongst Christians, and God's approval.

Clement of Rome

22 February

Psalm 48:3   2 Samuel 12:5-7   James 3:10-14

Where would we have been without this Church? Who would have handed down to us, across twenty centuries, the teaching of our dear Lord Jesus? Who would have encouraged us in the truth, reassured us in the path we had undertaken?

The Church already was founded before we appeared on the scene, and had we not come on the scene would have gone on being saints and sinners, capable of high ideals and base enormities, the dwelling place of peace and a jungle of violence.

But one thing is sure: if we should fail, overwhelmed by our sins and our faithlessness, the Church will not have failed. The 'little remnant' will have arrived none the less. God Himself is the guarantor.

Carlo Carretto, I, Francis

23 February Polycarp *(see p.256)*

Psalm 61:5   2 Kings 2:6   2 Corinthians 13:5

Christ, and only Christ, was the All in All. Paul was saying that Christ living in a believer was an observable fact, and that new believers could learn by observing more mature believers. Paul spoke of a Lord who could be practically followed – and lived – with the help of the lives of those gone before.

That which had been a spring of life within me now leaped boldly, laughing in my spirit, sending my doubts scurrying in disarray and confusion. I laughed at my fleeting doubts. 'Are you so shocked that what Paul preached actually worked? Are you horrified that Paul expected Christ to be seen in Him? Much of what you call humility is a form of religious pride!'

Malcolm Smith, Follow Me

24 February

Psalm 61:4   Isaiah 60:1   Matthew 16:28–17:8

In this momentary lifting of the veil, a foretaste of the Resurrection glory, the true meaning is given – the glory of such humiliation. Here faith is given a glorious icon. Each detail is a stroke of the brush, a precious gem.

The true external value of the God who in Christ hides Himself in identifying Himself with us in all our fragility, insignificance even to death, is the God who by so doing transforms our nature with His own glory and majesty. By the way of solidarity and temptation He leads us into glory. He 'transfers us from the kingdom of darkness into the kingdom of His Son.'

Roland Walls, The Royal Mysteries

25 February

Psalm 61   Song of Songs 3:1-4   1 Corinthians 2:9-10

In speaking of this desire ... I feel a certain shyness. I am almost committing an indecency. I am trying to rip open the inconsolable secret in each one of you – the secret which hurts so much that you take revenge on it by calling it names like nostalgia and romanticism and adolescence, the secret also which pierces with such sweetness that, when, in every intimate conversation, the mention of it becomes imminent, we grow awkward and affect to laugh at ourselves, the secret we cannot hide and cannot tell.

C.S. Lewis

26 February

Psalm 125:2   Song of Songs 8:6   John 16:15

The love of Christ is not a different love from the eternal fire in the heart of God or that which flows between the three persons of the Trinity. We are loved passionately by God. The self-sacrificing love between the three persons is the joy at the centre of God. What is the response from us to such love? To silently wonder. We enter into the ebb and flow of this divine love. The Holy Spirit enables us to know something of the reality of this love in the depths of our heart.

Ralph Wouldham

27 February

Psalm 122:8   Daniel 6:19-23   Philippians 1:3-5

In solitude we can come to the realisation that we are not driven together but brought together. In solitude we come to know our fellow human beings not as partners who can satisfy our deepest needs, but as brothers and sisters with whom we are called to give visibility to God's all-embracing love. In solitude we discover that community is not a common ideology, but a response to a common call. In solitude we indeed realise that community is not made but given.

Henri J.M. Nouwen, Clowning in Rome

28 February

Psalm 127:2   Isaiah 58:10-11   Luke 2:15-20

Do you ever start thinking,
'Lord, do I really have to love these people?
Oh, I can't take it any more?'
Do you ever want to peg out?
   does it ever let up?
   is the war ever over, Lord?
   when is it going to get easy?

Jesus said His yoke is easy,
   and His burden is light.
He never said there won't be a yoke or burden
   but that's alright.
The yoke is going to hold you,
   and a burden's made to bear.
Lord, when the load gets heavy on me,
I know You'll be there; I know You'll be there.

I tried to speak the truth in love today
   to someone walking the wrong way;
   it fell on stony ground.
It seems the more I try to follow You,
   the more the enemy rages:
   he's not going to win.

I know You'll be there, I know You'll be there.

*Larry and Pearl Brick,
from the* See-Through Servant *album*

29 February

Psalm 138:8   Song of Songs 4:12   Mark 6:30-32

My island teaches me new truths, or deepens the truths I already know. Like life, the island is never the same. Who of us has not known those 'naked days' when we feel the world is against us, that its prying eyes strip us naked and leave us crucified: days when we feel we could give anything for a little privacy; days of sorrow and pain when we want to hide and have no place to hide?

But if one reads the Scriptures and comes across its lovely poetic words about a 'garden enclosed', a 'fountain sealed', and wonders about it all, then my island will reveal the secret of those holy words, and it will lead gently to contemplation, which is the key to that garden. Someday, unseen and unheard, the Bridegroom will come into such a garden. Then one will understand what it is to be all His.

Catherine de Hueck Doherty, I Live on an Island

March
Ask for the old paths

1 March David *(see p.231)*

Psalm 61:2-3   Proverbs 18:20   Ephesians 1:18-21

Jeremiah 6:16 tells us to 'ask for the old paths' and the commentary on these pages will largely be the stories and prayers of the Celtic saints.

We begin by slowly examining the much-used Celtic discipline of putting on St Patrick's Breastplate, calling on God to protect His servant.

> I bind unto myself today
>   the strong name of the Trinity
> by invocation of the same,
> the Three in One and One in Three.
> I bind this day to me for ever,
> by power of faith, Christ's Incarnation,
> His baptism in the Jordan River;
> His death on Cross for my salvation;
> His bursting from the spicèd tomb;
> His riding up the heavenly way;
> His coming at the day of doom;
> I bind unto myself today.

Translation in verse by Mrs C.F. Alexander

2 March Chad *(see p.286)*

Psalm 34:7-8   Isaiah 6:1-3   Matthew 25:15-23

In 2 Kings 6:15-17 Elisha's servant has his spiritual eyes opened and can see what the man of God knew all along, the presence of angels defending them. 2 Samuel 5:23-24 tells us of David's army not moving until given the signal of the sound of angelic hosts marching overhead. Patrick knows himself to be in the company of all those who love and serve his God, all ranks of angels, earlier saints and elders, Old Testament men of faith, martyrs and monastics. All that matters is God's approval.

> I bind unto myself the power
> of the great love of the Cherubim;
> the sweet 'Well done' in judgement hour;
> the service of the Seraphim,
> Confessors' faith, Apostles' word,
> the Patriarchs' prayers, the Prophets' scrolls,
> all good deeds done unto the Lord,
> and purity of virgin souls.

3 March

Psalm 3:3-4   Job 38:4-13   John 1:3-5

All of nature is invested with the loving care of an infinitely creative God. Each act of creation reflects some aspect of His love and strength. God is BIG, but still cares about every detail of what He has created, and so He cares for us. We can look to Him for direction. Jesus was able to say that He spoke what He was given to speak [John 8:26] and if we too can be sensitised to what is from Him [John 10:4-5] we will find the fear of the Lord is indeed the beginning of wisdom [Proverbs 15:31-33].

I bind unto myself today
the virtues of the starlit heaven
the glorious sun's life-giving ray,
the whiteness of the moon at even,
the flashing of the lightning free,
the whirling wind's tempestuous shocks,
the stable earth, the deep salt sea,
around the old eternal rocks.

I bind unto myself today
the power of God to hold and lead,
His eye to watch, His might to stay,
His ear to hearken to my need,
the wisdom of my God to teach,
His hand to guide, His shield to ward;
the word of God to give me speech,
His heavenly host to be my guard.

4 March Owini *(see p.253)*

Psalm 139:11-12   1 Kings 18:21   Romans 13:11-14

Patrick's life really was in danger at the time he first prayed the Breastplate, but all the solitaries and people of prayer know that the biggest battles can be the ones inside – 'fightings and fears, within, without'.

> Come swiftly, O Lord, to the dark moments when we are lost. Make us aware of Thy presence. Strengthen us to resist the urges and pulls to deeper darkness. Stir us to move away from the dark moments of sinfulness toward the light of Thy forgiveness. Come quickly, O Lord, as we call – or forget to call – and keep Thou close to us and keep us close to Thee this day and night and as far as the days and nights stretch before us, through Christ. Amen.

James W. Kennedy, Holy Island – A Lenten Pilgrimage

Against the demon snares of sin,
the vice that gives temptation force,
the natural lusts that war within,
the hostile men that mar my course;
or few or many, far or nigh,
in every place, and in all hours,
against their fierce hostility,
I bind to me these holy powers.

5 March Piran *(see p.256)*

Psalm 91:4-8   Daniel 1:20   Luke 10:18-20

When Patrick arrived at Tara it was Easter Eve and he lit a fire so he could keep vigil. God had arranged it that by this timing he would be brought to give an account of the hope he had in Christ, for it was also a Druid festival for which every fire in the land must be put out in preparation. Patrick's Easter light shone boldly, so he was brought before the king.

Against all Satan's spells and wiles,
against false words of heresy,
against the knowledge that defiles,
against the heart's idolatry,
against the wizard's evil craft,
against the death-wound and the burning,
the choking wave and poisoned shaft,
protect me, Christ, till Thy returning.

When King Laeghaire tried to have Patrick killed as he left Tara, it was from jealousy, for Patrick had preached to many and turned them to Christ away from the magic and old religion of the Druids. The would-be murderers saw only a company of stags pass by. It would seem that the Breastplate prayer was answered!

6 March Baldred *(see p.223)*   Billifrith *(see p.225)*

Psalm 139:5-8   Deuteronomy 33:27   Luke 23:33-34

> Christ be with me, Christ within me,
> Christ behind me, Christ before me,
> Christ beside me, Christ to win me,
> Christ to comfort and restore me,
> Christ beneath me, Christ above me,
> Christ in quiet, Christ in danger,
> Christ in hearts of all that love me,
> Christ in mouth of friend and stranger.

Christ beneath me

Beneath are the everlasting arms – and they bear the print of the nails. No matter how far I have sunk, He descends to lift me up. He has plumbed all the hells of this world that He may lift us upwards. He is our firm support.

David Adam, The Edge of Glory

7 March

Psalm 96:11-13   Jeremiah 33:3   1 John 1:1-5

The mighty God, the Everlasting Father, the Prince of Peace, Wonderful, Counsellor, the One who said 'I Am that I Am, that is My Name', comes when we call. He comes, but not because we are lords and He our slave. The God who comes awaits our signal, our vigil fire lit to welcome His coming. He longs to be with us, to love and protect us. The Breastplate prayer ends as it begins; like the interweaving of Celtic design it really has no ending, only eternity in which the design brings us back to the same place, more secure in the knowledge that our life is eternal and interlocked with His own.

I bind unto myself the name,
the strong name of the Trinity;
by invocation of the same,
the Three in One, and One in Three,
of whom all nature hath creation;
Eternal Father, Spirit, Word:
praise to the Lord of my salvation,
salvation is of Christ the Lord.

8 March Senan *(see p.260)*

Psalm 23:3-4   Joel 2:25   John 4:28-30

'I know the plans I have for you, says the Lord, to give you a future and a hope' [Jeremiah 29:11]. God can take events of the past and weave them so skilfully into a new plan for us that not only do we find there is a future for us after all, but it is as if there have been no wasted years.

Christ behind me

> There He walks in your past. He walks in all the dark rooms you pretend are closed, that He may bring light. Invite Him into your past. Experience His forgiveness, His acceptance of you. Offer especially all that you are ashamed of ... all that you wish to forget ... all that still pains and hurts you ... all the hurt you have caused others. Walk there in the places you are afraid of, knowing that He walks with you and will lead you on!

Christ before me

> He forever goes before us to prepare a place for us. He is on the road we tread. Wherever life is leading us, He has gone before. Perhaps we have no clue about what lies ahead; we know who is ahead of us, so the future is not quite unknown.

David Adam, The Edge of Glory

9 March

Psalm 139:15-17   Isaiah 66:3-4   Hebrews 11:24-25

The future is not a foregone conclusion. But when we give God permission to intervene and bring about His will in us, still again and again He offers us choices, perhaps between one good and another. This is so that we can create through our choices, enabling Him to bring into being things He had long ago planned for us. He constantly plans for me in love, and in His mercy He never allows me to see the might-have-beens that only He could see.

In one of Charles Williams' poems he describes the images of possibilities as carved in stone and rock hidden for ever under the sea unless our choices call them into being, until they become visible and become realities:

> Before the making of man or beast
> the Emperor knew all carved contingent shapes...
> These were the shapes only the Emperor knew.
> Sideways in the cleft they lay,
> and the seamews' wings everywhere flying,
> or the mist, or the mere slant of the things
> seemed to stir them;
> then the edge of the storm's shock over us
> obliquely split rock from rock...
> Did you not see, by the dolorous blow's might,
> the contingent knowledge of the Emperor
> floating into sight? ... the sculpture,
> the living sculpture, rose and flew!

From Taliesin through Logres

10 March

Psalm 148:3-8   Joel 3:14-16   Acts 26:16-18

Patrick placed all these things in prayer as a shield between him and those who sought to take his life. It worked; they passed through unseen, Patrick and his companions, including a young boy called Benignus. The ambush party waiting for them saw only 'a company of stags with a little fawn running behind them'. Coincidence? The escape at Tara enabled Patrick to continue his mission in Ireland. Perhaps you can replace 'Tara' with the name of where God has you, as you pray:

> At Tara today in this fateful hour,
> I place all heaven with its power,
> and the sun with its brightness,
> and the snow with its whiteness,
> and fire with all the strength it hath,
> and lightning with its rapid wrath,
> and the winds with their swiftness
>   along their path,
> and the sea with its deepness,
> and the rocks with their steepness,
> and the earth with its starkness:
> all these I place, by God's almighty help
>   and grace,
> between myself and the powers of darkness.

11 March

Psalm 94:16-20   Genesis 12:1-3   Luke 9:60-62

Columba was from an Irish royal family, but chose the life of a monk. Nonetheless he managed to quarrel with King Diarmait, chief of the kings of Ireland, over two incidents. Diarmait had executed a relative of Columba, named Curnan, for accidentally killing another young man during a hurling game, and had imprisoned Columba for giving him sanctuary. He also ruled that a hand-copied book of Psalms must stay in Clonard monastery with the original from which Columba had copied it. Columba told his kinsmen and soon they and neighbouring clans went to war to avenge the injustice. Thousands of men were killed or wounded, and Columba poured out his grief to a holy man called Laisren. The penance he gave Columba was to leave Ireland and to go as a missionary. 'Rest not until as many souls are won for Christ's Kingdom as you have caused to fall by the sword,' he said. Columba and his friends came first to Oronsay, then sailed to Iona from which no glimpse of Ireland could be seen. There he looked back to make sure.

'Every time I saw those hills across the water I should want to go home, and one day the want might have been too strong for me,' he thought. They call that place the Bay of the Coracle where Columba's boat is supposed to have come to land.

12 March Paul Aurelian *(see p.254)*

Psalm 84:9-11   1 Chronicles 15:23-28   John 14:2-3

Columba established a fine missionary base on Iona, and he and his monks travelled far over the sea in their frail coracles, preaching the Gospel in the Orkney and Shetland Islands, in the Faroes and the Hebrides. One evening in June in the year 597 he went out into the fields where the brethren were working and called them to him. 'The time is near for me to be parted from you,' he told them. 'At dawn tomorrow I shall yield up to the Lord the precious thing with which He has trusted me for so many years.' The monks knew that he meant his soul, and they were very sad, but Columba himself was full of joy. The last text he copied out was Psalm 34, verse 10: 'they who seek the Lord shall want no manner of thing that is good.'

> Almighty Father, Son and Holy Ghost,
> eternal, ever-blessèd, gracious God,
> to me, the least of saints, to me allow
> that I may keep a door in Paradise;
> that I may keep even the smallest door,
> the furthest door, the darkest, coldest door,
> the door that is least used, the stiffest door,
> if so it be but in Thine house, O God!
> if so it be that I can see Thy Glory,
> even afar and hear Thy voice, O God!
> and know that I am with Thee – Thee, O God.
>
> *W. Muir, the 'Prayer of Columba'*

13 March

Psalm 104:23   Isaiah 43:20-21   Colossians 3:17

> The first two years of Columba's residence in Iona were spent in learning the language, tilling the soil, training followers, and generally organising the community. The days were filled with prayer, study, and manual labour, and in this last Columba, with his great spiritual and intellectual gifts, was always ready to share. In dairy, granary, or in the fields, each worshipped God in his appointed task, and made his toil a sacramental thing ... The secret of the early Celts lay in this, that they linked sacrament with service, altar with hearth, worship with work.
>
> F.M. McNeill/Troup

For us, too, it is important to discover the rhythm of praying as we work and through our work. Sometimes a simple manual task can even assist the praying heart in its focus. Prayer-baskets were woven simply out of reeds as monastics framed their prayers. The simplest task can become for us a prayer-basket.

14 March

Psalm 72:1-4   Jeremiah 31:21   1 Corinthians 2:2-5

> King Oswald, a man beloved of God, when he was about to give battle to the heathen, set up the sign of the holy cross, and kneeling down, asked God that He would grant His heavenly aid to those who trusted in Him in their dire need. It is told that, when the cross had been hurriedly made and a hole dug to receive it, the devout king with ardent faith took the cross and placed it in position, holding it upright with his own hands until the soldiers had thrown in the earth and it stood firm. Then he summoned his army with a loud shout, crying, 'Let us all kneel together, and ask the true and living God Almighty of His mercy to protect us from the arrogant savagery of our enemies, since He knows that we fight in a just cause to save our nation.'

The whole army did as he ordered, and advancing against the enemy at the first light of dawn, won the victory that their faith deserved. To this day they called this place Hefenfelth meaning 'the heavenly field'.

Bede

The cross at Heavenfield was set up as a waymark, and the Kingdom of Christ began to come in Northumberland.

15 March

Psalm 127:1   Isaiah 28:9-11   1 Corinthians 3:1-2

When King Oswald originally asked the brothers of Iona to send someone to teach the Faith of Christ to his people, they sent him a man of a more austere disposition. Meeting with no success in his preaching, for the people refused to listen to him, he returned home and reported to his superiors that he had been unable to teach anything to the nation to whom they had sent him because they were an uncivilised people of an obstinate and barbarous temperament. The Scots fathers, therefore, held a great conference to decide on the wisest course of action, for although they regretted that the preacher whom they had sent had not been acceptable to the Northumbrian folk, they still wished to meet their desire for salvation. Then Aidan, who was present at the conference, said to the priest whose efforts had been unsuccessful,

'Brother, it seems to me that you were too severe on your ignorant hearers. You should have followed the practice of the Apostles, and begun by giving them the milk of simpler teaching, and gradually instructed them in the word of God until they were capable of greater perfection and able to follow the sublime precepts of Christ.'

All who were at the conference paid close attention to all he said, and realised that here was a fit person to send to instruct the ignorant and unbelieving, since he was particularly endowed with the grace of discretion. They therefore consecrated him, and sent him to preach.

Bede

16 March

Psalm 126   Exodus 4:11-17   1 Corinthians 14:20-21

On Aidan's arrival, the king appointed the island of Lindisfarne to be his base, as he asked. As the tide ebbs and flows, this place is surrounded by sea twice a day like an island, and twice a day the sand dries and joins it to the mainland. The king always listened humbly and readily to Aidan's advice, and diligently set himself to establish and extend the Church of Christ throughout his kingdom. And while Aidan, now their bishop, who was not yet fluent in their language, preached the gospel, it was most delightful to see the king himself interpreting the word of God to his thanes and leaders; for he himself had obtained perfect command of the Scottish tongue during his long exile.

Bede

Bede also tells us that other helpers came from Scotland, proclaiming the word of God with great devotion in all the provinces under Oswald's rule. Many were baptised, and churches were built in several places. People flocked gladly to hear the word of God – not just when it was Aidan preaching and their beloved king standing by his side as interpreter, his own eyes glowing at the privilege of proclaiming the truth he loved.

17 March   Patrick *(see p.253)*   Joseph of Arimathea *(see p.245)*

Psalm 121:7-8   Isaiah 35:8   Acts 8:35-40

How many times must Aidan have looked up at the Cheviots and said to himself, 'I will lift up my eyes unto the hills ... my help comes from the Lord who made heaven and earth.' Bede tells us that he walked almost everywhere, and all who accompanied him, monks or lay-folk, were required to meditate, that is, either to read the Scriptures or to learn the Psalms. This was their daily occupation wherever they went. They also lived what they taught and this was the highest recommendation of their belief. He never cared for any worldly possessions, unless it was so he could give them to assist the poor. Always travelling on foot, unless it was absolutely necessary to ride, in town or country this gave Aidan the opportunity to stop and speak with whoever he met as he went, be they high or low in status. If they were heathen, he urged them to believe and be baptised; if Christians already he would strengthen their faith and inspire them by word and example to live a good and generous life. The Cheviots stand and remember. Even so the Lord will not forget to be our shield, preserving the comings and goings of His own. A causeway shall be there and a way ...

18 March

Psalm 72:12-13   Proverbs 21:13-14   James 2:17-18

Oswald at length brought under his sceptre all the kingdoms and provinces of Britain speaking the four languages of British, Pictish, Scottish and English. Although he wielded supreme power, Oswald was always wonderfully humble, kindly and generous to the poor and strangers. The story is told how on the Feast of Easter one year, Oswald sat down to dine with Bishop Aidan. A silver dish of rich food was set before him, and Bishop Aidan had just raised his hand to bless the food when the servant who was appointed to relieve the needs of the poor came in suddenly and informed the king that a great crowd of needy folk were sitting in the road outside begging alms of the king. Oswald at once ordered his own food to be taken out to the poor, and the silver dish to be broken up and distributed among them. The bishop, who was sitting beside him, was deeply moved to see such generosity, and taking the king's right hand, exclaimed, 'May this hand never perish.'

Bede

Later events proved that his prayer was heard, for when Oswald was killed in battle, his hand and arm were severed from his body, and, says Bede over 200 years later, 'remains uncorrupted to this day'.

19 March

Psalm 63:1-4   Jeremiah 6:16   1 Timothy 2:8

> It is said that Oswald often remained in prayer from the early hour at which prayers were said, known as Lauds, until dawn, and that through his practice of constant prayer and thanksgiving to God, he always sat with his hands palm upwards on his knees. It is also said, until the saying became a proverb, that 'his life closed in prayer', for when he saw the enemy forces surrounding him and knew that his end was near, he prayed for the souls of his soldiers, saying as he fell, 'God have mercy on their souls.'
>
> *Bede*

> Express again the reality that God is there.
> There for your life. There in your prayer.
>
> Between each thought and each action
> place the Presence.
> Between each encounter and event
> place the Presence.
>
> *David Adam*

20 March   Cuthbert *(see p.231)*   Herebert *(see p.240)*

Psalm 49:1-3   Isaiah 58:6-8   2 Timothy 2:2

> Aidan, Bishop of Lindisfarne, 'cultivated peace and love, purity and humility; he was above anger and greed, and despised pride and conceit; he set himself to keep and to teach the laws of God, and was diligent in study and prayer. He used his priestly authority to check the proud and powerful; he tenderly comforted the sick;

he relieved and protected the poor. To sum up what could be learned from those who knew him, he took pains never to neglect anything that he had learned from the writings of the apostles and prophets, and he set himself to carry them out with all his powers.'

Bede

It was Aidan who would free slaves whenever he was able, and a number of these became his closest disciples. It was he who broke ground winning people for Christ across Northumberland, and always learning himself, imparted to others the life he had embraced and carried as a torch.

> O Lord, I pray that in You,
> I'll break ground both fresh and new.
> As a student make me stand,
> break the hardness of the land
> with Your forgiving Father-hand.

Paul Stamper

21 March Enda *(see p.236)*

Psalm 78:70-72   2 Kings 2:8-14   Hebrews 12:22-23

On the night when St Aidan died, a boy was taking his turn to stay awake with sheep upon the Northumbrian hills. As he watched the flock with friends, he looked up from time to time at the great belt of stars which is called the Milky Way, and thought to himself that that was the pathway by which the souls of the dead go to heaven. And while he was gazing upwards, he saw a sudden vision. He has described it for us in graphic words:

> Methought I saw a dazzling radiance shine suddenly out of the darkness, and in the midst of the streaming light a choir of angels descended to earth and lo! they were bearing away as in a globe of fire a happy soul.

That boy was named Cuthbert, who afterwards was to become one of the most famous of the bishops of Lindisfarne. The vision that he saw is known as the Passing of St Aidan.

Cuthbert was an orphan and lived with a widow called Kenswith who loved him as though he had been her own son.

> He longed to be a soldier, but also wanted to serve God. At the age of fifteen he mounted his horse and carrying the weapons he had trained himself to use, set off for adventure, intending to dedicate his strength to God. His horse led him to the door of the Abbey of Melrose, where Eata, one of Aidan's disciples, in turn discipled him.

22 March

Psalm 107:23-30   Jonah 1:4-15   Mark 4:36-41

> In Aidan's school were four brothers, the youngest of whom was called Chad. Chad eventually came to have charge of the Abbey at Lastingham, and ruled over the same in love and peace. From him his monks learned gentleness and humility. One brother whose name was Trumhere noticed that if a gale arose while Chad was reading or doing anything else he would at once call upon God for mercy, and pray Him to have mercy upon mankind. And if the wind increased in violence, he would close his book and prostrate himself on the ground praying even more earnestly. But if there was a violent storm of wind and rain, or the earth shook with thunder and lightning, he would go to the church, and say prayers and psalms continuously until the tempest had passed. When questioned why he did this, he told his monks, 'Do you not know that it is the Lord who moves the air, raises winds, darts lightnings, and thunders from heaven to incite the people to fear Him, and to put them in mind of the future judgement? Wherefore it is indeed a time for us to show due fear and love.'

23 March Ethilwald of Farne *(see p.238)* Felgild *(see p.238)*

Psalm 103:19-22   Exodus 3:2-5   2 Timothy 4:7-8

Chad was eventually sent as Bishop of Mercia, and built a cathedral and monastery at Lichfield and with humility, simplicity and gentleness reached out to the people in that whole area. His influence spread and continued over the next two and a half years. Then one day he was alone in his oratory, and Brother Owini working outside heard the sound of sweet and joyful singing coming down from heaven to earth. It approached the building, then entered the oratory filling the place and the surrounding air. Half an hour later the song rose through the roof and returned to heaven with inexpressible sweetness. Owini had stood astonished, now Chad opened the oratory window and bade him run to fetch seven other brothers, then he urged them to be faithful and constant, announcing that soon he was to leave them. Owini remained behind after they were blessed and asked Chad about the singing. 'Since you were aware of it already I will tell you if you promise not to speak of it yet,' Chad answered. 'They were angelic spirits summoning me to the heavenly reward and in seven days they have promised to return for me.'

Bede

Earth is crammed with heaven,
and every common bush afire with God,
but only he who sees
takes off his shoes.

Elizabeth Barrett Browning

24 March Oscar Romero *(see p.259)*

Psalm 89:15-16   Ezekiel 34:11-12   James 5:16

When Cuthbert was made prior at Melrose he did not restrict his teaching and influence to the monastery, but worked to rouse the ordinary folk far and near to exchange their foolish customs for a love of heavenly joys. He often used to leave the monastery, sometimes on horseback but more frequently on foot, and visit the neighbouring towns, where he preached the way of truth to those who had gone astray. Cuthbert was so skilful a speaker and had such a light in his face, and such a love for proclaiming his message that none presumed to hide their inmost secrets, but openly confessed all their wrong-doing for they felt it impossible to conceal their guilt from him. He gladly undertook the task of visiting and preaching mainly in the villages that lay far distant among high and inaccessible mountains which others feared to visit, and whose barbarity and squalor daunted other teachers. He taught with patience and skill, and when he left the monastery it would sometimes be a week, sometimes two or three, and occasionally an entire month before he returned home, remaining in the mountains to guide the peasants heavenward by his teachings and example.

Bede

25 March

Psalm 55:22   Proverbs 16:1-3   Colossians 3:12-15

When Cuthbert came as prior to Lindisfarne he handed on the monastic rule by teaching and example, but some of the monks preferred their old way of life to the rule. He overcame these by patience and forbearance, bringing them round little by little through daily example to a better frame of mind. At chapter meetings he was often worn down by bitter insults, but would put an end to the arguments simply by rising and walking out, calm and unruffled. Next day he would give the same people exactly the same admonitions, as though there had been no unpleasantness the previous day. In this way he gradually won their obedience. He was wonderfully patient, and though overwhelmed by sorrow at these monks' recalcitrance, he managed to keep a cheerful face.

He urged his people to lift up their hearts and give thanks to the Lord God more by the yearnings of his own heart than by the sound of his voice. Often as they were pouring out their sins he would be the first to burst into tears, tears of sympathy with their weakness.

Bede

26 March

Psalm 91:14   Isaiah 35:7   Ephesians 6:10-13

Cuthbert was determined to do battle for Heaven, but did not underestimate the strength of the challenge. 'If I could live in a tiny dwelling on a rock in the ocean,' he lamented, 'surrounded by the swelling waves, cut off from the knowledge and the sight of all, I would still not be free from the cares of this fleeting world nor from the fear that somehow the love of money might snatch me away.' Not till he had first gained victory over our invisible enemy by solitary prayer and fasting did he take it on himself to seek out a remote battlefield farther away from his fellow men. Eventually he moved onto the Inner Farne a few miles out south-east of Lindisfarne. The island was haunted by devils; Cuthbert was the first man brave enough to live there alone. But when the man of God came, he ordered the evil spirits to withdraw, and the island became quite habitable.

Bede

27 March

Psalm 5:11-12   Isaiah 43:10-11   Revelation 1:8

God to enfold me, God to surround me,
God in my speaking, God in my thinking,
God in my sleeping, God in my waking,
God in my watching, God in my hoping,
God in my life, God in my lips,
God in my soul, God in my heart,

in my sufficing, and in my slumber,
God in mine ever-living soul.

Carmina Gaedelica

As He is He was: as He was He is.
He shall be as He is and was,
the Eternal forever so be it Amen.
The Forever Eternal so be it Amen.

David Adam,
The Edge of Glory

28 March

Psalm 22:14-17   Isaiah 53:5   John 21:19-20

A fourteenth-century hermit we know only as the Monk of Farne was one of the people to inherit Cuthbert's call to a solitary life on the Inner Farne. These extracts are from his writings:

> All day long I stretched out my hands on the cross towards thee, O man, to embrace thee; I bow down My head to kiss thee when I have embraced thee, I open My side to draw thee into My heart after this kiss, that we may be two in one flesh. There can be safety for thee nowhere else but in Me, when the day of wrath and judgement comes. See, I have shown thee the sign thou didst beg; know then how much I love, and fly quickly to me.

> ...precisely because I am a sinner, I have fled to Thee; since there is nowhere I can flee from Thee save to Thee. Thou dost stretch out Thine arms to receive me and bend down Thy head to kiss me; Thou dost bleed that I may have to drink, and open Thy side in Thy desire to draw me within ... I will gladly run to Thee albeit a sinner, albeit unclean, for with Thee there is merciful forgiveness; Thou wilt wash me in Thy blood, and I shall be made whiter than snow. I will enter into Thee and not stay without, for outside Thee there is no salvation.

29 March

Psalm 15:2-4   Micah 6:8   3 John 5-6

> Just as a table without bread is a needy one,
> so absence of charity is ruin to the soul,
> for the soul walks by love, and the man who
> does not love abides in death.
>
> *The Monk of Farne*

> Whoever does not love does not know God, for God is love.
>
> *1 John 4:8*

> If I give away all my possessions, and if I hand over my body so that I may boast, but do not have love, I gain nothing.
>
> *1 Corinthians 13:3*

It is not what we give of ourselves or our resources that is the measure of how we love, but what we hold back.

30 March

Psalm 16:6   Genesis 18:1-8   Matthew 25:34-40

Celtic rune of hospitality

> I saw a stranger yestere'en.
> I put food in the eating place,
> drink in the drinking place,
> music in the listening place,
> and in the sacred name of the Triune
> He blessed myself and my house,
> my cattle and my dear ones,
> and the lark said in her song

often, often, often,
goes Christ in the stranger's guise.

Kenneth MacLeod

31 March

Psalm 72:6-7   Isaiah 26:3-4   John 21:21-22

> Deep peace of the running wave to you
> Deep peace of the flowing air to you
> Deep peace of the quiet earth to you
> Deep peace of the shining stars to you
> Deep peace of the Son of peace to you.

Fiona Macleod

April
The inward journey

1 April Mary of Egypt *(see p.250)*

Psalm 86:11   Proverbs 5:1   Hebrews 12:11

Many years ago Paul and Mary Cullity placed a copy of *The Inward Journey* by Gene Edwards into Andy Raine's hand and said, 'You must read this – you'll hate it!'

What the book itself had to say was that sooner or later you will reach the conclusion that the Christian life is *mostly* about suffering so you might as well be prepared for it instead of being taken by surprise.

This month we will be using passages from Gene Edwards' book for our daily notes, describing what a believer 'might expect to encounter experientially on his way down the road toward transformation'.

2 April

Psalm 86:16   Proverbs 3:13-14   Luke 14:28-30

Gene Edwards talks of the reason he wrote *The Inward Journey*:

> I was a very ignorant new Christian when I wandered into the huge bookstore of the Ridgecrest Baptist Assembly grounds in North Carolina. As I entered the store I was absolutely awed by the endless, infinite array of books and the myriad categories they were divided into. Dazed, I walked over to the clerk behind one of the counters and asked, 'Where do you keep the books for new Christians?' She looked at me rather puzzled, weighed my question, and replied, 'Well, there's no such section.' Then she asked, 'What is it you're interested in?' This still ranks as

one of the most incongruous questions ever asked me. I didn't have the slightest idea what there was to be interested in.

Three decades have now passed. I suppose during the years I have read about as many books as a man can afford to buy, borrow or copy.

Until this day I still pick up literature marked 'for the new Christian' and with great disappointment find it either inane, useless, traditional, cranial, old, shallow, irrelevant or carrying within its covers the curse of scholarship. That question still haunts me, 'Where are the books for new Christians?'

3 April

Psalm 135:4-6   Genesis 32:24-31   Revelation 19:16

It took a lifetime of God at His best to break that man, and even then ... only when He touched him at the strongest point in his life.

Jacob says,
'That broken hip?
An angel did me a favour.'

4 April   Martin Luther King Jr *(see p.246)*

Psalm 133   1 Kings 5:17   1 Peter 2:5

Come with us to a quarry in King Solomon's time...

After the stone is cut free from the earth it is pulled here to the flat of the earth. The stone is then cut to an exact, predetermined size, chiselled with large, coarse instruments until it has some semblance of shape, then cut with finer chisels. Next it is coarse sanded, then it is fine sanded, and last polished.

When the stonemason is finished, the stone is flawless. From here the stone is taken to a distant city and to a building site.

All these stones will be taken to that city. Each is destined to be taken to an already determined place. It is interesting that when this happens each stone fits perfectly into its place. They fit so perfectly in fact, that they appear to be *one* stone.

5 April

Psalm 48:8   1 Kings 6:7   Revelation 21:18-21

There are enough stones here to build a city! A very large city. Can you hear the masons? They are beginning to return to their work over there. Hear the hammers? The chisels? One day, when all these stones are completed, they will be taken to the site, near the house. There they will be taken through a door, and from there to the builders' site itself, where the stones are being reassembled. Reassembled, but this time into a house ... almost as one vast stone.

At that site, on *that* side of the door, there will be no hammer, no chisel, no mason work at all. It is here, on this side of the building site where all cutting, chiselling, sanding and polishing *must* take place. Here! Not there. All the thud of hammer and falling of axes, the grating of chisels and the grinding of sand ... is done *here*! It is the plan of the Masterbuilder that all the business of making rough rock into perfectly fitting, polished stone be accomplished in the stone quarry. *There*, there, beyond this place, beyond that door, is only the assembling together of what has been done *here*.

6 April

Psalm 87   Isaiah 62:12   Revelation 21:9-11, 23

This particular house is very large.

Large enough to be a city, for it shall be a house for God to live in…

> 'A quarry, I live in the midst of a quarry. Called Earth.'
>
> The real quarry – you are down there somewhere, being chiselled on by God, man and circumstances. But not you alone. Every believer who has ever lived, those who lived before His visitation and all those who are yet to come, one day you all will be lifted out of this quarry through that door … Then shall no hammer be heard, for all of that is done in the quarry. Nor shall you be there as an endless array of stones. But together you will be assembled in one place, as one. A living city … the bride. The New Jerusalem.

7 April   Roland Walls *(see p.264)*

Psalm 102:25-27   Genesis 22:7-8   1 Peter 1:18-20

The angel Messenger takes Christian to see the secret God had prepared in Himself before the beginning of time –

> Just before him, lying in a pool of blood,
> lay the cold, dead and mangled form of a
> snow-white lamb.
> For
> He was slain
> before the foundation
> of the world.

8 April

Psalm 17:15   Job 19:23-26   James 5:10-11

We usually learn about Him only during periods of adversity. Few, if any, of us really seek after a deep, intimate relationship with the Lord except (1) just before, (2) during, and (3) right after those periods of calamity, disaster, catastrophe, suffering and pain! That's true of the very sinful, the very religious, and ... well ... the rest of us!

I challenge the idea that suffering is first of all a punishment for our sins. If that were true, then every believer on earth would be hiding under a rock somewhere.

Job lowered his voice, 'It appears we have a God who has supreme confidence in His own judgement. Nor can He be persuaded to show a great deal of interest in explaining Himself. He keeps His counsel to Himself, it appears; nor is He perturbed in the least that we're perturbed about His not being perturbed. But,' said he, raising his index finger in a gesture of discovery, 'I didn't need to learn anything else. I saw Him. Getting questions answered seems rather a paltry thing in comparison to having seen Him.'

Christian stood there for a long time. 'It's hard to realise that that was the man Satan went after with such a vengeance!'

'Shhh,' said the angel, Messenger. 'He knows nothing of that!'

9 April   Dietrich Bonhoeffer *(see p.225)*

Psalm 46:5   Daniel 2:44-45   Romans 8:18

Perhaps we should place the sign on the wall somewhere in our homes:

**Church life may be
hazardous to your health.**

The Lord knows something we don't: The Fall has left *all* of us in dire straits. Most of us are either extremely sinful or extremely religious. Or both! And further, I suspect that neither one of those states pleases God more than the other. Neither impresses Him. What *He* does in us impresses Him!

In the quarry which is Earth each stone was in a different stage of completion. A rough stone was just being pulled free of the mother mountain.

10 April

Psalm 27:13   Genesis 39:11-23   Romans 8:28

Visit Joseph, and what do you hear?

– a groan, followed by laboured breathing
from the cell's captive.

'They meant it to me for evil
but *He* meant it to me for good.'

11 April

Psalm 90:10, 12   1 Chronicles 29:11-16   2 Corinthians 3:18

See the Quarry: Earth!

Christian, there is but one place you will ever learn to follow Him, to worship Him, to obey Him, to love Him.
Only one place, one time ... to love Him.
Only one opportunity to be changed into His image.
The place is there ... the time ... your 70 years.

12 April Aldwin *(see p.221)*

Psalm 27:7-8   Isaiah 28:13   Philippians 3:7-10

Everyone should be warned: 'Give your life utterly to Christ and you will eventually suffer much more than you can now comprehend.' But there is no way a man can communicate to daring young Christians the amount of suffering they will encounter in one lifetime. Again and again they have been cautioned, in every way known. Yet, each time that sovereign hand of God has fallen on one of them and he (or she) has truly entered into the fellowship of Christ's sufferings, he is always surprised how hard, how unbearable, is the cross.

For better or worse at the beginning they did not have the good sense to run out the door. These were young Christians who loved the Lord, who would not be stopped, not even by the cross.

13 April

Psalm 2:11-12   Deuteronomy 4:23-24   Hebrews 12:28-29

Our emotions sometimes author one of the greatest problems of our Christian life: to create a God in its own image, a loving, sweet, and precious God who wouldn't dare declare war on a person's dominant emotions. The emotions do not have a franchise on this project. The intellect often sculpts out a God in its own image, a God who is very intelligent, rational, reasonable, very logical, very scriptural, very boxable and definable, and having erected this mind-made God in the centre of life, will vow and declare that this, and this alone, is the true and living God.

14 April

Psalm 44:17-26   Isaiah 54:11   John 21:17-22

What kind of Christian can best endure suffering? That Christian doesn't exist.

I could handle your problems easily. You could handle mine with a yawn. But it didn't happen that way. I got the ones I couldn't handle; so did you.

15 April

Psalm 141   2 Samuel 15:10-14   Acts 14:1-7

Many a Christian worker has raised up a work that perhaps was worthy to be called 'church life' or 'body life'. Once built, problems developed. He fought tooth, tong and nail to preserve his work. Why? I wonder. Why fight to preserve it? It will stand if it is Christ. If part of it stands, and that part is really Christ, then having nothing but that little part surviving is far better than a large work that has to be held together by reason, logic, theology, fear, accusation, doctrine or whatever. In my judgement, the worker might seriously consider stepping back, even out – dying to his work, letting the fire fall on that work and seeing just how much of it can survive.

16 April

Psalm 133:2   Ruth 1:16-18   Acts 2:42-47

There are many great success stories around, but those works very rarely reflect the bride of Jesus Christ. Sometimes she seems to be as elusive as her Lord. Rarely do you see her beautiful and whole, gathering somewhere in the city. Rarely will you ever gather in a place where you will sense the deep work of

Christ in the corporate body of people. Being with a people who have been made one ... and whose oneness – tested by the long trek of time – is found in nothing, absolutely nothing, but Christ. Such a people is rare, exotically rare. Rare because that glorious work which the Father did in the Son was so rare.

17 April

Psalm 69:20   Genesis 50:17-20   Luke 23:1-2

Another way to know that the Lord has gained some ground in your life: when you can accept criticism, even if viciously served, without a sense of resentment and with no need to retaliate.

Joseph said about his brothers, if you remember, that 'they meant it to me for evil but *God* meant it to me for good'.

18 April

Psalm 121   Proverbs 14:29-30   Matthew 10:24-27

Christian workers especially have a tendency to talk of anything that opposes their little world and their little work as being from the devil. (My, how much of that attitude I have witnessed in these last 30 years.) Such an accusation on the part of a worker, 'I'll tell you, this whole thing is of the devil,' surely makes it rough on the poor brother who is really causing the problem. He wakes up to find all his friends now thinking he's the devil ... or a reasonable facsimile.

It's an uncomfortable feeling, is it not, to be sitting out there in a meeting and hear that what you are doing is 'the devil's work'. I hope you survive; but frankly the chances are very slim that you will. Sure, I wish Christian workers wouldn't talk that way. Such talk has clubbered my blood for a generation. But they do. For centuries past they have and for whatever centuries lie ahead they will continue to. If the day comes that someone says of you, '*This* is of the devil', I admonish you, check your heart, check your mouth, check your motives. Get clean, get your motives pure, surrender your will, opinions, desires and hopes to the Lord. Then lift up your head to the hills and know that all things are permitted from the hand of the Lord. Sorrow, joy, hope and fear. Refuse to accept *even* this as from the hand of the Lord and chances are you will get bitter. A bitter Christian is a devastated Christian.

19 April

Psalm 119:8   Proverbs 3:5-6   Matthew 16:24

One brother wisely said, 'The cross is usually exactly the opposite of what we thought it was.'

When suffering comes your way, there is one thing that you certainly will do: you will ask the Lord, '*Why* has this happened?' There is something else almost as certain.

You will receive no answer.

If the 'why' could be removed, dear brother, most of the transforming power of the cross would disappear. The 'why' factor of the cross is perhaps its sharpest, most effective, most deadly aspect. Remove the 'why' factor of the cross and there really isn't much suffering involved in it.

20 April

Psalm 141:8   Daniel 3:14-18   Acts 12:1-7

Then what of those who are delivered, and delivered instantly from their sufferings? And what about this matter of exercising faith and therefore being delivered?

Sitting over there near you are two Christians. One is doing great, the other is in great pain; yet, the second seems to be just as worthy as the first. Why do his afflictions persist? Is it a lack of faith? What a quandary. What are we to believe? Of the two, who is closer to God? Has the afflicted brother failed in faith? Will the proper exercise of faith always triumph over affliction?

He who has been delivered by his faith has triumphed. He who is not delivered, yet faithfully (though weakly) yields – this one has also triumphed!

And if the truth is known, there is yet a third brother, the one who suffers and yet cannot find the strength to yield gloriously. He is only willing not to become bitter under the strong hand of God. He has no glorious story of healing or yielding, but it may just be that the pain he is going through is great enough and the work of God strong enough to penetrate past all his grumblings and groanings and change the inner man. Maybe, just maybe, even this one has triumphed!

21 April

Psalm 1:2-3   Isaiah 32:20   Matthew 24:32

I have observed through the years that most Christians have little understanding of the word 'season'. Our Lord is a seasonal God; He comes, He departs. His faithfulness never changes, but His seasons do! There are seasons when the tree is green, there are seasons when it is dry, and seasons when, for the life of us, the thing looks dead. Now, does this mean you are serving some capricious God who comes and goes by whim? Or, could it be, that it is only through *seasons* that true growth may come?

Paul said, 'Does not nature teach us?' Fruit from a tree comes to us as a result of three or four seasons.

The Christian *and* the Lord's body both need rain and sunshine, cold and hot, wind and doldrums.

22 April

Psalm 90:14   1 Kings 18:41-44   2 Timothy 4:2

Seasons of joy, seasons of sorrow, times when the Lord is so real it seems any activity you undertake is a spiritual experience.

Seasons of dryness, when things are so bleak that even a plateful of Sinai sand would be considered a feast! And are not these seasons from the hand of God? If so, what is His goal in the matter? He is taking you to that place where you can be a man for all seasons. Where seasons don't faze you ... no, not even the glorious ones. An old apostle said it so well to a young man. 'Be ready in season, be ready out of season.'

We are all very subject to seasons; yet these seasons are there to make us eventually seasonless. There is only one way you are ever going to learn to triumph over all seasons, and that is to go through each and every season ... many times. When you can reckon the sound of abundant rain and the hot blowing of a dry spell exactly the same, then you will be nearing the land of maturity.

23 April

Psalm 57   1 Samuel 27:1   James 5:13

A story about David, one of the authors of the Psalms. The angel Messenger takes Christian to meet David where he is squatting as a fugitive on a narrow ledge in the mountains.

'Wait here,' ordered Messenger.

Christian paused and looked down. They were on a narrow ledge high on a mountainside.

'Who goes there?' came a frightened cry.

'A friend,' replied the calm voice of Messenger.

'How did you find me? Do others know of this place?'

'Your secret is ours alone, and will remain so.'

'What do you want of me?' came a slightly more confident voice.

'A moment ago, as we approached, were you singing?' enquired Messenger of the man squatting in front of a small cave on the side of the mountain ledge.

'Yes, I often do. There is little else that I can do. Things I feel here, deep inside me – I often write them down.'

'That goatskin bag beside you – are your writings in there? I would like to show them to my young friend.'

Christian balanced himself carefully as he squatted precariously before the open bag of scrolls. One by one he opened them and read.

'It's the entire book of Psalms!' he declared, as he watched Messenger for some hint of explanation.

'No – not all of them. Perhaps one third.'

'Why have you shown them to me?'

'No great reason,' came the reply, as Messenger lifted the sack and turned away. 'Although,' he added almost as an afterthought, 'I thought you might be interested in seeing the music room in which they were penned.'

24 April

Psalm 102:1-4   2 Samuel 12:16-23   Hebrews 11:14-15

What can you do, in your hour of hurting, that might please your Lord? My guarded answer is: very little.

You can rejoice. That's one possibility. You can yield to Him. With joy you can offer up to Him the situation and say, 'Lord, I know this is from Your hand.' But the chances are you are not going to get anywhere near that. So what can you do in the midst of adversity? You can kneel; you can weep, and weep, and weep. *This* you can do.

There is one thing you must not do. Complain if you must, groan if you must, and get angry if you must. But oh, dear brother, stay far distant from bitterness, and from blaming others. Do that and you are dangerously close to forfeiting all future spiritual growth.

25 April

Psalm 37:37   Jeremiah 29:11   Mark 4:37-38

Is it possible to know if there is true brokenness in a man? I think so.

Such a man is not in rebellion toward anything:

1. nothing in his circumstances,
2. nothing that has to do with what other people inflict upon him,
3. and certainly not anything that God chooses to lay within his life.

He is at peace in all three circumstances.

26 April

Psalm 60:3   Isaiah 55:1-2   Matthew 9:17

Some of the wine they sipped was restored wine, and some of it was new wine, but for that little band of believers, *it was all new*.

Not one drop of that wine did they ever sip except by experience.

27 April

Psalm 41:9-13   Exodus 17:10-12   Colossians 1:23-25

If you become a worker, remember the words of that man there in that forsaken cell and make them your own: 'To suffer for the church, to suffer *in her place*, for this I was made a minister!'

On some future occasion when things are really getting rough you might remember those words. Keep reminding yourself of this, 'For *this* I was made a minister.'

28 April

Psalm 22:1-8   Isaiah 53:6-7   Matthew 5:11-12

The Lord did not complete His suffering. It has been given to the church to complete the sufferings of Christ. Suffering not yet filled up waits out there for you. You see, the body is also Christ. The body, which is the church, is part of that Christ. There is suffering out there yet to be endured, yet to be known, yet to be embraced by that part of Christ which is called the body. We all thank God that no one member of that body will ever have to know and endure all the sufferings that Jesus Christ experienced while living on earth. But each one of us – because we are in some mysterious way one with Him – will taste some part of His experience of suffering.

One within your fellowship may know *ridicule*. Another will partake of *physical* pain, another will know *rejection*, perhaps someone else may taste what it means to be *vilified* and verbally, socially crucified. And perhaps, just perhaps, there will be one within your fellowship who will touch that awful thing which Christ touched in that last moment on the cross: the dark night of the spirit.

There is one aspect of the cross that none of us will ever know – praise God! We will never know what it means to be the sin-bearer. That is one thing which I will never experience, nor will you. He and He alone has experienced that. He experienced the one thing that none of us should have escaped, and the one thing which He need never have known. He became the sin-bearer and thereby took suffering that was truly mine.

Now you must step into your place in the body of Christ, and you must receive and you must bear some segment of the suffering which is Christ's – that is, that part of Christ which is the church.

29 April

Psalm 3:3 Song of Songs 8:5-7 2 Corinthians 1:6-7; 2:4

If you ever see a great work of God,
something joyous,
alive and real,
something of Christ,
something that *is* Christ,
something enduring,
then you may be certain of one thing:
some lonely saint
silent, alone
went to the cross,
suffered, died
and fell into the earth.

And for what did that someone die?
for that lovely harvest,
that work of God
which now you see
and declare to be so beautiful.
There must be another day,
and another body of believers.
A day when someone else
must fall into the earth
and die.
And that someone may be you.

30 April

Psalm 18:41   1 Kings 18:42-43   Luke 22:41-44

If you cannot *cherish* what it is the Lord is doing in your life, at least do not *waste* what He is doing in your life. Lay down the self-pity, and with all the strength and grace that He allows you, yield to His work. If you cannot make it up within you to yield totally to your Gethsemane (most of us can't) then at least yield up to the light the dark feelings of resentment and bitterness that are trying to hatch inside you.

One day you are going to come to the conclusion that serving the Lord is mostly crying ... and suffering ... and agonising. What can you do in that sad hour? Nothing really, except bend over double and absorb into your being those sufferings, sufferings which really belong to the church. In that hour, bear her sufferings for her. And if you happen to look up, you will see her going on her way, gloriously rejoicing. She will be oblivious to the fact that she is, at that moment, so very glorious because you have suffered.

May
Crossroads

These readings are extracted mainly from three sources:

* *The Secret Jesus* by Aidan Clarke, which is about the role of the followers of Jesus in linking His presence and their world through prayer.
* *Inside the Mind of Unchurched Harry and Mary* by Lee Strobel, which deals with the difficulty that some Christians have in relating to ordinary people who happen not to be believers.
* *God: What the Critics Say*, edited by Martin Wroe, which is an anthology of quotations.

1 May

Psalm 38:15-17   Jeremiah 6:16   John 1:38-39

Go to the busiest crossroads you know, and try to notice everything: all the people, the cars, the buses, the colours, the noises, the clouds, the birds, the spaces. Notice the impatience.

Now picture the cross on which Jesus died as a crossroads of people, time and place; a physical crossroads through which at some time all people pass. Understand the cross as a meeting-place of all history with God, the source of all love, forgiveness and peace.

Aidan Clarke

Can You remember who I was?
Can You still feel it?
Can You find my pain?
Can You heal it?

Then lay Your hands upon me now
and take this darkness from my soul.
Only You can light my way;
only You can make me whole once again.

From Crossroads *by Don Maclean*

Remember in prayer all those who are at a particular crossroads in their own life, especially anyone close to you or with whom you have spoken in the last day or so.

Here is another prayer which can be said over and over again – perhaps with ten repetitions – at the crossroads, at home, or wherever you pray:

I praise You, Jesus,
Son of the living God.
The power of the Holy Spirit is with You to heal.
Blessed are Your death and resurrection;
and holy beyond all telling is the name of Jesus.
Holy Jesus, have mercy on us.
Fill us with grace and truth.
Give us power to become the children of God,
and protect us always and everywhere
by the loving power of the name of Jesus.
Amen.

Aidan Clarke

2 May

Psalm 44:8   Jeremiah 1:6-7   John 1:23, 29

What I believe about Jesus could not be contained in a thousand books. I believe in Jesus more than I believe in the pen with which I am writing these words. I cannot, however, expect you to believe my beliefs. Imagine you meet me in a café and I introduce you to a friend. I say, 'This is Jesus.' I do not then give you a list of things you must believe about his family and a thick book to memorise before I let you speak to him. I don't ask you to believe in him – because you can see him for yourself. I ask you only to trust him and to get to know him.

Aidan Clarke

3 May

Psalm 30:11   Jeremiah 2:9   Matthew 5:14-16

The witness of Aidan

One word, one light, one person,
one life He loved enough
for Him to die.
And the love that died,
His love that burns inside me,
impels me on the road
to seek for Christ in the stranger's face
or feel the absence of His touch.

Do you love Christ?
King Jesus, is He yours?
Then love God more,
and burn with love:
hold fast the light He gives.
Live thou for Him.
Believer, hold Him high,
that all may see the light of Jesus
in a son of man.

One word, one light, one person,
one life He loved enough
for Him to die.
And the love that died,
His love that burns inside me,
impels me on the road
to seek for Christ in the stranger's face
or feel the absence of His touch.

Do you love Christ?
King Jesus, is He yours?
God knows the emptiness:
deep cries to deep.
Receive the life He gives:
live now for Him.
Believe and be baptised,
then all will see
the life of Jesus in a son of man.

One word,
one light,
one person on the way.

Neil Arnold and Andy Raine

4 May

Psalm 33:18-22   Jeremiah 13:23   John 1:12

We need to clarify for the unchurched that intellectually believing in Christ is only part of the answer. One way is to use a Bible verse that provides a spiritual equation that spells out with math-like efficiency what it really means to become a Christian.

As I recite John 1:12, I ask them to listen for the active verbs: 'Yet to all who received him, to those who believed in His name, He gave the right to become children of God.'

Those verbs make up the equation: **believe + receive = become**.

To believe is intellectually to agree that Christ sacrificed Himself to pay for the wrongs we've committed. That's important, I tell them, but don't stop there. Some people sit in churches for years, stuck at this point, and they wonder why their spiritual life is stagnant. The next verb in the equation is critically important, too. We need to receive God's free offer of forgiveness and eternal life. We have to claim it for our own, because until we do that, it's not ours; it's just something we know about in our head. So it's necessary for us to admit our wrongdoing, turn away from it, and humbly accept Christ's payment on our behalf.

That makes sense, doesn't it? Jesus said, 'I have not come to call the righteous, but sinners.'

Lee Strobel

Faith is work.
It is a struggle.
You must struggle
with all your heart.
And on the way God
will ambush you.

Walter Wangerin, novelist

5 May

Psalm 68:35   Jeremiah 14:20-22   Luke 18:11

Christianity is the only co-operative society that exists for the benefit of non-members.

William Temple

'Tour-bus Christians' drive comfortably through life as they gaze out the window at others who are elbow-deep in the daily adventure of serving God and working among spiritually needy people.

Tour-bus Christians are insulated from the real-world activity and excitement of God's work. They may avoid some of the pain that's involved, and they may protect themselves from the difficulties and struggles, but there's no real adventure on a tour bus. They miss out on the excitement of living at the edge of expectation. They don't experience the tremendous counter-cultural truth that the more a Christian pours himself out serving others in God's name, the more God will fill him to overflowing. The adventure comes when you tell the tour bus to stop, and you jump off and say:

'Lord, I want to get into the fray. I want to play a role in the biggest adventure story of all time. Use me to make a difference. Use me to impact a young person for You. Use me to solve someone's problem. Use me to soothe someone's pain. Use me to answer someone's prayer. Use me to feed someone who's hungry. Use me to rescue a child. Use me to bring someone to You. Use me to ease someone's loneliness. Use me to raise a godly family.

'Use me to deepen someone's faith. Use me to cheer someone on. Use me to help a broken person understand that he's precious in Your sight. Use me to touch lives in Your name.

'I don't want to just observe cathedrals through my bus window; I want to roll up my sleeves and build one! Lord, use me to build a living cathedral dedicated to Your glory.'

Lee Strobel

6 May

Psalm 42:4-5   Jeremiah 23:18   Matthew 5:14-16

Many whom God has, the church does not have; and many whom the church has, God does not have.

Karl Rahner, theologian, parodying St Augustine

Who is the target of most of our communication of the gospel? Who are we seeking to reach? Some churches or ministries are 'seeker-driven', fashioning their approach to bring and effectively speak to secular individuals. They seek to reach unchurched non-Christians and turn them into devoted followers of Christ.

Sometimes the focus is unchurched Christians – those who claim a relationship with Jesus, but are not committed to any group of believers.

Another concern would be reaching churched unbelievers, individuals who attend a place of worship but for whatever reason remain untouched by the Gospel.

Then there are many churches whose main target, whether they want to admit it or not, is churched Christians. The content, language and style of all we present should be appropriate to our intended audience.

Lee Strobel

7 May

Psalm 71:1   Jeremiah 6:14   John 1:40-51

When we talk about Christianity being true the unchurched person of today shrugs with disinterest. 'You have your truth, I have mine.' What he wants to know is, 'Does it work?' We need to help him to understand the absolute and unchanging truth of Christ, but we should also explain how Christ is available to help him in practical ways to heal his hurts and help him deal with everyday living. We need to communicate that Christianity isn't just for the tomorrow of his eternity but also for the today of his life. Christianity does work.

The God of the Bible offers us supernatural wisdom and assistance in our struggles, difficulties, and recovery from past hurts. But we need to communicate that the reason it works is because it's true. Because Christ, at a point in history, had the power to overcome the grave, we can have access to that same kind of supernatural power to cope with the difficulties that face us day to day.

And because the Bible is God's revelation to His people, it contains a kind of practical and effective help that's unmatched by mere human philosophers.

Some people get mixed up in this area. One prominent nature worshipper in North Carolina says she doesn't want to hit a deer while driving at night, so:

As she sets out in her car, Anne imagines a blue light circling her vehicle clockwise three times, then silently chants, 'Three times around, three times about / a world within, a world without.' Then she adds a silent prayer to Artemis, a goddess of the hunt, 'to protect the deer and tell them I'm coming. I imagine this as a psychic warning system.' Anne believes wholeheartedly in this practice. 'It works!' she says. 'I have a friend who's hit twelve deer in five years. I've never hit one.'

Can you see how muddled thinking can lead to false conclusions? To deduce on the basis of a few missed deer that a belief system is valid turns logic on its head. As far as Christianity is concerned, we're not saying it's true because it works; we're saying Christianity is true and therefore it works.

Lee Strobel

8 May

Psalm 42:11   Jeremiah 21:8   2 Corinthians 11:3-4

Imagine your soul as being like the Tyne Bridge. There are busy times and quiet times. The job of the bridge is not to ask what is in the cars or lorries but simply to bear their weight for a few seconds and then allow them to go on their way. There is no problem when the flow of traffic is even, but when breakdowns and bottlenecks occur, the fights and the impatience begin. Your soul too has to take the weight and let it go. The suffering becomes prolonged only when you do not acknowledge its existence and let it pass on. Then it sits on your soul like a judgement.

The time to repair the bridge is in the night when the traffic is light. Your prayer in quiet times gives you the strength to cope with the heavy, busy times. You dig, patch and repair in the night. As a result the world can flow over your soul in the day without congestion. You must allow the flow of faith, love, healing, hope, joy and light to pass through you into the world. You must allow the flow of hatred, darkness and sin to flow from the world through you to God.

All of this is done by prayer, and by forgiveness of yourself, of others and perhaps even of God Himself for what you feel He has done to you. Little by little, you grow in the power of prayer, in the ability to bear the weight and accept the contradictions of the two-way flow between God and the world.

Aidan Clarke

9 May

Psalm 124:7   Jeremiah 24:7   Matthew 10:29, 31

Sit somewhere where you can see birds. (If that is not possible then imagine a crowd of seagulls in the sky, floating on the wind, wheeling, crying out their lonesome call of forgotten summers.) As you count the birds associate them each with the name of Jesus and the year of your life. The first bird you will tag 'Jesus, when I was 1' (or, if you prefer, do this in random order so it might be 'Jesus, when I was 17'). Whether you knew it or not Jesus was alongside you in every year of your life, and able to see without any distortion, but with full awareness of our joy and pain. He is with us now. If, as you label the birds and name the years, any hurtful event comes to mind, it is vital to lift it up and let it fly to God with as much love as you can manage in the name of Jesus.

Aidan Clarke and Andy Raine

Repeat or write the following prayer for yourself or for someone else:

Jesus, bless my conception.
Jesus, bless my time in the womb.

May the peace of the birth of Jesus be on my birth.
I present my whole being to Jesus.
May Jesus be in all the suffering of my life.
May Jesus heal me by His stripes.
Jesus, crown me with glory, praise, honour and thanksgiving.
Jesus, teach me to carry my cross and follow You.
Lord Jesus, receive my spirit.
Jesus, bless me in my daily death.
Jesus, bless me in my final death.
Jesus, give me a power of resurrection in each day of my life.
Jesus, be with me all my days.
Jesus, fill me with the Holy Spirit.
Jesus, lead me from earth to heaven.
Jesus, make me the person I am meant to be.

Aidan Clarke

10 May

Psalm 70:4   Jeremiah 29:13   Matthew 27:55

I read a story about a boy who lost a dog in New York City. As he walked up and down the streets, systematically and slowly, a friend complained that he wasn't even looking for the dog.

He answered, 'I'm not looking for him. I'm letting him find me. Sooner or later he will discover the trail I am putting down and follow it until he comes to me.'

In the same way, Jesus is not looking for converts. He has set down a trail which different people pick up at different points and follow until they find Him. The person who prays is also not looking for converts but setting down a track which others will find and follow to Jesus. Maybe a perfect evangelist is one whose work and love is never recognised, who is never acknowledged or thanked by anyone this side of the grave. May Jesus bless the millions who pray in secret.

Aidan Clarke

11 May Comgall *(see p.231)*

Psalm 60:4　Micah 5:2　Luke 24:32

I read Isaiah 53 in the Old Testament and found it to be an absolutely uncanny description of Jesus being crucified – and yet it was written more than 700 years before the fact. In all, there are about five dozen major prophecies concerning the Messiah, and the more I studied them, the more difficulty I had in trying to explain them away.

My first line of defence was that Jesus may have intentionally manoeuvred His life to fulfil the prophecies so that He would be mistaken for the long-awaited Messiah. For instance, Zechariah 9:9 foretold that the Messiah would ride a donkey into Jerusalem. Maybe when Jesus was getting ready to enter the town, He told His disciples, 'Go fetch me a donkey. I want to fool these people into thinking I'm the Messiah because I'm really anxious to be tortured to death!'

But that argument fell apart when I read prophecies about events that Jesus never could have arranged, such as the place of His birth, which the prophet Micah foretold 700 years in advance, and His ancestry, how He was born, how He was betrayed for a specific amount of money, how He was put to death, how His bones remained unbroken (unlike the two criminals who were crucified with Him), how the soldiers cast lots for His clothing, and on and on.

That was impressive enough. Stoner analysed forty-eight prophecies. His conclusion was that there would be one chance in ten to the 157th power that they would come true in any one person in history. That's a number with 157 zeros behind it!

I did some research and learned that atoms are so small that it takes a million of them lined up to equal the width of a human hair. I also interviewed scientists about their estimate of the number of atoms in the entire known universe. I concluded that the odds of forty-eight Old Testament prophecies coming true in any one individual are the same as a person randomly finding a single predetermined atom among all the atoms in a trillion trillion trillion trillion billion universes the size of our universe!

Jesus said He came to fulfil the prophecies. He said, 'Everything must be fulfilled that is written about Me in the Law of Moses, the Prophets and the Psalms.'

Lee Strobel

12 May

Psalm 49:15   Job 19:25   1 Corinthians 15:3-8

The evidence for the resurrection is that Jesus was killed by crucifixion and was stabbed with a spear; He was wrapped in bandages containing seventy-five pounds of spices; He was placed in a tomb; a huge rock was rolled in front of the entrance (according to one ancient account, so big that twenty men couldn't move it); and the tomb was guarded by highly disciplined soldiers.

Yet, three days later the tomb was discovered empty, and eye-witnesses proclaimed to their death that Jesus had appeared to them.

Who had a motive to steal the body? The disciples weren't about to conceal it so they could be tortured to death for lying about it. The Jewish and Roman leaders would have loved to have paraded the body up and down Main Street in Jerusalem; certainly that would have instantly killed this budding religion that they had spent so much time trying to squelch.

But what happened is that over a period of forty days, Jesus appeared alive twelve different times to more than 512 people: to sceptics like Thomas and James, and sometimes to groups, sometimes to individuals, sometimes indoors, sometimes outdoors in broad daylight. He talked with people and even ate with them. Several years later, when the apostle Paul mentioned that there had been eyewitnesses to the resurrection, he noted that many of them were still alive, as if to say to first-century doubters, 'Go confirm it with them if you don't believe me.'

In fact, if you were to call to the witness-stand every person who actually saw the resurrected Jesus, and if you were to cross-examine each one of them for only fifteen minutes, and if you did this around the clock without any breaks, you would be listening to first-hand testimony for more than five solid days.

Lee Strobel

13 May

Psalm 23:1-4   Deuteronomy 32:1-4, 9-10   James 2:23

There is a friend that sticks closer than a brother.

Proverbs 18:24

God is my best friend.
He cares about the things I care about.
He loves me even when I'm unlovable.
He is always there to listen and advise;
when I need to talk things over.

God is my heavenly Father.
He holds me in the palm of His hand.
He watches over me as the apple of His eye.
He wants me to grow up to be like Him.

God is my rock.
He is my refuge when I'm afraid,
my strength when I am weak,
my sure footing when I stumble.

God is my shepherd.
He finds me when I'm lost.

He gives me rest when I'm tired.
He leads me when I don't know
which way to go.

Sally Jo Shelton

14 May William Walcher *(see p.263)* Elfwy *(see p.235)*

Psalm 70:5   Hosea 14:9   Matthew 9:10-12

God is my physician.
He mends my heart when it is broken.
He restores my peace of mind when I'm upset.
He heals my body when I'm sick.

God is my Saviour.
He forgives me when I let Him down.
He delivers me when I'm in danger.
He saves me even from
the trouble I bring on myself.

God is my source.
He is my bread when I'm hungry,
my water fountain when I'm thirsty,
my bank when I'm broke.

God is my Lord.
He is the Ruler of my thoughts,
the inspiration of my words,
the initiator of my actions.

God is my everything.
Who is He to you?

Sally Jo Shelton

All your creatures

15 May

Psalm 148:7-13   Genesis 9:12-17   1 Corinthians 13:1; 14:7

> All God's children got a place in the choir;
> some sing low, some sing higher,

Creation in all its fascinating variety, each creature in its uniqueness, and human souls at prayer: woven in a complex pattern of interdependence...

> Let only Your will be done in me,
> as in all Your creatures.

Charles de Foucauld,
'Prayer of Abandonment'

The purpose of living is not to learn to make prayer, but to become prayer; to live in and for God according to the divine call, wholly surrendered to the Spirit's activity in the soul for the glory of God.

Fr Gilbert Shaw

16 May Brendan *(see p.226)*

Psalm 84:11   Jeremiah 31:18-19   Matthew 22:37

> PRAYER
> is the turning of our whole mind,
> our whole being,
> towards God.

Fr Gilbert Shaw

17 May

Psalm 84:2, 12   Proverbs 17:17   Luke 10:30, 33-34

Healing prayer

At every moment of our existence
You are present to us, Father,
in gentle compassion.
Help us to be present
to one another,
so that our presence
may be a strength
that heals the wounds of time
and gives hope that is for all persons
through Jesus, our Lord and Brother.

Weston Priory, Vermont

18 May

Psalm 84:3, 5   Genesis 28:11-12   John 4:34-36

He is my King;
in my heart He's hid.
He is my joy all joys amid.
I am a drop in His ocean lost
His coracle I, on His wide sea tost,
a leaf in His storm.

The book of His praise
in my wallet slung,
the cloak of His friendship round me flung,
hither and thither about I'm blown,
my way an eddy, my rest a stone,
and He my fire.

My meat His work
and my drink His will,

He is my song, my strength, my skill,
and all men my lovers in good and ill,
through Him my desire.

Marjorie Milne of Glastonbury,
Rhymes from a Lindisfarne Monk

19 May

Psalm 18:6, 10-11   Malachi 4:2   John 14:1-6

In the crack of the wind
I trace His feet;
and none in His coming was e'er so fleet,
so sweet.
Often my heart is a heavy stone
mock'd, trodden under
and spat upon,
my way a mirk and I alone,
alone:

Then in my heart flames
a climbing star
as His pilgrim feet come flashing far
to bring me where the blessèd are.
By Him I am fed, and healed and shriven;
He is the cleft in the dark sky riven
whereby I may leap to the bending heav'n
through the storm.

Marjorie Milne of Glastonbury,
Rhymes from a Lindisfarne Monk

20 May

Psalm 23:2-4   Genesis 22:7-8   Hebrews 13:12-13

The lambs were weary and crying
with a weak, human cry.
I thought on the Lamb of God
going meekly to die.

Up in the blue, blue mountains
dewy pastures are sweet,
rest for the little bodies,
rest for the little feet.

But for the Lamb, the Lamb of God,
up on the hill-top green,
only a Cross, a cross of wood,
two stark crosses between.

All in the April evening,
April airs were abroad;
I saw the sheep with their lambs
and thought on the Lamb of God.

Katharine Tynan Hinkson,
'All in the April Evening'

21 May   Godric *(see p.239)*

Psalm 22:2   Job 5:7   Revelation 4:8

Let God's name be glorified
and held in honour
in the world He chose to create.
May He establish His Kingdom
in our lives each day
and in the days ahead.
May His Kingdom come quickly

and without delay.
Amen. Let it be so.

May His great name be praised for ever,
glorified, exalted, honoured and proclaimed.
May His name, the name of the Holy One,
be praised, and recognised in all its greatness.
Bless God whose glory is beyond all blessing,
past our ability to praise.
His glory touches us more deeply
than any word of consolation in this world.
Amen.

Let there be great peace from heaven
upon us and all God's people.
Amen. Let it be so.

May He who sends peace from heaven
cover us with peace,
and give peace to all His people.
Amen. Let it be so.

*Adapted from the Kaddish, a Jewish prayer said
often during the first year of a bereavement*

In *A Jew Today* by Elie Wiesel the one remaining member of a Jewish family says to God:

Master of the Universe, I know what You want – I understand what You are doing. You want despair to overwhelm me. You want me to cease believing in You, to cease praying to You, to cease invoking Your name to glorify and sanctify it. Well, I tell You: No, no – a thousand times no! You shall not succeed! In spite of me and in spite of You, I shall shout the Kaddish, which is a song of faith, for You and against You. This song You shall not still, God of Israel.

We pray to God because He has too much to answer for to be allowed simply to disappear, because we have to protest against Him as well as to Him, and because the only alternative is despair, or silence.

22 May

Psalm 148:7-13   Job 38:4-7   Romans 1:19-20

My dear King, my own King,
without pride, without sin,
you created the whole world,
eternal, victorious King.
King of the Mysteries,
You existed before the elements,
before the sun was set in the sky,
before the waters covered the ocean floor;
beautiful King,
You are without beginning and without end.

King, You created the land out of shapeless mass,
You carved the mountains and chiselled the valleys,
and covered the earth with trees and grass.
King, You measured each object
and each span within the universe:
the heights of the mountains
and the depths of the oceans;
the distance from the sun to the moon,
and from star to star.

And You created men and women
to be Your stewards of the earth,
always praising You for Your boundless love.

From The Celtic Psalter (ninth century)

Gift from the sea

The rest of May's readings are from *Gift from the Sea* by Anne Morrow Lindbergh.

23 May

Psalm 130:6   Lamentations 3:25-26   Matthew 11:28-30

> The beach is not the place to work; to read, write or think. I should have remembered that from other years.
>
> Hopefully, one carries down the faded straw bag, lumpy with books, clean paper, long-overdue unanswered letters, freshly-sharpened pencils, lists and good intentions. The books remain unread, the pencils break their points, and the pads rest smooth, unblemished as the cloudless sky. No reading, no writing, no thoughts even – at least, not at first. One becomes, in fact, like the element on which one lies, flattened by the sea: bare, open, empty as the beach erased by today's tides of all yesterday's scribblings.
>
> The mind begins to drift, to play, to turn over in gentle careless rolls like those lazy waves on the beach. One never knows what chance treasures these easy unconscious rollers may toss up on the smooth white sand of the conscious mind. But it must not be fought for or – heaven forbid! – dug for. No, no dredging of the sea bottom here: that would defeat one's purpose. The sea does not reward those who are too anxious, too greedy or too impatient. To dig for treasures shows not only impatience and greed, but lack of faith. Patience, patience, patience is what the sea teaches.
>
> Patience and faith. One should lie empty, open, choiceless as a beach – waiting for a gift from the sea.

24 May

Psalm 121:1-2   Jeremiah 32:28-41   Romans 7:22-25

I want singleness of eye, a purity of intention, a central core to my life that will enable me to carry out all my obligations and activities as well as I can. I want, in fact – to borrow from the language of the saints – to live 'in grace' as much of the time as possible. I am not using this term in a strictly theological sense: by grace I mean an inner harmony, essentially spiritual, which can be translated into outward harmony. I am seeking, perhaps, what Socrates asked for in the prayer from the *Phaedrus* when he said, 'May the outward and inward man be one.' I would like to achieve a state of inner spiritual grace from which I could function and give as I was meant to in the eyes of God.

There are times when one seems to carry all one's tasks before one lightly, as if borne along on a great tide. And in the opposite state one can hardly tie a shoe-string. It is true that a large part of life consists in learning a technique of tying the shoe-string – whether one is 'in grace' or not.

I believe most people are aware of periods in their lives when they seem to be 'in grace' and other periods when they feel 'out of grace', even though they may use different words to describe these states.

25 May

Psalm 16:5-8   2 Kings 4:4-5   John 4:14

Certain environments, certain modes of life, certain rules of conduct are more conducive to inner and outer harmony than others. There are, in fact, certain roads that one may follow. Simplification of life is one of them.

I mean to follow a simple life. But I do not. I find that my form of life does not foster simplicity: the life I have chosen as wife and mother entrains a whole caravan of complications. It involves food and shelter, meals, planning, marketing, bills and making ends meet in a thousand ways. It involves friends, my husband's, my children's and my own, and endless arrangements to get together: letters, invitations, telephone calls and transportation hither and yon.

What a circus act we women perform every day of our lives. It puts the trapeze artist to shame. Look at us! This is not the life of simplicity, but the life of multiplicity that the wise warn us of. It leads not to unification but to fragmentation.

Distraction is, always has been, and probably always will be, inherent in women's lives. We must be open to all points of the compass; husband, children, friends, home, community; stretched out, exposed like a spider's web to each breeze that blows, to each call that comes. How difficult for us, then, to achieve a balance in the midst of these contradictory tensions; and yet how necessary for the proper functioning of our lives. How much we need, and how arduous of attainment is that steadiness preached in all rules of holy living. How desirable and distant is the ideal of the contemplative, artist, or saint – the inner inviolable core, the single eye.

With new awareness, both painful and humorous, I begin to understand why the saints were rarely married women. I am convinced it has nothing inherently to do, as I once supposed, with chastity or children. It has to do primarily with distractions. The bearing, rearing, feeding and educating of children; the running of a house with its thousand details; human relationships with their myriad pulls – women's normal occupations in general run counter to creative life, or contemplative life, or saintly life.

Woman instinctively wants to give, yet resents giving herself in small pieces. I believe that what she resents is not so much giving herself in pieces as giving herself purposelessly. What we fear is not so much that our energy may be leaking away through small outlets as that it may be going 'down the drain'. Purposeful giving is not as apt to deplete one's resources: it belongs to that natural order of giving that seems to renew itself even in the act of depletion. The more one gives, the more one has to give – like milk in the breast.

26 May Bede *(see p.224)*

Psalm 43:3-4   Proverbs 25:4   Romans 12:2

The problem is: how to remain in the midst of the distractions of life; how to remain balanced, no matter what centrifugal forces tend to pull one off centre; how to remain strong, no matter what shocks come in at the periphery and tend to crack the hub of the wheel. What is the answer? There is no easy answer; no complete answer. I have only clues – shells from the sea.

One answer, and perhaps a first step, is in the simplification of life; in cutting out some of the distractions. But how? Total retirement is not possible. I cannot permanently inhabit a desert island. I cannot be a nun in the midst of family life. I would not want to be. The solution for me, surely, is neither in total renunciation of the world, nor in total acceptance of it. I must find a balance somewhere, or an alternating rhythm between these two extremes: a swinging of the pendulum between solitude and communion, between retreat and return. In my periods of retreat, perhaps I can learn something to carry back into my worldly life.

One cannot collect all the beautiful shells on the beach. One can collect only a few; and they are more beautiful if they are few. My life at home, I begin to realise, lacks this quality of significance, and therefore of beauty, because there is so little empty space. The space is scribbled on; the time has been filled. There are so few empty pages in my engagement pad, or empty hours in the day, or empty rooms in my life in which to stand alone and find myself. Too many activities, and people, and things. Too many worthy activities, valuable things and interesting people. For it is not merely the trivial that clutters our lives, but the important as well. We can have a surfeit of treasures and excess of shells – where one or two would be significant.

27 May

Psalm 131   1 Samuel 16:7   Matthew 23:26-28

It is a difficult lesson to learn today – to leave one's friends and family and deliberately practise the art of solitude for an hour, or a day, or a week. For me, the break is the most difficult. Parting is inevitably painful, even for a short time. It is like an amputation, I feel. A limb being torn off, without which I shall be unable to function. And yet, once it is done, I find there is a quality to being alone that is incredibly precious. Life rushes back into the void, richer, more vivid, fuller than before. It is as if, in parting, one did actually lose an arm. And then, like the starfish, one grows it anew; one is whole again, complete and round – more whole, even, than before.

28 May

Psalm 143:6-8   Isaiah 55:1-3   John 16:32

It is not the desert island, nor the stony wilderness, that cuts you off from the people you love: it is the wilderness in the mind, the desert wastes in the heart through which one wanders lost – a stranger to oneself and estranged from others too. If one is out of touch with oneself, then one cannot touch others. How often in a large city, shaking hands with my friends, I have felt the wilderness stretching between us. Both of us were wandering in arid wastes, having lost the springs that nourished us, or having found them dry. Only when one is connected to one's own core is one connected to others, I am beginning to discover. And for me the core, the inner spring, can best be refound through solitude.

We are all, in the last analysis, alone. How one hates to think of oneself as alone. How one avoids it – it seems to imply rejection or unpopularity.

We seem so frightened today of being alone that we never let it happen. Even if family, friends and movies should fail, there is still the radio or television to fill up the void.

Women, who used to complain of loneliness, need never be alone any more. We can do our housework with soap-opera heroes at our side. Even day-dreaming was more creative than this: it demanded something of oneself and it fed the inner life. Now, instead of planting our own dream blossoms, we choke the space with continuous music, chatter and companionship to which we do not even listen. It is simply there to fill the vacuum. When the noise stops there is no inner music to take its place.

We must re-learn to be alone.

29 May

Psalm 23:1-3   Micah 7:14-15   John 12:43

If it is our function to give, we must be replenished too. But how? Everyone should be alone sometime during the year, some part of each week, and each day. If they were convinced that a day off, or an hour of solitude, was a reasonable ambition, they would find a way of attaining it. As it is, they feel so unjustified in this demand that they rarely make an attempt.

The world does not understand, in either man or woman, the need to be alone. How inexplicable it seems. Anything else will be accepted as a better excuse. If one sets aside time for a business appointment, a trip to the hairdresser, a social engagement, or a shopping expedition, that time is accepted as inviolable. But if one says: I cannot come because that is my hour to be alone, one is considered rude, egotistical or strange. What a commentary on our civilisation, when being alone is considered suspect; when one has to apologise for it, make excuses, hide the fact that one practises it – like a secret vice!

Certain springs are tapped only when we are alone. The artist knows he must be alone to create; the writer, to work out his thoughts; the musician to compose; the saint, to pray.

The problem is not entirely in finding the room of one's own, the time alone, difficult and necessary as this is. The problem is more how to still the soul in the midst of its activities. In fact the problem is how to feed the soul. I must try to be alone for part of each year, even a week or a few days; and for part of each day, even an hour or a few minutes, in order to keep my core, my centre, my island-quality. Unless I keep the island-quality intact somewhere within me, I will have little to give my husband, my children, my friends or the world at large.

30 May

Psalm 39:5-7   Jeremiah 17:7-8   Ephesians 4:22-24

The tide of life recedes. The house, with its bulging sleeping porches and sheds, begins little by little to empty. The children go away to school and then to marriage and lives of their own. Most people by middle age have attained, or ceased to struggle to attain, their place in the world. That terrific tenacity to life, to place, to people, to material surroundings and accumulations: is it as necessary as it was when one was struggling for security or the security of one's children? Many of the physical struggles have ceased, due either to success or failure. Does the shell need to be so welded to its rock? Married couples are apt to find themselves in middle age, high and dry in an outmoded shell, in a fortress which has outlived its function.

Perhaps middle age is, or should be, a period of shedding shells: the shell of ambition, the shell of material accumulations and possessions, the shell of the ego. Perhaps one can shed, at this stage in life one's pride, one's false ambitions, one's mask, one's armour. Was that armour not put on to protect one from the competitive world? If one ceases to compete, does one need it? Perhaps one can at last in middle age, if not earlier, be completely oneself; and what a liberation that would be!

So beautiful is the still hour of the sea's withdrawal, as beautiful as the sea's return when encroaching waves pound up the beach, pressing to reach those dark rumpled chains of seaweed which mark the last high tide.

We have so little faith in the ebb and flow of life, of love, of relationships. We leap at the flow of the tide and resist in terror its ebb. We are afraid it will never return. We insist on permanence, on duration, on continuity; when the only continuity possible, in life as in love, is in growth, in fluidity – in freedom in the sense that dancers are free, barely touching as they pass, but partners in the same pattern. The only real security is not in owning or possessing, not in demanding or expecting, not in hoping even. Security in a relationship lies neither in looking back to what it was in nostalgia, nor forward to what it might be in dread or anticipation, but living in the present relationship and accepting it as it is now.

31 May

Psalm 147:4-5   Genesis 26:12   Matthew 13:32

When we start at the centre of ourselves, we discover something worthwhile extending toward the periphery of the circle. We find again some of the joy in the now, some of the peace in the here, some of the love in me and thee which go to make up the kingdom of heaven on earth.

The waves echo behind me. Patience – Faith – Openness are what the sea has to teach; Simplicity – Solitude – Intermittency. But there are other beaches to explore. There are more shells to find. This is only a beginning.

June
Desert Fathers

The sayings of the Desert Fathers and Mothers are our topic this month.

No introduction is really necessary as their words speak for themselves.

As an old Pentecostal preacher used to say:

Watch the witness, brother –
watch for the witness!

Of the books about the lives and sayings of the Desert Fathers one of the best is *The Wisdom of the Desert* by Thomas Merton.

1 June

Psalm 103:1-5   Isaiah 43:18-21   2 Corinthians 5:16-17

Abba Poemen said about Abba Pior that every single day he made a fresh beginning.

Abbot Joseph asked Abbot Pastor: 'Tell me how I can become a monk.'
  The Elder replied: 'If you want to have rest here in this life and also in the next, in every conflict with another say, "Who am I?" and judge no one.'

2 June

Psalm 6   Exodus 21:12-24   Matthew 5:38-48

Abba Isaiah said:

> When someone wishes to render evil for evil, he is able to hurt his brother's conscience even by a single nod.

A brother who was insulted by another brother came to Abba Sisois and said to him:

'I was hurt by my brother, and I want to avenge myself.'

The old man tried to console him and said: 'Do not do that, my child. Rather leave vengeance to God.'

But he said: 'I will not quit until I avenge myself.'

Then the old man said: 'Let us pray, brother.' And standing up he said: 'O God, we no longer need you to take care of us since we now avenge ourselves.'

Hearing these words, the brother fell at the feet of the old man and said: 'I am not going to fight with my brother any more. Forgive me, Abba.'

3 June   Kevin *(see p.246)*

Psalm 57   Jeremiah 17:9-10   Luke 21:8-15

They said of one monk that the more anyone despised or vexed him, the more he would run towards them saying:

> Such men are a cause for progress for zealous people; while those who praise deceive and trouble the soul. Indeed, it is written, 'Those who call you blessed are deceiving you.'

Abba Antony said:

> The time is coming when people will be insane, and when they see someone who is not insane they will attack that person, saying: 'You are insane, because you are not like us.'

4 June   Eadfrith *(see p.234)*   Petroc (Pedrog) *(see p.256)*

Psalm 131   Nehemiah 1:4-11   Luke 17:7-10

They said of Abbot Pambo that in the very hour when he departed this life he said to the holy men who stood by him:

> From the time I came to this place in the Desert, and built me a cell, and dwelt here, I do not remember eating bread that was not earned by the work of my own hands – nor do I remember saying anything for which I was sorry, even until this hour.
>
> And thus I go to the Lord as one who has not even made a beginning in the service of God.

5 June

Psalm 12   Ecclesiastes 5:10-15   Matthew 5:38-42

Once some robbers came into the monastery and said to one of the Elders: 'We have come to take everything that is in your cell.'
And he said; 'My sons, take all you want.'
So they took everything they could find in the cell and started off. But they left behind a little bag that was hidden in the cell, the Elder picked it up and followed after them, crying out: 'My sons, take this, you forgot it in the cell.'
Amazed at the patience of the Elder, they brought everything back into the cell, and did penance, saying: 'This one really is a man of God.'

6 June

Psalm 111   1 Samuel 30:21-25   Luke 12:22-34

One of the Elders had finished his baskets and had already put handles on them, when he heard his neighbour saying: 'What shall I do? The market is about to begin and I have nothing with which to make handles for my baskets.'

At once the Elder went in and took off his handles, giving them to the brother with the words: 'Here, I don't need these, take them and put them on your own baskets.'

Thus in his great charity he saw to it that his brother's work was finished whilst his own remained incomplete.

7 June

Psalm 104:10-30   Ecclesiastes 3:1-14   Luke 7:31-35

Once Abbot Antony was conversing with some brethren, and a hunter who was after game in the wilderness came upon them. He saw Abbot Antony and the brothers enjoying themselves, and disapproved. Abbot Antony said: 'Put an arrow in your bow and shoot it.'

This he did.

'Now shoot another,' said the Elder. 'And another, and another.'

Then the hunter said: 'If I bend my bow all the time it will break.'

Abbot Antony replied: 'So it is also in the work of God. If we push ourselves beyond measure, the brethren will soon collapse. It is right therefore, from time to time, to relax.'

8 June

Psalm 106:24-27   Exodus 16:1-3   Mark 8:14-21

One of the Elders used to say:

> In the beginning when we got together we used to talk about something that was good for our own souls, and we went up and up, and ascended even to heaven.
>
> But now we get together and spend our time in criticising everything and we drag one another down into the abyss.

9 June   Columba *(see p.230)*

Psalm 51:1-12   Job 9:14-15   John 8:1-11

There was a fornicating monk who kept a woman in his cell, so indiscreetly that word began to get around about it. Some of the monks living nearby decided to do something about it, and they asked Abba Ammonas who was visiting the region to go with them.

The offending monk, seeing them coming, hid the woman in a large water jar. This was spotted by the Abba when they all went into the cell. The Abba sat on the jar, while the others searched the room. They could find nothing, and went away ashamed. When they had gone the Abba got up and took the culprit's hand and simply said to him: 'Brother, pay attention to yourself.'

10 June

Psalm 52   Amos 5:21-24   Matthew 7:21-23

Abba Agatho used to say:

> If you are able to revive the dead, but not be willing to be reconciled to your neighbour – it is better to leave the dead in the grave.

There was a certain Elder who, if anyone maligned him, would go in person to offer him presents, if he lived nearby. And if he lived at a distance he would send presents by the hand of another.

11 June

Psalm 127:1-2   Zechariah 13:7-9   1 Corinthians 3:5-15

As the Elders said:

> The reason why we do not get anywhere is that we do not know our limits, and we are not patient in carrying out the work we have begun. But without any labour at all we want to gain possession of virtue.

Abba Pastor said:

> The virtue of a monk is made manifest by temptations.

12 June

Psalm 25:8-15   Deuteronomy 6:10-25   Luke 23:34

Abba Pastor said:

> A man must breathe humility and the fear of God just as ceaselessly as he inhales and exhales air.

Abba Alonius said:

> Humility is the land where God wants us to go and offer sacrifice.

One of the Elders was asked: 'What is humility?' He answered: 'If you forgive a brother who has injured you before he himself asks pardon.'

A brother asked another of the Elders: 'What is humility?'

The Elder answered him: 'To do good to those who do evil to you.'

The brother asked: 'Supposing a man can't go that far, what should he do?'

The Elder replied: 'Let him get away from them and keep his mouth shut.'

13 June

Psalm 132:1-5   Proverbs 12:11   Luke 10:38-42

A brother came to visit Abba Sylvanus at Mount Sinai. When he saw the brothers working hard, he said to the old man: 'Do not work for food that perishes, for Mary has chosen the good part.'

Then the old man called to his disciple: 'Zachary, give this brother a book, and put him in an empty cell.'

Now when it was three o'clock the brother kept looking out of the door to see if someone would call him for the meal. But nobody called him, so he got up, went to the old man, and asked: 'Abba, didn't the brothers eat today?'

The old man replied: 'Of course we did!'

'Then why didn't you call me?' he asked.

The old man replied: 'You are a spiritual person, and do not need that type of food; but since we are earthly, we want to eat, and that's why we work. Indeed, you have chosen the good part reading all day long, and not wanting to eat earthly food.'

When the brother heard this he repented: 'Forgive me, Abba.'

Then the old man said to him: 'Mary certainly needed Martha, and it is really by Martha's help that Mary is praised.'

14 June

Psalm 53:1-4   Job 11:14-15   2 Corinthians 9:6-15

Once some brethren went out to visit the hermits who lived in the desert. They came to one who received them with joy, and seeing they were tired, invited them to eat before the accustomed time, and placed before them all the food he had available.

But that night when they were all supposed to be sleeping the hermit heard the visitors saying: 'These hermits eat more than we do.'

Now at dawn the visitors set out to see another hermit – and as they were starting out their host said: 'Greet him from me, and give him this message: Be careful not to water the vegetables.'

When they reached the other hermitage they delivered this message. The second hermit understood what was meant by the words. So he made the visitors sit down and weave baskets, and sitting with them he worked without interruption. And in the evening when the time came for lighting the lamp, he added a few extra psalms to the usual number, after which he said to them: 'We do not usually eat every day out here. But because you have come along it is fitting to have a little supper today for a change.'

Then he gave them some dry bread and salt, then added: 'Here's a special treat for you.'

Upon which he mixed them a little sauce of vinegar, salt and oil, and gave it to them. After supper they got up again and said more psalms, and kept praying till almost dawn, at which the hermit said: 'Well, we can't finish all our usual prayers – for you are tired from your journey. You had better take a little rest.'

And so when the first hour came they all wanted to leave the hermit – but he would not let them go. He kept saying: 'Stay with me a while. I cannot let you go so soon, charity demands that I keep you for two or three days.'

But they, hearing this, waited until dark, and then under cover of night they made off.

15 June

Psalm 37:1-11   Song of Songs 2:8-17   Luke 22:45-46

A certain brother went to Abbot Moses in Scete, and asked him for a good word. And the Elder said to him:

Go, sit in your cell
and your cell will teach you everything.

An Elder said:

The monk's cell is that furnace of Babylon in which the three children found the Son of God. But it is also the pillar of cloud out of which God spoke to Moses.

16 June

Psalm 19:7-11   Amos 6:1-7   James 1:22-25

Abbot Pastor said:

If you have a chest full of clothing, and leave it for a long time, the clothing will rot inside of it.

It is the same with the thoughts in our heart. If we do not carry them out by physical action, after a long while they will spoil and turn bad.

17 June

Psalm 98:1-3   Genesis 28:13-15   Matthew 6:25-34

One of the brothers asked an Elder, saying: 'Would it be all right if I kept two pence in my possession, in case I should get sick?'

The Elder, seeing his thoughts, and that he wanted to keep them, said: 'Keep them.'

The brother going back to his cell, began to wrestle with his own thoughts saying: 'I wonder if the father gave me his blessing or not?'

Rising up he went back to him: 'In God's Name, tell me the truth, because I am all upset over these two pence.'

The Elder said to him: 'Since I saw your thoughts and your desire to keep them, I told you to keep them. But it is not good to keep more than we need for our body. Now these two pence are your hope. If they should be lost, would not God take care of you?'

Cast your care on the Lord, then, for He will take care of us.

18 June

Psalm 139:1-18   Judges 16:20-22   Luke 12:1-7

One of the Fathers said:

> Just as it is impossible for a man to see his face in troubled water, so too the soul unless it be cleansed from alien thoughts cannot pray to God in contemplation.

Another of the Elders said:

> When the eyes of an ox or mule are covered, then he goes round and round turning the mill wheel. But if his eyes are uncovered he will not go round in the circle of the mill wheel. So, too, the devil if he manages to cover the eyes of a man can humiliate him in every sin. But if that man's eyes are not closed he can easily escape the devil.

19 June

Psalm 1:1-3   Deuteronomy 6:4-6   Luke 19:11-27

A brother asked one of the Elders: 'What good thing shall I do?'

The old man replied: 'God alone knows what is good. However I heard it said that someone inquired of Abbot Nisteros, a friend of Abbot Anthony, and asked: "What good work shall I do?" And that he replied: "Not all works are alike. For scripture says that Abraham was hospitable and God was with him. Elijah loved solitary prayer and God was with him. And David was humble and God was with him. Therefore, whatever you see your soul desire according to God, do that thing and you shall keep your heart safe."'

20 June

Psalm 25:8-12   Jeremiah 9:1-6   Luke 14:7-11

Abba John the Little said:

> We have abandoned a light burden, namely self-criticism, and taken up a heavy burden, namely self-justification.

Abba Silvanus said:

> Woe to the person whose reputation is greater than his work.

A brother came to see Abba Theodore, and started to talk and inquire about things which he himself had not tried yet. The old man said to him:

> You have not found a boat, or put your gear into it, and you haven't even sailed – but you seem to have arrived in the city already! Well, do your work first; then you will come to the point you are talking about now.

21 June

Psalm 50:7-23   Hosea 6:4-6   Luke 12:1-4

Once the Rule was made in Scete that they should fast for the entire week before Easter. During this week, however, some brothers came from Egypt to see Abba Moses, and he made a modest meal for them.

Seeing the smoke, the neighbours said to the priests of the church at that place: 'Look, Moses has broken the Rule and is cooking food at his place.'

Then the priests said ... 'When he comes out we will talk to him.'

When the Sabbath came the priests, who knew Abba Moses' great way of life, said to him in public: 'Oh, Abba Moses, you did break the commandment made by the people – but you have firmly kept the commandment of God!'

22 June

Psalm 51:3-6   Isaiah 55:6-7   Matthew 9:9-13

Abba Milos was asked by a soldier whether God could forgive a sinner. After instructing him at some length, the old man asked him: 'Tell me, my son, if your cloak was torn would you throw it away?'

'Oh no!' he replied, 'I would mend it and wear it again.'

The old man said to him: 'Well, if you care for your cloak, will God not show mercy on His own creature?'

Abba Sarnatas said:

> I prefer a person who has sinned if he knows he has sinned and has repented, over a person who has not sinned and considers himself to be righteous.

23 June

Psalm 119:89-96   Exodus 19:3-8   Hebrews 5:7-10

It was said about Abba John the Little that he went away to an old Theban in Scete who lived in the desert. Once the old man took a piece of dry wood, planted it, and said to John: 'Water it every day with a bottle of water until it bears fruit.'

The water was so far away from there that John had to go out late in the evening and come back the next morning. Three years later, the tree came to life and bore fruit. Then the old man took some of the fruit to the church, and said to the brothers: 'Take and eat the fruit of obedience.'

24 June Bartholomew of Farne *(see p.223)*

Psalm 26:1-8   Ruth 3:1-11   John 20:10-18

Abba Pastor was asked by a certain brother: 'How should I conduct myself in the place where I live?'

The Elder replied: 'Be as cautious as a stranger; wherever you may be, do not desire your word to have power before you; and you will have rest.'

Amma Sara said:

> If I prayed to God that all might be inspired because of me,
> I would find myself repenting at the door of every house.
> I would rather pray that my heart be pure towards everybody.

25 June

Psalm 37:30-31   Proverbs 13:1-3   James 3:1-12

It was said about Abba Agatho that for three years he carried a pebble around in his mouth until he learned to be silent.

Abba Poemen said:

> Teach your mouth to speak what is in your heart.

Abba Isidore of Pelusia said:

> Living without speaking is better than speaking without living.
> For a person who lives rightly helps us by silence, while one
> who talks too much merely annoys us.

26 June

Psalm 85:9   Micah 6:6-8   Matthew 9:9-13

One of the brethren sinned, and the priest told him to leave the community. So then Abbot Bessarion got up and walked out with him saying: 'I too am a sinner.'

27 June

Psalm 118:25-29   Isaiah 5:20-21   Luke 18:9-14

Once two brothers were sitting with Abbot Poemen, and one praised the other brother saying: 'He is a good brother, he hates evil.'

The old man asked: 'What do you mean he hates evil?'

And the brother did not know what to reply. So he said: 'Tell me, father, what is it to hate evil?'

The father said: 'That man hates evil who hates his own sins, and looks upon every brother as a saint, and loves him as a saint.'

28 June   Irenaeus *(see p.243)*

Psalm 41:1-3   Isaiah 58:6-12   Luke 10:25-37

A brother asked one of the Elders: 'There are two brothers of whom one remains praying in his cell, fasting six days at a time and doing a great deal of penance. The other takes care of the sick. Which one's work is more pleasing to God?'

The Elder replied: 'If that brother who fasts six days at a time were to hang himself up by the nose – he could not equal the one who cares for the sick.'

29 June

Psalm 113   Proverbs 2:1-8   2 John

Amma Theodora said:

> A teacher ought to be a stranger to the love of domination, and a foreigner to vainglory, far from arrogance, neither deceived by flattery, nor blinded by gifts, nor a slave to the stomach, nor held back by anger, but rather should be patient, kind, and as far as possible humble. She ought to be self-disciplined, tolerant, diligent and a lover of souls.

30 June

Psalm 150   Jeremiah 15:15-21   Matthew 24:4-14

The Holy Fathers came together and spoke of what would happen in the last generation. One of them called Squirion said: 'We now desire to fulfil the commandments of God.'

Then the Fathers asked him: 'What about those who will come after us?'

He replied: 'Perhaps half will desire to keep God's commandments, and will seek the Eternal God.'

And the Fathers asked: 'Those who come after these, what shall they do?'

He replied and said: 'The men of that generation will not have the desire of God's commandments. At that time wickedness will overflow and the charity of many will grow cold. And there shall come upon them a terrible testing. Those who shall be found worthy in this testing will be better than we are and better than our fathers.'

July
Pilgrimage

1 July

Psalm 120:1   Micah 4:1-2   Luke 2:40-47

This month's notes are on the subject of pilgrimage, a journeying to a particular place, in the expectation that such a journey will have deep significance. It may be to a place with personal memories, or a holy place where for generations people have prayed and sought God. Everyone's starting point and journey is different, inside – and outwardly.

(The psalms we are using this month are the Psalms of Ascent used by pilgrims on their way to Jerusalem.)

All kinds of people go on pilgrimage of one sort or another, not all of them believers; it is a chance for things to move, to change, perhaps even for God to break into their lives.

Canterbury

> ...and they were pilgrims all that towards Canterbury meant to ride ... I soon was one of them in fellowship and promised to rise early and take the way to Canterbury.
>
> *Geoffrey Chaucer*

2 July

Psalm 120:2-4   Job 1:6-8   Luke 4:1-13

Inner Farne

> Then I saw that there was a way to hell even from the gate of heaven, as well as from the City of Destruction. So I awoke, and behold it was a dream.
>
> *John Bunyan*, Pilgrim's Progress

In general we pray, 'Lead us not into temptation', but at the same time the Spirit of God may draw us into a deserted place to be tested.

The island of Inner Farne which was Cuthbert's 'lonely battlefield' had the reputation of being just such a place. Geoffrey of Coldingham, in the twelfth century, writes:

> Farne, which was formerly the fortress of devils, is now a cloister and a school of saints ... It always contains, indeed it actually forms, men of virtue, because when someone is led by the Spirit into the desert, he must expect to be tempted by the devil. Consequently he either cultivates sanctity or else he leaves this holy place. And the strength of temptation is greatly increased by the island's poverty and the cold caused by the sea. ...There is a continual assault from the waves and ceaseless conflict with them. Sometimes the island is completely covered with foam, which flows in from the sea and is blown over it by the wind, and this is a great mortification to those who live there, and it makes them cold and afraid...

3 July Thomas *(see p.262)*

Psalm 120:5-7   Zechariah 8:3-5   Luke 15:13-20

Derry

One sort of pilgrimage is to go back to a place full of memories, of joy, of childhood. Many things will have changed, not least ourselves, and it is a bitter-sweet experience.

This song talks of one man's return to Derry during the troubles:

> But when I returned
>   how my eyes were burned
> to see how that town had been brought
>   to its knees
> by the armoured cars
>   and the bombed-out bars
> and the gas that hangs on to every tree.
> Now the army's installed
>   by the old gas-yard wall
> and the damned barbed wire
>   gets higher and higher.
> With their tanks and their guns,
>   oh my God, what have they done
> to the town that I loved so well?

T.S. Eliot writes:

> You are not here to verify,
> instruct yourself, or inform curiosity
> or carry report. You are here to kneel
> where prayer has been valid. And prayer is more
> than an order of words, the conscious occupation
> of the praying mind, or the sound of the voice praying.

4 July

Psalm 121:1-3   Habakkuk 3:16-19   John 10:14-26

The high places

The life of the praying person is a journey farther up and farther in, to places God Himself has spoken about to the attentive heart. On one such occasion the Shepherd said to Much-Afraid,

> When you continue your journey there may be much mist and cloud. Perhaps it may even seem as though everything you have

seen here of the high places was just a dream, or the work of your own imagination ... But you have seen *reality*, and the mist which seems to swallow it up is the illusion. Believe steadfastly in what you have seen. Even if the way up to the high places appears to be obscured and you are led to doubt whether you are following the right path, remember the promise, 'Thine ears shall hear a word behind thee, saying, This is the way, walk ye in it, when ye turn to the right hand and when ye turn to the left.' Always go forward along the path of obedience as far as you know it until I intervene, even if it seems to be leading you where you fear I could never mean you to go.

Hannah Hurnard, Hind's Feet on High Places

5 July

Psalm 121:4-7 Song of Songs 7:11-13 Romans 13:9-10

Little Gidding

In 1620 Nicholas Ferrar, his mother, brother and brother-in-law with their families restored a derelict village church at Little Gidding. There they said the daily office of prayer. They were Church of England, and tried to combine the monastic values with normal family life.

For many people the name 'Little Gidding' is at first familiar because of the poem of the same name by T.S. Eliot published as one of his *Four Quartets*. He seems in these verses to capture something of the nature of pilgrimage – the precise directions to somewhere often awkward to find; and you're not sure quite why you came or what it was you're looking for. If you find it, or it finds you, words cannot easily convey what has happened but it becomes part of the journey that continues.

Not waiting for You, climbing up the hill,
I slip and stumble. Still, Your hand
upon my shoulder is so strong;
and every boulder sings a song of love
while, high above,

Your laughter draws me on and on;
and ever since that morning
there has been no right or wrong, but love.

From Hillclimbing for Beginners
Trevor Sandford, Water into Wine band

Wherever He may guide me,
no want shall turn me back;
My Shepherd is beside me,
and nothing can I lack.
His wisdom ever waketh,
His sight is never dim,
He knows the way He taketh,
and I will walk with Him.

Anna L. Waring

6 July

Psalm 121:8   Zechariah 6:8   Acts 26:19

Bamburgh

On the mainland opposite Lindisfarne is Bamburgh, the ancient capital of Northumbria. Here we think of the faithful King Oswald, and of Aidan.

The beach itself seems timeless, and full of memories...

The castle towered above them and before them were the sands, with rocks and little pools of salt water, and seaweed and the smell of the sea and long miles of bluish-green waves breaking for ever and ever on the beach. And oh, the cry of the seagulls! Have you heard it? Can you remember?

C.S. Lewis

It was one summer's evening, years ago, at Bamburgh on the Northumbrian coast, that we received the call to ministry.

Sitting on the rocks, gazing out to sea and the Farne Islands,
I saw a vision of people being rescued and brought safe onto
the rock.

Roy Searle

I saw a picture of Northumbria, dark, but with beacons of light
growing and pushing back the darkness, then bands of people
travelling around the area, fanning into flame what God already
was doing in the area.

Don Bridge

7 July Boisil *(see p.225)*

Psalm 122:1   Ezra 5:1-2   Mark 1:35-36

Old Bewick

Beside the little road from Eglingham to Chatton is a stone Celtic cross, and carved beneath it are the joyful words,

> I was glad when they said to me,
> Let us go to the house of the Lord.

A narrow drive leads to a tiny chapel hushed with prayer, where twice a month communion services still are held, but day by day people make their way to be alone, to be quiet.

At Easter in 1988 with adults and children we sang and processed up that little path to place a wooden cross from Heavenfield in the hut by the church gate. This hut was to be used as a *poustinia*, a silent place for prayer.

> Come, occupy my silent place
> and make Thy dwelling there.
> More grace is wrought in quietness
> than any is aware.

John Oxenham

You do not realise it yet, but the preaching of the Gospel emanates from the *poustinia*, creates a unity with God, then causes a confrontation with the world.

Catherine de Hueck Doherty, Poustinia

8 July

Psalm 122:2   Ezra 3:11-13   Luke 19:12-26

Cair Paravel

Fill this place, Lord, with Your glory! Let what happens here in our day be as great as what happened in the past. But don't let us build monuments to the past. If the foundations were sound, we have hope to build again. We want to work, we must not die. Let Your tender mercies come unto us that we might live again.

C.S. Lewis in his book *Prince Caspian* has the children exploring the place they have been taken to:

> 'Have none of you guessed where we are?' said Peter.
> 'Go on, go on,' said Lucy, 'I've felt for hours that there was some wonderful mystery hanging over this place.'
> '...we are in the ruins of Cair Paravel itself,' said Peter.

The place may have a powerful significance, but it is God's purposes that must be made visible and tangible. When we say, 'I'm in charge of these ruins,' it must mean we are guardians of a vision, not curators for the department of ancient monuments.

9 July

Psalm 122:3-9   2 Kings 4:4-5   Luke 1:46-53

Medjugorje

Since June 1981 six young people from the village of Medjugorje in the former Yugoslavia claim to have been having visions of Mary, the Lord's mother. She urges them to prayer especially for peace, to love of Jesus and faithfulness to the gospel, and to Scripture.

David du Plessis, a well-known Pentecostal, was one of the many who have visited there:

> In my two days in that town I never heard an unkind word or criticism of anyone. The love, unity and fellowship I saw there are only possible in the power of the Holy Spirit. I am quite prepared for God to perform miracles in the twentieth century. And if one of these miracles involves messages delivered by the mother of Jesus, I believe God is capable of that. I saw young people reading the Bible. The priests told me that thousands of Yugoslavians, including atheists and Moslems, have accepted Jesus Christ. They told me that their church is crowded to capacity every single day, and on weekends there are so many people waiting outside that they sometimes have fifty priests hearing confessions. The Mother has encouraged the people to confess their sins and to accept Christ's forgiveness. The whole place is charged with the love of God. You can feel it and you can see it.

The village is in Croatia, and their priests have at times been imprisoned. Despite harassment by the police, there is great peace in the hearts of the villagers and young people. The only spectacular thing most visitors see is the lives of the people, which are really quite impressive. The pilgrims, like the villagers, are moved to repent, to convert their whole lives. Most return home dedicating themselves to prayer, fasting and spiritual growth.

Jim Wallis writes:

> The powers and principalities of this world are aware that prayer and its results are the most revolutionary of acts. That is why they consider those who pray to be a threat. Prayer is an action in itself, a potent political weapon to be used in spiritual warfare against the most powerful forces of the world.

10 July

Psalm 123:1 Genesis 5:24 Acts 1:7-11

Walsingham

In the tiny Chapel of the Ascension at Walsingham the depiction of the ascension comes, at first, as something of a shock: a pair of feet sticking out from a large white cloud on the ceiling. It brings home to us the absurdity of the situation ... a cloud received Him from our sight. God took Him – and what a way to go! He is gone ahead to prepare a place for us, and in 'a way that baffles description' – it is as simple as that.

> Help us to understand that the pilgrimage of this life is but an introduction, a preface, a training school for what is to come. Then shall we see all of life in its true perspective. Then shall we not fall in love with the things of time, but come to love the things that endure.
>
> *Peter Marshall*

> ...they have left their house and home, and turned pilgrims, seek a world to come, and they have met with hardship in the way and they do meet with troubles night and day.
>
> *John Bunyan*

> He walks with God
>   who turns his face to Heaven,
> and keeps the blest commands
>   by Jesus given;
> his life upright,
>   his end untroubled peace.
>
> *Dorothy Ann Thrupp*

11 July

Psalm 123:2-4   Isaiah 7:14   Matthew 2:1-11

Haddington

The annual pilgrimage to Haddington in Scotland would be quite an occasion. Time for ecumenical liturgy, for buses and sandwiches and quiet excitement. Then suddenly the moment as you looked at the scene of Mary holding up her child and the royal visitors kneeling before Him: the wonder of it all, He came right down to me!

> In the white falling snow
> the pilgrim travels on.
> his face towards the sun.
> Beyond the open road he travels on
> past the lamp shining windows
> and faces by the fire
> before the midnight hour,
> for Christmas time has come around again...
>
> *Chris Simpson* 'Seasons'

> Say, shall we yield Him, in costly devotion,
> odours of Edom and offerings divine?
> Gems of the mountain and pearls of the ocean,
> myrrh from the forest or gold from the mine?
>
> Vainly we offer each ample oblation,
> vainly with gifts would His favour secure;
> richer by far is the heart's adoration,
> dearer to God are the prayers of the poor.
>
> *R. Huber*

T.S. Eliot in his 'Journey of the Magi' writes as if he were one of the pilgrims who came from so far away. To us their significance lies in the moment of their arrival, their kneeling, their gifts and adoration. For them, there is also a problem, for they return where they came from, but changed, no longer at ease as they were before.

12 July

Psalm 124:1-5   Isaiah 35:3-4   Revelation 5:11-12

Patmos

'Your task is a simple one, walk with Me,
  show Me to those who have seen Me,
and to those who have been near,
  but are afraid,' says the Lord.

And as he spoke he no longer looked to them like a lion; but the things that began to happen after that were so great and beautiful that I cannot write them.

From The Last Battle *by C.S. Lewis*

John, at the end of his Gospel, says, 'I suppose the world itself could not contain the books that would be written.'

Then, once again, he was chosen to describe the indescribable: not just what he had felt and touched, but what he had seen in a vision.

Liz Bell shared with us some of her memories of a visit to Patmos where John the Apostle was exiled, and where he received his Revelation:

Worship in the cave itself – this small cave some 2,000 years ago gave shelter to the beloved disciple of Jesus. Patmos – God's love just drenched the place like the 'thousand stars'. We walked two or three miles in the pitch dark down a rocky track with our candles, singing for joy and hearts burning with love.

On our final day we went looking for the Holy Well where God had provided the spring:

All men from all lands, kneel before you go.
Bend down low, lost son, sad daughter,
   bend down and drink;
I am the water of the well.

13 July

Psalm 124:6-8   Isaiah 43:18-21   Revelation 12:7-12

Coventry

Satan, in case you want me
  then you will find me
    in the Presence of God,
and in that presence you cannot follow
  'cos I'll be resting
    in the Spirit of God,
and there is no fellowship
  twixt darkness and light;
and there is no compromise
  twixt wrong and right.
    I'm gonna keep my life bright!

Satan, you're not forgotten,
  we're out to get you, so tell me
    how does it feel?
Have you seen Coventry – at the Cathedral?
  there is an angel,
    and you are under his heel.

From Star Wars of Darkness and Light
by Bill Davidson

14 July

Psalm 125:1   Genesis 37:19   1 Corinthians 11:1

Assisi

He was born in the small town of Assisi in the year 1182. Even today, as you walk through the Umbrian countryside, the peace of St Francis seeps into your soul and you begin to believe that perfect joy is possible. When the light of the Spirit was dying out all over the world, this man, this little man, this one man re-enkindled the flame. He was only 45 years old when he died, but he left behind a Dream to dream and a Journey to challenge every man.

Murray Bodo

In Assisi the past is not history,
but the life of Francis is now,
    just as Christ is now.
And because Francis holds Christ's hand
    and so do we: there is no time-gap.

Norma Wise

I dreamt I saw a procession of saints, holy men and bishops in their fine robes and rich clothes. Behind them walked many poor people. And the poor had their eyes on the ground, searching it to be certain they could see the footprints of Jesus there and step in them. At the very back of the line was a little man, not very handsome and dressed in rags, but his head was held back, for his eyes were on heaven all the time. Poor fool. Poor, poor fool.

From the play Poor Fool
by the Northumberland Theatre Company

There have been thousands of footsteps
    around Assisi, but through them all
the footsteps of Francis
    seem freshly there, unaltered,
        calling out for us to walk in them,
            and learn.

Brenda Grace

15 July

Psalm 125:2   Genesis 28:16-17   Ephesians 3:16-19

The house with golden windows

This is a story told of a young boy who lived with his parents in a cottage on a hillside, overlooking a wide valley. His greatest joy was to sit on the doorstep on summer evenings, and gaze across the valley to a house miles away on the opposite hillside, for, just as the sun was sinking in the west, the windows of that house would burst into flame, shining dazzlingly with golden light. How perfectly happy the people must be who live there, he thought! One day he packed sandwiches and set off to find the house with the golden windows, but it was farther off than he expected, and it was already towards sunset as he climbed steeply uphill. To his disappointment the house was a plain cottage after all, and the windows ordinary windows. The good people there offered him supper, and made up a bed in the kitchen, for it was too late now for him to return. That night, in his dream, he asked directions of a girl about his age. 'The house with the golden windows? Yes, I've seen it.' And she pointed. He woke to the early song of the birds. Drawing the curtain aside he looked out. There far across the valley, was his own house – and, wonder of wonders, its windows flashed with gold in the brightness of the morning sun.

> And the end of all our exploring
> will be to arrive where we started
> and know the place for the first time.

T.S. Eliot

16 July

Psalm 125:3-5   Numbers 17:1-11   John 21:15-17

Glastonbury

Glastonbury is a place of legend and pilgrimage. Its Christian history is very early, and Joseph of Arimathea is said to have visited there, and given witness to Christ.

Other legends say that Patrick and Brigid came there, either of which is possible. Its connections with Arthur and Merlin have fascinated Christians and pagans alike. Today it is a place of deep spiritual hunger, and conflict at times.

Pray for the believers in that town, because as the song says:

> It's hard to dance
> with the Devil on your back.

Pray that their love of Christ will grow ever stronger.

The most important thing in my life
   is that I chose to follow Jesus.
No-one makes me.
   I chose to.
I have chosen to follow Him
   because He loves me
and love makes all the difference.

Ann Kiemel

The ancient Glastonbury carol says:

The bells of Paradise, I heard them ring.
And I love my Lord Jesus above everything.

17 July

Psalm 126   Jeremiah 31:21   Luke 23:26

Heavenfield

Many a commemorative cross stands by roadside or in field, but few as significantly as that which stands at Heavenfield. It reminds us of good King Oswald, returning from Iona to unite his land, and win its people to Christ. He did not shirk his responsibilities, but fulfilled them with honesty and faith, as a Christian first, and only secondly as a king. We can only imagine with what mixture of emotions he knelt before the cross that day.

God has a place for you to fill,
but it will take all of you to fill it.

Hugh Redwood

He walks with God who, as he onward moves,
follows the footsteps of the Lord he loves,
and keeping Him for ever in his view,
his Saviour sees and His example, too.

Dorothy Ann Thrupp

I'm going where He goes –
out into the world
of lonely people.

Ann Kiemel

If this is not a place
   where tears are understood,
      then where can I go to cry?

Ken Medema

18 July

Psalm 127   Amos 9:13-15   Hebrews 12:1

Iona

The mountaineer and the fisherman and the shepherd of the Isles live their lives in lonely places, and the winds and waves bear to them messages from the unknown beyond.

Wilkie

This, then, is the Iona of Columba.

There is the bay where the little, sea-tossed coracle drove ashore. There is the hill – the Hill of Angels – where heavenly visitants shone before him. There is the Sound across which the men of Mull heard vespers sung by hooded monks – heard the Lord's song sung in a strange land. There is the narrow strip of water across which holy men came to take counsel, sinners to do penance, kings to be crowned. The little island speaks with a quiet insistence of its past – for was it not at once the fountain and the fortress of the faith, at once the centre of Celtic learning and of Christian charity?

Troup

In Iona of my heart, Iona of my love,
instead of monk's voice
   shall be lowing of cows;

but ere the world shall come to an end
Iona shall be as it was.

Attributed to Columba

How wonderful it is to walk with God
along the road which holy men have trod.

Theodore H. Kitching

Follow the example of good men of old,
   and God will comfort you and help you.

Columba

19 July

Psalm 128   Proverbs 20:24-25   Matthew 18:18-20

Renewing of vows

Go back to the old wells, to the sweet waters. Isaac dug the wells again which they had used in his father's day. Returning to 'the old wells' may mean the renewing of a promise. Many couples in particular renew their vows, or return to places that for them hold important associations.

The union of your spirits here
   has caused Him to remain,
for wherever two or more of you
   are gathered in His Name
   there is love.

Noel Paul Stookey

We seek a clear light to shine
   upon our troubled way.
We ask You to give us clearer directions.
Where we have missed the way
   and wandered far, bring us back
      at whatever cost to our pride.
Take away our stubborn self-will,

for we know that in Your will alone
is our peace. We seek that peace.

Peter Marshall

20 July

Psalm 129   Esther 3:13; 4:7; 8:6   Matthew 25:35-37

Dachau

If I said 'Yes, I forgive, but I cannot forget,' as though God, who twice a day washes all the sands on all the shores of all the world, could not wash such memories from my mind, then I know nothing of Calvary love.

Amy Carmichael, If

Not every pilgrimage is a pleasantly inspirational experience! Art Katz in his testimony-book *Ben Israel* writes of his visit to the concentration camp at Dachau:

> I was totally unprepared for what greeted me at this museum of death ... the gas rooms with the jets still in the ceiling. Here my brother-Jews had been herded like cattle into cars. Women and children. Stripped naked. Old men and young boys. Why was the ear of God silent to the shrieks and prayer of these helpless, innocent ones who were slaughtered like cattle? My stomach turned sick and my eyes blurred with tears ... Outside were the conveyor belts where the bodies were dispatched to the giant ovens ... the mutilated bodies were slowly and systematically fed into the flames. The huge smokestacks never ceased their ugly belching – twenty-four hours a day as the ovens were stoked with the House of Israel.

And later, on the train that took him on his way...

> In an instant the truth dawned: Katz, except for the accident of birth, the caprice of time and place, you might have been born a German Aryan. It could have been you stoking bodies into the

ovens. He shuddered and looked long into the blue eyes of the German man opposite.

'I have been to Dachau,' he said quietly.

21 July

Psalm 130   Jonah 3:5-10   2 Corinthians 7:8-10

Darmstadt

> In my dream, behold I saw a man clothed in rags, standing in a certain place, with his face from his own house, a book in his hand, and a great burden upon his back. I looked, and saw him open the book, and read therein, and as he read he wept and trembled...
>
> *John Bunyan*

Repentance is seen by many as unfashionable and outmoded. Like sin, it is not to be talked about. But John the Baptist and Jesus himself made it central to their teaching of the Kingdom of God.

In Darmstadt, on State Highway 3 between Frankfurt and Heidelberg, stands a small chapel. Its building was the first of many victories for the sisters in establishing their Land of Canaan. Basilea Schlink and her community of Mary Sisters believed for the land, the finance, the permission, and with each obstacle, they sought deeper repentance lest any inward attitude blocked the release of God's blessing. Repentance is at the heart of their community, repentance, the joy-filled life.

> As Christian walked on he came to a hill which grew steeper and steeper. The load on his back was very heavy as he climbed. Near the top there was a cross, and just as Christian came to the cross his burden fell from his back. It rolled and tumbled down the hill until it fell into a dark hole, and he saw it no more.
>
> *John Bunyan*, Pilgrim's Progress

22 July

Psalm 131:1   1 Samuel 16:14-23   Acts 16:23

A place of quiet

He walks with God
 who speaks to God in prayer,
and daily brings to Him his daily care.

Dorothy Ann Thrupp

In every man lies a zone of solitude
 that no human intimacy can fill:
  and there God encounters us.

Brother Roger of Taizé

Speak to me, Lord, give me Your peace.
Show me the way to go.
I need Your love, I need Your strength,
all of my needs You know.

Be by my side, be in my heart.
Be in my every prayer.
Filling my life, filling my soul,
all of the time be there...

Give me Your love
 – give me Your peace...

Ros Robertson

23 July John Cassian *(see p.228)*

Psalm 131:2   Isaiah 35:1   Mark 6:30-31

St Cuthbert's Island

St Cuthbert's Island adjoining the shore of Lindisfarne is a wonderful parable of quiet, for it is always in sight of the main island, and yet for hours and hours at a time it is completely cut off. It seems designed especially to experience a day of solitude, long enough to limit your freedom, but not as inaccessible as the life of the true hermit.

Here Cuthbert, and almost certainly Aidan before him, escaped from the pressures of community and of missions and turned their face towards God.

> Thank you, Lord, that You have set aside places,
> special trysting places where we can meet with You.
>
> *Alistair Eberst*

> How wonderful it is to talk with God
> when cares sweep o'er my spirit like a flood;
> how wonderful it is to hear His voice,
> for when He speaks the desert lands rejoice.
>
> *Theodore H. Kitching*

We've all got little cells in our hearts, little hermitages that God wants to fill. For some there's a physical place of silence. It's hard to be silent. It's hard to stop. To know God in the quiet is worth a lot – it's there we'll get our vision and our peace to come through whatever hits us.

24 July

Psalm 131:3   Isaiah 6:1-9   Revelation 4:6-11

Santiago de Compostela

Jennifer Lash, in her book *On Pilgrimage*, tells a story about Gustava's son Cornelius, who had said to her as she left to go on pilgrimage to Santiago de Compostela, 'I hope you find what you are looking for.'

> At the end of her journey I asked her what she had found. 'I have sown seeds,' she said. 'Now I must go home, live and work and wait for the harvest. I'll tell you in two years.'
>
> As we ate together Gustava was full of tales; eager with all the adventures, but she was also very happy to be going home. Certainly it had been difficult, sometimes grim. How had she coped? 'I trained myself to remember the faces of the children; they were so clear, as if they were with me.'
>
> I asked Gustava why she had gone. 'For my sins,' she replied smiling. Never has anyone seemed so loving, open, caring and sinless. Gustava is a Catholic. She explained to me that, although you may be absolved of sin, the sin is itself a separation from God. She had wanted to work through that separation. 'Also I wanted to thank,' she said, 'thank for my life and health and my immediate family and I wanted to pray for two particular people.'
>
> I thought of Cornelius's remark to his mother. One is always looking. Perhaps finding is simply looking further. 'Looking' is life. Maybe a pilgrimage puts that 'looking' into keener focus.

25 July

Psalm 132:1   Ruth 1:16   John 15:11-12

Weston Priory

Whenever we go to New England we make a point of visiting Weston Priory in the Vermont hills. The peacefulness of the place itself, the wooden chapel, the beautiful songs of the brothers at prayer...

> Peace I leave with you, My friends...
> I have called you now...

and their involvement in the Sanctuary movement and God's heart for justice...

> Because of our belief in God as Spirit
> we choose to affirm and encourage
> the prophetic voices
> that recognise both the sin
>   and the need of our time.
>
> Because of our belief in
>   the Church as community
> we choose to have no superiors or
>   inferiors among us.
> We choose to be a community
>   that dances and sings,
> in spite of the tendencies of our times
> to despair and cynicism.

Renewal of baptismal vows, Weston Priory

> Be glad with dance and song,
>   let joy ring free:
> God's love renews our hope.

Philip Franckiewicz, Weston

This renewal of hope is spoken of also in this description of life in another community:

This morning during the common prayer I suddenly became aware of the quality of my brothers and I am moved to the depths of my heart. They give their life – all their life. They pay dearly the price of their commitment. I know that better than any. Then I can no longer say if my admiration is for my brothers or for Christ who has to set his mark on them.

Brother Roger of Taizé

26 July

Psalm 132:2-9   Zechariah 8:1-3   John 12:20-25

Taizé

Thou art the Way, none other dare I follow.

Arch R. Wiggins

My failure to understand made me sad, and by way of comforting myself I read my Bible. In this way I followed the main road for five days.

The Way of a Pilgrim

Each year thousands of pilgrims make their way to Taizé in France, most of them young people, and a large proportion not Christians in any recognised sense. Their time there is carefully prescribed, but non-directive. Their own conversations, the communal prayer, and the ecumenical life of the brothers all have a profound impact.

Some people come to Taizé in a last attempt to find something in the Church. Are my words going to drive them away for good, and without any hope?...

And to find some kind of reply, I search deep within myself for some word, some image. And maybe it is I who am most surprised of all by the words I utter...

It is the thirst that I sense in the young people on the hill.

For them, as for every generation, it is strong to the point of anguish...

Brother Roger of Taizé

I went with the flow of the crowd. The bells started. The footsteps hastened. Outside the church various young people stood about with large signs, saying 'Silence' in a variety of languages, swinging from their necks. People gathered up worn sheets of music from a small table. In many languages on panels outside the church there was this notice:

Be reconciled all who enter here; parents and children, husbands and wives, believers and those who cannot believe, Christians and their fellow Christians.

Jennifer Lash, On Pilgrimage

27 July

Psalm 132:10-18   Numbers 6:25   2 Corinthians 4:6

The Via Dolorosa

In the middle of a busy conference in Jerusalem two of us took a short while to wander through the narrow streets of the Old City. Glancing above me I saw a Roman numeral on the wall, and realised suddenly that we were upon the Via Dolorosa, only yards from the spot where tradition has it that a woman called Veronica held out a cloth to wipe the face of Jesus as He struggled under the weight of His cross.

Look on the face of Jesus Christ, you will find it *is* still the answer; no hurt you have experienced can have taken you to the place He has not been. He has been wounded. The hurt on His face, in His eyes. The healing for you will be as you also look into His face.

Faith builds a bridge
   across the gulf of death.
Death's terror
   is the mountain faith removes.

John Bunyan

Christ of the human road,
>   let us reach out to touch You,
>   and, sweet Christ,
>   show us Your lovely face.
>   As we see Your face by faith,
>   we learn to become like You,
>   Lord Christ,
>   that the world may see Your glory.
>   Show us Your lovely face.

28 July

Psalm 133   Isaiah 30:15   Mark 9:1-8, 14-19

Roslin

In the village of Roslin in Midlothian you would eventually find the Community of Transfiguration. A condemned property with minimal facilities and an enclosure with several wooden huts, and one larger hut serving as a chapel. It is ironically appropriate, for was it not on the mount of transfiguration that Peter wanted to build huts to remain there in the reflected glory of the face of Jesus? It was possible to visit Roslin on retreat, for a day or longer on your own in one of the huts, shut in with God and with yourself.

> The things that come out of a man are they that defile him, and to get out of them a man must go into himself, be a convict, and scrub the floor of his cell.
>
> *George MacDonald*

> I undervalue my silence too much. Too often I move from action into silence instead of the other way about.
>
> *R. Morrison*

> When you come down from the mountain air, be on your guard against catching cold.
>
> *Hugh Redwood*

At Roslin, the other usual visitors were wayfarers, fed and given shelter in the house.

> ...thanking him for his kindly hospitality, I went on my way;
> where to, I did not know myself.
>
> The Way of a Pilgrim

29 July

Psalm 134:1   Isaiah 49:8-9   John 2:5

Clonfert

Nearby the ancient Clonfert Cathedral, old farm-buildings have been rebuilt and new buildings erected to serve the needs of Emmanuel House of Providence. In the land where Brendan walked and prayed, the work of prayer and evangelising goes on today. The bell above the main house, and the beautiful circular oratory, are what draw your attention. The laughter of the children and their running feet on the gravel. A car arrives with a middle-aged couple who walk to the silent oratory, writing the name of a troubled friend in the book of prayer-intentions. A whole camp for young people or for families, a school retreat or prayer-meeting. A cross of reconciliation.

I asked Ken Wise to put into words what his visit to Clonfert had been like:

> When you walked through the gates you knew you had come to a different place, a very godly place. It's not just friendliness, there's a presence there. We went not knowing what to expect. It seemed to be that God's presence was all round the place. I admit I was apprehensive, but when we got there it was totally different.
>
> Ken Wise

How wonderful it is to walk with God
along the road that holy men have trod.
How wonderful it is to hear Him say:
Fear not, have faith
'tis I who lead the way.

Theodore H. Kitching

30 July

Psalm 134:2   Joshua 5:13-15   Matthew 28:17

Lindisfarne

> Down the wide open road
> the pilgrim travels on,
> his face towards the sun,
> beyond the open road he
> travels on.
>
> And the waves steal the footprints
> of the summer from the sand;
> beneath the silver moon
> the North wind blows the
> fading leaves again.

Chris Simpson, 'Seasons'

And now perhaps our travels will bring us again to the Holy Island of Lindisfarne like so many, pilgrims and tourists alike. Most will venture over only between the tides when the island is an island in name only. The tide comes in and the place becomes quieter. With tourist and holidaymaker less in evidence, islander and island speak, and smile, then leave us to thoughts of our own. It has always been that way.

> Here was a sequence both of access and inaccessibility. There were hours when the tide closed it for prayer.

Ronald Blythe

> The tide did now its flood-mark gain,
> and girdled in the Saint's domain;
> for, with the flow and the ebb, its style
> varies from continent to isle;
> dry-shod, o'er sands, twice every day,
> the pilgrims to the shrine find way;
> twice every day, the waves efface
> of staves and sandalled feet the trace.

Walter Scott

31 July Ignatius of Loyola *(see p.242)*

Psalm 134:3   Genesis 32:29-31   Philippians 3:10

La Verna

Never forget: 'If a man wishes to come after Me, he must deny his very self, take up his cross, and begin to follow in My footsteps.'

> Hold Thou my feet,
>   let there be no returning
> along the path which Thou
>   hast bid me tread.
>
> *Arch R. Wiggins*

Francis wished with all his heart to stand beneath the cross of Christ, assuring Him of his love, that he would be there with Him, ever present on the hill of Calvary throughout the ages till the Risen Christ returned in all His glory and the cross would be no more! It was with such an intention that Francis had made his final journey to the top of La Verna, that holy mountain far to the north of Assisi. There on that mountain he had asked in fear and trembling that Christ would let him experience and share some of His sufferings on the cross. It was as if his whole life had begun and ended there. La Verna was the impossible Dream and eternal journey come true. And yet it remained only as a memory, except for the wounds of Jesus in his feet and hands and side. And they, of course, made all the difference between the poor man who walked up the mountain and the poor man who limped down.

Murray Bodo

August
Iona

1 August

Psalm 137:4-6   Deuteronomy 3:23-27   Philippians 2:8-11

In February 1992 twelve men went together to the island of Iona to pray. This month we ask you to journey there with us in prayer. Iona was home to Aidan; and Oswald lived there for years also, but chiefly it is Columba's story we will recall.

> Dun I is the homeland mountain, that brooded over the first church, and the huts of Columba's brothers.
>
> Margaret Cropper

We walked up to the top of Dun I to pray and there we sang 'Jesus, we enthrone You', and discovered someone else had laid out small stones there on the ground, declaring JESUS IS LORD.

Next day we stood with Ken from Belfast, near the place where Columba landed and looked to be sure he could no longer see his native Ireland, and there again we prayed and sang, 'Jesus, Lord of all, Name above all names'.

> Cul ri Erin, the back turned towards Ireland;
> farewell to the known and dear,
> advance to the unknown,
> with its formidable hazards,
> its sharp demands.

2 August

Psalm 96:10-13   Genesis 28:11-12   Ephesians 6:18

Columba and his brothers lived in simple huts, praying for each other, and for all those far and wide whose lives they were to influence.

> A central hut upon a rising ground served as Columba's cell. He watched in prayer for the small company assembled round, and for the mighty int'rests everywhere, which claimed his anxious heart. The stone was here which served him as a couch for needful sleep.
>
> *Richard Meux Benson*

Columba, disdaining the luxury of straw, used to lie on a stone, with another rounded stone for a pillow. A stone with a Celtic cross on it is preserved in Iona Cathedral and legend says that this is the very stone used by Columba for his pillow.

> Remember the holy places, the Cathedral, full of gracious light, and the stillness of the stone, with its carven capitals, its timeworn arches, its store of patterned grave stones, and the hard pillow where Columba laid his head.
>
> *Margaret Cropper*

3 August

Psalm 133:1-2   1 Chronicles 12:1, 18   John 21:8-10

Some stories tell of Columba being exiled from Ireland because of so many being killed in a battle fought on his behalf. He vowed to win as many lives for the Kingdom's sake.

In this poem by Fiona Martin, who was warden of Bishop's House, Iona, more monks from Ireland are arriving to join Columba's community:

Columba's bay

Sea-polished stones
did you welcome them
as they waded ashore,
guiding with calloused hands
coracles among the rocks?
And did the sucking sea
tug at their feet as
Erin tugged at their hearts?

With what dismay did they
remember the oaks of Derry,
warm hearths and friends?
Cold the cry of seagulls,
curious the bobbing seals,
bleak the mists of
moorland and machair.

Then through the gloom,
glowing as the day dawns,
a fire – and, dimly seen,
arms outstretched in greeting,
Columba stands. Beside him,
some fish, some bread, and
breaking upon their spirits the
reminder of another Man,
another place...

Fiona Martin

4 August

Psalm 48:9-13   1 Kings 8:55-58   Philippians 4:4-6

Columba divided his monks into three classifications. There were the 'Seniors' who were engaged in intellectual activities, the conduct of worship, and the copying of manuscripts in the scriptorium. The 'Working Brothers' performed and taught the outdoor farm labour, fishing, and sealing on the shore of Erraid, a nearby island where seals congregated. The 'Juniors' were young learners or novices, candidates for monastic vows. All had to work hard, and participate in all the hours of worship.

Edward W. Stimson

Columba's monastic rule, eventually used by many similar communities, required that the monks own nothing but bare necessities, live in a place with but one door, centre conversation on God and God's Testament, refuse idle words and the spreading of rumour and evil reports, and submit to every rule that governs devotion. They were to prepare always for death and suffering, offer forgiveness from the heart to everyone, pray constantly for anyone who has been a trouble, put almsgiving before all other duties, not eat unless hungry, or sleep unless tired, pray until tears came, and labour to the point of tears, as well, or if tears 'are not free', 'until thy perspiration come often'.

James H. Forest

5 August Oswald *(see p.277)*

Psalm 29:3-11   Exodus 19:18-19   Revelation 12:10-12

John tells us there will be one loud voice in heaven – but whose?

Columba when singing in the church with the Brothers, raised his voice so wonderfully that it was sometimes heard five hundred paces off, and sometimes one thousand paces. But what is stranger still: to those who were with him in the church, his voice did not seem louder than that of others; and yet at the same time persons more than a mile away heard it so distinctly that they could mark each syllable of the verses he was singing, for his voice sounded the same whether far or near. It is however admitted that this wonderful character in the voice of the blessèd man was but rarely observable, and even then it could never happen without the aid of the Holy Ghost.

But another story concerning the great and wonderful power of his voice should not be omitted. It is said to have taken place near the fortress of King Brude (near Inverness). When the saint himself was chanting the evening hymns with a few of the Brothers, as usual, outside the king's fortifications, some Druids coming near to them, did all they could to prevent God's praises being sung in the midst of a pagan nation. On seeing this, the saint began to sing: 'My heart overflows with a goodly theme; I will address my verses to the King, and my tongue will be the pen of a ready writer ...' [Psalm 45:1]. And in the same moment his voice was, in a marvellous manner, so raised in the air like a terrible peal of thunder, that both the king and the people were filled with intolerable dread.

Adamnan

6 August

Psalm 24:7-10   Proverbs 8:3-12   Acts 12:7-11

One significant interview on Kingdom business was Columba's meeting with King Brude, and on this journey he was accompanied by his friends, Abbot Comgall of Bangor and Kenneth, later abbot of Agaboe, who were visiting him at the time...

> In the first weariness of the saint's journey to King Brude, it happened that the king, uplifted with royal pride, acted haughtily, and would not open the gate of his fortress on the first arrival of the blessed man.

Adamnan

> Brude the Pictish King awaits him proudly – 'We cannot heed his message. Let him bring what words he likes! Him and his words we fling in scorn away! Bar well the gates' – Vain pride!

See angel hosts this monk encompassing!
Columba's hand invoked the Crucified!
That great voice shook the walls,
   and quick the gates flew wide!

R.M. Benson

And ever after from that day, so long as he lived, the king held this holy and reverend man in very great honour, as was due.

Adamnan

In an account parallel to Adamnan's in the Latin *Life of Comgall*, it was Comgall who made the sign of the cross to break open the locked gates, Columba forced the door of the king's house in the same manner, and when the king threatened them with a sword, Kenneth caused the king's hand to wither until he believed in God. Unfortunately, none of the accounts tell us much we would like to know about Columba's successful mission, the real conversion of King Brude, the securing of the deed to Iona, and the favour of Brude upon the evangelising of his kingdom. Yet all of these things surely took place.

Edward W. Stimson

7 August

Psalm 97:1   Isaiah 52:7   Galatians 6:14

The conflict must be long. Through many a year
Columba's feet those distant hills must tread,
strengthen'd by penance still to persevere;
oft 'neath their sores the rocky path grew red:
in winter oft the snow became his bed:
but love still bound him to the Crucified.

R.M. Benson

The names of ninety churches and monasteries are associated with Columba's name; thirty-seven of these are in Ireland, but fifty-three are in Scotland and the Western Isles. Even if allowance for error is made, the number of his foundations, especially in the Western Isles and on the western coast, is tremendous, from Wigtown in the south to Butt of Lewis in the north and as far west as Saint Kilda. From these Christian colonies the light of the Gospel spread far and wide throughout the area.

Reeves and E.W. Stimson

8 August

Psalm 36:5-6   1 Kings 18:43   1 Corinthians 2:1-5

For most monastic centres the visible characteristics of landscape have altered in the course of only a few generations.

> With Iona the case is very different. We may be sure that what we now see is very much what Columba saw. Its distinctive features depend upon the enduring sea ... Nothing, therefore, can be more certain than that, when we look upon Iona, or when we range even the wide horizon which is visible from its shores, we are tracing the very outlines which Columba's eye has often traced, we follow the same winding coasts and the same stormy headlands, and the same sheltered creeks, and the same archipelago of curious islands, and the same treacherous reefs – by which Columba has often sailed.

From Iona *by the Duke of Argyll (1878)*

9 August

Psalm 107:29-30   Proverbs 25:25   Acts 27:15

Columba's journeys in the coracle amidst the lakes

...His hide-bound boat
bore him and his where lofty forests frown
reflected in the lake. With joy they float,
their hearts aye buoyant with the truth they own.
No sunlit breeze has ere such glory known.
Yea, when the stormy waters have denied
their progress, still in prayer they labour'd on.
They sang that heav'n might hear!

Their song was mightier than the howling wind:
from the deep cavern of the soul it sprang,
as taught by God, and form'd by Him to find
mysterious echoes. While the strugglers sang,
demons took flight, and angel-trumpets rang,
op'ning men's weary hearts in regions wild
to hail the strangers' tidings. Awed they hung
on words so new, so welcome.

R.M. Benson

10 August

Psalm 90:9-12   Isaiah 2:5   Matthew 25:1-7

The memories cling – shadows of time long past,
when king and Viking, from the storm of battle,
in thee with hero-saints found peace at last.

Amid the strife, the gloom, of warring ages,
held by thy sons, the torch of Truth flamed high,
lighted for anxious men the shadowed valley,
blessed with new hope the nations far and nigh.

Fled have the years – the kings and kingdoms vanished.
Unchanged art thou: and of a changeless clime,
Dear storied isle, art thou not ever speaking,
beyond the reach, beyond the realm of time?

S. Dixon, Iona

Jesus bids us shine with a pure, clear light
　...burning in the night.
Jesus bids us shine first of all for Him;
well He sees and knows it
　if our light is dim.

Jesus bids us shine then for all around.
Many kinds of darkness in this world abound.
　...so we must shine.

Susan Warner

11 August Clare *(see p.230)*

Psalm 55:22　Isaiah 62:1　Acts 5:14

A few places in the world are held to be holy, because of the love which consecrates them, and the faith which enshrines them. One such is Iona ... It is but a small isle, fashioned of a little sand, a few grasses salt with the spray of an ever-restless wave, a few rocks that wade in heather, and upon whose brows the sea-wind weaves the yellow lichen. But since the remotest days, sacrosanct men have bowed here in worship. In this little island a lamp was lit whose flame lighted pagan Europe. From age to age, lowly hearts have never ceased to bring their burthen here. And here Hope waits. To tell the story of Iona, is to go back to God, and to end in God.

Fiona Macleod

Many churches in the region of the Picts trace their origin to the Religious Houses settled by Columba:

> Thus through the hills long clothed in heathen night
> Columba's rule took root with wid'ning sway.
> New homes of love beneath its mystic light
> learnt by Iona's discipline to pray.
> New hearts obey. The hallowing skies
> send benedictions down, with God's own life to rise.

R.M. Benson

12 August

Psalm 31:14-24   Genesis 12:1-3   2 Corinthians 11:26-29

> Alone with none but Thee, my God,
> I journeyed on my way:
> What need I fear, when Thou art near
> O King of night and day?
> More safe am I within Thy hand
> than if a host did round me stand.
>
> The child of God can fear no ill,
> His chosen dread no foe:
> we leave our fate to Thee, and wait
> Thy bidding when to go.
> 'Tis not from chance our comfort springs,
> Thou art our trust, O King of kings.

Columba

13 August

Psalm 103:20-21   Genesis 28:16-17   Luke 2:20

Columba seems to have been no stranger to visits from angels, and was often aware of their comings and goings, especially to protect someone in danger or escort a departing soul heavenward, even when these occurrences were at a distance, such that Adamnan says later 'news' from far away would confirm to have happened at the exact time he had been aware of the event. He spoke of them seldom, but was often in the company of angels as he prayed.

> Hard vict'ries inly won,
> make strong the soul
> to breathe the sov'reign peace
>   which angels share:
> Unnumbered hosts
> strengthen the loving soul that perseveres!

R.M. Benson

One day, on Iona, he commanded his brothers to allow him to go alone, unfollowed, to the Machair, the western plain. There on a little hill he was met by many angels who were clothed in white and flew at great speed. We know this because one disobedient monk spied on the meeting, and thereby cut it short!

The site of this story is still recognisable today on Iona:

> One little hill-top is not rocky,
> but rounded, green, distinctive:
> the hill where Columba spoke with
> holy Angels.

Margaret Cropper

14 August

Psalm 71:5-8   Amos 3:7   Philippians 1:20-26

Columba explains to Lugne and another man called Pilu on Iona that, 30 years after his arrival from Ireland, his time at last has come to die; his angel escort awaits – but the prayers of others have intervened and caused God to rearrange the departure date!

> My sons, I pray'd that God would not delay
> to call me hence, for thirty years are run.
> I pray'd that He would end my toilsome way.
> I know His goodness when my work is done,
> nor dare I grieve if still that toil lives on.
> God heard my prayer. The angels came.
>   They stand
> on yonder rocks to bear me to God's Throne.
> But still four years they wait!
>   So God's command
> yields to the Church's prayers,
>   that rise throughout the land.
>
> *R.M. Benson*

But they urged Him strongly saying, 'Stay with us, because it is almost evening and the day is now nearly over.' So He went in to stay with them.

Luke 24:29

15 August   Mary, mother of Jesus *(see p.249)*

Psalm 84   2 Kings 23:4   Luke 17:7-10

> ...to me, the least of saints, to me, allow that I may keep a door in Paradise.
>
> *From the 'Prayer of Columba',*
> *trans. by W. Muir*

One duty of a door-keeper is to stand guard against all that is harmful; another is to welcome whoever may come as a guest.

> The One who was no less than God
> took on the flesh of lowly man
> and came to wash the feet of clay
> because it was Your holy plan;
> and I, no greater than my King
> would ever seek a place
> of humble service in Your house.
>
> Oh, let me be a servant,
>   a keeper of the door!
> My heart is only longing
>   to see forevermore,
> the glory of Your presence,
>   the dwelling of the Lord.
> Oh, let me be a servant,
>   a keeper of the door.

Twila Paris

> ...if so it be that I can see Thy glory,
> even afar, and hear Thy voice, O God.

From the 'Prayer of Columba',
trans. by W. Muir

16 August Brother Roger of Taizé *(see p.257)*

Psalm 23:4-5   Genesis 49:29-33   Matthew 20:17a

On Whitsun Eve, Diarmit conducts Columba to bless the barn. It is now four years later, and Columba says to him:

> This Saturday will be a Sabbath indeed to me; for it is to be the last of my laborious life on which I shall rest from all its troubles. During this coming night, before the Sunday I shall, according to the expression of the Scriptures, be gathered to

my fathers. Even now my lord Jesus Christ deigns to call me; to whom, this very night, and at His call, I shall go. So it has been revealed to me by the Lord.

Adamnan

They both were hush'd
   in one absorbing thought
God gave: God takes:
   and death can never break
the bond of love which God's own hand
   has wrought.
Silent they homeward turn.
   No words could make
fit utterance for that love which in
   such silence spake.
Columba's soul was gazing on the Lord:
his weary body scarcely could go on,
   though leaning on Diarmit.

R.M. Benson

17 August

Psalm 102:7   Exodus 15:11   Luke 1:47-50

According to a legend related in the Old Irish life of Columba, it was revealed to him that a human sacrifice would be necessary for the success of his mission, and Oran, one of his twelve companions, offered to be buried alive. Three days later when the grave was opened Oran is said to have opened his eyes, and begun to comment, 'Death is no wonder, nor is hell as it is said.' Columba is said to have wondered what he would say next, and promptly buried him again! (In truth, Oran was not the name of one of the twelve, but of a man buried fifteen years before Columba landed.)

Remember Relig Oran, graveyard of kings,
its narrow deep carved doorway,
   the rough grey walls,

Relig Oran where the dead of Iona,
    king and crofter together sleep their sleep.
Remember the Nunnery, once the sheltering home
of women who loved God, now to their honour
    set with a flower garden, lavish, sweet,
its broken ruins sprouting valerian
    red and white, in every angle and coign.

Do not forget the buildings that are no more,
where the first monks kept fast and feast.
And over the Causeway,
    lost among the hilltops,
is one remaining, the solitary's cell.

Margaret Cropper

Here we came in prayer and pilgrimage, made our muddy way to the hermit's cell, said a Benedicite, and sang an Adoramus Te, murmured a Magnificat in the nunnery ruins, and in Oran's chapel proclaimed, 'Who is like unto Thee, O Lord among the gods?' The stone walls echoed: 'let me be a sweet, sweet sound in Your ears'.

18 August

Psalm 139:6-12   2 Samuel 15:21   Revelation 12:11

The White Sands of Iona skirt its north-western shore. They are of unusual whiteness, and are composed of the powdered shells of innumerable land-snails. The stretch of sand known as Tràigh Bhàn nam Manach (White Strand of the Monks) is believed to have been the scene of the third slaughter of Iona monks by the Danes, and the hard steep rock at the northern extremity is said to have been stained with the blood of the victims.

Here I stand, looking out to sea
where a thousand souls have prayed
and a thousand lives were laid on the sand...

Iona

Precious in the sight of the Lord is the death of His saints.

Psalm 116:15

The white strand of the monks

Sea-sharp winds
shriek between rocks,
hurling gulls seaward,
shredding their thin cries,
clawing fragile clouds
till, remnant-torn,
their sharp tears
spatter matted heather,
and cleft rocks
bleed by a white strand
where wide-eyed monks
trembling wait.

Fiona Martin

19 August

Psalm 22:4-5   Genesis 44:16-17   1 Corinthians 10:15-16

Kenneth Macleod speaks in the same breath of Iona and of the Holy Grail, that cup which Christ blessed at His last supper, and which Joseph of Arimathea is often portrayed as holding at Christ's wounded side to catch the drops of His blood. There is at once a simplicity, a deep mystery, and a faith that goes beyond purely rational considerations that is at the heart of the experience which is Iona, and as with the Grail, if the mystery it points to is Christ Himself and a love for Him, then perhaps that is what matters most, through the ebb and flow of many a tide.

To Iona

For their sake who lived and died in thee,
sang their faith and taught their joy to me,
for their sake I bow the knee,
Iona the blest,
isle of my heart, my grail.

Kenneth Macleod

Thou grail-lit Iona

My heart's own shrine
where only lives what seemed to die,
my Grail-lit Isle,
ebb-tide, flow-tide, Christ is nigh.

Kenneth Macleod

20 August Oswin *(see p.253)*

Psalm 123:2   Numbers 24:16-17a   Revelation 22:16-18

The nunnery on Iona (now ruined) was established at the beginning of the thirteenth century, and the nuns were at first Benedictine, then later of the Augustinian order.

Dawn in the nunnery

Day breaks behind the Bens of Mull
streaming across the restless Sound
blessing with shy shadows
pillars and the ruined arches of
the Nunnery.

Holy place of ancient silence
basking in prayers of countless years
etching in the early sky

a benediction while a North wind snatches
the Abbey bell.
With deep compelling resonance it sounds
evoking in hearts a hidden longing
echoes of a vocation long-locked
within the rosy glow of this rough granite –
a sacred call.

Eyes uplifted, elated in expectation,
our sinful human-ness suffused with
transforming grace, we glimpse
in fleeting simplicity of soul
our Morning Star.

Fiona Martin

21 August

Psalm 48:1-3, 12-14   Isaiah 61:4   2 Peter 3:8-9

The woodwork on the buildings of the small village gathered near the pier is so weathered that it makes them look as timeless as seagulls. At a monkish distance to the north, amid wide fields grazed by the island's sheep, the monastery looks as it must have looked when the Benedictines finished the premises 700 years ago: the plain square tower of St Mary's Cathedral and the austere rectangular masses of the adjoining buildings are all of enduring grey stone with deep-cut windows under steep slated roofs. So solid does the monastery appear that it is hard to picture the ruined state it was in for four centuries after the Scottish Parliament outlawed the monastic life in 1561. Had that Act of Suppression come two years later it would have been a full thousand years since the first monks landed on Iona and began spreading the Christian faith in Scotland.

James H. Forest,
Sojourners *magazine, May 1980*

The Celtic monks, knowing that same restlessness and provocation which issues from the Almighty, depicted the Holy Spirit both as a dove *and* a wild goose. But where in our contemporary devotions are there glimpses that God, in the twentieth century, can be expected to surprise, contradict, upset or rile us in order that the kingdom may come?

John L. Bell & Graham A. Maule

...and I say a prayer,
that the Wild Goose will come to me.

Iona, 'Here I stand'

22 August

Psalm 51:18   Haggai 1:2-5   Matthew 17:24-27

In 561 Columba arrived on Iona with his twelve; in 1938 MacLeod arrived with another band of twelve, half craftsmen without jobs, half students for the ministry. They built a wooden shed to live in by the fallen monastery and began the work of rebuilding.

MacLeod recounts that the group needed money with which to get its project started. 'I wrote to the richest man I knew. He replied that I should go see a psychiatrist at once. Then I asked – me a pacifist, mind you – Sir James Lithgow, a builder of warships at his Govan shipyard. He was interested, but asked if I would give up my pacifism if he gave me the £5,000. I said "Not on your life." "Then," he said, "I will give you your £5,000." ' Materials were hard to obtain: 'The war was on and the government commandeered all timber. But a ship coming from Canada struck a storm and jettisoned its cargo of lumber in the Atlantic. The timber floated 80 miles, finally landed on Mull, *opposite Iona* – and all the right length! It roofs the Iona library today.'

James H. Forest

23 August

Psalm 101:4-5   Proverbs 30:12-13   John 8:3-9

'Pray for me. I ask you, my brothers and sisters, to pray for me.' If ever you go to a black church that's a phrase you'll hear almost every person use when they stand up or come forward to testify – sometimes it's just like punctuation, not heartfelt at all, but it's still an important reminder.

If you attend Mass you will say, 'I ask … all the Angels and Saints and you, my brothers and sisters, to pray for me to the Lord our God.'

And George MacLeod, founder of the Iona Community, as he quotes the old spiritual, echoes the same words:

> It's not my brother or my sister
>   but it's me, O Lord:
> standing in the need of prayer.
> We are so warm in our own self-esteem
> that we freeze the folks around us.
> We get so high in our own estimation
> that we stand isolated on a mountain top
>   of self-righteousness.
> That is why You came: Lord Jesus:
> not to save the lecherous but to turn
>   the righteous to repentance.
> And it is me, O Lord.

From Where Freedom is and Laughter

24 August

Psalm 25:4   Jeremiah 29:12-13   Luke 5:1-3

Iona is a small, rocky island in the Scottish Hebrides. Three and a half miles long and a mile and a half broad, it is not imposing. Why is it a magnet for so many people today? Why do they come, in fulfilment of St Columba's prophecy that to this small island homage would be paid by rulers and commoners?

Some come because of its history – tempestuous, bloody, thrilling and profoundly significant. They come to capture the spirit of St Columba and the Celtic Church. They come to the ancient burial ground of Scottish and Norwegian kings, asking where the graves of Duncan and Macbeth can be found...

Others seek the fabled beauty of Iona – a Hebridean jewel in the Atlantic: the changing colours of the dancing sea, the whiteness of the sand and the quietness, the quietness.

The peace of Iona whispers to many. Iona has been described as 'a thin place', only a tissue paper separating the material from the spiritual. Many people have tried to express the experience – and have come back again and again.

Ron Ferguson, Chasing the Wild Goose

Let us speak for a while of the blessed island,
Iona, thrust out a little from the land,
like Peter's boat,
   where Christ can speak with men.
The Sound that separates it changes colour
and mood, from the pearl-like glimmer
   of quiet dawns,
to deep sapphire, emerald-edged at noon;
and so, by grey, by silver, to dusk again,
to the white summer tides
   of the long light nightfall.
This is an island of contrast,
   of fierce forbidding rock
jutting out into Atlantic breakers,
   and flower spangled turf
where sheep and cattle graze.

Margaret Cropper

Iona has cast its spell on the sons of men. In early times, it heard the sweet songs of God sung by Saint Columba and his followers. In later days, greater men than we have found there what they sought. This island set apart, this mother land of many dreams, still yields its secret, but it is only as people seek that they truly find. To reach the heart of Iona is to find something eternal – fresh vision and new courage for every place where love or duty or pain may call us. And whoever has so found is ever wishful to return.

G.E. Troup

Many may visit; only a few can stay, remain on Iona. Pray that those who leave may be faithfully planted as mustard seeds of hope in the world. Pray that those God wants there for His purposes may be drawn to Iona, and others kept firmly away.

25 August Ebba *(see p.235)*

Psalm 127:1   Exodus 35:30–36:1   John 15:26

From the morning service at Iona Abbey

Almighty and everlasting God, who of old didst fill the builders of Thy tabernacle with Thy spirit, in wisdom, in understanding, and in beauty, vouchsafe, we beseech Thee, Thy grace and blessing to us Thy servants: enlighten, purify, direct and sanctify us: accept and establish our work for the honour of Thy house and service: grant us the powerful aid of Thy Holy Spirit in all our undertakings, that we may promote Thy glory and further Thy Kingdom: through Jesus Christ our Lord. Amen.

God asks, 'Who will go for me?
   Who will extend my reach?
And who, when few will listen
   will prophesy and preach?
And who, when few bid welcome,
   will offer all they know?
And who, when few dare follow,
   will walk the road I show?'

John L. Bell and Graham Maule,
'The Wild Goose of Iona'

Please pray today for the work of the Iona Community in Glasgow, and elsewhere in the world.

26 August Ninian *(see p.318)*

Psalm 91:1-7   Daniel 2:20-22   1 Timothy 4:1-2

> Jesus called the twelve disciples together and gave them power and authority to drive out all demons and to cure diseases.
>
> *Luke 9:1*

> For in the Name of the Lord Jesus Christ, by virtue of his prayers, he cured men suffering from the attacks of various diseases; and he alone, God helping, drove out from this our Island (Iona) which now has the Primacy, malignant and innumerable hosts of demons warring against him, seen by bodily eyes and beginning to bring deadly diseases upon his Monastic Society.
>
> *Adamnan*, The Life of Saint Columba

> I feel no conflict here.
>
> *From 'Iona',
> a song on the album by Iona*

Do pray for the protection of the work God has raised up on the island of Iona. Many people journey there each year, tourists and pilgrims, seekers of all kinds, many of whom have rejected what they have seen of Christianity so far. How crucial is the witness of those they meet there! Others journey there to the pre-Christian power sources of druidism and magic, for Iona is the focus of much attention from those interested in what is loosely termed 'new age'. Pray for much wisdom for the Christians they will meet on Iona and who engage or interact with them. For all who seek to minister or have been given responsibility at the Abbey, Camas or Macleod centres, or at the Catholic prayer-house or at Bishop's House, we pray protection from weariness and discouragement, from division and argument, from deception and lies of every kind.

What good are our prayers? A painting I love shows a boy shooting paper aeroplanes at the sky. Coincidence or not, in the exact place his paper aeroplanes were aimed the thick cloud has cleared as if a window were opened to the deep of the heavens.

> O Isle from whence the Light streamed far
>   and wide
> God guard thee from all evil.

Bessie J.B. MacArthur

Pray for all who are part of the tapestry of Iona's life today:

> teaching truth to the living,
> chanting consolation to the dying,
> and battling to the death
>   with paganism
>   for possession of the Isles.

Kenneth Macleod

27 August

Psalm 148:1-8   Daniel 3:9-18   Acts 28:2

An Iona Benedicite

> O ye angels of the Lord, bless ye the Lord,
>   praise Him and magnify Him for ever.
> O ye Saints of the Isles, bless ye the Lord.
> O ye Servants of Christ who here sang
>   God's praises and hence went forth
>   to preach, bless ye the Lord.
> O ye souls of the faithful, who rest in Jesus,
> O ye kindly folk of the Island,
> O ye pilgrims who seek joy and health
>   in this belovèd Isle, bless ye the Lord.
> O ye sheep and hornèd cattle,
> O ye lambs that gambol on the sward,

O ye seals that glisten in the waters,
   bless ye the Lord.
O ye ravens and hoodies,
O ye rooks that caw from the sycamores,
O ye buzzards that float on the
   wind-currents, bless ye the Lord.
O ye gulls that fill the beaches with
   your clamour,
O ye terns and gannets that dive
   headlong for your prey
O ye curlews and landrails,
O ye pied shelduck and Bride's ghillies,
O ye dunlins that wheel in unison over
   the waves, bless ye the Lord.

E.D. Sedding

28 August Pelagius *(see p.255)* Arthur Burt *(see p.226)*

Psalm 148:9-14   Daniel 3:19-25   Luke 19:37-40

O ye larks that carol in the heavens,
O ye blackbirds that pipe at the dawning,
O ye pipits and wheatears,
O ye warblers and wrens that make
   the glens joyful with song,
O ye bees that love the heather,
   bless ye the Lord.
O ye primroses and bluebells,
O ye flowerets that gem the marsh with colour
O ye golden flags that deck Columba's
   Bay with glory, bless ye the Lord.
O ye piled rocks fashioned by Nature's
   might thro' myriad ages,
O ye majestic Bens of Mull,
O ye white sands and emerald shallows
O ye blue and purple deeps of ocean,
O ye winds and clouds, bless ye the Lord.

> O all ye works of the Lord, bless ye the
> Lord, praise Him and magnify him
> for ever.
>
> E.D. Sedding

29 August

Psalm 45:1   Ecclesiastes 3:1-3   Mark 4:30-33

Iona: If you have a good map of Scotland you will find it among the Inner Hebrides off the south-west tip of Mull, a comma of land separated by a strait the width of an exclamation point.

But from today's Iona there are still offshoots, including one founded by John Oliver Nelson, Kirkridge, in Bangor, Pennsylvania, for Nelson once spent a summer laying slate tiles on the roof of the Iona abbey refectory. 'This place was the start of my life,' he says of Iona. 'This is home.'

It is home for many. Still, Iona Community remains small. As big in the eye of the world as is the island itself on a world map. Small as a mustard seed, you might say. Small, but potent and marvellous.

St Columba must be glad with the sight of it, but little surprised. He had a gift for seeing the future and knew one day there would be nothing left of his foundation, but he saw beyond that time to its restoration. Poet as well as prophet, he left his prophecy as poem:

> Iona of my heart,
> Iona of my love,
> instead of monks' voices
> shall be lowing of cattle.
> But ere the world comes to an end,
> Iona shall be as it was.

James H. Forest

30 August

Psalm 102:13-22   Amos 9:14-15   Revelation 12:17

Columba's prophecy

'Vast throngs I see in realms far, far away –
with stubborn pride they challenge Christ's
    appeal:
and thou, dear home,
    through plunged in long decay,
shalt rise anew thine ancient fires to feel,
leading the last long war with holy zeal!
But oh! let none thy blessing dare to claim
who shirk the law of strife! Messiah's heel
must feel the serpent's bruise,
    strong through Christ's name
by vigil, fast, and prayer,
    the serpent's pride to tame.'
His utt'rance ceased,
    but still his eye looked on
as if in distant skies his mind could read
the mysteries of the future.

R.M. Benson

31 August   Aidan *(see p.221)*

Psalm 5:11-12   Genesis 12:2   Hebrews 12:14-17

Please continue to pray for Iona, for the Community, and for our friends at the Hostel and Bishop's House – our month of thinking of Iona draws to a close, but their work goes on...

Iona, of all these things guardian and keeper,
keeper of men's souls from age to age,
Iona, where men come to discover God,
you sent by adventurous hearts over swaying
    waters

a word of truth to the nations of old times;
send that word today, by your countless
    pilgrims,
who carry away across the gleaming sound
a blessed intimation, a stir in the breast,
a measure of beauty, a kindness in the heart,
a hallowed secret, shaping the long years.

Margaret Cropper, June 1950

Farewell, then, to Iona. In old days, when they said goodbye in the Gaelic, they said something lovely, but so charged with meaning. When husband parted from wife, mother from child, lover from her who was 'half his sight', they remembered that days might be dreary, friends few, and life hard. But they looked into each other's eyes, and the words always came – 'The blessing of God go with you, and the blessing of Columba.'

G.E. Troup

September
In the shadow of Aidan

1 September

Psalm 22:31   Genesis 49:33   Matthew 28:19-20

Introduction

These reflections on the life of Aidan were written by the Revd Kate Tristram, who lives and works on Holy Island. They were inspired by *The Shadow of the Galilean* by G. Thiessen, a book about Jesus – though Jesus does not appear directly in it. He is entirely seen through the eyes of others. His 'shadow' is the impact He made on them.

Someone wrote: 'History is the lengthened shadow of a man.' Certainly, the story of Holy Island is the lengthened shadow of St Aidan: Lindisfarne would not have become 'Holy' Island without him.

So, over the following days, we will try to see Aidan through the eyes of some of those who met him, who knew him directly, or who knew him through others. Allow these witnesses to speak for themselves.

2 September

Psalm 121:5-8   Jeremiah 1:8-9   Luke 22:35

Brother Corman

I am Brother Corman, a monk of Iona.

I was the first to be sent from Iona to Northumbria, when King Oswald asked us to send a mission. I was obedient; I was even eager. It seemed a wonderful opportunity – a great new field of evangelism opening up to us.

Yet, somehow, it didn't work out for me. I just couldn't get on with the Northumbrians. They were so ignorant and so obstinate. Perhaps I got impatient, but I had so much to give, so much to teach. But they wouldn't take it from me.

So, I went back to Iona and we held a meeting at which I reported back to my fellow monks.

Then Aidan spoke. I've known him for years; I like him. But I hadn't expected him to come forward. 'Brother,' he said to me, 'perhaps you were too eager, too demanding. Perhaps the gentle approach would have been better.'

At that, all the monks turned to him and said, 'All right – you go and try!'

I struggled to say the right thing, the Christian thing. I said, 'God bless you, brother; may you succeed.' And I thought, 'Little do you know!'

So Aidan went, and I stay here on Iona.

3 September

Psalm 113:5-8   Deuteronomy 15:11   Luke 1:46-55

King Oswald

I am Oswald, King of Northumbria. I already knew Aidan before he came here: he was a young monk when I was a boy in exile on Iona. I had been bitterly disappointed when Corman went home. So, when Aidan and his monks arrived, I said, 'Thank God you've come. I'll give you any bit of land you choose for your monastery. I'll help you in any way I can. Just call on me.'

And so he did. I even taught him the English language – me, who never taught anyone anything except how to hold a sword! But Aidan supported me too. He helped me to see how to be a practical Christian and turn my faith into action. I'll never forget the look on my hungry warriors' faces when I gave our Easter dinner away to the poor! But Aidan was thrilled. He's genuine through and through, is Aidan. There's no difference between what he teaches and what he is.

4 September

Psalm 119:30-32   Proverbs 15:23   2 Timothy 2:7

The first traveller

I am a British Christian. My family were Christians when Ireland was still in pagan darkness. I belong to the ancient church of this land. I didn't like the thought of this Irish missionary upstart. I thought he was a puppet of the English king, whom I hate.

When I saw him coming down the lane I would have passed by in silence. But something about him, something in the way he looked at me, made me stop. 'Are you a Christian?' he asked, gently.

'Of course,' I said, huffily.

'That's good to hear,' he said. 'Now will you try to be a better one?'

I don't know why I didn't explode with anger, but I didn't. Suddenly I actually wanted to be a better Christian. And suddenly I wanted to know Aidan better and hear what he had to say.

5 September Teresa of Calcutta *(see p.262)*

Psalm 53:2   Isaiah 61:1   Matthew 28:19-20

The second traveller

I am English; and I used to be pagan. When I saw Aidan coming down the road I thought, 'Here comes that foreigner the king thinks so highly of, with his strange religion. But

I don't want any new-fangled ways. The old gods are good enough for me.'

But Aidan stopped when he got to me and said, 'Are you a Christian?'

'No,' I said, 'and I don't want to be either.'

Then he said, 'Will you tell me what you do believe?'

And for some reason I wanted to talk to him; and we talked. All that he said was new to me – about Jesus, who came to show us what God is like. Then he said, 'Would you like to hear more? Would you go to a meeting in your village if I arranged one?'

I said, 'Yes.' So I went, and what I heard convinced me. Aidan's monks convinced me too, by the sort of people they were. They didn't ask me for anything; they just wanted me to know the truth. Now I am a Christian.

6 September Madeleine L'Engle *(see p.247)*

Psalm 119:50   Isaiah 37:14-24, 33-34   Matthew 21:22

The woman of Bamburgh

My husband and I live in Bamburgh; we're just ordinary townsfolk. Of course, we see the king often, coming from and going to his castle. We often see Bishop Aidan as well. We're Christians. But it can be dangerous, living so close to the royal court: the king's enemies tend to have a go at us.

I'll tell you about something that happened a little while ago. Our enemy, the King of Mercia, actually got right to the gates of the town, and we were besieged. He was building a fire so he could burn us out; and because of the way the wind was blowing we had no chance to escape. Truly, we were between the devil and the deep blue sea.

Desperately we gazed out to sea; and there, of course, was the Farne Island, and on it Bishop Aidan, on retreat. He was looking at Bamburgh: he could see what was happening. As we looked at him he raised his hands and began to pray. He looked so calm, standing there praying. Then, quite definitely, we felt the wind change, gathering force until it blew the smoke and flame away from us. The Mercian enemies just disappeared; we never saw them again that day.

Of course, it was Aidan that did it. Or rather, it was God; but God listens to Aidan's prayers. He is a real man of God.

7 September

Psalm 107:23-30   Numbers 23:19-20   Romans 8:28

The monk Cynemund

I never knew Aidan, though I rather wish I had. I am a monk of Jarrow, and my name is Cynemund. This story was told to me by a friend, a monk called Utta. I'm sure it must be true, since it happened to Utta himself – and he is now the worthy Abbot of Gateshead.

Anyway, when King Oswy decided to marry the princess Eanflaed from Kent, Utta was asked to be in charge of the party escorting her up here to Northumbria. Of course, they intended to travel from Kent by sea. Sea travel is generally thought to be easier, but Utta was a bit nervous at the thought of the long sea voyage. So he went to Aidan and asked him to pray for them. Aidan produced a little bottle of holy oil and said, 'You will meet a storm, quite a bad one. But don't panic. Remember: when the storm is at its worst, pour a little of this oil onto the waters.'

That was exactly what happened. There was a storm, so bad that the sailors despaired of saving their boat and their lives. But Utta produced his oil and poured it out – and the storm calmed down.

Just like the Gospels, isn't it? Yes, I do wish I had met the man in whom the Spirit of God worked like that.

8 September

Psalm 147:10-11   Esther 6:7-9   Matthew 25:34-40

The beggar

I am a rich man now – but I used to be a beggar, one of the lowest of the low. You'll wonder how things changed.

Well, one day I was out on the road and I saw coming towards me that strange bishop the King is so fond of. What was especially strange was that he had a horse. Generally he walked, or so I'd heard. And what a horse! A noble beast indeed, and all done up in gold and silver and fine leather. I thought, 'What wouldn't I give for a little bit of that horse's harness!'

Religion had never done me any good; but I'd try anything once, so when I got level with the bishop I held out my hand and said, 'Alms, for the love of God.'

He looked round as if thinking what he could give, and then he said, 'Of course. Have this horse.'

'What?' I shrieked. 'All of him?'

And then he smiled. 'All four legs of him,' he said; 'and the trappings as well.' I just stood there dumbfounded, and then he said, 'Take him, but remember this: the horse is a son of a mare, but you are a son of God.' Then he walked on.

Since then, I've been rich, but I'm different in other ways too. I give to beggars now – it's great to have something to give. And I mean to learn more about this God whose son I am.

9 September

Psalm 34:1   Proverbs 8:14-17   Matthew 25:21

Abbess Hild

I am Hild, Abbess of Whitby. It was not Aidan who converted me to Christianity. I was converted by Paulinus while I was still a girl at the court of my great-uncle King Edwin. I am very grateful to Paulinus, who gave me a good start in the Christian life.

But it is to Aidan that I owe the fact that I am here today. I was a mature woman when I first met him, and I knew that I wanted to be a nun. In fact I had decided to go to a religious house in Gaul, where my sister had already taken the veil. But Aidan persuaded me to give up this idea. 'Your country needs you,' he said. 'The women of Northumbria need you. The church of Northumbria needs you. I need you.' So I stayed, and eventually I came here to Whitby.

I generally know my own mind and stick to it. So what was it about Aidan that made me change it and agree to stay? I think it was the realisation that he spoke the simple truth. He did not try to dominate me or flatter me. He just said I was needed. He genuinely believed that women could be called and that women could be educated; and I saw, without conceit, that he needed someone like me.

I said I was grateful to Paulinus; I don't know if I'm exactly grateful to Aidan. It's not been an easy life. But not a single day passes in which I don't at some point think of him – the one who changed the direction of so many lives, including mine.

10 September

Psalm 116:15   2 Kings 13:14, 20-21   Acts 6:15

The carpenter

It's a funny thing: wood usually burns, but here's a bit of wood that won't.

I'm a carpenter, and so was my father before me. There's a team of us here at Bamburgh, and we're rebuilding this wooden church that was accidentally burned down a few weeks ago. This sort of thing often happens, what with using so many candles, and my dad told me it happened once before, in his day, to the earlier church on this very spot. It all burned, he said, except for one beam. That's the beam I've got in my hands at this moment: a second fire, and still it hasn't burned!

But there's a story about this beam. They say that when Bishop Aidan was taken with his last illness, he was leaning against the wooden wall of the little church here, and it was against this beam that he died. That's why it won't burn. Well, there are stranger things!

Of course, I didn't know Bishop Aidan. He was well before my time. But all I've heard about him has been good. I'll tell you one thing: he may have died, but his work hasn't. That can't be destroyed, any more than this beam. Round here, we're all Christians now, and proud of it.

11 September

Psalm 141:2-4, 8   Amos 3:3   1 Corinthians 13:12

St Wilfrid

I am an old man now, Wilfrid by name: you've probably heard of me. I've had a long, exciting and, indeed, tempestuous life. And now, soon to die, I'm going over the whole story. I've told a lot of it to my friend Eddius, who is keen to write my life. But I never told him what is now in my mind about those early days at Lindisfarne, where all my opportunities began.

Sometimes it seems only yesterday that I first went to Lindisfarne as a pageboy of 14 years, attending a sick nobleman. I joined the school there, learned to read and write, learned Latin – indeed, learned the foundations of my faith. Aidan was still alive then, though he died two or three years later. Yes, of course I thought he was wonderful, and I still do. But ... he died, and my own particular call led me to Rome; and there I fell in love with Rome – and all the wealth that Rome had to give.

I suppose two men could hardly have seemed more different than Aidan at the height of his powers and I at mine. Yet, I wonder. Yes, I have fought for power and privilege, as he never did. Yet the deepest truth about me was that I strove for the gospel as I saw it, and that was the deepest truth about him too. So, in that greater light which I am soon to enter, where Aidan already is, my hope is that we shall both be seen to have served the same God, and there will be friendship between us.

12 September

Psalm 48:1-3   Haggai 1:13-14   Hebrews 11:4-5

Bishop Lightfoot

My name is Joseph Barber Lightfoot. I'm Bishop of Durham in these days of good Queen Victoria. I'm sitting here in my study, trying to write a sermon about St Aidan.

Of course, it's not difficult to tell his story: all we know comes from Bede, and Bede's account makes very easy reading. What I'm searching for is some way of summing up his work and his importance in Christian history – some words that people will remember. He was a great missionary, of course, but not the only one. For instance, there was Augustine down in

Kent – most southerners know about him. Yet Aidan was so single-minded, so tireless in his work; and after him so much of the country was converted by those he trained. So much of the country ... so much of England...

Ah! Now I have it, the sentence I am looking for: 'Augustine was the apostle of Kent, but Aidan was the apostle of England.'

13 September

Psalm 113:3   2 Kings 2:11-14   2 Timothy 4:7-8

Conclusion

And now we let them go, these shades we have conjured up to speak to us from the past.

We are left with St Aidan's shadow: the impact he made on those who knew him, and on the Christian history of our land.

Today we, the people of Lindisfarne, the people of Northumbria, the people of England, thank God for our apostle; for those he taught; for those he inspired; for the Christian faith we hold; for the Church to which we belong; for the means of grace; and for the hope of glory.

14 September

Psalm 49:1-3   Isaiah 58:6   Matthew 25:37-40

Prayers

Aidan was the champion of the poor,
the liberator of slaves,
but also the friend of kings.
We pray for all Christians
entrusted with responsibility,
that they may be blessed with true friends,

and that they may faithfully witness
to the power of God and the love of Christ.

We pray for ourselves:
for the gift of friendship,
and of faithfulness,
and that we would be freed from selfishness.

We will journey with the kind-hearted Saviour.
If we have fed the hungry from our own table
God will feed us with all good gifts.

15 September

Psalm 27:4   Daniel 2:20-23   Luke 6:38

> Aidan, you held back nothing,
> no reserve in your giving to Him
> who gave all for you.
> All you asked in your journeying
> was a place of quiet
> to gaze into the face of God.
> You have come at last
> to the source of all wisdom.
>
> Aidan, in the presence of God, pray for us.

16 September

Psalm 122:8-9   Isaiah 41:1, 4-6   John 3:8

> Lord, we pray for Iona,
> the island which was always home for Aidan.
> We pray that there the wind of the Spirit may blow,
> that there the cause of Christ may triumph,
> that there the work of God may prosper.

Lord, we pray, as Aidan did,
for the holy island of Lindisfarne,
cradle isle where nature,
work and prayer would meet as one;
the place to which Aidan
and his companions came,
led by Christ,
there to build a home for restless souls,
a beacon to shed forth the light of Christ.

For this is peace; this is God.

17 September

Psalm 89:13-15   Isaiah 9:7   1 Corinthians 14:8

In practical ways

Lord of my heart,
give me courage to strengthen me
that, among friends or enemies,
I may always proclaim Your justice.

18 September   George MacDonald *(see p.248)*

Psalm 143:5-6   Isaiah 49:15-16   1 Timothy 2:8

Hands, Lord —
Your gift to us.
We stretch them up to You.
Always You hold them.

Your hands,
scarred,
became a sign
of Your love
no time can erase.

Your hands,
which have us
inscribed on their palms,
pour down blessing
on the details of our days.

Laurel Bridges

19 September

Psalm 22:26-28   1 Chronicles 29:11-14   Mark 6:2-4

O Son of Mary,
how wonderful
Your friendliness to me!
How deep! How unchanging!
Help me to pass it on.

Help me to find my happiness
in my acceptance
of what is Your purpose for me:
in friendly eyes; in work well done;
in quietness born of trust;
and, most of all,
in the awareness
of Your presence in my spirit.

Come, Lord Jesus, come as King.
Rule in our minds: come as peace.
Rule in our actions: come as power.
Rule in our days: come as joy.

Thy Kingdom come among us. Amen.

20 September

Psalm 65:9-10   Genesis 1:11   John 20:6-10

Follow the example of good men of old

Where young and old with gladness dance with Me
I'll give My house of hospitality.
Don't store false treasure.
Follow their example, these good men of old;
and buy My field – with moth-strewn gold.
True men and women who responded:
these were empty vessels, filled with treasure
hidden deep within them by My hand.

Freely you have received,
so freely you must give your plans to Me,
right from the start; then you will truly live.

Good men of old learned not to say,
'I'm *sorry* I believe.'
I look not for wary, reluctant
followers on the fringe.
Instead I shall allow, in full community,
My waymarks to proclaim My truth, My name;
empty vessels standing low awaiting
the ebb or flow, from My deciding, guiding hand,
of waters hidden deep within the land.

'Son, they have little wine at this feast.'
And at her request the jars are filled,
even the best.
The water now offered is made choicest wine.
And the Father surely smiles.

Oh to respond, empty vessels,
as good men of times past,
and carry this vintage refreshment
to those coming last!

Ken Lydon

21 September Henri Nouwen *(see p.252)*

Psalm 24:7-10   Genesis 19:2-3   Luke 19:15-16

In hospitality

There is a door to which you have the key,
and you are the sole keeper.
There is a latch no hand can lift save yours.
No ruler, nor warrior, writer, thinker:
but only you.
O heart, hurry now and welcome your King
to sit by the warmth of your fire.

22 September

Psalm 119:73   1 Samuel 17:33-37   Ephesians 4:10-13

In obedience

When the shadows fall upon hill and glen;
and the bird-music is mute;
when the silken dark is a friend;
and the river sings to the stars:
ask yourself, sister,
ask yourself, brother,
the question you alone have power to answer:

O King and Saviour of all,
what is Thy gift to me?
and do I use it to Thy pleasing?

From Hebridean Altars

23 September Adamnan *(see p.221)*

Psalm 139:13-18   Jeremiah 29:11   1 John 4:18-19

Often I strain and climb
and struggle to lay hold
of everything I'm certain
You have planned for me.
And nothing happens:
there comes no answer.
Only You reach down to me
just where I am.
When You give me no answer
to my questions,
still I have only to raise my arms
to You, my Father
and then You lift me up.
Then because You are my Father
You speak these words of truth
to my heart:

'You are not an accident.
Even at the moment of your conception,
out of many possibilities,
only certain cells combined,
survived, grew to be you.
You are unique.
You were created for a purpose.
God loves you.'

24 September

Psalm 8:9   Ecclesiastes 3:11-13   Matthew 20:25-28

God, our God,
Your design for each of us
is perfect in its friendliness.

There is a purpose in all things;
and whoso finds it
wins strength to bear.

For even the Son of Man
did not come to be served,
but to serve,
and to give His life for many.

25 September Cadoc *(see p.227)*

Psalm 25:17   Isaiah 40:28-31   2 Timothy 4:9-10

O Holy Christ,
bless me with Your presence
when my days are weary
and my friends few.

26 September

Psalm 143:8   1 Kings 18:43   Luke 14:10-11

How many times a day do I say,
'Why am I here?
What here can stir my gifts to growth?
What task of greatness awaits me
that I have long neglected?

'Have I missed Your voice, O God?
Here I am:
send me!
Please!'

'I have prepared a place for you,' says the Lord,
'that is for you, and only you, to fill.
First of all, come to My table,

and ask that you might serve,
looking even for the lowest tasks.
When the work of service is done,
then you may look for your own place at table.
But do not seek the most important place
in case it is reserved for someone else.
The place I have appointed is where you will be happiest.'

27 September

Psalm 37:8-9, 11   Ecclesiastes 7:8   Luke 17:7-10

> Make this the prayer of your heart:
>   Lord, show me the right seat,
>   find me the fitting task
>   give me the willing heart.
>
> Commit your way to the Lord.
> Be still before the Lord
> and wait patiently for Him.
> Do not fret – it only leads to evil.

28 September

Psalm 131:1-2   1 Kings 19:19-21   Mark 14:32-40

> Help me to know that the secret of contentment
> lies in organising the self
> in the direction of simplicity.
>
> Unless You have another task for me,
> keep me vigilant in prayer.

29 September Michael and All Angels *(see p.251)*

Psalm 31:14-16   Exodus 3:14-15   Revelation 22:13

In the present moment

Hurry is an unpleasant thing in itself, but also very unpleasant for whoever is around it. Some people came into my room and rushed in and rushed out and even when they were there they were not there – they were in the moment ahead or the moment behind. Some people who came in just for a moment were all there, completely in that moment.

Live from day to day, just from day to day. If you do so, you worry less and live more richly. If you let yourself be absorbed completely, if you surrender completely to the moments as they pass, you live more richly those moments.

I do not think it is lack of time that keeps me from doing things, it is that I do not want enough to do them.

Anne Morrow Lindbergh,
Bring Me a Unicorn

30 September

Psalm 84:8-11   1 Chronicles 16:27-29   2 Corinthians 3:18

May everything in this my being
   be directed to Thy glory
and may I never despair.
For I am under Thy hand,
and in Thee is all power and goodness.

Dag Hammarskjöld, Markings

October
With understanding

1 October

Psalm 119:1-4   Nehemiah 8:2-6   Matthew 22:37-38

This month we will be reading slowly through Psalm 119, the longest psalm, which gives thanks for God's laws which give understanding and bring life. We pray God will teach us to obey Him, to honour Him, and to praise Him with understanding.

In John Irving's novel *The Cider House Rules* the rules are carefully posted up where everyone can see them, but it makes no difference because the people who have to keep them cannot read. The rules still apply, and so do the penalties for breaking them. God's laws are in-built in our world, so lack of understanding is dangerous.

In *Winnie the Pooh* by A.A. Milne, Owl is instructing Pooh Bear to follow the customary procedure:

'What does Crustimoney Proseedcake mean?'
    said Pooh.
'For I am a Bear of Very Little Brain,
    and long words Bother me.'
'It means the Thing to Do.'
'As long as it means that, I don't mind,'
    said Pooh humbly.

The word of God challenges us,
    Do you seek Him with all your mind?
And we respond,
    Amen. Lord have mercy!

2 October

Psalm 119:5-8   Nehemiah 8:8   1 Corinthians 6:9-11

The one with the gift of making things clear brings understanding, and imparts life.

The rules are there for your protection and you know they make sense. People break God's rules, and are damaged in consequence. How we need to explain, to help others understand! People need the Lord. We can encourage them to find God and His ways in their life. What He has done for us He can do for them, too.

We can be part of the process, fully given to the purpose of the Lord Christ.

An old Celtic song expresses it this way:

> As You reach out to bless mankind,
>   I feel Your embrace drawing me close.
> I rise with You, dear Jesus, and You
>   rise with me.

3 October   Thérèse of Lisieux *(see p.262)*

Psalm 119:9-11   Nehemiah 8:9-10   Romans 12:2

The word God speaks can be hidden in our heart as a secret weapon, to protect us from sinning against Him. His words alter our understanding and slowly renew our mind, changing our way of thinking.

First of all, His word may make us sad for we realise how far we fall short of His intentions for us; but He urges us to feed on His word with joy, and be strengthened. If our thinking is shaped by His word we may be protected from many unnecessary hurts, and destructive ambitions. That is why the Psalm pays particular attention to the young man and the cleansing of his ways before habits of sin and wilfulness become deeply ingrained.

Abba Isaiah, one of the Desert Fathers, said to beginners who were off to a good start, obediently following the tradition of the fathers:

Just as the young branches can easily be corrected and bent, so can beginners who are obedient.

4 October Francis of Assisi *(see p.238)*

Psalm 119:12-16   Nehemiah 8:11-12   1 Corinthians 14:14-15

'I will not forget Your word,' says the Psalm. There's not a whole lot of point in hearing or reading the words of God if we immediately forget what has been said.

James 1:22-25 says that the person who does that is like someone looking in a mirror, then forgetting what they look like, but that the perfect word of God gives freedom if we continue to act on it.

We should pray and praise with the Spirit, but also with understanding; it's not a case of one or the other. The two ways of praying go together; they are not opposites. Praying with understanding does not mean speaking our mind to God. Instead, we pray first only as the Spirit gives us the ability, and in doing that we find we have understanding we did not have before. Even our ability to pray is His gift to us. As we hear from God we begin to have wisdom and understanding.

A fool may talk, but a wise man speaks.

Ben Johnson

5 October

Psalm 119:17-24   2 Kings 6:15-17   Luke 4:1-13

All of us use only a fraction of our brain-power, to say nothing of how little we develop our five senses. Often when one sense is impaired, others become more finely tuned. An artist with quadriplegia may manipulate a paintbrush with the mouth, or a person who is blind may develop a keen sense of hearing.

How many of us go through life with our spiritual eyes unseeing, or fast closed? And how is our spiritual hearing? Can we distinguish the voice of the deceiver from that of the Shepherd?

O God, Your words are my counsellors. Yours is the voice I'll listen to.

> In the steep common path of our calling,
> be it easy or uneasy to our flesh,
> be it bright or dark for us to follow,
> be Thou a shield to us from the wiles
> of the deceiver,
> from the arch-destroyer with his arrows
> pursuing us,
> and in each secret thought our minds
> get to weave
> be Thou Thyself on our helm and at
> our sheet.

From Carmina Gadelica

6 October

Psalm 119:25-32   1 Chronicles 4:9-10   Philippians 3:13-14

Remove from me the way of lying. Lying is not always even deliberate untruth. It may be to not report accurately, but act as if we were certain of the facts. It may be that to choose the way of truth is to be careful never to exaggerate, to be known as a person of our word.

People should be able to say, 'They said so, so it must be the case.' Being in the right is beside the point.

As Hugh Redwood has said, 'Don't bend the truth when you hammer it home!'

The last verse of this section of the Psalm is powerful:

> I will *run* the way of Your commandments when You enlarge my heart.

If my heart is enlarged I'll not have time to hold back, nor will I carry things that hamper my progress.

Do you love Christ,
King Jesus, is He yours?
Then love God more
and burn with love.
Hold fast the light He gives,
live thou for Him.
Believer, hold Him high...

'Aidan'

7 October

Psalm 119:33-40   Isaiah 53:3   John 8:43-46

Turn away, O God, the reproach I fear. It can matter a lot what other people say, those who speak wrongfully against me.

> Who steals my purse steals trash,
>   'tis something, nothing,
> 'twas mine, 'tis his,
>   and has been slave to thousands.
> But he that filches from me my good name
> steals that which not enriches him,
>   and leaves me poor indeed.

Iago from Othello

Even in the poverty of reproach Christ can meet us, and He is all in all.

> Thou, Lord, alone, art all Thy children need
>   and there is none beside;
> from Thee the streams of blessèdness
> proceed;
>   in Thee the blest abide.
> Fountain of life and all-abounding grace,
> our source, our centre and our dwelling place!

Mme Guyon

8 October

Psalm 119:41-48   Genesis 41:14-16   Matthew 10:18-20

By seeking out Your precepts I will walk at liberty! I will speak of You before kings and rulers, standing unashamed.

> As the evening wore on, the men became impatient. The chief complained, 'You refuse to co-operate with us. You refuse to tell the truth. We will imprison you for life.' A chill went down my spine. Life imprisonment in the nation of Albania! More grace was going to be needed to accept this than to accept the death sentence.
>
> For the last time they asked me the question. 'Who sent you to Albania?' Again I replied that I was a Christian who lived and served God, that I had come at His command, and that I was prepared to bear full responsibility for my actions. I had known, when I crossed the border, the possible implications of what I was doing.
>
> One of the interrogators then asked an interesting question: 'Are there other people like you who are doing what you are doing?' Without realising the impact of my reply, I said that yes, there were hundreds who were responding to the call of Jesus Christ to go to the uttermost parts of the earth – to the areas that have never heard – to reach the entire ... Undisguised fear was written on his face as he asked a further question, 'You mean others like you will come to Albania?'

Reona Peterson,
Tomorrow You Die

9 October

Psalm 119:49-56   Job 35:9-11   James 5:13

In the night Your song will be with me, will be with me, in the night. A song keeps singing in my heart for I am Yours and You, Lord, are mine, and all my times are in Your hand.

Lord of my heart,
> give me vision to inspire me,
that working or resting,
> I may always think of You.
Lord of my heart,
> give me light to guide me, that,
at home or abroad,
> I may always walk in Your way.

From Robert van de Weyer's anthology, Celtic Fire

With Your inspiration
the pilgrim is fired,
is filled with courage
to tackle the way.

He treks through Tear Valley
and makes it a spring,
a blessing, like early
rain bringing new life.
He takes the path inward
to stand before God.

From The Othona Psalms

10 October Paulinus *(see p.254)*

Psalm 119:57-64   Ezekiel 37:2-4   Romans 8:19-23

The earth is full of Your steadfast love, but now teach *me* Your commands. It is me that is out of step, out of tune, discordant and jarring.

> The brightest colour upon His palette is of no use to the Artist
> if it refuses to blend with the others.

Hugh Redwood

We need to find our place in God's purpose, receptive and open to His direction and inspiration; and all creation waits as it were on tiptoe in excited anticipation of what can happen if we assume the destiny for which we were created, and stand as 'sons of God'. We become 'Christ-carriers'.

> Believer, hold Him high
> that all may see
> the light of Jesus
> in a son of man.

'Aidan'

11 October

Psalm 119:65-72   Genesis 37:23-24; 50:20   Acts 5:29-39

Poor Joseph fell foul of his brothers' jealousy. In the bottom of his pit it took a lot of imagination to believe any good could ever come of it.

> Anyone who strives to climb out of a pit will not pray that its sides shall be smooth.

Hugh Redwood

> Withdraw not Thy hand, O my God, from me here,
> O Chief of the chiefs, O withdraw not Thy hand.

From Poems of the Western Highlanders

When things seem really bad we might need to hesitate before assuming it's against us and out to get us. As Gamaliel pointed out, we need to be careful *just in case* it's God we'd be fighting in rejecting it.

> Great questions stand unanswered before us, and defy our best wisdom. Though our ignorance is great, at least we know we do not know. When we don't know what to say, keep us quiet.

Peter Marshall

12 October Wilfrid *(see p.265)*

Psalm 119:73-78   Jeremiah 18:1-6   Romans 8:25-26

> O God, forgive the poverty and pettiness of our prayers. Listen not to our words, but to the yearning of our hearts. Hear beneath our petitions the crying of our need.
>
> *Peter Marshall*

God, You hear within us the groanings so deep they cannot even be uttered. Let Your tender mercies come unto us that we may live again.
   'Can I not do with you as the Potter?' says the Lord God.
   Lord, help me to realise that I am Your project.

> Have Your own way, Lord, have Your own way,
> You are the Potter – I am the clay
> Mould me and make me after Your will
> while I am waiting, yielding and still.
>
> *Adelaide A. Pollard*

'Can I not do with you as the Potter?'
'Yes.'

13 October

Psalm 119:79-80   2 Kings 10:15   Galatians 6:10

> It is your business and others' to go forth, confronting them face to face, for that is the only way of bringing them to Me. For when you are face to face with them, you love them, and once you love them, then I can speak through you.
>
> *From* Molchanie
> *by Catherine de Hueck Doherty*

His love that burns inside me
impels me on the road
to seek for Christ in the stranger's face
or feel the absence of His touch.

'Aidan'

Make friends of God's children;
help those who are weak;
forgetting in nothing,
His blessing to seek.

William D. Longstaff

Oh the comfort, the inexpressible comfort of feeling safe with a person; having neither to weigh thoughts nor measure words, but to pour them all out, just as they are, chaff and grain together, knowing that a faithful hand will take and sift them, keep what is worth keeping, and then, with the breath of kindness, blow the rest away.

Dinah Maria Mulock Craik

If your heart is right with my heart,
    give me your hand,
the right hand of fellowship,
the right hand of brotherhood.
If your heart is right with my heart,
give me your hand.

14 October

Psalm 119:81-88   Judges 6:11-14   Hebrews 12:11-12

The story is told of a man who tripped and fell off a cliff. Clutching at the grasses on the edge of the cliff he found himself for a moment or two able to hang on and delay his fall.

'Is there anyone up there?' he cried out desperately. 'Yes,' came the reply, but no further response. 'Who are you? Why don't you help me?'

shouted the man. 'I'm God,' said the Voice, 'and I will help you. But you must do exactly as I say.' 'OK,' whispered the man, 'what have I to do?' 'First, *let go!*' 'Is there anybody else up there?' called out the man.

Poor fearful little Gideon had to do something just like that to become the mighty man of valour God saw him as. Against an army which far outnumbered them, God's solution was to cut back even further on numbers!!

> With decrease thou shalt have increase. Count not as men count. Do not look into thy hand and say, 'I have not enough,' for with less, even with decrease, nothing shall be impossible to thee. Like with the army of old – I can do more even with less.

15 October Teresa of Avila *(see p.261)*

Psalm 119:89-95   Deuteronomy 17:19   Revelation 1:3; 5:2-5

Oh well, I guess it has been settled in heaven, and yet I would have died had my trust not been in Your word.

> Prayer is not the privilege of a few. It is a reality easily accessible, for tiny children as for old men. It finds expression in innumerable ways.
>
> *Brother Roger of Taizé*

> Delightful I think it to be
>   in the bosom of an isle
>   on the crest of a rock
>   that I may see often
>   the calm of the sea,
> that I may pore on one of my books
>   good for my soul,
> a while kneeling for beloved heaven,
>   a while at Psalms,
>   a while meditating upon the
>   Prince of Heaven.
>
> *Columba*

Little do men perceive what solitude is...

> For a crowd is not company,
>> and faces are but a gallery of pictures,
>> and talk but a tinkling cymbal
>>> where there is no love.

Francis Bacon

16 October Gall *(see p.239)*

Psalm 119:96   1 Samuel 2:18-21   Matthew 5:48

Those of us who are unfamiliar with Greek can apparently miss out on the subtleties of meaning in many New Testament passages.

I am told that one such verse is that which says, 'Be perfect even as your Heavenly Father is perfect.' The two words used for 'perfect' are slightly different. The one is perfection in a limited, finite way, the other infinite.

What this means is that Jesus' command to be perfect is attainable (at least on a good day!). We are asked to be as perfect as we can be, even like He is as perfect as He can be. We are being asked to eat our dinner like our Daddy, not to eat our Daddy's dinner. As we grow, so does our capacity for such food.

> ...like an onion: except that as you go in and in, each circle is larger than the last.

C.S. Lewis

17 October

Psalm 119:97-104   Proverbs 2:1-6   Luke 2:40-47, 52

Oh how I love Thy law! It is my meditation, all the day. 'I have more understanding than all my teachers...' Jesus had this, not because He was God, but because He was receptive in His human life to the Voice and direction of His Father. As a boy He had apparently not experienced the anointing of the Holy Spirit yet, but even so by saturating Himself in Scripture He was filled with understanding. Nor did He consider Himself unteachable, unable to learn from others.

Aidan of Lindisfarne had a similar love of Scripture, and especially the Psalms which he would memorise, and speak by heart as he travelled on foot with his companions. In Eastern Europe and elsewhere, when copies of the Bible are hard to come by, believers naturally treasure the word, and memorise as much as possible. No authority can remove the word hidden in your heart; it can be meditated upon all day long.

> If we practised silence a little bit more, then when we did speak we'd have something to say.
>
> *John Skinner*

> I weave a silence on to my lips
> I weave a silence into my mind
> I weave a silence within my heart
> I close my ears to distractions
> I close my eyes to attractions
> I close my heart to temptations.
>
> Calm me, O Lord, as You stilled the storm
> Still me, O Lord, keep me from harm
> Let all the tumult within me cease
> Enfold me, Lord, in Your peace.
>
> *David Adam*

18 October

Psalm 119:105-112   Isaiah 30:20-21   Hebrews 4:12-13

'Your word is a lamp to my feet'; where I am standing now, and the step just before me that I need not hesitate over. 'Your word is a light to my path', shining a little way ahead, giving me glimpses of direction to reassure me and give me purpose. You shine faithfully upon my life, but You cannot and will not take the steps for me – it is I who must walk in Your way and become the expression of Your will.

O Lord, give me wisdom. I dare not take a step without You. When I cannot see all of the way forward, help me to trust that You will whisper in my heart or in my ear calling me back when I might step to right or left of what You intend for me. When there are snares for my feet, help me to find the way through, and continue with a rejoicing heart to the end.

> When we do not know what to do, let us ask of Thee, that we may find out. We dare to ask for light upon only one step at a time. We would rather walk with Thee than jump by ourselves.
>
> *Peter Marshall*

Be Thou my vision, O Lord of my heart.

Attributed to Patrick

19 October

Psalm 119:113-117   Isaiah 55:8-9   Ephesians 1:3; 2:6-7

Uphold me that I may live and not be ashamed of my hope. Hold me up and I shall be safe.

> Give me a calm and confident trust in Thee. Make me willing to live just one day at a time. May my heart re-echo to Thy promise that only as I rest in Thee can the desires of my heart be given to me. And now help me to do my part in placing a guard around my thoughts, by resolutely refusing to return to my old haunts of distrust. I thank Thee for Thy love for me and for Thy help. Amen.
>
> *Peter Marshall*

My greatest struggle is the struggle not to struggle.

Arthur Burt

What the soul has to do in the time of quiet is only to be gentle and make no noise ... Let the will quietly and prudently understand that one does not deal successfully with God by any efforts of one's own.

Teresa of Avila

I knew a man who always said 'Keep looking down,' 'You mean keep looking up, don't you?' 'No! No! We are seated together with Christ in heavenly places!'

Arthur Burt

Keep looking down, we're seated in the heavenlies,
    God's mighty power has raised us over all.
Keep looking down, above all principalities,
    for we have 'died and risen with the Lord.'
And in His name we have authority,
    and in His name we shall prevail,
And in His name we dare to face the enemy
    and in His name we cannot fail.
    Keep looking down!

Jimmy Owens

20 October

Psalm 119:118-120   Nehemiah 8:9   James 3:3-7

Man can control all kinds of things, but the tongue may be the hardest of all. Once a word is out of our mouth, it is hard to call it back. Regret will not achieve this.

God's rulings are not negotiable, either. When we ignore them we hurt ourselves and usually others as well. When we see the damage we cause them we are aware of our sin, and rightly are frightened of God. His forgiveness frees us, but if we become sensitised to His approval, and ask for the sense of the 'fear of the Lord' this can help us begin to know wisdom, *and* guard our tongue.

The man who never minces his words is responsible for a lot of indigestion.

Hugh Redwood

The fear of the Lord can help us also to be directed in the particular path that will best help us in our own journey with God. The paths may be as varied as the people! Specific obedience is what is required.

The way depends on where we live: one may go north, the other south, yet both will get to the city.

Hugh Redwood

Pour down upon us from heaven
the rich blessing of Thy forgiveness;
Thou who art uppermost in the City,
be Thou patient with us.

Grant to us, Thou Saviour of Glory,
the fear of God, the love of God and
   His affection, and the will of God
   to do on earth at all times
as angels and saints do in Heaven;
each day and night give us Thy peace.
Each day and night give us Thy peace.

From Carmina Gadelica

21 October Tuda *(see p.263)*

Psalm 119:121-128   1 Kings 3:12-13   Matthew 22:15-22

O Lord, teach us to number our days that we may apply our hearts unto wisdom. Time is short, and no one of us knows how little time he has left. May we be found using wisely our time, our talents, and our strength.

Peter Marshall

Help us to know judgement and justice, Lord. When Your judgements come, then stand by me, and teach me Your statutes so I can understand what justice really is.

Lord, You know I am Your servant, so give me understanding. Protect me from deception. Give me wisdom. When people try to trick me or confuse me with their questions and clever arguments, help me to see their heart. Help me to know when to say nothing. Help me to know when to answer what they are saying. Help me to know when it is an unspoken question that I should be answering.

Teach me to recognise the moments when You wait to intervene, so I can say, 'It is time – *You* work now, Lord!'

22 October

Psalm 119:129-132   Habakkuk 2:14   John 7:37-39

Jesus stood up and said, 'Whoever is thirsty, let them come to Me and drink, and drink, and drink.'

O Lord, Your word enters and lets in the light. It gives understanding to the simple.

Open-mouthed and longing we come to You. To whom else shall we go? You have the words of eternal life. We have believed, some of us recklessly, some of us hesitantly, but we have believed, and have come to know that You are the only one who can satisfy our thirst.

> I am an emptiness for Thee to fill;
> my soul a cavern for Thy sea.
>
> *George MacDonald*

23 October

Psalm 119:133-135   Isaiah 58:6-10   Romans 6:16-18

'Be sure your sins will find you out,' the proverb says. But listen to Hugh Redwood's comment on that:

> Much better it would be, no doubt,
> if Sin could always find us out.
> This is the question: Why does Sin
> so very often find us in?

Lord, order my steps in Your word. Don't let *any* iniquity have dominion over me; let no sin rule over me. Shine Your face on me, Your servant.

Lord, be Lord of all of me. I want You to be the Master, not my independence, my wrong actions and attachments, my wrong attitudes. None of these should master me.

> Do now for me what I cannot do for myself. Break the habit patterns, reverse the direction of my negative thoughts, lift from me once again all anxieties and apprehensions.

Peter Marshall

24 October

Psalm 119:136   Isaiah 5:1-4   Luke 13:34; 19:41

Centuries ago, Demonax the Cynic said this:

> Probably all laws are useless; for good men do not need laws at all and bad men are made no better by them.

We can see that he has a point – up to a point! But the writer of the Psalms says, 'Streams of tears flow from my eyes because Your law is not obeyed.' For this to be our response we need to have compassion for those who do not take heed of God's law. For this to be our response we need to be touched with the sorrow of God's heart, and long to comfort Him. For this to be our response we need to believe that the law of God is good, and just, and given to care for and tend the people He loves.

Does it move us to tears that the law of God is abandoned, ignored, or even scorned? Does it move us to action when we realise that most people have little concept of what the laws of God are? Is our heart under Kingdom rule? or do we have divided loyalties, as if we were citizens of two kingdoms, obeying whichever rule of conduct happens to suit us at the time?

'What more could I have done for you than I have done?' says the Lord, 'for I have loved you!'

And Jesus wept.

25 October

Psalm 119:137-140   2 Kings 10:16-17   Matthew 23:1-13

> Often in the past, Lord, I have come to Thee with heavy heart
> and burdened life. And Thou hast answered my prayers and
> graciously lifted the burden from me. Yet with a strange
> perversion, I still refuse to leave my burdens with Thee. Always
> I gather them up – those heavy bundles of fears and anxieties –
> and shoulder them again.
>
> *Peter Marshall*

Some of the strongest words You speak, Lord, are those condemning
    people who put heavy loads on the backs of others,
    people who delight in seeing others weighed down
        by their guilt and failure,
    people whose eyelids judge even their friends.

Your house should be built of living stones, not sinking ones. Jesus,
the prophecies about You said that the zeal for Your house consumed
You. May that zeal consume us, too. Help us to destroy everything
that gets in your way, but to do so with a pure heart.

> My soul is dry dust,
>   choking worldly ambition.
> My soul is wet earth,
>   bearing rich fruits of grace.
> My soul is a flame of fire,
>   blazing with passionate love.
>
> *From* The Black Book of Carmarthen

26 October Cedd *(see p.229)* Eata *(see p.234)*

Psalm 119:141-143   Jeremiah 9:23-24   Matthew 11:25-26

> 'I am small and despised.'
> 'Yes, but have I not said, "Do not despise the day of small things!"?'
>
> *Amy Carmichael*

> I'd rather be a little thing climbing up
> than a big thing tumbling down.
>
> *Old Sunday-school song*

> The man to whom little is not enough will not benefit from more.
>
> *Columbanus*

27 October

Psalm 119:144   Deuteronomy 32:47   Luke 7:1-7

> Many a man has grown upright because his tendrils have clung to a cross.
>
> *Hugh Redwood*

By Your cross and resurrection You have redeemed the world.

Say but the word, give me understanding, and I shall live. I shall not die, but I shall live and proclaim what You have done, Lord. Just say the word, Lord. Speak it to me. There is a power within the word You speak which is greater than the word itself. Give me understanding. Only You can impart revelation. People may explain to me, but only You can reveal it to me, even then, in a way that makes me realise it.

Realise that word within my heart. Realise Your word in my life.
Make it real, Lord, in me. Let Jesus the Living Word become
flesh again, and live among us, spoken through our lives to a
world that is dying for want of the knowledge of Him.

Send forth Your word and heal them. Let Your glory be over all
the earth.

Arthur Burt, Andy Raine

28 October

Psalm 119:145-152   Habakkuk 2:1, 3   Romans 10:13-15

Each of the sections of this, the longest of Psalms, has an initial letter as its title, following the Hebrew alphabet. Like the month, the alphabet and the Psalm are nearing the end. This section, 'Koph', speaks of a mature response to dependency and prayer in difficult circumstances. The soul cries out to God and waits in silent dependency on Him.

If we are the witness to Christ in today's market places, where there are constant demands on our whole person, we need silence. If we are to be always available, not only physically, but by empathy, sympathy, friendship, understanding ... we need silence. To be able to give joyous, unflagging hospitality, not only of house and food, but of mind, heart, body and soul, we need silence.

Catherine de Hueck Doherty

Sometimes God will wake us in the night to watch with Him and see things from a new perspective. Sometimes it's the only time He can be sure of getting our complete attention. Sometimes that is the time, the exact time, when our prayers are needed.

29 October

Psalm 119:153-160   Jonah 2:5-7   Romans 8:11

Your word was true from the beginning. Every one of Your righteous judgements endures for ever. Quicken me. Restore me to life. Lord, I believe.

Hal Lindsey is the author of *The Late Great Planet Earth* which (for a short time!) enjoyed immense popularity amongst Christian readers of some years ago. The following incident is from a subsequent book, *The Terminal Generation*.

> A nurse came up to me after I'd just spoken and said, 'Hal, will you please come and meet a soldier I brought over from the veterans' hospital? He accepted Christ as His Saviour and Lord as a result of my reading your book to him. It really took courage for him to come here tonight – he's in great pain because both arms and legs have been amputated. He lost them in Vietnam.' When I walked up to the wheeled stretcher on which he was lying, the young man looked up with a radiant face and said, 'Tell me, Hal, will my new body have arms and legs?' While choking back tears I turned to Philippians 3:20 and 21 and read:
>
>> But our citizenship is in heaven. And we eagerly await a Saviour from there, the Lord Jesus Christ, who, by the power that enables Him to bring everything under His control, will transform our lowly bodies so that they will be like His glorious body.
>
> 'Jim,' I said, 'your body will be like Jesus Christ's glorious body. We know that His resurrection body is perfect, so we know that yours will be, too.'

30 October

Psalm 119:161-168   1 Samuel 26:1-25   Titus 3:1-2

Great peace have they who love Your law; nothing offends them.
   Lord, do I love Your way? Is it great peace that I experience? or just medium-sized peace?
   Am I easily offended? easily tripped up? easily stumbled?
   Give me the peace that never returns evil for evil.

> Peace and comfort can be found nowhere except in simple
> obedience.
>
> *François Fénelon*

31 October All Hallows' Eve *(see p.222)* Bega *(see p.224)* Reinfrid *(see p.257)*

Psalm 119:169-176   Nehemiah 8:12   Philemon 4-7

This month we have read Psalm 119 and prayed: 'Give me understanding according to Your word.'

> Father, I know now, if I never knew it before, that only in You
> can my restless human heart find any peace. For I began life
> without knowledge, but full of needs. And the turmoil of my
> mind, the dissatisfaction of my life all stem from trying to meet
> those needs with the wrong things and in the wrong places.
>
> *Peter Marshall*

I have strayed like a lost sheep. Seek your servant. Lord, You have found me, loved and fed me. Now I must send something to others for whom nothing has been prepared.

It is everyone's duty to pray to God for their friends. And for all their friends, whether they are numerous or few. To make a habit of it may be to impose considerable demands upon time and memory, but it is not merely worthwhile, it is a matter of supreme importance. If you've only a handful of friends, it won't take long, and, if you're one of the lucky ones, with more friends than you can remember all at once, card-index them. Pray for them in instalments, but pray for them. Nobody knows what they may be doing if they pray for a friend tonight.

Hugh Redwood, God in the Shadows

November
Chosen people

1 November All Saints *(see p.222)*

Psalm 39:13   Deuteronomy 7:6   Acts 22:11-16

An unknown poet once wrote:

> How odd
> of God
> to choose
> the Jews!

This month we will be looking at the life and calling, tradition and history of God's very own chosen people, and seeing what we can learn.

When Tevye in *Fiddler on the Roof* is warned by the constable of the coming *pogrom* that will be a new wave of trouble for the Jewish community he turns to heaven, and says: 'Dear God, did You have to send me news like that? It's true we are the Chosen People. But once in a while can't You choose someone else?'

Dave Berg (of *Mad* magazine) asks:

> *Chosen for what?* Chosen to lead in the Path of Righteousness? Maybe. Chosen to be a Light unto the World? Maybe. Chosen to bear witness to my Friend, Whose name is *God*? Maybe. *Or* Chosen to take the *blame* from all the *blame throwers* for everything that goes wrong in the world ... the old story tells of a wise man talking to his bigoted acquaintance and he says, 'You're right, all the trouble in this world is caused by the Jews – *and the bicycle riders*!'

The bigot asked, 'Why the bicycle riders?'

The wise man says, '*Why the Jews?*'

2 November

Psalm 98:6-7   Micah 7:19   1 Corinthians 15:50-54

Rosh Hashana is the name of the Jewish new year festival, and on the first day of the new year a ceremony called 'Tashlich' takes place near a source of water. The ceremony originated in Germany in the fourteenth century in a non-Jewish custom – fish were fed with breadcrumbs as a sign of cleansing from sins. Now the prayer used is one which is based on the prophet Micah's words: 'and cast all thy sins into the depths of the sea'.

Corrie ten Boom, whose family loved and protected the Jews during the Nazi occupation of Holland, has said:

> When God forgives our sins, He separates them as far from
> us as the east is from the west, buries them in the bottom
> of the deepest sea, and puts up a sign for the Devil, saying,
> NO FISHING!

3 November

Psalm 118:20-28   Leviticus 23:39-43   John 7:37-46

The Feast of Tabernacles or booths (Succot) is the context for John's Gospel chapters 7 to 9.

During the Feast the procession carrying water from the pool of Siloam would circle the Temple and pour their libations on the altar, and this was done seven times on the last day of the Feast. Palm-branches and fruit were waved before God and Psalms 113 to 118 always sung.

Bonfires were lit, and men of piety danced, holding lighted torches and singing songs and hymns to the accompaniment of harps, lyres, cymbals and trumpets played by Levites.

The Talmud

In the evening of the final day of the Feast there was a magnificent sight as the lamps were lit in the Court of the Women. Light streamed forth so that the Temple shone with an incredible brightness of light. It seems that this was the moment that occasioned Jesus' amazing statement:

I AM the Light of the world.

4 November

Psalm 119:96-106   Jeremiah 31:33-34   2 Timothy 3:14–4:3

Simchat Torah, the Rejoicing of the Law, is not a biblically prescribed feast, but occurs immediately after Succot.

The Scrolls of the Law are taken out of the Holy Ark and carried in men's arms. Fathers dance with their children, and women throw sweets on them. According to tradition, the synagogue must be encircled seven times or more. The festival is celebrated on the day on which the reading of the Torah is completed and begun again from Genesis. The Torah is read on an annual cycle, so the Jewish community created a great festival of joy on a day that could have been only a day of tedious re-rolling of the community's scrolls from the end to the beginning. We might also ask, is it not a great cause for rejoicing to complete a reading of the Scriptures by the community and to have the opportunity to begin reading again?!

Daniel Juster in his study *Jewish Roots* asks whether the early Messianic Jews would have had an ark:

I believe they did. We historically know that they read the Torah (i.e. Genesis to Deuteronomy). In the first century Torahs were kept in an ark! Did they keep the New Testament Scriptures in the Ark? We do not know. However, we do know that ancient eastern churches that stem back to the Syrian church have ark-like structures in which they keep the Scriptures.

Among some of the Orthodox Hasidic communities today this celebration soars into great heights of joy and energy. For Messianic Jews there is further cause for rejoicing – all true believers in Messiah are accounted righteous and have the joy of God's own Torah written on our hearts by His Spirit.

> So GOD went to Moses and said,
> 'I have a commandment for you.'
> 'How much is it?'
> 'Nothing.'
> 'Good, then I'll take ten.'
>
> *David Berg*, My Friend GOD

5 November

Psalm 9:1   Deuteronomy 6:4-9   Matthew 22:35-38

A *mezuzah* (Hebrew for 'doorpost') is a cylinder of metal or wood put aslant on the right-hand doorpost of the house. Inside is a rolled fragment of parchment on which is a summary of the Deuteronomy command: 'Remember God and love him with your all.'

Anyone going in or out is obliged to remember it and may stretch out their hand towards it, and kiss the hand. In such a house the whole course of life ought to be subject to the authority of God's word.

A tale is told of a Gentile buying a house from a Jew, and noticing the *mezuzah*, asking its significance. 'This is a *mezuzah*,' the Jew explained. 'Inside the case you see is a scroll on which are written the most sacred and holy words of the Jewish law.'

When the transaction was completed, the purchaser of the house was interested to see if the *mezuzah* would be taken with the outgoing family. But no, the *mezuzah* stayed, and every day he saw it on his way in or out, until finally his curiosity would hold no longer. With a small screwdriver he removed the case, opened the tiny parchments with trembling fingers, and read:

'HELP! I am being held prisoner in a *mezuzah* factory.'

To spiritualise the story mercilessly – we too are prisoners, faced day to day with the question, 'Do you seek HIM with all your heart, and with all your soul, and with all your mind, and with all your strength?'

Amen. Make us Your captives, Lord, for only then can we be free.

6 November Illtyd *(see p.243)*

Psalm 46   1 Kings 17:9-16   John 10:1-27

The Feast of Dedication mentioned in John's Gospel is more commonly known as Hanukkah, and usually occurs close to Christmas time. It recalls the days of the Maccabees who led the Jewish people in revolt against their Syrio-Greek oppressors during the inter-testamental period. The accounts of these events will be found in translations of the Apocrypha, or in editions of the Scriptures which include deutero-canonical texts.

Jesus' words are about being a good, true shepherd, and are intended as a contrast to the evil shepherd who had compromised their religious practices with those of pagan Greek culture.

The candlestick used during the eight days of Hanukkah has eight stems, lit by an extra candle called the shammas. It recalls how, when the Temple was rededicated after the victory of the Maccabees and the Menorah was lit, they found only enough oil to keep it alight for one day (and this original Menorah was supplied by oil). Only the prescribed oil could be used and it took eight days before it could be prepared. Miraculously the one day's supply was enough for the eight days.

The lighted *Hanukiah* in Jewish households of today should be placed in a window so everyone can see it. An additional candle is lit on each day of the festival.

This song 'Maoz Tzur' is a traditional one sung after the candles are lit:

Rock of Ages, let our song
praise Thy saving power;
Thou, amidst the raging foes
wast our shelt'ring tower.
Furious they assailed us
but Thine arm availed us,
and Thy word broke their sword
when our own strength failed us.

7 November Willibrord *(see p.265)*

Psalm 42:7   Jonah 1:17–2:2   Matthew 12:38-41

'Jonah was in the belly of the fish.'

Many people will say: 'That is impossible, that is a fable.' But God, who can make fishes 100 feet long, says that it is possible. (Can you make a fish one inch long?) And God can do an even greater miracle: Christ says that as Jonah was three days and nights in the stomach of the fish, so He would be three days and nights in the heart of the earth, in the grave, and then rise from the dead. Jonah says inside the fish: 'Salvation is of the Lord!' Salvation, in Hebrew, is Yeshua, or Jeshua; that is the Hebrew name for Jesus...

Professor Samuel Schultz argues that there is no room for the idea of a harsh vindictive God of justice in the Old Testament to be contrasted with a God of love and mercy in the New. Love and mercy are always offered before judgement is rendered. Yeshua's warnings concerning judgement in the New Testament are as severe as anything in the Old, even if we argue that the highest personal revelation of God's love is seen in Yeshua!

Incidentally, the 4 April 1896 *Literary Digest* gave a story of a Mediterranean whale that demolished a harpoon boat.

> Two men were lost ... One was found alive in the whale's belly
> a day and a half after it was killed. James Bartley lived with no
> after effects except his skin was tanned by the gastric juices.

8 November

Psalm 111:9; 109:13   Exodus 3:13-15   Luke 1:47-64

> The Jews would not willingly tread upon the smallest piece
> of paper in their way, but took it up, for possibly, said they,
> the name of God may be upon it. Though there was a little
> superstition in this, yet truly there is nothing but good religion
> in it, if we apply it to man. Trample not on any; there may be
> some work of grace there, that thou knowest not of. The name
> of God may be written upon that soul thou treadest on: it
> may be a soul that Christ thought so much of as to give His
> precious blood for it; therefore, despise it not.
>
> *Samuel Taylor Coleridge*

> The letters JHWH are a jumble of Hebrew consonants, and a
> better translation than Jehovah is 'The Lord'. The name of God
> is so awful, so unpronounceable, that it has never been used
> by any of his creatures. Indeed, it is said that if, inadvertently,
> the great and terrible name of God should be spoken, the
> universe would explode.
>
> *Madeleine L'Engle*

The Scriptures recognise how important a name is; it denotes someone in particular, and affirms that they have significance.

> The God who created and formed you says this, Do not be
> afraid for I have redeemed you. I have called you by your name.
> You are mine.
>
> *Isaiah 43:1*

One of the strongest curses ever framed is that someone's name be cut off, remembered no more.
Madeleine L'Engle writes:

> ...we live in a world which would reduce us to our social security
> numbers. Area codes, zip codes, credit card codes, all take
> precedence over our names. Our signatures already mean so little

that it wouldn't be a surprise if, soon, we, like prisoners, are known only by our numbers. But that is not how it was meant to be.

Survivors of the concentration camps still have numbers branded on their bodies; they bear the mark of a system that needed to dehumanise them.

9 November

Psalm 17:10, 14-15   Deuteronomy 15:7-11   1 Corinthians 13:3

Stooping to help somebody. This position is called *Mitzvah*, a good deed. This, they say, *nudges God* right to the *Book of Golden Deeds*. And God writes down the *Mitzvah* in *diamond-studded letters ten feet high*.

In the twelfth century Moses Maimonides devised eight ways to nudge God for a *Mitzvah* while performing *charity. Each one higher than the other*. The highest degree is to make the man who needs charity *self-supporting*. The next highest degree is where the one that *gives* and the one that *receives* are *not* aware of each other. The third Inferior degree is where the *recipient* knows the *giver*, but the giver does *not* know the recipient. A lesser Mitzvah is when the poor man knows to whom he is indebted, but the giver does not know to whom he has given. The fifth degree is where the giver puts alms into the hands of the poor without being asked. The sixth degree is where he puts money into the hands of the poor *after* being asked. The seventh degree is where he gives *less* than he should, but does so *cheerfully*. The eighth degree is where he gives *resentfully*.

But there's a *catch* to all these *Mitzvahs*. It's best illustrated by an old story about a Rabbi, who was so addicted to golf that he even snuck off on the *High Holy Day* to play. That day he made a *hole in one*. As he danced about with exultation, there was a rumble of thunder and a clap of lightning, and God's voice boomed down on him. '*So who are you going to tell?*' That's the *catch* when you earn a *Mitzvah*. '*So who are you going to tell? If you do, you'll lose it.* The question is, what have you *done* for someone today, that you *didn't have to do* ... and whom *didn't you tell?*'

Dave Berg, My Friend GOD

10 November

Psalm 89:19-29   1 Samuel 20:28-42   Mark 14:22-24

It is important to the understanding of the story of David and Saul to understand that David and Jonathan, Saul's son, had entered into a covenant relationship with each other.

This agreement was far more than a friendship or business contract – in some ways its significance was equal to or greater than that of marriage. It involved a vow that was binding for life, sealed by the shedding of blood, an exchange of possessions, a covenant meal of bread and wine with the promise:

> This bread is my body, all my strength is yours and this wine my blood which I will shed willingly on your behalf. Your enemies become my enemies, too. All I have is yours by right.

Abram and God made such a covenant, and on the strength of it God could demand the surrender of his only son. Jesus spoke out His part of a similar covenant at the Seder meal with His disciples, and we know that even if we are faithless He remains faithful.

When Saul suspected David and Jonathan had become covenant-brothers he was angry because whether Jonathan lived or died David became king by right if he should so choose.

11 November   Martin of Tours *(see p.248)*

Psalm 68:1, 3   Esther 3:1-6   Luke 1:51-55

Purim, which commemorates the deliverance of the Jews from the hands of Haman through Esther the queen and her uncle Mordecai, is the feast of reversals. It reminds us that eventually the Evil One's machinations will be tolerated no longer and all shall be well and all manner of things shall be well.

> Purim is the nearest thing Judaism has to a carnival. The Talmud gives leave to a worshipper to drink on this day until he cannot tell the difference between 'Blessed be Moredecai' and 'Cursed be Haman'. To the credit of many otherwise non-observant Jews, they often do their best to comply. In Israel a public street festival not unlike Mardi Gras has sprung up, with the name As'lo Yoda, the Talmud word for 'until he cannot tell the difference'.
>
> The day before Purim is the Fast of Esther, a sunrise-to-sundown abstention. At sundown thesynagogues fill up. The marked difference between this and all other occasions of the Jewish year is the number of children on hand. Purim is the children's night in the house of the Lord. It always has been, and the children sense their rights and exercise them.
>
> They carry flags and noisemakers, the traditional whirling rattles called 'groggers', which can make a staggering racket. After the evening prayers the reading of the Book of Esther begins, solemnly enough, with the customary blessing over a scroll and the chanting of the opening verses in a special musical mode heard only on this holiday. The Reader chants through the first and second chapters and comes at last to the long-awaited sentence,
>
> 'After these things, the king raised to power Haman the Agagite' – but nobody hears the last two words. The name 'Haman' triggers off stamping, pounding, and a hurricane of groggers. The Reader waits patiently. The din dies. He chants on, and soon strikes another 'Haman'. Bedlam breaks loose again. This continues, and since Haman is now a chief figure in the story, the noisy outbursts come pretty frequently. The children, far from getting tired or bored, warm up to the work. They do it with sure mob instinct; poised silence during the reading, explosions on each 'Haman'. Passages occur where Haman's name crops up several times in a very short space. The children's assaults come like

pistol shots. The Reader's patience wears thin and finally breaks. It is impossible to read with so many interruptions.

He gestures angrily at the children through the grogger storm and shoots a glance of appeal to the rabbi. This, of course, is what the children have been waiting for ... Thereafter to the end it is a merciless battle between the Reader and the children. He tries to slur over the thick falling 'Haman's, they trip him every time with raucous salvos. He stumbles on to the final verse, exhausted, beaten, furious, and all is disordered hilarity in the synagogue. It is perhaps not quite fair to make the Reader stand in for Haman on this evening, but that is approximately what happens.

Herman Wouk, This is my God

12 November

Psalm 107:43   Deuteronomy 33:3   John 15:15b-16

Rabbinic disciples were people who were attached to a particular person and who then themselves decided to follow and accept the teachings of that person. To become a disciple was entirely up to the individual: they chose to follow a rabbi and accept his teachings until they felt able to leave and establish independent status as teachers themselves. Jesus was different. He chose his disciples.

Keith Whitehead, Emmaus Community

In this light it is interesting to look again at the story of Mary and Martha. The contrast between them is not just that between contemplative and active. The expression 'sit at the feet of' is not just a description of what would make a good snapshot of Lazarus, Mary and Martha to put in the family album: Mary sat listening to Jesus, looking up into His face. Instead it is the equivalent of Saul of Tarsus studying for a prolonged period under Rabbi Gamaliel. When Jesus disputed with other teachers he often argued from the rabbinical principle, 'From the minor case to the major', or as Arthur Burt would say, 'The greater includes the lesser'. So if circumcision could be performed on the Sabbath to make a minor member of the body whole before God, then miraculous power could be used on the Sabbath to heal and make a whole body whole. Or if the commandment said to not commit adultery, the greater which included this would say 'not even in your heart'. The greater includes the lesser, but the small things mattered, too.

> I have a friend you can go to with
> your small problems.
> My friend's name is
> GOD.
>
> *Dave Berg*

13 November

Psalm 39:2   Isaiah 61:1-3   John 20:1-16

As a young Dutch-Jewish refugee Johanna-Ruth Dobschiner found an illustrated children's Bible in the home she was evacuated to, and re-read the familiar stories of Noah, Abraham, Isaac, Jacob, Joseph, Moses and Pharaoh, Joshua, Saul, David, Solomon, Haman, Jeremiah, Isaiah, and Malachi...

> Almost unconsciously I entered a part of history previously unknown to me, yet strangely familiar. It still dealt with the people of Israel but new characters had entered the scene, names I had never been taught, names which had never been mentioned at home or in school lessons. Scenes which took place in Synagogue and Temple, according to this Bible, registered a blank when searching my memory. Yet all the stories were so obviously Jewish ... One person outshone all others in these stories – a prophet born in Israel. As the weeks and months passed by, his life became part of mine. The readings about him and incidents concerning him became more important to me than anything else in my own environment. I found I could tolerate my isolation without frustration, always longing for the next opportunity to learn more about him for he had become my hero.

Then the cross:

> While still reading of his agonies, in myself I wished for him to show the power that was his, and free himself from that cross. I knew he would do it, and as I read on I waited eagerly for the moment when this would be described ... Instead, 'It is finished.' I had lost the one I loved dearly, although I had never met him, except within the pages of this book. Now all was lost to me.
>
> According to the custom of my people I mourned for him seven days. My thoughts were wholly centred on my loss and a deep sense of depression settled upon me. I was weepy, edgy, moody and unhappy. True, I had suffered disappointment, but why not act as an adult and read the remaining pages of the book?
>
> The first day of the week, and Mary finds his grave empty, the body stolen. What next! Having fought back her tears for so long, Mary now gave way to her grief. She felt as I had done during these past ten days, and again I joined in her sorrow.
>
> ...and then continued reading...

J.R. Dobschiner, Selected to Live

14 November

Psalm 78:3-8   Isaiah 62:1   Romans 11:26-29

The atmosphere of the New Testament carried on the spirit of the Hebrew Scriptures pervasively and profoundly – but Rabbinic Judaism replaces revelation with human reason, and this development was well under way even before the coming of Jesus, and culminated in the rejection of Him and the witness of His Jewish apostles by the first-century Jewish religion leadership. Rabbinic Judaism is the child of the first-century Pharisees who added the prayer of condemnation against Jewish believers and Jesus to synagogue liturgy. This all took place long before the Church had become infiltrated by paganism and begun to reject its Jewish roots.

Sometimes in John's Gospel and other places we are confused by the phrase 'the Jews' being used to condemn the religious establishment, Pharisees, Sadducees and religious leaders: were not John and the other writers also Jews? Americans abroad are called 'Yanks', but in the Southern United States 'Yankee' is used as a sectional term to refer to the North. Galilean Jews referred to Judeans as 'the Jews' since 'Judean' and 'Jew' in Greek are the same word.

Such condemnations were after all in-house criticisms and not intended as ammunition for generations of anti-Semites.

Anti-Semites never quote any of the following:

- John 4:22 'Salvation is of the Jews'
- that Jesus was, is and forever will be a Jew descended from Jacob!
- that 'the common people (Jews) heard Him gladly'
- that many wept openly at His death and
- that the priestly establishment feared all of Jerusalem following Him (Luke 20:19; 22:2)
- that myriads of Jews did follow Him (Acts 21:20)
- that Jewish apostles spread the good news of Yeshua throughout the world.

The proper scriptural response is gratitude and love. Paul says, 'It is not you who support the root, but the root supports you' [Romans 11:18].

15 November

Psalm 137:4   Genesis 18:16-33   2 Peter 3:9-17

> Let me tell you an old Hebrew legend:
>
> It is written that as long as GOD can find 36 *just men*, He'll keep this world going.
>
> They are called 'Lamed Vornicks' meaning 36.

It is also rumoured that GOD sends out a prophet in every generation to find these 36 *just men*. So far there are only 35 names on that list. Now I'm not claiming to be a prophet. But somewhere, reading these words at this very moment is the 36th *just man*!

Now the world is saved

Dave Berg

Elie Wiesel writes:

One of the Just Men came to Sodom, determined to save its inhabitants from sin and punishment. Night and day he walked the streets and markets protesting against greed and theft, falsehood and indifference. In the beginning, people listened and smiled ironically. Then they stopped listening: he no longer amused them. The killers went on killing, the wise men kept silent, as if there were no Just Man in their midst.

One day a child, moved by compassion for the unfortunate teacher, approached him with these words:

'Poor stranger, you shout, you scream, don't you see that it is hopeless?'

'Yes, I see,' answered the Just Man.

'Then why do you go on?'

'I'll tell you why. In the beginning, I thought I could change man. Today, I know I cannot. If I still shout today, if I still scream, it is to prevent man from ultimately changing me.'

16 November Celtic Advent Begins *(see p.229)*

Psalm 40:7   Isaiah 58:9   Hebrews 10:7

God desires to look at us with open face and say, 'Here I am, and I am here for you.' The Hebrew word for this is '*Hineni*' – and there are familiar stories of people responding to God in this way. *Hineni* means 'I'm ready, Lord; I'll go if You send me; I'm listening, Lord, tell me what You would have me know.'

'Abraham!'
 'Hineni,' he replied.
 'Take your son, your only son Isaac, whom you love, and go to the region of Moriah. Sacrifice him there.'
 'Hineni?'
 'The fire and the wood are here, where is the lamb for the sacrifice?'

God called to Moses from the bush that was burning, 'Moses! Moses!'
 And Moses said, 'Hineni.'

A voice called in the night. The child Samuel gave answer: 'Hineni – what do You want?'

'Whom shall I send, and who will go for Me?' said the voice from the midst of the throne.
 And Isaiah responded, 'Hineni.'

Lord God, help us to be willing and available, open to your call, to say, 'Hineni, Adonai. Here I am.'

17 November Hild *(see p.291)*

Psalm 105:26-38, 43   Exodus 7:20-24   Acts 7:36

The plagues, although grievous physical trials to the Egyptians, represent far more:

The plagues undercut faith in the Egyptian gods and show the powerlessness of the Egyptian gods to protect Egypt from the God of Israel. The Nile, for example, is a 'god'; it turns rancid. Hupi is the frog 'god' and Egypt is given enough frogs to feast on frogs' legs for decades to come! The sun is a chief 'god'; it is blotted out by darkness. Most alarming is the death of the first born – especially Pharaoh's own first born – who would have been considered an incarnation of the sun god!

Egyptian religion was a very sophisticated pagan ritual of magic and superstition. Egypt was the most powerful nation of that age. Therefore, the exodus of this enslaved people was truly a defeat of paganism, of all false gods, of all superstition and magic, a defeat authored by the one Creator – God!

The defeat of Egypt and its gods by the Israelites could only lead to the conclusion that God is the Lord of all the earth. The exodus of Israel struck terror into the hearts of the decadent, utterly corrupt Canaanite people whom Israel was to conquer.

Daniel Juster, Jewish Roots

18 November

Psalm 136:1-12   Exodus 13:1-15   Mark 14:14-16

The family is gathered for the Seder meal, and a young boy asks the question that demands the recounting of the story of the miracle of the exodus, a story rehearsed from generation to generation.

> 'Why is this evening
> different from all other evenings?'

> 'Because we were once slaves
> of the Pharaoh of Egypt;
> but the Lord heard our voice:
> He felt our sorrow
> and understood our oppression;

with His outstretched arm
He led us out of Egypt.
Then we were at last set free.
Blessèd is the Lord
who promised salvation to Israel:
he has kept His promise
and kept the Covenant
He established with Abraham.'

19 November

Psalm 16:9-11   2 Chronicles 30:2-5   1 Corinthians 5:7-8

Jesus and his disciples celebrate the Passover meal a full day earlier than they should, since he knows that if they waited it would not be possible, and He has so desired to share the feast with them, and will not be disappointed. (They are only one day out, after all, and in 2 Chronicles we read how God blessed the reinstitution of Passover even when by force of circumstance His people were a whole month out from the correct date.) Jesus would be on trial all night and nailed to the cross around nine the next morning. Six hours later He died at the exact time when the Passover lambs were also killed. At the sunset the Preparation would be over and the Passover Feast would begin which must be observed as Sabbath [Leviticus 23:4-8] known as the first day of unleavened bread. Any leaven is carefully hunted for and swept out of a Jewish home before these seven days begin. The soldiers are urged to break the legs of crucified men so they will die more quickly and be removed before the Feast Sabbath begins: Jesus is already dead by now. He is carried hastily to a borrowed tomb, observed by the women. Between the Feast and the usual weekly Sabbath they have time to prepare the spices for His embalming, then early on the first day of the week, when it is already 'the third day since all this took place' they hurry to the tomb and find him gone. Death could not hold Him.

20 November

Psalm 147:14   Leviticus 23:9-11   James 1:17-18

On the fourteenth day of that month the Passover lamb was prepared. After sunset it was eaten, and this began the Sabbath which was a high holy day, the first day of unleavened bread. On the next day, the sixteenth, the day after this Sabbath day when no work was done, a priest would search for the first sprouts of grain in the ground, carry his find back to the Temple and wave them before the Lord as the 'first fruits'.

Another seven times seven days, a sabbath of sabbaths, makes fifty days, 'pentecost', and by then the grain will have ripened until an armful can be gathered – but for now it is just an early sign of life, first fruits from the earth.

21 November

Psalm 80:7-19   Genesis 4:10   2 Timothy 2:2-7

During the fifty days between First Fruits and Pentecost (or Weeks) occurs another more modern marked day on the Jewish calendar. This is Holocaust Day – Yom Ha Shoah – the Day of Calamity which recalls the destruction of European Jewry under the unspeakable horrors of the reign of the Nazis. The day is marked in both synagogues and larger communities by services which include memorial prayers, readings from concentration camp poetry and literature, and recommitment to the survival of Israel.

> My heart still beats inside my breast
> while friends depart for other worlds.
> Perhaps, it's better – who can say? –
> than watching this, to die today?
>
> *Eva Pickova, age 12, Auschwitz*

Then they came for the Jews and I didn't speak up because I was not a Jew.

Pastor Martin Niemöller

22 November   C.S. Lewis *(see p.247)*

Psalm 121:3, 5-8   Genesis 24:34-58   Hebrews 11:5-16

> O Lord our God
> and God of our fathers!
> Mercifully direct and guide our steps
> to our destination,
> and let us arrive there
> in health, joy and peace!
> Keep us from snares and dangers,
> and protect us from enemies
> that we might meet along the way.
> Bless and protect our journey!
> Let us win favour in Your eyes
> and in the sight of those around us.
> Blessèd are You, O Lord,
> who hear and grant our prayers!

Praying with the Jewish Tradition,
trs. Paula Gifford

23 November   Columbanus *(see p.231)*

Psalm 65:9-13   Leviticus 23:15-22   Acts 2:1-2

The temple priest returns to the grain field, now full and rich with a very ripe crop of grain, ready for harvest. He cuts and gathers enough to make two loaves. Back in the temple, he beats and presses the seed, grinding it to flour, adding water to fashion loaves from the dough and slips them into the depths of a fired oven. He waits. It is now about eight in the morning. Soon the loaf will be ready to lift out from the oven, take to the altar and lift up to God. Then the day of Pentecost will have fully come.

Meanwhile at a house somewhere in the city people are praying, and the presence of God bursts upon them. The Day of Pentecost is fulfilled. Harvest is here. The church is born.

Gene Edwards

24 November Eanfleda *(see p.234)*

Psalm 126   Ruth 3:18; 4:13-16   John 10:16

Shavuot or Pentecost speaks of harvest fulfilling the promise of the first fruits. At Shavuot the Book of Ruth is read for the main action of the story takes place around harvest-time.

God called the Jewish people into relationship with Him in order that they might in turn reveal His nature, His character and His greatness to the other nations and be a light to the world.

The story of God's care and mercy towards Ruth who was a Moabitess makes beautiful reading, and reminds us that God's choice of Israel as His peculiar people was in the nature of a First-Fruits festival – the full harvest must embrace all peoples.

25 November

Psalm 19:1-6   Judges 21:16-25   1 Corinthians 7:9-12

The last chapters of the book of Judges can be summed up in the final verse: they all did what seemed right in their own eyes. It is a pantomime of neglect, abuse, reprisals, massacre, hasty oaths and back-pedalling.

The 600 Benjamite men were given 400 virgins from Jabesh Gilead – the only survivors respectively from both areas, but that left 200 Benjamites still needing wives, and all the other Israelites had sworn not to give their own daughters to a Benjamite.

Instead, they turned a blind eye, and let the Benjamites hide nearby when the young girls came out to dance through the vineyards at harvest-time. We read of no complaints: their families were satisfied, the couples returned to larger portions of land, and were never able to be divorced. However hastily, some of the couples at least had chance to decide for themselves who'd be carried off by whom. Today 'Tu B'Av' is celebrated as the Festival of Love.

At a Jewish wedding ceremony the marrying couple exchange vows under a very special canopy known as a 'hupah'. The rods at the four corners are either able to stand on the ground or are held by the groom's attendants. The top of the canopy is his own prayer tallit (a fringed shawl). The symbolism is that he is taking the bride under his roof and she is becoming part of his house.

> A song shall be heard in the cities of Judah
> and in the streets of Jerusalem
> a song of joy, a cry of gladness
> a song of the Bridegroom,
> a song of the Bride.
>
> *Jeremiah 33:10-11*

26 November

Psalm 116:3-4   Ecclesiastes 12:14   Luke 21:21

In AD 70 before the fall of Jerusalem there were several divisions within Judaism – Pharisees, Sadducees and Essenes were the most prominent sects. Nazarene Jews (Jewish believers in Jesus) were another section of the Jewish community. But when the Roman armies approached Jerusalem to quell Israel's rebellion, these Nazarenes fled the city, taking up residence in Petra. They thereby avoided terrible destruction and slaughter by the Roman army. The rest of the Jews distrusted them thereafter and assumed there was treachery afoot. Why did they flee? In Luke 21 and Matthew 24 Jesus predicted that Jerusalem would be surrounded by enemies. His followers were commanded, whenever they saw this beginning to occur, to 'flee to the mountains'. They were not traitors; they were simply following their Yeshua's teaching.

Amazingly, this date, Tisha B'av, was exactly that of the destruction of the first Temple; now 656 years later the second Temple was destroyed (and in 1492 it was on this day the decree of Expulsion of Jews from Spain took effect). This date is still marked by mourning customs.

Now some people argue that, with the birth of modern Israel, mourning for the fall of Zion has become an anachronism.

But the Jewish national memory is long. It is not likely that the given date of the capture of Jerusalem and the ruin of two temples will be forgotten.

In the twelfth century the Crusades set out to free the Holy Land from Arab-Islamic control. The cry then went out that it was inconsistent to seek to rid the Holy Land of infidels when there were infidel Jews within the midst of the lands of Europe. Hence Crusaders held their crosses high as they pillaged and destroyed Jewish lives and property throughout Europe on their way to the Holy Land. Many were burned alive or tortured. Bad theology easily kills – as surely as obedience to the words of Jesus brought life to the Nazarenes at Petra. There is a tendency to read Scripture in such a way that we assume all the negative words to Israel are still addressed to Israel, and that anything nice to say will be transferred to the 'church'.

We may validly receive from Scripture a subjective answer or a word with real prophetic significance to us. What we cannot do is disregard its original intention. ('Upper and Nether Springs' speaks about Northumberland for us, but we are not saying that was the author's original intention, only that God has quickened such an understanding of these passages in addition to their own factual meaning.)

27 November

Psalm 30:1-5   Job 2:7-13   John 11:32-40

Jewish custom was to mourn for the dead three full days and nights known as 'days of weeping' which were followed by four 'days of lamentation' thus making seven days. One rabbinical notion suggested that for three days the person's spirit wandered about the sepulchre hoping to re-enter the body, but when corruption set in the spirit left. For this reason loud lamentations began on the fourth day. When the seven-day mourning period was over, and the visitors had left, the mourner returned to a quiet period of less intense mourning for

30 days, then 11 months to progressively come out of mourning. Close relatives make a practice of saying 'the Kaddish' often in the eleven months – a prayer of praise to God and longing for His Kingdom. Its wording is parallel to that of the Lord's Prayer and is often used at other times, as well.

> Glorified and sanctified be the Great name of God in the world which He created according to His will. May He establish His Kingdom during your days and during the days of the whole house of Israel at a near time speedily and soon. Say, Amen. May His Great name be praised for ever, glorified and exalted, extolled and honoured, and praised and magnified be the Name of the Holy One, blessed be He, whose glory transcends, yea is beyond all blessing and praise and consolation which is uttered in the world. Say, Amen. May there be great peace from heaven upon us and upon all Israel. Say, Amen. May He who makes peace from the heavens grant peace upon us and upon all Israel. Say, Amen.
>
> *The Kaddish*

David Kossoff in his book *A Small Town is a World* tells of Rabbi Mark sitting by the death-bed of his friend old Mendel. Mendel sensed the Rabbi's grief and made jokes. But then when his breathing grew shallow he asked the Rabbi for one last wish, his voice by now rather faint. 'Anything, old friend,' said Rabbi Mark, bending forward to hear the words. 'When it's all over,' said Mendel, 'and it's time to lift me into my coffin, promise not to hold me under my arms ... I'm ticklish.'

A prayer upon waking:

> The soul You gave me is pure, my Lord: You gave it life and You preserve it within me, and at the end, when the time comes, You will take it away, only to give it back to me one day. But as long as that soul is in me it will worship You, O Lord my God, the God of my fathers, from whom one day the dead will receive back their souls.

One Jew exclaimed to his friend:

'You should live to be 120 years and a couple of months.'
'Why a couple of months?'
'So you shouldn't die suddenly.'

28 November

Psalm 104:19-23   Isaiah 45:3-7   Mark 1:21-32

> Evening comes when You call,
> and all nature listens to You
> because You hold it all.
> And now You hold me.

Annie Herring and Matthew Ward

> Blessed are You, O Lord our God, King of the universe! At Your word night falls. In Your wisdom You open heaven's gates, You control the elements and rotate the seasons. You set the stars in the vault of heaven. You created night and day. You cause the light to fade when darkness comes and the darkness to melt away in the light of a new day. O ever-living and eternal God, You will always watch over us, Your creatures. Blessed are You, O Lord, at whose word night falls.

From The Talmud

> In name of the Lord Jesus,
> and of the Spirit of healing balm,
> In name of the Father of Israel,
> I lay me down to rest.

From Carmina Gadelica

The rest of the seventh day is a memorial of creation, but also a sign of the covenant between God's people and Himself. If a king were to ratify a treaty or agreement this would bear a sign, usually an image of the gods he owed allegiance to, but Israel was commanded to not make any such image – instead the sabbath itself would be the sign, and a representation of His nature. Only Israel had a seven-day cycle of weeks. We do not sense today how unique Israel truly was, for the seven-day week has since become the practice of the world.

Adapted from Jewish Roots

29 November

Psalm 45:1   Leviticus 26:2-4   Romans 8:26

There is a story told about a Jewish farmer who, through carelessness, did not get home before sunset one Sabbath and was forced to spend the day in the field, waiting for sunset the next day before being able to return home.

Upon his return home he was met by a rather perturbed rabbi who chided him for his carelessness. Finally the rabbi asked him: 'What did you do out there all day in the field? Did you at least pray?'

The farmer answered: 'Rabbi, I am not a clever man. I don't know how to pray properly. What I did was simply to recite the alphabet all day and let God form the words for Himself.'

When we come to celebrate we bring the alphabet of our lives. If our hearts and minds are full of warmth, love, enthusiasm, song and dance, then these are the letters we bring. If they are full of tiredness, despair, blandness, pain and boredom, then those are our letters. Bring them. Spend them. Celebrate them. It is God's task to make the words!

Ronald Rolheiser

30 November

Psalm 116:7   Isaiah 49:15-16   2 John 12

If my lips could sing as many songs
as there are waves in the sea:
if my tongue could sing as many hymns
as there are ocean billows:
if my mouth
filled the firmament with praise:
if my face
shone like the sun and moon together:
if my hands
were to hover in the sky like powerful eagles
and my feet
ran across mountains as swiftly as the deer:
all that would not be enough
to pay You fitting tribute,
O Lord my God.

Unknown author

December
Deeper life

1 December Charles de Foucauld *(see p.229)*

Psalm 43:3   Genesis 5:22-24   Hebrews 11:15-16

This month's notes are on the subject of the call to a deeper life.

One dynamic of that call is the sense that where we really belong is somewhere else, that we have heard something inside us calling us to 'Come away'. We belong to a different Kingdom: our home is another country.

It often is like this:

'Follow Me.'
'Yes, Lord, I'll follow You … But, Lord…'
'Yes?'
'Where to? Where will I be going?'
'With Me.'

From time to time the sense of alienation from everything around us may be strong, the sense of being a stranger, someone on a journey; but the stranger can see things through different eyes from those of people who live in that one place all the time.

This world is not my home…

2 December Jean Donovan *(see p.233)*

Psalm 86:2-4   Job 23:8-14   Matthew 10:9-20

It is a terrible risk to follow even a Friend into the unknown. It is made worse by the fact that He so often seems to disappear or go ahead instead of staying close by.

The instructions He gives us should make it so much easier to continue on the journey: but what instructions?

- 'Don't provide extra for yourself in case I let you down.'
- 'Don't worry what to say.'
- 'I will be there when you need Me, even if it's only at the last moment.'

Instructions like these leave us incredibly vulnerable, but they are only examples of what He really is asking from us: that we choose intentionally, deliberately to make ourselves vulnerable and to walk in that vulnerability!

3 December

Psalm 22:6-7   Exodus 4:2-3a   Matthew 26:6-13

God tells Moses to throw down even the one thing he still holds in his hand.

Jesus, having come to our world as a human being, becomes more humbled still, His life taken from Him in the ugliest of executions – what a waste it looked! His life was poured out in intentional uselessness, like the expensive ointment the woman poured on His head.

Some of us are indignant at the waste, like Judas was.

Some of us are envious of her – at least she had the ointment.

We would like to have something to give, to pour out for love of Him, but we don't have even that. It seems we don't have anything.

Nothing to offer except our uselessness, and our choice to be with Him: and that is a choice that no one but Him is likely to put any value on.

4 December

Psalm 139:9-10   Job 4:12-13   1 Thessalonians 4:11

In the face of all kinds of pain we find that often there is nothing to say, but it's impossible to be still.

A woman whose child had been killed in an accident talked about her reactions. No one could say anything that would help, she said, and God was silent too – as if He knew better than to try to say anything.

The Scripture says to be still and know that He is God, but she couldn't be still, not at all.

But even when you don't talk to God or have any stillness of your own to bring Him, you can still be met by God in His stillness.

That's what she discovered, and that eventually 'the stillness becomes part of you'.

5 December

Psalm 139:5   Song of Songs 8:5a   Mark 1:35

We are asked to follow in the footsteps of our Lord when they are not clear in the road, and even when that road runs through desert.

Going into the desert we are never quite sure what to expect. Being alone can be peaceful, or frightening, or just a dull nothing. But coming out of the desert we find that we are leaning on Him in a new way.

The Russian word *poustinia* only means 'desert', but is the name given to the wooden hut where someone is shut away for time alone with God.

It is a typical experience for the person undergoing *poustinia* to feel nothing is happening at all, but as they emerge they find others waiting, pressing them to share what God has given them in the *poustinia*.

And they will not be disappointed.

6 December

Psalm 90:12   Song of Songs 2:10-15   Ephesians 4:26, 32

It is important to remember that the deeper life is in fact a deepening of our own relationship with God.

Our experience of other relationships tells us that it is perfectly possible to be with another person for hours day after day without consciously spending time together. In some relationships there may be a deliberate policy of avoiding being together.

Being in relationship with God can be very similar, avoiding time alone, or filling that time with anything at all that can distract from the real question of how much love there is in our heart for Him, and how much being together with Him is a priority, first love for Him freshly rekindled, the relationship still deepening.

Are you there for Him?

7 December   Diuma *(see p.232)*

Psalm 139:13-18   Song of Songs 4:9   Ephesians 5:31-32

The pilgrim worried that sometimes he would not have much time to care for his love-relationship with God. Then the Lord spoke to him, and answered his unspoken question:

Do you have only one minute? Hem it with quietness. Do not spend it in thinking how little time you have. I can give you much in one minute.

The pilgrim sat by the water, and his dear Lord said to him:

As the ripples of the river glance up to the light, let your heart glance up to Me in little looks of love very often through the day.

Amy Carmichael

The old couple sat with each other in peaceable silence, and no signal was needed for the kettle to go on, or the tea to be poured, the fire tended to.

'What do you find to do all the time, after all these years?' someone asked the old lady, 'don't you ever tire of each other's company?'

'Oh no,' she replied, 'you see, it's like this: I looks at him, and he looks at me, and we're happy together.'

8 December

Psalm 39:13   Isaiah 5:1-2   Luke 22:54-62

Jesus turned and looked at Peter. Everything was in that look: disappointment, love, forgiveness. One look, and he was perfectly known, perfectly discovered.

> Take me often from the tumult of things into Thy presence. There show me what I am and what Thou hast purposed me to be. Then hide me from Thy tears.

From Hebridean Altars

9 December

Psalm 139:17-18a   Genesis 17:3-6, 15-17   Philippians 3:12, 14

> The thoughts of the son ran thus: 'My hopes painted beautiful pictures, but they are fading one by one.'

> His Father said: 'Destroy all those pictures. To watch them slowly fading is weakening to the soul. Dare then to destroy them. You can if you will. I will give you other pictures instead of those your hopes painted.'

Amy Carmichael

God doesn't see me the way I do either; I look all the time into a distorted mirror that exaggerates some features and makes others disappear. God sees a true picture of me with all my faults and limitations, but more than this He sees a picture of all the possibilities and potential I hold.

'Just let Me get my hands on this one,' He thinks, 'and then just wait and see what the finished picture will be.'

Sometimes God gives us glimpses of that picture to encourage us and spur us on. For me it is a long process, but in the end it is all about becoming God's picture of me.

10 December

Psalm 139:14-17   Jeremiah 18:3-6   Philippians 3:12-14

'I am His project' – those were the words on Mary Alice's bookmark, but they were the belief of her heart, too, and however great the problems in her life He would continue to work on that project and bring the work to completion.

Paul, the Apostle, had a similar understanding and so he knew that though he was in Nero's prison he was not Nero's prisoner, but the prisoner of Christ Jesus. Any other arrest or imprisonment was irrelevant. A light shone in the cell.

In the late evening a believer looked over the day and was discouraged, but his Father spoke to comfort him.

> In the early morning did you not bear your beloved ones on
> your heart? Did you not offer to Me every hour of the day, every
> touch on other lives, every letter to be written, everything to
> be done? As the hours passed over you perhaps you did forget;
> but is it My custom to forget?

Amy Carmichael

Lord, You never forget me, even though often I forget: I am Your project.

11 December Thomas Merton *(see p.251)*

Psalm 40:17   1 Kings 19:9   Romans 8:27

God is not easily impressed – but then He never asks us to try to impress Him. It is as if He turns to us when we are consumed with our own unworthiness and are tempted to avoid meeting with Him, then He cuts across all our excuses and says: 'Relax, I already know you.'

Amy Carmichael captures the feeling of such an exchange in her book *His thoughts said ... His Father said...*

> The son said, But I am not successful.
> His Father said, At the end of the day will
>   My word be,
> Come, thou good and successful servant?
> If only thou wilt walk humbly with thy God it will be,
> Come, thou good and *faithful* servant.

We are not called to be successful, but faithful – relax!

12 December Finnian of Clonard *(see p.238)*

Psalm 38:8   Jonah 1:17–2:1   Matthew 6:6

John Skinner's story of the novice monk has impressed upon many of us the words of counsel the novice is given:

> Go to your cell,
> and your cell will teach you everything.

The cell is the place of being shut away with God, and with yourself. This may be a physical place or just a choice to be opened to Him in an interior way. We know it is exactly what we need, but avoid time alone and find other things to address in order to delay it...

The son felt fenced in. His Father took him to the fence and bid him look; he looked and he did not notice a hedge of thorn or a barbed wire entanglement; he saw a fence of feathers.

'With His feathers shall He make a fence for you.' The son remembered how once he had said, 'There are days when little things go wrong, one after another, and I am distracted by much serving. Such days are very trying.' Then the Father had said, 'On such days take to yourself the words of your Saviour which you so often have given others. Let them be your solace and your tranquillity. But tell me, when you are under pressure, do you turn first to your companions or to Me? Your companions listen and respond, but you never tell Me about it. Let Me see your face, let Me hear your voice.'

Amy Carmichael

13 December

Psalm 40:12   Numbers 13:30-33   Luke 4:1-13

Each of us has triggers that activate irrational fears, psychological monsters that seem overpowering to us but which probably would be no problem to someone else.

It may be a temptation to do the right thing the wrong way, or a lie thrown in our path by the enemy that anyone else would laugh at for its foolishness.

The common denominator is the same – it is a giant bigger than our own courage, and it comes out when we're alone. All of us have monsters of some kind, nightmares from our past or from our subconscious, unwelcome 'visitors'.

But it was the Spirit who drove Jesus into the desert, God who instructed the Israelites to subdue and drive out the giants, and He is bigger than any giant or monster the enemy may resuscitate or invent.

Sometimes He'd rather the nightmares appeared and came out into the light to be recognised for what they are, and be robbed of their power to surprise us.

14 December John of the Cross *(see p.243)*
Catherine de Hueck Doherty *(see p.232)*

Psalm 91   1 Samuel 5:1-4   Luke 4:1-13

While we avoid facing up to our personal 'monsters' they actually have more power to intimidate us.

That is why giving them a name is important – it begins to define them, to make them a known quantity.

Fears need naming, and so do temptations; and lies brought into the light lose their power to destroy.

15 December

Psalm 38:4   Exodus 2:11-14   Matthew 5:21-22

Years ago I saw an old black and white film about a man with amnesia. Slowly, as the pieces of the murder-mystery come together he begins to realise that although he does not remember it, the truth is that he is the murderer the police are looking for.

The film made quite an impression on me because I was used to films and programmes where the 'good guys' and the villains were clear from the beginning.

From that time on whenever a murder report came on TV, or was in the papers, my instinct was to have immediate sympathy for the murderer, rather than the victim or their family!

All of us have murder in our hearts from time to time, and lots of other unpleasant things. If looks could kill we'd leave plenty of corpses in our wake, some days.

God's concern is not just for the regulating or modifying of our outward behaviour, but for an ongoing change in our hearts.

16 December

Psalm 137:3   Nehemiah 2:2   John 21:24

When Adrian Plass decided to write the story of a quiet but remarkable Church Army officer turned vicar he called it *A Smile on the Face of God*. It was a story with lots of loose ends, unanswered questions and memorable incidents, a story to make you cry or make you laugh at other times.

Most of the Christian 'testimony' books you see are about apparent success stories which, even if their contents are true, miss out most of the failures and bad times and ordinary days. But suppose it was your story that was being told, what are the memorable incidents? What impact has God made on your own story? And have you brought a smile to His face?

17 December   Antiphon Day *(see p.223)*

Psalm 66:10-13   Daniel 3:26-27   2 Corinthians 4:6-7

A terrible fire ravaged the whole building, and when, afterwards, she went back to inspect the remains of her office all she could do was shake her head and be grateful that she had not been in the building at the time. Certainly none of the files of papers had survived.

With one backward glance her eye fell on a tiny blackened vase still standing on the charred remains of her desk. She had a new office now in a different place and was able to move in there instead. Well, little vase, she said, you and me have survived and you shall come with me into my new office.

It stood in the usual place on the corner of her new desk, but when people came in she noticed a difference in their reaction. Before, they would say,

'Oh, what a beautiful vase.'

Now, since it had been through the fire, they said,

'Oh, what beautiful flowers.'

18 December Samthann *(see p.260)*

Psalm 33:18   Lamentations 3:55-57   Luke 18:13

Francis, the great saint of Assisi, considered himself the most worthless of men, and the greatest of sinners.

The more the brightness of God's presence shone upon his heart the more his sin seemed black in comparison. (We may remember that Isaiah had a vision of God in His holiness, and immediately exclaimed, 'Woe is me – I am ruined, for I am a man of unclean lips and my eyes have seen the King.')

Brother Masseo ran after Francis crying, 'Why after you? Why after you? Why is the whole world following after you?' and Francis was able to only laugh that God had chosen him because no more worthless creature could be found on whom to set His mercy.

> A pilgrim looked at the reflection of a mountain in still water.
> It was the reflection that first caught his attention.
>
> But presently he raised his eyes to the mountain. Reflect Me,
> said his Father to him, then others will look at you. Then they
> will look up, and see Me. And the stiller the water the more
> perfect the reflection.
>
> *Amy Carmichael*

19 December

Psalm 139:23-24   Proverbs 15:16-17   1 Corinthians 13:1-3

God doesn't care so much about our outward actions, however sincere, as He does about the heart, its motives, and especially the love for Him that is carried there.

Works of charity may help others, demonstrations of courage and idealism may inspire others to faith and action, but these and even miracles of faith can still flow through a life where the love of Christ has grown cold. If I have not love I am nothing.

I should look to my own heart, and ask how much love for him it holds.

20 December

Psalm 42:8   Song of Songs 7:10-13   Philippians 4:12

There are times when our times with God seem boring, predictable and routine.

Will we become so discouraged by this that we give up spending time consciously in His company?

Will we persist in the routine of the relationship and hope that the feelings return?

Or will we endeavour to be flexible in our times with Him, keeping the time together varied, finding afresh what pleases Him?

The relationship should grow deeper over the years, not become stale.

21 December

Psalm 40:1, 5   Hosea 2:14-15   Matthew 13:31-32, 44

Be prepared to give God time, just because He matters. Give time for the relationship to develop, and be rooted even more deeply in your life.

Everything in me felt like saying, I am not worthy that You should come under my roof, but instead I said, 'When will You come to me? I want to wait here with a perfectly-kept heart for I know Your words give me life for ever...'

> As my thoughts were thus occupied, I found myself on the shore of the sea. And I took a grain of sand from the miles of sand about me and I held it in my hand. Then I knew that my desire for the presence of my Lord was like a little grain for smallness in comparison with my Lord's desire to come under

my roof; for that was like the measure of the measureless
sands. And as my thoughts followed this great thought,
Jesus my Lord answered and said to me,
'With desire I have desired to come to you.'

Amy Carmichael

22 December

Psalm 1:1-3   Jeremiah 17:7-8   Matthew 13:3-6

Our roots need to go deeper than circumstances. It is possible to be rooted deeper than catastrophe.

In the Nazi detention centres many of the Jewish people taught classes, prepared musical concerts, shared reminiscences that would be life-increasing and sustaining. Some gave up instead, and had no will to live. In life or in death, it is important to plant, to invest ourselves, and to glorify God.

His thoughts said:

> My longing is to heal the broken and the weak, to defend the
> maimed, and to lead the blind to the sight of the glory of the
> Lord. My choice is to be a corn of wheat and fall into the ground
> and die. Then why these waverings?

His Father said:

> Too much of your surface is exposed to the breath of every wind
> that blows. You must learn to dwell deep.

And the son who had wavered answered humbly,

> Renew within me a settled spirit.
> Establish me with Your directing Spirit.
> My heart is fixed, O God, my heart is fixed.
> I will sing and give praise.

Amy Carmichael

23 December

Psalm 88:13-14   Genesis 8:22   Romans 8:38-39

The soul goes through many seasons, seasons of new life and promise, of full fruit, of loss and then of apparent deadness with hope for new life again. The secret is to appreciate the value of these changes and gain the benefits of each and not become too discouraged.

In Murray Bodo's story of the life of Clare of Assisi, *A Light in the Garden*, some of these seasons of the soul are touched upon:

> The lives of Francis and Clare are themselves seasons of every soul, and it has something to do with Assisi in the spring becoming summer, surrendering to the gentle mists of fall, lying seemingly dead in winter, and waiting for the poppies of another spring ... You choose your vocation in life over and over again. It is not a decision made once for all time when one is young. As Clare grew in experience and in understanding of her commitment, she had to say yes again and again to a way of life that was not exactly the life she expected at the beginning.

Amy Carmichael writes:

> The soul remembered how when she was a very little child she had sympathised with the grey sea. The blue sea was a happy sea. The green sea, when the waves thereof tossed themselves and roared, was a triumphant sea. But the grey sea looked anxious. So the child was sorry for the grey sea. Grey weather she abhorred. Something of this feeling was with her still. Grey weather was not among the things for which she gave thanks. Then God her Father said to her:
>
>> All weathers nourish souls.

24 December Christmas Eve *(see p.112)*

Psalm 140:1-3   Job 37:5-13   John 17:15

'Each day has enough trouble of its own,' Jesus taught in the Sermon on the Mount. He meant it. He was realistic enough to recognise that this world is too often a place of suffering, for now still in the grasp of the World Hater, the prince of this world.

A day will come when sorrow will be no more and death itself be destroyed, but until then there will always be some poorer than others, some bereaved, mistreated, abused. We must do all we can to protect and to heal, but even the miracles we see are only signs of the Kingdom. That Kingdom is at the same time 'already' and 'not yet'. We are not exempt from trouble, injustice, violence and suffering, just because we are believers. He will allow some of these things to touch us also, even though it is not Him that visits them upon us.

Jesus, who understood that it was necessary for Him to suffer, still questioned, Was there no other way? Job wondered what was going on and in this life was never told what had happened in the courts of heaven over his story of trials. We know that no test is beyond what we can endure, but why this random, faceless violence unleashed at times in our society? The cross begins with an unanswered 'Why?' – and Christ also shouldered the cross.

25 December Christmas Day *(see p.114)*

Psalm 139:12   Isaiah 45:3, 7   1 Corinthians 4:5

> Do not be afraid to walk in darkness, for I am uncreated light.
> I will cause you to look on darkness and not be afraid.

This was a word spoken to John Skinner many years ago, but it is a word worth hearing for many of us.

It will be necessary for many of us to look on darkness, and when that happens it is important that it be robbed of its power to frighten us. There are many kinds of darkness. The darkness of sin should not surprise us, and when we confess it, and yield it to God, we no longer need carry its guilt.

The darkness of despair and of unanswered questions may require that we reach out and hold His hand in the darkness, even by faith, and just keep on walking.

26 December Stephen *(see p.260)*

Psalm 94:18-19   Song of Songs 1:5   Luke 7:45-47

'I am dark, but comely,' says the old translation of the words of the Shulamite girl in the Song of Songs.

God, who loves us, is a realist. He knows our faults and disadvantages, but through all of that He loves us, He sets His love upon us and wants to shout to all around about the beauty that He sees in us.

How can we be down on ourselves, or count ourselves worthless when He was willing to give everything in order to claim our love?

The knowledge of that love is enough to make that beauty shine from us which till now only He could have seen and no one else would have guessed at. It comes from within.

27 December John the Beloved *(see p.244)*

Psalm 51:6   Jeremiah 17:9-10   1 Corinthians 4:4

When it is just me who has been wronged my lips should most often be silent. And I must see to it that in the hidden person of the heart there is always the gentleness of Christ.

Words of complaint can be so destructive. Let this be my rule:

> Silence, unless the reason for speech will bear the searchlight of Eternity.

Often our heart seems clear and in order, and only the Holy Spirit can begin to make us aware of our self-righteousness, self-conceit, mixed motives and avoidance of unpleasant home-truths.

C.S. Lewis in his poem 'As the Ruin Falls' expresses the idea that it is only foolish talk when he says that he loves someone, since he must recognise that he is 'mercenary and self-seeking' through and through. He wants the one he loves, and God and any or all of his friends to provide exactly what he wants. He 'loves' them precisely because it suits him very well to do so. I think we all know what he means...? Having confessed how flawed our love is, we still choose to love and to offer that love as sincerely and truly as we know how.

28 December Holy Innocents *(see p.241)*

Psalm 130:2-3   2 Samuel 12:5-7a   Romans 12:3

One of the questions in the Ignatian *Spiritual Exercises* asks,

> What would I say to someone else in circumstances like my own? What counsel would I give them?

It is very easy for us to be hard on another person, even judgemental in our reactions, but make allowances when we are the offender.

David is very cross with the man Nathan tells him about, and only then can Nathan turn round and say: The man is you!

We should not think too highly of ourselves – we're only as high as we are at our lowest moment, except perhaps by the grace of God which lifts us from the miry clay.

Some people have the opposite problem and can be far more generous and forgiving toward other people, but will never have a good thought or word for themselves.

Let the love of God be reflected in your love for yourself and others. With God in the equation our potential for good is limitless.

29 December

Psalm 138:3   Isaiah 6:5-7   Romans 8:18-25

His thoughts said:

> I am not what I am meant to be, or what others think I am.

His Father said:

> It is written, 'He restores my soul. The Law of the Lord is perfect, restoring the soul.' Let some word of Mine restore you. Did you think you had a Father who did not know that His child would need to be restored? I will restore health to you: I will heal you of your wounds. I will restore comfort to you. I will restore to you the joy of My salvation. I will renew a right spirit within you. I will not cast you away from My Presence. Child of My love, trust your Father. If the Spirit speaks some word in your heart, obey that word. And, before you're even aware of it, you will know that you are restored.
>
> *Amy Carmichael*

Going deeper in God always involves knowing yourself, including your own sinfulness. That doesn't mean we should be stuck there, we need to look for breakthroughs, keys to unlock areas of persistent defeat.

30 December

Psalm 38:8-21   Ruth 1:18-22   Acts 16:23-25

One of the best things about the book of Psalms is that we find that we are not the first person in the world to complain to God, or feel like the prayers come back unheard or that our rivals should be beaten to a pulp, or that the bad guys always win.

Scripture was never intended to be handed to other people as a placebo or as ready-made easy answers. God has many answers for us, but they are rarely easy, and even when freely offered they were often costly...

> But still the son felt like a long shore on which all the waves of pain of all the world were beating. His Father drew near to him and said, 'There is only one shore long enough for that. Upon My love, that long, long shore, those waves are beating now; but you can be one with Me. And I promise you that there shall be an end, and all tears shall be wiped from off all faces.'

Amy Carmichael

31 December John Wycliffe *(see p.265)*

Psalm 138:8   1 Kings 9:4-7   2 Corinthians 10:5

Not to make judgements about other people's light, but to obey the light given to you is all that concerns you.
　　Lord, what shall this man do?
　　'What is that to you? *You* follow Me!'

So cast down your imaginations – don't try and work it out. It won't be like what you read in books.

Be real with God.
Don't try to relive someone else's journey.

　　'What is that to you? *You* follow Me!'

the Finan series of Daily Readings

THE FINAN SERIES OF DAILY READINGS

January
Be Thou my vision

1 January New Year *(see p.115)* Telemachus *(see p.261)*

Psalm 123:2   Exodus 33:18-23   Mark 8:24-25

Be Thou my vision,
O Lord of my heart...

The studies this month are prepared by Amund Karner, and based around the words of the song 'Be Thou My Vision'. It is an old Irish Celtic poem, set to music in the nineteenth century, and still found in many hymn books.

I ask not to fly from the world but to be involved with the world. I am in the world but also in the presence of Jesus. I listen for His word to a broken world. He sees my brokenness and the brokenness of the world around me. I stand in God's presence looking at Him, listening to Him, bringing to Him the things of the world that have filled my vision. I listen for His word. Be Thou my vision, O Lord.

2 January

Psalm 131:1-3   Ezekiel 36:26   Matthew 15:11, 15-20

> Be Thou my vision,
> O Lord of my heart...

Do you respond first of all with your head, or with your heart? Or do you just give a gut reaction? It varies from time to time; and we are very different from each other. The mind can be a very heartless thing in its responses. But the heart 'has a mind of its own'. At the end of the day we need a place of rest inside ourselves to return to.

Focus your gaze, and then, when the arrow of your attention is released, it will hit the mark and find Him.

> The aim: Him.
> The glory: His.

> He is my vision,
> and the Lord of my heart!

3 January

Psalm 103:1-6   Exodus 3:1-14   Philippians 3:1-9

> ...naught be all else to me,
> save that Thou art.

Everything else is nothing. Pile it all up, and what does it amount to? Nothing, really. Then turn around and instead see I AM. I am what? No, just I AM. His very name is a statement of reality. God IS, and everything else is an irrelevance in comparison. I AM is in the here and now, in the present moment, and present at this moment.

In His presence, in His power, live a moment at a time: live that moment fully. To try to live a holy life is to be crushed by the immensity of the task, but a whole life consists of a series of such moments.

> ...naught be all else to me.

4 January   Juniper *(see p.245)*

Psalm 42:8   Daniel 6:10-11   Philippians 4:8

> *Thou my best thought*
> *in the day and the night...*

All kinds of things fill our thoughts. But when we think of Him, sanity enters the picture. It is as if the conductor takes his place at the rostrum: all the discordant sound, the tuning up and fidgeting, turns to silence; and then a melody, a full-bodied score in many parts, comes to birth in the very place where there had been chaos and confusion.

> Lord, I think many things.
> I have many thoughts.
> Let me not forget You,
> nor lose sight of You,
> even for a moment:
>
> Thou, my best thought.

5 January

Psalm 16:7   2 Samuel 22:7-16   Galatians 6:17

> *Thou my best thought*
> *in the day and the night...*

The night can be a time that makes us uneasy. It is a time to feel isolated, a time of darkness, of the unknown. And darkness is the covering of God: it is where He lives. He is light; and the light in darkness is a greater light than a light at day. It is in the dark we can see stars, not in the daytime. But it is at night, in the early hours, when most people are likely to die. But we do not talk about that. Nowadays, we are sanitised from much suffering and death. It happens in the specialised places – hospitals, nursing homes. It is removed from us, and we lose part of our perspective on life.

But we need darkness – for is not God closer to those who suffer? Have you not felt closer to God at the times of suffering than at the other times when everything has been going well for you? Who is it the doctor visits? The one who is well, or the one who is ill?

Do not go looking to have pain happen to you, but do not always hurry out of its path when it comes. Remember, when we think of Him, it is in the day *and* the night.

6 January Three Kings' Day *(see p.263)*

Psalm 119:105-112   1 Samuel 3:3-4   Acts 2:16-18

> *...waking or sleeping,*
> Thy presence my light.

Joel promised dreams to the people: and we are living in the time of this promise, the time of the dream. Dream on, and let God speak through your dreams.

> Lord, in the multitude of my thoughts,
> Thy comforts delight my soul.
> Waking or sleeping,
> it is Thy presence which enlightens me.

7 January

Psalm 139:11-12   Exodus 33:14-15   1 John 2:3-11

> *...waking or sleeping,*
> *Thy presence my light.*

In a book called *It's All Right to Cry* this quotation is to be found: 'Nobody is wise who does not know the darkness. I appreciate the dark hours of my existence in which my senses are sharpened.'

8 January

Psalm 18:28-29   Daniel 3:23-25   John 8:12

Be Thou my vision,
O Lord of my heart;
naught be all else to me
save that Thou art.
Thou my best thought
in the day and the night;
waking or sleeping,
Thy presence my light.

9 January

Psalm 51:6   Proverbs 4:5-9   Ephesians 1:17

*Be Thou my wisdom,
be Thou my true word...*

Wisdom cannot be learnt with just the head; to temper its logic the heart must also be engaged. Wisdom is not in short supply, surprising as it may seem. We have not, precisely because we forget to ask.

Wisdom is to be desired more than gold. Solomon asked for wisdom; and God was very pleased that he did not ask for riches. However, having asked for wisdom, he got riches too.

Lord of my heart,
be Thou my wisdom.
Be at the beginning of all I speak,

of all that I begin.
Be Thou my true word.

10 January

Psalm 139:7-12   2 Kings 6:16-17   Romans 8:38-39

*I ever with Thee,
and Thou with me, Lord...*

'I am with you always,' He says. He is all around His people, as strong and reliable as the mountains. He wants us to be with Him, prepares a place for us to share, comes to our place, to our ordinariness, shares bread and wine at table. The commonplace is given great significance because of His presence.

Jesus often turned up in unexpected places and in unexpected ways. When we do not see Jesus around us, it is often because we do not look well enough.

Open my eyes to see...
I ever with Thee,
and Thou with me, Lord.

11 January

Psalm 40:7   Zechariah 4:1   Luke 15:20

*Thou my great Father,
and I Thy true son...*

We can never be at peace till we have performed the highest duty of all, till we have arisen and gone to our Father. If we come from God, nothing is more natural than to want Him; and when we haven't got Him, to try to find Him.

May the one Father make us all clean at last, and when the right time comes, wake us out of this sleep into the new world, which is the old one, when we shall say as one that wakes from a dream 'Is it then over, and I live?'

George MacDonald

12 January

Psalm 32:4-9   Jeremiah 1:5   Galatians 4:4-7

> Thou my great Father,
> and I Thy true son...

God is nearer to you than any thought or feeling of yours ... Do not be afraid. If all the evil things in the universe were around us, they could not come inside the ring that He makes about us. He always keeps a place for Himself and His child, into which no other being can enter.

George MacDonald

God prepares good works for us to walk in, and will not give His child any gift that is less than the best.

God has plans for us, plans for good – good, not evil – but when we walk outside His will He is still there, pulling us back to Himself. We are His sons if we do His will.

We do, because we know it will please Him, not to win His love. The love is freely given and quite undeservedly. And it is only fitting that such a great Father should have in me a true son.

13 January   Hilary of Poitiers (see p.240)   Kentigern (see p.245)

Psalm 131:2   Jeremiah 17:7-8   Luke 2:25-38

> Thou in me dwelling,
> and I with Thee one.

In 1 Thessalonians 4:11 we are told to study to be quiet or study to be still. This stillness must begin in the heart. It is a decision, an active choice, to become still, to still your soul. Sometimes, it is as if there is a bunch of monkeys in the tree-which-is-your-mind; and you will not still them by shouting. If you speak quietly and gently – just as you would to a petulant child – peace will result. The mind is like a child, always wanting more, something new; each thing it sees it wants.

> It is stillness I need, Lord,
> and Thou in me dwelling.

14 January

Psalm 4:4   Isaiah 32:17   Galatians 2:20

> Thou with me dwelling,
> *and I with Thee one.*

Stillness is not simply silence, but an attitude of listening to God and of openness towards Him.

From the Philokalia

> Thou in me dwelling,
> and I with Thee one.

15 January   Ita *(see p.54)*   Paul of Thebes *(see p.254)*

Psalm 24:8   Jeremiah 38:1-6   1 Corinthians 13:12

We become drowned in the detail of our despair; and it is precisely then that we must turn our focus away to the larger picture, which is hidden from us. We trust, and we believe now that we will see then. We believe now that God is still working, and that we will understand one day.

> Be Thou my breastplate,
> my sword for the fight;
> be Thou my armour,
> and be Thou my might,
> Thou my soul's shelter,

and Thou my high tower;
raise Thou me heavenwards,
O Power of my power.

16 January

Psalm 119:11   1 Samuel 17:38-39   Ephesians 6:14, 17

Be Thou my breastplate,
my sword for the fight...

The breastplate protects the heart; all the ways to the heart are covered; righteousness is the breastplate. This is being right, or made right, able to stand in confidence. Unlike David, we will find that the armour our King provides fits us perfectly.

Great God,
be Thou my breastplate.

17 January   Antony of Egypt *(see p.223)*

Psalm 51:6   Jeremiah 31:33   2 Corinthians 10:4-5

Be Thou my breastplate,
my sword for the fight...

The fight in which we find ourselves is the fight against the powers in the heavenlies. The tools for the fight are the ones provided for us by God, our job being to use them. We need to know our weapons. We also have a fight in our own lives in the realm of our thoughts and our wilfulness. The revelation of God must be drawn from its scabbard at our side and its point directed even at our own breast, keenly cutting even between soul and spirit, between our own thoughts and the quiet wisdom of God.

Be Thou my sword for the fight!

18 January

Psalm 34:7   2 Chronicles 20:15-22   2 Corinthians 10:3

be Thou my armour,
and be Thou my might...

Whether we sit, walk or stand, we fight for God. The battle belongs to the Lord. Let Him fight for you – do not put your hand outside His protection.

Amma Sarah turned to the ascetic life, living in the desert, but was for 13 years tempted by lust. It was said that she never prayed that this warfare should cease, but instead she said, 'O God, give me strength.'

When tempted, do not try to fight on your own – let God fight for you. In admitting our weakness, we allow God to be our strength.

Be Thou my armour,
and be Thou my might.

19 January

Psalm 131:1   Zechariah 4:6   2 Corinthians 4:7-8

be Thou my armour,
and be Thou my might...

God made the world out of nothing, and it is only when we become nothing that God can make anything of us.

Martin Luther

Thou, my true might.

20 January

Psalm 144:1-2   Deuteronomy 29:5   John 10:29

Thou my soul's shelter,
and Thou my high tower...

The Lord is a refuge that is strong, and a very present help. In a shelter you are passive and the shelter does the 'work' of sheltering. You have to stay in the shelter and not venture out. In the shelter you can rest and be quiet, you are looked after and are safe. Even though the Israelites walked through the wilderness for 40 years, their clothes did not wear out, nor did their shoes need mending. The Lord was their protection and defender.

Thou my soul's shelter,
and Thou my high tower.

21 January

Psalm 137:4   2 Kings 2:1   Colossians 1:11

raise Thou me heavenwards,
O Power of my power.

His power is at work in us, and if only we set our mind on the things which concern Him, we will see this power in operation. The power of God makes great works possible, but is just as operative in the small, perhaps unnoticed, things of life.

The power of God is great, yet He gives of it freely for His purposes. We have to wait for the power. There is no time for delay, as the Spirit has already come; the waiting is to prevent us dashing ahead, reliant on our own ability instead of His enabling. Even when works of power or 'miracles' occur, these only confirm the message: 'Look heavenward!'

The works of power are a signpost which says, 'Go, in this direction, to God.' But it was never intended that we worship the signpost!

Raise my gaze heavenward,
Great Power of my power.

22 January

Psalm 23:4   Exodus 20:3   Galatians 2:20

*Riches I heed not,
nor man's empty praise,
Thou mine inheritance
through all of my days.
Thou and Thou only
the first in my heart;
High King of Heaven,
my treasure Thou art.*

Death is implicit in this verse. There is so much of us to die; but it needs to die completely if we are to live in the newness of life which comes with a definite break between the old and the new. It is not superficial dying that is called for, but the utter death of every aspect of our life. God is jealous, and wants us to shut Him out of nothing.

Do you love the Lord with all your heart? He accepts us as we are now, and slowly moulds us towards His image of what we can be. He knows us as we will be, and works to conform us to that image.

23 January

Psalm 73:26   2 Kings 5:20-27   Philippians 2:3

*Riches I heed not,
nor man's empty praise...*

Outward esteem, the praises of those round about us, their flattery and compliments, soon prove hollow, if they are all we have to feed upon. Looking good, looking clever, looking busy can consume much of our energy as we compete for medals in people-pleasing. We judge strangers by the clothes they wear. In some circles cleverness and intellectual ability are regarded highly. Being busy attracts praise.

But are we doing what God wants us to be doing? Whose approval do we really want?

The answer to that question will determine the values we live by. Listen to this comment from a devout Hebridean soul:

> Though we prospered little,
> yet we were rich in faith and unfearingness.

From Hebridean Altars

24 January

Psalm 16:5-6   2 Kings 2:9-16   Ephesians 1:13-14

Thou mine inheritance
through all of my days.

In *Hebridean Altars* there is recounted the concern of a mother for her daughter who was about to leave and make her life in a faraway city, 'where gold weighs more than love, and folk are too busy to think of the sun or sea'. The mother prayed a blessing upon her, and sought in this way to impress upon her the richness of her true heritage, before other values could cloud her mind.

> Jesus, draw Thou nearer and shield my soul,
> Thou mine inheritance now and always.

25 January

Psalm 51:6   Jeremiah 17:5-10   Luke 10:30, 33-34

Thou and Thou only,
the first in my heart...

We live in a world where mental ability is rewarded. But the heart is not trained; it just muddles along. Soon we know more and more, and understand less and less. Sophisticated media reports bring information about wars and disasters right into our living room; but we are less affected than previous generations would have been by reports of a mishap in a neighbouring village.

Yet compassion reaches out across barriers of status, class or ability, and reaches out to the person who is hurting. Compassion does not depend upon knowledge or learning; the 'Samaritan' only needs to know where the sore is, so he can anoint it with oil.

If something in us is still able to respond a little, then all is not lost. The heart is alive and kicking, able to be coaxed into generosity, able to prioritise its focus. Love of God should be the first priority, for true love of self and of neighbour both flow from this.

Do I love Thee, the living God,
with all my heart?
Amen. Lord, have mercy.
Thou, and Thou only.

26 January

Psalm 45:1   Hosea 2:23   revelation 19:11-16

High King of heaven,
my treasure Thou art.

The Lord is High King. We need to be careful not to forget this, not to treat Him with contempt, just because He does not lash out at us when we fail to respond as He wishes. In olden times the Israelites did not value what God was doing for them. We should not disappoint Him, as they did in their day. God is love, but because of our weakness and foolishness and unresponsiveness, that love is no stranger to anger and pain.

> My heart runs to You,
> my Lord, my High King,
> High King of heaven.

27 January

Psalm 45:10-15   Song of Songs 4:16   Matthew 6:19-21

> High King of heaven,
> *my treasure Thou art.*

Do I count all things as loss for the sake of knowing Him? Is He what I treasure the most, so that my heart and heaven are already one? What do I value most in my life? What is it that I spend most of my time thinking about? Am I careless in my relationship with God? Do I neglect to spend time cultivating this relationship? Do I treasure it? Do I set as much value on it as He has on me?

Pelagius, in the company of his fellow bishops, looked at a beautiful woman who passed by them, while the others looked away discreetly. Pelagius apparently profited from a long, hard look, for he launched into the following outburst:

> What do you think, beloved brothers, how many hours does this woman spend in her chamber giving all her mind and attention to adorning herself for the play, in order to lack nothing in beauty and adornment of the body: she wants to please all those who see her, lest those who are her lovers today find her ugly and do not come tomorrow.

> Here we are, who have an almighty Father in heaven offering us heavenly gifts and rewards, our immortal Bridegroom who promises good things to His watchmen, things that cannot

be valued, which eye has not seen, nor ear heard, nor has it entered into the heart of man to know the things that God has prepared for them that love him.

What else can I say? When we have such promises, when we are going to see the great and glorious face of our Bridegroom which has a beauty beyond compare, upon which the cherubim do not dare to gaze, why do we not adorn ourselves and wash the dirt from our unhappy souls, why do we let ourselves lie so neglected?

My treasure Thou art,
O High King of heaven.

28 January Canaire *(see p.228)*

Psalm 22:4   Isaiah 25:7-8   Revelation 2:10-11

*When battle is done,
grant heaven's joy to me...*

The picture is one of a team game where each competitor must complete the obstacle course for themselves, but on reaching the finish line is greeted excitedly by other team members, and then turns to cheer on those who are still to complete the race. In heaven the angels rejoice whenever a single competitor sets out. The rewards are great, but so are the difficulties. Each trophy of victory is at a cost beyond our imagination.

The loud cry resounds:
'It is finished!'
When all is accomplished, Lord,
grant heaven's joy to me!

29 January

Psalm 119:105   Genesis 1:2-3   Revelation 21:1-3, 22-23

grant heaven's joy to me,
bright heaven's Sun.

We are reaching the end of the song; and the end refers back to the beginning and rounds off the story: as it was in the beginning, is now and ever shall be.

In the beginning was darkness; and God spoke to dispel the darkness, as His first act of creation. At the end, the darkness is gone, for He Himself is the light in the new Jerusalem, bright heaven's Sun.

30 January

Psalm 46:1-4   Ezekiel 36:26-27   Romans 8:28

Christ of my own heart,
whatever befall...

Love goes into God's presence,
while at the gate
Reason and Knowledge
must remain
and for an audience wait.

Angelus Silesius

What can separate us from God's love? Wherever we go, we find it there; and if we do not see it, we need to trust in its presence.

Only with your heart can you see clearly. The most important things are invisible to the eye.

Antoine de Saint-Exupéry,
The Little Prince

The love between God and you is very intimate and private. It is personal and secret. It is like the relationship of a couple who are truly intimate. Your bedroom is a place of closeness, honesty, openness and remaining vulnerable. You don't always need to talk. You can, occasionally, just be there, touching each other, holding hands. Christ of my own heart, look not on the outer courts, but on the inner – then You will see. The King's bride is all beautiful within.

31 January

Psalm 17:15   Job 19:25   Hebrews 12:2

still be Thou my vision,
Thou Ruler of all.

In his poem 'Little Gidding', T.S. Eliot says that we shall not cease our exploring until we 'arrive where we started, and ... know the place for the first time'.

'Be Thou my vision' ... and so it is that we come back to the beginning of our looking – 'Sir, we would see Jesus.' To be conquered by love – a love that overcomes each of us.

Every time the disciples looked at Jesus, or Jesus looked at them, they saw more.

Still be Thou my vision,
O Ruler of all.

February
Doorkeepers

1 February Brigid's Day *(see p.267)*

Psalm 138:3   Leviticus 9:24   Matthew 22:8-10

Brigid was famous not only for the perpetual fire that burned at her monastery in Kildare, but for her hospitality and welcome.

Brigid's feast

I should like a great lake of finest ale
for the King of kings.
I should like a table of the choicest food
for the family of heaven.
Let the ale be made from the fruits of faith
and the food be forgiving love.

I should welcome the poor to my feast,
for they are God's children.
I should welcome the sick to my feast,
for they are God's joy.
Let the poor sit with Jesus at the highest place,
and the sick dance with the angels.

God bless the poor,
God bless the sick,
and bless our human race.
God bless our food,
God bless our drink;
all homes, O God, embrace.

2 February

Psalm 146:7-8   Isaiah 58:6-7   Mark 11:1-2, 7-11

> O that I had in the desert a traveller's lodging-place, that I might leave my people and go away with them!
>
> *Jeremiah 9:2*

> He was a friend to man,
> and lived in a
> house by the side of the road.
>
> *Homer*

One Celtic brother called Cronan moved his whole establishment to Roscrea after a royal visitor had been unable to find him in Sean Ross. 'I shall not remain in a desert place,' he said, 'where strangers and poor folk are unable to find me readily. But here, by the public highway I shall live, where they are able to reach me easily.'

This urge to dispense hospitality to the wayfarer and the indigent led to the founding of Christian settlements along the main roads of Ireland.

3 February

Psalm 84:5   2 Kings 4:8-10   Matthew 21:12-17

> There are hermit souls that live withdrawn
> in the peace of their self-content;
> there are souls like stars that dwell apart,
> in a fellowless firmament;
> there are pioneer souls that blaze their paths
> where highways never went;
> but let me live by the side of the road
> and try to be a friend.
>
> *Adapted from Sam Walter Foss*

4 February

Psalm 143:2   2 Kings 4:11-17   John 11:1-53

> Let me live in a house by the side of the road,
> with people passing by –
> the ones who are good, and the ones who are bad,
> as good and bad as I.
> I would not sit in a scorner's seat,
> or hurl the cynic's ban;
> let me live in a house by the side of the road
> and be the friend I can.

Adapted from Sam Walter Foss

5 February

Psalm 143:8   2 Kings 4:18-24   John 12:1-3

> I see from my house by the side of the road
> by the side of the highway of life,
> those who press with the ardour of hope,
> and others who faint with the strife.
> But I turn not away from their smiles nor their tears –
> both parts of an infinite plan.
> Let me live in a house by the side of the road
> and be the friend I can.

Adapted from Sam Walter Foss

6 February

Psalm 143:10   2 Kings 4:25-37   Romans 12:15

> I know there are brook-gladdened meadows ahead
> and mountains of wearisome height;
> that road passes on through the long afternoon
> and stretches away to the night;

but still I rejoice when the travellers rejoice,
and weep with the strangers that moan,
nor live in my house by the side of the road
like someone who dwells alone.

Adapted from Sam Walter Foss

7 February

Psalm 142:5   Jeremiah 9:23-24   Luke 2:3-7

Let me live in my house by the side of the road,
where all manner of folk go by.
They are good, they are bad, they are weak, they are strong,
wise, foolish – so am I.
Then why should I sit in the scorner's seat
or hurl the cynic's ban?
Let me live in my house by the side of the road
and be the friend I can.

Adapted from Sam Walter Foss

8 February   Elfleda *(see p.235)*

Psalm 141:4   Daniel 1:3-4   Acts 17:23-25

It is a sin against the Holy Spirit stubbornly to refuse to learn from other people who know about life in today's world. We can ask them for a drink, as Jesus did at the well in Samaria: he did not hesitate to listen to the Samaritan woman (when His own people would have nothing to do with her people).

We have a message for the world; but we need the world too. Without understanding the world we have no relevant language in which to share that message. Moreover, the world helps us understand ourselves better, especially our need to be open to the newness of the Gospel.

Adapted from Jean-François Six

9 February Teilo *(see p.261)*

Psalm 82:3-5   Esther 4:14   1 Corinthians 14:8-10

We are alive today, not in Paul's time. The men and women we meet have different ideas from those of the Jews and pagans he met. It is the ideas of today's people, and what is important to them, that must be confronted with the good news. These values will not be destroyed, but set on fire by the life of the Risen Jesus. Pope Paul VI said: 'It is not a good thing to be promised to the world or unite ourselves with its thoughts, customs and tastes; but instead we should study it, love it and serve it.'

Yes, it is important to understand the world, to love and serve it so much, in its unique culture, as to become bilingual.

Adapted from Jean-François Six

10 February

Psalm 144:3-7   Micah 4:4   Galatians 3:26-29

I heard about a king who owned a castle in the sky
where serfs and kings were all the same and nobody ever had to die.
I heard all wealth and power was shared with the common man;
and other serfs said, 'Seems to me like a dream in a wonderland.'
And as the years went by I still had doubts about it all,
but something burned down deep inside so I searched for the castle wall.
I said 'Hey, King, can you see me from your castle in the sky?
There's just no way to look inside 'cos the walls are much too high!
Won't you come down from your castle into my wishing well?
Tell all the sunken memories they've each got a dream to tell.'
And though you may not understand, it's just my way to say:
castle kings and poor men's dreams fill your life only with toil and pain.

And finally I met a serf who seemed a lot like me.
He said, 'I am the castle king, won't you come and I'll set
   you free?'
He took me to the castle moat, and the bridge was quickly drawn.
I fell in shame to hide my face as the serf turned to take the throne.
And he came down from his castle into my wishing well,
picked up the sunken memories with each their dream to tell.
And though no one else could, he understood the words I had
   to say,
the castle king changed everything; now I walk with him every
   day.
In all my dreams I'd never seen the serf with a smiling face,
but now it's true, I'm telling you, for the serf and the king
   embrace.

Tim Sheppard

11 February Caedmon *(see p.321)*

Psalm 143:7   Ecclesiastes 9:3   John 1:29

The capacity and tendency to *not* believe is truly 'the sin of the world'. This is more crucial than a narrow and childish idea of sin where the individual does something they are told they should not, then feels guilt and blame, creating a prison of self-centred delay in having it put right. That is not the sin of the world although it gives it power and strength. Being prince of your own illusion, deluding yourself about yourself, about others and about God – that is the sin of the world.

(It is important that I do more than confess my sins – I must confess that I am a sinner. I must not just receive forgiveness, but live as a forgiven person.)

To believe in the Risen Christ is to believe that through the 'yes' of Jesus, God breaks through and gives birth to a new humanity. Up to the moment of this 'yes' people were primarily locked in incredulity. Jesus comes to break this circle and this human propensity to 'non-believing'. He opens hearts to trust in God who then responded and who does not cease to respond now to us through the Risen Christ.

Jean-François Six

12 February

Psalm 85:13   1 Kings 18:21   Mark 9:23-24

The fool says in his heart, 'There is no God.'

Psalm 14:1

The believer can only perfect his faith on the ocean of nihilism, temptation and doubt; he has been assigned the ocean of uncertainty as the only possible site for his faith. On the other hand the non-believer is not to be understood undialectically as a mere man without faith.

Just as we have already recognised that the believer does not live immune to doubt but is always threatened by the plunge into the void, so now we can discern the entangled nature of human destinies, and say that even the non-believer does not represent a rounded and closed existence. However vigorously he may assert that he has long left behind him supernatural temptations and weaknesses, and now accepts only what is immediately certain, he will never be free of secret uncertainty.

Just as the believer is choked by the salt water of doubt constantly washed into his mouth by the ocean of uncertainty, so the non-believer is troubled by doubts about his unbelief, about the real totality of the world which he has made up his mind to explain as a self-contained whole. He can never be absolutely certain of the autonomy of what he has seen and interpreted as a whole; he remains threatened by the question whether the belief is not after all the reality which it claims to be.

Just as the believer knows himself to be constantly threatened by unbelief which he must experience as a continual temptation, so for the unbeliever faith remains a temptation, and so a threat to his apparently permanently closed world.

Joseph Ratzinger, Introduction to Christianity

13 February

Psalm 85:7   Jeremiah 29:13   John 14:6

Two men please God: one who serves Him with all his heart because he knows Him, one who seeks Him with all his heart because he knows Him not.

Panin

14 February

Psalm 144:11   Isaiah 40:28-31   Luke 15:20

Speaking of younger people today, some really are unbelieving: that is they have recognised that the God of Jesus, this God of tenderness actually exists – and they refuse Him.

Others are not really unbelievers as such since they have rejected only the picture of God they have seen portrayed through certain Christians now or in history.

Adapted from Jean-François Six

If you are running away from a wrong picture of God, does that take you further away from Him or closer to Him?

15 February

Psalm 22   Isaiah 53:6   Luke 22:40-45

Jesus experienced the extreme of dereliction. Pronouncing on the cross the first words of the psalm, 'My God, my God, why have You deserted me?' Jesus wants to express the meaning of the whole psalm.

But how can we fail to see that this psalmody of Jesus on the cross is the expression, once more, of a temptation overcome, of a despair outrun? Faith, trust, hope are not natural to humanity: religion, law, sentence, are. But to reveal, in the very heart of failure and at the hour of death, amid human clamour and the silence of God, that God is Love, is that not the true, intense and free acknowledging of God? And is it not a turning of the back, in manner more victorious than any other, on the temptation of unbelief? Evil, wretchedness and failure are, in effect, the first grounds of unbelief and this is understandable: how can one not curse God and despair when evil is there and heaven seems empty? Jesus overcame this temptation.

The cry that Jesus uttered on the cross – 'a loud voice' says the Scripture – must not be romanticised but, rather, taken in its precise texture.

Jean-François Six

16 February

Psalm 139:12   Exodus 32:32   Galatians 6:2

> Truly, You are a God who hides Himself, O God of Israel, the Saviour.
>
> *Isaiah 45:15*

Thérèse of Lisieux underwent profound changes in her experience of faith during the Easter of 1896: before that time she thought that atheism was a flaunted position, a sham. 'I could not believe that there really were godless people who had no faith at all: it was only by being false to their own inner convictions that someone could deny the existence of heaven.'

Finally, her eyes were opened to realise that unbelievers
really exist. She experiences the sense of the darkness, such
impenetrable darkness, a darkness which cannot recognise the
King of Light. 'But here I am, Lord, to whom Your divine light
has made itself known.' She finds herself in a situation which
seems absurdly contradictory. She does not cease to participate
in the light of the faith and at the same time she participates
in the darkness in which unbelievers live. She is immersed in
suffering never experienced previously and in joy greater than
she ever felt before. She thinks that if Jesus has made her see
the reality of unbelief and has made her participate in the night
of unbelief, it is only so that she may turn the tables: so that
she may live this state of darkness for the sake of unbelievers
themselves. And, consequently, for her it is a new joy that she
had never experienced until then – the joy of not living the joy of
faith so that precisely these 'others', these unbelievers who do
not know this joy, might finally attain to it: 'What does it matter,
that I should catch no glimpse of heaven's beauties, here on
earth, if that will help poor sinners to see them in heaven?'

Jean-François Six (abridged)

17 February Finan *(see p.238)* John Hyde *(see p.241)*

Psalm 78:19   Job 22:2-7   Luke 4:1-3

Passing through the valley of tears, they make it a place of
springs.

Psalm 84:6

The night Thérèse experiences is a sharing of life with Jesus and
unbelievers at one and the same time. From the moment she
recognises the existence of genuine unbelievers she reckons
herself as their companion.

'Lord, one of Your own children, to whom Your divine light
has made itself known ... by way of asking pardon for these
brothers of mine, I am ready to live on a starvation diet as long

as You will have it so.' Her concern is to remain with those who eat the bread of unbelief: she does not want to 'rise from this appetising meal'. She is prepared, she says, to remain there as the last one until 'all those who have no torch of faith to guide them catch sight, at least, of its rays'.

This manner of sharing the bread of unbelief is at the same time a manner of breaking bread with Jesus, of sharing the Eucharistic table: for it is Jesus who has led her to this table of unbelievers. Of this she is certain. For Thérèse, the perfect joy is to find herself among unbelievers and, eating at their table, to be shaken by their questions while remaining in the faith.

'I find it difficult to believe in the existence of anything except the clouds which limit my horizon. It is only then that I realise the possibilities of my weakness; find consolation in staying at my post, and directing my gaze towards one invisible light which communicates itself, now, only in the eye of faith.'

Jean-François Six

18 February   Colman *(see p.230)*

Psalm 84:5-7   Job 23:10   Philippians 4:11-12

The more a human being advances in the Christian faith, the more they live the presence of God as an absence, the more they accept to die to the idea of becoming aware of God, of fathoming Him. For they have learned, while advancing, that God is unfathomable. And from then on the presence of God assumes value in their eyes only against the backdrop of absence. The mystic, in his long and complicated pilgrimage, experiences alternately the presence and absence of God. But, by degrees, the absence of God is felt more and more and the mystic understands that this absence is now the norm. Thus the mystic is someone who has had a long-term confrontation with God, like Jacob in the struggle that he waged all through the night, someone who does not cease to confront God. God always precedes us, we see Him only from behind, He walks ahead, He is ahead of us. What the mystic experiences – and every Christian is a mystic because it is not the great illuminations that are the mark of the mystic but the night, an everyday night – is a kind of distancing from God in proportion to advances in the deepening of their faith.

Jean-François Six

19 February

Psalm 84:1-4   1 Chronicles 15:23-24   Mark 14:32-37, 50-52

Almighty Father, Son and Holy Ghost,
eternal, ever-blessèd, gracious God,
to me, the least of saints,
to me allow that I may keep a door in Paradise,
that I may keep even the smallest door,
the farthest door, the darkest, coldest door,
the door that is least used, the stiffest door,
if so it be but in Thy house, O God;
if so it be that I may see Thy glory,
even afar, and hear Thy voice, O God
and know that I am with Thee, Thee, O God.

From the 'Prayer of Columba',
trans. by W. Muir

20 February

Psalm 145:3, 14   Isaiah 12:3-4   John 13:14-15

I saw a door open in heaven.

Revelation 4:1

God the Lord has opened a door
Christ of hope, Door of joy!
Son of Mary, hasten Thou to help me:
in me, Lord Christ, let there be joy.

Celtic Prayer

The One who was no less than God
took on the flesh of lowly man,
and came to wash the feet of clay
because it was Your holy plan.
And I, no greater than my King,
would ever seek a place
of humble service in Your house
to gaze into the light that is Your face.

Twila Paris

21 February

Psalm 142:2   Isaiah 26:2-3   Luke 2:29-30

He had been recently converted to Christ, and thrilled with the wonder of the truths he so newly had grasped – that one day all his trials would be over, that in heaven everything would be different. But then one Sunday in the meeting he heard them sing a song he had not heard before: 'Sweeping through the gates of the New Jerusalem'. 'Aw, no!' he said, 'I thought I'd be done with all that!' His workaday occupation? He was a road sweeper!

Some years ago my sister remarked, 'When I was younger and heard older folk say that they'd been the church treasurer or organist, or a Sunday-school teacher, for thirty or more years in the same place, I used to think: How boring! how unimaginative! Now I realise how much faithfulness it takes not to get offended, not to get fed up – but to continue year after year in the task God has allotted.'

22 February

Psalm 85:11   1 Chronicles 17:16   Matthew 25:1-4

I dreamed I saw my name in lights
and spoke Your word for all to hear.
I dreamed my name was recognised
by people far and people near.
But I have come to understand

like David long ago,
that humble service in Your house
is still the greatest dream a heart can hold.

O let me be a servant,
a keeper of the door.
My heart is only longing
to see for evermore
the glory of Your presence,
the dwelling of the Lord.
O let me be a servant
a keeper of the door.

Twila Paris

Ye servants of the Lord,
each in his office wait,
observant of His heavenly word
and watchful at His gate.

Let all your lamps be bright,
and trim the golden flame;
gird up your loins, as in His sight,
for aweful is His name.

Watch: 'tis your Lord's command;
and, while we speak, He's near;
mark the first signal of His hand,
and ready all appear.

O happy servant he,
in such employment found!
He shall his Lord with rapture see,
and be with honour crowned.

Christ shall the banquet spread
with His own royal hand,
and raise that faithful servant's head
amid the angelic band.

Philip Doddridge

23 February   Polycarp *(see p.256)*

Psalm 84:4   Isaiah 40:9   John 1:35-39

I stand by the door.
I neither go too far in, nor stay too far out,
The door is the most important door in the world –
it is the door through which folk walk when they find God.
There's no use my going way inside and staying there,
when so many are still outside, and they, as much as I,
crave to know where the door is.

Samuel Moor Shoemaker

24 February

Psalm 143:6   Isaiah 59:9-10   Acts 9:10-20

And all that many ever find
is only the wall where a door ought to be.
They creep along the wall like blind men,
with outstretched, groping hands,
feeling for a door, knowing there must be a door,

Yet they never find it...
so I stand by the door.

Samuel Moor Shoemaker

25 February

Psalm 84:12   1 Chronicles 23:2-5   Acts 12:5-16

The most tremendous thing in the world
is for people to find that door – the door to God.
The most important thing anyone can do
is to take hold of one of those blind, groping hands,
and put it on the latch – the latch that only clicks

and opens to that person's touch.
People die outside that door, as starving beggars die
on cold nights in cruel cities in the dead of winter –
die for want of what is within their grasp.
Others *live*, on the other side of it – live
because they *have* found it,
and open it, and walk in, and find Him...
So I stand by the door.

Samuel Moor Shoemaker
(altered for emphasis)

26 February

Psalm 84:3   Isaiah 65:17-19   John 14:2

Go in, great saints, go all the way in –
go way down into the cavernous cellars,
away up into the spacious attics –
it is a vast, roomy house, this house where God is.
Go into the deepest of hidden casements
of withdrawal, of silence, of sainthood.
Some must inhabit those inner rooms,
and know the depth and heights of God,
and call outside to the rest of us how wonderful it is.
Sometimes I take a deeper look in,
sometimes venture in a little farther;
but my place seems closer to the opening...
So I stand by the door.

Samuel Moor Shoemaker

27 February

Psalm 84:10; 85:8   Joel 3:14   John 21:2-5

There is another reason why I stand there.
Some people get part way in and become afraid
lest God and the zeal of His house devour them;

for God is so very great, and asks of you your all;
and these people way inside only terrify them more.
Somebody must be by the door to tell them that they are spoiled
for the old life, they have seen too much:
once taste God, and nothing but God will do any more.
Somebody must be watching for the frightened
who seek to sneak out just where they came in,
to tell them how much better it is inside.

The people too far in do not see how near these are
to leaving – preoccupied with the wonder of it all.
Somebody must watch for those who have entered the door,
but would like to run away.
So for them, too, I stand by the door.

Samuel Moor Shoemaker (altered)

28 February

Psalm 143:5   Nehemiah 8:10   John 4:28-38

I admire the people who go way in.
But I wish they would not forget how it was
before they got in. Then they would be able to help
the people who have not yet even found the door,
or the people who want to run away again from God.
You can go in too deeply, and stay in too long,
and forget the people outside the door.

Samuel Moor Shoemaker

29 February

Psalm 84:10-12   2 Kings 23:4   Luke 14:10-11

As for me, I shall take my old accustomed place,
near enough to God to hear Him, and know He is there,
but not so far from others as not to hear them,
and remember they are there, too.

Where? Outside the door –
thousands of them, millions of them.
But – more important for me –
one of them, two of them, ten of them,
whose hands I am intended to put on the latch.
So I shall stand by the door and wait
for those who seek it.
'I had rather be a door-keeper...'
So I stand by the door.

Samuel Moor Shoemaker

March
Small beginnings

The readings this month are largely quotations gathered as we have reflected on our experiences as the Northumbria Community.

1 March David *(see p.231)*

Psalm 119:25-26   Ecclesiastes 7:8   Matthew 13:44

> The Desert Fathers' creative subversion, their simple and radical renunciation, cut powerfully through the subtleties of religion and reminded ordinary people that behind all the argumentation was the simple gospel challenge: 'If anyone wants to be a follower of Mine; let him renounce himself, take up his cross and follow Me' [Matthew 16:24].
>
> *William McNamara*

2 March Chad *(see p.286)*

Psalm 17:15   1 Kings 19:11-12   Luke 7:40-43

> The monk is not defined by his task, his usefulness; in a certain sense he is supposed to be useless, because his mission is not to do this or that job but to be a man of God.
>
> *Thomas Merton*

3 March

Psalm 71:2-3   Isaiah 58:8   Luke 15:11-32

For this is the wonder of God, that when we walk in the light of His countenance, the very shadows of our life are charged with healing power.

Hugh Redwood, God in the Shadows

4 March   Owini *(see p.253)*

Psalm 119:27-28   Proverbs 15:16   Luke 12:16-21

Christianity has to be disappointing, precisely because it is not a mechanism for accomplishing all our human ambitions and aspirations; it is a mechanism for subjecting all things to the will of God.

Simon Tugwell

5 March   Piran *(see p.256)*

Psalm 144   Song of Songs 2:15   Luke 16:19-31

Community is a terrible place, a place where our limitations and egoisms are revealed to us. When we begin to live full time with others we discover our poverty and our weakness, our inability to get on with others ... our mental and emotional blocks; our affective and sexual disturbances, our frustrations and jealousies ... and our hatred and desire to destroy.

Jean Vanier

6 March Baldred *(see p.223)*   Billifrith *(see p.225)*

Psalm 63:1-8   Ruth 3:10   Matthew 13:45-46

To worship God *means* to serve Him. There are two ways to do it. One way is to do things for Him that He needs to have done – run errands for Him, carry messages for Him, fight on His side, feed His lambs, and so on. The other way is to do things for Him that you need to do – sing songs for Him, create beautiful things for Him, give things up for Him, tell Him what is on your mind and in your heart, in general rejoice in Him and make a fool of yourself for Him the way lovers have always made fools of themselves for the one they love ... Unless there is an element of joy and foolishness in the proceedings, the time would be better spent doing something useful.

Frederick Buechner

7 March

Psalm 35:19-24   Genesis 4:10-16   Luke 18:9-14

And I will restore your judges as at the first, and your counsellors as at the beginning. Afterwards you shall be called the city of righteousness, the faithful city.

Isaiah 1:26

If the Catholicism that I was raised in had a fault, and it did, it was precisely that it did not allow for mistakes. It demanded that you get it right the first time. There was supposed to be no need for a second chance. If you made a mistake, you lived with it and, like the rich young man, were doomed to be sad, at least for the rest of your life. A serious mistake was a permanent stigmatisation, a mark that you wore like Cain.

I have seen that mark on all kinds of people: divorcees, ex-priests, ex-religious, people who have had abortions, married people who have had affairs, people who have made serious mistakes with their children, and countless others who have made serious mistakes. There is too little around to help them.

We need a theology of brokenness. We need a theology which teaches us that even though we cannot unscramble an egg, God's grace lets us live happily and with renewed innocence far beyond any egg we may have scrambled.

We need a theology that teaches us that God does not just give us one chance, but that every time we close a door He opens another one for us.

Ronald Rolheiser, Forgotten Among the Lilies

8 March Senan *(see p.260)*

Psalm 65:13   Isaiah 60:22   Mark 4:2-9, 13-20

A sense of direction was fixed in my soul. Before me lay the road of life: much of it hidden, obscure, but my destination was clear, a full view of certainty. Heaven was ahead. Its gates were open, Jesus was there. Stretched between me and that glorious goal was a lifetime of service in the Lord's harvest fields.

Heaven would have to wait. I knew now what I wanted more than anything else, even more than heaven itself. I looked up, kneeling by my bed, tears streaming down my face.

Oh Jesus, here's my life. Add to it or take from it what You will, only there is just one thing I would ask, dear Lord. Please, when I have finished my life's work in Your fields, let me meet You with my arms laden down with golden sheaves. Oh, don't let me meet You empty handed. Give me, dear Lord, precious souls for my hire. When I reach heaven, however long that may take, give me the joy of bringing many others with me.

Jean Darnall, Heaven Here I Come

9 March

Psalm 85:13   Isaiah 61:1-4   Luke 14:15-24

What is both Good and New about the Good News is the wild claim that Jesus did not simply tell us that God loves us even in our wickedness and folly and wants us to love each other the same way and to love Him too, but that if we let Him, God will actually bring about this unprecedented transformation of our hearts Himself.

What is both Good and New about the Good News is that mad insistence that Jesus lives on among us not just as another haunting memory but as the outlandish, holy, and invisible power of God working not just through the sacraments but in countless hidden ways to make even slobs like us loving and whole beyond anything we could conceivably pull off by ourselves.

Thus the Gospel is not only Good and New but, if you take it seriously, a Holy Terror. Jesus never claimed that the process of being changed from a slob into a human being was going to be a Sunday-School picnic. On the contrary. Child-birth may occasionally be painless, but rebirth never. Part of what it means to be a slob is to hang on for dear life to our slobbery.

Frederick Buechner

10 March

Psalm 34:18   Isaiah 30:17   Luke 14:7-11

True discretion is impossible without true humility. Self-deception is unlikely when a person is humble enough to submit to the judgement of another.

John Cassian

11 March

Psalm 142   Song of Songs 8:8-9   Matthew 7:24-27

The man who fashions a visionary ideal of community demands that it be realised by God, by others and by himself. He enters the community of Christians with his demands, his own law, and judges the brethren and himself accordingly. He acts as if he is the creator of community, as if it is his dream which holds the community together. When things do not go his way, he calls the effort a failure. When his ideal picture is destroyed, he sees the community going to smash. So he becomes first an accuser of his brethren, then God, and finally the despairing accuser of himself.

Dietrich Bonhoeffer

12 March   Paul Aurelian *(see p.254)*

Psalm 144:1-8   Isaiah 28:10   Matthew 13:52

The renewal of the church will come from a new type of monasticism, which has only in common with the old an uncompromising allegiance to the Sermon on the Mount. It is high time men and women banded together to do this.

Dietrich Bonhoeffer

13 March

Psalm 144:9-15   Ezekiel 17:22-24   Matthew 13:31-32

Dynamic and erratic, spontaneous and radical, audacious and immature, committed if not altogether coherent, ecumenically open and often experimental, visible here and there, now and then, but unsettled institutionally. Almost monastic in nature but most of all ... enacting a fearful hope for human life in society.

William Stringfellow

14 March

Psalm 85:1-7   1 Kings 18:44-45   Matthew 25:1-13

Looking down I saw Scotland, England, Wales and to the Northwest, Ireland. The treetops upon the hills and the clustered clouds hid the people. Suddenly small, flickering lights appeared. They were scattered all over the isles. I came closer to the land. The light was firelight. There were fires burning from the top of Scotland to Land's End on the tip of Cornwall. Lightning streaked downward from the sky above me. I saw it touch down with flashing swiftness, exploding each of the fires into streams of light. Like lava, they burned their fiery path downward from the top of Scotland to Land's End. The waters did not stop them, but the fire spread across the seas to Ireland and to Europe.

Then the Lord said: I will penetrate the darkness with a visitation of My power. With lightning swiftness I will release the power of my Spirit through a renewed people who have learned how to be led by the Spirit. They will explode with a witness that will touch every part of society in Britain. I'm strategically placing them to touch the farms, villages, towns and cities. No one will be without a witness whether they be children in the schools, farmers in the fields, workers in the factories and docks, students in the universities and colleges, the media, the press, the arts or government.

I seemed to see an army of all types of people moving into the continent with a compassionate ministry – participating, caring communities involved with each other at a grass-roots level, sharing the love of God everywhere. I saw the empty cradles of Europe, her churches, holding a new generation of Christian leaders.

Jean Darnall, Heaven, Here I Come

15 March

Psalm 85:2-9   Joshua 14:6-14;   Matthew 5:19

> A student is not above his teacher, nor a servant above his master. It is enough for the student to be like his teacher, and the servant like his master.
>
> *Matthew 10:24-25a*

O Lord, I pray that in You
I'll break ground both fresh and new.
As a student let me stand,
break the hardness of the land
with Your forgiving Father-hand.

Paul Stamper, 'Student Song'

16 March

Psalm 85:8-12   Isaiah 58:11-12   Luke 17:7-10

Lindisfarne:
a point on earth – where land and sea,
God and the willing soul still meet
in total, timeless harmony;
a church – where the sanctuary
lamp has flickered throughout the ages,
telling the presence of Christ
to sunshine and storm, saint and sinner;
a house – where love draws the traveller in;
a haven created by loving people that
renews the spirit of love
in world-weary souls.

Sheila M. Whittle

17 March Patrick *(see p.253)*   Joseph of Arimathea *(see p.245)*

Psalm 137:4   Genesis 12:1-2   Matthew 9:16

Jacques Ellul quotes a second-century Christian apologist describing the believers of his day:

> Though they are residents at home in their own countries, their behaviour there is more like aliens; they take full part as citizens, but they also submit to everything as if they were foreigners. For them, any foreign country is a motherland and any motherland is a foreign country.

18 March

Psalm 122:7-8   1 Samuel 2:18-19   Matthew 25:14-30

> If you want your dream to be,
> build it slow and surely.
> Small beginnings,
> greater ends.
> Heartfelt work grows purely.
>
> If you want to live life free,
> take your time, go slowly.
> Do few things,
> but do them well:
> simple joys are holy.
>
> Day by day,
> stone by stone,
> build your secret slowly.
> Day by day,
> you'll grow too;
> you'll know heaven's glory!

Donovan, 'Simple Joys',
from the film Brother Sun, Sister Moon

19 March

Psalm 145:3-7   1 Chronicles 22:19   Mark 4:26-29

Years ago a small seed
was planted deep into the
heart of hopeful souls.

Over the years that seed grew
and spread itself to other souls
during Easter Workshops
and companionships.

Now that plant flourishes
in many hopeful souls
all working together as one.

Last Easter, buds
could be seen on every bough
of that widely spread plant.

The people of the Nether Springs
prepared themselves to flower
in their base founded by God.

This base was God's aim
for the Northumbria Community,
even though
they never knew it until now.

Anne Louise Haggerstone
(1992)

20 March Cuthbert *(see p.231)*   Herebert *(see p.240)*

Psalm 63:1-2, 7   Proverbs 1:7   Mark 13:33-37

> The world gives itself
> up to incessant activity
> merely because
> it knows of nothing
> better.
> The inspired man
> works among
> its whirring wheels
> also; but he knows
> whither the wheels
> are going,
> for he has found
> the centre
> where all is
> stillness...
>
> *Paul Brunton*

21 March Enda *(see p.236)*

Psalm 27:13   Nehemiah 2:17-18   Matthew 21:28-32

> Observe, admire and obey may be given as the novice's watchwords. The ideal must not remain an ideal, but has to be realised at whatever the cost. The cost is heroism.
>
> *John Cassian*

22 March

Psalm 63:1-8   Proverbs 9:10   Matthew 18:10-14

> Those who lean on Jesus' breast hear God's heartbeat.
>
> *Fr Amphilothius, hermit of Patmos (1889–1970)*

23 March   Ethilwald of Farne *(see p.238)*   Felgild *(see p.238)*

Psalm 121:3-4   Ecclesiastes 3:1-3   Matthew 9:17

> PERPETUAL CHANGE
> is here to stay!

24 March   Oscar Romero *(see p.259)*

Psalm 118:17-21   Malachi 4:2   Matthew 22:1-14

> To confess your sins to God is not to tell Him anything He does not already know. Until you confess them, however, they are the abyss between you. When you confess them, they become the bridge.
>
> *Frederick Buechner*

25 March

Psalm 145:10-12   Song of Songs 5:10, 16   Luke 10:29-37

> A Christian is one who points at Christ and says, 'I can't prove a thing, but there's something about His eyes and His voice. There's something about the way He carries His head, His hands, the way He carries His cross – the way He carries me.'
>
> *Frederick Buechner*

26 March

Psalm 149:5   1 Kings 17:10-16   Matthew 13:47-50

Who knows how the awareness of God's love first hits people. Every person has his own tale to tell, including the person who would not believe in God if you paid him. Some moment happens in your life that you say Yes right up to the roots of your hair, that makes it worth having been born just to have happen. Laughing with somebody till the tears run down your cheeks. Waking up to the first snow. Being in bed with somebody you love.

Whether you thank God for such a moment or thank your lucky stars, it is a moment that is trying to open up your whole life. If you turn your back on such a moment and hurry along to Business as Usual, it may lose you the ball game. If you throw your arms around such a moment and hug it like crazy, it may save your soul.

How about the person you know who as far as you can possibly tell has never had such a moment – the soreheads and slobs of the world, the ones the world has hopelessly crippled? Maybe for that person the moment that has to happen is you.

Salvation is a process, not an event.

Frederick Buechner

27 March

Psalm 71:2-3   Proverbs 16:8   Matthew 25:31-46

'Your sins are forgiven,' Jesus said to the paralytic, then, 'Rise' – whereupon the man picked up his bed and went home.

Matthew 9:2-7

It is as hard to absolve yourself of your own guilt as it is to sit in your own lap. Wrongdoing sparks guilt sparks wrongdoing *ad nauseam*, and we all try to disguise the grim process from both ourselves and everybody else. In order to break the circuit we need somebody before whom we can put aside the disguise, trusting that when He sees us for what we fully are, He will not run away screaming with, if nothing worse, laughter. Our trust in Him leads us to trust His trust in us. In His presence the fact of our guilt no longer makes us feel and act out our guiltiness. For a moment at least the vicious circle stops circling and we can step down onto the firm ground of His acceptance, where maybe we'll be able to walk a straight line again.

Frederick Buechner

28 March

Psalm 145:1-3   2 Samuel 6:5, 14-15   Luke 18:1-8

Dynamos of praise

O my child, lean upon Me; for I am your helper; I am your shield and your buckler. Yes, I am your strong tower and support. No evil shall befall you, for you are surrounded and protected by My presence, and no evil can touch Me. Yes, let your heart rejoice in Me, and occupy your heart with praise. There is no need that I will not fulfil as you praise and worship – both your needs and the needs of others.

Some have contemplated the power of faith and of prayer, but only rarely have I revealed to people this far greater power of praise. For by prayer and faith doors are opened, but by praise and worship great dynamos of power are set in motion, as when a switch is thrown and an electric power plant such as Niagara is thrown into operation. Praying for specifics is like requesting light for individual houses in various scattered places, while worshipping and praise flood the whole area with available current.

I do not discount prayer (petitions). I only show you a more marvellous way – a faster means of bringing more help to more people with less elapse of time. So many need Me. So little time is available. Turn loose your praises, and in proportion to your liberality, you shall see My generosity expressed, and in infinite magnitude.

Labour not to analyse each need. Leave the diagnosis and the mechanics of it in My hands. Complexities are as nothing to Me. They exist only in your mind, sown by the enemy, to dull your faith. Ignore all this. Weigh nothing, unless you inquire of your own heart how much love for Me is there. Hold Me closely, nor let Me go. I will surely bless you, and I will make you a blessing.

I will make you a blessing. Think not to take a blessing to someone, or hope that I will send a blessing. Lo, I will make you as My ambassador, to be yourself a sweet savour of life and grace. Through your saltiness shall others be made thirsty. Through your joy shall others be made to long after reality.

Frances Roberts, Come Away, My Beloved

29 March

Psalm 140:12   Genesis 50:21   Luke 11:5-13

In the early days of the Northumbria Community's life at Hetton Hall, John Skinner, while walking near the stable block, where holes were being knocked in the walls, prayed, 'How are we going to pay for all this? And what about all the mission work? It's all too much – You know what a worrier I am! What can You do?'

The Lord seemed to stand before him, wearing only a simple, seamless, homespun garment. He said, simply, 'I am poor, too.' He paused, then added, 'But I will go to the Father for you.'

30 March

Psalm 121:8   Job 42:12-13   Matthew 21:33-46

The Covenant of Community, profound as it is, can never guarantee that a certain person will always stay physically close to another. It guarantees only that there will always be someone there, inspired by the same Spirit.

Jean Vanier, Man and Woman He Made Them

31 March

Psalms 133   Exodus 34:21-22   Matthew 13:24-30, 36-43

A time to gather

A time to gather, a time to reap
the fruits we've planted, hoping to bear peace.
The seeds have fallen so many months ago:
the harvest of our life will come.

In tenderness is life's beauty known;
and as we listen the morning star will shine.
The days go by; why not let them be filled
with new and surprising joys?

A time for kneading love's leaven well,
to open up and go beyond ourselves;
And as we reach for this moment, we know
that love is a gift born in care.

A time for hoping and being still,
to go on turning away from brittle fear.
A time to come back with all of one's heart
and bending to another's call.

This is our journey through forests tall;
our paths may differ and yet among them all
life's dreams and visions sustain us on our way
as loving gives birth to joy, gives birth to joy.

Gregory Norbert, Weston Priory

April
Abandonment

This month's readings are taken from the letters, prayers and meditations of Charles de Foucauld.

1 April Mary of Egypt *(see p.250)*

Psalm 9:2   Isaiah 40:9   Romans 1:15-16

> You are powerful over Your creatures, You can do all things in me. Give me a right mind, give me the wisdom that You promise to all who ask for it. Convert my heart and let me glorify You to the utmost till my last breath and through all eternity. I ask this in the name of our Saviour Jesus Christ. Amen. Amen. Amen.
>
> *Je veux crier l'Evangile*
> *toute ma vie.*
> (I would shout the Gospel
> all my life.)

2 April

Psalm 6:1-4   Isaiah 40:2   Romans 7:19

> What shall I tell you about my soul? It is still more or less as you knew it, I still have a lot to do about humility, obedience, charity, meditation too, and many other things; it seems to me that where my soul is concerned I lose rather than gain; I ought to admit this as a tragic certainty; the only thing, basically, that prevents me from doing so, that prevents me from admitting this sad fact, is my huge desire for it not to be true.

I have no humility, no simplicity. What a huge sheet of paper I would need to enumerate all that I have too little of and all that I have too much of!

3 April

Psalm 42:7   Isaiah 40:1   Romans 12:15

When we love, what is sweeter than to give something to the loved one, especially to give Him something we hold dear, to suffer for love of Him, to give Him our very heart's blood. And then not only have we offered something to our Lord Jesus – our tears – but it is so marvellous that He lets us offer Him these on behalf of each other.

4 April Martin Luther King Jr *(see p.246)*

Psalm 1:2   Ruth 3:7   John 12:3

When one loves one longs to be for ever in converse with him one loves, or at least to be always in his sight. Prayer is nothing else. This is what prayer is: intimate intercourse with the Beloved. You look at Him; you tell Him of your love; you are happy at His feet; you tell Him you will live and die there.

5 April

Psalm 91:1-7   Ruth 3:14a   Matthew 14:23

She had a sister named Mary, who sat at the Lord's feet and listened to what He was saying.

Luke 10:39

O my God, thank You for letting me be at your feet! How divinely good You are! You love me. It seems madness to think it. You, perfect God, love me, a poor evil, cowardly creature, falling a thousand times a day. No, it is not madness, it is truth, the truth of Your Divine Heart, and Your love is far beyond our love and Your heart far beyond our hearts.

Whilst everything sleeps, drowned in silence and darkness, I live at the feet of God, unfolding my soul to His love, telling Him that I love Him, and He replying that I will never love Him, however great may be my love, as much as He cherishes me. What happiness to be allowed to spend these nights with God.

Teach me to prolong these hours in which I watch alone at Your feet. Everything sleeps, no one knows of my happiness nor shares it. I rejoice through the solitude of the night in Your presence, O my God.

6 April

Psalm 27:3-4   Isaiah 40:4   John 10:10

Let us try with all our strength to occupy our minds with only God. Even whilst doing our tasks we must keep our eyes fixed constantly on Him, never detaching our heart from Him, only keeping our attention on our tasks as much as is right and necessary, never our hearts. God must be the King of our minds, the Lord of our minds, so that the thought of Him never leaves us, and we speak, think and act always either for Him or guided by the love of Him. Let our souls be thus a house of prayer and not a den of thieves. Let no stranger enter in, no profanity even in passing. Let it always be occupied with its Beloved. When one loves, one never loses sight of that which one loves.

7 April Roland Walls *(see p.264)*

Psalm 5:1-3   Lamentations 2:19a   Mark 1:35

Let us do what our Lord did and rise early in the morning, whilst everything is at rest in silence and darkness, when sleep envelops everything in torpor, in profound quiet. Let us rise and watch with God, lifting our hearts to Him, laying our souls at His feet, and at this early hour when intercourse is so secret and so sweet let us fall at His feet and enjoy converse with our Creator. How good He is to let us come to His feet whilst all is sleeping. Whilst all is sleeping in silence and shadow, let us begin both our day and our prayers. Before our working day begins let us pass long hours praying at the feet of our Lord.

8 April

Psalm 31:1-2   Isaiah 40:28-29   Mark 1:38

During the many occupations that fill the day our minds must be constantly fixed on God, and our eyes always turned towards Him either by using ejaculatory prayer or simply by turning our thoughts to Him. It matters little what means we use, so long as the soul gazes on her Beloved.

The hours given up entirely to prayer will give us the strength, with God's grace, to keep ourselves in His presence through the rest of the day and give up all our time to what is called 'perpetual prayer'.

9 April Dietrich Bonhoeffer *(see p.225)*

Psalm 6:9   Isaiah 40:27   Mark 15:34

We must speak to God with perfect simplicity, telling Him all our thoughts, even our complaints. Since our sufferings are allowed by Him we may make our plaint to God as our Lord did, but we should complain with all reverence, love, submission, unbounded and loving conformity to His will.

10 April

Psalm 30:10-12   Isaiah 40:25-26   Luke 22:43

The more you suffer, the more you are tempted, the more you need to pray; prayer now alone can strengthen you with help and consolation. Let not pain and fierce temptation paralyse your prayer. The devil does all he can to prevent you praying at these times. But rather than give in to weak human nature which absorbs the soul in its pain so that it sees nothing else for the time, turn your eyes to our Lord and speak to Him standing so near. He is with you, looking on you lovingly, listening for your words. He tells you to speak, that He is there to hear you, that He loves you and you have not a word to say to Him, no look to give Him. What ingratitude! Look at Him, speak to Him without ceasing. The deeper your agony, the deeper you must bury yourself in the Heart of your Beloved, and cling to His side with ceaseless prayer.

11 April

Psalm 4:7-8   2 Chronicles 30:8a   Luke 23:46

Father, into Thy hands I commend my spirit.

Luke 23:46

This is the last prayer of our Master, our Beloved. May it be ours. And not only ours at our last moments, but at all times.

> My Father, I commend myself to You;
> I give myself to You;
> I leave myself in Your hands.

My Father, do with me as You wish.
Whatever You do with me,
I thank You.
I accept everything.
I am ready for anything.
I thank You always.
So long as Your will is done in me
and in all creatures,
I have no other wish, my God.

I put my soul into Your hands,
giving it to You, my God,
with all my heart's love,
which makes me crave
to abandon myself to You
without reserve,
with utter confidence,
for are You not my Father?

12 April Aldwin *(see p.221)*

Psalm 16:1   Habakkuk 2:4   Matthew 9:22

It is the rarest virtue of all to have real faith, faith that inspires all one's actions; and faith in the supernatural which tears the mask from the world and sees God in everything; which makes all things possible; which takes all meaning out of such words as worry, peril, fear; which makes us pass through life calmly, peacefully, happily, like a child holding its mother's hand; which gives the soul perfect detachment from all material things, showing it their emptiness and puerility; which gives to prayer the confidence of a child asking something he deserves from his father; a faith to which all is falsehood except to do the will of God.

It will help us to regard all other living things as aids to the winning of Heaven, for we can always give God praise for them, or use them, or renounce them.

Faith will show us the greatness of God and our littleness. It will make us undertake whatever is pleasing to God without hesitation or false shame or fear and without looking back. Ah! such faith is rare indeed. My God, give me this faith; my God, I believe, help Thou my unbelief; my God, let me believe and love.

I ask it in the name of our Lord Jesus Christ.

13 April

Psalm 23:3-4   Proverbs 3:11-12   Luke 11:11-12

You are a Father, all powerful and infinitely wise and good and tender. You say to us as Your children, so frail we are and hardly able to walk except with our hands in Yours, 'All that you ask I will give you if only you ask with confidence.'

If we ask You for dangerous playthings You refuse them in goodness for us, and You console us by giving us other things for our good. If we ask You to put us where it would be dangerous for us to be, You do not give us what is not for our good, but You give us something really for our welfare, something that we would ask for ourselves if our eyes were open.

You take us by the hand and lead us, not there where we would wish to go, but there where it is best for us to be.

14 April

Psalm 8:3-4   Isaiah 40:6-8   Romans 11:33-34

All created beauty, all beauty of nature, the beauty of the sunset, of the sea lying like a mirror beneath the blue sky, of the dark forest, of the garden of flowers, of the mountains and the great spaces of the desert, of the snow and the ice, the beauty of a rare soul reflected in a beautiful face, all these beauties are but the palest reflection of Yours, my God. All that has ever charmed my eyes in this world is but the poorest, the humblest reflection of Your infinite beauty.

15 April

Psalm 139:7-10   Isaiah 40:5   Romans 11:36

Those creatures in whom I admire a reflection of His perfections, on whom there falls a little ray of the infinite sunshine, are outside me, far removed from me, distant and separate, whilst You, who are perfection, beauty, truth, infinite and essential love, You are in me and around me. You fill me altogether ... there is no particle of my body that You do not fill, and around me You are nearer than the air in which I move. How am I blessed! What happiness to be united so completely to perfection itself; to live in it, to possess it living in myself! My God, You who are in me, in whom I am, let me know my happiness.

Give me a perpetual sense of Your presence, of Your presence all around me, and at the same time that loving fear one feels in the presence of Him one loves passionately, and which makes one, in the presence of one's Beloved, keep one's eyes on Him with great desire and firm purpose to do all that may please Him and be good, and gently fear to do or think anything that may displease or harm Him.

In You, by You, and for You. Amen.

16 April

Psalm 7:17   Isaiah 40:18-20   1 Corinthians 13:12

I know You enough to show me that I should love You without measure.

I rejoice that I shall know You better in Heaven; and, seeing Your beauty, I shall love You more and more.

17 April

Psalm 139:23   Ezekiel 36:26, 33-36   Mark 1:40-41

Compassion to weep for Your sorrows: truly this would be a great grace. Of myself I am incapable of drawing tears from this heart of stone at the thought of Your cross, so horribly hard is it. But I ask from You the gift of compassion, so that I may give it to You. Turn my stony heart to a compassionate one and give me grace to kiss Your footprints with the tears You would have me shed from my soul and from my heart. I must have zeal for souls, a burning love of souls which have all been bought at the same price.

18 April

Psalm 22:31   Zechariah 9:9   Luke 14:8-10

Charles de Foucauld here quotes the words of Abbé Huvelin, who was instrumental in bringing him to God. These words, from a sermon, are addressed to Christ:

> You took always the lowest place
> and did it so completely that no one
> ever since has been able to wrest it
> from You.

19 April

Psalm 16:11   Isaiah 40:13-14   Matthew 5:11-12

As they left the council, they rejoiced that they were considered worthy to suffer dishonour for the sake of the Name. And every day in the temple and at home they did not cease to teach and proclaim Jesus as the Messiah.

Acts 5:41-42

Faith is that which makes us believe
from the depths of our souls
all the truths that the Gospel holds.

The just man lives truly by his faith, for it replaces for him the greater part of his natural senses; it so transforms all things that the senses are of little use to the soul, which through them is only deceived, whilst faith shows it realities. Where the eye sees but a poor man, faith sees Jesus. Where the ear hears curses and persecution, faith sings: 'Rejoice and be joyful.' The touch feels only blows and stonings; but faith says, 'Be glad that you are deemed worthy to suffer for the name of Christ.' Our taste perceives only a wafer of unleavened bread; faith shows us our Saviour Jesus, God and man, soul and body.

20 April

Psalm 18:28-29   Isaiah 40:21-24   2 Corinthians 11:26-30

The senses hold suffering in horror. Faith blesses it as a gift from the hand of Jesus, a bit of His cross which He lets us carry. The senses take fright at that which they call danger, at all that might mean pain or death; but faith is afraid of nothing; she knows nothing can happen to her but what is the will of God. Thus in everything that may happen, sorrow or joy, health or sickness, life or death, she is content and fears nothing. The senses are anxious about the future and ask how shall we live tomorrow, but faith feels no anxiety. He who lives by faith has his soul full of new horizons open before him, marvellous horizons lit with a new light, and with a divine beauty surrounded with new truths of which the world is not aware. Thus he who believes begins a new life opposed to that of the world, to whom his acts seem like madness. The world is in the darkness of night, the man of faith is in full light.

21 April

Psalm 3:3-5   Isaiah 40:3   2 Corinthians 12:9-10

I was lowly and disdained. Seek, ask for and love those occupations which degrade you, such as sweeping dung or digging the ground, whatever is most lowly and common; the more you make yourself lowly in these ways, the more you will be like Me. Even if you are thought mad, all the better. Thank Me infinitely. I was thought mad, that is a point of resemblance between us. If you should be stoned and reviled and cursed in the streets, all the better. Thank Me, for it is a great grace. Did they not do the same to Me? You should rejoice that I make you like Myself in this. But you must not bring this treatment upon yourself by eccentricity or strange behaviour. I did nothing to be so treated; I did not deserve it in any way, and yet I was so treated. So do nothing to deserve ill-treatment, but if I give you the grace to undergo it, thank Me for it. Do nothing to prevent it or stop it. Act as I should have done. Do only good, but give yourself to the lowest, humblest task; show yourself to others, by your dress, your lodging, your friendliness with the humble, the equal of the humblest.

22 April

Psalm 18:35   Isaiah 40:11   1 John 4:16

He who loves has his Beloved always in his mind; that time to him is well spent that is spent in contemplating Him, and the time to him is wasted in which He is out of his sight. He counts as profitable only those hours in which he contemplates the only thing that to him has any reality. All else is for him emptiness and nothingness. Let your soul melt into Mine, immerse yourself in Me, lose yourself in Me. Think how often I have told you to hope for the day when you will lean for ever on My breast. And since I allow it I tell you now to begin to live this life, in silence, lay your head upon My breast and so accomplish your pilgrimage.

23 April

Psalm 4:1-4   Isaiah 40:15-17   1 John 4:19

O my God, You are there before me. What will You that I think or that I say to You out of the depths of my heart?

'I do not ask you to think a great deal, but to love a great deal,' the Holy Spirit answers. 'Adore Me, love Me, contemplate Me; tell Me and repeat over and over again that you love Me, that you give yourself to Me, that you long for all My children to give themselves to Me and love Me.'

All is sleeping, all is at rest. Thank You, my God, for calling me to adore You and love You. Hold my eyes open and set wide the gates of my soul. Let me lose and sink myself in the contemplation and love of You.

24 April

Psalm 31:7   Isaiah 40:12   Matthew 14:22-23

Trust nothing, yourself least of all; but in Me have that perfect confidence that banishes fear. Remember how many storms I have quieted by a word, making a great calm to follow. Remember how I held up Peter walking on the waters. I am always as near to all people as I was then to him, and as ready to help and succour in all that is for the good of the soul. Be confident, faithful, courageous; have no fear for your body and soul, for I am there, loving and all-powerful. Never forget that I am there. In this life the tempest never ceases, and your boat is ever ready to sink. But I am there, and with Me it will never be wrecked.

25 April

Psalm 40:8   Song of Songs 8:7   Matthew 22:36-38

The greatest commandment is to love God with all your heart and all your soul and all your strength. It means to love Me as your King, above everything, as much as you can, as much as the grace I give you makes it possible to love Me.

What does loving mean? To one soul God may give this feeling, to another that feeling. First and foremost is the longing to see, to know, to possess the Beloved; the longing to be loved by Him, the longing to please Him, to do Him some good; the desire to praise Him, admire Him, imitate Him; the desire to be approved by Him, to obey Him in everything, to see Him pleased, to see Him possessed of all that is good and to His glory; the longing, in a word, for all that is for His good; the wish to suffer for Him, to share His labours, His life, His conditions; to conform one's soul entirely to Him; the wish to give oneself to Him, to live only for Him; the longing to labour for His service, to share the pain of His sufferings, the joy of His joy, the pain of those things that grieve Him, and in union with Him to rejoice in those things that please Him.

All these sentiments are the effect, result, outcome of love. They belong to love and are part of love, but they are not all love itself. A single one of them is really the essence of love – that is to desire passionately and above all things the well-being of the Beloved, to that degree that all else means nothing to one, that one lives only for the accomplishment of this desire.

26 April

Psalm 18:1-2   2 Samuel 7:20   Luke 11:13

Prayer is the cry of our hearts to God. So it must be something perfectly natural, perfectly genuine, the expression of the deepest things in our heart. It is not your lips that should speak, nor your mind, but your will. Your will manifested, spread out before your Father, true, naked, sincere, simple, and presented before Him by you. This is what prayer should be. This needs neither a long space of time nor many words, nor many thoughts. It varies: sometimes it will be longer, sometimes quite short, according as your heart's desire prompts you.

Prayer, in the widest sense of the word, may be either a silent contemplation or one accompanied by words. The best prayer is the most loving prayer. The more it is laden with love, the more the soul holds itself tenderly and lovingly before its God, the more acceptable is that prayer.

27 April

Psalm 123:1   1 Kings 8:59-61   1 Thessalonians 5:17

My children, what I ask for you in your prayer is love, love, love. Besides the time that you should consecrate entirely to prayer every day, you should lift up your hearts to Me as often as possible. When at work, you can, whilst giving yourself up to it, either keep Me constantly in your thoughts as is possible in purely manual labour, or perhaps you will only be able to lift your eyes to Me from time to time, whenever you can. It would be sweet and right to contemplate Me always, never to lose sight of Me – but this is not possible in this world, for ordinary folk; it is only possible in Heaven. What you can and should do is to lift your hearts to Me as often as you can during the time that is not taken up solely with prayer; lift the eyes of your soul up to Me as often and as lovingly as you can, and whilst you are at work keep the thought of Me as much present to your mind as is compatible with your work.

28 April

Psalm 52:8   Isaiah 40:30-31   1 Thessalonians 5:18

> We must not trouble about health
> or life any more than a tree
> troubles about a leaf falling.

29 April

Psalm 7:8-10   Job 42:2, 5   1 Thessalonians 5:21

Six months before his death Charles de Foucauld wrote to Louis Massignon:

> As for Jesus' love for us, He has proved it clearly enough for us to believe in it without being able to feel it.
>   To feel we loved Him and He loves us would be heaven.
>
> But heaven is not, except at rare moments and in rare cases, for us here below.

30 April

Psalm 34:13   Isaiah 49:15   1 Thessalonians 5:23-24

On the day of his murder Charles de Foucauld was writing a letter to his cousin:

> It seems we do not love enough. How true it is we shall never love enough. But the good Lord who knows from what mud He has fashioned us and who loves us more than any mother can ever love her child, He who never lies, has told us that none who come to Him shall ever be rejected.

May
To a young disciple

This month's readings are a development of Columbanus' *Letter to a Young Disciple*.

1 May

Psalm 138:6   Isaiah 28:11   Matthew 20:25-27

Be helpful when you are at the bottom of the ladder and be the lowest when you are in authority

Too many of our models for authority are ones of hierarchy or domination. We think of rulers and leaders as those who are over other people and supported by them. Instead of a pyramid model where the few dominate the many, in God's Kingdom it is more helpful to picture a huge saucer into which is thrown all the people of God in all their giftedness, from the least to the greatest. Those more strongly gifted for ministry will not rise to the top, but sink to the bottom where they may undergird and provoke the rest of the people of God.

One true example of Christian humility was King Oswald of Northumbria who himself willingly worked as interpreter for Aidan so that his people might receive the gospel.

2 May

Psalm 2:10-12   Daniel 1:3-9   Matthew 17:24-27

Be simple in faith but well trained in manners

When Augustine came to Kent he summoned bishops and teachers from the Celtic Church in Wales to a conference at which they would discuss working together in the process of evangelisation. He remonstrated with them to change their traditions for Roman ones, but also prayed over a blind man who was duly healed.

To the second such conference the Welsh sent seven British bishops and many learned men. Before the second meeting they consulted a hermit for direction. He answered, 'If he is a man of God, follow him.' They asked how they could tell. The hermit reminded them that Jesus said He was meek and lowly of heart. If Augustine were the same it would be obvious that he himself bore the yoke of Christ and was offering it to them, but if he were harsh and proud this was not God's doing and they should disregard him. The test should be this, that the British party arrive later than Augustine and his party, then observe whether he stood to greet them or insolently remained seated.

Not only did he remain sitting down, but began to lay conditions upon their fellowship, that they should change the manner of their calculation of the date of Easter, their monastic tonsure, and their way of baptising. They recognised that under such circumstances he despised already what they stood for and would do so even more if they gave in to his demands. For want of manners much healthy co-operation in the gospel was thus forfeited.

3 May

Psalm 16:5-6, 8   Proverbs 26:17, 20-22   John 21:15-22

Be demanding in your own affairs but unconcerned in those of others

Isaiah 58 speaks of the possibility of being guided continually by the Lord, of being a watered garden – a spring with waters that never fail – but insists that the condition for this happening is the taking away from our midst the pointing finger that accuses our brother, saying 'It's all *your* fault!' or 'Look what you have done' or 'You are a disgrace to us all.'

If we attend to ourselves, are demanding of obedience from ourselves, if we remove the plank from our eye, then, should we notice the splinter in our brother's eye at all, we will willingly help him remove it – at his request – and without needing to see it through a magnifying glass.

4 May

Psalm 19:12-13   1 Samuel 20:8-17   John 15:15

Be guileless in friendship, astute in the face of deceit

A friend is someone you can be yourself with. Trying to be someone we are not will not win us friendship. Our need to impress is the enemy of any true beginning. But when we know ourselves to be accepted, a true friend can help us uncover any areas of self-deceit, and love us into deeper reality.

When we are aware that another person has lied to us, deceived us, betrayed our trust or deliberately misled us, if we are wise we will not easily trust them again. We are required to show them love, to meet them with forgiveness – but trust should be earned. To close our heart to that person would be contrary to forgiveness, but to allow their behaviour to go unchecked may not be in their best interest. Here our response should be discerned carefully.

5 May

Psalm 132:1-5   Proverbs 17:17   1 Peter 5:8

Be tough in times of ease, tender in hard times

When things are hard, often we are more reliant on God, leaning on Him in our hardship. When things become easier we tend to be more self-assured, blasé and independent. It is important then to keep our promises, and not forget the lessons we have learnt – or soon we may find ourselves having to learn them a second time. When outward circumstances are not checking us it is important to find appropriate disciplines to stop us becoming lazy or unfit. We never know how suddenly we may be called upon, or how we may regret wasted days of opportunity.

But when we are weary, heavy-laden, and when circumstances press upon us, Jesus counsels us to allow Him to be yoked beside us, shouldering much of the weight. When times are hard it is the wrong time for recriminations – gently we should ease one another's burdens.

6 May

Psalm 139:12   Isaiah 30:20-21   Titus 1:15-16

Keep your options open when there is no problem, but dig in when you must choose

Too often the Christians are hiding out in their mission citadels peering out, cautiously preparing to run out quickly and lasso some poor passer-by, claim them for God and haul them back into the safety of the citadel. This is called making a difference in the world…? What happened to the promise that 'greater is He who is in you than he that is in the world'?

We are not asked to live a blinkered or protected existence in a safe, ivory-towered environment. We are sent to walk confidently with a pure heart into the world of people and culture and pain and pressure. It need not contaminate us, if only we live the life that has taken root deep inside of us. God wants to plant us in places where we can make a difference and be His presence – not in any self-conscious way.

There may be times when we need to speak out, opt out, explain our beliefs are different from those around us – but we should not provoke confrontations or become defensive. These times, when they happen, may lead to miracles or to persecution – or both.

7 May

Psalm 119:71, 113-117   Isaiah 50:4-5   Romans 5:3-5

Be pleasant when things are unpleasant, and sorrowful when they are pleasant

A container that is brim-full of sweet waters cannot spill bitterness no matter how sharply it is jostled. Unpleasant situations can drive us closer to God, and to each other, if we let Him into them. We learn so much in these times that some mature souls are sad to see a pressure-cooker situation come to an end. They have learnt that it is a mistake to be at ease with ease. It is important to be kind to someone when we know they are under pressure, and when things are difficult for us it is equally important that we do not become difficult for other people!

Jim Wallis of the Sojourners Fellowship says that his favourite theologians are always under six years of age. One such child heard their parent's apology: 'I'm sorry I shouted at you, honey, it's just that I am really under pressure just now.' The child responded: 'So being under pressure makes you yell at small children? I think you really have a problem...'

8 May

Psalm 119:165-168   Genesis 13:5-9   1 Corinthians 12:3

Disagree where necessary, but be in agreement about truth

Jesus said, 'He who is not against us is for us.' There is no excuse for division and antagonism between believers or groups of believers. It is possible to disagree strongly or deeply and still affirm that we hold fundamental truths in common, and that we are still family. Barnabas and Paul could not agree as to the wisdom of taking John Mark on mission again. In consequence they then worked separately, still extending the Kingdom but through different geographic areas. Who knows if this diminished or increased their overall effectiveness? Similarly, after the Council of Whitby in 664 Bishop Colman returned to Iona with all the Irish monks and about 30 native to Northumbria who chose to go to Scotland rather than remain and implement the council's decision. Even Bede refers to Colman as 'a man of innate prudence and good sense'. After a short stay on Iona, Colman and his brothers went to Ireland and he founded two monasteries there.

The first of these monasteries was at Inis-bo-finde off the west coast of Ireland. The Northumbrians settled well, but complained that each summer the Irish monks travelled the countryside, and were not around to bring in the harvest but were content not to travel during the winter! Colman then built a second monastery on the Irish mainland for these Northumbrians, which in time grew but later conformed more to Roman practice than Celtic. Bede does not tell us the nature or purpose of the journeyings of these Irish monks who had come from Lindisfarne.

9 May

Psalm 104:13-34   Nehemiah 8:9-11   Colossians 3:19

Be serious in pleasures, but kindly when things are bitter

Our God is one who turned gallons of water into wine at a wedding, the extravagant Creator who plants flowers in places no one but Him is likely to find. No wonder He tells us that whatever we do we should do with all our hearts, and show consideration for those in trouble of all kinds. Jewish culture reflects this celebration of life, and so do the stories of the Celtic saints. This story from a 'Life of Brigid' is a good example:

There was a certain man biding in Lassair's church, and his wife was leaving him and would neither eat nor sleep with him. Brigid blessed water for him and said 'Put that water over the house, and over the food, and over the drink of yourselves, and over the bed in your wife's absence.' When he had done thus, the wife gave exceeding great love to him, so that she could not keep apart from him, even on one side of the house; but she was always at one of his hands. He went one day on a journey and left the wife asleep. When the woman awoke she rose up lightly and went after the husband and saw him far from her, with an arm of the sea between them. She cried out to her husband and said that she would go into the sea unless he came to her.

10 May

Psalm 119:165-166   Proverbs 18:19-21   1 Corinthians 6:1-8

Be strong in trials, weak in dissensions

Too often we are weak in trials, but very strong in dissent. Often it takes two parties to make a quarrel; but if I am determined not to take offence easily, the quarrel can be averted. Why is the other person picking a fight, anyway? What has upset them? Was it me? Was it my lack of thoughtfulness, or a lack of love on my part? Or has someone else upset them?

If we tried more often to be weak, vulnerable and forgiving, unpleasantness would be more readily averted and we would win our brother. Sometimes we would even win our cause. Sadly, we too often care more about being right than acting rightly. Trials may not be enjoyable, but the joy of the Lord may sustain us and hold us together through all kinds of trying circumstances.

11 May Comgall *(see p.231)*

Psalm 37:8   Proverbs 10:17-19   James 1:19-20

Be slow to anger, swift to learn, slow also to speak, as St James says, equally swift to hear

> Be quick to hear the hard words that people bring to you. Then be slow to react. Don't rush into denial, retaliation and rationalisation. Our challenge is to convert the energy once used by our self-defence machines into listening power, vulnerability power and contemplation power. We need to say to ourselves, 'Before I flare up, I'm going to quiet myself and listen. I'm going to be quick to hear, slow to speak, and slow to anger. I'm going to search for the truth in what this person is saying, and learn from it.'
>
> *Bill Hybels*

> We were given two ears and one mouth to use in that proportion. Jesus never commanded us to engage in theological debates with strangers, flaunt four-inch crosses and Jesus stickers or throw out Christian catch-phrases. But He did tell us to work and live in such a way that when the Holy Spirit orchestrates opportunities to speak about God we will have earned the right.
>
> *Bill Hybels*

12 May

Psalm 17:2   Deuteronomy 32:34-36   Colossians 3:13-14, 17

Be up and doing to make progress, slack to take revenge, careful in word, eager in work

It should never be said of Christians that as workers they are half-hearted, careless, tardy, irresponsible, whiney, or negligent. Behaviour like that embarrasses God. It brings reproach on Him. At work Christians should epitomise character qualities like self-discipline, perseverance, and initiative. They should be self-motivated, prompt, organised, and industrious. Their efforts should result in work of the very highest quality. Why? Because they're not just laying bricks; they're building a wall for God's glory ... They're not just driving a tractor; they're ploughing a straight furrow for God's glory ... Christians must strive every day to be beyond reproach in all their marketplace dealings and practices.

Bill Hybels

13 May

Psalm 15:1-2, 4a   Proverbs 8:13   Matthew 5:6

Be friendly with men of honour, stiff with rascals

C.S. Lewis in his *Reflections on the Psalms* says that provided someone is rich and powerful it seems people will treat them as a celebrity – far from disapproving of their misdeeds, the notoriety adds to their charm, and instead of shunning them even Christians can be drawn into admiring such people.

What is *our* behaviour? Whose approval matters to us? What is the standard against which we measure people and their behaviour? Do we think as citizens of another Kingdom? Or just use Christian jargon on the outside?

14 May William Walcher *(see p.263)* Elfwy *(see p.235)*

Psalm 41:1   Ezekiel 3:8-9   Matthew 12:17-21

Be gentle to the weak, firm to the stubborn, steadfast to the proud, humble to the lowly

Columbanus in his letter instructs the young disciple how to behave towards different sorts of people or how to behave towards the same people when they are in a different stage or have a particular attitude.

With the weak it is appropriate to be gentle, encouraging and strengthening them, following the example of Christ who would not crush the bruised reed. When someone is stubborn it is important not to give way to them, but remain firm and immovable. They will not then overpower you and get their own way; instead they recognise you will not be intimidated by their attitude. Your face will be strong enough to meet their gaze fair and square without becoming angry and obstinate in turn. When they back down or become reasonable you will have won their respect. A proud person is one who sets a wrong value on themselves, who thinks too much or too little of themselves, constructing a fearfully exaggerated self-image as out-and-out success or hardened failure. They project a belief, but you *are*.

Their self-image fluctuates: you remain constant, yet are growing slowly. Their attitude changes to show their 'best side': your focus remains steady. Circumstances may help to humble us, but can equally make us resentful, bitter and proud: it is all our choice how we respond, whether we choose to humble ourselves under the mighty hand of God or are resistant.

15 May

Psalm 131:1   Judges 7:4-7   Philippians 4:5

Be ever sober, ever chaste, ever modest

The words of the letter here remind us of Jesus' remarks about the happy servant who is found sober and diligently going about the Master's business when his Master returns unexpectedly. It is not exam technique that is required here, but preparation for continuous assessment.

16 May Brendan *(see p.226)*

Psalm 69:9a   Isaiah 59:12-19   Titus 2:14

Be patient as far as is compatible with zeal

Zeal is defined as ardour, energy, fervour. Patience is well and good, but not if it swamps zeal and extinguishes its direction and energy. Where it is not possible to direct that zeal into action it can be channelled into urgency of prayer, grasping the right arm of God by the elbow to reach out to open doors of opportunity fastened tight shut because of our prayerlessness.

When zeal abates or evaporates we need to discern whether we were wrongly counselled to 'have patience' or whether the original fervour was misplaced and immature and would have energised some misdirected scheme embraced in rash enthusiasm. It still remains true that it is easier to alter the course of an already moving vehicle than to push-start one that has forgotten how to even let its engine tick over. We need hearts consumed with passion to activate the coming of the Kingdom, that will not rest till its brightness appears as the noonday sun.

17 May

Psalm 116:12   2 Chronicles 31:20-21   2 Corinthians 9:6-7

Never be greedy, but always generous – if not in money, then in spirit

Bede describes the lifestyle of Colman and his community on Lindisfarne:

> They owned no wealth apart from their livestock, since any money they received from the rich was at once given to the poor. They had no need to save money or provide accommodation in order to receive the rulers of the world, who only came to the church for the purpose of prayer and to hear the word of God. King Oswy himself, whenever the opportunity allowed it, came with only five or six thanes, and went away

after completing his prayers in the church. Even if it chanced that they had a meal there they were content with the simple daily fare of the brothers, and asked for nothing more.

Bless, O Lord, my kitchen with Thy right hand!
My kitchen, the kitchen of the white God.
Mary's Son, my Friend, cometh to bless my kitchen.
My Prince, may we have abundance with Him!

Traditional, attributed to Brigid

18 May

Psalm 119:164   Daniel 6:10   Matthew 25:1-13

Be timely in fasting, timely in the night-offices, discreet in duty

Dave Cape, in his book *On the Road with Jesus*, tells of how he walked across South Africa with a towel, a basin and a cross, washing the feet of people he met and witnessing to the love of God. Often the journey seemed pointless, and only obedience kept him there:

We were faithfully to do the things that we told people we did. For example, we would have a regular daily schedule, and on the days designated for my being out on the road, I would ensure that I was out there on time and for a particular time-span. Some days would be extremely hot, making walking a test of endurance; other days would be cold, or windy, and people who accompanied me or met with me would often express surprise at my being out in those extreme conditions.

19 May

Psalm 119:54   Isaiah 42:4   Acts 17:11

Be persistent in study, unshaken in turmoil, joyful in suffering

Bede says of Aidan:

> He cultivated peace and love, self-discipline and humility. His heart had the mastery over anger and avarice, and was contemptuous of pride and vainglory. He spared no effort in carrying out and teaching the commands of heaven, and was diligent in his reading and keeping of vigils.

20 May

Psalm 91:4b-5   Proverbs 15:1   1 Thessalonians 5:21-22

Be vigilant in the cause of truth, cautious in time of strife

In the event of a dispute it is especially important to establish what is the truth, but great discretion and wisdom is needed. Not all of us are anointed with wisdom, as Solomon obviously was when he threatened to slice a baby in two in order to identify the child's mother [1 Kings 3:16-28].

Brigid was presented with a case of similar difficulty, but God intervened to assist her.

> At an assembly of Irishmen held in Teltown a woman brought with her a child who she claimed had been fathered by Bishop Bron. Bron, one of Patrick's community, denied the child was his. Brigid asked the woman how she had conceived, and charged her not to speak falsehoods. The woman accused Bron yet again.

Then tumour and swelling filled her tongue so she was unable to speak. Brigid made the sign of the cross over the child's mouth, and asked: 'Who is your father?' The infant answered: 'A wretched, miserable man in the outskirts of this assembly, that is my father.' So Bishop Bron's good name was saved.

21 May Godric *(see p.239)*

Psalm 1:1   Jeremiah 4:22   John 10:1-10

Be submissive to good, unbending to evil

Our society teaches us to be suspicious of what is good, and to listen passively to whatever is evil. It is imperative that we learn to be teachable and submissive if God is to use us. But even the suggestions of the Thief must be given no opportunity to remain. The difficulty may come in deciding which voice is whose. And time spent with the Shepherd is the surest way of recognising His voice, and of knowing when an impostor is seeking to pursuade us. The true Shepherd would not say that; *He* does not come to steal, kill or destroy.

22 May

Psalm 145:3-7   Genesis 22:14-18   Romans 12:16-18

Be gentle in generosity, untiring in love, just in all things

Bede speaks of Bishop Colman and his predecessors Aidan and Finan:

> The sole concern of the teachers of those days was to serve God, not the world, and to feed the soul, not the belly. The religious habit, therefore, was held in great respect at that time, so that whenever a cleric or monk appeared he was welcomed gladly by everyone as a servant of God. Even if one was discovered passing on the roads they would run up to him and bow their heads, and were glad to be signed with the cross by his hand or blessed by his lips; and they paid close heed to such

men's exhortations. On the Lord's Day they gathered eagerly in the church or monasteries, not to get food for their bodies but to listen to the word of God; and if a priest came by chance to their village the people at once came together, eager to receive from him the word of life. The priests and clerics themselves visited the villages for no other reason than to preach, baptise, visit the sick and, in sum, to care for their souls; and so free were they from any taint of avarice that none accepted grants of land and estates for building monasteries unless compelled by the secular rulers!

Bede, History of the English Church and People

Lord, daily order my steps that I might be transformed into Your likeness; imperfect as I am, make me a mirror that reflects Your uncompromising love. Covenant-keeper, make me like You.

Dave Cape

23 May

Psalm 145:14-17   Job 29:11-13a   Matthew 26:11

Be respectful to the worthy, merciful to the poor

It is no sin to have wealth, but it is sinful to be attracted to wealth. It is the love of money, not money itself, which is the root of all evil.

Aidan, dining one Easter with King Oswald, was himself ill at ease with the feast set before them. Just then a servant arrived to say that many poor people had arrived at the castle asking for alms. Oswald with a wave of his arm ordered their own meal to be taken away and fed to the people outside, and the silver plate broken and distributed between them. Aidan was so overcome that he exclaimed, 'May the hand that did this never perish.'

Any society or 'civilisation' may best be judged by the way it treats its weakest members.

24 May

Psalm 107:43   Joshua 6:25   Ephesians 4:26b

Be mindful of favours, unmindful of wrongs

Caedmon of Whitby seemed to know he was about to die for he asked to be taken to the sick-house, and there he and his attendant talked and joked in good spirits with each of the other occupants until after midnight. Then Caedmon asked for the Eucharist. Taking it in his hand he asked if their hearts were all at peace with him, and they had no complaint, quarrel or ill-feeling towards him. They all replied that their hearts were entirely at peace with him and quite without anger, and they asked him in turn to be at peace with them in his heart. He quickly replied: 'My heart is at peace, little children, with all God's servants.' Then he received communion, and then enquired how long it was till the brothers had to awake to sing their nightly praises to the Lord. They replied, 'It will not be long.' 'Good,' he said, 'then let us wait for that hour.' He signed himself with the cross, laid his head on the pillow, slept for a while, and so ended his life happily, peaceably, in silence.

Bede

25 May

Psalm 119:19   Proverbs 22:29   Philippians 2:4

Be a lover of the ordinary man, and do not wish for riches

Bede says of Aidan, 'He showed the authority befitting a bishop in rebuking the proud and mighty, and was merciful in bringing comfort to the weak and relief and protection to the poor.'

Bill Hybels remarks that in the marketplace 'profits, quotas, sales reports, balance sheets, budgets and competition' are what matter, not people: they have become the lowest priority.

In the marketplace we need to make time to express interest in others – in their spouse, kids, health, problems, goals, frustrations, hobbies, holidays, and dreams. Competitors don't care about these things, but brothers and sisters do.

We also need to be helpers in the marketplace. That may mean offering to take up slack in another's workload. It may mean staying late to help a partner finish a report, or occasionally working through lunch to help someone meet a deadline.

Bill Hybels

26 May Bede *(see p.224)*

Psalm 116:10-11   Proverbs 22:11, 24-25   Matthew 10:16

Instead, cool down excitement and speak your mind

When people submerge their true feelings in order to preserve harmony, they undermine the integrity of a relationship. They buy peace on the surface, but underneath there are hurt feelings, troubling questions, and hidden hostilities just waiting to erupt. It's a costly price to pay for a cheap peace, and it inevitably leads to inauthentic relationships ... No one says anything 'unsafe'. They never discuss misunderstandings, reveal hurt feelings, air frustrations or ask difficult questions ... Offences occur, but nobody talks about them. Doubts about the other's integrity creep in, but they're never dealt with. In time such relationships deteriorate.

Bill Hybels

Denying our true feelings is not advisable, but calmness can achieve reconciliation more easily than raised voices or recriminations.

Cuthbert had difficulty in teaching the Rule to some of the monastics of Lindisfarne. At chapter meetings he was often worn down by bitter insults, but would put an end to the arguments simply by rising and walking out, calm and unruffled. Next day he would give the same admonitions, as though there had been no unpleasantness the previous day. In this way he gradually won the love and obedience of the brothers.

How do you respond when someone says something uncomfortable to you? Do you overcome your natural human instinct to reject it? Do you listen and seek the truth in the other person's concerns? Or do you get angry? Do you slip into denial, retaliation or rationalisation?

Well, do you?

27 May

Psalm 16:3   Proverbs 27:17   James 3:1

Obey your seniors, keep up with your juniors, equal your equals, emulate the perfect

In other words, do not lag behind or become competitive. Show respect to everybody, especially those who have been on the road longer than you. Look especially to those who do not seem to have become embittered or suspicious or sarcastic. Take note of those who seem to carry around the presence of Jesus, learn the secret of their relationship with Him.

28 May

Psalm 19:13   Proverbs 25:6   Hebrews 12:12

Do not envy your betters, or grieve at those who surpass you, or censure those who fall behind, but agree with those who urge you on

Herebert the anchorite of Derwentwater had long had Cuthbert as a spiritual friend and would visit him once a year 'with a desire to be ever more enflamed, by the help of his teaching, with longing for the things of heaven'.

On one such occasion Cuthbert said to Herebert, 'Whatever need you have, ask me now, for I am certain that the time is at hand for me to leave aside this earthly tabernacle.' Herebert begged him that they pray God that in His mercy as they had served Him together on earth, they might pass together to heaven and behold His grace.

They never saw each other again on earth, but both died the following 20 March, companions again.

29 May

Psalm 53:1-4   Ecclesiastes 4:10   1 Thessalonians 3:13
Though weary, do not give up

I continued to press on, limping, my feet aching, slipping, sliding, desperately wanting to sit down, chilled to the marrow. Even in this sopping wet state I could feel the hot tears welling in my eyes. Eventually I cried out to God and said, 'God, what is this all about? Why am I out here? What am I doing here? Am I crazy?' Then came the still, small voice of the Spirit as I sensed the Lord saying, 'No, David, I am just teaching you to endure; I am just checking you out.'

Finally after some six hours Carol arrived to collect me and I could hardly bend down to get into the car. I looked at her and said, 'If I were a quitter, today would be the day I quit,' but as Carol turned the car, I knew once again the Lord was saying, 'No one, after putting his hand to the plough and looking back, is fit for the Kingdom of God.'

Dave Cape, On the Road with Jesus

All good soldiers keep on fighting.
Don't grow weary in well-doing.
Just keep looking unto Jesus,
'cause when this age comes to an end,
I've read the book, and we win!

Reba Rambo and Dony McGuire

30 May

Psalm 56:8   Ezra 3:11-13   Philippians 4:4-6

Weep and rejoice at the same time – out of zeal and hope

At Hackness a nun called Bega was resting when she heard the chapel bell tolling, summoning the sisters to pray for a departing soul. She saw the roof gone and all flooded with light and the soul of abbess Hild being escorted to Heaven by many angels. She opened her eyes to realise she was sat amongst the other sisters, and it was a dream. Running to her own abbess, Frigyth, she announced that Hild had been taken from them. The sisters hurried to chapel where they sang psalms until a messenger arrived to bring news of the death of Abbess Hild which to the messenger's surprise was no surprise to them at all. The reality of the joy of her passing mingled with all their sadness at her loss.

Bede

31 May

Psalm 119:31-32   Isaiah 40:28-31   Hebrews 10:38

Advance with determination, but always fear for the end

When Brigid was out with her sheep she saw Nindid the scholar running past. 'What are you running like that for? and what are you seeking?' she said. 'I am going to heaven,' he replied. Brigid begged him to pause and pray with her that her passage there might be easy. 'I can't stop now,' he said. 'You see, the gates of heaven are open now and who knows how long it may be before they shut.' But he stayed and together they prayed an 'Our Father' for him and Brigid – and for the many thousands she would drag through the gates behind her.

From the Life of Brigid

As Christians we need to be reliable in both word and deed and not to compromise on that which we promise the Father and others we will do. Being out on the road far from familiar surroundings, we find ourselves continually tempted by the enemy's weapons of mediocrity and compromise. Some days would be extremely hot, making walking a test of endurance, other days would be cold or windy, and people who accompanied me or met with me would often express surprise at my being out in those extreme conditions. My reply would simply be: The weather might have changed, but God hasn't changed His mind. He didn't tell me to walk if the sun was shining or if it wasn't raining, or if it was a beautiful calm day without any wind; He simply said, 'Go.'

Dave Cape, On the Road with Jesus

June
Jesus of the scars

1 June

Psalm 22:16   Isaiah 52:15   Luke 24:30-40

Question: What are the only man-made things in heaven?
Answer: The wounds in the hands, feet and side of Jesus.

> If we have never sought, we seek Thee now;
> Thine eyes burn through the dark, our only stars;
> we must have sight of thorn pricks on Thy brow;
> we must have Thee, O Jesus of the scars.
>
> *Edward Shillito*
> *(written towards the end of World War I)*

2 June

Psalm 129:3-4   Isaiah 50:6-9   1 Peter 2:22-24

Jesus' hands and feet were not just anyone's hands and feet, but the signs of His real bodily presence. They were the hands and feet of Jesus marked with the wounds of His crucifixion. It is of great spiritual importance that Jesus made Himself known to His disciples by showing them His wounded body. The resurrection had not taken His wounds away but, rather, they had become part of His glory. They had become glorified wounds.

Jesus is the Lord who came to save us by dying for us on the Cross. The wounds in Jesus' glorified body remind us of the way in which we are saved. But they also remind us that our own wounds are much more than roadblocks on our way to God.

They show us our own unique way to follow the suffering Christ, and they are destined to become glorified in our resurrected life. Just as Jesus was identified by His wounds, so are we.

Henri Nouwen

3 June   Kevin *(see p.246)*

Psalm 109:30-31   Lamentations 1:12   Revelation 1:7

In the Cross of Christ God says to us, 'That is where you ought to be. Jesus my Son hangs there in your stead. His tragedy is the tragedy of your life. You are the rebel who should be hanged on the gallows. But lo, I suffered instead of you, and because of you, because I love you in spite of what you are. My love for you is so great that I meet you there, there on the Cross. I cannot meet you anywhere else. You must meet me there by identifying yourself with the One on the Cross. It is by this identification that I, God, can meet you in Him, saying to you as I say to Him, *MY BELOVED SON.*'

Emil Brunner

4 June   Eadfrith *(see p.234)*   Petroc (Pedrog) *(see p.256)*

Psalm 22:7-9   Jeremiah 29:13-14   Luke 22:61-62

Hast thou no scar?
no hidden scar on foot, or side, or hand?
I hear thee sung as mighty in the land,
I hear them hail thy bright ascendant star:
hast thou no scar?
Hast thou no wound?
Yet, I was wounded by the archers, spent;
leaned Me against the tree to die, and rent
by ravening beasts that compassed Me, I swooned:
Hast thou no wound?

No wound? No scar?
Yet, as the Master shall the servant be,
and piercèd are the feet that follow Me:
but thine are whole. Can he have followed far
who has no wound, no scar?

Amy Carmichael

5 June

Psalm 116:1-2   1 Chronicles 4:9-10   John 12:24

From prayer that asks that I may be
sheltered from winds that beat on Thee;
from fearing when I should aspire;
from faltering when I should climb higher;
from silken self, O Captain, free
Thy soldier who would follow Thee.

From subtle love of softening things;
from easy choices, weakenings.
Not thus are spirits fortified;
not this way went the Crucified.
From all that dims Thy Calvary,
O Lamb of God, deliver me.

Give me the love that leads the way,
the faith that nothing can dismay,
the hope no disappointment tire,
the passion that will burn like fire.
Let me not sink to be a clod:
make me Thy fuel, flame of God.

Amy Carmichael

6 June

Psalm 69:13   Ephesians 3:14-17   2 Corinthians 5:14-15

> Love's as hard as nails.
> Love is nails:
> blunt, thick, hammered through
> the medial nerves of One
> who, having made us, knew
> the thing that He had done:
> seeing (with all that is)
> our cross, and His.
>
> C.S. Lewis

7 June

Psalm 32:5   Micah 7:8-9   Galatians 6:14

> Knowing God without knowing our own wretchedness makes for pride. Knowing our own wretchedness without knowing God makes for despair.
>
> Knowing Jesus Christ strikes the balance because He shows us both God and our own wretchedness. Jesus is a God whom we can approach without pride and before whom we can humble ourselves without despair.
>
> Blaise Pascal

8 June

Psalm 37:23-24   Job 42:7-9   Matthew 16:21-26

Deny yourself

> Peter did not understand. Jesus did not come to be a great healer and miracle worker; nor did He come to be king. He came to show God's character, which is mercy and

compassion. He healed people; but His purpose in coming to earth was to go to the cross. We all accept that now, because it is history. We know about the resurrection. We have the benefit of hindsight. The disciples did not, and they were shocked.

But what about the Messiah's followers? Their expectations of Him had just been radically altered, and Jesus was about to do the same to their expectations of themselves. The followers of a king are in for a good time – power, prestige, influence – that is what everyone wants. But if the king is going to die, what of his followers? Before they had time to think it through, Jesus let them know: *'If any man will come after Me, let him deny himself and take up his cross, and follow Me.'*

Maurice Barratt

9 June Columba *(see p.230)*

Psalm 71:1-4   Hosea 6:1-3   Philippians 3:7-11

When we say 'Christ has died', we express the truth that all human suffering in time and place has been suffered by the Son of God who also is the Son of all humanity and thus has been lifted up into the inner life of God Himself. There is no suffering – no guilt, shame, loneliness, hunger, oppression, or exploitation, no torture, imprisonment, or murder, no violence – that has not been suffered by God. There can be no human beings who are completely alone in their sufferings, since God, in and through Jesus, has become Emmanuel, God with us. The Good News of the gospel, therefore, is not that God came to take our suffering away, but that God wanted to become part of it.

Henri Nouwen

10 June

Psalm 27:1   Isaiah 9:2-7   John 18:25

In Him was life, and the life was the light of all people. The light shines in the darkness, and the darkness did not overcome it.

John 1:4-5

A Light came out of darkness;
no light, no hope had we,
till Jesus came from Heaven
our light and hope to be.
Oh, as I read the story
from birth to dying cry,
a longing fills my bosom
to meet Him by and by.

Yet deeper do I ponder,
His cross and sorrow see,
and ever gaze and wonder
why Jesus died for me.
And shall I fear to own Him?
Can I my Lord deny?
No! Let me love Him, serve Him,
and meet Him by and by.

William A. Hawley

11 June

Psalm 28:1   Isaiah 64:1   Hebrews 11:13-15

Is there no balm in Gilead?

Jeremiah 8:22

The heavens frighten us; they are too calm;
in all the universe we seem to have no place.
Our wounds are hurting us, where is Thy balm?
Lord Jesus, by Thy scars, we claim Thy grace.

Edward Shillito

12 June

Psalm 39:7   Genesis 18:23-32   Luke 19:40-41

One of the Just Men came to Sodom, determined to save its inhabitants from sin and punishment. Night and day he walked the streets and markets protesting against greed and theft, falsehood and indifference. In the beginning, people listened and smiled ironically. Then they stopped listening: he no longer even amused them. The killers went on killing, the wise kept silent, as if there were no Just Man in their midst.

One June a child, moved by compassion for the unfortunate teacher, approached him with these words: 'Poor stranger, you shout, you scream, don't you see that it is hopeless?' 'Yes, I see,' answered the Just Man. 'Then why do you go on?' 'I'll tell you why. In the beginning, I thought I could change man. Today, I know I cannot. If I still shout today, if I still scream, it is to prevent man from ultimately changing me.'

Elie Wiesel

13 June

Psalm 147:3   Zechariah 13:6   John 20:19-27

If when the doors are shut, Thou drawest near,
only reveal those hands, that side of Thine;
we know today what wounds are, have no fear,
show us Thy scars, for we know the countersign.

The other gods were strong, but Thou wast weak;
they rode, and Thou with cross didst stumble to a throne;
but, to our wounds, only God's wounds can speak,
and no god has wounds, but Thou alone!

Edward Shillito

14 June

Psalm 86:8, 11 Isaiah 53:4-5 1 Corinthians 1:23

> I see Your hands,
> not white and manicured,
> but scarred and scratched and competent,
> reach out –
> not always to remove the weight I carry,
> but to shift its balance, ease it,
> make it bearable.
> Lord, if this is where You want me,
> I'm content.
> No, not quite true. I wish it were.
> All I can say, in honesty, is this:
> If this is where I'm meant to be,
> I'll stay. And try.
> Just let me feel Your hands.
> And, Lord, for all who hurt today –
> hurt more than me –
> I ask for strength and that flicker of light,
> the warmth, that says You're there.

Eddie Askew, Many Voices, One Voice

15 June

Psalm 22:1-2 Song of Songs 3:2 John 20:13

The nursery poem ends with the exclamation:

> God's in His heaven,
> all's right with the world.

Our experience tells us that, whether God's in His heaven or not, all is certainly not right with the world. Perhaps He is not there after all – that is how it seems.

In Buechner's novel *The Final Beast* a young minister whose wife has recently died listens ironically to one of his little daughters praying seriously to 'Our Father who aren't in heaven'. He feels he cannot correct her very easily.

16 June

Psalm 42:3   Lamentations 1:16   Matthew 24:8, 19

Fear

Today the ghetto knows a different fear:
close in its grip, death wields an icy scythe.
An evil sickness spreads a terror in its wake,
the victims of its shadow weep and writhe.

Today a father's heartbeat tells his fright
and mothers bend their heads into their hands.
Now children choke and die with typhus here,
a bitter tax is taken from their bands.

My heart still beats inside my breast
while friends depart for other worlds.
Perhaps, it's better – who can say? –
than watching this, to die today?

No, no, my God, we want to live!
not watch our numbers melt away.
We want to have a better world.
We want to work – we must not die!

Eva Picková, aged 12
(died in 1943 in Auschwitz)

17 June

Psalm 10:1   Isaiah 45:3-6   John 20:27-29

> Strike the thick cloud of unknowing with the sharp dart of longing love, and on no account think of giving up.
>
> *From* The Cloud of Unknowing *(c. 1370)*

After the Second World War the following words were found written on the wall of a Nazi concentration camp:

> I believe in the sun, even when it isn't shining,
> I believe in love, even when I feel it not,
> I believe in God, even when He is silent.

18 June

Psalm 103:10-12   Micah 7:18-19   Ephesians 3:14-19

The remarkable Dutch lady Corrie ten Boom, you may recall, lost her beloved sister, Betsy, in a Nazi concentration camp during the last war. The Ten Boom family had harboured Jews at their home in Holland, and the Gestapo exacted a terrible price.

Corrie was spared, and survived the horrors of the awful camp at Ravensbrück. Afterwards she dedicated her life to witnessing for Christ by conducting meetings and writing several books about her experiences. Eventually, a motion picture of her life story was made. It was called *The Hiding Place*. Corrie tells of a very moving incident which happened during one of her testimony meetings in Germany, after the war. She had just finished speaking to the German congregation about the love of God and how He can forgive even our worst sins. 'In fact,' she declared, 'God takes our sins and casts them into the deepest ocean.' After the service, as people were leaving the church, she noticed a balding, heavy-set man, in a grey overcoat making his way towards her as she stepped off the platform. As he drew closer, her blood ran cold, for she instantly recognised him as one of the cruel, wicked guards from Ravensbrück where both she and Betsy had been so inhumanely treated. Now this guard stood before her with an outstretched hand.

19 June

Psalm 130:7b   2 Kings 10:15   Romans 5:5

The man began to speak to Corrie. 'A fine message, Fräulein! How good it is to know that, as you say, all our sins are at the bottom of the sea. You mentioned Ravensbrück in your talk. Well, I was a guard there.' It was obvious to Corrie that he had not recognised her. But she had never forgotten his face. The man continued: 'You know, since that time I have found Christ as my Saviour and I know that He has forgiven me for all the terrible things I did. However, I would like to hear you say it too, Fräulein.' Again he reached out his hand. 'Will you forgive me too?'

Corrie stood, looking into the face of her former tormentor, a man responsible for the death of her sister. She recoiled in anger and contempt as the terrible memories came flooding back. Hatred welled up within her. How could she forgive this man? She held her own hand behind her back as she wrestled with the awful contradictions raging inside her. Love and forgiveness had been her message to others. But right now it seemed impossible to practise it herself. One of her favourite sayings was: 'Forgiveness is not an emotion; it is an act of the will.' Poor Corrie, her emotions had failed her. All that remained now was her will.

Silently, she lifted up a prayer to heaven. 'Jesus, please help me. I can stretch out my hand. I can do that much. You supply the feeling.' Awkwardly, hesitatingly, she reached out her hand. Suddenly her prayer was answered, for immediately her heart was filled with the love of God for this man. 'I forgive you, my brother!' she cried. 'With all my heart I forgive you too.'

20 June

Psalm 86:5   Micah 6:8   Matthew 18:23-25

Forgiveness is very easy to talk or even write about, but we need the power of the Holy Spirit to actually forgive. For the Christian, forgiveness is not optional. It is mandatory.

Henry Ward Beecher said, 'We are most like beasts when we kill. We are most like men when we judge. We are most like God when we forgive.' Go ahead – stretch out that hand of forgiveness to someone today. Write that letter, make that call, as God for Christ's sake has forgiven you. And always remember the words of Corrie ten Boom: 'Forgiveness is not an emotion. It's an act of your will.'

21 June

Psalm 116:10-11   Jeremiah 6:14   Colossians 2:4

'It will be all right in the end,' someone says. Will it? Maybe. But often that is not the case. 'There is a purpose in all this,' says another. This implies that God intended this awful situation, that He approves of suffering. (Especially if, as sometimes happens, we bring trouble onto ourselves, it would be insulting God to suggest that the wreckage was His idea in the first place.)

All that we deeply experience is significant (even if it was not what we or God intended to happen!).

What we can say truthfully in a bad and trying situation is this: 'This is not without significance.'

But, especially in times of deep suffering, easy answers that come glibly off the tongue are insulting, hurtful and insensitive.

22 June

Psalm 130:4 1 Kings 1:49-53 Matthew 6:14-15

Jesus' prayer was, 'Father, forgive them;
they know not what they do.'
A prayer born in death, writhing with pain.
A prayer risking faith, facing the sorrow.
A prayer living in hope, seeing the future.

My prayer was, 'God, how can I forgive them?
They do know what they did.'
A prayer saying, 'It still hurts.'
A prayer wanting vengeance.
A prayer seeking direction.

My prayer became, 'God, help me forgive them;
they know what they did.'
A prayer saying, 'They were wrong.'
A prayer wanting reconciliation.
A prayer seeking courage.

My prayer became, 'God, forgive them;
they know what they did.'
A prayer that wrestled with injustice.
A prayer that acknowledges weakness.
A prayer that found hope in God's love.

My prayer remains, 'God, forgive them;
they know what they did.'
Because forgiving recreates life from death.
Because forgiving cleanses the healing wound.
Because forgiving builds the bridge of freedom.

Jared P. Pingleton,
The Role and Function of Forgiveness

23 June

Psalm 143:3-4   Lamentations 3:27-31   Mark 14:33-37

To be human is to be lonely. To be human, however, is also to respond. The human person has always responded to this pain.

Sometimes it has moved us to greater depth of openness towards God and others, to fuller life, and sometimes it has led us to jump off bridges, to end life; sometimes it has given us a glimpse of heaven, sometimes it has given us a glimpse of hell; sometimes it has made the human spirit, sometimes it has broken it; always it has affected it. For loneliness is one of the deepest, most universal, and most profound experiences that we have.

Even if you are a relatively happy person who relates easily to others and who has many close friends, you are probably still lonely at times. If you are a very sensitive person, the type who feels things deeply, you are probably, to some degree, lonely all the time.

Ronald Rolheiser, The Restless Heart

24 June   Bartholomew of Farne *(see p.223)*

Psalm 84:4-6   Ecclesiastes 2:22-23   1 Corinthians 10:13

I have most invariably found that the very feeling which has seemed to me most private, most personal and, hence, most incomprehensible by others, has turned out to be an expression for which there is a resonance in many people. It has led me to believe that what is most personal and unique in each of us is probably the very element which would, if it were shared and expressed, speak most deeply to others.

Carl Rogers

25 June

Psalm 18:29   Isaiah 59:1-2   Ephesians 2:14-18

> We knock fists against the walls that wall us off from brothers.
> Give them to hear us. Give us to hear the terrible needs that
> beat like hearts behind brothers' walls.
>
> We knock fists against the walls that wall us off from You. Hear
> us and know the loneliness of lives walled up in flesh and rib.

Frederick Buechner, The Final Beast

26 June

Psalm 143:10   Jeremiah 29:11   Ephesians 5:15-19

> Lead me, Lord, lead me by Your Spirit,
> make Your will clear for my future.
>
>> For it is You, Lord,
>> You, the wounded healer
>> who makes my heart sing
>> and my feet dance for joy.
>
> Fill me, Lord, fill me with Your Spirit,
> Spirit of love, Spirit of joy and peace.
>
> Be my Rock, be my Rock of refuge,
> of courage and strength for my journey.
>
> Heal me, Lord, heal me by Your Spirit,
> my every wound, my every need and want.
>
>> For it is You, Lord,
>> You, the Wounded Healer
>> who makes my heart sing
>> and my feet dance for joy.

27 June

Psalm 27:1-6   Isaiah 42:5-7   Luke 22:47-48

Why did it have to be a friend
who chose to betray the Lord?
And why did he use a kiss to show them
that's not what a kiss is for?
Only a friend can betray a friend,
a stranger has nothing to gain,
and only a friend comes close enough
to ever cause so much pain.

And why did there have to be a
thorny crown pressed upon His head?
It should have been a royal one,
made of jewels and gold instead.
It had to be a crown of thorns
because, in this life that we live,
for all who would seek to love
a thorn is all this world has to give.

And why did it have to be
a heavy cross He was made to bear?
and why did they nail His feet and hands?
His love would have held Him there.
It was a cross, for on a cross
a thief was supposed to pay,
and Jesus had come into this world
to steal every heart away.
Yes, Jesus had come into this world
to steal every heart away.

Michael Card

28 June Irenaeus *(see p.243)*

Psalm 119:80   Isaiah 1:6   Philippians 2:5-8

It is because of the refusal to be vulnerable that, far too often, instead of enjoying friendship and intimacy with those around us, we find ourselves fencing with each other, using our talents, achievements, and strengths as weapons.

To be vulnerable in the true sense does not mean that someone must become a doormat, a weakling, devoid of all pride, going out of his way to let others know all of his faults and weaknesses. Nor is vulnerability to be confused with the idea of 'letting-it-all-hang-out', or any other form of psychological strip-tease. To be vulnerable is to be strong enough to be able to present ourselves without false props, without an artificial display of our credentials. In brief, to be vulnerable is to be strong enough to be honest and tender. Like Jesus, the person who is vulnerable is a person who cares enough to let himself be weak, precisely because he does care.

Ronald Rolheiser, The Restless Heart

29 June

Psalm 38:9   Song of Songs 5:8   John 4:13-14

In the beginning God was alone, but, wanting to share His infinite love and life, He posited for Himself a creature, the human being, with whom He could potentially share that life. We, as human persons, are therefore nothing other than possible partners that God has posited for Himself in order that He might share His life in dialogue, love, and beatific vision. Now, if we are to be capable of such a dialogical love relationship with an infinite God, this implies some pretty astonishing characteristics on our part. We must not only be free personal beings, capable of receiving and responding to such love and yet retaining our freedom and self-identity, but we must be open to the infinite itself as well, beings who are capable of receiving infinity itself in love and vision. Because of our capacity for the infinite, we are unable to achieve complete satisfaction and fulfilment in this life. We are by our very structure both blessed and condemned to be lonely and insatiable, restlessly striving to fill a space within ourselves which is infinitely deep. We are lonely because of the way God has made us, and our loneliness is very good, albeit painful, because it keeps us focused on the very purpose for which we were created.

Ronald Rolheiser

30 June

Psalm 31:1   Isaiah 54:4-5   Hebrews 2:9-10

O Tree of Calvary,
send Thy roots deep down
into my heart.
Gather together the soil of my heart,
the sands of my fickleness,
the stones of my stubbornness,
the mud of my desires;
bind them all together,
O Tree of Calvary;
interlace them with Thy strong roots;
entwine them with the network
of Thy love.

Chandran Devanesen

July
The city without a church

These readings are extracted from *The City Without a Church* by Henry Drummond.

1 July

Psalm 149:1-4   Joel 3:17-18   Revelation 21:10, 22

John, in his Revelation, holds up to the world the picture of a city without a church as his ideal of the heavenly life. By far the most original thing here is the simple conception of heaven as a city. The idea of religion without a church – 'I saw no temple therein' – is anomalous enough; but the association of the blessed life with a city – the one place in the world from which heaven seems most far away – is something wholly new in religious thought. All other heavens have been gardens, dreamlands: passivities, more or less aimless. Even to the majority among ourselves, heaven is a siesta and not a city.

The heaven of Christianity is different from all other heavens, because the religion of Christianity is different from all other religions. Christianity is the religion of cities. It moves among real things. Its sphere is the street, the marketplace, the working life of the world.

2 July

Psalm 90:17   Proverbs 2:21   Revelation 21:22

If the future life were to be mainly spent in a temple, the present life might be mainly spent in church.

But if heaven be a city, the life of those who are going there must be a real life. Christ's gift to us was life: a rich and abundant life. And life is meant for living. An abundant life does not show itself in abundant dreaming, but in abundant living – in abundant living among real and tangible objects and to actual and practical purposes.

3 July   Thomas *(see p.262)*

Psalm 48:1-3   Micah 4:1-2   Acts 4:32-35

When Christianity shall take upon itself in full responsibility the burden and care of cities – the Kingdom of God will openly come on earth. People do not dispute that religion is in the church. What is now wanted is to let them see it in the city.

4 July

Psalm 87:3   Isaiah 65:17-19   Revelation 3:12

One Christian city, one city in any part of the earth, whose citizens from the greatest to the humblest lived in the spirit of Christ, where religion had overflowed the churches and passed into the streets, inundating every house and workshop, and permeating the whole social and commercial life – one such Christian city would seal the redemption of the world.

5 July

Psalm 122:6-8   Isaiah 35:2   Hebrews 11:10

John saw his city 'descending out of Heaven'. It was, moreover, no strange apparition, but a city which he knew. It was Jerusalem, a 'new Jerusalem.' The significance of that name has been altered for most of us by religious poetry: we spell it with a capital and speak of the New Jerusalem as a synonym for heaven. Yet why not take it simply as it stands, as a new Jerusalem? Try to restore the natural force of the expression – suppose John to have lived today and to have said, 'I saw a new London'? Jerusalem was John's London.

6 July

Psalm 122:6-8   Nehemiah 4:7-9   Hebrews 13:14

In every city throughout the world today, there is a city descending out of heaven from God. Each one of us is daily building up this city – or helping to keep it back.

7 July Boisil *(see p.225)*

Psalm 50:2   Isaiah 9:2-3   John 9:5

The city has no need of sun or moon to shine on it, for the glory of God is its light, and its lamp is the Lamb.

Revelation 21:23

This light, John saw, would fall everywhere. It was irresistible and inextinguishable. No darkness could stand before it. One by one the cities of the world would give up their night. Room by room, house by house, street by street, they would be changed.

8 July

Psalm 147:2-3   Isaiah 10:1-3   James 1:27

> And the name of the city from that time on shall be: The Lord is There.
>
> *Ezekiel 48:35*

People complain of the 'indefiniteness' of religion. There are thousands ready in their humble measure to offer some personal service for the good of others, but they do not know where to begin. Let me tell you where to begin – where Christ told His disciples to begin: at the nearest city. I promise you that before one week's work is over you will never again be haunted by the problem of the indefiniteness of Christianity. You will see so much to do, so many actual things to be set right, so many merely material conditions to alter, so much pure unrelieved uninspiring hard work, that you will begin to wonder whether in all this naked realism you are on holy ground at all.

9 July

Psalm 26   Ezekiel 36:35-36   Luke 19:40-41

In all seriousness I make this definite practical proposal: believe in your city. What else? In Jesus Christ. What about Him? That He wants to make your city better; that that is what He would be doing if He lived there. What else? Believe in yourself – that you, even you, can do some of the work which He would like done, and that unless you do it, it will remain undone. How are you to begin? As Christ did. First He looked at the city; then He wept over it; then He died for it.

10 July

Psalm 84:7   Jeremiah 31:38-40   Colossians 1:15-20

Where are you to begin? Begin where you are. Make that one corner, room, house, office, as like heaven as you can. Begin? Begin with the paper on the walls, make that beautiful; with the air, keep it fresh; with the very drains, make them sweet. Abolish whatsoever makes a lie – in conversation, in social intercourse, in correspondence, in domestic life. This done, you have arranged for a heaven, but you have not got it. Heaven lies within: in kindness, in humbleness, in unselfishness, in faith, in love, in service. To get these in, get Christ in. Teach all in the house about Christ – what He did, and what He said, and how He lived. Teach it not as a doctrine, but as a discovery, as your own discovery. Live your own discovery.

Then pass out into the city. Do all to it that you have done at home.

11 July

Psalm 100:3   Genesis 18:30-32   Matthew 5:13-16

The righteous are concerned about justice for the poor; but the wicked do not want to know.

Proverbs 29:7

The good person out of the good treasure of the heart produces good, and the evil out of evil treasure produces evil; for it is out of the abundance of the heart that the mouth speaks.

Luke 6:45

By far the greatest thing a man can do for his city is to be a good man. Simply to live there as a good man, as a Christian man of action and practical citizen, is the first and highest contribution anyone can make to its salvation. Let a city be a

Sodom or a Gomorrah, and if there be but ten righteous men in it, it will be saved. Simple, old-fashioned Christianity did mighty work for the world in that it produced good men. It is goodness that tells, goodness first and goodness last. Good men even with small views are immeasurably more important to the world than small men with great views.

12 July

Psalm 40:8   Proverbs 31:8-9   1 John 3:17-18

Any experiment that can benefit by one hairbreadth any single human life is a thousand times worth trying.

13 July

Psalm 87:5-6   1 Samuel 16:7   Matthew 13:33-34

Material blessedness when held up as the whole gospel for the people is as hollow as the void of life whose circumference it even fails to touch.

External reforms – education, civilisation, public schemes, and public charities – have each their part to play. Any experiment that can benefit by one hairbreadth any single human life is a thousand times worth trying. But those whose hands have tried the most, and whose eyes have seen the furthest, have come back to regard first the deeper evangel of individual lives, and the philanthropy of quiet ways, and the slow work of leavening others one by one with the Spirit of Jesus Christ.

14 July

Psalm 40:17   Exodus 4:13-16   Matthew 18:1-4

Next to its love for the chief of sinners, the most touching thing about the religion of Christ is its amazing trust in the least of saints.

15 July

Psalm 106:3   Isaiah 1:17   Matthew 13:33-34

My plea is for the city. But I plead for good men, because good men are good leaven. If their goodness stop short of that, if the leaven does not mix with that which is unleavened, if it does not do the work of leaven – that is, to *raise something* – it is not the leaven of Christ. The question for good people to ask themselves is: 'Is my goodness helping others? Is it a private luxury, or is it telling upon the city? Is it bringing any single human soul nearer happiness or righteousness?'

16 July

Psalm 73:24   Judges 6:11-15   John 15:12-15

'Speak, Lord, Your servant is listening.'

1 Samuel 3:10

If you ask what particular scheme you shall take up, I cannot answer. Christianity has no set schemes. It makes no choice between conflicting philanthropies; decides nothing between competing churches; favours no particular public policy; organises no one line of private charity. Christianity is not at all carried on by committees.

As Christ's friends, His followers are supposed to know what He wants done, and try to do it – this is the whole working basis of Christianity. Next to its love for the chief of sinners, the most touching thing about the religion of Christ is its amazing trust in the least of saints.

17 July

Psalm 51:13   Isaiah 55:1-2   John 4:4-10

Each village along the highway Christ walked had someone waiting to be helped. His pulpit was the hillside, His congregation a woman at a well. His work was everywhere; His workshop was the world. One's associations of Christ are all of the wayside. We never think of Him in connection with a church.

18 July

Psalm 109:25   Isaiah 53:2-5   Matthew 11:18-19

He was the Son of Man. This was the highest life ever lived. So simple a thing it was, so natural, so human, that those who saw it first did not know it was religion, and Christ did not pass among them as a very religious man. It is certain that the religious people of His time not only refused to accept this type of religion as any kind of religion at all, but repudiated and denounced Him as its bitter enemy.

19 July

Psalm 144:14-15   Isaiah 58:3-5   James 1:22-27

The truth is, people will hold to almost anything in the name of Christianity: believe anything, do anything – except its common and obvious tasks.

20 July

Psalm 107:8-9   Hosea 11:10   John 1:14

> I saw no temple in the city, for its temple is the Lord God the Almighty and the Lamb.
>
> *Revelation 21:22*

It is because to large masses of people Christianity has become synonymous with a temple service that other large masses of people decline to touch it. It is a mistake to suppose that the working people of this country are opposed to Christianity: the working men would still follow Christ if He came among them.

21 July

Psalm 122:6, 8-9   Isaiah 60:1-2, 11   Matthew 23:13-15

In many lands the churches have literally stolen Christ from the people; they have taken Christianity from the city and imprisoned it behind altar rails.

22 July

Psalm 127:1   Amos 5:21-24   Acts 7:48-50

Nine men are striving to get people to go to church for each one who is striving to make people realise that they themselves are the church.

23 July John Cassian *(see p.228)*

Psalm 107:7   Isaiah 66:1-2   Revelation 21:22

> I have said that were it mine to build a city, the first stone I should lay there would be the foundation-stone of a church. But if it were mine to preach the first sermon in that church, I should choose as the text: 'I saw no church therein.' I should tell the people that the great use of the church is to help people to do without it.

24 July

Psalm 125:1-2   1 Kings 6:7   1 Corinthians 13:10

> As a channel of nourishment, as a stimulus to holy deeds, as a link with all holy lives, let everyone use the church, and to the utmost of their opportunity. But beware of mistaking its services for Christianity. What church services really express is the *want* of Christianity. And when that which is perfect in Christianity is come, all this, as the mere passing stay and scaffolding of struggling souls, must vanish away.

25 July

Psalm 133:1   Micah 6:8   1 John 4:16-21

> The only preparation which multitudes seem to make for heaven is for its judgment bar. What will they do in its streets? What have they practised of love? How like are they to its Lord? Earth is the rehearsal for heaven. The eternal beyond is the eternal here. The street-life, the home-life, the business-life, the city-life in all the varied range of its activity, are an apprenticeship for the city of God. There is no other apprenticeship for it.

26 July

Psalm 107:31, 43   Genesis 28:16-17   Colossians 3:23

The daily round is so very common, our ideas of a heavenly life are so unreal and mystical that even when the highest heaven lies all around us, when we might touch it, and dwell in it every day we live, we almost fail to see that it is there.

27 July

Psalm 107:35-37   Isaiah 40:3-5   Revelation 1:9-19

When John's heaven faded from his sight, and the prophet woke to the desert waste of Patmos, did he grudge to exchange the heaven of his dream for the common tasks around him? Was he not glad to be alive, and there?

28 July

Psalm 122:2-4   Joel 2:25-26   Hebrews 11:8-10, 14-16

Traveller to God's last city, be glad that you are alive. Be thankful for the city at your door and for the chance to build its walls a little nearer heaven before you go. Pray for yet a little while to redeem the wasted years. And week by week as you go forth from worship, and day by day as you awake to face this great and needy world, learn to 'seek a City' there, and in the service of its neediest find heaven.

29 July

Psalm 61:1-5, 8   Job 23:3-6   Luke 7:7

Lord, I have nothing;
help me to give even what I do not have.
Lord, I feel nothing;
help me not to be jealous, that You may
use me to touch others' hearts.
Lord, I am weary;
help me to remember that You
have been weary, too.
Lord, I need refreshing;
help me to refresh others and to forget
about my own needs.
Lord, I can't see the way ahead;
help me not to get in the way
of those who can.
Lord, I am disappointed;
help me not to bring disappointment to others.
Lord, I have no one to help me;
help me to trust in You.
Lord, I can't see You;
yet You see me –
help me to remember that.
Lord, I am not worthy to receive You,
but only say the word and I shall be healed.

Hugh Barney

30 July

Psalm 28:7-8   Isaiah 43:2   2 Corinthians 4:16-18

The worship of men and women spending themselves in compassionate action would have an air more of desperation than formality. They would stagger into church utterly drained of goodness, unable to face another day unless their numbed spirits were re-sensitised and their strength renewed. They would be too hoarse to sing, too stiff to kneel, and too dog-tired to take away any long exhortations from the pulpit. They would await the reading of the lesson with something akin to dread as God presented them with yet more impossible demands. Every false word in the service would stand out like a sore thumb and pretentiously ornate language would be heard no more. Instead, they would gasp out a simple litany exposing the horror and pain and misery they had shared, asking God to show them Jesus in it.

Colin Morris

We meet You in the brokenness of the world and the cries of the hungry for bread. Enable us to be the bread that *You* break which provides life for the world. And when we come again to Your table, Lord, ourselves broken, may we once more become the bread of sincerity and truth, as You become for us the Bread of Life.

Alan Jenkins

31 July Ignatius of Loyola *(see p.242)*

Psalm 68:9-10   Ecclesiastes 11:1-6   Luke 19:20-24

Those who do not believe in Jesus laugh at the prophecies He made but did not keep; but those who do believe, wait. Some, in the first few centuries of the Christian era, fled to the deserts of Egypt, there to weave mats one day, unweave them the next, waiting prayerfully for Jesus to come again. Others, realising that Jesus will come when He will come, and not a moment before, set about to market the mats woven in the desert and to witness to their faith in the marketplace.

William Griffin, Endtime

August
What gives you the right?

1 August

Psalm 27:7-10   Deuteronomy 5:16   Mark 7:9-13

God's laws are there to protect us. Whether we have good or bad parents or, like most of us, something in between, it is important for us to honour and bless them. Sometimes it is necessary for a person to forgive a parent who has already died, and, even if it *is* only from one side, to make their peace.

No person can be to us *all* that we need, and only God is able to be Alpha and Omega and all in between, to fill in the gaps where other people fail or disappoint us: God is never a disappointment.

Judgements we have made against our parents may condemn us, and resentment can tie *us* up and cause us all kinds of damage as well as not freeing *them*. Often physical healings can be held back until resentments and bitterness are dealt with.

God can walk with us through all our memories until they become the peaceable Kingdom.

2 August

Psalm 44:1-7   Judges 1:8-13   Romans 8:14-18

Othniel already knew Achsah – they were cousins. And if he had not wanted to marry her he would not have taken the city for Caleb: to take the city was to ask for her hand. We know from Judges 3:8-11 that later Othniel would rise up and rescue his people, and finally be made the first judge over them.

We cannot know God to be our Father until we are adopted. He wants to adopt us, and accept us into His family; but that cannot happen unless we agree. It is the Spirit of God who brings us the assurance that the transaction is complete; that we are accepted as one of His and heir to all He has.

God is wealthy and willing; but we must help also to dispel the lie put about by the enemy telling people: 'We are *all* God's children.' It is not true, and believing that it *is* may prevent others from ever truly becoming children of God.

3 August

Psalm 126   Joshua 15:17-19   Luke 11:5-13

Caleb had given his daughter Achsah a dark land for her dowry – a desert. It was not enough. She had confidence in her father, and she had become an asker. She got off her ass, came to her father and said, 'You've given us this land; now give me also springs of water that the land might be irrigated.' The father gave her upper springs and nether springs.

If we ask our Father to give us the gift of the Holy Spirit, we need not have any anxiety that we will receive some counterfeit gift. How can it be serpent or scorpion we receive, if it is God Himself we are asking? We ask with confidence: it is enough that by simple faith we can claim what He is more than willing to give, and begin to thank Him.

4 August

Psalm 146:5-7   Genesis 27:1-36   Luke 15:25-31

In the familiar story of the prodigal son, the father turns to the elder son, and says, effectively, 'You are always with me, and all that I have is yours. All you had to do was ask. Have you been with me this long, and still you don't know me?'

And Jesus says to us:

Extravagance to a wild and careless degree is the characteristic of My Father and Me. I was never precise, calculating and sensible when it came to giving life and love for you on that dark hill. That is why I have the reputation (in Heaven anyway!) of being the most extravagant person ever to walk the dust paths on this planet ... You cannot hoard yourself up for a rainy day, son, and justify it in the light of My teaching. You must give yourself extravagantly, for security in the wisdom of your own economic prowess is directly opposite to the extravagance of My Father who revels in feeding birds, cultivating grass and inventing flowers simply because ... because ... because He enjoys doing it.

Phil Streeter

5 August Oswald *(see p.277)*

Psalm 105:4-8   Genesis 32:22-32   Matthew 11:12

Jacob wrestled with someone, probably with God Himself. He would not let the one he was wrestling with go – unless He blessed him. He wrestled with God and found his own identity in the process.

Perhaps what God really requires is not so much an upright man as one who is reckless, and determined to press into Him whatever the cost. This is probably the meaning of the verse in Matthew 11 (and also in Luke 16:16) about the violent gaining of the Kingdom.

Jacob emerged a broken man, but with a whole new identity; and all of Israel is called by his name to this day. The name means 'prince with God', or 'prince of God', 'soldier of God' or 'God-wrestling'.

Do we prevail with God? Have we wrestled with Him enough to have also embraced who He says we are able to be? Do you seek Him with all your strength?

6 August

Psalm 51   2 Samuel 11   Mark 2:3-12

David stayed behind at home, when his place was with his men. This created the opportunity for temptation. Each wrong step made the next more inevitable. And Joab was dangerously aware of what David was about. It is important to realise that through all this time the extraordinary worship David had instituted in Israel continued. There was continuous praise before the ark of God with no veil between. This happened 24 hours a day for well over 30 years. Things did not grind to a halt just because of David's sin. And eventually David would go and sit in God's presence, waiting for answers in his self-inflicted predicament.

The same God is worthy of all our devotion – He who alone has power to forgive sin, and who can say, 'Gather up your bed, and walk again.'

7 August

Psalm 40:9-14   2 Samuel 2:13-32   Matthew 5:21-26

Rivalry and jealousy and party-spirit: all these things can easily lead to unpleasantness and violence. When all of this escalates it is hard for it to stop, and it seems the only way is for someone to speak out for non-violence as Abner did. The fruit is peace: a ceasefire, for a time, until the need to retaliate re-emerges, and the focus of the anger is an Abner or a Martin Luther King or an Oscar Romero.

Joab used his position of power as security, assuming he would go unpunished. David curses him, but lets it pass. Joab, after all, is 'family', and he was defending his own family honour. This story happens before David's adultery with Bathsheba, but both have something in common: Joab and David think themselves in positions of such power that they are outside the law and need pay no heed to consequences.

8 August

Psalm 119:129-136   2 Samuel 20:4-13   Hebrews 4:14-16

Joab has no right to remove a man just because he stands in his way, but relies on the fact that David is unable to point the finger, having requested Uriah's death in the same way.

Jesus, when He died, caused a veil between people and God to tear from top to bottom. (It was fastened at the top, so it even ripped the hard way!) This means we can come boldly into the presence of God to confess our failure and difficulties. We have the *right* to enter boldly because of trust in His death and in His dying love. He has the right to say to us, 'I know what you feel like, I know how hard it is,' because God did not cheat: He was born as one of us, and experienced trials like our own. He has every right to say, 'Hold on, it's possible for you to make it through.'

9 August

Psalm 72:1-14   1 Kings 2:1-6   John 14:27-30

David is dying and entrusts his throne to Solomon. Chief among his unfinished business is the task of holding Joab accountable for his murders.

Jesus can truthfully say that Satan has no case against Him, since He has consistently made the right choices all along. Satan has no legal right over Him – no one takes His life from Him: He even co-operates with the betrayal that has been engineered to bring about His death.

There is a traditional story [see also Easter Eve, p.141] in which Death gloats to the Prince of Hell that he has captured Jesus of Nazareth. Now, finally, he will take revenge on the one who released Lazarus from his clutches. 'Oh no,' screams his colleague. 'Don't you know what that means? He will come here, and none of our prisoners will be able to be secured. He can even preach to them if He wants to!'

The Old Testament men of faith in their place of waiting begin to feel restless and excited ... 'Lift up your heads, you gates,' they say, 'that the King of glory may come in.'

10 August

Psalm 62:5-8   Joshua 20:1-6   John 8:3-11

In God's provision, places of refuge were to be set up for the protection of those who had killed someone without it being premeditated murder. There they could find sanctuary from anyone who wanted to avenge the death. There they could be secure.

When David was fleeing from Saul for his life, he and his followers hid in a cave called Adullam. Other people hurried to join him there: 'all those in debt, all those who were discontented, all those who were in distress'. These became David's mighty men whose great exploits we read about in 1 Samuel 22.

We all need places where we can feel safe, where past misdeeds can be put behind us, where no one will condemn us. Then maybe we can go and do great things – and perhaps even go and sin no more.

Jesus did not pretend the past had never happened, but He seemed to find ways of not letting it be the end.

Now is where we are standing, and today is, let us not forget, the first day of the rest of our lives.

11 August   Clare *(see p.230)*

Psalm 25:7-14   Hosea 3:1-3   1 Corinthians 6:15-17

The prophet Hosea was married to Gomer, whom he loved dearly but who was often unfaithful to him. Out of this experience, Hosea was able to speak to the people about how God feels when they run away from His love, and how He remains faithful.

God made us; and for us to function as intended we should consult the Manufacturer's instructions. Sometimes the handbook is out of reach, but it holds the answers or, at least, the explanation. God's intention for sex was that it be part of the bonding of a permanent relationship: that one body and one spirit go together. When a person gives him or herself to a number of partners that person is joined to each of them; and, as each walks away, that person feels more and more fragmented.

God can heal that fragmentedness and release the bonds of the past. These can be cut right through. His laws are there for our protection.

12 August

Psalm 53:1-4   Genesis 5:21-31   John 2:1-11

Enoch is known as a prophet, and the Scripture tells us that he walked with God from the time his son was born. This was obviously a turning-point in his life. Perhaps the naming of his son was his very first prophecy. The name he gave his son means 'After him it shall come', and his son was Methusaleh. The 'it' would seem to be speaking of judgement. God had spoken through Enoch that this must come. God is so reluctant to bring that judgement that the guy with the prophetic name saw his own son die of old age, and was the oldest man who ever lived. The exact year he died, there came the great flood. The delaying of it was certainly extreme; but then God rarely does anything by half-measures.

> No, Jesus. You are by no means economical. Even the picnic on the hill resulted in twelve basketfuls of left-overs. It wasn't six bottles of well-water that You changed into wine, but SIX THIRTY-GALLON stone jars full! Once again, sheer extravagance!
>
> *Phil Streeter*

13 August

Psalm 139:23-24   Malachi 3:16-17   Matthew 13:24-30

While we were still sinners Christ loved us. He sees potential in the most unlikely lump of stone. But that potential cannot even begin to be released until we acknowledge Him. He has paid the price for the whole quarry! Will we surrender to His purpose and allow Him to wash us clean, then chip away at all that would get in the way, and hone the surfaces until He can see His own reflection in the jewel of our lives?

We need to desire this uncomfortable process; not only for ourselves, but for those for whom we have the responsibility of praying.

When He returns to make up His jewels, what will He find? Stones, resistant, hard and rough? Or gems, prepared and radiant with His glory? The final day will reveal it all. Willing and unwilling remain side by side until then. In the field which is the world, and also in the ground of my heart, wheat and weeds grow together.

Without walls

A hurting world is around us, and we hide behind our freshly decorated walls, and pretend it does not exist, or that we do not know what it is to hurt. We are challenged to come out and be *without walls*.

14 August

Psalm 50:2   Hosea 10:12b   2 Corinthians 4:6-7

> We are called to intentional, deliberate vulnerability.
>
> *The Rule of the Northumbria Community*

I had a vision of a house. Every time a crack appeared in the wall, or damage in the house, I dashed out to repair it as quickly as I possibly could, like most of us do, so that the inside of the house was protected and kept safe from the weather and the storms. And the Lord said to me, 'This is what your Christian life is like. Whenever any cracks appear in the wall that has been built up around about you over the years by the world and by yourself you dash out and you fill in the cracks so that no one is able to see what is inside. But I want the world to be able to see what is inside. I want to be able to come in through the cracks into your life and I am not going to fill them up either, I am going to flow in and out of these cracks. So when you see the cracks appear in your life, do not rush out and fill them in. Let Me come in.'

David Mattches

15 August Mary, mother of Jesus *(see p.249)*

Psalm 18:49   Job 34:2-8   Matthew 9:10-11

The accusation made about Jesus is that He mixes with the wrong kind of people. He has friends that respectable people would be ashamed to be seen with. It is not even as if He can keep these friends hidden away in a different world; some of them follow Him around, and the circles begin to overlap. He recognises that how rich and successful, how presentable someone is, how much 'street-cred' someone has, does not matter: the rich can be very needy, and the poor can be selfish. Inside, we are all weak and prone to failure; it would be unwise for any of us to cast the first stone. Jesus was a friend of sinners, and we need to be, too. He made Himself of no reputation, and we need to be a little less protective of our own.

16 August Brother Roger of Taizé *(see p.257)*

Psalm 104:34   Exodus 4:2-3a   Colossians 3:17, 23-24

God asks the question: 'What is that in your hand?' We respond incredulously. Surely He knows, so why need He ask the question? He draws our attention to the very thing in our reach, and asks us to lay it at His feet – our ability or treasured possession – all at His disposal. But then little can become much when we place it in the Master's hands. In the book of Acts we read of a woman called Dorcas (or Tabitha) who had won the hearts of all around by her use of the gift she had for sewing. It may be that God will make use of our cooking or baking or hill-walking or love of sports or whatever ... to glorify Him. Remember the picture of the juggler who would practise his juggling and gymnastics before the altar in the church? A favourite Christmas song also tells the story of a little drummer boy:

I have no gifts to bring,
to lay before the King.
Shall I play for Him?

Then He smiled at me –
me and my drum.

17 August

Psalm 24:1   Ecclesiastes 10:19   Matthew 9:9-10

Matthew had met Jesus and wanted all his friends to meet the Master too. What could he do? He could do the one thing he really knew how to do well – he could throw a party. People always enjoyed his parties. So he threw a big party and invited everybody – Jesus could do the rest.

Why can we not just do the same – lay aside time-consuming religious activities, and spend time with people we like, instead?

18 August

Psalm 15   Proverbs 11:24-25   John 13:7, 15

But the Comforter shall teach you.

John 14:26

We have sought not to supply the Holy Spirit with a timetable and a specification of what we require. He has a way of dealing with such impudence, and invariably has the last laugh. What, then, are to be our priorities? To be available. To be accepting without being sentimental. The demands made upon us are only possible to meet if matched by openness to the Spirit. In the power of the Spirit, therefore, we make ourselves available. We are prepared to be vulnerable, to be sensitive enough to try to protect others who may not understand what we understand, and to be willing to spend and be spent in the service of Christ the King.

Norman Motley, Letters to a Community

19 August

Psalm 18:49   Esther 4:10-16   John 15:15

The story of Esther is a remarkable picture to us of what it is to be a bridge of peace. Esther took the opportunities that came her way, and as a result was in a position of particular influence.

The famous Irish legend is that if you ask anyone for directions they'll reply, 'The way to Kilkenny? That's very easy, but you wouldn't start from here!'

Suddenly Esther is made to realise that she, and only she, is in the very place the directions start from. She is in a unique position. Esther identifies with the people she has come from. She speaks their language, knows their hearts, but also can speak on their behalf. She is prepared to risk her very life to do so.

Each of us has a position of influence no one else could occupy; but it is essential that we identify ourselves with people.

> Sometimes we build up walls instead of bridges of peace and we ask Your forgiveness, O Lord.

Carey Landry

20 August   Oswin *(see p.253)*

Psalm 86:9   Proverbs 9:13-17   John 4:27-30

The woman came running into town shouting, 'I've found a man! I've found a man!' What was new about that? This woman was partial to men, had been married four or five times. Her reputation never seemed to cause her any difficulty in finding a new replacement. 'This man is different from any I've ever met – He told me all about me. Come on, everybody, I want you all to meet Him. He's a prophet – no, more than that...' She ran around shouting and calling out until everyone came out of their houses to see this man, and hear Him speak. And no one spoke like this man. He told stories that made you feel that heaven itself had opened and God Himself was near. Life would never be the same again.

21 August

Psalm 15:1-3   Proverbs 12:15   Luke 18:9-14

There is an over-used joke which tells of the man being shown around heaven by St Peter. He sees a small group of people sitting in a circle in one corner facing inwards. 'Who are they?' he asks. 'Shhh,' says Peter, 'they are the Baptists' [or Catholics, or Pentecostals, or whatever, depending on who is telling the joke] 'and they think they are the only ones here!'

Perhaps C.S. Lewis was thinking of this joke when he described the dwarves in *The Last Battle.* In the story they also went through the stable door that led into Aslan's country, but instead of the beautiful sunshine they saw only darkness; instead of fresh flowers they smelt filthy stable-litter. The proverb says that there is none so blind as those who will not see.

Sometimes our eyes can become so damaged we are unable to see even if we tried. If we want Him to, Jesus can make us see again – maybe tentatively at first, so that we see people who only look like trees walking, then eventually so we can see all people clearly – with His help.

22 August

Psalm 40:15   Proverbs 25:6-7   1 Peter 2:9

We are 'peculiar'. We have chosen not to go with the majority. We shall pray and reflect on the life of Christ: most people don't do this. We shall worship and receive God's gifts in His sacraments: most people don't do this. We shall be in a minority: we shall be odd. There will be no danger for us in that, as long as we don't begin actually to *like* being odd. We can see there, of course, the danger of wanting to withdraw into the small group of like-minded people, and to build the barricades to keep out those who are not sufficiently odd in *our* variety of oddness. That is the way to create sects and divisions, in which each is sure of his own chosenness and pours scorn on that of the others. In fact, we have to find a balance. It is our faith that God loves all, and all to Him are welcome. But there has probably never been a time in history when the majority of people were seriously seeking Him!

Kate Tristram

23 August

Psalm 104:34   Proverbs 15:31-32   Matthew 9:11-13

A hospital exists for the benefit of its patients. It is nonsense to complain that having patients admitted interrupts the smooth running of the hospital. The Church exists for the benefit of its non-members, to be salt for the earth, not for the sake of impressing more salt. Why is it, then, that the greater proportion of the Church's activities seem designed to be as off-putting as possible to the casual unchurched observer? At best they are user-friendly only to the initiated. Jesus said He did not come to call those who already thought they were right, but He came to call those who knew they were bad and selfish to be turned upside down.

24 August

Psalm 18:25   2 Samuel 22:30   Hebrews 11:30

There is an invisible line that is crossed when someone gives their heart to the Lord and passes from darkness to light, from being close to the Kingdom to being a subject of the King of kings. At the time someone crosses this line it may be so invisible they do not notice it at all, until afterwards they look back and see the distance they have travelled. Gratitude is appropriate; awareness of how momentous this transition has been is also appropriate. What is not appropriate is the building of a monument to that moment of remembered or unremembered transition; especially if this monument is a wall running the length of a friendship or a marriage. When a wall does appear we should be the ones who can reach over it, or leap over it, and affirm those relationships.

If the love inside is real it will break through any dividing wall and embrace those we care for, without us needing to deny or defend what we have experienced.

25 August Ebba *(see p.235)*

Psalm 15:1-3   Proverbs 17:17; 18:24   Matthew 11:19

Who are my friends? Are they Christians or not? Or some of each? If my friends are mostly Christians I am in danger of disappearing into a little Christian ghetto which will not be good for me.

My contact with non-Christians should not remain superficial – friendship, when it happens, comes from a mutual liking, beyond having just interests in common. It means being glad to spend time together; it means developing trust.

Friendship requires honesty. Friends do not need you to be 'up' all the time – instead they enable you to be more vulnerable.

26 August Ninian *(see p.318)*

Psalm 40:15   Nehemiah 2:12   1 Peter 2:11-12

There has probably never been a time in history when the majority of people were seriously seeking God.

Our Bible sets before us the idea that God may use a minority to serve the majority. Church history says the same. It is because of the faithfulness of the few, not the many, that the Christian faith has come down the ages to us and we have the chance to know God in this way. It has always been so. If God has called us and we want to respond to Him, then we must be faithful to our own vision, whatever the many think. But we must do it with open hearts and open arms, not safeguarding our fewness, our specialness. And we must do it in healthy laughter directed at ourselves, because really it is so ridiculous to think that God has chosen us for anything at all, even though it is true.

Kate Tristram

27 August

Psalm 24:1   Proverbs 20:12   Mark 7:24-28

What we are called to do is *be*. Our whole being should be saturated with the presence of God. People who choose to be around us become familiar with this. They will not have unrealistic expectations of us, since we do not pretend to be anything we are not. We are simply ourselves, distinct individuals who have an awareness of the reality of God. That fact of His reality has affected our lives in various ways that are contagious, but do not need defending. We can include our friends in our normal activities and conversation, of which God is a natural part. This need not and must not be self-conscious in any way. Any distancing or request for discretion on our part will come from our friends. We must only exercise the sensitivity necessary to relate to any person, not assume there are barriers in place which do not necessarily exist. Children will often be our teachers in this regard. They have no artificial concepts of spiritual or secular, of Christian or 'worldly' – they are happy to love God and get on with it, and talk freely with whoever they please.

28 August   Pelagius *(see p.255)*   Arthur Burt *(see p.226)*

Psalm 18:29-36   Proverbs 27:9   2 Corinthians 4:2

Do not have ulterior motives. We must be prepared to love someone as they are, not in the hope that eventually they will become a Christian. Obviously if we love them we want the best for them, and so desire that they have a relationship with God themselves; but if we could not go on loving them just the same, even if they never 'came through', our love is conditional and inadequate. Suppose we help our neighbour with his garden 'because it's a good witness'. That is not really good enough. We should do it because we want to, because we care, and that is a practical way of caring (then it *will* be a good witness). The neighbour is surprised, and questions in himself why you are doing this. If it is because you want to, that may impress him. But if next day you invite him to church, he concludes that the garden was an excuse to get under his defences and make it difficult for him to say no when you invited him to church, since he then feels under an obligation to you. His initial delight that you should be so unselfish turns instead to distaste. What a disappointment – he thought just for a while that you might care about him or be wishing to be friendly. Obviously he was wrong.

29 August

Psalm 131:1-2   Proverbs 20:24, 27   Matthew 6:5

If someone really does not care whether they live or die it is hard to threaten them. If our identity lies in *whose* we are, and not just *who* we are, then even loss of reputation will only be a temporary setback. The need to be someone, to have clout, to command respect, to have prestige or position, these are shackles every bit as strong as those of materialism.

To be seen as holy, or spiritually mature, someone of depth, having a quiet authority: are these not also ambitions, or bolsters of our status?

If we can only reach the true poverty and yieldedness of not 'needing to be' anything (even a humble nothing), then we will truly be invisible. We will be unable to be bought by any pressure.

30 August

Psalm 24:1-6   Proverbs 15:23   Matthew 5:13-16

Jesus talked of Christians as the salt of the earth, and as a light for the world. The salt is not good if it loses its flavour; the light is not good if it is hidden. To be effective, salt must not be separate, but amongst the food where it is invisible, yet its influence pervades the whole. Light must not be blocked by anything, but set apart where it can be clearly visible. We are given two analogies that are almost opposite in their strategy – to show that there are times and situations which require one or the other approach. On the whole it seems there are two kinds of situation when we are required to actively set our light on a lampstand and avoid it being hidden. One of those is a direct confrontation in which the world insists upon us conforming to their standards (of darkness), but we refuse to compromise the truth we know. The second kind of situation is one where an encounter is not sustained, but a clear witness can still be given (like a person walking down a darkened street holding a candle). A polarisation of light and darkness is not usually desirable in long-term situations where we can instead build friendships, where people see how we really are on a day-to-day basis. Here we must be salt.

31 August Aidan *(see p.221)*

Psalm 16:6   Proverbs 11:12   Matthew 13:18-23

Imagine a long line running from −100 to +100 with a zero point somewhere in the middle:

−100 ———————————— 0 ———————————— +100

At one end, −100, is the most hardened sinner that ever lived, who is coincidentally an out-and-out atheist. At the other, +100, is the most saintly believer you could meet. Everybody else is on the line somewhere. Zero represents the point of initial surrender to Christ. Often we think that evangelism is about moving someone we meet from −40 to +10 in 20 minutes! Even when someone makes a commitment abruptly they may have already been at −2 and only needed a nudge over to +5. A nudge at the wrong time could have shot them back to −18.

When I use this analogy I am interested to see how people react. Some immediately apply it to the impact they have on friends or acquaintances. Others personalise it: 'Before what happened this week I must have been about −3, now I'm around +4.' 'I don't know where I am ... −10 maybe.' What we must not do is judge someone else's position. All that matters is that through being with us each person is drawn along the line, closer to Christ, and not knocked farther back.

September
Standing in the secret

These readings focus on intercessory prayer.

1 September

Psalm 97:1, 3   Esther 7:9-10   Matthew 8:2-27

Once, when Aidan of Lindisfarne was praying on the island that is known as the Inner Farne, he looked out across the short stretch of water that separated him from the mainland and saw that a fire had been lit close to the gates of the city of Bamburgh, where the king had his home and throne.

The ruthless Penda had been gathering forces against him for some time, so Aidan would be more alarmed than surprised. As the flames rose and threatened to devour Bamburgh, Aidan prayed, 'Lord, see what evil Penda does!' and in an instant the wind rose up and turned the fire away from the castle, wreaking havoc instead upon the perpetrators of the attack.

2 September

Psalm 149:4-9   Daniel 10:2-21   Revelation 12:7-9

Whatever you bind on earth will be bound in heaven, and whatever you loose on earth will be loosed in heaven.

Matthew 18:18

The implication in the story about Daniel and the angel is that Daniel's prayers made the difference, and, by him remaining constant in prayer until the answer came through, the blockage put up by the enemy was broken through.

Sometimes Satan will do all that he is allowed to do to thwart the purposes of God. We underestimate the contribution that our prayers can make in defeating the devices and schemes of the enemy. Territorial spirits do have influence on, or by default have jurisdiction over, areas and their inhabitants. But the faithful prayer of even one person can swing the balance in spiritual conflict in which they are involved.

We only *begin* to understand the significance and secret power of prayer, but the mystery is this: God is more than willing to act on our behalf, but our prayerlessness so often impedes His intervention.

God heard and answered Daniel's prayer immediately, but the enemy intercepted and delayed the answer. His persistence in prayer won the day.

> But I am not defeated and I will not be;
> God sends *His* angels, and they fight for me.

Priority

An ancient prayer says:

> St Michael the Archangel,
> defend us in battle;
> be our safeguard against
> the wickedness and snares of the devil.
> May God rebuke him, we humbly pray,
> and do thou, O Prince of the heavenly host,
> by the power of God, cast into hell
> Satan and the other evil spirits
> who prowl through the world,
> seeking the ruin of souls.
> Amen.

3 September

Psalm 53:2   Isaiah 55:8-9   2 Corinthians 10:5

Too often when we come to pray we have fixed ideas as to what the subject for our intercession will be – or if God gives us the subject we again lapse into our own thoughts, ideas and preconceptions instead of letting the Spirit teach us what to pray. We need to take authority over our own thoughts, however good, in case they prove to be an impediment to God's directives and burden.

Wordless prayer can often be effective, too. Some of the times when we 'worry' for hours on end for no apparent reason, about a person who normally we would rarely think of, may turn out to be the closest to real intercession we have ever come.

4 September

Psalm 62:8   1 Samuel 7:5-9   Mark 14:35-41

Sometimes it is important to pray and keep praying until we feel released to stop. It may be that at that precise time the breakthrough has come and our prayer is answered or the answer set in motion. Often if the date and time is logged in an intercession diary, it can be confirmed that this was exactly when prayer was needed. On other occasions the burden may be given us to carry only for a little while and then put on someone else in their turn.

Jesus in Gethsemane said, 'Could you not watch with Me for one hour?' An hour may often seem an eternity. But at the end of that night He was to say, 'The hour is come.' His disciples had slept at the crucial hour when He needed their support.

One man did watch with Him from a distance, a young man who had followed so hurriedly he had only had the chance to wrap a sheet around him and not lose sight of Jesus and the others. When Jesus was arrested he left in even more of a hurry, without even his sheet!

That young man who watched as Jesus prayed is usually believed to have been John Mark, the Gospel writer.

5 September   Teresa of Calcutta *(see p.262)*

Psalm 63:3   1 Samuel 12:23-24   1 Corinthians 7:3-5

Columba's friend, Lugne, had a problem in that his wife refused to share his bed any longer, so much had she come to find him and his attentions repulsive. She was prepared to care for all his other physical needs, or, if Columba so advised, to leave him and become a nun altogether. Columba would not hear of it, but instead suggested that all three of them fast from eating, and pray for the next 24 hours.

She agreed to try it, since the impossible or difficult might be altered by the prayer of faith. Accordingly all three prayed, and Columba stayed awake all night also, interceding for them.

She must have been well satisfied, on this occasion at least, for when next morning Columba asked Lugne's wife if she was willing to go to a convent she would on no account hear of it, and stayed happily with her man till the end of their days.

6 September   Madeleine L'Engle *(see p.247)*

Psalm 63:4   Exodus 17:8-16   1 Timothy 2:8

It was as if he were the conductor. When Moses raised his stick the Israelites were advancing loudly; if he let it fall they pulled back. I wonder how gradually or how soon he realised the connection.

They could not afford to take a hammering, so soon Aaron and Hur came to his rescue! The arms still are raised, and the rod; but now they will see it through together, and the stone can support his weight.

At times, we are the only one who can stand in our place of relationship and responsibility; but to know the support and prayer of others makes it bearable and possible. There may be others, especially leaders, who need our support and loyalty, or who need our prayers, just to hold their arms up, because how they hold out greatly affects what happens for lots of people and their lives.

7 September

Psalm 25:5-9   Haggai 2:9   Romans 12:9

From generation to generation the same problems may dog a particular area in a way that defies physical or sociological explanation – it is as if the place has a memory. Often in praying for a place the themes of its significant history will provide clues – keys to throw off all kinds of bondage. A trifling series of events may happen that unknowingly repeat a pattern; and it is as if there is a resonance with what parallel events have been before, and the effects are out of all proportion in consequence.

A prosperous city may owe its wealth, for example, to slave trading – an injustice that could be repented for vicariously.

A place with a long-ago history of sectarian rivalry will often have disproportionate difficulty in setting up contemporary inter-church projects.

Today's oppressive atmosphere may have causes in what has happened before anything in living memory. Because this has often been found to be the case, we can anticipate this and do research, but it is important not to look just for negatives. There are positive and spiritually powerful events and places whose significance we can explore. This is part of our spiritual inheritance. There may even be prayers, and prophetic words waiting to be fulfilled – waiting for us to experience the reality of them in our generation.

8 September

Psalm 110:7   Jeremiah 31:21   2 Peter 1:12-15

What do we mean by 'memory-stones'?

Joshua had stones placed by the edge of the Jordan river which God had parted to let His people cross dry-shod. The intention was that future generations could ask the meaning of the stones and be taught of God's faithfulness.

Celtic preachers would often set up a stone cross as their preaching point, and there the people would gather to be taught the word of God. Some of these crosses have carved pictures of a number of the Bible stories as part of their design.

Memory-stones can be landmarks, signposts, waymarks to guide the lost, to point them to tried and proven paths. The ruined remains of ancient buildings also are memory-stones – like the Western Wall of the Temple of Jerusalem, often called the Wailing Wall. Often the physical stones show us approximate sites, especially in Celtic Christianity where the original structures were almost always wooden. But the ancient ruins we are called to repair, and the broken altars we are called to restore, may not be of any concern to the Department of the Environment or the National Trust.

The stones, like us, cry out for a renewal of the faith that first secured their presence on 'this small earth of sea and land, this small space on which we stand'.

9 September

Psalm 48:12-13   Joshua 14:6-12   Acts 16:6-10

To walk and pray predisposes us for all kinds of things to happen. We may be led to a place or building and claim its use for God. We may pray healing in an area that has known great distress. We certainly can pray quietly for the people who live and work in that area, even at the same time as we are exposed to new impressions of it. Two walking together gives the opportunity to pray aloud in turn, discreetly giving the impression of talking one to the other. Often God's heart for a place will come upon us under these circumstances, and we become aware of the needs of the people round about, and what can be done to be part of meeting such a challenge.

Sometimes such a walk enables us to be in the path of an event, encounter or difficulty. Praying does not exempt us from involvement – remember Jesus' story of the man set upon by thieves, and the ones who saw and passed by! Aidan and his companions walked, saying the Psalms or reading Scripture as they went, but whoever they met he would challenge to love God more or, if they did not yet know Him, to believe and be baptised as His follower.

10 September

Psalm 5:11-12   Genesis 13:11-13; 18:17-33; 19:27-29   Ephesians 2:2

Abraham is not frightened to bargain with God and agree a fair arrangement – the figures may be negotiable, the terms can be made more favourable, perhaps?

God proves willing to bend a little, or even a lot, but at the end of the day the justice of His judgement is all the more vindicated.

Can we reason with God in such a way? and plead mercy for those in danger of well-deserved disaster? Do we care enough to try? and do we believe it could make any difference at all?

God relies on our prayer to take the limits off His activity in our world. We are not called to prayer in order to pander to His vanity, but in order to make a real difference in the earth.

11 September

Psalm 111:2, 10   Amos 3:7   2 Corinthians 10:3-5

Sometimes we will be led to pray things that make no sense to our natural mind. Later events could eventually help us to understand why it was necessary for us to pray the way we did.

For our own reference it will usually help to keep a record of these things, a kind of intercessory diary. If we then pray and get it wrong, at least we will have begun to be in motion and can be more easily redirected than if we had made no move at all!

God's government is a moral government; its directions are partially determined by people's free choice. It is as if the will of God is the path down a ski-slope with much twisting and turning necessary to negotiate a clear run to the finishing line. Many of the obstacles only appear when the descent is already in progress.

We need to listen to the Holy Spirit who can activate us to pray and intercede. Our prayers are part of the process of removing obstacles or alerting other skiers.

12 September

Psalm 3:8   Proverbs 10:22   Romans 15:2

We are called to bless even our enemies. How much more should we pray a blessing on others in the Body of Christ! – especially those we disagree with, or who hold a different view from our own.

If we ask a blessing on them, it is up to God to decide what He can and cannot bless in what they are and what they are doing.

We are not asked to understand each other first. If there are some elements in the church who really aggravate us it may be more useful to pray a blessing on them than to interact in a critical spirit. As we pray we begin to realise just how much God cares about them.

We can pray blessings on non-Christian folk, too. It is like pouring glitter over a home-made Christmas card – wherever the glue-stick has prepared the card the glitter will stick, the rest only rolls off; and even a little of the glitter can be enough to spell out a clear message.

13 September

Psalm 68:17-19, 28   Judges 13:15-18   Matthew 18:10-14

The book *Angels on Assignment* by Charles and Frances Hunter suggests that the prayers of a believer can have powerful effects upon the life-circumstances of family members who have no knowledge of God or love for Him. If the believer does not pressurise the family, but prays instead, angels of God can contrive all kinds of situations which independently challenge the person prayed for and which create some opportunity for them to respond to Jesus. Prayer can often accomplish this much, but no prayer, no angels, not even God Himself, can force that person to surrender – God will not overrule another person's will, without their permission. He can only begin the process again.

Augustine, who so strongly stresses God's power to intervene in the life even of so unwilling a convert as he, was actually able to be so arrested because of the persistent prayer of a believing mother.

14 September

Psalm 45:6   Isaiah 9:6-7   Luke 23:26, 38

In 1983 a core-group of leaders and other representatives met in preparation for the next Easter Workshop. Amongst other things it would be the first time we would have substantial numbers of Catholics and non-Catholics all together, and we were anxious to smooth the way for those not used to mixing with people from such different backgrounds.

This first meeting was not going well – several people were acting defensively. Alan Andrews picked up a guitar and began to sing his song:

> The King is among us
> and His glory shall be seen
> as we learn to ... touch each other.

Later in the day we would sing it again, and cry, holding hands; but now we sat thoughtfully in a circle staring at the coffee table. I reached behind me for a small wooden figure that was on the mantelpiece above the fireplace and put it in the centre of the coffee table. It was a figure of Christ carrying His cross, painfully stumbling along the road to Calvary.

Alan still was singing, but now I heard the words as if for the first time:

> And the government shall be upon His shoulder;
> His kingdom shall never cease.

Christ still intercedes for us, and feels the pain of our sin and division: the cross which was always on the heart of God is still the throne He rules from.

15 September

Psalm 36:5   Jeremiah 33:3   Revelation 3:8

A number of years ago, Andy Raine's friend Nigel painted a beautiful picture of a boy shooting lots of paper aeroplanes into the sky. They are all being directed at the same place high in front of him, and each falls to the ground again. The ground is covered with snow, and the sky with thick cloud – but in one place a clearing has appeared and the deep blue of the night sky can be seen through it. It has become a gateway to heaven.

So often our prayers, and other initiatives taken in blind obedience to the Spirit, seem as pointless as shooting paper aeroplanes into the sky – but the eyes of faith know that it is no coincidence that that will be the place where the clouds clear and heaven penetrates earth's concerns.

Broken gold

The following readings and prayers are about meeting God in everyday life, and offering that life to Him.

16 September

Psalm 65:8-13   Leviticus 27:30   1 Corinthians 16:2

> Man offers the first-fruits of his labour to the Creator of everything in the universe, stars and cornstalks and grains of dust. This is not to say however that man is simply a brutish breaker of furrows, but he labours well in a variety of trades also, with stone and with loom and with oar and with harp and with law-book and with sweet ordering of words and with prism, towards some end which is likewise a kind of harvest. Well he knows that he could not call himself man at all unless he labours all his time under the sun to encompass the end for which his faculties were given him. This end, whatever the

nature of his occupation, is his harvest time; and he would be a poor labourer that would not wish, among all that broken gold, to offer back a tithe or a hundredth into the hands that formed the original fecund dust.

George Mackay Brown, Magnus

17 September

Psalm 104:24-25   Isaiah 42:10   Acts 27:15

Praise and gratitude to You, Holy Father,
who created the skies and heaven first
and after that created the big wet sea
and the heaps of fish in it swimming closely.

*An ancient hymn
from the Great Blasket Island, Ireland*

Dear God,
be good to me.
The sea is so wide
and my boat is so small.

A prayer of the Breton fishermen

18 September   George MacDonald *(see p.248)*

Psalm 51:1-2   Proverbs 18:10   John 14:1-6

O Father everlasting,
with house of many rooms,
with You may I live,
with You may I live.

Son of the living God,
ancient and eternal King,
in You may my dwelling be,
in You may my dwelling be.

Holy Spirit of power,
in that clear pool of grace,
wash away my sins,
wash away my sins.

'Manchan of Liath's desire'
(tenth century)

19 September

Psalm 72:6-7   Proverbs 3:7-8   1 John 5:20

God to enfold me,
God to surround me,
God in my speaking,
God in my thinking.

God in my sleeping,
God in my waking,
God in my watching,
God in my hoping.

God in my life,
God in my lips,
God in my soul,
God in my heart.

God in my sufficing,
God in my slumber,
God in mine ever-living soul,
God in mine eternity.

From Carmina Gadelica

20 September

Psalm 63:6-7   Ezekiel 36:26-27   John 8:12

In the latter half of the nineteenth century Alexander Carmichael recorded, in the *Carmina Gadelica*, the prayers and traditions of the people of the Scottish Highlands and Islands which had never been written down before. An old man, whom Carmichael described as 'poor, aged and lonely', explained his night ritual:

> I do now as my mother was doing when I was a child. Before going to bed I place the bar upon the leaf of the door, and I make the cross of Christ on the bar and on the door, and I supplicate the great God of life, the Father of all living, to protect and comfort me this night ... After that I put out my light and then I go to bed, and when I lie down on my pillow I make the cross of Christ upon my breast, over the tablet of my hard heart, and I beseech the living God of the universe:
>
> May the Light of lights come
> to my dark heart from Thy place;
> may the Spirit's wisdom come
> to my heart's tablet from my Saviour.

21 September   Henri Nouwen *(see p.252)*

Psalm 115:13   Micah 5:2, 4   Luke 2:16-20

> May God's blessing be yours,
> and well may it befall you.

Celtic insight

The rest of the readings for this month are variously about the Celtic Church or the everyday culture of Celtic Christians, mostly from the Western Isles of Scotland. Their way of seeing can teach and inspire us.

22 September

Psalm 24:7   Isaiah 53:12   Acts 1:9-12

> And if I go and prepare a place for you, I will come again and will take you to Myself, so that where I am, there you may be also.
>
> *John 14:3*

Martin Reith, in his 1991 lectures on *Celtic Spirituality* at Bishop's House, Iona, cites a quotation from O'Laoghaire in *Irish Spirituality*. The words are originally in Irish and date from around 700; the subject is the Ascension of Christ:

> When the people of Heaven welcomed their heart-love, O Mary, your beautiful Son broke into tears before them.

23 September   Adamnan *(see p.221)*

Psalm 119:66-67, 71   Isaiah 40:3-4   Matthew 3:1-6; 4:12-17

> If anybody enters the path of repentance
> it is sufficient to advance a step every day.
> If you practise repentance,
> if your heart is meek,
> your way will be straight
> to the King of the Kingdom of heaven.
>
> *From the Rule of Comgall*

24 September

Psalm 127:3   Isaiah 11:1-2   Luke 1:41-48

The Christ-child's lullaby

> There was once a shiftless laddie in the Isles who had lost his mother, and that is a sad tale, but had got a stepmother in her place, and that is sometimes a sadder one.

On an evening he brought home the cattle for the milking, and if they gave little milk that time, and likely it was little they gave, who was to blame for it but the poor orphan?

'Son of another,' said his stepmother in the heat of anger, 'there will be no luck on this house till you leave!' But whoever heard of a luckless chick leaving of its own will?

...But leave the shiftless laddie did, and that of his own will, and ere the full moon rose at night, he was on the other side of the ben.

That night the stepmother could get neither sleep nor ease; her bed was like a cairn of stones in a forest of reptiles. 'I will rise', she said, 'and see if the night outside is better than the night inside.' She rose and went out, with her face towards the ben; nor did she stop until she saw and heard something which made her stop.

What was this but a woman, with the very heat-love of heaven in her face, sitting on a grassy knoll and song-lulling a baby-son with the sweetest music ever heard under moon or sun; and at her feet the shiftless laddie, his face like the dream of the Lord's night. 'God of the graces!' said the stepmother, 'it is Mary Mother and she is doing what I ought to be doing – song-lulling the orphan.' And she fell on her knees and began to weep the soft warm tears of a mother; and when, after a while, she looked up, there was nobody there but herself and the shiftless laddie side by side.

And that is how Christ's Lullaby came to the Isles:

> My love, my dear, my darling thou,
> my treasure new, my gladness thou,
> my comely beauteous babe-son thou,
> unworthy I to tend to thee.
>
> Hosanna to the Son of David,
> my King, my Lord and my Saviour!
> Great my joy to be song-lulling thee –
> Blessed among the women I.

Kenneth McLeod, The Road to the Isles

25 September Cadoc *(see p.227)*

Psalm 100:2-3   Jeremiah 23:4   John 21:16

The waiting crook

There was once a saint in Moidart who was always putting taunt upon himself as being the least of all the brethren, and the most useless. And one day he said within himself: 'No work that I am fit for has ever come to me; I will now take me to the hill, and let the Good Being himself choose a track for me.' On the third day he came to a great wooden cross partly decayed, standing on the edge of the peat moss. He knelt at the foot of the cross, and when he opened his eyes again, what saw he there but a shepherd's crook lying on the heather, as if it had dropped out of a hand. He took up the waiting crook, and, hurrying on, he now came to a village here and a settlement there which had waited long for the man with the crook.

Kenneth McLeod, The Road to the Isles

26 September

Psalm 71:6-7, 18-19   Deuteronomy 34:8, 10   Acts 20:24-25, 28

Lines from the poem of keening for Columcille (Columba of the Church), high saint of the Gael, by Blind Dallan Forgaill, Chief Poet of Ireland:

> It is not a little story, this is not a story of a fool.
> It is not one district that is keening, nor grief of one harpstring.
> He, our rightful head, God's messenger, is dead.
> The teller of words who took away our fear, does not return.
> The learned one who taught us silence is gone from us.
> Good his death: he went to God: angels met him.
> He knew the way he was going.
> He gave kindness for hatred, he broke the battle against hunger,

healer of hearts, satisfier of guests,
shelter of the naked, comfort of the poor,
their soul's light, a perfect sage who believed Christ.
Nor went any from this world who more steadfastly bore
  the cross.
IT IS HIGH HIS DEATH WAS...

27 September

Psalm 38:9   Isaiah 40:3-4   Matthew 6:6

The wilderness and the solitary place shall be glad for them,
and the desert shall rejoice, and blossom as the rose. It shall
blossom abundantly and see the glory of the Lord and the
excellency of our God.

Isaiah 35:1-2

As church and state in the Roman empire got married after
the toleration edict of 312, heroic virtue was exchanged for
compromise with the world, and the inevitable result was
insipid mediocrity. Men, and women, finding no challenge in
the cities, began to flock to the Egyptian and other deserts. This
was a bold encounter with the realities of existence, a challenge
to all accepted norms in society, a facing of the shadow side
of the human personality, and ultimately confrontation with
objective evil.

The Desert Fathers were essentially solitaries, expressing
their love for their neighbours by total self-oblation to God, by
continuous prayer, and by handcraft work for the poor. Their
lives reveal an extraordinary humility, gentleness, tenderness,
sensitivity and compassion ... And a firm grasp of Bible
teaching seems to have been based on the principle that you
don't ignore what you don't like.

Martin Reith, Celtic Spirituality

28 September

Psalm 31:3-6, 14-19   Proverbs 22:24-25, 28   Mark 9:35-42

The theology and observances of the ascetics of the Syrian and Egyptian deserts brought new choices for Christians. People could opt for an 'ordinary' life in the world, living the faith within the normal structures of human and political life, or could withdraw from everyday concerns and pursue their Christian vocation either as a solitary or as a member of an intentional community. This radical new alternative was obviously particularly attractive in a time of social upheaval.

The Eastern monastic tradition took hold among the Celts, many by this time living in the western parts of Britain and in Ireland, and linked by a common group of languages. From it emerged a very distinctive and dynamic form of Christian life and expression.

The faith of the Celtic Church was orthodox, and differed from the continental Church only in matters of emphasis. They would have no difficulty in recognising each other as fellow Catholic Christians. Where they differed was in priorities, style and organisation. The Celtic Church inhabited a monastic ethos which shaped its life, and gave it a different 'feel' from the mainstream continental Church.

What had happened was that while the Benedictine form of Christian organisation was directly under the authority of the Pope, Celtic Christianity, though entirely orthodox, had developed its own distinctive style, untouched by continental influences. New arrangements for the dating of Easter and styles of tonsure had bypassed the Irish and Scots, who were the conservatives in the matter.

Ron Ferguson, Chasing the Wild Goose

29 September — Michael and All Angels *(see p.251)*

Psalm 27:11   1 Kings 12:13   1 Corinthians 3:9-15, 20-23

Computing the date of Easter had been a perpetual problem for the Church since the first century. In 541 at the Synod of Orleans, new Easter tables were adopted but in the chaos of the times (there was a century and a half when migrating barbarian hordes had cut the Celtic Churches off from contact with Rome), no word of the change had reached Ireland. But when communications were restored Rome tried to insist that the clergy of the universal Church used the same identifying tonsure and the same date for Easter. Old habits die hard and the Celtic clergy would not conform.

At the Synod of Whitby in 664 King Oswy and the Northumbrians accepted the Roman system. Unfortunately Wilfrid of York, who argued the Roman cause, had spent much time in Gaul and picked up, it seems, some of the acrimony which had been directed against St Columbanus. Wilfrid won the argument but in such a way that the Iona missionaries felt slighted and they withdrew from England and many English monks went with them. They finally settled in the West of Ireland forming an English community in Mayo. The Britons of Strathclyde and the Picts soon followed Northumbria's example and most of Ireland also accepted the new dating. But Iona clung to the old way.

The ninth Abbot of Iona was Adamnan MacRonan and in 688, after visiting Jarrow and talking to Bede's Abbot Ceolfrid, he accepted the Roman practice. But many of the Iona monks refused to follow him, denouncing him as a traitor to the Founder. It was this bitter controversy which led him to write his master work *The Life of St Columba* to show his devotion to him. So perhaps we should be grateful.

After Adamnan died a faction set up a counter-Abbot and for decades there were two Abbots, two tonsures and two Easters on the Island. Finally it was an Englishman, St Egbert, who brought them to celebrate Easter together again in 729. Iona was the last Scottish abbey to conform.

Reginald B. Hale, The Magnificent Gael

30 September

Psalm 126:3, 5-6   Ecclesiastes 3:1-2   1 Corinthians 3:6-8

'The making of the bread, is it not the gladsome thing!'

And yet the reaping-song of the Gael has never been the purely joyous gladness of the young mavie which has never known the sorrow of the empty nest or of the deserted wood. To the singing of the harvest-song goes the life of a year, or of all the years – the summer that is gone, the winter that is coming; the ones who have sown but are not here to reap; the ones who will sow when the reapers that are have been forgotten; the Good Being who makes the sun shine and the corn ripen. There may be the breath of a sigh in that song, but there is also in it a whole storm of rapture.

Gladness must come to its own some time; for the sorrows, there are all the times. To the harvest-field go we, then, for life as it ought to be. The sickle is fate, the hand that holds it is ours, and for once we will be the conqueror. Cut we down a sorrow here and a pain there, bind them, and make them our slaves. Sure, then, this is the glad day, and the beautiful world, and the brave life – what we shall afterwards dream of in the long winter night.

Kenneth McLeod, The Road to the Isles

October
Parting and planting

1 October

Psalm 25:12-14   Ezekiel 36:26   Luke 6:45

Let Your tender word wear a hole in the hardness of our hearts; so as we hear Your word frequently our hearts will be opened to rightly fear God.

The Desert Fathers

2 October

Psalm 57:7-8   Isaiah 41:9-10   Ephesians 4:25-32

God be with us
on this Thy day;
to us and with us,
on this Thy day.

Grant us forgiveness,
grant us Thine own forgiveness,
Thou merciful God of all.

3 October   Thérèse of Lisieux *(see p.262)*

Psalm 107:10-14   Isaiah 49:6   John 1:9

> And now You're here –
> the light is shining where
> the darkness used to be –
> and all the world
> is a different place...
>
> ...and every single day a fresh beginning.

From The Song of Simeon

4 October   Francis of Assisi *(see p.238)*

Psalm 85:10-11   Exodus 24:16-18   Matthew 6:6

Many of the Celtic monasteries also had a place apart – a cell, retreat, or *dysert* – in which a monk or nun could retire when he or she needed to be alone. Sometimes the Celtic saints chose a cave for shelter and reflection, as did Columban and Ninian of Whithorn (362–432). Others moved to a hill or mountaintop to fast and pray. Many, as is clear in the stories of Aidan, Columcille, and Cuthbert, seemed especially drawn to be near the ocean's waves. Whatever their reasons for treasuring silence and seeking the solitary life, the early Christian Celts shared what the scholar John Ryan calls a 'surprising combination of apostolic and anchoretical ideals.'

E.C. Sellner, Wisdom of the Celtic Saints

> Spirit's wisdom,
> start up music from my Saviour in my heart!
> Be the peace of the Spirit mine this night.
> Be the peace of the Son mine this night.
> Be the peace of the Father mine this night.
> The peace of all peace be mine this night,
> each morning and evening of my life.

From Martin Reith, God in our Midst *and* Celtic Vision *(ed. Esther de Waal)*

5 October

Psalm 138:1-3   2 Samuel 22:31-37   Acts 12:6-10

> This day God gives me
> strength from high heaven,
> sun and moon shining,
> flame in my hearth.
> Flashing of lighting
> wind in its swiftness,
> deep of the ocean,
> firmness of earth.
>
> God's way is my way,
> God's shield is round me.
> God's host defends me,
> saving from ill.
> Angels of heaven,
> drive from me always
> all that would harm me.
> stand by me still.
>
> *James Quinn (based on St Patrick)*

6 October

Psalm 28:3-5   Genesis 2:18-24   Galatians 3:28

The close ministerial association of male Celtic missionaries with women met with vehement condemnations from Church authorities on the Continent. Judging from protests against the practice, missionaries evidently travelled quite frequently with women companions, some of whom helped with the celebration of the Eucharist. Below is a sixth-century letter written by bishops in Gaul to Irish missionaries:

> Through a report made by the venerable Sparatus, we have learned that you continually carry around from one of your fellow-countrymen's huts to another, certain tables upon which you celebrate the divine sacrifice of the Mass, assisted

by women whom you call *conhospitae*: and while you distribute
the Eucharist, they take the chalice and administer the blood
of Christ to the people. This is an innovation, an unheard-of
superstition ... For the love of Christ, and in the name of the
church united and of our common faith, we beg you renounce
immediately upon receipt of this letter, these abuses of the table.
We appeal to your charity, not only to restrain these little women
from staining the holy sacraments by administering them illicitly,
but also not to admit to live under your roof any woman who is
not your grandmother, your mother, your sister, or your niece.

7 October

Psalm 1:1-3   Leviticus 6:12-13   1 Peter 3:7

Canaire (or Cannera) lived and prayed for many years in a cell she had built near Bantry Bay. Shortly before her death she decided to visit Senan's island home. Considering her words to Senan about his lack of hospitality, she may well have been the first Irish feminist! She also evidently had a positive effect on the older man, for early legends say that Aidan of Lindisfarne was a disciple of Senan, and he certainly, as we have seen, was a significant mentor for both women and men.

Canaire died about the year 530. Her feast day is 28 January. The site of her partially submerged grave is marked with a simple flag and can still be seen in the waters off Scattery Island.

> Canaire the Pious, a holy woman living in the south of Ireland, set up a hermitage in her own territory. One night, while she was praying all the churches in Ireland appeared to her in a vision. It seemed as if a tower of fire rose up to heaven from each side of the churches. The highest of the towers of fire, and the straightest toward heaven was that which rose from Inis Cathaig (Scattery Island). 'Fair is Senan's cell,' Canaire said. 'I will go there, that my resurrection may be near it.' She went immediately, without guidance except for the tower of fire, which she saw continuing to blaze day and night until she arrived. Now when she had reached the shore, she walked upon the sea as if

she were on smooth land until she came to Inis Cathaig. Senan knew that she was coming and went to meet and welcome her.

'Yes, I have come,' Canaire told him.

'Go to your sister who lives on the island east of this one, so that you may be her guest,' said Senan.

'That is not why I came,' said Canaire, 'but to find hospitality with you on this island.'

'Women cannot enter on this island,' Senan replied.

'How can you say that?' said Canaire. 'Christ is no worse than you. Christ came to redeem women no less than to redeem men. Women as well as men can enter the heavenly kingdom. Why, then, should you not allow women to live on this island?'

'You are persistent,' said Senan.

'Well then,' Canaire replied, 'will I get what I ask for? Will you give me a place to live on this island and the holy sacrament of the Eucharist?'

'Yes, Canaire, a place of resurrection will be given you here on the brink of the waves,' said Senan. She came on the shore then, received the sacrament from Senan, and immediately went to heaven.

From E.C. Sellner, Wisdom of the Celtic Saints

8 October

Psalm 118:17-18   Jeremiah 6:16   Philippians 1:21-24

As I put off from me my raiment,
grant me to put off my struggling.
As the haze rises from the crest of the mountains,
raise then my soul from the mist of death.

I will lie in my bed
as I would lie in the grave
with Thine arm beneath my neck,
Thou Son of Mary victorious.

Traditional prayer from God in our Midst *(ed. Martin Reith)*

9 October

Psalm 135:19-20   Ezekiel 47:12   Luke 24:46-48

Ciaran of Clonmacnois lived from about 512 to 545. He was one of the great monastic founders called the 'Twelve Apostles of Ireland' educated by Finnian at Clonard. Following in his mentor's footsteps, Ciaran established one of the largest, richest, and most important monastic centres of learning in the entire Celtic church. Ciaran also seems to have had a great capacity for friendships. He had a broad network of friends and advisors scattered throughout the early Irish church, including Columcille of Iona (a fellow student), Finnian of Clonard (his tutor), Enda of Aran Islands (a mentor), Senan of the Scattery Island (a colleague), and Kevin of Glendalough (a close friend).

Ciaran founded the monastery of Clonmacnois on the banks of the Shannon River in late 544. Less than a year later, on 9 September 545, he died unexpectedly at the age of 33.

The vision of the great tree

Ciaran went to the island of Aran to commune with Enda. Both of them saw the same vision of a great fruitful tree growing beside a stream in the middle of Ireland. This tree protected the entire island. Its fruit crossed the sea that surrounded Ireland and the birds of the world came to carry off some of that fruit. Ciaran turned to Enda and told him what he had seen. Enda, in turn, said to him: 'The great tree is you, Ciaran, for you are great in the eyes of God and of all humankind. All of Ireland will be sheltered by the grace that is in you, and many people will be fed by your fasting and prayers. Go in the name of God to the centre of Ireland, and found your church on the banks of a stream.'

E.C. Sellner, Wisdom of the Celtic Saints

10 October Paulinus *(see p.254)*

Psalm 72:8-14   Deuteronomy 6:5-6   Luke 16:10

The three things that most please and displease God

St Brendan once asked Ita what were the three works most pleasing to God, and the three works most displeasing to Him. Ita answered, 'Three things that please God most are true faith in God with a pure heart, a simple life with a grateful spirit, and generosity inspired by charity. The three things that most displease God are a mouth that hates people, a heart harbouring resentments, and a confidence in wealth.'

St Brendan and all who were there, hearing that opinion, glorified God in His chosen one.

11 October

Psalm 91:1-2   Isaiah 52:13-15   Matthew 5:5

Jesu,
Thou humble King of the meek and poor,
who wast brought low and crucified so sore,
do Thou defend and shield me for this night,
my soul on Thine own arm, O Christ, to lie.
Keep me as the apple of an eye,
hide me under the shadow of Your wing.

From Praying with Highland Christians
and Psalm 17:8

12 October Wilfrid *(see p.265)*

Psalm 63:1-3   Genesis 12:1   Acts 1:8

Whatever the reason, many of the early Christian Celts shared the desire to travel. In contrast to the *red martyrdom* of giving one's life up for Christ or the *green martyrdom* of participating in severe penitential practices, they faced the *white martyrdom* of living years far from home and hearth for the sake of the gospel. (The Celts had a specific word, *hiraeth*, for the extreme yearning for home associated with this latter form of martyrdom; because of their deep love of family, it was considered the hardest of all to endure.) Beginning with St Patrick, Celtic missionaries chose this way of life out of deep devotion to Christ.

E.C. Sellner, Wisdom of the Celtic Saints

13 October

Psalm 37:1-9   Exodus 16:8-11   John 16:33

Here are two different translations of St Columba's last reported words of blessing:

> I give to you, my children, these final words: 'Be at peace with one another, bound together by mutual and unfeigned love. If you do this, according to the example of the ancient fathers, God, who gives strength to the righteous, will bless you: and I, abiding with Him, shall intercede for you. Not only will God provide all things needed for this present life, but He shall prepare for you the blessings of eternity.'

> These, O my children, are the last words I address to you – that ye be at peace, and have unfeigned charity among yourselves; and if you thus follow the example of the holy fathers, God, the Comforter of the good, will be your Helper, and I, abiding with Him will intercede for you: and He will not only give you sufficient to supply the wants of this present life but will also bestow on you the good and eternal rewards which are laid up for those that keep His commandments.

14 October

Psalm 150   1 Chronicles 16:8-11   Acts 1:14

Life in David's community in Wales

When labour in the fields was finished they returned to the monastery and spent the whole of the day until the evening in reading, writing or praying. When evening came, and the stroke of the bell sounded, whether only the tip of a letter or even half the form of the same letter was written, they rose quickly and left what they were doing. In silence, without empty talk or chatter, they went into the church. When they had finished chanting the psalm, with voice and heart in complete harmony, they humbled themselves on bended knees until the appearance of the stars in the heavens brought the day to a close.

Patrick Thomas

15 October   Teresa of Avila *(see p.261)*

Psalm 119:26-32   Isaiah 53:3, 7a   Matthew 24:1-5

Becoming part of David's community in Wales

It was the custom that anyone who yearned for this manner of saintly life and asked to join this monastic community first remained for ten days at the door of the monastery, as if rejected and also silenced by words of abuse. If he put his patience to good use and stood there until the tenth day, he might be admitted and first put to serve under the elder who had charge of the gate. After he had toiled there for a long time, and many conflicts within his soul had been reconciled, he was finally judged fit to enter the brethren's society.

16 October Gall *(see p.239)*

Psalm 119:66-70   Deuteronomy 7:9-13   John 14:12-13

The parting words of David of Wales to his friends

My brothers and sisters, be joyful, keep your faith and belief, and perform the small things which you have learned from me and have seen in me.

17 October

Psalm 91:14-16   Judges 6:36-40   Matthew 26:29

The parting of friends

Maedoc and Molaise of Devenish were comrades who loved each other very much. One day they were praying at the foot of two trees. 'Ah Jesus!' they cried. 'Is it your will that we should part, or that we should remain together until we die?' Then one of the two trees fell to the south, and the other to the north. 'By the fall of the trees,' they said, 'it is clear that we must part.' Then they told each other goodbye and kissed each other affectionately.

Maedoc went to the south and built a noble monastery at Ferns in the centre of Leinster, and Molaise went north to Lough Erne and built a fair monastery at Devenish.

18 October

Psalm 2:3-4   Ecclesiastes 3:1-2   John 4:23

Recognising time as a reality made holy by a loving God, the Celtic saints valued the daily, the routine, the ordinary. They believed God is found not so much at the end of time when the reign of God *finally comes*, but *now*, where the reign is already being lived by God's faithful people. Theirs was a spirituality

characterised by gratitude, and in our stories we find them
worshipping God in their daily work and very ordinary chores.

E.C. Sellner, Wisdom of the Celtic Saints

Labour and rest, work and ease,
the busy hand, and then the stilled thought:
this blending of opposites
is the secret
of the joy of living.

From Hebridean Altars

19 October

Psalm 40:10   Isaiah 63:7   John 14:27

Hild lived until she was 66. These were among her last words:

As long as you are in good health, serve God with all your
might. When you are ill, remember all His mercies with
thankfulness, and above all things live in Christian love and
peace with one another and with all.

Keep within me
a stillness
deeper and sweeter
than a forest's
in mid of winter.

From Hebridean Altars

20 October

Psalm 32:1-2   Job 1:21-22   Matthew 7:12

Caedmon composed his songs only that they might be useful
to the soul, and their solemn beauty did even more for the
conversion than for the delight of his countrymen. Many were

moved by them to despise this world, and turn with ardent love to the divine life. He died as poets seldom die. At the very beginning of his illness he desired his bed to be made in that part of the infirmary which was assigned to the dying, and, while smiling and talking cheerfully with his brethren, asked for viaticum. At the moment when he was about to administer communion to himself, from the pyx brought from church according to the usage of the period, and while holding in his hands the Holy Eucharist, he asked all those around him, if any one had any grudge against him, or any complaint to make. All answered, 'No.' Then said he, 'I, too, my children, have a mind at peace with all God's servants.'

A little while after he had received from the venerable Sacrament, as they were about to waken the monks for Matins, he made the sign of the Cross, laid his head on the pillow, and fell asleep in silence, to awake no more.

21 October Tuda *(see p.263)*

Psalm 101:3-7   Ezekiel 33:30-32   Matthew 25:41-45

Father of Israel,
forgive all that in each of us
is unprepared for Christ's coming:
our insensitivity to others;
our ignoring of the stranger;
our lack of attention to Your Word.

David Adam

22 October

Psalm 131:1-3   Micah 6:8   Matthew 25:35-40

Cuthbert's last message to his brothers:

> Always preserve divine charity among yourselves, and when you come together to discuss your common affairs let your principal goal be to reach a unanimous decision. Live in mutual harmony with all other servants of Christ. Do not despise those faithful who come to you seeking hospitality. Receive them, put them up, and set them on their way with kindness, treating them as one of yourselves. Do not ever think yourselves better than the rest of your companions who share the same faith and follow the monastic life.

23 October

Psalm 34:1-2   Proverbs 6:6-11   Luke 18:1-8

Cuthbert's words on the night of the passing of Aidan's soul into heaven:

> How wretched we are, given up to sleep and laziness so that we never see the glory of those who watch with Christ unceasingly! What miraculous things I have seen after so short a vigil!

24 October

Psalm 136:23-24   Zephaniah 3:17   Romans 8:35-39

> I am calmed because I know You love me.
> Because You love me, nothing can move me from my
>   peace.
> Because You love me, I am as one to whom all good
>   has come.

From Hebridean Altars

25 October

Psalm 25:3-7   Proverbs 3:5-8   Luke 18:9-14

> Deliver me from self-trustfulness.
> In the frequent days in which I must do battle with
>   my self for foe,
> arm me with a constant trust in Thee.
>
> *From* Hebridean Altars

26 October   Cedd *(see p.229)*   Eata *(see p.234)*

Psalm 27:1-4   Deuteronomy 6:6-11   1 Thessalonians 1:4-10

> Lord, You love us to stand in Your sight upright
> and with such a gentleness in us that
> some other will yearn to win its power.
>
> *From* Hebridean Altars

27 October

Psalm 80:4-7   Isaiah 54:6-8   Revelation 7:13-17

> When mystery hides Thee from the sight of faith and hope;
> when pain turns even love to dust;
> when life is bitter to the taste and our song of joy
> dies down to silence;
> then, Father, do for us that which is past our power to do for
> ourselves.
> Break though our darkness with Thy light.
> Show us Thyself in Jesus suffering on a Tree,
> rising from the grave,
> reigning from a throne with all power and love for us unchanging.
> So shall our fear be gone
> and our feet set upon a radiant path.
>
> *From* Hebridean Altars

28 October

Psalm 107:23-30   Ecclesiastes 3:1-8   Matthew 8:23-27

Guthfrid of Lindisfarne relates an incident in the life of Ethilwald, who was Cuthbert's successor as hermit on Inner Farne for 12 years before he died on that same island:

> 'I came with two brothers to Farne Island,' he said, 'wishing to speak to the most reverend Father Ethilwald. We were greatly inspired by his discourse, and when we had asked his blessing and were returning homewards, while we were in the middle of the sea, the calm weather that was favouring our crossing suddenly changed. There followed a storm of such ferocity and violence that the sail and oars were useless, as we expected nothing but death. Having struggled unavailingly against the wind and waves for a long time, we looked back to see whether it were practicable to fight our way back to the island we had left, but found the storm equally violent on all sides, so that there was no hope for escape. But as we looked into the distance we saw Father Ethilwald, the beloved of God, come out of his cell on Farne to watch our progress, for he had heard the roar of the gale and raging of the sea, and had come out to discover what would happen to us. When he saw us in distress and despair, he fell on his knees to the Father of our Lord Jesus Christ, and prayed for our safety. Directly his prayer was ended, the raging sea grew calm, the severity of the storm lessened on all sides, and a following wind bore us over the sea toward land. As soon as we reached the shore and dragged our small boat out of the water, the wind that had dropped a while for our sakes at once began to blow again, and continued strongly all that day. So we realised that the short interval of calm had been granted by the mercy of heaven at the prayer of the man of God so that we might escape.'

29 October

Psalm 8   Genesis 1:1-5   John 12:23-28

On the day of Bede's death he was still working, but, too weak to write, had a younger monk take down the words he dictated. The final chapter of the book he was writing was not finished, so the younger brother, Wilbert, said to him, 'Dear master, there is one sentence still unfinished.'

'Very well,' replied Bede, 'write it down.'

Soon the younger man said, 'Now it is finished.'

'You have spoken truly,' affirmed Bede. 'It is well finished.'

30 October

Psalm 88:9-14   1 Kings 8:54-56   Mark 11:25

> A monk once questioned Abbess Samthann about ways of praying. He wondered whether a person should pray lying down, sitting or standing. She replied: 'In every position, a person should pray.'

E.C. Sellner, Wisdom of the Celtic Saints

31 October   All Hallows' Eve *(see p.222)*   Bega *(see p.224)* Reinfrid *(see p.257)*

Psalm 139:7-10   Jeremiah 16:18-20   Ephesians 6:18

> Fervently I pray Thy strong protection:
> hold Thou me firmly in Thy hand.

November
The house that John built

See also 'A litany of saints', p.326.

1 November All Saints *(see p.222)*

Psalm 94:17   Exodus 20:18-21   John 14:1-4

At the Council of Whitby in 664 Colman readily acknowledged not only the fidelity of the brothers from Lindisfarne and their disciples to the teachings of Columba, but that the apostle John had fathered the branch of the Church to which they owed allegiance. The same easy familiarity and respect is present amongst many of us especially in the Northumbria Community when such names as Columba, Brigid or Cuthbert are mentioned.

> This is Jesus, the Carpenter King
> who came from God to show us His heart.
> He died, but returned from the jaws of the grave
> and promised His friends He would always be with them.
> The fire of His love would remain in their heart.
> And this is the House that God built.

2 November

Psalm 25:14   Jeremiah 31:20   Revelation 1:12-18

> This is John the beloved one
> who followed Jesus as the Way,
> embraced the Truth and shared His life;
> and at the supper of the Lord

leaned closer to Him, heard His words;
for those who lean on Jesus' breast
hear the heart of God.
And this was the heart that John heard.

When years had passed, and he was old,
on Patmos island he was held
a prisoner for his love of Christ;
but watching in his lonely cave
he saw the shape of things to come,
of things in heaven and on earth
a Revelation!

Sweet punishment to him – the solitude
that drove him deeper into God,
enfolded by the Spirit till he saw
the Lord with eyes of fire, and hair like wool,
and heard His voice like thundering waterfall:
and this was the heart that John heard.

3 November

Psalm 26:1-2   Jeremiah 31:21   Mark 1:16-18

Repentance

Great Light, thank You for waking me
from my long, selfish sleep.
Lead me, my King.
I am ready to follow.

Stephen Lawhead, Merlin

4 November

Psalm 25:6   Jeremiah 31:3   Mark 1:19-20

The seeking of love

It is possible to search for love and find it. More often, I think, love finds us when we are not even searching ... Love has found us ... we cannot turn it away.

Stephen Lawhead, Merlin

5 November

Psalm 26:3   Jeremiah 31:22   John 13:23

When a man whose marriage was in trouble sought his advice, the Abba said, 'You must learn to listen to your wife.'

The man took this advice to heart and returned after a month to say that he had learned to listen to every word his wife was saying.

Said the Abba with a smile, 'Now go home and listen to every word she isn't saying.'

Anthony de Mello, One Minute Wisdom

6 November   Illtyd *(see p.243)*

Psalm 45:10-11   Micah 4:2-4   Luke 7:44-46

This is an Amma, Desert Mother,
one who left the city's crowds
to find a place of solitude
to seek God only, face to face,
to know her God and to be known
and truly seen,

yet loved and claimed as His,
a warrior who has faced herself
and lived to tell the tale
of love that frees and draws and heals.

She is not alone, for many others
seek the desert and its wisdom, and
as others showed the way of Christ to *them*
so *they* each will show to each who seeks
the Way, by leaning, like beloved John,
on Jesus' breast and listening for His heart.
So many come; so many learn;
so many come to love and lean;
they say,
This is the house that love built.

7 November   Willibrord *(see p.265)*

Psalm 45:12-15   Micah 4:5-8   Luke 8:1-3

To a woman who complained about her destiny the Abba said,
'It is you who make your destiny.'

'But surely I am not responsible for being born a woman?'

'Being a woman isn't destiny. That is fate. Destiny is how you accept your womanhood and what you make of it.'

Anthony de Mello, One Minute Wisdom

8 November

Psalm 45:16-17   Micah 2:12-13   Luke 8:11-21

The Abba, while being gracious to all his disciples, could not conceal his preference for those who lived 'in the world' – the married, the merchants, the farmers – over those who lived in the monastery.

When he was confronted about this he said, 'Spirituality practised in the state of activity is incomparably superior to that practised in the state of withdrawal.'

Anthony de Mello, One Minute Wisdom

9 November

Psalm 111:1-5   2 Kings 6:1-4   Matthew 25:37-40

This is Martin, a soldier's son
who chose to follow Christ instead
and not the gods of war.
He tore his cloak in half, one night,
to wrap some poor uncared-for soul
in warmth and care against the bitter cold.
Next night, in dreams, he heard *in singing*
the voice of heaven saying,
'Martin, you have clothed Me with this cloak.'

At twenty-six he built his first community of hermits,
living simply, loving God;
and this was the life that Martin taught,
and this was the house that love built;
and this was the heart that John heard;
and this was the way that God made.

10 November

Psalm 139:4   Daniel 12:10   Matthew 3:8-11

Ninian returned to Scotland from his travels and studies in Europe. At Whithorn he and a team of skilled builders built a gleaming white stone monastery which was famous throughout the land for education and learning, prayer and mission.

Sometimes he liked to visit the shepherds and herdsmen who tended the flocks and cattle belonging to the monastery. Once he had all the animals gathered into one place so he could pray a blessing on them. Last of all he came to the cattle and with his staff drew around them a circle of protection. Everyone ate, listened to Ninian, then went off to their sleep. The cattle remained, and were noticed by thieves. No wall. No hedge. No ditch. No barking dogs! Just lots of cattle waiting to be carried away!

The thieves rushed inside the circle Ninian had drawn. The bull of the herd rushed at the men, and attacking their leader, pierced his belly with its horns so that the life was torn from him, and so were his entrails. The bull's hoof tore at the earth and dug its imprint into a stone there, so that place became known as 'The Bull's Print'.

Meanwhile, Ninian finishing his prayer came past that place and saw the man lying dead and the other thieves running hither and thither nearby. He prayed to God to restore the man to life and then to health, and ceased not his tears and entreaties till it was so. The other men, his companions, had found themselves unable to leave the confines of the circle, until begging Ninian's forgiveness and being scolded by him he bade them depart. And only then could they cross the circle.

11 November Martin of Tours *(see p.248)*

Psalm 139:5   Daniel 7:9   Matthew 5:14-16

> This is Ninian who went to Rome
> to study the faith, but on his way home
> to Britain visited Martin at Tours,
> and was greatly encouraged, and learnt from his love.
> He raised up in stone a Scottish foundation
> called Candida Casa, the 'White House' no less!
> It gleamed like a beacon, and so did its message
> as Ninian travelled to preach to the people
> the message of love and the kindness of Christ.
> He taught them, as well, to seek God's protection
> by drawing around them a circle of prayer;

and this was the circle that Ninian drew,
and this was the life that Martin taught;
and this was the house that love built;
and this was the heart that John heard;
and this was the way that God made.

12 November

Psalm 139:1   Daniel 11:33-35   Matthew 5:33-37

To the disciples' delight the Abba said he wanted a new shirt for his birthday. The finest cloth was bought. The village tailor came in to have the Abba measured, and promised, by the will of God, to make the shirt within a week.

A week went by and a disciple was despatched to the tailor while the Abba excitedly waited for his shirt. Said the tailor, 'There has been a slight delay. But by the will of God, it will be ready by tomorrow.'

Next day the tailor said 'I'm sorry it isn't done. Try again tomorrow and, if God wills, it will certainly be ready.'

The following day the Abba said, 'Ask him how long it will take if he keeps God out of it.'

Anthony de Mello, One Minute Wisdom

13 November

Psalm 126:1   Exodus 3:2-6   Luke 15:20

This is Patrick, of Cumbria born,
his father and grandfather Christians and priests;
but God has no grandchildren, no hangers-on.
Faith must be *more* than, 'Oh yes, *I* know *that*.'

Patrick was captured and taken for slavery
to Ireland, where always he still dreamed of home
and the prayers of his family, Christ's cross and protection.
And now Patrick prayed like he'd never before!
God heard; he escaped, and came safely to Britain.
Now when he dreamed it was Ireland he saw;
and he knew God had called him to go with the gospel,
to redeem from the darkness her people for God.
The presence of Christ would be his protection:
Christ under, above him, before and behind,
between him and each eye, between him and each word.
He challenged the druids (and some received Jesus)
then family by family won Ireland for Christ.
And this was the prayer that Patrick made;
and this was the circle that Ninian drew,
the life that Martin taught,
that love built,
the heart that John heard,
the way that God made.

14 November

Psalm 127:3-4   Exodus 4:13   Luke 15:28-31

To a visitor who claimed he had no need to search for Truth because he found it in the beliefs of his religion the Abba said:

There once was a student who never became a mathematician because he blindly believed the answers he found at the back of his maths book – and, ironically, the answers were correct.

Anthony de Mello, One Minute Wisdom

15 November

Psalm 131:1-3   Exodus 4:29-31   John 14:8-9

'Every word, every image used for God is a distortion more than a description.'
'Then how does one speak of God?'
'Through Silence.'
'Why, then, do you speak in words?'
At that the Abba laughed uproariously. He said, 'When I speak, you must not listen to the words, my dear. Listen to the Silence.'

Anthony de Mello, One Minute Wisdom

16 November   Celtic Advent Begins *(see p.229)*

Psalm 146:7-8   1 Samuel 25:18, 20, 32   1 John 4:19-21

This is Brigid who loved the poor,
and gave away all she could spare
and would have given everything
if everything was hers to share.

She gave her *love* to God as well.
In her community at Kildare,
all souls were welcome there to feast
on simple food, and ale, and love of Him
who gave unstintingly for us
His love, His heart, His dying blood.
Her *utmost* love was love *returned*.
And this was the way that Brigid lived,
the prayer that Patrick made,
the circle Ninian drew,
the life that Martin taught,
the house that love built,
the heart that John heard,
the way that God made.

17 November   Hild *(see p.291)*

Psalm 119:24   Isaiah 45:15   Romans 8:15-19

Our work in creation

I have not lost my way – it is just that so many ways open
before me that sometimes I hardly know which way to choose.
To decide for one is to decide against another. I never imagined
it would be this hard.

Now you know. The higher a person's call and vision, the more
choices are given them. This is our work in creation: to decide.
And what we decide is woven into the thread of time and being
for ever. Choose wisely, then, but you must choose.

Stephen Lawhead, Merlin

18 November

Psalms 119:26-31; 120:7   Isaiah 48:17-20   Romans 5:1-5

This is Columba who followed the Lord,
and chose to be monk instead of High King;
but when wronged against let his clan become angry,
and bloodshed and war followed swiftly in slaughter.

So, sailing from Ireland, at least he determined
to win for his Lord as many in lives
as the deaths he had caused.
Iona was his harbour, foundation and shortmooring
as tirelessly he laboured to win souls for his Master.
Columba now the gentle, Columba of the church.

And this was the peace Columba found,
the peace of Christ,
the way that Brigid lived,
the prayer that Patrick made,
the circle Ninian drew,

the life that Martin taught,
the house that love built,
the heart that John heard,
the way that God made.

19 November

Psalm 119:32-33   Isaiah 45:18   Romans 8:31

My all-in-all

Great light, mover of all that is moving and at rest, be my journey and my destination, be my want and my fulfilling, be my sowing and my reaping, be my glad song and my stark silence. Be my sword and my strong shield, be my lantern and my dark night, be my everlasting strength and my piteous weakness. Be my greeting and my parting prayer, be my bright vision and my blindness, be my joy and my sharp grief, be my sad death and my sure resurrection!

Stephen Lawhead, Merlin

20 November

Psalm 119:67, 77   Isaiah 49:15-17   Romans 6:1-2, 5

One of the disconcerting – and delightful – teachings of the Abba was: 'God is closer to sinners than to saints.' This is how he explained it:

God in heaven holds each person by a string. When you sin, you cut the string. Then God ties it up again, making a knot – and thereby bringing you a little closer to Him. Again and again your sins cut the string – and with each further knot God keeps drawing you closer and closer.

Anthony de Mello, One Minute Wisdom

21 November

Psalm 5:3   Isaiah 55:4   2 Thessalonians 2:16-17

This is Oswald, who learned to pray
that God would *be* with him in each new day
and when, as king, Northumbria was his,
back to Iona he sent messengers to ask
that someone come without delay
to help him win his people for the Lord.

And this was the work that Oswald loved,
the peace Columba found, the peace of Christ,
the way that Brigid lived,
the prayer that Patrick made,
the circle Ninian drew,
the life that Martin taught,
the house that love built,
the heart that John heard,
the way that God made.

22 November   C.S. Lewis *(see p.247)*

Psalm 112:2, 4-5   Isaiah 58:10-11   Matthew 7:26

This is Aidan, strong and good,
who challenged all to love God more,
believe, and truly follow Him with generous heart;

and this was the message that Aidan lived,
and this was the work that Oswald loved,
the peace Columba found, the peace of Christ,
the way that Brigid lived,
the prayer that Patrick made,
the circle Ninian drew,
the life that Martin taught,
the house that love built,
the heart that John heard,
the way that God made.

23 November Columbanus *(see p.231)*

Psalm 18:46   Isaiah 6:8   Matthew 13:45-46

This is Hild who was challenged by Aidan
to found a rule and live its power,
and influence leaders, and care for the humble,
and be just where God called her to be.

And this was the Yes that Hild said,
the message that Aidan lived,
the work that Oswald loved,
the peace that Columba found, the peace of Christ,
the way that Brigid lived,
the prayer that Patrick made,
the circle Ninian drew,
the life that Martin taught,
the house that love built,
the heart that John heard,
the way that God made.

24 November Eanfleda *(see p.234)*

Psalm 19:1-3   Isaiah 11:2-3   Matthew 13:35

One apostolic characteristic is calling out the gifts of others. The wise leader recognises the importance of being aware of what God is doing, and then co-operating with it. Aidan had done just this with Hild, challenging her to return to Northumbria and trusting God in her to be equal to any eventuality she might face.

When Caedmon suddenly exhibited the ability to compose wonderful songs celebrating God as Saviour and Creator, Hild was eager to encourage, release and commission him to instruct the people through his songs. God in him, and the Spirit upon him, would be equal to the task.

25 November

Psalm 19:4a   Isaiah 27:2-3, 6   Matthew 13:34

The language of the heart

> The surest way to the heart is through song and story ... I do not know why this should be, but I believe it to be true ... Perhaps it is how we are made; perhaps words of truth reach us best through the heart, and stories and songs are the language of the heart.
>
> *Stephen Lawhead*, Merlin

> The shortest distance between a human being and Truth is a story.
>
> *Anthony de Mello*, One Minute Wisdom

26 November

Psalms 17:10; 18:37   Isaiah 5:1-4   Matthew 13:33

Hild and Wilfrid were both intelligent, able and devout Christians. Both had been exposed to Christian teaching and usage more in the Roman tradition before encountering its counterpart in the vibrancy and simplicity of the Celtic Church.

Hild was more than happy to acknowledge her indebtedness to all who had shown her the way of Christ, but openly embraced and sided with the Celtic way. To her way of thinking Wilfrid had been schooled by the best, learning even from Aidan himself on Lindisfarne, but used them only as a stepping-stone on his own journey that led him to embrace the Roman way. He sneered at the Celtic Church's 'ignorance' and 'awkwardness', misrepresenting the issues involved to the king at the Whitby synod, and effectively betrayed those who had raised and sought to nurture him. Hild as a Christian may have had to forgive Wilfrid, but nonetheless did all she could to thwart his further aggrandisement and to block his influence.

27 November

Psalm 115:17-18   2 Kings 2:10-12   Hebrews 13:7

> This is Cuthbert who, watching sheep,
> saw light in the sky as Aidan died.
> He dedicated his life to God
> in prayer,
> in love and solitude.
>
> He sought to reconcile his brothers,
> protecting in his prayer
> the house that John built,
> and Columba taught,
> and the *yes* that Hild said,
> which was the message Aidan lived,
> the work that Oswald loved,
> the way that Brigid lived,
> the prayer that Patrick made,
> the circle Ninian drew,
> the life that Martin taught,
> the house that John built,
> that love built,
> that God made.

28 November

Psalm 36:7-9   Proverbs 17:1   Matthew 7:25

King Oswy needed the Whitby synod to settle once and for all which way Easter should be calculated. A small enough matter, but emotive because of conflicting loyalties involved and declared.

Colman spoke with pride for the Celtic side declaring their loyalty to John the apostle who had ruled that Easter continue to be calculated in accord with Jewish reckoning. It had always been so, and Columba and others before and since had not seen fit to question this. It would do well enough.

Wilfrid, instead of arguing for the expectancy of united practice of some kind, spoke rudely of Columba and deprecatingly of the entire Celtic tradition. His six years on Lindisfarne had apparently not taught him to respect his betters, nor his time away taught him manners.

Instead he employs an ingeniously simplistic argument: 'Peter holds the keys to the kingdom of heaven, yes? And you suggest that the king today make a decision that will honour John in precedence over Peter?'

Oswy the king felt left with no choice. It was not wise for someone who had lived a life that was at best only intermittently holy to risk the displeasure of the door-keeper of heaven itself.

Wilfrid thus in Northumbria brought devastation on much that had been built by Oswald and Aidan in the name of John and Columba. What would remain, or be built again in the same spirit of the gospel?

29 November

Psalm 88:8-9   Proverbs 15:18, 20, 33   Hebrews 12:14-15

So in Northumbria the Church had officially fallen to Roman control and usage. Those who left travelled to Iona and on to Ireland where the Celtic ways persisted in places for hundreds of years.

But those like Hild and Cuthbert, who had supported the Celtic side at the Whitby council but chose to remain in Northumbria, had difficult tasks ahead. For the sake of peace and unity all must conform to the rulings now being introduced. Cuthbert especially would persuade those under his care to embrace ways and regulations he had no innate sympathy for, either.

It is amusing to notice the characteristically uncontrollable aspects of Celtic Christianity appearing through the cracks even after the reorganisation. In later years, for example, Cuthbert is finally persuaded to leave his hermitage on Inner Farne to be a bishop. But he agrees only because it is in line with unfulfilled prophecy in his life. Even then, he has a quiet word with his friend who is Bishop of Lindisfarne, and without consulting anyone else the two men swap bishoprics to keep Cuthbert closer to home. In their generation at least, Roman standardisation may have triumphed, but had certainly not won.

The Wild Goose still flew.

30 November

Psalm 119:65   Proverbs 3:13, 17   Colossians 3:15

So, is there a house that John built – today? Is it being built again? If so, it will be through leaning as beloved John did on the breast of Jesus, through hearing His heart-cry and uniting our hearts with His. It will not be through the establishing of some radical alternative structure that breeds schism or becomes another fast-decaying denomination awaiting fossilisation. It may be through living in a way that is recognisably different, as Hild and Cuthbert and the others did, working in and alongside the structures presented to them – with simplicity and fervour. If the structures fall, so be it – whatever is of lasting value will endure.

As Columba said to his community when he was dying:

See that you be at peace among yourselves,
my children, and love one another.
Follow the example of good men of old,
and God will comfort you and help you
both in this world
and in the world which is to come.

And this was the peace that Columba found:

the peace of Christ.

December
Enter in

These readings are extracted from *Poustinia* by Catherine de Hueck Doherty, used with permission of Fr Robert Wild, Madonna House, Combermere, Ontario. Copies of the book may be obtained from the Northumbria Community (contact details on p.836).

Please note: In a few places the wording of the original text has been altered slightly just to add some explanation or to enable the quotes to stand alone.

1 December   Charles de Foucauld *(see p.229)*

Psalm 27:8   Isaiah 41:17-20   Mark 6:31-32

> I am about to do a new thing; now it springs forth,
> do you not perceive it? I will make a way in the wilderness
> and rivers in the desert.
>
> *Isaiah 43:19*

May the risen Lord lead each of you into the desert of your heart, and speak to you there in His Spirit, and show you there the radiant mercy of His Father's face. Then may He lead you to His brothers and sisters who are everywhere awaiting your love.

2 December   Jean Donovan *(see p.233)*

Psalm 138:1-5   Deuteronomy 32:10-14   Hebrews 11:38

The word 'poustinia' is Russian meaning 'desert'. It is an ordinary word. If I were a little Russian girl, and a teacher during a geography lesson asked me to name a desert, I might say

'Saharskaya Poustinia' – the Sahara Desert. That's all it really means. It also has another connotation, as so many words have. It also means the desert of the Fathers of the Desert, who in ages past went away from everything and settled there. In the Western sense of the word, it would mean a place to which a hermit goes and, hence, it could be called a hermitage. The word to the Russian means much more than a geographical place. It means a quiet, lonely place that people wish to enter, to find God who dwells within them. It also means truly isolated, lonely places to which specially called people go as hermits, and would seek God in solitude, silence and prayer for the rest of their lives.

However, a poustinia was not necessarily completely away from the haunts of men. Some people had reserved, in their homes, a small room to which they went to pray and meditate, which some might call a poustinia. Generally speaking, however, a 'poustinik' (a person dwelling in a poustinia) meant someone in a secluded spot.

It was considered a definite vocation, a call from God to go into the 'desert' to pray to God for one's sins and the sins of the world, also to thank Him for the joys and the gladness and all His gifts.

3 December

Psalm 57:7-11   Song of Songs 4:12, 15   Revelation 7:7-15

It seems strange to say, but what can help modern man find the answers to his own mystery and the mystery of Him in whose image he is created, is *silence, solitude – in a word, the desert*. Modern man needs these things more than the hermits of old.

If we are to witness to Christ in today's marketplaces, we need silence. If we are always to be available, not only physically, but by empathy, sympathy, friendship, understanding and boundless 'caritas', we need silence. To be able to give joyous, unflagging hospitality, not only of house and food, but of mind, heart, body and soul, we need silence.

True silence is the search of any person for God.

True silence is a suspension bridge that a soul in love with God builds across the dark, frightening gullies of its own mind, the strange chasms of temptation, the depthless precipices of its own fears that impede its way to God.

True silence is the speech of lovers. For only love knows its beauty, completeness, and utter joy.

True silence is a garden enclosed, where alone the soul can meet its God. It is a sealed fountain that He alone can unseal to slake the soul's infinite thirst for Him.

4 December

Psalm 89:1-2   Lamentations 2:19   Matthew 6:16

There was no big fuss about going into a poustinia. From some village, from some nobleman's house, from some merchant's house – from any part of our society in Russia – a man would arise. (Of course only God knows *why* he did arise.) He would arise and go into the place (as the Russians say) where heaven meets earth, departing without any earthly goods, usually dressed in the normal dress of a pilgrim. In summertime, this garb was a simple hand-woven shift of linen of the kind ladies wear these days, only it came down to his ankles. It was tied in the middle with an ordinary cord. He took along a linen bag, a loaf of bread, some salt, a gourd of water. Thus he departed, after, of course, taking leave of everyone in the household or in the village. Some didn't even do this. They just stole away at dawn or in the dark of the night leaving a message that they had gone on a pilgrimage and maybe would find a poustinia to pray to God for their sins and the sins of the world, to atone, to fast, to live in poverty and to enter the great silence of God.

5 December

Psalm 16   Isaiah 58:6-12   Revelation 21:1-7

True silence is a key to the immense and flaming heart of God. It is the beginning of a divine courtship that will end only in the immense, creative, fruitful, loving silence of final union with the Beloved.

Yes, such silence is holy, a prayer beyond all prayers, leading to the final prayer of constant presence of God, to the heights of contemplation, when the soul, finally at peace, lives by the will of Him whom she loves totally, utterly and completely.

This silence, then, will break forth in a charity that overflows in the service of the neighbour without counting the cost. It will witness to Christ anywhere, always.

Availability will become delightsome and easy, for in each person the soul will see the face of her Love.

Hospitality will be deep and real, for a silent heart is a loving heart, and a loving heart is a hospice to the world.

6 December

Psalm 48:1-3, 8-14   Jeremiah 1:4-9   Mark 9:9-27

Then one of the seraphs flew to me, holding a live coal that had been taken from the altar with a pair of tongs. The seraph touched my mouth with it and said: 'Now that this has touched your lips, your guilt has departed and your sin is blotted out.' Then I heard the voice of the Lord saying, 'Whom shall I send, and who will go for us?' And I said, 'Here am I; send me!'

Isaiah 6:6-8

Who were these men and women of Russia? Why did they go into 'the desert'? Who were they spiritually?

They were people who craved in their hearts to be alone with God and His immense silence.

The mountain of God's silence – covered with the cloud of His mysterious presence – called these future poustinikki in that awesome yet loving way.

To go into the poustinia means to listen to God. It means entering into *kenosis* – the emptying of oneself. This emptying of oneself, even as Christ emptied Himself for us, is really a climbing of this awesome mountain right to the very top where God abides in His warm silence. It also means to know 'how terrible it is to fall into the hands of the living God' ... and yet how delightful, how joyful, and how attractive! So attractive, in fact, that the soul cannot resist. That is why the Russians say that he who is called to the poustinia must go there or die because God has called him to this mountain to speak to him in that awesome silence, in that gentle, loving silence. For God has something to say to those whom He calls to the poustinia, and what God says to them the poustinikki must repeat as a prophet does.

Humanly and psychologically speaking he is reluctant to speak, as every prophet was reluctant; but to him too comes the angel with the coal of fire, that invisible angel that cleanses his mind, his mouth, and his lips (symbolically speaking) and watches that man or woman arise and start on this awesome pilgrimage.

7 December   Diuma *(see p.232)*

Psalm 107:4-5   1 Kings 19:9-13   Mark 1:35

Silence is not the exclusive prerogative of monasteries or convents. Simple, prayerful silence is everybody's silence – or if it isn't, it should be. It belongs to every Christian who loves God, to every Jew who has heard the echoes of God's voice in his prophets, to everyone whose soul has risen in search of truth, in search of God. For where noise is – inward noise and confusion – there God is not!

Deserts, silence, solitudes *are not necessarily places but states of mind and heart*. These deserts can be found in the midst of the city, and in the everyday of our lives. We need only to look for them and realise our tremendous need for them. They will be small solitudes, little deserts, tiny pools of silence, but the experience they will bring, if we are disposed to enter them, may be as exultant and as holy as all the deserts of the world, even the one God Himself entered.

For it is God who makes solitude, deserts, and silences holy.

8 December

Psalm 119:97-106   Daniel 2:1-23   Luke 2:19

> He said to me, 'Mortal, eat this scroll that I give you and fill your stomach with it.' Then I ate it; and in my mouth it was as sweet as honey.
>
> *Ezekiel 3:3*

Into the poustinia the poustiniks brought one book only – the Bible. They read it on their knees, impervious to or even perhaps uninterested in any purely academic question. To them the Bible was the incarnation of the Word and they felt a lifetime wasn't enough in which to read it. Every time they opened it they believed with a tremendous deep faith that they were face to face with the Word.

Yes, the poustinik reads the Bible on his knees. He doesn't read it with his head (conceptually, critically) except in the sense that the words pass through his intelligence, but the intelligence of the poustinik is in his heart. The words of the Bible are like honey on his tongue. He reads them in deep faith. He doesn't analyse them, he reads them and allows them to stay in his heart. He may read only one or two sentences or maybe a single page in one day. The point is that he puts them all in his heart like Mary did. He lets them take root in his heart and waits for God to come and explain them which inevitably He will do when He finds such deep and complete faith.

9 December

Psalm 89:8-16   Lamentations 3:40-41   Galatians 5:18-25

Deserts, silence, solitude.

For a soul that realises the tremendous need of all three, opportunities present themselves in the midst of the congested trappings of all the world's immense cities. But how, really, can one achieve such solitude?

By standing still!

Stand still, and allow the strange, deadly restlessness of our tragic age to fall away like the worn-out, dusty cloak that it is – a cloak that was once considered beautiful. The restlessness was considered the magic carpet to tomorrow, but now in reality we see it for what it is: a running away from oneself, a turning from that journey inward that all men must undertake to meet God dwelling within the depths of their souls.

Stand still, and look deep into the motivations of life.

Stand still, and lifting your hearts and hands to God pray that the mighty wind of His Holy Spirit may clear all the cobwebs of fears, selfishness, greed, narrow-heartedness away from the soul: that His tongues of flame may descend to give courage to begin again.

10 December

Psalm 63:1-7   Isaiah 61:8-9   Matthew 6:5-6

From the moment their poustinia was built, from the moment of their closing its door upon themselves, not only they but the whole of humanity entered into that cabin with them.

When he closed the door for the first time he entered the very essence of the novitiate of God's love, for in this wondrous, extraordinary, awesome, beautiful, tremulous silence of God he would learn to know who God is.

God would reveal Himself to the poustinik in a fullness that He rarely communicates even to those who live in a religious community.

Everyone is a pilgrim on the road of life. Some – and there are more than we know of – are like the poustinikki, truly seeking the Absolute – God!

So I think the poustinia will begin slowly to attract many such people who will arise now here, now there ... and go seeking to find a place where they can enter into the silence of God and meet his Word – Christ – in that silence.

11 December   Thomas Merton *(see p.251)*

Psalm 5:4-5, 8-12   Exodus 19:1-9, 17-20   Romans 16:25-27

Thus the hermit, the poustinik, learns to know God. Not learn *about* Him, but learn *of God Himself through God Himself*.

For in the tremendous silence into which this poustinik entered, God reveals Himself to those who wait for that revelation and who don't try to 'tear at the hem of a mystery' forcing disclosure.

Now the poustinik lies prostrated, waiting for God to explain, as God did to the disciples of Emmaus, whatever God wants to explain to him. All he knows is that his heart too will burn within him as did the hearts of those disciples.

12 December Finnian of Clonard *(see p.238)*

Psalm 127:1   1 Chronicles 17:4-10   Mark 1:17

The person who follows the call to the poustinia and who leaves everything behind relies on the help of others. He becomes in reality a beggar. In Russia, when a village knew that a hermit was going to dwell in some abandoned hut, or one that he would come to beg them to help to build, they were glad. It meant that there was someone praying for them.

So the poustinik usually selected a secluded spot in a clearing in the woods. The hermit really sought the hidden places of his world – mountains, forests, woods – places where he was really alone with God.

Thus his human horizons were somewhat limited so that his spiritual horizons could grow without distractions.

13 December

Psalm 118:19-29   1 Kings 17:7-16   Matthew 7:8

I have set before you an open door.

Revelation 3:8

The poustinik also occupied himself with some work, like weaving baskets. People came to visit him, for a Russian hermit has no lock or latch on his door except against the wind. Anyone at any time of day or night can knock at his door. Remember, he is in the poustinia not for himself but for others. He is a connecting bridge between people and God and God and the people, and God speaks through him. The East believes that the poustinik is such a channel, so they come to him, and he must always be available.

He also must share food with anyone that comes. They may refuse, but it must always be offered. He may just have a piece of bread, but he will break it in half or into as many parts as there are people. Thus the second aspect of this strange life is hospitality, the sharing of what he has, the offering of it at any moment.

Hospitality above all means that the poustinik is just passing on whatever God has put into his empty hands.

He gives all that he has, and is:
words, works, himself, and his food.

14 December   John of the Cross *(see p.243)*
Catherine de Hueck Doherty *(see p.232)*

Psalm 34:6   Deuteronomy 15:16-17   Matthew 25:5-7

He gives of His works

A poustinik lives not far from a village. It is hay-making time, the weather turns stormy, and his help is asked. Immediately the poustinik drops everything or anything he might be in the middle of doing – prayer, garden, reading, whatever it may be – and spends all his time on the hay.

For we believe in Russia that if I touch God I must touch humanity, for there is really no distinction. Christ incarnated Himself and became man, so I must, like Christ Himself, be a person of the towel and the water. That is to say, wash other people's feet as Christ did, and washing other people's feet means service.

I cannot pray if I don't serve my brother. I cannot pray to the God who incarnated Himself when my brother is in need. It is an impossibility. It would be like the priest, the Levite, who passed the man beset with robbers, and that I cannot do.

So sometimes a poustinik might spend a month, six weeks, working for the various needs of the villagers and never think even for one minute about the fact that he is supposed to be in a poustinia, reading the Bible, or praying, because *he is in the poustinia of his heart always*, especially when serving others.

15 December

Psalm 132:16   Micah 6:6-8   Matthew 18:1-5

If you ever see a *sad* hermit or poustinik, then he is no hermit at all. The most joyous persons in Russia are the ones who have the eyes of a child at 70 and who are filled with the joy of the Lord, for they who have entered the silence of God are filled with God's joy. Yes, the life of a poustinik should be truly joyous with the quiet joy of the Lord and this will be visible. He will have the eyes of a child even if his face is old. You cannot fool people as to such things as the presence of love and joy in a human being.

16 December

Psalm 4:8   Genesis 28:10-22   Matthew 8:20

The poustinia must be almost stark in its simplicity and poverty. It must contain a table and a chair. On the table there must be a Bible. There should also be a pencil and some paper. In one corner area a basin and pitcher for washing up. The bed, if bed there be, should be a cot with wooden slats instead of a mattress, a couple of blankets or quilts and a pillow if absolutely necessary. This is all that should be offered in the way of bedding. Drinking water, a loaf of bread, which will be divided into three parts, one for breakfast, one for lunch and one for dinner. For those not accustomed to eating their bread with water, there are the makings for tea and coffee.

Prominent in the poustinia is a cross without a corpus, about six feet by three feet, which is nailed to the wall, and an icon of Our Lady in the eastern corner with a vigil light in front of it.

The cross without a corpus is a symbol of one's own crucifixion on it, for those of us who love Christ passionately want to be crucified with Him so as to know the joy of His resurrection.

17 December Antiphon Day *(see p.223)*

Psalm 139:15-16   1 Kings 9:1-3   Hebrews 8:10-11

The poustinia can never simply be a place of rest – sleeping, recreation, a 'change of pace'. The poustinia is a holy place, so holy that one trembles when one enters. It is not an eating place, nor a sleeping place. It is God's place.

The desert, of course, is the symbol of austerity, poverty, and utter simplicity. It is God who leads the soul to the desert, and the soul cannot remain in the desert long unless it is nourished by God. Therefore, it is a place where we fast from bodily food and even spiritual food, such as reading all kinds of books, for we enter there to meet our God with the only book in which He is fully accessible: the Bible.

Let your poustinia be a quiet, secret garden enclosed, for it is a hallowed place, a holy place where the soul enters to meet its God.

18 December Samthann *(see p.260)*

Psalm 131   Ezekiel 11:5   2 Corinthians 3:12-16

The one who goes to the poustinia for the first time will experience a certain amount of interior noise.

The first time one of the staff went she said to me on returning, 'Boy, that was a terrible experience! You know what happened to me?'

I said, 'Yes, I think I do. But tell me anyway.'

She said, 'All my thoughts buzzed in me like flies. I was thinking that my jeans needed stitching, that the garden needed weeding. I thought about everything except God.'

I said, 'Oh, that's perfectly natural.'

It takes a long time for the person of today to close the wings of his intellect and to open the door of his heart.

19 December

Psalm 95:8-9   Deuteronomy 7:17-24   Hebrews 2:14-18

At all costs the desert must be a place of utter simplicity. No books, no curtains, no pictures, except for an icon. And don't let us kid ourselves into thinking a poustinia must always be in the country, must always be a log house, or a shingled farmhouse. No, this would be a false idea of the poustinia – the desert – for the desert, the poustinia can be located everywhere, for fundamentally it is interiorised. If you have a spare room in the house or a large closet, it will do.

Truly the desert will strip you. The Lord of the desert will do that, too. Truly you will be tempted even as He was tempted. You will suffer as He has suffered, but you will also be filled with tranquillity – the tranquillity of God's order.

20 December

Psalm 17:1-2   Proverbs 3:3-6   John 13:23-25

For those of you who go into the poustinia, this is the essence of it:

> to fold the wings of your intellect.

In the civilisation of the West everything is sifted through your heads. You are so intellectual, so full of knowledge of all kinds. The poustinia brings you into contact first and foremost with solitude. Secondly, it brings you in contact with God. Even if you don't feel anything at all, the fact remains that you have come to have a date with God, a very special rendezvous. You have said to the Lord,

'Lord, I want to take this 24, 36, 48 hours out of my busy life and I want to come to You because I am very tired. The world is not as You want it, and neither am I. I want to come and rest on Your breast as St John the Beloved.

'That is why I have come to this place.'

21 December

Psalm 132:7-9   Leviticus 25:17   John 13:33-34

The West values itself for its ability to produce things. Priests, nuns and lay people tend to evaluate themselves interiorly by what they *produce*. Priests especially do not realise that their presence is enough. I often tell priests who work in parishes that one of the best things they can 'do' is simply walk around their neighbourhoods and be present to their people. If they don't do something, they feel that they are wasting their lives away. So it is with the poustinik. There is an inability to realise that the presence of a person who is in love with God is enough, and that nothing else is needed. That doesn't mean that the poustinik's assistance in definite ways cannot be helpful to the community. But it does mean that one should be perfectly at peace even (should I say especially?) when one hasn't got 'something to do'.

22 December

Psalm 37:4-7a   Song of Songs 8:6-7   1 Thessalonians 3:6-10

Prayer is the source and the most intimate part of our lives. The life of prayer – its intensity, its depth, its rhythm – is the measure of our spiritual health, and reveals to us ourselves. With the ascetics, the desert is interiorised, and signifies the concentration of a recollected spirit. At this level, where man knows how to be silent, true prayer is found. Here he is mysteriously visited.

There should be no break in our prayer. Why should my heart be removed from God just because I am talking to you? When you are in love with someone, it seems the face of the beloved is before you when you drive, when you type, and so on. Prayer is like that. If you fall in love, then it is impossible to separate life and breath from prayer. Prayer is simply union with God. Prayer does not need words. When people are in love they look at each other, look into each other's eyes, or a wife simply lies in the arms of her husband. Neither of them talks. When love reaches its apex it cannot be expressed anymore. It has reached that immense realm of silence where it pulsates and reaches proportions unknown to those who haven't entered into it. Such is the life of prayer with God. You enter into God and God enters into you, and the union is constant.

23 December

Psalm 119:105   Proverbs 6:23   Revelation 4:4-10

The call to be a poustinia in the marketplace

'Go into the marketplace and stay with Me. Be a light to your neighbour's feet. Go without fear into the depth of men's hearts. I shall be with you. Pray always. I shall be your rest.'

The face of this apostolate, this call, would be to daily reveal more and more the face of Christ. The face of this apostolate would be Nazareth. Nazareth, where He spent His hidden life. Nazareth, where the days were humdrum and ordinary, where no visible results were forthcoming except tables and chairs.

Nazareth, where the Son of God was simply the son of Mary and Joseph to all the people around him. Nazareth, where He lived as we will have to live, in the company of Mary and Joseph, and from them learn the silence of the heart. Nazareth, the preparation of His entrance into the desert, which was already a kind of desert situated in a small village of Galilee.

Our house of prayer in the marketplace would continue to intensify its very ordinariness and simplicity, bearing with people who will not understand why they are *producing so little*. They will have to accept the fact that people will say of them what others said of Jesus:

'Can anything good come out of Nazareth?'

Through their prayerful, hidden and seemingly unproductive life, God will prepare those involved in the house of prayer for new contacts and new works according to *His* plan and not *theirs*. Subtle temptations will come as the devil will try to twist the meaning of their vocation. He will suggest how impossible it is to form a community of love, to really become a poustinia in the market place with its door open. The essence of such a house will be that its members really bear with one another,

and cover themselves with humility, compassion and love
toward one another. The devil will attack with all sorts of logical
arguments and prove that it is *just not possible*.

24 December   Christmas Eve *(see p.112)*

Psalm 22:24   1 Samuel 3:1-10   Acts 9:3-19

The poustinia in the marketplace begins with prayer, much
prayer. It does not mean that you are not doing the work
you have been doing. No. But you must understand that the
poustinia *begins in your heart*. It is not a place, a geographical
spot. It is not first and foremost a house or a room. It is within
your heart. It is implementing the prayer of St Francis. That is
the work of the poustinik in the marketplace, to be hidden as
Christ was hidden in Nazareth.

When this work of the Holy Spirit is really allowed to take place
in a human heart, the person is utterly indifferent as to where
geographically he is situated. It is possible to live in a lovely
house while inwardly, spiritually, you are clad like John the
Baptist in animal skins and eating locusts and wild honey.

If this inner poustinia, this stripping of oneself, this kenosis,
is begun, it means that you kneel before the Lord and say,

'Here I am, Lord, do with me as You will. Speak for Your servant
is listening. Lord, I thank You for all You have given me, for all
You have taken away from me, for all You have left me.'

When you have done that, you will have begun to understand
the poustinia in the marketplace.

25 December Christmas Day *(see p.114)*

Psalm 145   Ezekiel 36:38   Luke 17:20-21

Suppose that you were married and became pregnant. Would you stop cooking for your husband? Would you stop doing the laundry, the cleaning, stop going to meetings on racial justice and school affairs? No. You'd go about your daily business. The only difference between you and everyone else would be that you were carrying a child. Your womb is a poustinia for the child, and you carry him wherever you go. Wherever you go you are pregnant with Christ, and you bring His presence as you would bring the presence of a natural child. For when a woman is with child, people give her special attention. They smile, they offer her a comfortable place to sit down. She is a witness to life. She carries life around with her.

I don't know if I have succeeded in giving you a clearer idea of what this kind of poustinia of the marketplace is. It is not a matter of retiring to a basement! You live in the marketplace and carry the poustinia within you. That is your vocation. You are pregnant with Christ. You are Christ-bearers. You are poustinia bearers.

Where? In the marketplace.

To whom? To anyone whom you meet there, but especially to those you are mandated to be with.

This eliminates, I hope, all notions of being recluses, of withdrawing from the marketplace.

26 December Stephen *(see p.260)*

Psalm 86:1-12   Ecclesiastes 1:10-11   John 11:5-7

We must follow Christ in the rhythm of His own life, the rhythm of solitude and action. What is needed in our days is to retire to solitude and silence, to hear the voice of God, to glorify

Him and pray to Him, and then to return to the secular world. Tragically the West keeps brushing this aside and saying,

'Yes, that's basically true – but let's get down to action!'

27 December John the Beloved *(see p.244)*

Psalm 105:42-45   Nehemiah 2:17-18   Philemon 20-21

If a Russian built a poustinia next to the village, he automatically knows that he is part of that village. He doesn't have to be told that he is now part of that community.

Being part of the community is not a matter of geography.

If your spiritual director says that you should spend three days in the poustinia, you spend three days. If he thinks you should spend four, you spend four. If he thinks you should come out of the poustinia for a while altogether, you come out. *Wherever you are in obedience, you are part of the community.* It is not a matter of being inside or outside the poustinia.

28 December Holy Innocents *(see p.241)*

Psalm 41:1-12   Genesis 3:8-10   1 Corinthians 13:12

Poustinia in the hospital – October 21, 1973

A room, a bed, two chairs:
stark, naked room of pain,
a room set all apart
for just that pain, in a desert more real
than the deserts of sand and heat.
Poustinias indeed where man meets his God,
face to face,
    both crucified.
Gone are all subterfuges, excuses, rationalisations.

Now man enters into the truth of God.
All his masks are torn and man becomes
what he truly is.
Poustinias in a hospital of Golgotha
on which the crucified God is planted
in the midst of crucified men.
Now is the moment of meeting.
Now is the moment of speaking.
But no words are needed in
the poustinia of a hospital room.
Only the steps of the Father
and the light
of the Spirit
that comes
like a gentle breeze
in the spring,
consoling,
assuaging,
making clear
all that was unclear
so that
in a stark,
naked
room of pain
joy enters.
The sick arise
and dance with Christ.

29 December

Psalm 23   Genesis 5:21-24   Revelation 3:1-6

As I sit here and try to rethink and meditate on what I have written about the poustinia, I honestly wonder if I can say 'Amen' just yet. My purpose was to explain the poustinia vocation as found in Russia, in my own life and in the life of the Madonna House. But, when you come right down to it, the poustinia is not a place at all – and yet it is. It is a stage, a vocation, belonging to all Christians by baptism.

It is a vocation to be a contemplative.

There will always be 'solitaries', or should be. But the essence of the poustinia is that it is a place within oneself, a result of baptism, where each of us contemplates the Trinity. Within my heart, within me, I am or should be constantly in the presence of God. This is another way of saying that I live in a garden enclosed where I walk and talk with God (though a Russian would say 'where all in me is silent and where I am immersed in the silence of God'). It's as if I were sitting next to God in complete silence, although there are always many other people around. (Like a husband and wife being in a private silence and solitude even though they are at a party and the room is filled with people.)

How stumbling words are! How inadequate the similes! Yet the poustinia is something like this to me: a state of contemplating God in silence.

30 December

Psalm 39:1-3   Deuteronomy 11:18   John 1:1-18

The poustinia is within, and one is forever immersed in the silence of God, forever listening to the word of God, forever repeating it to others in word and deed. Thus everything that I have said about the physical poustinia, about trying to adapt it to the West, can be said about every Christian everywhere. The poustinia is this inner solitude, this inner immersion in the silence of God. It is through this inner, total identification with humanity and with Christ that every Christian should be living in a state of contemplation. This is the poustinia within oneself.

I don't know if all this makes any sense. It does to me. It is only in identifying with Christ, it is only by plunging into the great silence of God within myself, that I can love others and identify with them.

It is by listening to the great silence of God, and having this strange, passive dialogue in which I become aware of the silence which is the speech of God – it is only by listening to this that I am able to speak to my brother. It is only by listening to this silence that I can acquire the ingenuity of love, the delicacy of Christ in my human relationships.

In this silence I become identified with Christ, I acquire a listening heart.

31 December John Wycliffe *(see p.265)*

Psalm 97:1-6   Exodus 3:1-6   Acts 2:1-11, 16-21

The poustinia is a state of constantly being in the presence of God because one desires Him with a great desire, because in Him alone one can rest. The poustinia is walking in this inner solitude, immersed in the silence of God. My life of service and love to my fellowman is simply the echo of this silence and solitude.

Inwardly I identify myself with God and with humanity. Jesus Christ Himself conducts me into this inner silence, into that solitude which speaks so loudly to the Father under the guidance of the Holy Spirit.

Now I am immersed in the Trinity, in the fire of the silence of God (for the silence of God is always fire; His speech is fire). Now I become as one on fire with love of Him and of all humanity across the world. Now it is not I who speak. I speak what God tells me to speak. When my immersion into this immense silence has finally caught fire from His words, then I am able to speak. I can speak because His voice is sounding loudly and clearly in my ears, which have been emptied of everything except Him.

Now only His name is on my heart, constantly; it has become my heartbeat.

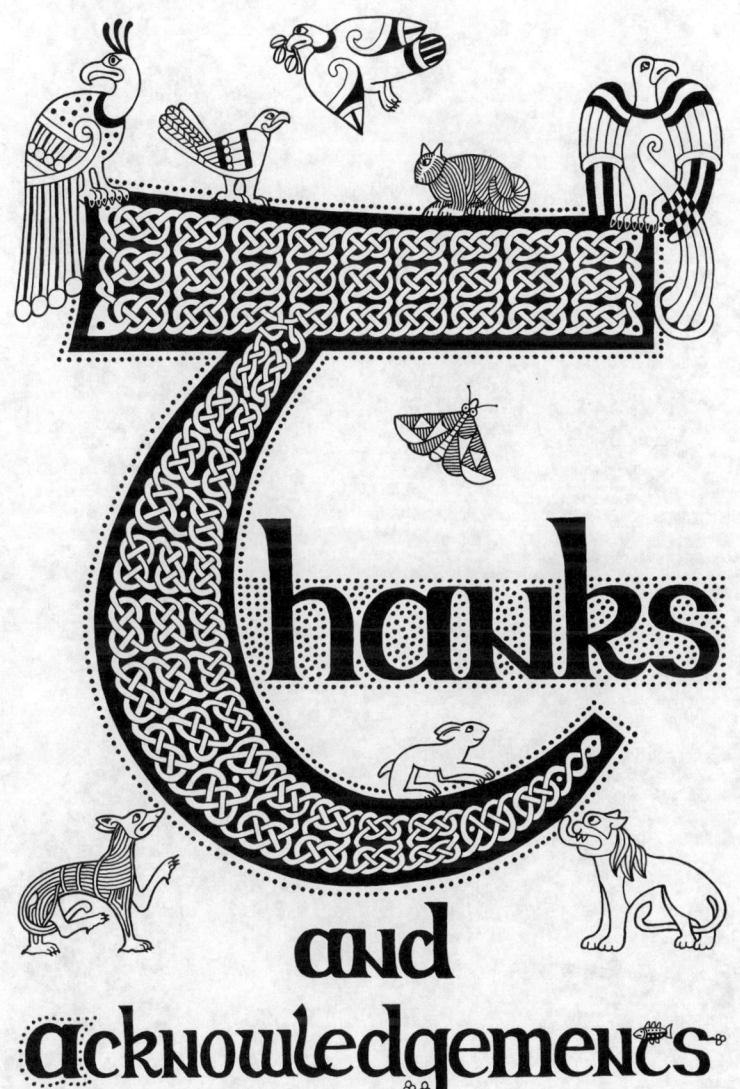

Thanks and Acknowledgements

CROSS-REFERENCES

This list of cross references is intended to help you find material relating to the saints, festivals of the church year and other topics, across both volumes of *Celtic Daily Prayer*. The two volumes are numbered continuously; page numbers i–836 are to be found in *Celtic Daily Prayer Book One: The Journey Begins*, and page numbers 837–1668 in *Celtic Daily Prayer Book Two: Farther Up and Farther In*.

Where the referenced material is found in the daily readings, only the name and date of the year of readings is given. The Aidan and Finan readings are in *Celtic Daily Prayer Book One: The Journey Begins*. The Colman and Eata readings are in *Celtic Daily Prayer Book Two: Farther Up and Farther In*.

Adamnan
Calendar, p.218
Biography, p.221
Finan readings, 29 Sept.
Peace, p.1066

Advent
Advent, Celtic, Calendar, p. 219
Advent, p.105 and p.985
Leading up to Christmas, p.207
Advent antiphons, p.108
Advent reflection, prayers and candle liturgy, p.985
Colman readings, 1–25 Dec.

Ageing (see also Mid-life)
Prayer from an older Companion, p.1037
Eata readings, 25, 27 July

Aidan
Calendar, p.217
Biography, p.57, 282
Meditation Day 16, p.41 and p.896
The Aidan Compline, p.57 and p.911
Introduction to Oswald – in practical ways, p.277
Aidan – in the power of the Spirit, p.282
Aidan readings 15, 18 Jan.; 16–18, 20–22 Mar.; 3 May; 1–12, 13–16 Sept.
Finan readings, 19, 23, 25 May; 15 July; 1, 9 Sept.; 4, 7 Oct.
Introduction to Follow the Example, p.1097
Peace, p.1066
Aldwin – in following the example of good men and women of old, p.1136
Colman readings, Intro.; 28 Feb.; 3, 5,

11, 15–18, 20–24 May; 17–20 Oct.
Eata readings, 13–14 July; 13–18 Sept.

Aldwin
Calendar, p.215
Biography, p.221
Meditation Day 10, p.892
Meditation Day 12, p.893
Aldwin – in following the example of good men and women of old, p.1136
Colman readings, 29 Jan.; 5, 7–9, 11, 13–16, 21–23, 26–29 Feb.; 3, 11 May; 31 Oct.

All Hallows' Eve
Calendar, p.218
Michael and All Angels, Calendar, p.218
Biography, pp.222, 251
'A confession of faith' in Coming into the light – rebirth, p.174
Light a candle in the darkness, p.121
Aidan readings, 5 Mar.
Michael liturgy – in joyful vigil and contesting against evil, p.1005
Reinfrid – in search of peace, p.1134

All Saints' Day
Calendar, p.219
Biography, p.222
A litany of saints, p.326
Light a candle in the darkness, p.121
A Hebridean grace, p.205
Introduction to Follow the example, p.1097

Angels, Michael and All
(see Michael)

Antiphon Day
Calendar, p.220
Advent Antiphons, p.108

Antony of Egypt
Calendar, p.213
Biography p.223
Aidan readings, 3, 7 June
Finan readings, 27 Sept.
Colman readings intro., 2, 9–10 June; 23 Oct.
Eata readings, 16 Aug.; Intro., 1–30 Nov.

Arimathea, Joseph of
(see Joseph)

Arthur Burt (see under B)

Ascension
Ascension, p.157
Aidan readings, 10 July

Assisi, Clare of (see Clare)

Assisi, Francis of (see Francis)

Aurelian, Paul (see under P)

Avila, Teresa of (see Teresa)

Baldred
Calendar, p.214
Biography, p.223

Baptism
Coming into the light – rebirth, p.174
For infant baptism see Christening.

Bartholomew of Farne
Calendar, p.216
Biography, p.223

Bede
Calendar, p.216
Biography, p.224
Finan readings, 29 Oct.
Before studying, p.1061

CROSS-REFERENCES   815

Aldwin – in following the example of good men and women of old, p.1136
Colman readings 5, 13, 21, 23, 26, 29, Feb.; 3 Mar.; 3, 11, May; 31 Oct.

Bega (sometimes spelled Begu)

Calendar, p.219
Biography, p.224
Finan readings, 30 May
Reinfrid – in search of peace, p.1134
Aldwin – in following the example of good men and women of old, p.1136

Bereavement

Walking with grief, p.190
Come now, p.191
A Caim, p.192
Aidan readings, 21 May; 27 Nov.
Caelan liturgy, p.192
Into my grieving, p.1050
In remembrance of a good mother, p.1051
When memories hold mixed emotions, p.1052
Taking courage, p.1053

Billifrith

Calendar, p.214
Biography, p.225

Birth

Coming into the light – birth, p.169
A blessing on a child, p.201
Just you, p.201
Child of calmer waters, p.1013
Prayer at a dedication or Christening, p.1014

Blessings

Ninian – in relating to the whole of life. A call to bless, p.318
Prayers for Blessing, p.199
Finan readings, 12 Sept.
Blessings, p.200
Colman readings, 10 Oct.

Boisil

Calendar, p.216
Biography, p.225
The Boisil Compline, p.68 and p.939
Colman readings, 22 Feb.; 22 Oct.

Bonhoeffer, Dietrich

Calendar, p.215
Biography, p.225
Finan readings, 11–12 Mar.
Eata readings, 4 Apr.

Boy to Man

About growing out of the father-wound, p.1014

Brendan

Calendar, p.216
Biography, p.226, 302
Brendan – in exploration of a vision, p.302
Aidan readings, 29 July
Finan readings, 10 Oct.
Small boat, great big sea Communion, p.955
Colman readings, 2 July; 25 Oct.
Eata readings, 14 Apr; 30 July

Brigid

Calendar, p.213
Biography, p.267
Brigid – in welcoming, p.267
Brigid's grace, p.205
Aidan readings, 21 Sept.
Finan readings, 1 Feb.; 9, 17, 31 May; 16 Nov.
A pub blessing, p.1091
Colman readings, 11 Mar.; 11 May; 13 Oct.
Eata readings, 26 July

Brokenness

A prayer in brokenness, p.181
The other side of pain (2nd stanza), p.1038

Brother Charles of Jesus
(see Charles)

Brother Roger of Taizé
(see Roger)

Burt, Arthur
Calendar, p.217
Biography, p.226
Aidan readings, 18 Feb.; Intro. June;
19, 27 Oct.

Cadoc (Cadog)
Calendar, p.218
Biography, p.227
Colman readings, 6–7 Mar.; 1, 7 July

Caedmon
Calendar, p.213
Biography, p.321
Caedmon – in declaration of a dream,
p.321
Finan readings, 24 May; 20 Oct.;
24 Nov.
Aldwin – in following the example of
good men and women of old, p.1136

Caim
Ninian – in relating to the whole of
life, p.318
A Caim, p.192
Caim prayer, p.203

Calcutta, Teresa of
(see Teresa)

Canaire
Calendar, p.213
Biography, p.228
Finan readings, 7 Oct.; 7 Nov.
Introduction to Follow the Example,
p.1097
Canaire – in celebration of woman,
p.1106

Cassian, John
Calendar, p.216
Biography, p.228
Finan readings, 10, 21 Mar.
Eata readings, 13 Feb.; 10, 12, 18 Aug.

Catherine de Hueck
(see Doherty)

Catherine de Hueck
Doherty (see under D)

Catherine Doherty
(see under D)

Cedd
Calendar, p.218
Biography, p.229
Cedd – in reflecting honestly,
p.1117
Colman readings, 18, 20 Feb.; 24 May;
Eata readings, Intro., 16–18 Sept.

Celibacy
Liturgy for a commitment to celibacy,
p.1023

Celtic Advent
Calendar, p.219
Biography, p.229
Advent, p.105 and p.985
Leading up to Christmas, p.207
A prayer in the preparation days of
Celtic Advent, p.989

Chad
Calendar, p.214
Biography, p.286
Chad – in willing service, p.286
Aidan readings, 22–23 Mar.
Colman readings, 18, 20 Feb.
Eata readings, Intro., 16–18 Sept.

Charles de Foucauld

Calendar, p.219
Biography, p.229
Meditation Day 4, p.29
Finan readings, 1–30 Apr.
Prayer of Abandonment, in Service of Healing with Eucharist, p.981
Introduction to Follow the Example, p.1097
Charles de Foucauld – in serving and stillness, p.1141
Eata readings, 30 Jan.

Charles of Jesus (see Charles de Foucauld)

Christening

Coming into the light – birth, p.169
A blessing on a child, p.201
Just you, p.201
Caelan liturgy, p.192
Child of calmer waters, p.1013
Prayer at a dedication or Christening, p.1014

Christmas Day

Calendar, p.220
Before a crib, p.108
After midnight, p.113
After it has grown light, p.114
Colman readings, 25 Dec.

Christmas Eve

Calendar, p.220
Before a crib, p.108
Christmas Eve, the long night, p.112
Leading up to Christmas, p.207
After midnight, p.113
Colman readings, 24 Dec.

Clare

Calendar, p.217
Biography, p.230
Aidan readings, 14 July; 23 Dec.
Finan readings, 18 Mar.

Clonard, Finnian of
(see Finnian)

Colman

Calendar, p.214
Biography, p.230
Finan readings, 8, 17, 22 May; 28–29 Sept.; 28 Nov.
Colman – in disappointment and the death of a vision, p.1121
Colman readings, Intro.; 24 May; 6 July; 21 Oct.

Columba

Calendar, p.216
Biography, p.230
Columba's blessing from Evening Prayer, p.25 and p.885
For a journey, p.200
Aidan readings, 11–13, Mar.; 18 July; 2–9, 11–17, 26, 29–31 Aug.; 15 Oct.
Finan readings, 19 Feb.; 5, 26 Sept.; 4, 9, 13, Oct.; 18 Nov.
Colman readings, 8 Jan.; 11 May; Intro., 2, 4, 6–8, 10–19, 22–31 July; 14–15 Oct.

Columbanus

Calendar, p.219
Biography, p.231
Finan readings, 1–31 May; 29 Sept.; 4 Oct.
Eata readings, 29 Feb.; 1–31 Mar.; 22 July

Columcille (see Columba)

Comgall

Calendar, p.215
Biography, p.231
Aidan readings, 6 Aug.
Finan readings, 23 Sept.
Colman readings, 6 July

Communion

Holy Communion, p.75 and p.947
Around a Table: a Family Breaking of Bread, p.950
Small boat, great big sea Communion, p.955
Celtic Communion Liturgy, p.963
Service of healing with Eucharist, p.973
Colman reading, 31 Dec.
Eata reading, 21 Mar.; 8 May; 10 Sept.

C.S. Lewis (see under L)

Cuthbert

Calendar, p.215
Biography, p.296
The Cuthbert Compline, p.60 and p.919
Cuthbert – into a desert place, p.295
Aidan readings, 21, 24–26 Mar.; 23 July
Finan readings, 26, 28 May; 4, 22–23 Oct.; 27, 29 Nov.
Introduction to Felgild – in persisting in prayer, p.1128
Aldwin – in following the example of good men and women of old, p.1136
Colman readings, 7, 22, 26, Feb.; 3, 11, 24 May; Intro, 22–24, 27–30 Oct.
Eata readings, 15–16 Apr.; 14 July; Intro., 21–22 Sept.; 11 Oct.

Darkness

A prayer in time of darkness, p.180
The shadow and the gift, p.1034
Help me, Lord, p.1041

David

Calendar, p.214
Biography, p.231
Finan readings, 14–16 Oct.
Colman readings, 1, 7–8, 10, 17–19 Mar.; 1 July

Death and dying

The shadow of death, p.187
Finan readings, 19 Nov.
Caelan Liturgy, p.192
A dying prayer, p.1050
Taking courage, p.1053
Eata liturgy, p.1124
Colman readings, 30 Nov.
Eata readings, 4, 24, 29 July

Dedication

Coming into the light – birth, p.169
A blessing on a child, p.201
Just you, p.201
Child of calmer waters, p.1013
Prayer at a dedication or christening, p.1014

de Hueck Doherty, Catherine (see Doherty)

Dewi (see David)

Dietrich Bonhoeffer (see under B)

Difficult times

Final prayer in About this Book, p.10
For those in trouble, p.182
In difficult times, p.1038

Distance

On separation from loved ones, p.180

Diuma

Calendar, p.220
Biography, p.232

Divorce

As I journey on alone, p.1026
A prayer after the disintegration of a relationship, p.1033

CROSS-REFERENCES

Colman – in disappointment and the death of a vision, p.1121
Colman readings, 1 Aug.
Eata readings, 13 June

Doherty, Catherine de Hueck

Calendar, p.220
Biography, p.232
Aidan readings, 29 Feb.
Finan readings, 1–31 Dec.

Donovan, Jean

Calendar, p.219
Biography, p.233
The way of the cross, section 5, p.131
Introduction to Follow the Example, p.1097

Eadfrith

Calendar, p.216
Biography, p.234

Eanfleda

Calendar, p.219
Biography, p.234
Colman readings, 21 Oct.

Easter Eve

The way of the cross, section 14, p.138
Easter Eve, p.141
Easter vigil, p.144

Easter

The way of the cross, sections 14–15, p.138–140
Aidan readings, 12 May
Eata readings, 8 Jan.

Eata

Calendar, p.218
Biography, p.234
Finan readings, 29 Nov.
Eata – in times of change, p.1124

Ebba

Calendar, p.217
Biography, p.235
The Ebba Compline, p.66 and p.935
Eata readings, 10 July; Intro., 20 Sept.

Elfleda

Calendar, p.213
Biography, p.235

Elfwy

Calendar, p.215
Biography, p.235
Meditation Day 10, p.34
Elfwy – in the heart of the shepherd, p.1139
Colman readings, Intro., 5, 8–14, 16, 24–25, 28–29 Feb.; 3 May; 31 Oct.

Enda

Calendar, p.215
Biography, p.236
Finan readings, 9 Oct.

Epiphany (see Three Kings)

Ethilwald of Farne

Calendar, p.215
Biography, p.238
Introduction to Felgild Compline, p.64 and p.929
Aidan readings, 8 Feb.; 28–29 Mar.; 18–19 May; 2 July
Finan readings, 28 Oct.

Farne, Ethilwald of

(see under E)

Fathers

About growing out of the father-wound, p.1014

Felgild

Calendar, p.215
Biography, p.64
The Felgild Compline, p.64 and p.929
Introduction to Follow the Example, p.1097
Felgild – in persisting in prayer, p.1128

Finan

Calendar, p.213
Biography, p.238
Meditation Day 18, p.42
Finan readings, 22 May

Finchale, Godric of
(see under G)

Finnian of Clonard

Calendar, p.220
Biography, p.238
Colman readings, 6–7 Mar.; 1–6 July
Finan Readings, 9 Oct.

Francis of Assisi

Calendar, p.218
Biography, p.238
Aidan readings, 29 Jan.; 14, 31 July; 18, 23 Dec.
Finan readings, 18 Mar.
Meditation Day 10, p.34 and p.892
Introduction to Follow the Example p.1097
Eata readings, 25–26 Apr.; 15 July

Gall

Calendar, p.218
Biography, p.239
Eata readings, 11, 14, 21 Mar.

George MacDonald
(see under M)

Girl to Woman

Liturgy of reflection for women, p.1018

Godric

Calendar, p.216
Biography, p.239
Colman readings, Intro., 24–31 May

Good Friday

Meditation Day 6, p.30
Meditation Day 25, p.46
The way of the cross, p.128
On Good Friday or at a crucifix, p.996

Graces

Graces, p.205 and p.1092

Harvest

Ninian – in relating to the whole of life, p.318
Harvest, p.161
Finan readings, 17 Sept.
Touching the Land, p.1000

Healing

Service of healing with Eucharist, p.973
Liturgy of the Holy Spirit, p.1077
When memories hold mixed emotions, p.1052

Henri Nouwen
(see under N)

Herebert

Calendar, p.215
Biography, p.240
Finan readings, 28 May

Hilary of Poitiers

Calendar, p.213
Biography, p.240
Colman readings, 9 Oct.

Hild

Calendar, p.219
Biography, p.291

Hild – in the right place, p.291
Aidan readings, 9, 22–28 Sept.
Finan readings, 30 May; 19 Oct.; 23, 24, 26, 29 Nov.
Introduction to Follow the Example, p.1097
Aldwin – in following the example of good men and women of old, p.1136
Colman readings, 3, 6–7, 17–19, 26 Feb.; 3, 11, 24 May; 19–21, 31 Oct.
Eata readings, Intro., 18–19 Sept.

Holy Innocents

Calendar, p.220
Biography, p.241
Colman readings, 28 Dec.

Hospitality

'For a guest room' in Brigid – in welcoming, p.272
Shabbat grace, p.205
Aidan readings, 21 Sept.
Finan readings, 1 Feb.
Colman readings, 1–30 Sept.

House-blessing

Brigid – in welcoming, p.267
A mezuzah prayer at the door, p.1063
Blessing for marriage and home, p.1063
Eata readings, 18 July

Hyde, John

Calendar, p.214
Biography, p.241
Introduction to Follow the Example, p.1097

Ignatius of Loyola

Calendar, p.216
Biography, p.242
A prayer in brokenness, p.181

Illtyd

Calendar, p.219
Biography, p.243

Innocents, Holy (see under H)

Irenaeus

Calendar, p.216
Biography, p.243
Colman readings, 2, 11 May; 23 Aug.; 6 Oct.

Irenée (see Irenaeus)

Ita

Calendar, p.213
Biography, p.54
The Ita Compline, p.54 and p.907
Finan readings, 10 Oct.
Introduction to Follow the Example, p.1097
Ita – in fostering courage, p.1109

Jean Donovan (see under D)

John Cassian (see under C)

John Hyde (see under H)

John of the Cross,

Calendar, p.220
Biography, p.243

John the Beloved

Calendar, p.220
Biography, p.244
Aidan readings, 12 July
Finan readings, 22 Mar.; 22 Apr.; 1, 5, 7, 27 Jul; 2, 28; 30 Nov.; 20 Dec.
Introduction to Follow the Example, p.1097
Colman readings, 4 Jan.; 25–26, 31 Mar.; Intro., 1–4, 11, May; 17, 30 July; Intro., 3–5 Oct.; Intro., 27 Dec.
Eata readings, 6 Jan.

John Wycliffe (see under W)

Joseph of Arimathea

Calendar, p.214
Biography, p.245
The way of the cross section 14, p.138
Aidan readings, 16 July; 19 Aug.

Journeying

Brendan – in exploration of a vision, p.302
On foot, p.199
For a journey, p.200
Till we meet again, p.200
Blessing on someone's journey, p.201
Journeying, p.1074

Juniper

Calendar, p.213
Biography, p.245
Meditation Day 29, p.50
Aidan readings, 29 Jan.; 14 July

Kentigern

Calendar, p.213
Biography, p.245

Kevin

Calendar, p.216
Biography, p.246
Finan readings, 9 Oct.

King, Martin Luther, Jr

Calendar, p.215
Biography, p.246
Introduction to Follow the Example, p.1097

L'Engle, Madeleine

Calendar, p.217
Biography, p.247
Aidan readings, 6 Feb.; 8 Nov.
Introduction to Follow the Example, p.1097
Eata readings, 4 Apr.; Intro.; 22 Dec.

Lent

Lent, p.123
Aidan readings, 21–22 Apr.

Lewis, C.S.

Calendar, p.219
Biography, p.247
Aidan readings, 28–29 Jan.; 25 Feb.; 6, 8, 12 July; 16 Oct.; 27 Dec.
Finan readings, 13 May; 6 June; 21 Aug.
Introduction to Follow the Example, p.1097
Eata readings, 4 Apr.; 5 May; Intro., 7, 13–21, 23–31 Dec.

Lewis, Jack (see above)

Lisieux, Thérèse of
(see under T)

Luther King, Martin Jr
(see under K)

Martin Luther King Jr
(see under K)

MacDonald, George

Calendar, p.217
Biography, p.248
Prayers for sleepless nights, p.185
Where earth and heaven meet, p.185
Courage, hope and peace, p.186
Aidan readings, 28 July; 22 Oct.
Finan readings, 11–12 Jan.
Eata readings, 4, 20 May; 3 July; Intro., 1–12, 27 Dec.

Madeleine L'Engle
(see under L)

Marriage

A marrying prayer, p.176
Don't shut me out, p.1030

Renewal of a marriage covenant, p.1031
Blessing for marriage and home, p.1063
Cherishing, p.1087
Colman readings, 30 Jan.

Marriage difficulties

In difficulties, p.178
The ultimate answer, p.179
Finan readings, 5 Sept.; 5 Nov.
A prayer after the disintegration of a relationship, p.1033

Martin Luther King Jr

(see under K)

Martin of Tours

Calendar, p.219
Biography, p.248
Colman readings, 5 Mar.; 11 May; 17 July; 9–10, 28 Oct.
Eata readings, 1 Sept.

Mary (mother of Jesus)

Calendar, p.217
Biography, p.249
The way of the cross sections 4, p.130; 12, p.137; 13, p.138
Aidan readings, 9 July; 20 Sept.
Finan readings, 24 Sept.
Advent Candle liturgy, p.987
Life-giving and living, p.1018
Colman readings, 11 Mar.; 25 May; 17 July; 4 Oct.; Intro., 25, 27, 29 Dec.

Mary of Egypt

Calendar, p.215
Biography, p.250
Finan readings, 6 Nov.

Maundy Thursday

Foot washing, p.125
Courage, hope and peace, p.186

Men

About growing out of the father-wound, p.1014

Merton, Thomas

Calendar, p.220
Biography, p.251
Aidan readings, 20 Feb.
Finan readings, 2 Mar.
Introduction to Follow the Example, p.1097
Colman readings, 8 Jan.; 27–30 Aug.; 16 Sept.
Eata readings, 12 Apr.; 11, 23 May; 6, 29 Aug.

Mezuzah

Aidan readings, 5 Nov.
A coming-home prayer, p.1062
A mezuzah prayer at the door, p.1063

Michael and All Angels

Calendar, p.218
Biography, p.251
Aidan readings, 13 July
Finan readings, 2, 13 Sept.
Michael liturgy – in joyful vigil and contesting against evil, p.1005
Eata readings, 29 Sept.; 14 Nov.

Mid-life

Mid-life appraisal and opportunity, p.183
Reaching mid-life, p.1033
Eata readings, 25, 30 July

Midsummer

Daybreak liturgy for the summer solstice, p.997
Seeing the sunrise, p.999

Mothers

Liturgy of reflection for women, p.1018
Mothering God, p.1036

In remembrance of a good mother, p.1051
A mother's prayer, p.1089

Mother Teresa (of Calcutta) (see under T)

Mungo (see under Kentigern)

New Year

Calendar, p.213
The opening door, p.115
A covenant service, p.116
Light a candle in the darkness, p.121
Telemachus – in peacefulness, p.1098

Ninian

Calendar, p.217
Biography, p.318
Ninian – in relating to the whole of life, p.318
Finan readings, 4 Oct.; 10–11 Nov.
Colman readings, 11 May; 10, 23, 29 Oct.
Eata readings, Intro., 1–10 Sept.

Noonday demons

Noonday demon prayer, p.1039
Eata readings, 29 Feb.

Nouwen, Henri

Calendar, p.218
Biography, p.252
Aidan readings, 27 Feb.
Finan readings, 2, 9 June
Colman readings, 10–11 Sept.

Oscar Romero

(see under R)

Oswald

Calendar, p.217
Biography, p.277
Oswald – in practical ways, p.277
Aidan readings, 14–16, 18–19 Mar.; 6, 17 July; 3, 17–20 Sept.
Finan readings, 23 May; 21 Nov.
A Celtic Communion, p.963
Introduction to Follow the Example, p.1097
Aldwin – in following the example of good men and women of old, p.1136
Colman readings, 11, 23–24 May; 16–17 Oct.
Eata readings, 10 July; Intro., 13 Sept.

Oswin

Calendar, p.217
Biography, p.253
Aidan readings, 8 Sept.
Aldwin – in following the example of good men and women of old, p.1136
Colman readings, 15 Feb.; 24 May.

Owini

Calendar, p.214
Biography, p.253
Meditation Day 21, p.44
Chad – in willing service, p.286
Aidan readings, 23 Mar.

Patrick

Calendar, p.214
Biography, p.70 and p.943
'Christ, as a light', in Morning Prayer, p.18 and p.867
The Patrick Compline, p.70 and p.943
'Declaration of faith' in Communion, p.79
A confession of faith, p.174
Aidan readings, 1–10 Mar.
Finan readings, 5 Oct.; 13 Nov.
Patrick – in resolute discipleship, p.1101
Colman readings, 11 May; 1, 6, 17 July; 11–12, 25 Oct.
Eata readings, 13 Apr.; 11 Sept.

Paul Aurelian

Calendar, p.214
Biography, p.254

Paulinus
Calendar, p.218
Biography, p.254
A baptismal prayer, p.174

Paul of Thebes
Calendar, p.213
Biography, p.254

Peace-making
Meditation Day 19, p.898
I am for peace, p.1066
Telemachus – in peacefulness, p.1098
Colman readings, 13–14 Mar.; 19 Apr.; 21 Dec.
Eata readings, 9, 12 June

Pelagius
Calendar, p.217
Biography, p.255

Pentecost
Invocation, p.xi
Liturgy of the Holy Spirit, p.1077
Song to the Holy Spirit, p.1081
Cedd – in reflecting honestly, p.1117
Colman readings, 27 Jan.; 29 Mar.

Petroc
Calendar, p.216
Biography, p.256
Colman readings, 13–14 Mar.

Pedrog (see Petroc)

Piran
Calendar, p.214
Biography, p.256
Daybreak liturgy, p.997
Piran – in following, p.1113

Polycarp
Calendar, p.214
Biography, p.256
Introduction to Follow the Example, p.1097
Colman readings, 1–2, 11 May; 5–6 Oct.

Reconciliation
The ultimate answer, p.179
Prayer for reconciliation, p.179
Reinfrid – in search of peace, p.1134

Reinfrid
Calendar, p.219
Biography, p.257
Meditation Day 10, p.34
Introduction to Follow the Example, p.1097
Reinfrid – in search of peace, p.1134
Colman readings, 31 Jan.; 3, 5–6, 8–11, 14, 16–20, 28, 29 Feb.; 3 May; 31 Oct.

Roger of Taizé
Calendar, p.217
Biography, p.257
Aidan readings, 22, 25–26 July; 15 Oct.
Eata readings, 13 Jan.

Roland Walls
(see under W)

Romero, Oscar
Calendar, p.215
Biography, p.259
Aidan readings, 10 Feb.

Saints
Saints, p.211–212
Calendar, p.213
Introduction to Follow the Example, p.1097
Colman readings, 23 Apr.; 5 May
Eata readings, 29 Oct.

Samthann
Calendar, p.220
Biography, p.260
Finan readings, 30 Oct.
Samthann – in stopping, p.1131

Senan
Calendar, p.214
Biography, p.260
Canaire, p.228
Finan readings, 7, 9 Oct.

Shabbat
Shabbat, p.89
The Welcoming of Shabbat, p.91
Havdala, p.97
Aidan readings, 28–29 Nov.
Colman readings, 28 July; 16, 18, 21–22 Aug.

Singleness
A prayer in brokenness, p.181
A prayer in 'the middle years' of opportunity, p.184
Singleness, p.1022
Liturgy for a commitment to celibacy, p.1023
As I journey on alone, p.1026
I wait and wait, p.1027
Reflections on being single, p.1028

Sleeplessness
Prayers for sleepless nights, p.185
Laying down and letting go, p.1041

Spiritual warfare
Meditation Day 6, p.30
Easter Eve reading, p.141
Aidan readings, 10 Mar., 13 July
Finan readings, 1–4, 6 Sept.
Michael liturgy – in joyful vigil and contesting against evil, p.1005
Patrick – in resolute discipleship, p.1101
Colman readings, 29 Mar.; 23 Oct.
Eata readings, 1–30 Nov.; 25–26 Dec.

Stephen
Calendar, p.220
Biography, p.260
Colman readings, 26 Dec.

Study
Finan readings, 16 Sept.
Before study, p.1061

Sunday after Easter
Thomas biography, p.262
Sunday after Easter, p.154

Taizé, Brother Roger of
(see under R)

Teilo
Calendar, p.213
Biography, p.261
Colman readings, 8, 18 Mar.

Telemachus
Calendar, p.213
Biography, p.261
Introduction to Follow the Example, p.1097
Telemachus – in peacefulness, p.1098

Teresa of Avila
Calendar, p.218
Biography, p.261
Blessing (Teresa's Bookmark) in Midday Prayer, p.20 and p.875
Eata readings, 30 Aug.

Teresa of Calcutta
Calendar, p.217
Biography, p.262
Finan readings, 8 July
Eata readings, 18 May

Thérèse of Lisieux
Calendar, p.218
Biography, p.262

Finan readings, 16–17 Feb.
Introduction to Follow the Example, p.1097
Eata readings, 13 Jan.

Thin places
Meditation Day 8, p.32
Where earth and heaven meet, p.185
Finan readings, 15 Sept.
Eata readings, 25 July

Thomas
Calendar, p.216
Biography, p.262
The Sunday after Easter, p.154
Introduction to Follow the Example, p.1097
Colman readings, 26 Apr.

Thomas Merton (see under M)

Three Kings' Day (Epiphany or Twelfth Night)
Calendar, p.213
Biography, p.263
Aidan readings, 11 July,
Finan readings, 16 Aug.
Colman readings, 23 Dec.

Tuda
Calendar, p.218
Biography, p.263

Walcher, William
Calendar, p.215
Biography, p.263
Colman readings, 11–12, 14, 22–25 Feb.

Walls, Roland
Calendar, p.215
Biography, p.264
Aidan readings, 24 Feb.; 28 July
Introduction to Follow the Example, p.1097
Colman readings, 11–12 Feb.
Eata readings, 1–31 Jan.

Weddings/Renewing of Vows
Awakening, p.162
A marrying prayer, p.176
Thigpen's wedding, p.176
Peace prayer for a wedding, p.177
Marriage blessings 1–3, p.178
Renewal of a marriage covenant, p.1031
Blessing for marriage and home, p.1063
Cherishing, p.1087
Eata readings, 8 July

Wilfrid
Calendar, p.218
Biography, p.265
Aidan readings, 11 Sept.
Finan readings, 29 Sept.; 26, 28 Nov.
Colman readings, 23–24 May; 21 Oct.
Eata readings, 18 Sept.

William Walcher
(see under Walcher)

Willibrord
Calendar, p.219
Biography, p.265

Women
Introduction to Shabbat, p.89
Finan readings, 7 Nov.
Liturgy of reflection for women, p.1018
I need some laughter, Lord, p.1035
Mothering God, p.1036
In remembrance of a good mother, p.1051
When memories hold mixed emotions, p.1052
A mother's prayer, p.1089
Canaire – in celebration of woman, p.1106

Wycliffe, John
Calendar, p.220
Biography, p.265

SOURCES AND ACKNOWLEDGEMENTS

This book is a new edition of *Celtic Daily Prayer*, originally published in 2000 to bring together into one volume the Community's earlier *Celtic Daily Prayer* (compiled by Andy Raine and John T. Skinner) and *Celtic Night Prayer*. The original work of revising, updating and expanding the two former books into one was largely undertaken by Andy Raine, with assistance from other Companions in Community. New material in this new edition has also been written mainly by Andy.

The following list gives further information to that already provided in the text about the sources of material used in this book. The authors and publisher acknowledge with thanks permission to reproduce copyright material included in this list. The Bibliography lists recommendations for further reading, and includes publications from which more extensive quotes are taken and which appear in a number of different places in this book. Every effort has been made to trace copyright holders, and the authors and publisher apologise to anyone whose rights have inadvertently not been acknowledged. This will be corrected in any reprint.

All illustrations and cover art © Francesca Ross. Used with permission. Music typeset by Michael Bennett.

Morning Prayer

'One thing': words from Psalm 27:4.
'To whom shall we go?': words from John 6:68 arranged by Jon Polce, and used with permission.
'Christ as a light': words of St Patrick, arranged by J. Michael Talbot, from the album, *Hiding Place* © 1990 Birdwing Music/Capitol CMG Publishing (Adm.

UK/Eire Song Solutions www.songsolutions.org). All rights reserved. Used by permission.
'Blessing': 'Peter's song for Marygate' by Peter Sutcliffe.

Midday Prayer

'Teach us, dear Lord': Psalm 90, words arranged by Jim Patterson, published by Youth With A Mission in *The Singing Word*.
'Blessing': by St Teresa of Avila ('Teresa's Bookmark').

Evening Prayer

'Watchmen': words from Psalm 130 by Larry and Pearl Brick from the album *See-through Servant* ©1989 Brick Publishing c/o R. Carlsen, 6209 John F. Kennedy Blvd., North Little Rock, AR 72115.
'Expressions of faith': translated for the British Council of Churches' Week of Prayer for Christian Unity 1988.
'In the shadow of Your wings': ©1985 Robert F. O'Connor, SJ and OCP, 5536 NE Hassalo, Portland, OR 97213, all rights reserved, used with permission.
'Blessing': St Columba of Iona.

Meditations

Day 6: from *If Only I Love Jesus* by M. Basilea Schlink ©Verlag Evangelische Marienschwesternschaft, Darmstadt, Germany.
Day 7: from M. Basilea Schlink and based on Revelation 12:10-11; 13:8b Psalm 138:8.
Day 9: follows a Francis Anfuso arrangement of Isaiah 58 up to verse 10.
Day 15b: from *Holy Island* by James Kennedy, Morehouse Publishing Company, Ridgefield, CT 06877, USA.
Day 17: from the album *Sing Psalms and Hymns* by Ekklesia.
Day 18: from the visitors' book at Marygate House, Holy Island.
Day 20b: Psalm 31:14-15, 211, words arranged by Marian Warrington, published by Youth With A Mission in *The Singing Word*.
Day 23c: from *Poems of the Western Highlanders* by Alexander MacNeill, published by SPCK.
Day 25: by Nathan Aldersley from *Salvation Army Songbook*, Salvationist Publishing and Supplies, London.
Day 27: from 'Arise, my love' by John and Ross Harding ©1975 Kingway's Thankyou Music, PO Box 75, Eastbourne, BN23 6NT, used with permission.
Day 28: arranged by Jonathan Asprey ©1975 Celebration/Thankyou Music, PO Box 75, Eastbourne, BN23 6NT.
Day 29: from *Juniper, Friend of Francis, Fool of God* by Murray Bodo, St Anthony Messenger Press, used with permission.
Day 30: from *House Like a Lotus* by Madeleine L'Engle © Farrar, Straus and Giroux Inc, New York. Based on a missionary hymn by D. T. Niles
Day 31: Edith Schaeffer, *L'Abri*, The Norfolk Press and Henry E. Walter.

The Aidan Compline

'Circle me Lord' from *The Edge of Glory* by David Adam (SPCK: London, 2011).

The Felgild Compline

'Calm me, O Lord' from *The Edge of Glory* by David Adam (SPCK: London, 2011).

The Cuthbert Compline

'As the bridegroom to his chosen', Johannes Tauler (1300–1361), translated by Emma Frances Bevan 1858.

Communion

'I make the cross': from *Hebridean Altars* (Wipf & Stock: Eugene, 2013).
'I know indeed': from *The Monk of Farne*. Dom Hugh Farmer, O.S.B (ed.) Darton, Longman and Todd: London, 1961.
'I praise the wounds': from *If I only love Jesus* by M. Basilea Schlink © Verlag Evangelische Marienschwesternschaft, Darmstadt, Germany.
'I pray you good Jesus': Bede.
Creed: from St Patrick's Confession.
'Listen Lord': John Bell, Iona Community © 1989 Wild Goose.
'O Lord, hear my prayer': Taizé.
'Through our lives': John Bell, Iona Community © 1993 Wild Goose.
'Look with kindness': from Eucharistic prayer of reconciliation No. 1, International Committee on English in the Liturgy (RC) 1974.
'O God, You are always': from Eucharistic prayers for children No. 1, International Committee on English in the Liturgy (RC) 1974.
'Almighty Father': W. Muir, *Prayer of Columba*.
'The power of Your love': by Geoff Bullock ©1990 Hillsongs, PO Box 74, Baulkham Hills, NSW 2153, Australia.

Shabbat

The Welcoming: Weston Priory, Vermont (adapt.)
'The day is not...' from an early Baptist monastery in Pennsylvania – our deep gratitude to the Community of the Holy Transfiguration in Australia for introducing us to this.
Song 'Shabbat Welcome' © Anna Raine from her CD *Ancient Paths*.
Shabbat Prayers: trad. adapt. Andy Raine.
Havdala; trad. adapt. Andy Raine except Cairn poem, blessing of children, 'We give thanks...' © Andy Raine.

Times and seasons

Christmas

'Though laid in a manger': from 'When wise men came seeking' by Richard Slater, *Salvation Army Songbook*, Salvationist Publishing and Supplies, London.

New Year

'Light a candle in the darkness': from Garth Hewitt, album *Alien Brain*, Word Music.

'Light one candle': song by Peter Yarrow © Silver Dawn Music, ASCAP House (NY) from Peter, Paul and Mary album *No Easy Road*.

'O God, You have been good': by Twila Paris, Starsong Records, Benson Corp., Nashville, USA.

Approaching Easter

'The basin and the towel': by Michael Card from 'Poiema', Word Records.

'Brother, let me be your servant': 'Servant song' by Richard Gillard, Scripture in Song, New Zealand.

'Knowing that...': by A. E. Whitham, *The Discipline and Culture of the Spiritual Life*, Hodder & Stoughton, London.

Sections 11, 12 and 13 of the 'The way of the cross' include passages from 'The Passion of Christ from a medical point of view' by C. Truman Davis, MD, MS of Mesa, Arizona.

Easter

Song of Moses: alternative title *The Horse and the Rider*, composer unknown; an arrangement is to be found in *Scripture in Song* music book Vol. 1, published 1976 by Marshall, Morgan & Scott.

Song of Miriam: Betty Pulkingham, Word of God Community, Ann Arbor, Michigan, from the album *Songs of Praise*.

'Come to the water': by John Foley, SJ © 1978 John Foley and North American Liturgy Resources, Phoenix, Arizona.

Sunday after Easter

Adapted from an original Greek Orthodox Liturgy.

Rites of passage

Birth

'We're giving her back to you': from the album *Enlistment* by Reba Rambo and Dony McGuire.

Marriage

'Thigpen's Wedding': Kemper Crabb from the album *The Vigil*, Starsong Records, Benson Corp., Nashville, USA.

Mid-life

'Middle age': by Anne Morrow Lindbergh from *Gift from the Sea*, Chatto & Windus, London.

The Shadow of Death: Caelan liturgy

Anita Haigh, 'We have come to seek you', copyright © Anita Haigh, Northumbria Community Trust.

Trad., 'I am bewildered', *Hebridean Altars* (Wipf & Stock: Eugene, 2013).

Nick and Anita Haigh, 'You're the voice that calms my tears' from the song 'Kyrie Eleison' © 2000 Break of Day Music (Adm. Song Solutions Daybreak www.songsolutions.org) All rights reserved. Used by permission.

Blessings and graces

Caim Prayer based on prayer by David Adam in The Edge of Glory, SPCK, London.

Follow the example

Aidan

Extracts taken from *A Scholar of Lindisfarne* by Gertrude Hollis, SPCK.
'Cry for the desert': by Twila Paris, Starsong Records, Benson Corp., Nashville, USA.

Brendan

I: Lyrics adapted by Chris Jones.
II: First stanza from 'Student Song' by Paul Stamper; 'I beseech': from Acta Sti. Brendani.
III: 'We were alone': from Dennis F. M'Carthy's *Voyage of St Brendan*.
VI: 'I thank you': words by St Columba of Iona; 'The journey' and 'There is a sense': from *The Magnificent Gael* by Reginald Hale; lyrics from Iona album *Beyond these Shores*.
IX: 'I Trust in Thee': from Psalm 31 arranged by Marian Warrington.
X: 'Return': from Dennis F. M'Carthy's *Voyage of St Brendan*.

Aidan series readings

Jan 2, 3: 'Inspired by love and anger' by John Bell and Graham Maule, The Wild Goose Worship Group of the Iona Community.
Jan 5, 21: The Methodist Covenant Service.
Jan 7–9: 'Don't shoot the wounded' by Chuck Girard. © Chuck Girard Ministry, PO Box 33226, Granada Hill, CA 91344, USA.
Jan 10–14: 'Stumbling blocks and stepping stones' by John Bell and Graham Maule, The Wild Goose Worship Group of the Iona Community.
Jan 25: from *The Singer* by Calvin Miller, Chatto & Windus, London.
Feb 5: from *When Jesus Looked o'er Galilee* by Catherine Baird, Salvationist Publishing and Supplies, London.

Mar 4: from *Holy Island* by James Kennedy, Morehouse Publishing Company, Ridgefield, CT 06877, USA.

April: *The Inward Journey* by Gene Edwards, Christian Books, USA. 1982.

May: *Inside the Mind of Unchurched Harry and Mary* by Lee Strobel, Zondervan, Grand Rapids, USA. 1993.

May: God: *What the Critics Say* by Martin Wroe, Hodder & Stoughton. 1992.

Jul 10: from the hymn *He walks with God who speaks to God in prayer* by Dorothy Ann Thrupp.

Jul 15: lines from T. S. Eliot's poem *Little Gidding* in 'Four Quartets', published in *Collected Poems 1909-1962*, Faber & Faber, London (see also Finan Series reading for Jan 31).

Jul 24 and 26: from *On Pilgrimage* by Jennifer Lash, Bloomsbury.

Jul 31: from *Never Forget* by Arch R. Wiggins, Salvationist Publishing and Supplies, London.

November: *My Friend God* by David Berg, SPI Books. 1972.

Nov Literat 22: from *Pure Crusade*, USA. 19 *Praying with the Jewish Tradition* 41. by Paula Clifford, SPCK. 1988.

December: *His Thofughts Said ... His Father Said* by Amy Carmichael, Christian

Finan series readings

Feb 3-7: from *Dreams in Homespun* by Samuel Walter Foss.

Feb 22: from *Keeper of the Door* by Twila Paris, Starsong Records, Benson Corp., Nashville, USA.

Feb 23-29: from the poem *I Stand by the Door* by Samuel Moor Shoemaker.

Mar 13: from *An Ethic for Christians and Other Aliens in a Strange World*, by William Stringfellow, Word Books, Waco, USA.

Mar 18: from Donovan's music for the film *Brother Sun, Sister Moon*.

Mar 28: from *Come Away My Beloved* by Frances Roberts, Kings Press, California, USA.

Mar 31: from *A Time to Gather* in the album *Spirit Alive* by Gregory Norbert, Weston Priory, VT 06161, USA.

May 18, 22, 29, 31: from *On the Road with Jesus* by Dave Cape, Kingsway Publications, 1993.

May 29: from *Keep on Fighting* by Reba Rambo and Dony McGuire in the album *Life in the Combat Zone*, 1991, RMR Records.

Jun 10: from *A Light Came Out* by William Hawley, Salvation Army Songbook, Salvationist Publishing and Supplies.

Jun 14: from *Many Voices, One Voice* by Eddie Askew, The Leprosy Mission.

Jun 16: from *I Never Saw Another Butterfly* by Eva Pickova, Word Music. 1969. State Jewish Museum, Prague.

Jun 18-20: adaption of Corrie ten Boom's story by D. Goudy.

Jun 26: hymn adapted by Fr Andrew A. Patenaude, MS (Father Pat of La Salette, New Hampshire).

Jun 27: *Why?* by Michael Card from his album *Scandalon*, Word Music.

July: *The City Without a Church* by Henry Drummond, Hodder & Stoughton. 1947.

Aug 18: from *Letters to a Community* by Norman Motley, Othona Community. 1986.

Sep 13: *Angels on Assignment* by Charles and Frances Hunter, Hunter Books, Houston, USA.

Sep 16: from *Magnus* by George Mackay Brown, Hogarth Press. 1973.

Sep 22: *Irish Spirituality*, Veritas Publications. 1981.

Sep 28: from *Chasing the Wild Goose* by Ron Ferguson, Fount. 1988.

BIBLIOGRAPHY

Adam, David. 1985. *The Edge of Glory*. Triangle/SPCK.
Adam, David. 1990. *The Eye of the Eagle*. Triangle/SPCK.
Adam, David. 1993. *Fire of the North*. SPCK.
Adam, David. 1997. *Flame in my Heart*. Triangle/SPCK.
Adam, David. 1999. *On Eagles' Wings*. Triangle/SPCK.
Adamnan. *Life of Saint Columba*. Llanerch. (Facsimile reprint, 1988.)
Bede. *A History of the English Church and People*. (Trans. Leo Sherley-Price 1968) Penguin Books.
Buechner, Frederick. 1965. *The Final Beast*. USA: Atheneum.
Buechner, Frederick. 1973. *Wishful Thinking: A Theological ABC*. USA: Harper & Row.
Carmichael, Alexander. 1992. *Carmina Gadelica*. Floris Books.
Carmichael, Amy. 1941. *His Thoughts Said, His Father Said*. Dohnavur/SPCK.
Carmichael, Amy. 1938. *If*. USA: Christian Literature Crusade.
Carmichael, Amy. 1987. *Toward Jerusalem*. Dohnavur/SPCK.
Darnall, Jean. 1974. *Heaven, Here I Come*. Marshall Morgan & Scott.
de Foucauld, Charles. 1930. *Meditations of a Hermit*. Burns & Oates.
de Foucauld, Charles. 1977. *Letters from the Desert*. Burns & Oates.
de Mello, Anthony. 1985. *One Minute Wisdom*. USA: Doubleday Image.
Doherty, Catherine de Hueck. 1974. *Poustinia*. USA: Ave Maria Press.
Hale, Reginald. 1976. *The Magnificent Gael*. Canada: World Media Productions.
Hybels, Bill. 1991. *Honest to God?* USA: Zondervan.
Lawhead, Stephen. 1988. *Merlin*. Lion Publishing.
Lewis, C.S. 1956. *The Last Battle*. The Bodley Head.
Lindbergh, Anne Morrow. 1955. *Gift from the Sea*. Chatto & Windus. USA: Pantheon Books.
Maclean, Alistair. 1937. *Hebridean Altars*. Hodder & Stoughton.
MacLeod, Kenneth. 1927. *The Road to the Isles*. Robert Grant & Son.

Marshall, Catherine (ed). 1966. *Prayers of Peter Marshall*. William Heinemann.

Merton, Thomas. *The Wisdom of the Desert*. Darley Anderson Books.

Nouwen, Henri. 1989. *Seeds of Hope*. Darton, Longman & Todd.

O'Donaghue, D. 1893. *The Lives and Legends of Saint Brendan The Voyager*. Llanerch. (Facsimile reprint 1994.)

O'Fiannachta/Foristal. 1988. *Saltair, Prayers from the Irish Tradition*. Dublin: Columba Press.

Quoist, Michel. 1963. *Prayers of Life*. Dublin: Gill & Son. USA: Sheed & Ward.

Redwood, Hugh. 1932. *God in the Shadows*. Hodder & Stoughton.

Rolheiser, Ronald. 1990. *Forgotten Among The Lilies*. Hodder & Stoughton.

Rolheiser, Ronald. *The Restless Heart*. Hodder & Stoughton.

Sellner, E.C. *Wisdom of the Celtic Saints*. Ave Maria Press.

Six, Jean-François. 1983. *Is God Endangered by Believers?* USA: Dimension Books.

Skene (ed.). *The Black Book of Carmarthen*. USA: AMS Press.

The Cloud of Unknowing (trans. C. Walters). 1961. Penguin Books.

van de Weyer, Robert. 1990. *Celtic Fire: An Anthology of Celtic Christian Literature*. Darton, Longman & Todd.

van de Weyer, Robert. 1995. *The Letters of Pelagius. Celtic Soul Friend*. Arthur James.

Wiesel, Elie. 1982. *The Testament*. Penguin Books.

Contact details for the Northumbria Community

For further information please see The Northumbria Community website:

www.northumbriacommunity.org

or contact the Community office at:

The Northumbria Community
Nether Springs
Croft Cottage
Acton Home Farm
Felton
Northumberland
NE65 9NU

Tel: 01670 787645 (from outside the UK: +44 1670 787645)

Email: **office@northumbriacommunity.org**

The Northumbria Community Trust
Registered Charity No: 1156630